ENGLAND
AND THE
CRUSADES

ENGLAND

AND THE

CRUSADES

1095–1588

Christopher Tyerman

THE UNIVERSITY OF CHICAGO PRESS   CHICAGO AND LONDON

CHRISTOPHER TYERMAN
is a lecturer at Hertford College, Oxford, and an assistant master at Harrow School.

THE UNIVERSITY OF CHICAGO PRESS, CHICAGO 60637
THE UNIVERSITY OF CHICAGO PRESS, LTD., LONDON

© 1988 by the University of Chicago
All rights reserved. Published 1988
Printed in the United States of America

97 96 95 94 93 92 91 90 89 88   54321

Library of Congress Cataloging-in-Publication Data

Tyerman, Christopher.
  England and the Crusades, 1095-1588 / Christopher Tyerman.
    p.   cm.
  Bibliography: p.
  Includes index.
  ISBN 0-226-82012-2
  1. Great Britain—History—Medieval period, 1066-1485.   2. Great
Britain—History—Tudors, 1485-1603.   3. Crusades.   4. England-
Church history—Medieval period, 1066-1485.   5. England—Church
history—16th century. I. Title.
DA176.T94 1988
942—dc19   87-30252
                                                            CIP

For Sarah

Contents

Preface

Writing a first book, the academic tyro inevitably and thankfully incurs heavy debts. It is a pleasure as well as an obligation to record my gratitude to those who have made this book so much better than I could have done alone. In particular I must thank the electors of the R. H. Murray Fellowship at the University of Oxford and the Rector and Fellows of Exeter College, Oxford, for providing the time and surroundings which made this work possible. For help on individual points, for discussion, and for opportunities to air some ill-formed views, I am extremely grateful to Dr. W. J. Blair, Dr. D. A. Carpenter, Mr. C. S. L. Davies, Professor R. B. Dobson, Dr. P. W. Edbury, Dr. P. R. Hyams, Dr. S. D. Lloyd, Mr. J. O. Prestwich, Professor J. S. C. Riley-Smith, and Mrs. J. Wallis. To avoid poaching or duplication, by mutual agreement I have not viewed Dr. Lloyd's thesis, *English Society and the Crusade, 1216–1307*, which fortunately is soon to be published by the Oxford University Press. To Mr. E. Christiansen I owe the introduction to my publishers, as well as guidance, encouragement, and inspiration over many years. Dr. P. H. Williams and Dr. P. A. Slack generously spared time to comment on a medievalist's excursion into early modern history. Dr. M. H. Keen read most and Dr. J. R. Maddicott the whole of the first draft. My debt to all of them, as critics and friends, is very great. What I and this book have gained from the intellectual companionship of Paul Slack and John Maddicott is immeasurable. As with the crucesignati themselves, I have made mistakes on my *iter*, not all of them redeemable by the help and advice of others. For such errors and all remaining blunders and follies I alone am responsible. Finally, I hope my sharpest, kindest critic, who has shared, suffered, tolerated, and eased the inner agonies and outward frustrations of authorship, will accept as some inadequate recompense the dedication of the work with which she has lived for so long.

I must thank the Trustees of the British Library for permission to reproduce MS Roy 2 A XXII on the cover and the Trustees of the National Gallery, London, for permission to reproduce the Wilton Diptych. Mrs. Gwendoline Butler kindly allowed me access to the papers of her late husband, Dr. L. H. Butler. Both the Trustees of the R. H. Murray Fund and the Rector and Fellows of Exeter College, Oxford, assisted with the expense of typing the manuscript of the book, which task was undertaken with patience by the staff of Tonedo, Ltd., Oxford. Thanks are also due to the staffs of the libraries in which this work gestated, in particular the staffs of the Bodleian Library, Oxford, the Venerable Order of St. John's Library, Clerkenwell, and the Assistant Librarian, Exeter College, Oxford. The evidence of the patience, friendliness, and skill of the staff of the University of Chicago Press is everywhere in the following pages.

Some Dates

1264–65	Montfortians wear crosses at battles of Lewes and Evesham; Popes Urban IV and Clement IV proclaim crusades against English rebels; royalists wear red crosses at Evesham
1268	The Lord Edward takes the cross
1270–72	Crusade of the Lord Edward
1287	Edward I takes the cross again
1290	Expulsion of the Jews from England
1291	Crusade of Otho de Grandson; fall of Acre to Egyptians; evacuation of the last Frankish possessions on the mainland of Syria
1300	Crosses worn by English soldiers in Annandale campaign
1307–14	Suppression of the Templars
1308–10	Hospitaller Crusade; Rhodes captured
1309	Headquarters of Teutonic Knights moved to the Baltic
1313	Edward II takes the cross
1329–36	Edward III negotiates for joint Anglo-French crusades to Spain and then the Holy Land
1330s onwards	Englishmen campaign against the heathen in the Baltic
1343–44	Siege of Algeciras attended by Henry of Grosmont
1365	Sack of Alexandria; Englishmen prominent in Christian force
1366	Englishmen join crusade of Amadeus VI of Savoy
1383	Bishop Despenser of Norwich leads crusade against schismatics in Flanders
1386	John of Gaunt's campaign in Spain designated a crusade by Urban VI
1390	Englishmen join the duke of Bourbon's crusade to Tunis
1390–91 and 1392–93	Henry Bolingbroke (later Henry IV) in Baltic and Holy Land
1395–96	Anglo-French negotiations for a crusade against the Ottomans
1396	Battle of Nicopolis
1409	Indulgences offered for the building of the Hospitaller castle at Bodrum
1410	Battle of Tannenberg
1428–29	Cardinal Beaufort's crusade against the Hussites of Bohemia preached in England
1453	Fall of Constantinople to Ottomans leads to renewed campaigns to raise money for crusade
1476	Crusade indulgence form is printed (first piece of printing in England to survive)
1481	Caxton prints the *Deeds of Godfrey de Bouillon*
1501	Indulgence campaign of Jasper Ponce
1511	English expedition under Lord Darcy against the Moors gets no further than Cadiz
1536	Pilgrimage of Grace

1540	Suppression of the Hospitallers in England (final disendowment, 1559)
1569–70	Revolt of the Northern Earls
1578	Thomas Stukeley leads papal crusade to Ireland, is deflected to Portuguese crusade in North Africa and killed at the battle of Alcazar; Irish enterprise continued by FitzMaurice and Sanders
1588	The Spanish Armada enjoys crusade indulgences
1639	Fuller publishes his *History of the Holy War*

Popes 1088 — 1590

Urban II	1088–1099	Alexander IV	1254–1261
Paschal II	1099–1118	Urban IV	1261–1264
*Theodoric**	1100	Clement IV	1265–1268
Albert	1102	Gregory X	1271–1276
Sylvester IV	1105–1111	Innocent V	1276
Gelasius II	1118–1119	Adrian V	1276
Gregory VIII	1118–1121	John XXI	1276–1277
Calixtus II	1119–1124	Nicholas III	1277–1280
Honorius II	1124–1130	Martin IV	1281–1285
Celestine II	1124	Honorius IV	1285–1287
Innocent II	1130–1143	Nicholas IV	1288–1292
Anacletus II	1130–1138	Celestine V	1294
Victor IV	1138	Boniface VIII	1294–1303
Celestine II	1143–1144	Benedict XI	1303–1304
Lucius II	1144–1145	Clement V	1305–1314
Eugenius III	1145–1153	John XXII	1316–1334
Anastasius IV	1153–1154	*Nicholas V*	1328–1330
Adrian IV	1154–1159	Benedict XII	1334–1342
Alexander III	1159–1181	Clement VI	1342–1352
Victor IV	1159–1164	Innocent VI	1352–1362
Paschal III	1164–1168	Urban V	1362–1370
Calixtus III	1168–1178	Gregory XI	1370–1378
Innocent III	1179–1180	Urban VI	1378–1389
Lucius III	1181–1185	*Clement VII*	1378–1394
Urban III	1185–1187	(Avignon)	
Gregory VIII	1187	Boniface IX	1389–1404
Clement III	1187–1191	*Benedict XIII*	1394–1423
Celestine III	1191–1198	(Avignon)	
Innocent III	1198–1216	Innocent VII	1404–1406
Honorius III	1216–1227	Gregory XII	1406–1415
Gregory IX	1227–1241	Alexander V	1409–1410
Celestine IV	1241	*John XXIII*	1410–1415
Innocent IV	1243–1254	Martin V	1417–1431

*(Popes in italics are considered to be antipopes.)

Clement VIII	1423–1429	Leo X	1513–1521
Eugenius IV	1431–1447	Adrian VI	1522–1523
Felix V	1439–1449	Clement VII	1523–1534
Nicholas V	1447–1455	Paul III	1534–1549
Calixtus III	1455–1458	Julius III	1550–1555
Pius II	1458–1464	Marcellus II	1555
Paul II	1464–1471	Paul IV	1555–1559
Sixtus IV	1471–1484	Pius IV	1559–1565
Innocent VIII	1484–1492	Pius V	1566–1572
Alexander VI	1492–1503	Gregory XIII	1572–1585
Pius III	1503	Sixtus V	1585–1590
Julius II	1503–1513		

Introduction

This book is not intended as a history of the crusades with English subtitles. Rather, it is a study of the effects of the crusade movement on the politics and society of medieval England and only looks from that perspective at the English, and occasionally Welsh, contributions to the crusading campaigns themselves. The stance is deliberately Western and domestic, for it is essential to the understanding of the significance of the crusades that their European and local dimension be appreciated, an aspect for long neglected by scholars and writers more interested in military expeditions, religious ideals, commerce, and European colonialism. The purpose is to show that the courtroom and council chamber no less than the battlefield bear witness to the importance of crusading, which was, as F. M. Powicke wrote over a generation ago, a political and economic function of society. The history of the crusades follows the contours not of any systematic theory or dogmatically organised canonical institution, but instead of changing devotional and secular aspirations and needs, of which crusading was as often a symptom as a cause.

The crusade meant different things to different people at different times; it both reflected and concentrated domestic developments in religious observance, military organisation, personal piety, social ambition, and financial administration in church and state. The aim here is to show that the crusade was an important aspect of English history in its own right, not an appendix or a distraction, a good story, a costly blunder of foreign policy, an aberration of religious hysteria, or an indulgence in vaunting ambition, although it was all of these as well. Participation in crusading exposed patterns of social, religious, and cultural behaviour often remote from the ideal itself. It refined popular and ecclesiastical attitudes to violence on the one hand and redemption on the other. It accelerated the development of techniques of raising money through extraordinary, compulsory national taxation and of recruiting men by paid contract, which were both of central importance to the growing political and institutional cohesion of the late medieval state. Responses to the crusade demonstrate how people behaved in facing some of the more difficult aspects of life: money, self-esteem, social repute, landlords, the church, God, and salvation. Although emerging from and running parallel to older theories of just and holy war, crusade ideology and rhetoric supplied a distinct impetus towards the creation of a quasi-religious ideology of nationalism which sustained English politicians and people into the sixteenth century and beyond.

The subject also provides a case study relevant to the wider history of the crusade movement itself. England may not have been typical (where is?) but its experience is illuminating. The justification for this approach lies in the hundreds, if not thousands, of named and unnamed men and women whose commitment, in thought, word, pocket, or deed, has survived as testimony that the crusade was a part of their environment. However, one battleground familiar to historians of the crusade will be avoided. It is not part of this work to pass judgement on the motives of those actively or passively involved in crusading. For one thing, evidence of private feeling and emotions is almost wholly lacking. For another, an individual's capacity to be moved by contradictory impulses is immeasurable; to allocate precise, let alone single, motives is to mislead. The only test of sincerity of interest in the crusade, or lack of it, is in the evidence of external actions and attitudes. It is not the purity of the enthusiasm of a person or group that matters so much as the importance of the crusade, popular or unpopular, exciting or mundane, for good or for ill, in their conscious lives. That is demonstrable and will be demonstrated.

A crusader, a *crucesignatus* or man signed with the cross, was someone who, with the approval of his local priest or other authoritative cleric, swore a vow to go to fight the enemies of the church, in the Holy Land or elsewhere. In public recognition and confirmation of his oath, the individual performed the liturgical rite of assuming the cross. This was often, perhaps usually, conducted as a sequel to that of receiving the scrip and staff of the pilgrimage. As a symbol of his having solemnly bound himself, the crusader wore on his garments a cloth cross, usually sewn onto the shoulder. Once the cross had been received, the crusader became, like the pilgrim, immune from various secular liabilities and enjoyed the spiritual privilege of full remission of confessed sins. Such, at least, was in crude outline the standard practice as it had developed by 1200. The reality was often less clear. Not all crucesignati fought, some in the twelfth century probably not even promising, let alone intending, to do so, and many never embarked on the journey, through

2

accident or design. Conversely, it is unlikely that everybody who fought in wars regarded by participants and contemporaries as crusades were in fact crucesignati, although probably most were. In terms of individual motive, objective, and action, therefore, the crusade presents a diverse picture.

Equally, as a religious institution the crusade was never unitary or monolithic in practice. It was a particular form of war, justified, according to circumstance, by pope or private conscience as being holy, and associated, initially by Pope Urban II in 1095, with the pilgrimage to Jerusalem; as such it was a religious exercise. The crusade had twin ancestors, in the militant secular mentality and growing religiosity of the early medieval warrior aristocracy, and in the monastic radicalism of the church reform movements of the tenth and eleventh centuries. It was the papacy that first fused holy war (one which, if conducted in a pure state of mind, was meritorious in the sight of God) with pilgrimage (a penitential act designed specifically to gain the executant remission of the penalties of sin and a better chance of Eternal Life). It was also the papacy that subsequently manipulated this construct most extensively and inventively. However, the tension between the individual's perception and official control was never resolved. Sustained by widely various religious and secular impulses and often barely reconcilable pressures of piety and social esteem, the institution of the crusade was only lent some legalistic cohesion by the thirteenth-century policies and legislation of popes and the legal codifications of canon lawyers. Alongside what could be called public or official crusades following the classical model of a campaign authorised by express papal edict, recruited by papally delegated agents, and conducted according to papal rules, there existed a continuing stream of private crusades, journeys by individuals or groups of pilgrims who had taken the cross outside the confines of any immediate general call to arms.

The failure of contemporaries clearly to distinguish between a pilgrimage and a crusade, ceremonially for about half a century and linguistically, in some cases, for four centuries after Urban II's speech launching the First Crusade, was neither coincidental nor solely a function of academic unease at the implications of a war that earned the soldiers indulgences instead of demanding penance; it mirrored reality. As a pilgrimage-in-arms the crusade, true to its prototype, had Jerusalem as its central, most potent, and most important goal, to such an extent that in the majority of instances even the papacy equated the spiritual and temporal privileges attached to a number of campaigns it directed at targets other than the Holy Land with those granted to pilgrim-crusaders to Jerusalem. If the canonists and papal apologists are

3

believed, formally this association was unnecessary, and a number of surviving rites for giving the cross do allow for destinations apart from the Holy Land; practically, however, for England the link was probably essential. English support for the crusade, at least in the first two centuries, was overwhelmingly concentrated upon the Holy Land enterprise.

If not unitary, neither was the crusade static. At the very time when ideology and practice were being constructed in the thirteenth century, the administration of the crusade took a new direction. Instead of depending upon active, personal participation, the spiritual benefits of the crusader, notably the indulgence, were made accessible to those who paid to redeem their crusader's vow. Within a few generations the indulgence began to be sold outright without any intervention of a pilgrim-crusader vow. The later Middle Ages, although short of crusading victories, witnessed, partly in the wider involvement in the movement made possible by selling indulgences, the tenacity of the ideal and institution in a recognisable and comprehensible form. This period also saw a potentially more significant development in the cross-fertilisation of the crusade with a new and ultimately all-conquering, yet in some respects derivative, phenomenon, the national war. The religious and secular energies that had gone into the efforts to secure the Holy Land or fight other enemies of the church far from home were translated, or perhaps were returned, to defending the *patria*. The emotions that inspired the crusader were in many ways equivalent to those that encouraged the national warrior: duty to a righteous and respectable cause sanctified by lay authority and the church, against an enemy characterised as being hostile to the cherished and familiar community of the national or religious faithful (the paradigm of the twelfth-century "Saracen" or the twentieth-century "Hun").

However, the triumph of nationalism should not be anticipated. Englishmen still took the cross in the late fifteenth century, and Tudor monarchs still found the vocabulary and the emotional and spiritual resonances of the crusade both intelligible and useful. As an institution of organised religion and a living intellectual force the crusade only ceased to occupy a place in English life in the late sixteenth century, a casualty of the religious and political reordering of social values during the Reformation. The time span of this book is, therefore, both deliberate and inevitable, embracing the history of the movement from its inception to its dissolution. The period, though long, possesses its own unity; Spanish recruits to the Armada in 1588 were offered crusade privileges explicitly associated with those granted to crusaders to the Holy Land. In England, the crusade was characteristic of the habitual, communal religion of medieval Catholicism, which derived its strength

4

from the aspirations and interests of the faithful as much as from the dictates of the clergy. By 1600 the concerns of the faithful were being articulated in a different idiom, one alien to the crusade.

England was not left unmarked by the experience of half a millenium. Some of English history's more colourful moments occured on crusade, most famously Richard I directing operations from his sickbed at Acre on the Third Crusade or Eleanor of Castille sucking the poison from the Lord Edward's wound eighty years later. The crusade appeared in numerous late medieval folktales and legends, such as the stories of Robin Hood or the Lambton Worm. Reputedly the oldest public house in England, *The Old Trip to Jerusalem* at Nottingham, dating, it is alleged, from 1189, commemorates the extensive English involvement in the Third Crusade. More certainly, the memory of the crusading military orders lingers in the names of places they once owned; in London alone there are the examples of the Temple, St. John's Wood, and Knightsbridge. Perhaps the crusade's most indelible imprint was on the literary and public records of medieval England, but it also left a trace on the English language. As a synonym for a just cause vigorously pursued, the term *crusade* has been widely adopted in the English-speaking world at least since the eighteenth century, to apply to a variety of issues: military, as in General Eisenhower's war memoir *Crusade in Europe;* social, as in Thomas Jefferson's 1786 call for a "crusade against ignorance"; religious; and political. Occasionally, the adaptation displays knowledge of the word's original implications. Thus in the London *Spectator* of 19 January 1985, a correspondent wrote, "Crusading rhetoric is all very well if one really is on the march to Jerusalem—it begins to jar a bit if it's clear that we're not going any further than Southend." This sentiment would not have disgraced a moralising preacher of six or seven centuries ago.

In view of all this, it is surprising that until recently there had been no study of England and the crusades. This book will be the first modern academic attempt at an account of the whole period. Yet the crusades in general have long held the historical and literary attention of British writers and, for just as long, they have been a subject of controversy. Since the sixteenth-century Protestant martyrologist John Foxe, the crusade has been analysed and judged. For Thomas Fuller, a moderate royalist Anglican in the mid-seventeenth century, as for Foxe, the "holy war" was tarnished with Catholicism: "Superstition not only tainted the rind, but rotted the core of this whole action." The theme of "savage fanaticism" was expounded most dazzlingly by Edward Gibbon a century later and was placed by him in a general philosophical attack on the damaging effects of irrationality and religion. This attitude was famously summed up by David Hume in his *History of Great Britain* (1761), when he described the crusades as "the most signal and durable monument to human folly that has yet appeared in any age or nation." The Protestant analysis and its rationalist heir still find powerful modern echo in the work of Sir Steven Runciman, whose epic three volumes on the movement end with a resounding condemnation of the crusades as "nothing more than a long act of intolerance in the name of God, which is the sin against the Holy Ghost."

Between Hume and Runciman the nineteenth-century British revival of medievalism in art, literature, and religion to a degree rehabilitated the image of the crusades, although not universally among the medieval enthusiasts. Walter Scott, for example, admired chivalry and set one of his novels, *The Talisman*, in the camp of the Third Crusade in Palestine, yet he was unhappy about the crusades and their associated intolerance; *Ivanhoe* exalts chivalry but casts the Knights Templar as hypocrites and villains. However, the tide of sentimental Gothicism proved irresistible. In works such as Kenelm Digby's revised *Broad Stone of Honour* (1828–29) or Henry Stebbings's *History of Chivalry and the Crusades* (1830), Catholic and Anglican apologists united in praising the crusades as the expression of virtues they hoped to instill in their readers. As an image of human greatness the crusade continued to inspire into the early twentieth century. The Oxford historian Ernest Barker, in his brilliant essay on the crusades written for the *Encyclopaedia Britannica*, chose "to give thanks for their memory" as examples of human devotion and daring.

Since the Second World War, judgement, let alone approval, of the crusades has been less prevalent among historians. The intellectual and emotional complexities of legitimate public violence and its outlined consequences for the sufferers, in particular the Jews, coupled with the retreat of European colonialism, have made crusading more approachable and less attractive to modern Western commentators. For some historians, the revival of a theology of Christian resistance and just war in Catholic South America, even though it lacks the authority of papal blessing, has revived an intellectual appreciation of the nature of crusading. More to the point, the range of sources for the crusaders' circumstances and environment has widened to include not simply the records of their deeds on campaigns and in the East, but also evidence of their domestic situation and the society from which they came. This less polemical, more humdrum material prompts new lines of enquiry that integrate the crusades even more firmly into the study as well as the reality of medieval Europe.

A consequence of these fresh insights is to shift the emphasis of investigation towards the place occupied by the crusade in society and away from the mere recitation of the military history of the movement. Thus it is not only the traditional chronological frame that needs adjustment. The themes of this book are not those of the success or failure of individual crusades or of the movement in general. Instead they concern the extent to which crusading penetrated the ordinary workings of English life, in political discussions at the highest level, private behaviour, the common law, the land market, the organisation of armies, social mobility, and the fortunes of individual families and of whole communities, most notoriously that of English Jewry. It may be a matter of regret, or, alternatively, relief, that Evelyn Waugh never pursued his idea, expressed in 1935, of writing a history of England and the Holy Places; what follows does not attempt to repair his omission, for it will deal with the reverse of what interested the novelist, namely the effect of the Holy Places, and the crusading brand of militant Christianity, on England.[1] The scope is broadened to include such diverse issues as anti-Semitism and the history of military uniforms, civil disobedience and the rise of nationalism. Yet even though this is inevitably a long book, there are gaps. Most notably, after the first chapter there has been no attempt to investigate in detail English migration and settlement in areas conquered by crusading forces, nor has there been space to include a full history of the military orders in England.

Although concentration is on the significance of the crusade in medieval England, wider perspectives may be gained on the nature and application of an ideal and habit that gripped imaginations for five hundred years. The crusades were important to England and to the rest of Europe. This book tries to indicate how, and to offer suggestions as to why, for centuries after the first summons in 1095, men and women contemplated leaving their homes at great personal cost and potential danger to travel to the furthest edge of the known world to capture or protect the Empty Tomb. As the crusade was a recension of Christian just and holy war, it is appropriate to begin the investigation with the genesis of that tradition and the origins of the crusade in England.

I

A New Way of Earning Salvation

At Clermont in central France in November 1095, Pope Urban II called upon the knights of western Christendom to go to the aid of their fellow Christians in the East and to liberate the Holy Sepulchre at Jerusalem. In two senses this call was not unexpected. In March 1095 at the Council of Piacenza, envoys of the Byzantine emperor, Alexius I Comnenus (1081–1118), had appealed to Urban for military aid against the Seljuk Turks who were occupying Asia Minor. Twenty years earlier, in the same context of help for Byzantium, Urban II's political mentor, Gregory VII, had proposed just such an expedition to combat the Moslems, relieve eastern Christendom, and visit the Holy Sepulchre. Urban planned his announcement at Clermont with care; however, nothing could have prepared him for its reception.

The response was immediate and massive. Within a year, armed contingents led by, among others, the itinerant preacher Peter the Hermit and lesser nobles such as the viscount of Melun, Walter the Penniless, and Emicho of Leiningen, had set out for the East on what historians have persistently misnamed the Peasants' Crusade. Except for less exalted leadership and their failure to reach their destination, these armies were more or less indistinguishable from the subsequent so-called Princes' Crusade. None of the early bands got further than western Asia Minor; many failed even to reach Constantinople. The armies of the greater lords fared better. Separate Frankish (i.e., northern or southern French-speaking) armies began leaving for the East in the late summer of 1096, commanded by important rulers such as Raymond, count of Toulouse; Robert Curthose, duke of Normandy; Stephen, count of Blois; Godfrey de Bouillon, duke of Lower Lorraine; his brother Eustace, count of Boulogne; Hugh, count of Vermandois, brother of the king of France; and Bohemund of Taranto, son of Robert Guiscard, the Norman conqueror of southern Italy.

Despite strained relations with a startled Greek emperor when these armies reached Constantinople in the winter and spring of 1096–97, the hostility of the Turks, and the unfamiliar environment of Asia Minor and Syria, these crusaders met with success. Nicea in Asia Minor was captured in 1097. After fighting their way across Anatolia, the Franks took and defended Antioch following an epic siege in 1098. Despite desertions and heavy casualties through combat and disease, and helped by reinforcements by sea, the crusaders, led by Raymond of Toulouse, captured Jerusalem on 15 July 1099, a victory they secured by defeating an Egyptian counterattack at Ascalon a month later.

With the Holy City and the vital strategic centres of Jaffa, the port of Jerusalem, Antioch, and Edessa (taken in 1098 by a splinter group led by Baldwin of Boulogne) in Christian hands, most of the surviving crusaders returned to the West, leaving behind a rump based on the retinues of the successful commanders who remained: Bohemund and the Italian Normans, at Antioch; the Lorrainers of Godfrey de Bouillon, who was succeeded by his younger brother Baldwin of Edessa in 1100, at Jerusalem; and Raymond of Toulouse and his Provençals, who sought a stronghold on the northern Syrian coast, finally settling on Tripoli, which Raymond invested in 1104 but which only fell to his successor in 1109. By 1124, when Tyre was captured, Frankish rulers controlled most of the Syrian coastline from Cilicia in the north to Ascalon (which only fell in 1153) in the south, as well as a narrow strip of hinterland including the lower Orontes valley, Galilee, Samaria, Judea, and parts of the desert east and south of the Jordan River and the Dead Sea towards the Gulf of Aqaba. It had been a most startling achievement which quite literally broadened the horizons of western Christendom.

ORIGINS OF AN IDEA

The implications of the First Crusade went much deeper than military success. The expedition summoned at Clermont inaugurated a new form of Christian war, in which service to Christ was at the same time military and meritorious, and in which warriors wearing the symbol of the cross enjoyed the temporal status and spiritual rewards of pilgrims. Although controversial, the idea of a holy war was already old. Six centuries earlier Augustine of Hippo had defined a Christian just war as possessing three qualities: defensive of the church, righteous in intent, and legitimate in authority. Although widespread dissemination of precise intellectual arguments may be doubted, popular perception of permissible violence had a long history, in England as elsewhere. Deriving much energy from the aristocratic values of a pre-Christian society, the virtues of the heroic warrior had been turned by the church in the seventh century into a code based upon defence of God's People and Laws, which could, with little contradiction, become aggressive, especially when God's People could be identified with a nation or with the church itself, pitted against a pagan foe. In Bede's account of the battles of Oswald of Northumbria in the seventh century, Oswald, "a man beloved of God," led his army, "small but strong in faith," to victory over Cadwalla of Gwynedd at the battle of Heavenfield (c. 633) only after he had erected a cross and prayed for God's aid, "for He knows that we are fighting in a just cause for the preservation of our whole race," the ensuing victory being attributed to his army's faith. Xenophobia and religion here strove together even though Cadwalla was himself a Christian. Oswald's death at Maserfield (c. 642) conformed to a different but related pattern, that of martyrdom. Killed by pagans, dying with prayers for his people on his lips (notice there were no prayers for his enemies), with the greatness of his faith soon to be revealed in miracles, Oswald became a popular saint on the continent as well as in England, his conduct as a warrior being integral to his appeal.[1] Although not the Christianity of the Beatitudes, his was a Christianity blessed by the church.

To fight the enemies of God was consistently regarded as virtuous, and contemporaries gave religious contexts to wars such as those waged by Charlemagne against the continental Saxons in the eighth century. Thus the Saxons were "hostile to our religion" and thought it "no dishonour to violate and transgress the laws of God and man."[2] Effective defence demanded retaliation, the theoretical justification for aggression being symbolised in the almost invariable attempts, as familiar to Charlemagne and the Saxons as to Alfred of Wessex and the Danes a century later, to suppress the defeated pagans' religion and impose Christianity upon them. In England, theories of holy war appear to have been crystalized by the resistance to the Vikings. When the homilist Aelfric wrote towards the end of the tenth century, "*Justum bellum* is just war against the cruel seamen [i.e., Vikings] or against other peoples that wish to destroy our lands," he was restating an ideology that had received practical application for over a century.[3] In Alfred's reign (871–99) West Saxon nobles may have fought the Danes with swords decorated by symbols of the Evangelists; under the year 883 the *Anglo-Saxon Chronicle* associates a military success at London with prayers and the despatch of alms to foreign shrines; frequently the *Chronicle* characterises the Danes as pagans or heathens, in contrast to Alfred's Christianity and contacts with Rome; in Asser's panegyric on Alfred, the king's religion predominates, and his image as a Christian warrior is thereby enhanced.[4] The efficacy of Alfred's policy depended less on intellectual niceties than on the blending of an ideal of the holy warrior with secular necessities and with the existing military habits and cultural expectations of his thegns.

These continued under his successors to determine literary responses to Danish attacks. The spirit of crusading is close by the hand of the author of the poem about the battle of Maldon (991), who portrayed the doomed hero Britnoth in the midst of the carnage thanking "his Creator for the day's work that the Lord had granted him" and who depicted Britnoth's loyal thegns praying to God "that they might take vengeance for their lord and work slaughter among their foes."[5]

It was Carl Erdmann's view that the overt Christianization of the emergent knightly class of the eleventh century provided an essential context for the promotion and acceptance of the crusade.[6] Yet many of the images and ideas which later found expression in crusading rhetoric, although not receiving universal academic approval, were available to an English audience well before the year 1000. In the prehistory of crusade ideology Aelfric's *Lives of the Saints* are prominent. Written in the vernacular in the late tenth century and addressed explicitly to a secular, aristocratic audience, Aelfric's homilies on St. Oswald, St. Edmund of East Anglia, and Judas Maccabeus provide strong testimony of the penetration of the ideal of "godes thegen," God's thegn who fought for his people and religion.[7] Aelfric presents two contrasting views of the Christian warrior and ruler. He retains the hagiography of the passive Christian martyr in St. Edmund, who deliberately throws away his weapons before facing his pagan tormentors. But this traditional image is allied with that of active resistance.[8] As in Bede, Aelfric's Oswald is shown fighting to win power as well as to defend his faith and people. Even the passivity of St. Edmund is balanced by the martyr's determination, against the advice of his bishop, to resist the heathen Danes whatever the odds. Edmund's patriotism, like Oswald's, complements his religion, but in his case significant emphasis is laid on the impossibility of a Christian ruler ever compromising with unbelievers.

Aelfric's gloss on Edmund's actions was derived directly from Abbo of Fleury's *Life* of Edmund, composed in England a few years before, and therefore reflects a wider intellectual tradition which unites English and continental, specifically Carolingian, experience. Recently Abbo's *Life* has been described as a "key text in the early ideology of the crusades."[9] It could be argued, however, that it goes little further than Bede or Alfred. A more striking model of holy war is that presented in Aelfric's poem on the Maccabees, based on the Book of Maccabees in the Apocrypha, which was later extensively plundered for Biblical analogies by crusade propagandists. Here there is no passivity in the face of the infidel threat: "We verily fight for ourselves against them, and for God's law."[10] The war waged by Judas Maccabeus is eminently just; it is an honourable outlet for ambitions of glory; it is at times aggressive (Judas taking the fight across the desert to his enemies); and it is bloodthirsty. Just as in Aelfric's poem on Oswald, Penda dismembers the saint's corpse by cutting off the head and right arm, so in identical fashion Judas mutilates his fallen enemy Nicanor—a detail not in the Apocrypha.[11] This mixture of sacred and profane foreshadows the crusade. Also like later crusaders, Judas is concerned with the remission of his soldiers' sins; to him the faithful appeal for armed help against the heathen who oppress them; and at his side angels from heaven ride into battle.[12] Aelfric is clear that before the final victory of Christianity many unbelievers shall perish "for their hardheartedness against the heavenly Saviour."[13] As for Judas himself

> Manyfold were his great battles;
> and he is as holy, in the Old Testament,
> as God's elect ones, in the Gospel-preaching;
> because that he ever contended for the will of the
> Almighty.[14]

Aelfric's respect for God's warrior was strong, and his view of the infidel unites his world with that of later, more famous expressions of Christian militancy and intolerance, such as the *Song of Roland*. In his poem on the Exaltation of the Cross he combines the image of the Christian warrior with images of the Holy City of Jerusalem and the Cross of Redemption, when the Emperor Heraclius fights "the enemy of God" to recapture the Holy Cross from the Persians and restores it, in simple humility, to Jerusalem, scene of Christ's Passion. It was this restoration, Aelfric maintained, that was commemorated on Holy Cross Day, 14 September, a day later especially associated with crusading.[15] Aelfric wrote to be understood by the wider lay community, and there is little reason to think his views eccentric or unpopular, even though they failed to receive full academic acceptance for another two centuries.

In one important respect, however, Aelfric displayed a mentality different from the crusader's. While repeating familiar explanations of just war, Aelfric interprets Judas's temporal battles as prefigurations of the more important spiritual warfare against the Devil instituted by Christ and waged by monks, "God's Champions in the spiritual battle, who fight with prayers not swords; it is they who are the soldiers of Christ."[16] Thus Aelfric stopped well short of the great volte-face of Urban II. The contrast can be put starkly. In 1070 the victors of Hastings, who had fought in a just cause against schismatics and oath-breakers under a papal banner given to Duke William specifically for this purpose, were forced to do penance for their part in the slaughter. On crusade after 1095 the carnage itself could be the penance. Even in 1070 an important distinction was drawn in the penalties imposed on monks who fought at Hastings: those who fought for gain were treated as murderers; those who fought in public war, as a duty, were given a penance of three years only. The key was right intention, for lay as much as monkish warriors.[17] After 1095, however, Christ of Peace, to the dismay of many, became a God of War, whose Sacrifice required direct, physical, and violent revenge, and whose temporal estate demanded forceful military defence by a Judas Maccabeus rather than by an Edmund, king and martyr. Aelfric might have understood St. Bernard's *De Laude Novae Militiae* (1128), a paean of praise for the ideals of the military order of Templars, but he would have rejected its fusion of the military and the monastic; for him the real conflict remained in the cloister, not on the battlefield, and the soldier could not compare with the monk either in the battle against Satan or in the search for individual salvation. This was the emphasis shifted by Urban II.

In the eleventh century the image of Jerusalem and the concept of holy war, the twin pillars of Urban II's call to arms, were familiar in England. A royal charter of 1093 used "the holy city, God's celestial Jerusalem" as a metaphor for the world redeemed by the death of Christ.[18] The English had been eager pilgrims for centuries, and in the eleventh century pilgrims to Jerusalem included important clerics like Abbot Withman of Ramsey (c. 1020) and Bishop Aldred of Hereford and Worcester, later archbishop of York (1058). Aldred's successor at Worcester, Wulfstan, had to dissuade a hermit at Malvern, Aldwine, from going to Jerusalem.[19] Laymen also made the journey: Harold Godwinsson's brother Sweyn died returning from the Holy Land in 1051–52; shortly after the Conquest, Ulf, a Lincolnshire landowner and friend of Bishop Aldred, departed for Jerusalem, possibly not intending to return, as he left a will disposing of his lands.[20] The Norman rulers of England, from whom Ulf may have been escaping, had an equally illustrious, if shorter tradition: William I's father, Robert the Devil, had led a large pilgrimage to the Holy Sepulchre in 1035 and had died on the return journey. This tradition of pilgrimage merged with the new concept of an armed pilgrimage, a crusade, but even after the Franks had secured the Holy Places in 1099 they remained distinct. The Englishman Saewulf who visited Palestine in 1102–3 was a pilgrim, not a crusader.[21]

Throughout the eleventh century the Christianization of the warrior ethic continued. The papacy elevated certain military campaigns into holy wars, such as Leo IX's war against the Normans in Italy in 1053, and the Norman invasions of Moslem Sicily in 1060 and of England in 1066. The figure of the holy warrior was increasingly familiar. In 1067 a benefactor of the Benedictine nuns of St. Amand, Rouen, was described as "miles christi," and William of Normandy himself fought at Hastings wearing relics round his neck.[22] Militant Christianity, enshrined in tales of Charlemagne or warrior saints, was in fashion in the Anglo-Norman world. According to Orderic Vitalis, Gerold, chaplain to the violent and worldly marcher baron Hugh of Avranches (d. 1101), tried to raise the moral tone of his master's household with stories of "the deeds of holy knights," including the martial saints Demetrius, George, Theodore, Sebastian, Maurice, and Eustace, and legends of William of Orange, the "holy athlete" who served God first in war against the Moors and later in the cloister (and who became a central figure in twelfth-century *chansons des gestes*).[23] Foreign cults of warriors arrived to join the indigenous saints even before the First Crusade allowed freer access to Eastern hagiography. Aelfric had celebrated St. George and St. Sebastian, and they, together with St. Maurice, were invoked in an English *laudes regiae* (c. 1084 x 1095) to guarantee "safety and victory to all English princes and armies." They were also among the saints the First Crusaders saw riding to their aid at the head of celestial battalions.[24]

There was personal contact with the East as well. For a generation the cousins of the Norman conquerors of England had been disputing control of southern Italy and the Adriatic coast with the Byzantine empire. In the armies facing the Norman Robert Guiscard and his son, the future crusader Bohemund, were the emperor's crack troops of the Varangian guard, dominated on this front by English refugees. Both Alexius I and his predecessor had relied in time of crisis on English mercenaries, the supply of whom continued or even increased as William I's reign progressed and the lot of the English aristocrat worsened. These Varangians derived not only from the drifting English exiles in Scandinavia but also from direct recruitment, witnessed by the Byzantine coins and seals dating from the third quarter of the eleventh century found in Winchester.[25] The presence of these Englishmen so close to the emperor possibly added to the tension and mistrust in relations between Alexius I and the crusaders, including the Normans Bohemund and Robert of Normandy, when they arrived at Constantinople in the winter and spring of 1096–97. Before the First Crusade, however, it had not only been Englishmen that the Greeks had hired. William of Poitiers hints that Duke William had been approached to help Byzantium against "the great power of Babylon." There is evidence of Byzantine recruitment in Normandy during the 1080s, and twenty years earlier Norman mercenaries such as Roussel de Bailleul had been an important element in Byzantine armies on the eastern frontier.[26]

THE FIRST CRUSADE

On the face of it, English involvement in the First Crusade was minimal and peripheral. One of the most striking features of the First Crusade was its self-consciously French character. Most of the planners and leaders thought of themselves as *Franci*. Contemporary observers ignored the lack of actual political or linguistic identity and pointed to an image of neo-Carolingian unity, a Frankish Christendom, as in the *Song of Roland*, beset by infidels. All four eyewitness writers who described the First Crusade saw themselves as Franks, even though they came from Provence, northern France, and southern Italy.[27] The preaching was concentrated in France and the Rhineland. On his tour in 1095–96 Urban II appeared deliberately to avoid Anglo-Norman lands. Although the *Anglo-Saxon Chronicle* talks rather formally of the great excitement in England provoked by Urban's sermon at Clermont, most modern historians have tended to share William of Malmesbury's opinion, expressed somewhat pompously forty years later, that only a faint murmur of "Asiatic events" crossed the "British Ocean."[28] Yet the First Crusade was not without its impact; it was later described by one English chronicler as the greatest event since the Resurrection.[29] References to Englishmen on the crusade of Peter the Hermit in 1096 are too vague to carry conviction. However, William II's brother, Robert Curthose, duke of Normandy, led an army to Palestine which included some who had English connections, like the Fleming Arnulf of Hesdin, who died at Antioch, and William Percy, who according to the traditions of his foundation, Whitby Priory, died at Montjoie, the hill outside Jerusalem where the crusaders had their first sight of the Holy City on 7 June 1099. Percy's crusade had tangible repercussions in England; before leaving he had endowed Whitby with additional estates, although whether through piety or in return for cash is unknown.[30]

Any narrow definition of the term "English," however, even in the sense of being "from England" distorts the nature of the cross-Channel Anglo-Norman aristocracy, especially at the highest levels. In Curthose's company were Ralph de Gael, former earl of Norfolk, with his wife and son; Edith, sister of William de Warenne, a great landowner in southern England; Philip of Bellême, son of Roger of Montgomery, the conqueror of Shropshire; Eustace of Boulogne, holder of an immense fief in southeast England; and Odo, bishop of Bayeux, half-brother of the Conqueror and for twenty years one of the most powerful men in England as well as Normandy. None were English by birth or tongue, but all had strong connections with Norman rule in England. The Anglo-Norman aristocracy was hardly distinct from that of northern France in general. Curthose's mother had been Flemish, and one of his companions on crusade was his brother-in-law, the count of Blois. The wife of another crusader, Baldwin of Boulogne, later king of Jerusalem (1100–1118), was an Anglo-Norman, Godehilde of Tosni, who was actually described by later writers as English.[31] The ruling classes in England were by no means isolated; their failure to participate reflected not ignorance but politics.

The most immediate impact of the crusade on England was financial. To pay for equipment and to ensure adequate cash for the journey, crusaders great and small were forced to sell, lease, or mortgage their lands and rights; Curthose was no exception. In an agreement probably engineered by Abbot Jarento of St. Bénigne, Dijon, the papal legate who crossed to England early in 1096, Robert pledged the duchy of Normandy to William Rufus for three years in return for ten thousand silver marks. The money was raised by taxation and was shipped across to Normandy in September, ready for Robert's departure.[32]

Historians have usually followed Orderic Vitalis in suggesting that Curthose was escaping the threat to his rule posed by Rufus.[33]This may be unfair. The agreement with Rufus was shrewder than at first it appears. Curthose needed a vast treasure to pay his way, guarantee his retinue's support, and establish his position in the allied crusader force. Ten thousand marks was just such a treasure, obtainable in no other way and equivalent, F. Barlow has estimated, of a quarter of Rufus's annual income (although as that income is unknown the calculation must be highly speculative).[34] In the event the money was used effectively, Robert maintaining a large contingent and exerting considerable military and political influence throughout the crusade. Without a treaty, Rufus could have annexed the duchy anyway, but the mortgage arrangement enabled Robert to secure his patrimony. In 1096 Robert was unmarried and without an heir of his body; the treaty at least provided that in the event of his failing to return, the duchy would be kept in the family, protected from potential interlopers like the king of France or the count of Anjou. Of course there was a risk that Rufus would refuse to restore the duchy on Robert's return, and Orderic suggests that Rufus had no intention of doing so. But in the circumstances of 1096 the agreement contained much to the brothers' mutual benefit.[35] Curthose, struggling to retain the undivided loyalty of the Norman barons, might have feared disinheritance at any time. Under the treaty, which was guaranteed by the pope, he could expect on his return to contest his rights backed by an enhanced reputation, papal sanctions, and the desire of neighbouring rulers and elements within the duchy to prevent Rufus dominating northern France. With such a coalition, Curthose's chances of outfacing his brother after the crusade may well have seemed greater than his chances of survival in 1096. In the event Curthose, determined not to default or give Rufus any excuse to withhold the duchy, obtained the pledge money from his new father-in-law, Geoffrey of Conversano, lord of Brindisi, on his return journey.[36] Rufus's unexpected death in August 1100 meant that the 1096 treaty was never tested, but that is no reason to assume its weakness.

Collection of the 1096 mortgage money in England caused resentment, and decades later the bad taste lingered in the mouths of monastic chroniclers. The rate of the tax (four shillings to the hide) was heavy and fell on laity and clergy alike, to the especial fury of clerical commentators. The need for bullion was supposed to have driven monks to strip their reliquaries and melt down their ornaments.[37] Church leaders were less outraged, the bishops of Winchester and Rochester assisting the assessment, and Archbishop Anselm agreeing to contribute even though he lacked the required cash and had to borrow two hundred marks from the Canterbury monks, in return for a grant of one of his manors for seven years.[38] The money was realised within six months. Collection was in the hands of the king's tenants-in-chief, whose own demesne land was exempt. They passed the burden down to their tenants. Earls, barons, and sheriffs despoiled their knights and villeins, reported one writer. A generation later William of Malmesbury explained that many clergy saw the only way to meet royal demands was to drive farmers off the land. In this manner the levy, and perhaps the reasons for it, penetrated down through the social hierarchy.[39] Before he paid, Anselm had to be persuaded, perhaps by the legate himself, to help the king raise the mortgage, and it is possible that the destination of the money weighed with the archbishop on the side of payment. The spread of information in this way may be one explanation for the dissemination of news of the crusade, in the absence of any evidence of organised preaching or publication of the crusade decrees of the Council of Clermont.[40] Another channel of information may have been the informal but extensive monastic network. But even if the tax of 1096 made people aware of the call to crusade, it may have deprived those below the highest ranks of the aristocracy of the means to answer. On the continent crusaders, eager to convert land into cash, looked to the church to supply the bullion, but in England in 1096 all available bullion was going to the king. Thus the mortgage permitted a prominent role on crusade for Robert Curthose, whilst helping determine that he would have few companions from England.

It is sometimes claimed that the circumstances of Norman England—the need to oversee newly acquired estates, the need to keep ahead of potential rivals, and the continuing opportunities to acquire land and status in Scotland and South Wales—negated the appeal of the crusade. This is only partly true. The idea that material gain was a prime motive for taking the cross in 1096 (or at any other time) is not supported by the evidence. Most crusaders intended, like Curthose, to return, and the majority of survivors did so after the battle of Ascalon in August 1099. Of itself, land hunger was neither a common nor a likely compulsion to men who would have had to mortgage, lease, or sell the land they already possessed in order to go on crusade. For excitement and military glory neither Scotland nor Wales competed as rival attractions. Robert FitzGodwin, who campaigned in Scotland in 1097 with Edgar Atheling, the erstwhile claimant to the English crown, received land in Lothian, an enhancement of status, and possibly some excitement in the process. None of these prevented him from making the journey to Jerusalem in 1102.[41] Crusading was not an equivalent to profiteering at home, but a complete alternative that could only be undertaken in specially favourable political circumstances. The reason for the lack of English aristocratic response was the absence of overt encouragement from the king, the great feudatories, and the church.

For the king the crusade had placed Normandy in his hands, thereby opening further avenues of expansion, into Maine for example. He had no time for Jerusalem. Royal priorities inevitably influenced not only the king's immediate entourage but also a wider circle of barons and knights who looked to royal patronage, favour, local offices, and pay to supplement their incomes. Men of ambition would think it unwise to absent themselves from the scene, even if they could afford to, just when new opportunities for advancement were appearing. Men of prudence may have lacked confidence in the integrity of their estates or political status during a long absence. Above all, the king himself gave no lead. Having had to swallow his pride and admit a papal legate to England as the price of the treaty with Curthose, Rufus did nothing to encourage a long legatine stay or to organise preaching.

Without royal initiative widespread enthusiasm would be difficult to excite; without ecclesiastical support, it would be almost impossible. Archbishop Anselm's attitude was distinctly lukewarm. Earlier in his career he had adopted the traditional monastic view that the way to Jerusalem lay in the cloister, a spiritual journey. In 1086 he had referred to terrestrial Jerusalem when trying to dissuade a young man from fighting in the East, calling on him to "renounce the Jerusalem which is now not a vision of peace but of tribulation," and he alluded prophetically to the "treasures of Constantinople and Babylon which must be seized with bloodstained hands."[42] A decade later he could hardly oppose the new policy of the pope whose recognition he had

18

championed, but there are no clear signs that he had fundamentally changed his priorities. Late in 1096 Anselm instructed the bishop of Salisbury to stop the abbot of Cerne from leading some of his monks to Jerusalem and to prohibit other monks in the diocese from doing the same. The ban, which echoed papal policy, was extended to the sees of Exeter, Bath, and Worcester and had the backing of the king.[43] Whilst canonically proper, Anselm's approach, and the lack of organised preaching, did nothing to create an atmosphere of enthusiasm. During the archbishop's exile at the papal court in 1098–99 his opinions changed—or were changed by his hosts—but even then his softened attitude applied only to laymen taking the cross. The coolness towards clerical involvement remained.[44] By no means alone in disapproving of monks leaving the cloister, Anselm, unlike other contemporary supporters of the reformed papacy, did little or nothing to arouse lay participation, at least until after the end of the First Crusade. It is perhaps significant that, in contrast to many historians of the time, Anselm's biographer and confidant, Eadmer, appears to have been uninterested in the crusade.

Some in England exerted themselves. The monks of Cerne acquired a ship costing thirty shillings. Others, distinct from Curthose's army, actually embarked for the East. When the crusaders arrived at Antioch in October 1097 they discovered, according to an eyewitness, Raymond of Aguilers, that the nearby seaport of Lattakiah had already been captured by a fleet from the West that included sailors from England, *angli*, whose presence was later noted by other chroniclers and in a letter of the citizens of Lucca in 1098. There is some confusion over the chronology of the fleet's movements, but it appears that from early 1098 at the latest English ships (thirty is Raymond of Aguilers's figure) were operating in the Levant, probably in concert with flotillas from the Italian ports of Lucca, Pisa, and Genoa, and possibly in cooperation with the Byzantine authorities in Cyprus. Raymond of Aguilers, who was in the crusader camp at Antioch, declares that the fleet had sailed from England via the Straits of Gibraltar. Many of the details are obscure, and are made more so by later writers, notably Albert of Aix and Orderic Vitalis, but it is reasonable to suppose that from the early stages of the siege of Antioch until after Easter 1100 (when the new Patriarch of Jerusalem, the former archbishop of Pisa, Daimbert, recorded with regret that most returned home) English ships and sailors played an important role in maintaining the lifeline of food and supplies between Byzantine Cyprus and the crusaders on the Syrian mainland, and that angli joined the march south from Antioch into Palestine in Spring 1099 and were present at the fall of Jerusalem on 15 July.[45]

These angli appear almost from nowhere. Accounts of eleventh-century pilgrimages suggest the use of the land routes to Constantinople or southern Italy, but before 1097 it is not possible to identify regular links between England and the Levant beyond the traffic in mercenaries to Byzantium. It has been suggested by J. Shepard that the English sailors in 1097–98 were themselves mercenary troops in the pay of Alexius I, sent to cover the advancing crusader forces as they penetrated hostile territory in northern Syria. The evidence for this attractive theory is, unfortunately, less than convincing, as it relies heavily on a fantastic if not fanciful account in a much later Norse saga, the *Edwardsaga*, of the arrival in Byzantium in the early 1090s of a fleet of English mercenaries. Even if the saga account has a kernel of truth—a big "if"—there seems no good reason or evidence to suppose that this contingent of putative Varangians continued to act together as a maritime force for many years. The argument is further vitiated by the assumption of the participation in the 1097–98 fleet of Edgar Atheling. In fact his involvement in the East must date from 1101–2, as he was in Scotland late in 1097. He was only associated by a later generation with the First Crusade. The closest contemporary sources make no connection between these English and the Varangians and if, as one account has it, they cooperated with Curthose, any such identification becomes less credible. It should also be noted that the letters of the citizens of Lucca and of Archbishop Daimbert mentioning the angli fail to link them to the Greeks.[46]

The most likely provenance of the English fleet was the ports of southern England, especially those of the Channel, which were in close contact with the continent and could hardly have been ignorant of crusade recruitment in France. Half a century later, despite a similar lack of apparent organised preaching in England, ports like Southampton, Hastings, Dover, London, and Ipswich provided significant contingents for the Second Crusade who acted in concert with groups from the other side of the Channel and North Sea. The pattern in 1096–97 could have been similar, although there is no evidence that it was. Equally, men from the southern ports probably had some experience of long-distance trade with the Bay of Biscay, Galicia, and the Iberian coast, with which they were certainly well acquainted in the early twelfth century.[47] A further clue to the identity of the angli is provided in the account by Ralph of Caen of their dealings at Lattakiah with Curthose, when they sought the duke's protection from local marauders. Ralph wrote in 1113, after Curthose's fall from power and imprisonment in 1106, and his hostile assessment of the duke's motives in going to Lattakiah—that he wished to escape the privations of the camp at Antioch—need not be taken too seriously. That Robert did leave the siege of Antioch at about the time Ralph said he did is confirmed by Raymond of Aguilers.[48] If, therefore, the Lattakiah episode can be credited it is likely that behind the chroniclers' description of angli lay men with Norman connections; Anglo-Saxon emigrés or refugees would have been less likely to seek protection from the duke of Normandy, and the investment required to mount such an expedition would have been found more easily in the Anglo-Norman rather than the Anglo-Saxon community.

THE GROWTH OF A TRADITION

The fall of Jerusalem in 1099 marked the end of the First Crusade but the beginning of the crusade movement. Immediately, new military expeditions embarked, and although they met with disaster in Asia Minor, the early years of the twelfth century saw a flood of pilgrims, merchants, and warriors eager to exploit the new spiritual and material opportunities offered by the conquest of the Holy Places. All had their welcome and some their reward in the new Frankish principalities which struggled to establish a secure presence in Syria and Palestine. The success of the crusade and the popularity of the Holy Land affected both intellectual attitudes to warfare and the behaviour of individuals.

The explosion of literary panegyric consequent on the capture of Jerusalem did more than Urban II's preaching to delineate and publicize this new form of holy war, which offered salvation as well as glory. The combination soon caught the imagination of clerical writers and laymen, despite the initial coolness of canon lawyers. The new synthesis of penitence and militancy did not, however, obliterate older perceptions; instead, traditional descriptions of and attitudes to holy war began to be penetrated by distinctive crusading motifs. From the start popes applied the privileges associated with the journey to Jerusalem to other areas of military endeavour, such as Spain, of which they approved. However, for much of the twelfth century crusading was not a systematic canonical institution or even theory but an imprecise set of attitudes and habits which became fused with older concepts of pilgrimage and just war.

The progress of the new ideal can be seen in works not specifically associated with crusading, as well as in those composed in praise of it. In the former, the tenacity of precrusading formulations of holy war is evident. According to Henry of Huntingdon, in 1138 troops from the north of England fought against the Scots at the battle of the Standard under the banners of local saints. They were granted absolution before the battle, their cause was declared "very just" by the bishop of the Orkneys, and they were promised release from all penalties of sin if they fell in defence of the patria. The bishop's speech to the soldiers combined secular patriotism and military pride with martyrdom and absolution.[49] Most of these themes had histories separate from the crusade. The immensely popular story of the First Crusade probably sharpened the emphasis of Henry of Huntingdon and other early twelfth-century writers on direct ecclesiastical blessing and grants of remission of sins to those killed, but there was nothing explicitly crusading about these features. By contrast, in Geoffrey of Monmouth's *Historia Regum Britanniae* (1136) a similar traditionalism is given added force by specifically crusading images. At the battle of Bath, Arthur promises, traditionally enough, to keep faith with God and to revenge his countrymen, and "with God's help" the pagan Saxons will be defeated. Then Archbishop Dubricius exhorts the troops, "You who have been marked with the sign of the Christian faith" (i.e., the cross) to follow in Christ's footsteps even to death: "If any one of you is killed in this war that death shall be to him as a penance and an absolution for all his sins."[50] This ideology is halfway between the bishop of Orkney's speech and a crusade sermon, the crusading overtones of the sign of the cross, the footsteps of Christ, martyrdom, and indulgence combining effortlessly with the older elements of prowess, religion, and patria. Although possessing no value as a historical source for the kings of Britain, Geoffrey's *Historia* does reflect the values of his own society, the author setting out to be popular; dedicatees of his *Historia* included King Stephen and Robert, earl of Gloucester and Waleran, count of Meulan, himself later a crusader.[51]

Geoffrey's use of crusade analogies in the 1130s is unsurprising, for by then the events of 1095–99 were widely known. So were the ideological glosses placed on these events by writers such as Baudri of Borgeuil, whose rewriting of the anonymous eyewitness account the *Gesta Francorum* formed the basis of the versions by the Anglo-Norman writers Orderic Vitalis and Henry of Huntingdon.[52] Most chroniclers felt the need to extol the wonders of the journey to Jerusalem. In the 1120s and 1130s Orderic devoted a whole book in his chronicle to it (book 9); William of Malmesbury, who derived his narrative from another eyewitness, Fulcher of Chartres, half of book 4 of his *Gesta Regum Anglorum*.[53] Not only did chroniclers maintain a keen interest in the affairs of the new Frankish states in the East, they were also instrumental in adding to the glamour of the First Crusaders themselves. As early as 1125 William of Malmesbury recounted fanciful tales of Godfrey de Bouillon cutting Turks in two and of Robert Curthose, still alive when William wrote, slaying the Moslem leader Kerbogha at Antioch (which he did not) and being offered the crown of Jerusalem (which he had not been). Orderic similarly presented a number of embroidered anecdotes.[54] By 1140 such stories had been incorporated into Gaimar's vernacular *L'Estoire des Engleis*.[55] In turn these chroniclers influenced western attitudes towards the Greeks and Moslems by their inclusion of hostile caricatures, such as the antagonistic descriptions of the Byzantines by William of Malmesbury and Orderic.[56] In helping to spread suspicion and intolerance, these writers played a not insignificant role in the hardening of western attitudes towards their neighbours.

Literature was not the only channel of influence. Even though there were no recruitment or preaching campaigns in England, at least until the visit in 1128 of the founder of the Templars, Hugh de Payens, and possibly not until the Second Crusade, men took the cross and set out on pilgrimages, often returning with concrete reminders of the Holy Land. An early instance of this was the endowment of Barnwell Priory by Pain Peverel with "most genuine relics in gold and precious topaz which he acquired on the Antioch campaign with Robert Curthose." Later in the century a visitor brought the former pilgrim and recluse Godric of Finchale relics from Jerusalem, much to the hermit's delight.[57] Within a century of the First Crusade England no less than the rest of western Europe was strewn with physical witnesses to the spiritual importance of the detritus of the Holy Places. Some relics could have a dynamic effect. At the siege of Lisbon during the Second Crusade in 1147 an Anglo-Norman priest, probably from East Anglia, brandished a portion of the True Cross in exhorting English crusaders to the final assault: "Adore Christ . . . who on this wood of the saving Cross spread out his hands and feet for your salvation and glory. Under this banner, only do not hesitate and you shall conquer."[58] And they did.

The reputations of the crusaders themselves not only encouraged the manufacture of legends but created a lasting popular impression parallel to the literary flights of fancy. One of Curthose's companions, the "most famous" Count Robert of Flanders, was eulogised by Henry of Huntingdon as having been "on a journey to Jerusalem because of which his memory will live for ever."[59] Such fame could pay dividends. According to Robert of Torigni, writing in Normandy a few years after the death of Curthose in 1134, the former duke was given especially pleasant conditions of custody by his brother Henry I after his defeat at Tinchebrai in 1106, because the king had decided to treat him "not as an enemy captive but as a noble pilgrim."[60] Conversely, those like Stephen of Blois or the Grandmesnil brothers, who deserted the besieged crusader army in Antioch in 1098 by letting themselves down the walls at night, were mocked as "clandestine rope-dancers" (*furtivi funambuli*).[61] Guilt and public opprobrium drove two of them, Stephen of

Blois in 1101 and Ivo of Grandmesnil in 1102, back to the Holy Land. Stephen's death at Ramlah in 1102 redeemed his reputation to the extent that forty years later he could be mentioned, perhaps with a touch of irony, by the English baron Brian FitzCount to Stephen's son Henry, bishop of Winchester, in the same breath as those crusaders who had kept faith.

Brian's remarks came in a letter he wrote (c. 1143) in response to an invitation by Bishop Henry to look back at what the bishop saw as Brian's treachery to his brother King Stephen.[62] Brian, a partisan of Matilda, replied with a stinging attack on the bishop's own failure to keep his oath to Matilda. He declared himself unafraid to review the past, choosing as his example "the worthy deeds of our famous ancestors" who had liberated Jerusalem from the pagans, having exchanged their castles, towns, wives and estates for pilgrimage.

> Count Stephen, your father, Count Robert of Normandy, Raymond, count of St. Giles, Bohemund, Robert, count of Flanders, Count Eustace of Boulogne, Duke Godfrey and many other magnates, knights and rich men. And you know that those counts were not like the count of Mohun [a former supporter of Matilda who had deserted to Stephen]. When I look back at those men who obeyed the command of the pope, who left so many and so much and who, as loyal knights [boni milites] captured Jerusalem by arms and assault and there established Godfrey, a good and legitimate king, and when I look back at your own command to men to help the daughter of King Henry [i.e., Matilda], I do not fear. . . ."[63]

For Brian FitzCount there was nothing artificial or contrived about the crusaders' reputations, which served as lively models of honour and fidelity. This secular admiration, couched in terms of knightly loyalty rather than religious virtue, may well express Brian's own views and stands as an important complement to the opinions of clerical authors. However, the First Crusaders provided more than a model of virtue; theirs was an example to be followed.

EARLY ENGLISH CRUSADERS

In the years after 1099 the tradition of crusading developed among Englishmen. Some of the names have survived, like that of "Harding of England" who arrived with a number of English ships at Jaffa in July 1102.[64] It is tempting to identify him with one Harding of Oxford, who sometime before 1109 also made the journey to Jerusalem, in preparation for which he had given the abbey of Eynsham two houses in Oxford.[65] But Harding was a common name. Others, however, can be recognised with greater certainty from a variety of documentary sources, mainly land deeds, and from chronicles. Although the number of tenants-in-chief embarking for Jerusalem at times other than the large crusades was always small, crusading appealed to almost all other sections of free society that could afford it. There were landowners, like Robert of Baskerville (c. 1109), Peter de Oburvilla (pre-1130), Philip of Braouse (pre-1126), Godwin Gilbert of Huntingdon (1133 x 1160), Philip Basset of Postwick (1147), Henry of Groxhill (1152), and the leaders of the English crusaders on the Second Crusade, Hervey of Glanvill, Simon of Dover, and Saher of Achelle; burgesses like Andrew of London (1147) and Roger of Cornhill (pre-1130); merchants like the future hermit Godric of Finchale (1102?) and the Viels of Southampton (1147); and clergymen such as Gilbert of Hastings, whom the crusaders installed as bishop of Lisbon in 1147.[66] The Anglo-Saxon tradition was represented by Edgar Atheling and Robert FitzGodwin (1102).[67] English ships sailed for the Holy Land in 1102, 1107, 1112 (when en route the English sailors were hired by rebels to fight against Queen Urracca of Leon-Castile), 1140 (or 1142 when crusaders from Southampton and Hastings joined an unsuccessful attack on Lisbon), and, famously, in 1147. In 1143 a number of Welsh crusaders were apparently shipwrecked and drowned in the Mediterranean.[68] Elsewhere, in 1124–25 a former sheriff of Shropshire, Reginald of Bailleul, found his way to Spain, his campaign with the Aragonese being described by Orderic in terms directly analogous to crusading.[69]

The motives of these men varied and it is dangerous to simplify. The *Gesta Stephani* claims that repentance moved two notorious men of violence, William Peverel of Dover and Philip, bastard son of Robert of Gloucester, to join the Second Crusade. To dismiss this as stereotyped clerical moralising is unsatisfactory. It may have been politically convenient for both men to absent themselves from England, but Peverel met his death on crusade and Philip had abjured "the spirit of cruelty" after a serious illness; they may have had genuine spiritual impulses. Equally, the same chronicler, picking up a theme already prominent in popular crusade literature, ascribed the general popularity of the Second Crusade to the desire of the "vigorous youth" of England for vengeance against the infidel.[70]

Political embarrassment was an obvious spur, as with Arnulf of Hesdin on the First Crusade and Waleran of Meulan on the Second. The one was a former rebel; the other was caught in a hopeless conflict of loyalties when England and Normandy, in both of which he held land, 25 were controlled by rival claimants. Some made a virtue of necessity, as did Ralph of Mandeville who, on going to Jerusalem in the 1140s or 1150s, raised money on English lands he apparently was abandoning anyway.[71] Individual motives could be mixed. Ivo of Grandmesnil went on crusade in 1102 both to avoid political unpleasantness and to purge his cowardice at Antioch, his crusade being a form of voluntary exile.[72] The crusade could provide satisfaction for specific crimes as well as for general sin; in 1128 a Welshman, Morgan, son of Cadwgan, went to Jerusalem to atone for fratricide.[73]

Godric of Finchale, on the other hand, after many years as a merchant, felt the need to improve his soul and to turn away from Mammon, his first crusade being a symbol as well as a ritual of repentance.[74] Piety should not be underestimated. Before his departure Godwin Gilbert granted his house and some land in Huntingdon to Ramsey Abbey, stipulating that if he died without an heir the abbey was to keep the property and inherit all his other land; even if he did leave an heir, the abbey was still to retain the property granted and receive half of the rest of his land and money. Godwin also hinted that he was contemplating becoming a monk himself.[75] Robert of Torigni's description of the 1140s as a time of increasing humility, penance, and contrition may be monastic hyperbole, but it was indeed a period of extensive lay patronage of the church. Increasing numbers of the laity were seeking the cloister or the hermit's cell and making generous provision for their souls.[76] The journey to Jerusalem fitted this pattern of religious investment and pious gestures. For the first time one shrine was so redolent of spiritual power, so publicized, and so popular that western Christians seemed to regard the pilgrimage to the Holy Sepulchre almost as an obligation, as compelling and certainly as attractive as the Moslem's mandatory *haj*, the pilgrimage to Mecca. There was a practical reason for this; as contemporaries were quick to notice, after 1099 the Holy Places were more accessible. The element of pilgrimage was the basis of the popularity of active crusading. Fulcher of Chartres, chaplain to King Baldwin I of Jerusalem, described the flotillas of pilgrims, "French as well as English, or Italians and Venetians" arriving in the earliest years of the twelfth century "timidly in single ships, or in squadrons of three or four." After landing at Jaffa "they came on to Jerusalem; they visited the Holy of Holies, for which purpose they had come." Fulcher lamented that so few pilgrims remained in the Holy Land.[77] Many pilgrims were crusaders as well.

On both occasions that Godric of Finchale visited Palestine his behaviour, as described by his biographer, was that of a pilgrim, seeing as many of the Holy Places as possible, imposing on himself severe physical privations, eating frugally, and praying often; in the church of the Holy Sepulchre he felt as if he had been made a new man. Yet on each occasion he had deliberately and formally taken the cross, which his biographer characterised in openly military terms, Godric being described as bearing on his shoulders the *Dominicae vexillum crucis*, the banner of the Lord's Cross. Godric the humble penitent was a crucesignatus, a crusader.[78] Evidently his biographer, Reginald of Coldingham, prior of Durham, in the second half of the twelfth century found no contradiction in this; nor presumably did Godric, as Reginald had obtained his information from the hermit himself and had sent the finished *Life* to him on his deathbed. Visitors to the Holy Land like Godric called themselves pilgrims because there was no other suitable word, but many of them were not content with the scrip and staff alone and took the cross expecting both to adore and to fight, probably in that order. The tradition of crusading was established as a form of pilgrimage by these crucesignati. Bound by few canonical conventions, their authorisation came from no specific papal command but rather from local priests and their own consciences. Any definition of crusading which seeks to place these early twelfth-century crusaders into a rigid or discrete canonical framework ignores the human reality.

Although Prior Reginald's description of Godric's two crusades makes it unlikely that, as some historians have suggested, Godric was the English seaman in whose ship Baldwin I sailed from Arsur to relieve the siege of Jaffa in May 1102, many pilgrims were prepared to fight.[79] In the same year, Robert FitzGodwin, who had come with Edgar Atheling, was killed defending Baldwin I at Ramlah, and the arrival in July of the fleet carrying Harding of England caused the Egyptians to withdraw from Jaffa. In 1103 the pilgrim ship taking Saewulf and his companions home, when set upon by a Moslem fleet from Tyre and Sidon, provided nearly two hundred fighting men, pilgrims "ready to die for Christ," who "seized their arms and fortified the turret of our ship." The Moslems withdrew only to have some of their own ships plundered by other Christians, possibly also pilgrims, from Jaffa. In 1112 and 1140 (or 1142) men who had taken vows to visit Jerusalem were directed towards battles in Spain.[80]

Not all pilgrims were crucesignati, but the crusader was always a *peregrinus*, a pilgrim. The interaction of the two elements is well illustrated by Albert of Aix's account of the appearance at Jaffa in 1106 or 1107 of a fleet manned chiefly by Englishmen, but including some Danes, Flemings, and Antwerpers.[81] On arrival these pilgrims, who called themselves "soldiers of the Christian faith," declaring that the cause of their journey was to worship at the Holy Sepulchre, asked the king for a safe-conduct to Jerusalem and back. Baldwin I supplied them with an armed escort. Having "redeemed their vows to God in the temple of the Lord's Sepulchre," they returned to Jaffa where they immediately offered a rather surprised Baldwin their military services. After some discussion an attack on Sidon was proposed, and the pilgrims' fleet was mobilized. However, the Moslem rulers of Sidon bribed the king, who postponed the assault on Sidon; the pilgrims thereupon dispersed and returned home. This sequence of events was repeated more than once, when eager visitors were greeted by more circumspect locals. Albert of Aix's "English knights" were keen to fight but, significantly, only after they had fulfilled their vows. Not yet had Jerusalem been separated from the pilgrim's vow nor had travelling and fighting alone become sufficient fulfillment of crusaders' oaths. On the Second Crusade, when such a severance was proposed to English crusaders in Portugal, a number of them objected strongly.[82]

Any potential crusader had to convert his assets into cash, and the commonest source of cash tended in the twelfth century to be religious houses. From the First Crusade numerous continental and, later, English charters show how crusaders sold, leased, or mortgaged property in return for loans or gifts of money.[83] Whilst the financial penalty to crusaders was heavy, the demand for bullion or specie provided favourable opportunities for those who possessed either and were staying at home. By his ability to exploit the resources of his kingdom, William Rufus acquired Normandy and at the time of his death may have been negotiating a similar deal with another putative crusader, the count of Poitiers.[84] In 1102 Robert of Meulan gave Ivo of Grandmesnil five hundred marks in return for Ivo's land for fifteen years.[85] However, religious houses were in the forefront of this business because they were repositories, if not of coin, then of precious metal or jewels. Monks melted down reliquaries and ornaments to pay the 1096 tax and perhaps, as on the continent, to subsidize crusaders. This market received regulation in Eugenius III's bull *Quantum Praedecessores* of 1146, but the pope was probably reacting largely to existing practice.[86] The mechanics and wider social significance of financing crusading are discussed in detail in a later chapter, but it is worthwhile to note here that the experience of the two generations after 1095 established the pattern for the future, defining in practice, if not in theory, what crusading was all about.

Most English crusaders intended to make a round trip to Jerusalem, but not all. Although he died en route, Ivo of Grandmesnil had no intention of returning, his contract with Robert of Meulan stipulating that at the end of fifteen years the crusader's son, Ivo the Younger, was to marry Robert's niece and receive his patrimony.[87] In the first half-century or so of the Latin states in the East, a number of men with the cognomen "Anglicus" appear as witnesses to charters in the kingdom of Jerusalem. A William Anglicus witnessed a charter of Baldwin III in 1144 and a namesake, possibly the same man, appeared on a charter of the master of the Hospital in 1146. At about the same time a John Anglicus attested a charter of the prior of the Holy Sepulchre. These men were probably clerics, the latter conceivably a canon of the Holy Sepulchre.[88] More influential and certainly from England was William, prior of the chapter of the Holy Sepulchre, who was appointed first Latin archbishop of Tyre in 1128, a man, so one of his successors wrote, of praiseworthy habits.[89] Another influential Englishman was Ralph, for thirty years until his death in 1174 chancellor of the kingdom of Jerusalem. He had been bishop of Bethlehem from 1156 and was a favourite of Queen Melisende, who had unsuccessfully tried to instal him as archbishop of Tyre in 1146. The chronicler William II of Tyre, Ralph's successor as chancellor, described him as very learned but very worldly.[90] Ralph, although holding no benefice before 1146, had risen to prominence in Queen Melisende's service in the 1140s. In the years after the Second Crusade he played an active role in the affairs of the kingdom as chancellor, diplomat, and even military commander, being wounded on campaign in Egypt in 1165. He was one of a number of enterprising English bureaucrats who took service abroad, a Levantine counterpart to men such as Thomas Brown, minister to Roger II of Sicily and later an official of Henry II in England's exchequer. It was under Bishop Ralph that the remarkable Byzantine mosaics were installed in the Church of the Nativity in Bethlehem. Archbishop William I of Tyre, and possibly the otherwise obscure William and John Anglicus, may well have been scions of noble families from which, B. Hamilton has suggested, the senior clergy of the kingdom of Jerusalem recruited men sent out by relatives or friends to make their ecclesiastical fortunes in this new market of preferment.[91] This colonial aspect is hinted at by the chronicler William of Tyre, who ascribed Ralph's elevation to the see of Bethlehem to his being a fellow countryman of the then pope, the English Hadrian IV.[92] As for lay settlers, there is no firm evidence that men from England settled in Outremer before about 1150, although it is not unlikely. It has been suggested that Robert FitzGodwin was given land in the East either by Godfrey de Bouillon or Baldwin I, but it is more likely that he arrived in Jerusalem only very shortly before his death in 1102.[93] Some Englishmen may have accepted the financial blandishments of Patriarch Daimbert and remained behind when the English and Pisan fleets left the Holy Land after Easter 1100.[94] Later it is clear that laymen of English extraction made their homes in the East, but of the earlier years of Christian occupation more cannot be said.

By the time of the Second Crusade (1146–49) active crusading had become established in many levels of English society, its traditions, legends, language, and appeal consolidated into a large and familiar literary topos. There was also a political dimension. Although not obviously an enthusiast himself, Henry I was inescapably involved. An ally and neighbour who also held large fiefs in England, Eustace, count of Boulogne, was the senior member of the ruling house of Jerusalem; in 1118 he had been suggested for, if not offered, the crown of Jerusalem. Henry's interest was more with the destiny of the county of Boulogne, which he secured after Eustace's death for his favoured nephew Stephen, but the Boulogne claim to Jerusalem could not be ignored. Of no less interest was the marriage of Count Fulk of Anjou to Melisende of Jerusalem in 1129, as it coincided with the alliance with Anjou whereby Fulk's son married Henry's daughter Matilda. It was through this marriage that Henry II, Henry I's grandson, derived his close relationship with the later twelfth-century kings of Jerusalem. Henry I was also touched by the affairs of Antioch when Raymond of Poitou, who was living at Henry's court, was invited (c. 1133), to become the husband of the Antiochene heiress.

If the tangled politics of Outremer could not fail to entwine the rulers of the West, neither could the needs of departing English crusaders. Royal consent was required for the territorial arrangements of Ivo of Grandmesnil and Peter *de Oburvilla*, whose nephew paid the exchequer five marks for the custody of his uncle's lands.[95] The flow of men was not all one way. In 1128 Hugh de Payens, founder of the Templars, visited Normandy and England, according to the Peterborough version of the *Anglo-Saxon Chronicle*, to raise troops to help the Holy Land.

The military orders had been created to serve the needs of the invigorated pilgrim traffic in Palestine. In 1118 Hugh de Payens and a few companions banded together under monastic vows to provide military protection for pilgrims on the road from Jaffa to Jerusalem. A decade later his Order of the Temple of Solomon, already enjoying the patronage of Baldwin II of Jerusalem, received papal approval and a rule of its own. At the same time Bernard of Clairvaux, who had been instrumental in obtaining recognition for the order, wrote his treatise *De laude novae militiae* celebrating this new form of monasticism, an order of knights dedicated to God's service and bound by monastic vows. The Order of St. John of Jerusalem, the Hospitallers, had begun as a charitable hostel in Jerusalem catering to the medical needs of pilgrims.

Receiving papal approval for their independence in 1113, the Hospitallers gradually assumed a military role similar to that of the Templars, until by midcentury the functions of the two orders in the defence of the Frankish principalities had become almost indistinguishable. Although neither order entirely abandoned its charitable duties of hospitality and protection, it was in their position as self-financing, independent professional soldiers that their chief importance lay. Free of all authority except the pope's, the two orders rapidly amassed property throughout Christendom and began to pursue vigorous and at times disruptive autonomous policies in the East. In time, their network of possessions in East and West and their international facilities for protection and security attracted them to the role of bankers as well as guards.

The visit to western Europe of Hugh de Payens in 1128 was the beginning of this process of securing international patronage outside the Holy Land which established the military orders as characteristic and unique creations of the crusade movement in England as in the rest of Europe.

Henry I gave money, and large numbers may have answered Hugh's appeal, apparently more than at any time since the First Crusade. According to the *Anglo-Saxon Chronicle,* when the crusaders reached Palestine the promised campaign failed to materialize, to their disillusion and resentment. However, this is contradicted by William of Tyre's story of how Hugh's recruits, whether or not they included angli, joined in an attack on Damascus in 1129.[96] In fact, recruitment was probably confined to France, even if Englishmen extended financial patronage to Hugh's mission and order.[97] No companion of Hugh from England can definitely be identified. However, Hugh did attract funds and arouse interest. Within a decade the Templars and Hospitallers were receiving grants of lands, rents, churches, mills, fisheries, and other property throughout the kingdom. The spread of pious and charitable grants to the new, specifically crusading, orders and others associated with the Holy Land confirms a general interest in the crusade and Outremer. Sometimes the links of patrons and the crusade were strong. Gilbert of Lacy, a patron of the Templars, joined the order; Saher of Achelle, leader of one of the contingents which embarked for Jerusalem in 1147, had given property to the Templars in Kent and Leicestershire; another benefactor, Roger of Mowbray, went on crusade to the Holy Land three times between 1146 and 1186.[98] Templar churches built in imitation of the Temple of Solomon (i.e., the al-Aqsa mosque) in Jerusalem began to appear, the Old Temple in Holborn dating from perhaps as early as 1135 and certainly before 1144. A round church had been built in Cambridge some years before by the Augustinian canons of the Order of the Holy Sepulchre on land given for the purpose by the abbey of Ramsey; the model in this instance was apparently, as with Hospitaller churches, the rotunda of the Holy Sepulchre.[99]

THE SECOND CRUSADE

In such ways was consciousness of and sympathy for the crusade, and especially for the Holy Land, established in England. The process bore fruit when in 1146 Eugenius III, in response to the loss of Edessa to the Moslem leader Zengi in 1144, appealed for a new general Christian effort to throw back Islam. A number of English tenants-in-chief and other landowners took the cross and joined the army of Louis VII of France in 1147. They included Waleran of Meulan, earl of Worcester, William of Warenne, Roger of Mowbray, William FitzGilbert of Clare, Philip of Gloucester, William Peverel, Philip Basset of Postwick, Hugh Tirel and Bishop Roger Clinton of Chester.[100]William of Aumale, whose father had been on the First Crusade, took the cross but because of age and obesity failed to depart.[101] Louis's crusade was a disaster. Casualties were high, Warenne and Peverel being among the dead, and nothing was achieved for the Holy Land.[102] Without Jerusalem as a military goal there was a certain aimlessness, especially once the crusaders reached the Holy Land. In the West the crusade had been seen by its principal propagandist, Bernard of Clairvaux, as a uniquely advantageous opportunity for laymen to achieve redemption. His revivalist preaching played down the image of Jerusalem and broadened the ideological and geographic parameters of the movement, authorising crusading attacks on the Wends. This may have been good theology, but it made for poor strategy and ignored the importance to crusading of pilgrimage, which placed Jerusalem as the emotional focus even when not the military objective. The one major success of Jerusalem-bound crusaders was the siege and capture of Lisbon in October 1147. Despite clerical assurances that the process rather than the goal of crusading was beneficial and secular inducements to stay in Portugal after the fall of the city, many pressed on the following spring to the Holy Sepulchre.[103]

The crusaders who assisted the king of Portugal in taking Lisbon came from Flanders, the Rhineland, and in particular from southern and eastern England—Norfolk, Suffolk, Kent, London, Hastings, and Southampton. There has survived an eyewitness account of this campaign, the first such by an English author, probably written by a chaplain in the entourage of Hervey of Glanvill, the leader of the East Anglian contingent and prominent local landowner in the area. This work, the

De Expugnatione Lyxbonensi, reveals the commitment of the middle ranks of society, lesser landowners, knights, burgesses, merchants, and priests, as well as the sophisticated organisation and self-regulation whereby the many small and not always harmonious groups of crusaders formed a sworn mutual association which bound them together under a series of agreed rules.[104]

The crusaders who assembled at Dartmouth in May 1147 from all over southern England constituted a specifically English contribution. Most of them, including some of their leaders, like Glanvill, were tied to lives and estates in England alone and lacked the continental dimension of their social superiors. By contrast, the crucesignati who were great Anglo-Norman feudatories, like Waleran of Meulan or William of Warenne, were in their careers and family associations as much, if not more, French than English. It was appropriate that they, unlike the crusaders at Dartmouth, should travel east with the king of France, who was almost as much their lord as the king of England.

The *De Expugnatione* contains three speeches on the subject of crusading, put into the mouths of the bishop of Oporto, Hervey of Glanvill, and a "certain priest," perhaps the author himself.[105] These illustrate some salient features of the mid-twelfth century crusading mentality, with which it is appropriate to conclude this chapter on the introduction of the crusade ideal into England. Although written by an eyewitness soon after the events described, it is unlikely that the speeches are verbatim reports. Rather, they are more or less formal reconstructions. However, the sentiments expressed by the three very, perhaps deliberately, different speakers bring close the flavour of mid-twelfth century crusade oratory. The bishop of Oporto was trying to deflect the crusaders from their journey to the Holy Land so they could assist in the capture of Lisbon, just as earlier crusaders had been induced to turn aside in 1112 and 1140. The essence of his appeal lies in the often quoted remark, "The praiseworthy thing is not to have been to Jerusalem but to have lived a good life while on the way." Therefore, despite much that was standard, the circumstances of the speech were peculiar. It is possible that the writer preserved something of the original, for the tone is pleading, even a little uncertain of the ethics of what is being proposed. The bishop, whose sermon is the most complex of the three, may have had some of the vocabulary of St. Bernard but lacked his self-confidence, which is perhaps a little surprising considering that the Spanish Reconquista had been associated with the Jerusalem crusade by the papacy and by some Iberian bishops at least since 1123–24. The bishop began by calling the crusaders God's People, who had left home on "a blessed pilgrimage" in order to obtain from God an eternal reward. As in St.

Bernard's preaching, the bishop's sermon emphasised repentance, the "new baptism," and spiritual rewards, insisting that the act of crusading was as efficacious as its completion. The familiar theory of holy war is described in terms of vengeance, defence, and recovery of homeland: "Sin is not in waging war but in waging war for the sake of plunder," and "When a war had been entered upon by God's will it is not permitted to doubt that it has been rightly undertaken." As an added incentive the bishop promised the crusaders money which, ironically in view of his earlier remarks, turned out to be plunder from Lisbon. In the acceptance of meritorious Christian violence coupled with the centrality of repentance, the bishop echoed St. Bernard. Yet he had to go further to disassociate the goal of the pilgrimage (Jerusalem) from the process of the crusade. In his dry and slightly involved academic exposition of the traditional theories of just war of Augustine and Isidore of Seville, the bishop called upon a longer heritage into which the crusade was accommodated, using citations from the late eleventh-century canonist Ivo of Chartres as the basis of his sermon. His message was essentially conservative, couched in a crusading context, but hardly comparable with later, especially thirteenth-century, apologia. The theory was still fluid and flexible, the crusade only one, perhaps not yet even the dominant, type of holy war. Yet the appearance of such a piece in written form anticipated growing ideological solidity, as the corpus of such works increased. In the dissemination of crusade ideas, chronicles like the *De Expugnatione* played their part both in the story told and in the preservation of some ephemeral literature of crusading.[106]

Hervey of Glanvill's speech is much less intellectual, its tone much more like that of Brian FitzCount's letter to the bishop of Winchester. Glanvill was pleading for the unity of the crusaders and the maintenance of their sworn association, and he too cited the example of their ancestors and appealed to their honour, pride, and hope of glory. To those reluctant to join the attack on Lisbon he urged "the counsels of honour," the secular obverse to the bishop's plea of religious duty. The speech of the unknown priest, made to English crusaders just before an attack on the walls of Lisbon, has a more robust, demagogic clerical style, filtering donnish ideology so that it could be immediately accepted by troops about to see action. In place of the carefully balanced, almost diplomatic arguments of the bishop of Oporto there are asserted commands, the intellectual arguments being whittled down to basic and emotive essentials. Holding a relic of the True Cross he urged confession and repentance; only the pure of heart could earn God's forgiveness for their sins. Reaching a crescendo of passion, with his audience beginning to "fall down upon their faces with groans and tears," the priest declared: "If it should happen that anyone signed with this cross should die, we do not believe that life has been taken from him, for we have no doubt that he is changed into something better. Here, therefore, to live is glory and to die is gain." This last phrase, borrowed from St. Paul, rang down through crusading history. St. Bernard was one of the first to use it in a crusade context in his letter to the English in 1146.[107] Perhaps that is where the priest got it from. At the end of the sermon many of the listeners received the cross.[108] This may be thought an odd thing to happen as most were presumably crucesignati already. Possibly this renewal of the vow reinforced morale and the confidence that they were doing the right thing, after all the earlier arguments. It also brought under the scope of indulgences those who may not have earlier taken the cross. Alternatively, it may indicate that for all the speech's vividness the author was adapting a standard crusade sermon, applicable with only minor adjustments to many different circumstances.

Formal or realistic or both, the *De Expugnatione*'s account of the sack of Lisbon brings us face to face with the experience of twelfth-century crusading. A variety of intellectual and emotional responses lay behind the well-turned epithets of the preachers: the conservatism of the bishop of Oporto, Glanvill's standard recital of knightly mores, and the more specifically crusading passion of the priest. The prosaic realities are also displayed: anxieties about the wives left behind, suspicion of foreigners, squabbles over precedence and booty, and the battlefield heroism of the seven young men from Ipswich who unflinchingly protected the crusaders' siege engine from fire.[109] It is hard, in the light of this and earlier evidence, to agree entirely with R. W. Southern that "the Crusade fell on dull ears in England" until the Third Crusade.[110] This remark could only apply to the great magnates, upon whom large-scale crusades depended for recruitment, organisation, and finance. It is true that the greatest landowners in England did not, in contrast to their French counterparts, join either the First or Second Crusades in any numbers. But among their tenants and vassals, men with few cosmopolitan connections or high political entanglements, but with a surer claim to being identified as English, active crusading had taken hold. In the experience of those who did embark for Jerusalem in the years before 1150 lies the true history of how the ideal became a habit of mind and action to be passed down to succeeding generations. In these years family traditions were established which later sustained the whole movement: traditions of the already great, the Percies or Mowbrays, or the less great—Hervey of Glanvill's brother Roger, his son Rannulf, and Rannulf's nephew Hubert Walter all in their turn became crucesignati.[111] The crusade, the new way of salvation, had become part of English life.

2

Henry II: The King over the Water?

Crusading in the years between 1149 and 1187 presents a paradox. Interest in the affairs of the East remained strong and contacts were close, yet the private commitment of those who went on crusade was matched by public inertia, a refusal by the rulers of the West to go to the aid of Outremer. Many English crucesignati and pilgrims went east in the generation between the Second and Third Crusades, including such influential figures as Roger of Mowbray, William of Mandeville, Henry of Lacy, Hugh of Beauchamp, William Marshal, probably Robert II of Leicester, and possibly the long-serving Justiciar Richard of Lucy. In 1160 the king's constable, Walter of Hereford, resigned his offices and departed for the Holy Land with a substantial personal retinue. Once in Jerusalem, he made contact with English Templars such as Gilbert of Lacy. Most, like Walter, intended to return, although not all: Hugh of Braimuster deliberately disposed of all his property before he left for Outremer.[1] Yet, despite regular and urgent appeals from the East for a new general expedition or *passagium*, and frequent protestations by Western rulers of their anxiety for the plight of Jerusalem, no direct, large-scale military assistance was forthcoming.[2]

In this, England was no different from the rest of western Europe. Indeed, regarding the highest ranks of the aristocracy, the great families surrounding the cosmopolitan court of Henry II, it is misleading to talk of any distinct English response. The accession of the count of Anjou to the English throne in 1154 ensured that his greatest vassals would continue, like their predecessors since 1066, to identify themselves with a French overlord and their cross-Channel estates rather than with any one geographic, let alone national, area. In 1188 the contingents for the Third Crusade were allocated crosses of different colours according to their overlords—Capetian, Angevin, or Flemish—not their nations—France, England, or Flanders. Nevertheless, the Angevin "empire," and especially England, does present a slightly different picture from its

36

neighbours. The important crusaders from Henry II's lands, unlike their counterparts from the great comital or ducal houses of the rest of France and Germany, such as Flanders, Burgundy, Blois, or Saxony, lacked the resources of power and wealth to organise any significant campaigns independent of the king. In the Angevin territories, such autonomous counts and dukes simply did not exist, as all such titles were in the hands of the king and his sons. The authority wielded by Roger of Mowbray or Hugh of Beauchamp was of a wholly lesser order than that of Thierry of Flanders, his son Philip, Henry of Burgundy, Henry the Lion of Saxony, or even the counts of Champagne, Blois, and Troyes; hardly surprising, then, that their crusades should differ in scale too. This dependence within the Angevin lands upon the king for money, men, and approval tended to make the contrast between private concern and public action starker.

One general reason for the dichotomy in response was disillusion with the Christian rulers of Outremer, whose behaviour, to western eyes, hardly conformed to the heroic images of the founding fathers. This alienation was exacerbated by contact. The Second Crusade had shattered the aura of sanctity and success reflected in Brian FitzCount's retrospect of the First Crusade. The reputations of Bohemund, Tancred, and Godfrey de Bouillon remained undimmed, but after 1148 the crusade movement had to cope with failure and the seeming abandonment of God's cause by God Himself.[3] St. Bernard's explanation, that the failure was due to Christians' sin, was hardly encouraging. At the end of the century the shrewd and critical William of Newburgh blamed the disasters squarely on the sins, not of Christendom, but of the crusaders themselves, concluding that "having achieved nothing of note they returned without glory."[4] A generation before, memories were even sharper. In 1169 a letter from the entourage of the exiled archbishop of Canterbury, Thomas Becket, criticised a plan for the crusade devised by Henry II and Louis VII of France as profitless and cited "the most wretched outcome" of the Second Crusade, "grievous to the church," as an illustration that "gifts offered from theft and wrong-doing are not pleasing to God."

It was still possible to win renown, or at least remembrance, as a crusader; Stephen of Mandeville's reputation was preserved by his son's grant of two mills to the priory of Montacute, in part to commemorate his father's death "in an engagement on the road to Jerusalem." Elsewhere, however, talk of crusading bred a mocking tone. Count William IV of Nevers had died on crusade in Palestine of a fever, but, as the same letter from the Becket camp commented, he was mourned as a holy warrior "who was not even killed by Parthian darts or Syrian swords, so that not even a hero's glorious death could bring him consolation; but widow's tears, poor men's sorrow and complaints of churches are thought to have snuffed him out ingloriously."[5] Arguably, the de-mythologising of crusading was inevitable and could have brought a welcome awakening of realism, had it not been that one of the causes of the failure of the Second Crusade perceived in the West was the treachery of the Latin settlers, the so-called *pullani*, whose luxury and greed became notorious. One result of such dissatisfaction was that Ralph Niger, a well-connected academic and former intimate of the household of Henry II's eldest son, writing during the preaching of the Third Crusade in 1188, could interpret the defeat of the Jerusalemites by Saladin in 1187 as a judgement of God "well deserved by their guilt." Sin had delivered Palestine to the enemy, "hardly surprising as that land was certainly more dissolute than any other." Ralph's view was, in part, shared by the pope.[6]

Such attitudes had been consolidated by the experiences of crusaders from the West. In 1148 the siege of Damascus had been abandoned amid conflicting rumours and mutual recrimination between crusaders and pullani, the memory of which, according to the Jerusalem historian William of Tyre in the early 1180s, still rankled and had led to a decline in the frequency and duration of crusading visits from the West. While William's testimony is hardly unbiased, accusations of the obstructive-ness of local Jerusalemite intrigues pepper western accounts of crusades in this period. Even though it obviously took time for each new cru-sader to adjust to local eastern attitudes and to immediate political and military realities, as the twelfth century progressed the pullani were perhaps increasingly insensitive to the need to placate the eager arrivals from the West. For instance, after the concerted effort by the patriarch of Jerusalem, Heraclius, to recruit a new crusade from the West in 1184–85, when the crusaders arrived in the Holy Land in 1186 they found there was no fighting to be done, as a truce had been struck with Sala-din. Most of the crusaders immediately went home.[7] Such frustration made it inevitable that appeals from the East were not greeted uncriti-cally. Henry II, reflecting on Patriarch Heraclius's embassy, confided to his chaplain, Gerald of Wales, that "if the patriarch or anyone else comes to us, they are seeking their own advantage not ours."[8]

R. C. Smail has identified cycles of appeals to the West roughly every five years between 1149 and 1187, comprising "crisis, newsletter, ap-peal, preparations."[9] All the important Jerusalem embassies visited Henry. But the view from his court did not necessarily confirm the sense of doom which the ambassadors hoped to convey. Not only had each successive crisis been contained, but, until the 1170s, the kings of

Jerusalem had, as often as not, been on the offensive. Despite the loss of Edessa (1144), the reign of Baldwin III (1143–62) had witnessed no apparent decline of Frankish power, and in 1153 the strategic strong-hold of Ascalon fell to the Christians. In the 1160s a series of aggressive campaigns into Egypt were conducted by Amalric I, during which he penetrated as far as Cairo. Only after the consolidation of Saladin's power in Egypt from 1169, his unification of Egypt with Syria after 1174, and the accession of the leper Baldwin IV to the throne of Jerusalem in 1174 did the strategic outlook for the Latin states take on the gloomy aspect so familiar to later historians, both twelfth and twentieth century. Even so, as late as 1177 western crusaders arrived in the Holy Land to find plans afoot for a new invasion of Egypt.[10] In the West, those of Henry II's courtiers who took up their pens as chroniclers or homilists recorded not only Christian defeats but victories as well. Baldwin IV's victory over Saladin at Montgisard in 1177 made quite a splash in western accounts and reinforced belief in the efficacy of divine support.

But the role of God in the affairs of the East also presented a difficulty for those appealing for help for the Holy Land. If, as commonly believed at the time, sin explained defeat, for eastern envoys to argue they were being defeated was a tacit admission of pullani sinfulness. If, however, they denied defeat, how could they successfully appeal for assistance? They were thus caught between incredulity and disdain. Perhaps only a don with the eccentric, if academically impeccable, opinions of Ralph Niger could have appreciated the point fully, but it is worth noticing that the enthusiastic crusaders of 1188–92 fought to avenge the insult to Christ and prove themselves worthy of his mercy rather than to aid the pullani, who continued to strike Anglo-French observers as a shifty lot.[11] Moreover, despite their military problems and pleas of weakness, the Jerusalemites gave every impression of great wealth. Ralph Niger, admittedly a hostile witness, expressed astonishment at the lavish os-tentation, the gold, silver, and perfumes of Patriarch Heraclius and his companions when they passed through Paris in 1184; a display, Ralph declared, no western ruler could match.[12] To be fair, Heraclius made it plain that he was not primarily after money but men. However, the trappings of pomp might not have helped his cause.

The irony of the situation was that with the accession of the Angevin dynasty to the English throne came a closer official concern with the affairs of the pullani and the politics of the Holy Land. Henry II's pater-nal grandfather, Fulk of Anjou, had become king of Jerusalem in 1131, and for the next fifty years kings of a cadet Angevin line ruled in Jeru-salem, the uncles and cousins of the king of England. At Henry's court there was considerable interest in crusading. Apart from the magnates who went to the Holy Land, royal clerks like Roger of Howden noted the passing events of Outremer in detail. Templars and Hospitallers were familiar figures in Henry's entourage; one of them, a Templar called Roger, being the king's almoner in 1177. The king was personally kept in touch with the eastern Mediterranean by a stream of embassies and correspondence from Jerusalem, Antioch, and Constantinople, as well as by his own agents. Henry himself was not indifferent to the plight of Outremer, in 1166 and 1185 authorising taxation, and in 1182 bequeathing money to help the Holy Land. However, despite frequent talk of going on crusade he did nothing until events forced his hand.[13]

Rumours of an impending crusade were circulated, no doubt deliberately, during the Becket dispute in the 1160s. In 1170 Henry gave a firm pledge to the archbishop of Tyre that he would embark on crusade. He did so again to the papal legates at Avranches in 1172 as part of his penance for the murder of his archbishop, and again at the treaty of Ivry with Louis VII of France in 1177. In the same year he held out the prospect of his own departure to the count of Flanders, and ten years later, before news of Hattin and the fall of Jerusalem had reached the West, he promised the same to Philip II of France.[14] Philip's refusal to believe Henry is scarcely surprising after such a sequence of false trails and broken promises; his cynicism echoed that of his father twenty years earlier. Hearing of Henry's supposed enthusiasm for a crusade, Louis VII was reported to have commented that he would not credit it "until he saw Henry's shoulders marked with the sign of the cross"; this sight was delayed until, in the wake of the news of Saladin's destruction of the kingdom of Jerusalem, Henry took the cross at Gisors in January 1188.[15] Until then anticipation was deliberately encouraged only to be as surely disappointed, for Henry II's responses were determined by the political problems he faced in the West. Such constraints constitute perhaps the most important reason for official western inaction.

The key to Henry's crusade policy lies in his diplomatic objectives, above all the need to maintain his empire intact. Specifically, this required ceaseless vigilance and care in his relations with the kings of France, Louis VII and Philip II, whose vassal Henry technically was as duke of Normandy and Aquitaine and count of Anjou. Early in his reign, Henry had been thwarted from asserting direct control over Toulouse by the intervention of Louis VII (1159). Thereafter, he recognised that he needed Louis's approval for the annexation of Brittany; his neutrality in Henry's endless problems with some of his vassals, especially in Poitou and central France; and his passivity in asserting Capetian claims on the borders of Normandy itself, notably in the Vexin. Of particular importance in the 1160s was Louis's acceptance of Henry's dynastic dispositions, in which all these problems came together. Louis's approval was finally given at Montmirail in 1169. Although not resolving all disputes between the two monarchs, this represented a considerable step towards the internal and external security of the Angevin lands. On the other side, Louis and Philip were always willing to make life difficult for their immensely powerful vassal. Both regularly championed the causes of malcontents in the Angevin "empire." The growing independence of Henry's unruly and ambitious sons presented the Capetians with even more scope for mischief. In 1173–74 Louis joined Henry's eldest son, the young Henry, and Eleanor of Aquitaine in a concerted attempt to destroy the old king's power; fifteen years later Philip II, in conjunction with Richard of Poitou, by now Henry's eldest surviving son, succeeded where his father had failed.

In these circumstances, Henry used the crusade as a means of keeping his French overlords talking, rather than plotting or fighting, as neither the pious Louis VII nor his more ruthless son could afford to be seen to oppose the cause of the Holy Land. However, the very tensions Henry hoped to ease by his promises to take the cross made it unlikely he would ever honour his pledges, especially as, despite triumphing over his enemies in 1174, the sources of conflict with overlord, family, and vassals remained. Diplomacy won Henry occasional freedom of manoeuvre; it did nothing to solve the underlying problems of maintaining unity, order, and authority throughout his huge dominions, which were his lifelong priorities.

If strained relations with the Capetians precluded any unilateral decision to go on crusade, more specifically between 1164 and 1172 the Becket controversy and its aftermath prevented the ecclesiastical and papal alliance necessary to organise a full-scale crusade. As the archbishop's supporters put it, "What will the expedition of Jerusalem profit which the kings have planned if peace is not first restored to the church?" Later the sworn commitment of 1172 was overtaken by the rebellion of 1173–74, which almost destroyed Henry's power, as he himself explained in a letter to King Amalric of Jerusalem.[16] The threat posed to Henry's authority and to the stability of his dominions by his "ferocious" sons never disappeared.[17] The accession in France of the fifteen-year-old Philip II in 1180 created a new set of difficulties, whilst at the very time of Heraclius's embassy in 1184–85 Henry was endeavouring to solve the problem of Ireland and to pacify his sons Richard and Geoffrey of Brittany.[18] Without a concerted peace with his French overlord, his own sons, and his vassals, a crusade by Henry would have been politically imprudent and would have placed at risk all that he had tried to achieve in establishing his rights within his territories. The reason Henry and his councillors gave for resisting Heraclius's appeal for help in 1185 was compelling. Henry was needed in the West; his duty, as his councillors made plain, lay in preserving peace and maintaining order and justice in accordance with his coronation oath.[19] As for Henry's sons, themselves potential leaders of a crusade, their policies were increasingly dominated by their hopes for the succession. In 1182–83 the young Henry, denied an independent role by his father in the West, threatened to seek it in the Holy Land. According to Gerald of Wales, in 1185 Prince John begged to be allowed to answer Heraclius's call for the help of one of Henry's sons, if the father could not go east. If true, John probably regarded Palestine as more glamorous than his ordained destination, Ireland. The more reliable Ralph of Diceto, however, specifically noted that, as none of Henry's sons were at the relevant meeting with Heraclius, it seemed to those present unsuitable to decide anything on their behalf.[20]

Suspicion of Jerusalemites and unpropitious political circumstances may have provided solid reasons for Henry's inactivity. But it is also plain that throughout his reign Henry used the prospect of his departure on crusade as a negotiating tactic, having little direct association with the military situation in Palestine or eastern requests for aid. As early as 1163, discussion of disputes with Louis VII were related to the needs of the Holy Land.[21] In 1168 Henry persuaded William of the White Hands, bishop-elect of Chartres, to convey to Louis an offer to accompany the French king to the Holy Land. Louis refused to believe a word of it, but the point of the exercise was noticed by a member of Becket's entourage, John of Salisbury: "Yet Louis was the more inclined from then on to enter an agreement with Henry."[22]

The portrayal by Bishop Gilbert Foliot of London of Henry as an enthusiastic crusader probably convinced few, but in the negotiations leading to the important conference at Montmirail in January 1169 the card was played with greater effect.[23] Henry discussed a crusade with Louis, and a story was put about that the English king wished to take the cross, if only a reconciliation with Becket could be reached. Although the rumours were later recognised by Becket's partisans as having been false, at the time the archbishop was sufficiently swayed by them to attempt a compromise. As it happened, negotiations foundered on Becket's obstinacy, but the crusade proposals helped detach Louis, if only briefly, from the archbishop's party. It was a significant achievement, as the Montmirail conference resulted in an Angevin-Capetian dynastic settlement.[24]

A year later Henry used the crusade to enlist the support of the archbishop of Tyre, the envoy from Jerusalem, in obtaining a settlement of the Becket problem and some territorial claims from Louis VII. Maximum effect was achieved by publicity, at which Henry was adept:

> To lend greater colour to his crusading zeal, Henry discussed peace with the church with the help of great men and men of religion and of his household . . . . he used the archbishop of Tyre's offices in this, laying before him first of all God and his Christianity . . . as his sureties in the presence of a gathering of archbishop, bishops, abbots, and many notables; and secondly he named his uncle, the king of Jerusalem.[25]

For the gambit to continue to work, however, Henry's proposals at some stage had to be precise; thus he was forced to give a hostage to fortune by setting a deadline for departure at Easter 1171.

The murder of Becket in December 1170 initially allowed Henry to delay further. However, reconciliation with the church inevitably included a renewed crusade commitment. At Avranches in May 1172, as part of his penance for his involvement in the murder, Henry swore to take the cross for a period of three years at Christmas and to depart the following summer unless his services were urgently required in Spain to resist the recent Moslem incursions, in which case the crusade would be postponed for the duration of the Spanish campaign. It may be noted that the Spanish enterprise was not regarded as a substitute for Holy Land crusade, merely a legitimate reason for postponement.[26] Possibly, Becket's murderers had already been sentenced to spend fourteen years with the Templars fighting the infidel in the Holy Land. Henry promised to provide enough money for the Templars to support two hundred knights for a year.[27] The immediate political advantages of the Avranches agreement were demonstrated during the Great Rebellion of 1173–74, when the pope lent his support to Henry against his sons and Louis VII in circumstances which made it impossible for Alexander III to insist on the fulfilment of Henry's crusade promise. Thirty years later an embittered Gerald of Wales claimed that, around 1175, the pope had allowed Henry to commute his crusade oath into one to found three religious houses, a redemption reminiscent of William of Aumale's in 1150.[28] Ralph Niger, another critic with close associations with the English and French courts, later recalled Henry's promises to Louis VII before Becket's murder and his oath at Avranches, "but by bribing the pope he flouted his vow and oath"; otherwise contemporary sources make little comment.[29] Henry seems to have got away with doing nothing.

Pope Alexander III may not have required a bribe to turn a blind eye. Until the treaty with the emperor Frederick Barbarossa in 1177 he needed allies. Both Henry and Louis could also have been useful in southern Europe, as fears persisted of further Moslem attacks in Spain and anxiety grew at the spread of heresy in southern France; in 1178 both kings apparently toyed with the idea of a campaign against the heretical Cathar *perfecti* of Toulouse.[30] Henry was prepared to keep the crusade in play, either through confidence or a lack of alternative ruses. In 1176, in order to delay the expedition east of the count of Flanders, Henry promised either his own participation or a contingent of troops.[31] At Ivry in September 1177 Henry bound himself to go on crusade with Louis VII, as part of a general settlement whereby the rights of each were to be respected and outstanding disputes put to arbitration. The key stipulation, which helped Henry undermine his disaffected vassals in France, was that of mutual protection of life, limb, and worldly honour. Details of the conduct of the crusade and the preservation of each king's lands in his absence were also agreed.[32] The chances of these terms being put into operation were limited. Louis was aging, soon to die, and his son was still a boy. Henry had the reverse problem; he was still active, but his sons were maturing and restless.

The crusade commitment persisted. Although when Henry renewed the Capetian treaty with Philip II in 1180 the crusade clauses were dropped, both kings reiterated their commitment to help the Holy Land in answer to Alexander III's appeal of January 1181. In the same year Henry tried to persuade the count of Bar to divert his crusading endeavours from Spain to the Levant.[33] In his later struggles with Philip, Henry persisted in striking the pose of a crusader when it suited him. At Châteauroux in 1187 he put on an elaborate performance for the benefit of the French negotiators. Tears streaming down his face, he declared, "Lords, friends and my kinsmen, I am a sinful man and have lived a bad life. But now I wish to amend my life and errors and desire where I still have time, to be reconciled with God. Because I now have the men and the money, if it pleases my Lord and the king of France, I shall go against the pagans." What he wanted, he said, was a two-year truce. On hearing of this scene Philip II was clearly entertained, smilingly teasing his returning negotiators with "You believed all that?"[34] Nevertheless he was prepared to give Henry the truce he wanted, chiefly no doubt because it suited his own interests; possibly also because in the struggle for loyal vassals and secure territory each ruler had to be seen to be a good lord, and Henry had appealed doubly to Philip as vassal and as penitent crusader.

As circumstances never combined to render a large-scale crusade feasible or even desirable for the kings of England and France, or even the papacy, Henry avoided concerted obloquy from his political rivals, who after all were themselves guilty of the same empty promises. As long as nobody else made a move towards answering the call to the East Henry could maintain some credibility as a potential crucesignatus, despite thirty years' prevarication. Writing in 1188–89, Gerald of Wales accepted Henry's crusading zeal as genuine, blaming his failure to act on the 1173–74 rebellion; he even described Henry as "the especial supporter of the land of Palestine."[35] Admittedly, this was written during Henry's lifetime in the midst of the preparations for the Third Crusade, but its tone, however fragilely apologetic, shows that Henry's reputation stayed in good shape. Henry's personal preferences and bitter experience may also have acted as disincentives. He was a reluctant warrior at the best of times, preferring, like his grandfather Henry I, to throw money rather than men at problems. He tried to avoid battles and disliked casualties. In reaction to Patriarch Heraclius's call to arms in 1185, Henry is supposed to have remarked angrily in private, "These clerks can incite us boldly to arms and danger since they themselves will receive no blows in the struggle, nor will they undertake any burdens which they can avoid."[36]

Unwilling to crusade in person, Henry was prepared to spend money instead. In 1166 and 1185 general taxes on revenues, moveables, and property were imposed by the English and French kings, although at low rates varying between a 120th for one year and a 240th in the four subsequent years, in 1166, and between a 100th for one year and a 240th in the three subsequent years, in 1185.[37] The wider significance of these levies belongs to the history of European taxation. On Henry II's Le Mans ordinance instituting the 1166 crusade tax B. Z. Kedar has remarked, "Le Mans . . . may claim the dubious distinction of being the birthplace of income tax."[38] For Henry's immediate purposes, these taxes signalled his willingness to convert sympathy into the expenditure not of his subjects' lives but of their money. Evidence of collection is sparse, but some money was collected at Tours, its disbursement prompting a serious row between Henry and Louis VII. There is also an entry on the 1167 Pipe Roll recording the dispatch by royal ship from Southampton of "alms granted for the eastern church," which may refer to the same levy.[39]

The fate of the 1185 tax is even more shadowy, although a chronicler from Laon in northern France claimed that in 1186 Henry sent three thousand pounds to the Holy Land.[40] The lack of outcry from English contemporary chroniclers at either levy suggests that their incidence caused neither especial hardship nor particular shock, despite their novelty. One important feature was the public nature of the imposition of the taxes. Both the 1166 and 1185 ordinances paraded the names of the great who were involved—the king of France, the bishops, the papal legate—and emphasised the breadth of consultation with prelates, earls, and barons, and their universal assent to the measures, a point noted by the archbishop of Canterbury in 1185.[41] Such general agreement was politically useful; it also signalled to a wide audience Henry's serious-ness, in refutation of the cynicism of Becket's friends or the disappoint-ment and bitterness of Patriarch Heraclius.

These taxes were exceptional responses to specific political circum-stances—the renewed papal call for a crusade in 1165 and the Jerusalem embassy of 1184–85. More common were Henry's personal offers of more modest help. According to the chronicler of Meaux Abbey in Yorkshire, the Avranches promise to pay for two hundred knights for a year would have cost Henry sixty thousand gold pieces (three hundred *aurei* each), perhaps equivalent to 600 pounds, although Smail has cal-culated, from an unspecified source, a sum "not less than £2,500."[42] In 1177, Henry gave the count of Flanders five hundred marks to help his crusade and a further one thousand marks for the defence of the Holy Land.[43] In his will of February 1182 Henry bequeathed twenty thousand marks to the Holy Land: five thousand each to the Templars and Hos-pitallers, another five thousand to be held jointly by the masters of the military orders for "the common defence of the land of Jerusalem," and a final five thousand for miscellaneous religious houses, lepers, re-cluses, and hermits in Palestine. Here, too, the king was careful to se-cure the widest publicity, obtaining a papal guarantee of the terms and placing copies of the will in Canterbury Cathedral (shades here of Becket and the unfulfilled Avranches terms), the treasury at Winchester, and "in his coffers" (*cofris suis*).[44] One of Henry's courtiers, Walter Map, preserved a garbled story of Henry promising a bishop of Acre sixty thousand marks, which he raised within a month "without oppressing anybody." Map's anecdote is too confused to be credited as fact, even though H. E. Mayer has tried to place the event in the spring of 1182; but in outline it is the sort of gesture Henry could have made at any time after 1165. Map's story embodies precisely the sort of public re-lations coup Henry was regularly attempting and illustrates that the pattern of royal behaviour towards the Holy Land had impressed itself on the minds of at least some observers.[45]

Public shows of generosity were evidently important. However, H. E. Mayer has gone so far as to suggest that Henry amassed, by regular annual payments from 1172, a treasure in Jerusalem worth at least thirty thousand marks by 1187. This frozen bank account was plundered in 1187 to pay for soldiers at Hattin, the ransoming of at least seven thousand captives from Saladin, and the defence of Tyre. The need to protect the Jerusalem hoard, it is argued, influenced events in the East in 1177 and 1187, and Henry's handling of his son in 1183 and of Patriarch Heraclius in 1185.[46] There is little doubt that Henry placed money on deposit with the military orders which was used in 1187. Unfortunately the evidence hardly permits any definite estimate of the size of the investment, still less of its exact provenance.[47]

If Henry had aimed at making political capital from the Jerusalem treasure, the lack of publicity is uncharacteristic. Nevertheless, Angevin money, much of it probably from England, played an important role in the defence of the kingdom of Jerusalem in 1187. But it must remain uncertain how much of it there was, how and when it reached the East, and under what terms it was held there. It is possible, for instance, that it came from the 1185 tax, which, according to F. A. Cazel's reckoning, could have raised thirty thousand marks (the sum mentioned for Henry's treasure by a Templar chaplain) and could have been transported east by the 1186 English crusaders. The Laon chronicler alternatively suggests that in 1186 Henry sent money with the patriarch and the Templars.[48] There is, however, no unambiguous evidence.

Henry's financial involvement may lack clarity but it conforms to the image of a king whose eastern commitments were subordinate to his western interest. He provided or promised to provide money to Jerusalem because it was expected of him and he could afford it. It was honourable without being extravagant or risky. Henry's generosity was usually calculated for its return. When in 1183 he gave William Marshal one hundred livres anjou to go on crusade, he received two horses and a pledge of loyalty in return. More spectacularly, in 1177 he supplied Adalbert V of La Marche with six thousand marks, twenty mules and twenty palfreys to help the count end his days on crusade, in return for which he received the whole county.[49] Stories of Henry's open-handedness, circulated by court gossips like Walter Map and Gerald of Wales, harmed neither Henry nor his exchequer.

Nevertheless, there was a consistency in Henry's crusade policy besides expediency and profit. For the Angevins, the affairs of Jerusalem were a family matter. Throughout the twelfth century the orbit of Angevin dynastic concern had been extended through a series of marriages to England, Aquitaine, Saxony, Flanders, Sicily, Brittany, and, with Count Fulk's marriage to Princess Melisende, Jerusalem. Henry's relationship with the Angevins of the Holy Land assumed increasing significance as the eastern line began to falter, popes urging Henry to follow in the footsteps of his Angevin predecessors.[50] After the death of King Amalric of Jerusalem in 1174 Henry's anxiety grew. As the closest heir of the new king Baldwin IV in the male line, Henry may already have been considered for the regency or even the crown by elements at Jerusalem. In 1176, when he got wind of the intention of Count Philip of Flanders to go on crusade that Christmas, he tried to delay the count's departure because, Roger of Howden recorded, he had been told that Philip intended to usurp the throne of the leper boy-king Baldwin IV. This was a credible threat, as Philip was, like Henry, a grandson of Fulk of Anjou. Moreover his brother Matthew had married the heiress to the county of Boulogne, Philip himself being the guardian of Ida, the current heiress to the senior branch of the house of Boulogne, from which the first three rulers of Jerusalem had sprung. The bait Henry used, perhaps pointedly, to delay Philip was a payment of five hundred marks in memory of Matthew of Boulogne.[51] Philip's presence in the East would have posed an even greater threat if the marriage contract between Melisende and Fulk had, like an earlier one between the royal families of Jerusalem and Sicily, provided for the reversion of the Jerusalem throne to the heirs of the Western spouse.

Mayer has suggested that Philip's crusade was conducted with an eye to safeguarding Henry's Jerusalem treasure. But in view of Philip's earnest attempts to remain independent between Angevins and Capetians, it is unlikely that Henry would have regarded him as the safest protector of his interests, especially given the suspicions of the count's dynastic motives. In the event William of Mandeville accompanied Philip, effectively dogging his movements, his presence, and that of his independent fund of between five hundred and one thousand marks, possibly explaining the ineffectualness of Philip's crusade. In Jerusalem the count was denied influence and made to look a fool, at least according to William of Tyre, an eyewitness who remarked on Mandeville's private influence on Philip's unhappy decisions.[52] According to Roger of Howden, Henry had promised to accompany Philip or to send knights "to defend our blood-relative [*consanguineus*] the king of Jerusalem."[53] From whom? Saladin or European interlopers like Philip of Flanders? If the latter, Mandeville could have been congratulated on a job of sabotage well done. It might have been no coincidence that the only action Philip of Flanders saw (or was allowed to see by hidden Angevin pressure) in 1177 was outside the kingdom, in the north with the count of Tripoli and the prince of Antioch.

The image of consistent behaviour based on perceived rights and responsibilities is reinforced by Richard I's actions in Palestine in 1191–

92. During negotiations with Saladin's brother in November 1191, Richard demanded the return of the kingdom of Jerusalem, so one contemporary reported in verse:

> And all belonging thereto when
> It was the leprous king's domain,
> And, as to that king had been done,
> He asked tribute from Babylon [i.e., Cairo].
> He [i.e., Richard] claimed this as his heritage
> By conquest of his lineage.[54]

In 1192 before he departed for Europe, after a year during which he assumed his right to dispose of the throne, Richard I saw his nephew installed as ruler of Jerusalem; a family affair indeed. Order and legitimacy held European society together, however precariously, and formed the twin pillars upon which the Angevins based their own rule in France and England. J. O. Prestwich has written of Richard I that he "fought his campaigns not to win territory but to defend or to recover the rights of the house of Anjou."[55] A similar judgement could be passed on Henry II, whose dynastic interest in Jerusalem had increasingly overt political repercussions in the last years of his reign.

W. L. Warren, writing of Henry's 1182 will, has remarked that since Henry "attempted no new venture, it may be said that, politically speaking, his reign was over by 1182."[56] Unfortunately, old ventures unachieved retained a nasty potential for embarrassment. In the winter of 1182–83, the king's eldest son, Henry, provoked another forlorn rebellion. Early in 1183 he vowed at the shrine of St. Martial at Limoges to take the cross, in a gesture his father attributed more to anger than to faith. Even so, the old king tried hard to persuade his son to change his mind. In Roger of Howden's account there followed a distinctly melodramatic scene, with the young Henry showing himself a worthy heir to the actor who was to shed crusader's tears for his sins at Châteauroux four years later. The young Henry insisted he had taken the vow to redeem the sins he had committed towards his father and added, for effect, that unless the old king stopped finding loopholes in the vow and obstructing his crusade, he would kill himself. The young Henry also revealed that, in fact, he had been a crucesignatus for some time but had kept this secret, hoping to be restored to his father's favour "because without his grace he did not wish to go on crusade." This overacting was answered in kind, King Henry offering to equip his son more lavishly than any other crusader to the Holy Land. In the event the young Henry died before redeeming his vow or making any signs of doing so. Nevertheless, on his deathbed he imposed its fulfilment on William Marshal, who, receiving his master's cloak with the red crusader's cross sewn on the shoulder, promised to bear it to Jerusalem. Consequently, instead of paying for a major military campaign to the Levant, Henry II supplied a mere one hundred l. anjou (about forty marks) for William Marshal's travelling expenses.[57]

This curious footnote to Angevin history contains elements of literary stereotype, yet is not intrinsically improbable. There is, for example, no reason to doubt that William Marshal went to the Holy Land as the young Henry's proxy. The prince as a crucesignatus might have hoped for ecclesiastical protection if his rebellion collapsed, and, in his repeated efforts to assert his supremacy over his brothers, a crusade, or even the status of crusader, could have enhanced his prestige. More directly, as Howden's account implies, young Henry looked to a crusade subsidy from his father as a measure of the financial and political independence long denied him. Whether King Henry would have allowed any of this must be open to doubt, but at least his son's death removed the prospect of an uncomfortably close, and almost certainly noisy, reminder of his own delicate crusade position.

There was no such escape in 1185 when Henry faced the direct entreaty of Patriarch Heraclius for his personal intervention in Outremer. However, the importance of this mission and its failure to entice any western ruler should not be exaggerated. The internal problems of the kingdom of Jerusalem and the increasing anxiety of the Jerusalemites at their chances of resisting Saladin may not have seemed so very different from the situation which had existed since the accession of the leper King Baldwin IV in 1174. As recently as 1183, the regent, Guy of Lusignan, had outfaced a large Moslem invasion force in Galilee.[58] With hindsight even of a couple of years, the reaction of western European rulers in 1184–85, particularly but not exclusively Henry II, seemed a great betrayal. At the time it was business as usual: protestations of sympathy, promises of further financial assistance, but refusals to act personally.[59] Although it is hard to see how they could have been expected to appreciate the fact, the western leaders' reactions were inappropriate, as the 1184–85 mission was more urgent than that of any of its predecessors. In the kingdom of Jerusalem the realisation of the deepening crisis had led in 1183 to an unprecedented income tax. Heraclius himself carried papal letters which explained to Henry II that Baldwin IV's illness had left Jerusalem effectively without a king and reminded him of his previous vows to go to the Holy Land. The patriarch also bore with him the keys of the Holy Sepulchre and of the Tower of David in Jerusalem and a banner of the Holy Cross for presentation to one—any one—of the western monarchs willing to help.

Some commentators saw these symbols as signifying that Heraclius was, with the support of the barons of Jerusalem, actually offering the throne of Jerusalem to whichever western ruler could be engaged. A more sober English witness, Ralph of Diceto, however, interpreted them as reminders (*memorialia*) of the Birth, Passion, and Resurrection of Christ, symbols less of authority than of the special obligations Christians owed the Holy Land, quasi relics to which, Ralph said, Henry displayed great devotion.[60] Heraclius proferred the tokens to Henry at Reading on 29 January 1185. However, an assembly of bishops, abbots, earls, and barons held at the Hospitaller priory at Clerkenwell in the third week of March strongly advised against Henry's leaving his kingdom. It is uncertain precisely what Heraclius wanted. Gerald of Wales, writing in 1189, stated that Henry had been offered the lordship and obedience of the kingdom of Jerusalem; others are less explicit.[61] If the patriarch had meant to depose Baldwin IV, the leper king himself knew nothing of it when he corresponded with Heraclius's mission.[62] On the other hand schemes to involve the princes of the West in deciding the future rule of Jerusalem were circulating in the East at the time. The new regent of Jerusalem, Raymond III of Tripoli, had only recently suggested that if Baldwin IV's designated heir, Baldwin V, should die, the pope, the emperor, and kings of England and France should be consulted on the succession. Perhaps some sort of immediate arbitration or advocacy was envisaged; in 1184 Pope Lucius III had described the Jerusalemites as seeking Henry's protection (*patrocinium*).[63] However, the concern of Henry's councillors lest the king depart suggests that a lengthy, even permanent, absence was contemplated.

Heraclius in England pitched his rhetoric high and made his gestures count, perhaps out of desperation. He had been peddling his keys and banner all across Europe without luck, one continental observer drawing a risible but slightly pathetic picture of Heraclius offering the crown of Jerusalem to almost any prince he met.[64] By the time he reached England he had little to lose, and he missed few tricks. He made great play with Henry's family relationship with the Angevins of Jerusalem and his dynastic responsibilities. He also pointedly visited Becket's shrine at Canterbury and claimed that he had personally learnt of the martyr's death from a vision experienced by a Jerusalem monk only a fortnight after the murder.[65] Supported by the shade of the dead archbishop, Heraclius reminded Henry of the Avranches oath in an evident, but risky, attempt to put moral pressure on the rarely bullied king. His efforts were unavailing, perhaps because his proposals rested on shaky foundations. It is difficult to see in whose short-term interests Heraclius was acting. Jerusalem politics were dominated by two factions, led respectively by Guy of Lusignan, husband to Baldwin IV's sister Sybil, and the king's cousin, Raymond III of Tripoli. If Heraclius had been successful in finding a western prince ready to go East, both factions would have suffered by having their wings clipped and their re-versionary interests frustrated by the presence of, if not a new king, then a recognised arbiter who would have the prestige, men, and money to dominate local politics (a role later played with some success during the Third Crusade by Richard I). Heraclius may have obtained a mea-sure of selfless agreement from the Jerusalem barons for the sort of arbitration proposed by Raymond of Tripoli, although in the light of the barons' previous and subsequent behaviour this must remain un-likely. Perhaps Heraclius and his companions, the masters of the mili-tary orders, represented a force of conciliation within the kingdom. If so, whatever solution they came up with was not assured of automatic acceptance in the East.

Heraclius's chief problem was even more damaging. Put simply, he had little attractive to offer a prince of the West. Baldwin IV was ill and likely soon to die, but he had a living nephew and two sisters already married and of child-bearing age. The patriarch could not, therefore, propose a repeat of the 1128 agreement whereby Fulk of Anjou had married Princess Melisende, Baldwin II's heiress. Without an offer or prospect of the crown, any position allocated to a prince from the West would have been similar to the equivocal and uncomfortable role, of responsibility without power, forced upon Philip of Flanders in 1177—not an appetizing inducement. Outremer politics were notorious in the West for their deviousness, and Heraclius's promises must have been too vague to conquer western disinclination to become involved in them. The pullani had exaggerated their weakness so often before that there was little Heraclius could say to contradict western cynicism; only the catastrophic events of 1187 could do that. The patriarch left England, if not hysterically invoking martyrdom as Gerald of Wales would have us believe, at least, in Roger of Howden's words, "greatly troubled."

Henry's response was not entirely negative. He travelled with Her-aclius to France to discuss details for Anglo-French financial help, and it may have been Heraclius's suggestion that the subsequent tax be assessed according to the model of the 1183 Jerusalem levy. Henry also paid at least £5 13s 4d towards the patriarch's expenses and gave per-mission for his vassals to take the cross. Both kings authorized crusade preaching.[66] A few English crusaders, including the Second Crusade veterans Roger of Mowbray and Hugh of Beauchamp, reached the Holy Land in 1186, and some stayed despite the truce with Saladin, to wit-ness the disasters of the following year.[67]

With the news of the annihilation of the Frankish army at Hattin in July 1187, the subsequent fall of almost all the Christian strongholds in Palestine, and the surrender of Jerusalem in October, coupled with the impetuous adoption of the cross by Richard of Poitou in November, Henry II's personal crusade policy could be said to have come to an end; thereafter he was the victim of circumstances. In the previous twenty years his behaviour towards the Holy Land had been conditioned more by his interests in the West than by concern for the needs of Outremer. There is no reason to doubt Henry's conventional piety, which imposed the obligation to help defend Jerusalem at a period when a holy end was the ambition of even the most temporally ambitious. Henry did not treat the subject flippantly. His anger at the young Henry's petulant assumption of the cross indicates his awareness that the cross could not be lightly borne. A crucesignatus ceased to be a normal layman; he escaped customary secular constraints but also abdicated a certain freedom of action to an often impatient, suspicious, and jealous church. For the king himself a sworn promise to take the cross sometime in the future was less restrictive and thus preferable. Nevertheless, it would be difficult to depict Henry II, as Bishop Foliot tried to, as an enthusiastic crusader. In a nice touch combining ingenuity and malice, Ralph Niger even suggested that Henry only agreed to take the cross in January 1188 because of the coincidence that Pope Gregory VIII, whose call to arms he was answering, was the same man before whom Henry had sworn to take the cross at Avranches in 1172, when the future pope was papal legate.[68] Even after taking the cross, Henry, true to the habits of a lifetime, treated the fate of his dynastic lands in the West as his priority, and his failure to fulfil his vow was widely commented upon.[69] His death in 1189, his vow unfulfilled, may in part explain why he appears to have been assigned more of the blame for the failure to respond to the 1185 appeal than was Frederick of Germany, Philip II, or the count of Flanders, all of whom were equally culpable. Unlike Henry they were spared to redeem their error by actually embarking on the Third Crusade.

Henry was not deaf to the call of Jerusalem but he treated it as one of many pressing obligations, one which, even in the face of the impassioned arguments of Patriarch Heraclius, failed to take precedence over his coronation oath, to his duty as a king. In pursuance of his destiny, Henry was unscrupulous. His crusade policy led him to manipulate men, money, and the emotional force of the ideal itself to serve the dominant purposes and mainspring of his life, the rule of his western dominions. It was only when his family's rights themselves seemed threatened in the Levant that he stirred himself for Jerusalem. Unlike his eldest son, Henry II displayed no recorded deathbed regrets at leaving his crusader's vow unfulfilled. What he did achieve for the crusade was accidental—the troops at Hattin, the ransoms at Jerusalem, and the defence of Tyre—but characteristic of a reign in which the crusade had been placed in the full glare of publicity and yet only words and cash had crossed the Mediterranean. The crusade was never Henry's chief priority. He nonetheless ensured its continued significance in England as elsewhere in his dominions, through his use of its diplomatic potential, his desire for information from the East, and his taxation for the Holy Land, which as surely as any preaching campaign brought the plight of Outremer to his people. Whatever else he may have done, Henry II did not—could not—forget Jerusalem.

APPENDIX

HENRY II's HOLY LAND TREASURE

The figure of thirty thousand marks is an admitted estimate (*ut dicitur*), by a Templar chaplain writing around 1191–92. There is no evidence how much the Templars spent on soldiers at Hattin. Chroniclers in Palestine some years after the Third Crusade reported that the Hospitallers spent thirty thousand besants on redeeming at least seven thousand Christians captured at Jerusalem (i.e., c. three thousand pounds); the defender of Tyre in 1187–88, Conrad of Montferrat, praising the use by the Hospitallers of Henry's money, did not specify the amount.[70] Western sources are suggestive without being very helpful. No accounts for the 1166 or 1185 taxes survive; chroniclers record that Henry sent one thousand marks in 1177 and another three thousand pounds in 1186. Gervase of Canterbury, whose figures are imaginative rather than credible, stated that the king had *offered* fifty thousand marks in 1185.[71] It is not clear that the money promised in 1172 was ever paid; its disappearance from subsequent discussions and Henry's failure to honour other Avranches stipulations arouse suspicion. Henry's will of 1182, to which Mayer attaches great significance, reveals the existence of unspecified previous grants to the military orders and a bequest of five thousand marks for the defence of Jerusalem. There is no evidence that this money was actually deposited or that any of the will's terms were executed. A later tradition that Henry had assigned forty-two thousand marks to Jerusalem in 1182 is based on a misunderstanding and conflation of Ralph of Diceto.[72] All the will demonstrates is that when contemplating the destiny of his soul, Henry was concerned about the Holy Land, whither he had already sent an unspecified sum of money, as yet unused.

The fullest eastern description, in the *Chronicle of Ernoul* (c. 1197), associates the treasure with the murder of Becket: "And so it was that after St. Thomas had been martyred, he [i.e., Henry] sent each year in the passage [i.e., the twice-yearly sailing to the East] great wealth to place in the treasury of the house of the Temple and Hospital in Jerusalem, intending that when he came there he would find a great store with which he could aid and succour the land." From this store, Ernoul reported, came the money for the Hattin soldiers, perhaps four thousand strong who fought on foot under the standard of the king of England. What the English knights Roger of Mowbray and Hugh of Beauchamp, who also fought at Hattin, thought of this is not recorded.[73] Ernoul's version of annual payments to a standing Jerusalem account receives scarcely any western corroboration at all. Ernoul, writing after the Third Crusade, describes the events of 1187 in essentially dramatic terms, with little adherence to chronology, none to objectivity, and hardly more to fact. The drama of Hattin, the fall of Jerusalem, and the defence of Tyre were inevitably enhanced if into the story could be worked one of the great twelfth-century causes célèbres, the expiation of Angevin guilt at the death of Becket. More precisely, since 1187 Henry's son Richard I had played the leading part in the revival of the Christian kingdom, and Henry's great-nephew Henry of Champagne had been ruler of Jerusalem. The Third Crusade had also established the cult of Thomas Becket in the East. English crusaders had founded an order of regular canons at Acre dedicated to St. Thomas; some, such as the Londoners, had adopted Becket as their especial patron, and on at least one occasion others had fought under a banner depicting the martyr.[74] Alone, Ernoul's comments are not proof that Henry II spent fifteen years quietly salting away a fortune in Jerusalem; such behaviour would, on the face of it, have been highly eccentric.

Gerald of Wales, the western witness to the importance of Henry's Jerusalem account, in whom Mayer places much reliance, is no more dependable. Even when writing in 1189, Gerald sustained an elaborate literary device in which Henry's rejection of the Holy Land in 1185 became responsible for the disasters of his last years, in particular John's failure in Ireland. Gerald wished to show Henry's glory fading and how "honour was changed into ignominy". It was a theme he tended long and lovingly, expanding on it with inventiveness and vitriol years later in his *Liber de principiis instructione.*[75] Gerald interpreted the events of 1185 as a refusal by Henry of the crown of Jerusalem and then presented this as the pivotal moment of his reign, the supreme test which Henry failed, causing his ruin. However, Gerald's literary determinism was not original, his account of Henry's fall from grace having a clear precedent. Henry of Huntingdon had explained how Robert Curthose, the heroic crusader, was brought low to end his days the prisoner of his noncrusader brother, by citing Robert's alleged (and fictitious) refusal of the crown of Jerusalem in 1099; Robert, like Gerald's Henry II, being doomed for that one act of rejection and cowardice.[76] With his own crusading credentials far from perfect, as he had eagerly sought to be released from his vow as soon as Henry II was dead, too much should not be pinned on Gerald's rhetorical constructs.

3

The Third Crusade

On 4 July 1187 the army of Jerusalem was annihilated by Saladin at the Horns of Hattin in Galilee. Its leaders were dispersed, slain, or captured. Within three months the kingdom, denuded of knights, was overrun; Jerusalem itself fell on 2 October. Of the chief Frankish strongholds, only Tyre remained, saved by the fortuitous arrival of Conrad of Montferrat. News of Saladin's victories provoked a reaction in the West which revealed the depth of emotion and sense of responsibility excited by the Christian occupation of the Holy Land and the fate of Jerusalem. The counterattack, which began in 1189, was led by the emperor, Frederick Barbarossa, who took the land route to Constantinople and Asia Minor. He was followed a year later by the kings of France and England, who travelled by sea. After a successful march across Anatolia to Cilicia, the huge German force broke up after the emperor drowned in the River Saleph in June 1190. Only a small remnant reached Palestine. By August 1189 Guy of Lusignan, the king of Jerusalem who had been held prisoner by Saladin since the defeat at Hattin, had begun to besiege the strategically vital port of Acre, the capture of which became the prime target of the crusade.

Contingents from all over Europe began to arrive from the summer of 1189. However, delayed by internecine Angevin feuding and the death of Henry II in July 1189, Richard I and Philip II only began their journey in July 1190. An advance guard under the archbishop of Canterbury reached Palestine that autumn, but the kings only arrived the following spring and early summer, having spent the winter refitting at Messina in Sicily. Before he reached Syria in June 1191 Richard I, in a lightning campaign, had conquered Cyprus from its independent Byzantine ruler, Isaac Comnenus. Acre finally capitulated to the united crusader armies on 12 July 1191. Within three weeks Philip II sailed for home leaving Richard in effective command, although his authority was rejected by some French and many local barons. Marching south towards Jerusalem, Richard repulsed Saladin at Arsuf (September 1191). After occupying Jaffa, Richard twice attempted to march inland to the Holy City, each time being forced back by the vulnerability of his supply lines and the realisation that, even if he could take Jerusalem, he would not be able to hold it. With Saladin failing to recapture Jaffa, it became increasingly clear as 1192 progressed that neither side could hope to establish a decisive military superiority.

Negotiations for a truce with Saladin were complicated by the separate, and at times competing, discussions held between the sultan and the local baronage who were supporting Conrad of Montferrat for their new king instead of Richard's preferred candidate, Guy of Lusignan. Finally, in August 1192 Richard and Saladin agreed to a three-year truce. The Christians were to retain control of the coastal strip from Tyre to Jaffa, the fortifications that Richard had started to build at Ascalon were to be dismantled, and Jerusalem was to stay in Moslem hands. Before returning to the West many crusaders took advantage of Saladin's offer of safe-conduct to visit the Holy Sepulchre, an opportunity Richard himself declined. Richard sailed from Acre on 9 October 1192.

The massive counterattack of 1189–1192, although resting upon popular enthusiasm, was a controlled exercise, responses tending to be methodical rather than miraculous. The individual's decision to stake his property and his life on the quest to regain the Holy Places remained fundamental, but the context of his actions was a deliberate and measured campaign to attract recruits and subsidies. The explosion of popular enthusiasm was not accidental. Crusading had become a recognised duty, established within the framework of habitual piety. Fanaticism was rare, and the stirring of the Holy Spirit now moved most obviously in official channels. Christian patriotism still inspired widespread fervour and deeds of consummate bravery, with thousands apparently willingly going to their deaths for the sake of the cross. The esprit de corps of the crusaders at the siege of Acre, on the march on Jerusalem, or at the defence of Jaffa mirrored the piety of the First Crusaders. Yet the organisation of the crusade was emphatically secular, not cynical or hypocritical, but calculated, well-planned, and professional, with the initiatives coming from the top.[1] The Third Crusade was also the first in which the participation of the English was crucial.

Pope Urban III had died of shock when news of the disaster at Hattin reached western Europe in October 1187. In November the more robust Richard, count of Poitou, became the first ruler north of the Alps to take the cross. Simultaneously the new pope, Gregory VIII, issued a resounding call to arms in his bull *Audita Tremendi*, and before the fall of Jerusalem itself was known to them the kings of England and France became crucesignati in January 1188, at last honouring the obligations loudly proclaimed for many years.[2] The Anglo-French expedition which set out two years later came to be dominated by the personality, followers, and resources of Richard I, whose superiority in men, money, and equipment was acknowledged even by hostile witnesses. England, with its experienced and ruthless central administration, by providing Richard with his own fleet and the capacity to support and transport by land and sea an army of many thousands to the edge of the known world, allowed him to translate ambition into action with unrivalled confidence and decisiveness.[3] The scale and administrative effectiveness of the preparations for the Third Crusade demonstrated the extent to which individuals and communities, as well as the royal government, could become involved in the process of crusading. For the first time crusading was a political priority, touching the lives of the many who never contemplated leaving their homes as well as the numerous minority who did.[4]

PLANS

First reactions to the news of Hattin were confused. Not everybody was carried away in the flood of outrage and self-pity. Ralph Niger insisted that the crusade was a distraction and an escape from more urgent problems facing Christendom at home.[5] Henry II himself was as suspicious of Richard's motives in precipitately taking the cross as he had been of the young Henry's in 1183. As then, he sought to bridle his son. According to William of Newburgh, despite verbal support Richard's example was followed by none of the great princes; it was winter and everybody was wondering how to react.[6] Until the Gisors conference in January 1188 Henry II kept everyone guessing.

Adoption of the cross suited Henry's purposes by temporarily diverting Philip's pressure on the strategically vital frontier province of the Vexin. Despite Gervase of Canterbury's claim that it was Philip, "younger but more devoted," who took the cross first, it is more likely that Henry took the initiative; he had most to gain, by stalling Philip's aggression and spiking the independence of his son. Roger of Howden's comment on events at Gisors, that "on that day those who had been enemies were made friends," was a distinct overstatement. Although the archbishop of Tyre presided over the ceremony he was assisted by different metropolitans for each king, the archbishop of Rouen for Henry and the archbishop of Rheims for Philip. This insistence on independence and parity was further emphasised by the conference's decision that each crusade contingent should bear crosses of contrasting colours:

red for the followers of the king of France, white for the Angevins, and green for the Flemish. This may have made military sense, but it spoke little of any spirit of unity or friendship.[7] Despite the rhetoric and ceremonial, the shared crusader status failed to restrain hostilities between Henry, Philip, and Richard in 1188–89. Although Richard was reported to have spared the lives of rebels in Poitou provided they took the cross, and despite his personal enthusiasm for the crusade, his immediate priorities were to secure his inheritance and then, as king, to defend his lands against Capetian incursions.[8] However, the crusade could supply a framework within which mutual guarantees of rights and protection could be negotiated. In this sense the treaty of Nonancourt in December 1189 between Philip and Richard was closely analogous to that of Ivry in 1177, although political animosities were merely deflected, not defused, and were transported intact wherever the Angevin and Capetian courts travelled, even to Palestine itself.[9]

Despite the continuing political bickering, serious preparations did begin after the Gisors meeting. Initially, Henry toyed with the idea of following the traditional land route of Godfrey de Bouillon, Louis VII, and Conrad III via central Europe, Hungary, and Constantinople. In April 1188 Archbishop Baldwin of Canterbury was forcing his unfit entourage to dismount and lead their horses up a steep valley in mid-Wales as training for the land journey to Jerusalem.[10] An experienced Angevin agent, Richard Barre, was despatched to Frederick Barbarossa, King Bela of Hungary, and the emperor of Byzantium, Isaac Angelus, requesting safe passage for the Angevin and Capetian armies and access to markets, an issue which had caused great ill-feeling between crusaders and the indigenous populations on the First and Second Crusades.[11] Despite favourable replies, the scheme was dropped, possibly on the news that Barbarossa himself had taken the cross and was planning to use the Danube route. This would have revived bitter memories of the Franco-German competition for supplies in 1147 and might have also raised the unwelcome prospect of the English king having to accept the precedence of the German emperor.[12] The decision to transport the Angevin crusade by sea might, therefore, have been fortuitous but in retrospect the choice was vital. After the sharp setbacks to Byzantine power in the Balkans and Asia Minor in the 1170s and 1180s, the sea offered greater speed and security, even the Germans who marched across Europe and Asia Minor in 1189–90 admitting, somewhat masochistically, that the sea provided a "short voyage which reduced the fear from hostile pagans," ideal for the lazy.[13] The use of ships allowed the Angevins strategic flexibility and a large measure of independence.

To raise funds and recruit crusaders Henry issued a series of ordinances at Le Mans at the end of January and at Geddington (Northamptonshire) on 11 February 1188, where the preaching campaign was opened by Archbishop Baldwin of Canterbury; by early March, it was in full swing. By the autumn of 1188 money was being collected and equipment gathered near the south coast in a show of urgency contrasting markedly with the sluggishness of Capetian preparations.[14] The administrative details had almost certainly been thrashed out during lengthy deliberations at Gisors in mid-January.[15] At Le Mans, shortly after, the details of collection of a crusade tax were published. The Geddington ordinances contained revised provisions for the tax and incorporated and expanded some of the papal measures announced in Gregory VIII's *Audita tremendi*.[16] All lay and clerical crucesignati were to enjoy a plenary indulgence of all confessed sins; those who did not take the cross were to pay for one year a tenth of their revenues and moveables, excluding books, clothes, jewels, clerical vestments, and furnishings, and the horses, arms, equipment, and clothing of knights. The usually well-informed William of Newburgh added that the corn of the current year was exempt, but that in the following year the tithe on corn was to be levied from non-crucesignati, and that the taxpayers would have the incentive of a partial indulgence.[17] Crusader clerics, knights, and serjeants were to receive the tax from their lands and vassals to assist their preparations, but exemption was explicitly denied those from town or country ("burgenses et rustici") who had taken the cross without permission (*licentia*), presumably either of their lord or their local priest.[18]

The pope had insisted that the Holy Land had been imperilled not only because of the sins of the Jerusalemites "but also our own and those of the whole Christian people." In response the Geddington ordinances included strict sumptuary restrictions and prohibitions on swearing and gambling. To avoid loose living, no women were to accompany the crusade except laundresses of spotless repute. Following the papal policy of the Second Crusade, crusaders were excused interest repayments and, in addition, they now were exempted repayment of all debts whilst on crusade. Both lay and clerical crusaders were permitted to mortgage their goods, the creditor to enjoy them for three years from the Easter of the year in which the crusader departed. If a crusader died on the journey, the money he was carrying was to be divided between general crusade purposes and the poor, including the maintenance of the deceased's followers. A number of the standard privileges outlined in *Audita tremendi*, such as ecclesiastical protection for crusaders' goods, lands, and families and immunity from law suits, were omitted from both sets of Angevin crusade decrees. Even so, Henry II's ordinances signalled the close partnership of church and state by which this and all subsequent English crusade efforts were sustained.

The decrees concerning the crusader's morals, his state of grace, mind, clothing, and body expose a tension inherent in the crusading movement. Churchmen who interpreted the Christian failures in the East as a consequence of sin had an ideal vision of a crusader as a man reformed and transformed by the act of assuming the cross, by which he abandoned sin and self-indulgence for the simple life of a penitent seeking salvation in a symbolic imitation of the suffering of Christ bearing his cross. Yet, as some preachers were aware, there was an evident contradiction between the mores of the pilgrim and the knight.[19] Wealth and the martial ethos, vital for the temporal success of any crusade, tended to stimulate vanity and display, not sobriety of behaviour or dress. In 1190 Richard I bought a number of scarlet robes in clear breach of the explicit 1188 ban, and his love of magnificent, even garish, dress was never displayed more lavishly than when he received the submission of Isaac Comnenus in Cyprus in 1191.[20] Extravagance was an intrinsic element of dominion. Despite fashionable exaltation of the poor as instruments of God's purpose, crusading was conducted by the rich, for whose prestige and authority ostentation was essential.

Neither were the physical conditions and social relationships within crusade armies conducive to abstinence, Ralph Niger's fears of the dangers of the cameraderie of camp life being fully justified.[21] Within six months of the crusade's departure more relaxed gambling regulations were imposed (October 1190), allowing knights and clerics to indulge in a limited, and kings in an unlimited way. Severe penalties for humbler gamblers were also announced, and it was made clear that gaming debts incurred during the crusade had to be honoured.[22] Morale was of great importance, and brawls over wagers and gambling could easily undermine discipline, especially as alcohol was a staple of a soldier's diet. The Messina decrees mentioned neither swearing nor dress, but it is improbable that there was moderation in either.

The absence of women intended by the ordinances was also inconsistent with the habits of soldiers. After the capture of Acre in July 1191

> the town was filled with pleasure. There were good wines
> and bountiful and many damsels beautiful.

Richard himself hardly abided by the letter of the 1188 decrees by taking his future wife and his sister with him from Sicily.[23] When the army set out for Jerusalem in August 1191 women were again banned except for the washerwomen,

> The good old dames who toiled
> And dames who washed the linen soiled
> And laved the heads of pilgrims—these
> Were as good as apes for picking fleas.[24]

Not all crusaders indulged themselves in the fleshpots of Acre. Many abstained from sex for love of God and died; according to the eyewitness Ambroise, "they had not perished thus/had they not been abstemious."[25]

The more directly disciplinary ordinances were reinforced by the rules drawn up for the Angevin fleet, which was to sail round the Iberian peninsula to join the main army at Marseilles or Messina. Justiciars were appointed to enforce draconian discipline. Murderers were to be drowned or buried alive; bloodshed was to be punished by mutilation, other violence by keelhauling. Those caught swearing were to be fined and thieves tarred and feathered, before being put ashore at the first opportunity.[26] Discipline was vital to military success; it had been the failure to impose order in his army that had caused the internal disintegration of Louis VII's crusade in 1147.[27] A rabble of drunken, swearing, fractious, gambling, and wenching crusaders, however enthusiastic for the cause, was a recipe for disaster. Occasionally discipline did break down, as at Lisbon in 1190 when a group from the Angevin fleet ran amok in a drunken spree of looting and raping. But even after periods of inactivity at Messina in 1190–91 and Acre in 1191, order was usually restored once campaigning restarted.[28]

The testamentary decree of 1188 seems to have worked. When Archbishop Baldwin died at Acre in November 1190, Hubert Walter, his executor and now head of the English advance guard, disposed of the archbishop's money in two ways: he paid the wages of twenty knights and fifty serjeants to act as sentries in the camp in accordance with Baldwin's wishes, and he subsidised the destitute.[29] The regulations were modified for the rest of the army at Messina. A man who died on crusade could dispose of his arms, horses, and clothing, and half his other goods at will, provided nothing was returned to his homeland; clerics could bequeath their chapel furnishings and books. The residue in both cases was to be administered by a committee of ten important spiritual and lay leaders for common use by the crusaders.[30] The resulting fund would channel the wealth of dead soldiers to help hold the army together when individuals began, as inevitably they did, to run

63

out of cash. This regulation was especially useful, as the Messina decrees also forbade sailors and serjeants to change masters without permission, in a measure perhaps aimed by the French at preventing Richard from outbidding Philip for men who had no money of their own left.[31] The central fund, whilst not competing with royal or princely treasures, could have eased the lot of the impoverished crusader without involving problems of allegiance.[32]

These nonfiscal provisions suggest that the conduct of the crusade was carefully planned by an intelligent, informed, alert, and confident government alive to the varied practical requirements of propaganda, finance, and discipline. In sharp contrast were the Capetian ordinances, which were apparently limited to decrees on debt exemption and the crusade tax, with the latter lacking the Angevin provision for central scrutiny and collection.[33]

RECRUITMENT

Some great men at Henry II's court had taken the cross in 1185, but until January 1188 few had followed Richard of Poitou's example. However, the crusade ordinances were to have a direct impact. On news of the tax on non-crucesignati, "all the rich men of his [i.e., Henry's] lands, both clergy and laity, rushed in crowds to take the cross."[34] The advantages for them were threefold: crusader privileges, exemption from the crusade tithe, and access to the tithe money of their noncrusading vassals and tenants. Others apparently took the cross "for the love of God and remission of sins, some out of respect of the kings themselves." Gerald of Wales later recalled that Henry II forced not only friends and servants to take the cross but also those of whom he was suspicious and his worst enemies. In 1207 a royal judge, Henry of Whiston, admitted to having taken the cross not out of piety but out of love and favour of Henry II, and William of Newburgh identified devotion, royal command, and the desire to ingratiate as the spurs to action.[35] The enthusiasm of *curiales*, magnates, and prelates was not impervious to temporal calculation. Richard of Devizes noted that only two of the English bishops who took the cross, Archbishop Baldwin and Hubert Walter, actually attempted to fulfil their vows, and he had some harsh words for those like the bishop of Norwich and the archbishop of Rouen who obtained absolution "having saluted Jerusalem from afar."[36] According to the monk of Bury St. Edmunds, Jocelin of Brakelond, his master, the efficient businessman Abbot Samson, on hearing of the loss of Jerusalem began wearing a hair shirt and underclothes, abstained from meat, and attempted to take the cross. Henry II was staying at

Bury with the bishop of Norwich in February 1188 when Abbot Samson appeared with cloth cross and a needle and thread, begging to be allowed to become a crucesignatus. He was refused on the grounds that it would be unwise if both the bishop and the abbot were absent from East Anglia at the same time. Samson, ever a vigorous defender of his abbey's immunities, may have been more concerned to avoid the crusade tithe. In the event neither bishop nor abbot went to the Holy Land.[37]

The responsibilities of high office were regarded as legitimate excuses by the pope no less than the king. Clement III allowed Richard I's officials Geoffrey FitzPeter, William Brewer, and Hugh Bardolf to lay aside the cross in 1189. Initially Rannulf Glanvill also managed to buy release from his vow, although with Richard's accession his political star began to wane and ultimately he led the Angevin vanguard which reached the Holy Land in October 1190, eight months before the king.[38] If Richard of Devizes is to be believed, Richard himself agreed to the archbishop of Rouen's abandoning the crusade in return for all the prelate's money. The archbishop's plea that priests should stay at home to guard their flock was seen by Richard of Devizes as a shameful excuse "that even the most wretched of mothers would bear with distrust."[39] Among the powerful or would-be powerful, devotion to the crusade was rarely blind. When Hugh of Le Puiset, bishop of Durham, took the cross in 1185, he too started to wear a hair shirt but not for long; as soon as he was offered the justicarship in 1189 he disentangled himself from his vows.[40] Similarly the accession of Richard disturbed the commitment to the crusade of *familiares* like Roger of Howden and Gerald of Wales, suddenly no longer at the centre of affairs. They reacted very differently. Roger found his way to Acre but Gerald, who had taken the cross in March 1188, quickly obtained absolution.[41]

Pragmatism should not be confused with cynicism. The halfhearted were, in any case, no use on campaign. According to the possibly romanticised account of Richard of Devizes, the king's experience with the archbishop of Rouen prompted him to purge his army at Messina of all except those able and cheerfully willing to bear arms.[42] Of these there was no shortage for, as the *Itinerarium* recorded, it was not a question of who took the cross but who did not, an impression reinforced by the extant literary, legal, and financial records. The eyewitness accounts of Ambroise, Richard of Holy Trinity, author of the *Itinerarium Ricardi Regis*, Hugh de Neville (who told his story some years later to Abbot Ralph of Coggeshall), Robert of Turnham (whose memories appear in the Meaux chronicle), and Roger of Howden, can be supplemented by the exchequer records on the Pipe Rolls, land charters of departing crusaders selling, leasing, or mortgaging property, and later assizes of *mort d'ancestor,* which reveal a number of crusaders who never returned.[43]

The scale of the operation was massive. Richard of Devizes calculated that the Angevin fleet which sailed round the Iberian peninsula was designed to carry 8,750 soldiers and sailors. Although these figures possess a suspiciously bureaucratic neatness, Roger of Howden mentions that on the ship carrying the contingent of Londoners there were eighty well-armed young men, which corresponds almost exactly with Richard of Devizes's estimate of the complement of one of the large transport ships.[44] In addition to the fleet, there was the king's own army, which caused the wooden bridge at Lyons to collapse in July 1190 under the weight of so many marching feet. It was large enough to divide at Marseilles, with one group led by Archbishop Baldwin, Hubert Walter, and Rannulf Glanvill sailing directly to Syria. The king was still left with sufficient household troops to fill ten large transports or busses and twenty galleys, perhaps 2,500 to 3,000 men.[45] Some ships' companies could, however, be tiny; Ivo of Vieuxpont reputedly arrived at Acre in October 1190 in a small boat with only ten companions and three sailors.[46] Philip of France's household troops had been planned to number 1,950. Richard's total force, which he marched overland to meet the fleet at Marseilles, was almost certainly larger, perhaps as many as 6,000 men. Richard's force, which embarked for the Holy Land from Sicily in April 1191, could, again on Richard of Devizes's computations, have numbered as many as 17,000 troops and seamen, a huge army for the period.[47] In addition were those who had left for the East before the kings. In May 1189 a fleet of thirty-seven heavily laden ships carrying crusaders from England (in particular London), Denmark, and Flanders sailed from Dartmouth and helped capture Silves for the king of Portugal in September before sailing on to Acre. Ralph of Diceto estimated the number on board as 3,500, the *Itinerarium* more fancifully as 12,000, of whom, it was claimed, scarcely a hundred lived to see the capture of Acre in July 1191.[48]

Calculations must remain speculative, but the preaching campaigns and political and financial incentives offered between 1188 and 1190 were clearly successful. Gerald of Wales alleged that three thousand Anglo-Normans and Welshmen took the cross in just two months in the spring of 1188.[49] Preachers emphasised penitence, pilgrimage, the cross, Jerusalem, indulgences, and the need to avenge the insult to God. The tales of Christian heroism which encrust contemporary accounts of the siege of Acre, as much as the enthusiasm of audiences listening to crusade sermons, attest the importance of such nonmaterial incentives.[50] Enthusiasm, however, needed to be fostered by careful management. Thus Gerald of Wales's adoption of the cross at Radnor in March

1188 had been prearranged in order to impress the audience at the first sermon of the archbishop's Welsh tour.[51] On the same journey Gerald's effectiveness was probably enhanced by his close family connections with many of the local magnates.[52]

The government attached considerable importance to the success of the recruitment drive. This was most obvious on the Welsh tour in Lent 1188, when the spiritual invitation was reinforced with a hint of political compulsion by the presence of the justiciar, Rannulf Glanvill, at the important opening sermon at Radnor, attended by the powerful Rhys ap Gruffyd. By pressing the Welsh princes to take the cross and by excommunicating those like Owain Cyfeiliog ap Gruffyd ap Maredudd who did not, Archbishop Baldwin, as Henry II's agent, was asserting royal influence in a potentially unruly province. Ecclesiastically, the political dimension was even clearer. Baldwin, who had previously visited Wales as papal legate in 1187, made a point of celebrating mass at the high altars of the cathedrals at Llandaff, St. David's, Bangor, and St. Asaph's, the first archbishop of Canterbury to do so, in a deliberate gesture to mark Welsh subservience to his metropolitan jurisdiction.[53]

As the central objective of royal government from 1189, the crusade attracted large numbers from the political and administrative elite: members of powerful families, such as the earl of Leicester and his son, the earl of Ferrers, Nigel of Mowbray, Bernard of St. Valery, Richard of Clare, Gerard of Furnival, Waleran of Forz, and Warin FitzGerold; former sheriffs like Drogo FitzRalph, Rannulf and Roger Glanvill, Gilbert Pipard, and Bertran of Verdun; royal friends like Andrew of Chavigny; royal agents like Robert of Sablé, Richard of Camville, and Eustace of Burnes with the fleet of Richard of Turnham (later governor of Cyprus); household officials like the seneschal William FitzAldelin, the chamberlain Ralf FitzGodfrey, and the clerk of the chamber, Master Philip of Poitou, later bishop of Durham; and the vice-chancellor Roger Malcael, who drowned off Limasol in April 1191 still wearing round his neck the royal seal, which was only recovered when a peasant found Roger's body washed ashore.[54] (Ironically, six months before at Messina, Roger had sealed a royal charter quitclaiming the king's right of wreck.)[55] The royal administration had gone to war just as surely as if the king was campaigning in Normandy instead of the Mediterranean. A constant stream of messengers kept Richard in touch with his dominions, and in return he sent a number of newsletters announcing, for example, the fall of Acre and his victory over Saladin at Arsuf. The journey between England and the Holy Land may, very exceptionally, have taken as little as two months, and sensitive issues were referred to the king who continued to be aware, if not in control, of events in his realm.[56] Even on crusade, Angevin government retained its coherence.

An exception was the advance guard which sailed directly to the Holy Land from Marseilles in August 1190, reaching Palestine two months later. Led by Archbishop Baldwin, to some an ineffectual figure despite his capacity to sustain rancorous relations with his cathedral chapter over many years, this contingent became isolated from the rest of the Angevin forces. A feeling of isolation is implicit in letters written from Acre both by the archbishop and by Hubert Walter, bishop of Salisbury, in the autumn and winter of 1190–91. In October Baldwin—possibly for local consumption—appeared to be expecting Richard and Philip any day; by the New Year Hubert was urgently warning that unless the kings arrived by Easter (which they did not) the siege would fail. Despite Hubert's own endeavours to improve their plight, the crusaders' morale at Acre remained very low and the bishop feared that money would run out.[57] It seems as if the English in the camp at Acre were beginning to suspect that they had been abandoned.

Why had they been sent ahead? There was most obviously the need to protect Angevin interests. Already Conrad of Montferrat had signalled the threat he posed to Guy of Lusignan's tenure of the throne of Jerusalem. Guy was a vassal of Richard's in France, and was married to Richard's cousin Sibyl. Once at Acre Baldwin did all in his power to block Conrad's advance on the crown, after Sibyl's death had compromised Guy's position. He refused to sanction Conrad's marriage to Sibyl's heiress, her sister Isabel.[58] Richard had planned a leisurely progress for himself; as the king's surrogate the archbishop could try to exert influence, even wield authority on the king's behalf. Against this it could be argued that the archbishop's companions were hardly men in whom Richard would have much trust: the former rebel the earl of Ferrers; the dismissed justiciar Rannulf Glanvill; his uncle Roger, who had just been relieved of the shrievalty of Cumberland by King Richard; Rannulf's nephew Hubert Walter, recently, in reverse of the family fortunes, made bishop of Salisbury; and Rannulf's steward and former vicegerent as sheriff of York, Reiner, who had also suffered in the political purge of 1189.[59] Nevertheless, while Rannulf and the earl of Ferrers died soon after reaching the Holy Land, Roger and especially Bishop Hubert continued to play active roles in the crusade after Richard's arrival at Acre.[60] Perhaps at Marseilles Richard had felt he could dispense with the Glanvill connection, which he had been battering since his accession, while at the same time their affinity could provide a useful adjunct to the archbishop's entourage.

For those close to the king, the crusade offered considerable scope for temporal advancement. Through his efficiency, loyalty, and skill in battle and diplomacy in the East, Hubert Walter laid especial claim to

the king's confidence and established himself as an almost indispens-
able royal minister, who was soon to be rewarded with the see of Canterbury and the justiciarship. It is also possible to ascribe the subsequent
preferment of Hugh of Neville to the heights of secular government as
chief forester, or of Philip of Poitou to the bishopric of Durham, to the
good account they rendered of themselves to the king on crusade.
Friendships, influence, and command structures built up during war
have often had a tendency to survive into peace, from Caesar to Chur-
chill. Crusading, which threw men together in small groups often sharing extreme danger, was no exception.[61]

Besides the households of the king and great magnates came the
most significant body of crusaders. According to Gerald of Wales's account of Baldwin's Welsh preaching tour in 1188, the crucesignati, with
the possible exceptions of a group of murderous Anglo-Norman archers
from St. Clear's and some notorious criminals from Usk, were overwhelmingly nobles or knights and their military households, "all of
them highly skilled in the use of the spear and the arrow, most experienced in military matters and only too keen to attack the enemies of
our faith at the first opportunity."[62] The pragmatic bias is confirmed by
other sources.[63] Common sense dictated that for an expensive military
campaign fighting men should be engaged, capable of equipping themselves or of being supported by others. Crusading, in particular when it
involved expensive passage by sea which denied opportunities to for-
age, was out of reach of the individual who could not raise the necessary
cash. Indeed, the indigent noncombatant was the bane of crusading
armies; he ate, but neither paid nor fought.

It could with justice be argued that the king and his most intimate
associates had closer ties with France than with England. But if the
supreme command was French and Anglo-Norman, many followers
were from England. The most characteristic English crucesignati were
local landlords, knights, and gentry, who like Ivo of Vieuxpoint travelled with their small groups of companions (socii), relations, vassals,
or neighbours. The groups of crusading coniurati who attacked the Jews
in England in Lent 1190 were of just such comfortable but not spectacular means. They were pillars of local society, like the Yorkshire landowners whose charters raising money from their lands or bestowing
local charity in preparation for their crusade have survived; men like
Walter the Black, Fulk of Rufford, John of Penigeston, Walter of Scotney,
the knight Roger, son of Richard Touche; or contacts of the great, like
Roger the Constable, seneschal to William of Mandeville. It has been
suggested that English knights were "far from enthusiastic" towards
the Third Crusade.[64] This is hardly born out by the evidence. Although

comparative figures of those who went on crusade and those who did not are unobtainable, it is indisputable that a considerable body of English knights took the cross and embarked to fulfil their vows.

Something of this is shown in the accounts for the 1190 scutage to pay for defence against the Welsh. Those who could claim that they or their knights were crucesignati received relief from the levy according to the number of knights' fees involved, their names and the amounts remitted being recorded by the sheriff and entered on the exchequer Pipe Rolls. For a customarily avaricious regime to exempt subjects was unusual in Angevin England. But it could be argued that crusader knights were in a sense going to serve the king in person, and therefore should be exempt from a tax levied as an alternative to personal military service, and that it was a moot legal point whether crucesignati or their property were liable to pay any tax at all. Exempt from the crusade tax of 1188, in the thirteenth century they frequently enjoyed immunity from noncrusading levies such as the fifteenth of 1225 or the tallage of 1235.[65]

The Pipe Rolls of 1190, 1191, and 1192 identify fifty-nine named crucesignati, sometimes grouped together under fiefs held directly from the Crown as, for example, the knights of the abbot of Bury St. Edmunds, of Richard, earl of Clare, or of the honour of Peverel, and sometimes itemised under a county, such as those from Bedfordshire. Frequently the Pipe Rolls failed to record individual names; thus "many knights" were mentioned as exempt in Staffordshire in 1190. When dealing with knights from a particular fief, the roll usually simply records the name of the lord with an indication that the exemption applied to his followers, such as those of Robert of Lacy in Yorkshire, Richard FitzWilliam in Sussex and Richard Basset in Northamptonshire.[66]

To calculate the total numbers of crucesignati exempted is hazardous. The standard rate of the Welsh scutage was ten shillings per knight's fee, half the customary rate, and on the three Pipe Rolls the total sum pardoned was £64 3s 6d. But rates of assessment varied according to the number or fractions of fiefs held. Thus one crusader, Osbert of Broy from Bedfordshire, was pardoned six pence; another, Robert of Stafford, thirty shillings. The geographic spread is impressive: Staffordshire, Essex, Hertfordshire, Berkshire, Yorkshire, Huntingdonshire, Norfolk, Suffolk, Sussex, Wiltshire, Bedfordshire, Northamptonshire, and London. From the Pipe Rolls alone, the number of knights taking the cross may be inferred as being in three figures.

These crusaders were often men of substance. Henry of Hastings was pardoned fifty shillings for his lands held of the abbey of Bury St. Edmunds and thirty shillings as a vassal of the earl of Clare, implying a considerable holding in East Anglia alone.[67] Some of those named in the exchequer accounts can also be traced to the Levant: Roger le Pole, one of Hubert Walter's knights who died at Acre, had been pardoned thirty shillings; William Malet, pardoned ten shillings, arrived with the main army at Acre in June 1191; and Simon of Odell, a Bedfordshire landowner pardoned thirty shillings, died at Acre sometime after the king's arrival and was buried at sea.[68] Elsewhere on the Pipe Rolls more can be discovered of the circumstances of these crusaders. Richard of Clare, who died almost as soon as he reached Palestine in October 1190, left debts in Saham Toney in Norfolk of £26 8s 8d, although, naturally, he was quit of repayment for the crusader's term of three years.[69]

Despite the formal ecclesiastical protection granted to crusaders' families, property, and possessions, crucesignati on the Third Crusade appointed guardians of their lands. In 1188 Geoffrey Hose from Wiltshire, who was to die on crusade, paid the exchequer one hundred pounds to hold his land in peace and be allowed to appoint a custodian.[70] Families of crusaders, however, could be left in financial difficulties.[71] In particular, wives left behind were vulnerable to neighbours' rapacity, and conjugal opposition to the taking of the cross was not unknown.[72]

From the crusader's point of view, the immediate problems concerned the mechanics of travel; few, if any, journeyed alone. Knights were grouped together by a combination of feudal, political, and dynastic relationships: the Glanvill affinity; William and Gilbert Malet and Osbert and Robert de la Mare, who appear in East Anglian scutage returns and who in all probability arrived together at Acre in June 1191; or the group of northerners arriving at the same time described simply as "the Stutevilles."[73] According to William of Newburgh, the massacres of the Jews during Lent 1190 at King's Lynn, Stamford, and York were led by groups of young crusaders who acted in concert and, at King's Lynn, fled together by ship with their ill-gotten booty.[74] The fleet which sailed from Dartmouth in 1189, like its predecessor of 1147, was organised "by common agreement"; like the persecutors of the Jews, its leaders were probably bound together by oaths as coniurati.[75] Such cooperation was imposed by the pressures of finance, throughout England land and rents being sold, leased, or mortgaged to raise the money for the travelling expenses.[76] It was the sight of the Jews at Stamford enjoying their wealth while the crusaders themselves lacked adequate funds which propelled resentment towards violence in 1190.[77] Convenience and prudence argued for a pooling of resources.

Another cohesive element was geography. The knights of Staffordshire could well have stuck together because of prior acquaintance. Not all crusaders were *familiares* of their social superiors. In the multinational, polyglot turmoil of the camp at Acre, men from the East Riding of Yorkshire stuck together. The parson of Howden, the chronicler and royal clerk Roger, witnessed a charter of John of Hessle, a local Yorkshire landowner. In his account of the siege, Roger placed in the catalogue of those who died at Acre in 1190 a list of names of crusaders from Lincolnshire and Yorkshire: Ralph, parson of Croxby, Richard of Legsby and his brother Berengar, Robert the Huntsman from Pontefract, Robert Scrope of Barton-on-Humber, Rannulf of Bradford, Walter Scrope, Walter of Kyme, and Walter of Ros. Some, like Walter of Kyme, were from respectable and powerful families, and all were probably of provincial or local importance, yet they appear incongruous in Roger of Howden's list beside Rannulf Glanvill, Bernard of St. Valery, Guy of Châtillon, and the count of Flanders. Possibly they were known personally to Roger; they certainly came from in and around the neighbourhood of his parish, their association in death testifying to the local origins of this vast enterprise.[78]

Of the plight of the entourages of the great and of the common soldiers, the poet Ambroise is eloquent. The squires, serjeants (mounted or not), and infantry at Acre, like their commanders, needed money for food and clothes; although many had exhausted their funds, originally they must have had some, either their own or their masters'. Ambroise reveals an army of well-trained and well-armed soldiers with barons, knights, and serjeants possessing fine equipment, in which mounted knights combined effectively with disciplined foot soldiers even before the arrival of Richard I.[79] Until a charity fund was established by Hubert Walter in the winter of 1190–91, crusaders paid for themselves. When famine and astronomic prices hit the camp they affected serjeants, foot soldiers and knights alike. The so-called poor were not necessarily of base social origins, for in 1190–91 at Acre poverty embraced

> men of worth
> And valour, men of noble birth
> Reared among wealth and gentleness,

crack troops who had simply run out of money; hence the urgency of Bishop Hubert's task of organising central funding and provisioning.[80] Those in the lowest social group on the Third Crusade were much like the foot-sloggers of any medieval army: they were not untrained serfs, and they fought for money. The first thing both Philip II and Richard I did on arrival at Acre was to offer new rates of pay to the troops.[81] The image of the peasant leaving his field to fight for the cross is a myth. Numerous land charters testify to the strenuous search for cash, even by the well-to-do; for as little as five marks Walter the Black had to

alienate two bovates of land (perhaps about thirty acres). Other crucesignati, like many in Wales in 1188, soon discovered that they could
not afford the journey.[82] Serfs, for reasons economic, financial, and legal,
did not go on crusade except in the service of their lords or as proxies.[83]

The 1188 ordinances assumed urban as well as rural participation.
The crusade tax, which in towns (or boroughs) was assessed on income
by direct royal investigation of the wealth of civic worthies (two hundred
from London, one hundred from York, etc.), was strictly imposed on
burgesses and would have provided as great an incentive for townsmen
to avoid payment by taking the cross as it did for the rural aristocracy.
London, at least, had a long tradition of crusaders. Sometime before
1130 the prosperous city merchant Roger of Cornhill, grandfather of
Henry of Cornhill, one of the chief organisers of the Third Crusade, had
gone to Jerusalem; in 1147 a London contingent led by one Andrew
joined the fleet which captured Lisbon, and a coiner, Hachard, had gone
to the Holy Land in the 1160s.[84] The urban patriciate was open to the
same emotional, spiritual, and material pressures as other social groups,
as their role in the Third Crusade demonstrated.

Men from London were in the fleet that sailed from Dartmouth in
May 1189 and took Silves from the Moors in September. A year later
another ship load of at least eighty Londoners embarked for Jerusalem,
their eventful voyage to Spain being recounted in some detail by Roger
of Howden. During a storm, St. Thomas Becket appeared to three men
on board to assure them of his protection, as well as that of St. Edmund
and St. Nicholas, and to calm the tempest. Later the ship was deliberately scuttled by local Christians in newly conquered Silves, in an attempt to persuade the Londoners to help the king of Portugal resist a
fresh Moorish invasion; this they agreed to do only after receiving assurances of full compensation.[85] The vision of Becket may be connected
with the story of William, chaplain to the dean of St. Paul's (i.e., the
chronicler Ralph of Diceto). He vowed to dedicate a chapel to St. Thomas
if he reached Acre in one piece on the 1189 journey, on which at least
one other member of the St. Paul's clergy, Ralph of Hauterive, also
travelled. London crusaders adopted Becket as their especial protector,
just as at home they carefully tended his legend and birthplace.[86]

The 1190 London group was led by Geoffrey the Goldsmith and William FitzOsbert, nicknamed Longbeard. The latter was a member of a
prominent city family and was later notorious as the demogogic leader
of civic agitation in 1196 against the harsh fiscal and judicial policies
of Hubert Walter; he paid with his life. Whether the king subsidised the
Londoners' ship in 1190 is unknown, but even if he did the need remained for individuals to raise their own funds. FitzOsbert resorted,

like his rural counterparts, to mortgaging property, in his case half a messuage in the parish of St. Nicholas of Acre in London, to his brother Richard.[87] However financed, the Londoners acted independently of other naval contingents and, if the precedents of 1147 and 1189 were followed, they possibly organised themselves into a commune, a form of self-government popular in twelfth-century London. Ultimately, however, in the Holy Land, the Londoners were probably absorbed into the main force. Beyond the appearance of one Augustine of London, who was given as a hostage to Saladin by the beleaguered garrison at Jaffa in July 1192, they vanish from sight. It is, however, unlikely that experienced merchants, businessmen, or artisans found themselves bereft of employment in the entrepreneurial life of the temporary city that was the camp at Acre.[88]

A final social group was the secular clergy who, like laymen, were encouraged by tax exemption and permission to mortage property, including their benefices, to join the expedition. If only two bishops actually reached the Holy Land, countless other priests joined them. All ranks of the clergy were represented, from the archbishop, the bishop of Salisbury, and the abbot of Ford, through the archdeacon of Colchester, to parsons, chaplains, clerks, and the vicar of Dartford.[89] The clergy were fully integrated into the crusading armies. They prayed, exhorted, and encouraged the crusaders, they wrote and witnessed their charters, they conducted negotiations with the enemy, and they buried the dead. They also fought. Hubert Walter took to the field in person displaying characteristic flair and determination as pastor, warrior, and general.[90] In Cyprus an "armed clerk," Hugh de la Mare, dared give King Richard military advice, receiving extremely short shrift for his temerity.[91] Ralph of Hauterive, archdeacon of Colchester, who rallied a rout in the dark days of July 1190, was a man, so it was said, "of renown in learning and fame in arms." Nephew of Bishop Gilbert Foliot of London, canon of St. Paul's, colleague of the historian Ralph of Diceto, who praised his martial prowess, sometime royal justice, and master of the schools at St. Paul's, Archdeacon Ralph was no termagant hedge-priest but an aristocrat of the church who shared the aptitude of his class for war, if not the instincts.[92] He, and others like him, were full participants in the communal effort. Perhaps no less important was the influence of the clergy beyond the battlefield and council chamber, in fashioning public perceptions of the crusade through sermons and more lasting literary descriptions. Contemporary and modern images of crusading were and are heavily dependent on accounts of the Third Crusade by eyewitnesses such as the parson of Howden and Ambroise (or his source), who was a clerk from Normandy, as well as on collections of documents and anecdotes by clerical observers in the West.

FINANCE

Success in war is not achieved by numbers alone and, as J. O. Prestwich has written, "to be *bellicosus* it was necessary to be also *pecuniosus*."[93] This was a truth well appreciated by Henry II and his son. Almost as soon as he heard the news from the East in the winter of 1187–88 Henry began to investigate potential sources of income. The idea of a new crusade tax on goods and revenues did not immediately occur to him. This is perhaps not surprising, as the precedents of 1166 and 1185 had depended upon the cooperation of the king of France, of which Henry could not have been sure until the Gisors meeting in January. Furthermore Henry had levied the last such tax only in 1185, and in the previous two years he had tallaged his royal demesne and the Jews in England; he may have doubted the wisdom or practicality of additional exploitation.[94] Instead his thoughts turned to the church. Before the end of 1187 Henry ordered the sequestration of the profits made from the pilgrims to Becket's shrine at Canterbury, so that, the king's agents informed the outraged monks, the money could be directed by the king to help Jerusalem and to redeem Christian captives. The king secured the approval of Archbishop Baldwin, who was more concerned lest the monks use their treasure to win a longstanding suit they had against him at the Papal Curia.[95] The monks ignored or discounted the official justification, but it may nevertheless have been genuine, as the king was at pains to emphasise that spending church treasure to aid Jerusalem was both pious and honest. By the end of January 1188 King Henry had decided to risk the much wider tax embodied in the Le Mans ordinance. Even so, his early caution was perhaps justified, in view of the subsequent failure of the tax in France, the refusal of the Scottish barons to have anything to do with it, and the barrage of verbal criticism it attracted from contemporary chroniclers. Once settled, however, Henry with energy and urgency set about collecting the tax which was soon dubbed in France the "Saladin" tithe.[96]

Whereas collection of the tithe in Capetian lands was put in the hands of those with local powers of high justice, Henry decreed that the tax in his lands was to be assessed and levied in each parish, in the presence of a tribunal including the priest, a Templar, an Hospitaller, serjeants and clerks of the king, and the local baron, bishop, and dean. There was no mention in England of the sheriff, possibly because the proceeds were directed to a separate department of receipt, not the exchequer, and the unit of administration was the diocese, not the shire.[97] Defaulters risked excommunication, and any disputes, such as attempted fraud, were to be settled by a jury appointed from the parishioners. In towns the system used for royal tallages was modified so that the rich of each city had to confront the king on stated occasions to be assessed by a jury.[98] Howden noted that bishops were to ensure that news of the tax was published in every parish on three consecutive days, 25–27 December, the term of parochial collection in the parishes being fixed for 2 February. However, these dates present difficulties, for the ordinances were published in January and February 1188, and the exchequer audit of Michaelmas 1188 noted three tithe payments—from the honour of Tickhill, the abbey of St. Mary's, Leicester, and the see of London.[99] It was unusual for the accounts of the tithe to be recorded on the Pipe Rolls, however the sums noted in 1188 were not of receipts but liabilities which had fallen on lands temporarily in royal hands. (One of those rendering account for the lands of the vacant see of London was Ralph of Hauterive, the future crusade hero.) Clearly collection had begun soon after the ordinances were promulgated. Howden himself elsewhere implied that clerks and laymen were appointed and despatched to each county at or soon after the council of Geddington in February 1188.[100] There would have been no reason for delaying collection for almost a year. In 1166, for instance, the crusade tax had been announced in May and the first term for collection fixed for early October.[101] On the other hand it might have seemed appropriate to collect the tithe at the end of the year in which it was levied, especially if the collectors were looking to include a full assessment of the yield of the 1188 harvest.[102] Alternatively, Howden copied into his version of the original decree instructions prepared later in 1188 to fix the final, rather than the sole deadline, or to encourage dawdlers to pay up. The fact that Gervase of Canterbury, who recorded the original Geddington decrees, mentions no fixed timetable may support this explanation.[103]

The Saladin tithe in Henry's lands differed both from its predecessors of 1166 and 1185 and from the Capetian levy of 1188. In contrast to the earlier taxes, the tithe was fixed at a set rate for one year only, instead of a sliding scale over several years. Royal scrutiny of the collection was increased both in town and country and a greater number of items— including clothes, books, weapons, and church treasures—were excluded from assessment than previously, perhaps to avoid the problems of a crude means test. In his lands Philip II exempted a number of religious orders; Henry was not so generous.[104] The 1188 tax was novel and consequently unpopular, despite the recognition of its honourable cause. Contemporary chroniclers with impressive unanimity condemned the harshness of assessment and the violence of collection. Roger of Howden, himself in 1188 a royal collector of forest fines, told of royal threats to imprison defaulters until they had paid the last farthing.[105] The outcry may have been tinged with hindsight, especially knowledge of the delay in the departure of the crusade, suspicion that the tithe money had been exhausted in the internecine feuding of 1188–89, and memory of Richard I's spectacular spree of venality and extortion in 1189–90. Some ecclesiastical observers objected to the prominent part played by the archbishop of Canterbury, the use of the episcopal rather than the shrieval organisation perhaps striking an especially jarring note.[106] The point all writers tacitly admit, however, is that whatever the resentment, taxpayers did contribute, a sign at least of Angevin administrative or coercive power.

By contrast Philip II had to abandon collection of the Saladin tithe in Capetian lands because of strong protests from his magnates, and he almost had to apologise for having proposed the levy in the first place. This humiliating failure of 1188–89 perhaps stung Philip into the important administrative reforms of 1190 which, borrowing some techniques from Anglo-Norman models, materially and later crucially improved Capetian financial resources.[107] Similarly, when on Henry's suggestion King William the Lion of Scotland tried to persuade his barons to pay the tithe, they gave him and the English ambassadors a very firm refusal, even though agreement might have brought the return of some castles lost to the English some years earlier.[108] Within Angevin lands, on the other hand, there appears to have been little obvious public refusal to pay, although a caveat should be entered here. The original tithe ordinance had been issued at Le Mans for Henry II's continental lands, but almost all the evidence of collection and receipts comes from England alone. Income from lands south of Normandy must always have been precarious, especially in 1188–89 when the southern provinces simmered with civil war. In the autumn of 1189 Richard I wrote to the papal legate, John of Anagni, urging him to further exertions in collecting the tithe from the dioceses of Poitiers and Limoges.[109] John was addressed as if he were de facto in charge of levying the tithe in these two dioceses, contrary to the Le Mans ordinances; the king was apparently relying on legatine authority to impose an order and effectiveness into the collection where secular power alone had failed. As the legate was asked to redouble his efforts to eradicate tax avoidance and fraud, collection had evidently run into trouble, not least that of timing. The example of the successful resistance in Capetian lands may have increased the difficulties in areas disputed by the two kings or in areas where the local lords were in revolt against the Angevins. Although Poitou was later said to have contributed to the 1190 crusade fleet, it must be doubted whether much was raised of the Saladin tithe south of the Loire.

In England the machinery worked more smoothly. The Pipe Rolls record payments from lands held by the Crown and account for administrative expenses such as wages of receivers and money spent on a chest in which to store receipts. A depository seems to have been established at Salisbury, only late arrears being paid into the exchequer, which dealt with the wages and other expenses of the Salisbury office.[110] This partial separation from the exchequer, in line with previous crusade taxes, was a physical demonstration of the uniqueness of the levy and of royal determination to use the proceeds for the crusade. Collection appears to have been rigorous, the assessment, as planned, including revenues, moveables, and crops. Inevitably there were problems. One crucesignatus, Robert of Cokefield, an influential East Anglian landowner, claimed the tithe from his manors of Groton and Semer in Suffolk in accordance with the 1188 decrees, only to be challenged by the ever-alert Abbot Samson of Bury St. Edmunds. Abbot Samson complained to the "justices appointed to collect the tithes" that Robert only possessed a life interest in the manors and so was ineligible to enjoy the tithe from those lands; a fact later recognised before the justices by Robert himself. The abbey hardly benefitted financially, as the abbot had been refused permission to take the cross himself, but the judgement reinforced the abbey's lordship. Robert did, however, receive the tithe from his hereditary manor of Cokefield. It appears from this case and from the evidence of collection from exchequer records and chronicles that, despite the right of crucesignati to the tithes on their noncrusading tenants' property, the king took it upon himself to collect the tax, the crusader presumably claiming his share from the collectors or the central depository; the same system seems to have operated for a crusade tax in 1201.[111] Judicial confusion apart, there was also the risk of peculation. One of those appointed by the king to collect the tithe, perhaps even one of the receivers at Salisbury, the Templar Gilbert "de Hogestan," was caught red-handed by his fellow collectors. Gilbert had been salting away such large sums that his colleagues had begun to notice that the cash in their charge was diminishing daily.[112]

Despite a tiny central administrative staff (the Pipe Rolls mentioning only ten tellers), a cumbersome system of local assessment, and inevitable logistic and legal difficulties in collection, the Saladin tithe proved sufficiently lucrative not only to arouse clerical fury but also to be used as a model for extraordinary national lay and ecclesiastical taxation for centuries to come. It evidently raised a considerable amount. The 1189 Pipe Roll recorded the transport of large sums of money from Salisbury: two hundred marks to Bristol (perhaps for the hire of ships), twenty-five hundred marks to Gloucester (possibly for horseshoes and iron from the Forest of Dean), and five thousand marks to Southampton, where considerable amounts were spent on preparations for the crusade in the following year. Elsewhere the same Pipe Roll entered payment for the carriage of twenty-five thousand marks to the king in France; money perhaps from the tithe, even if it might have been directed to noncrusading ends, conceivably a debt of twenty-four thousand marks to Philip II which King Richard honoured.[113] Gervase of Canterbury estimated the yield of the Saladin tithe at seventy thousand pounds, with the tallage on the Jews, raised at the same time for the same purpose, bringing in sixty thousand pounds. He was clearly wrong about the Jewish tallage, confusing the 1186 levy promulgated at Guildford with the tallage of ten thousand marks demanded in 1188, which was followed by a further impost of two thousand marks in 1190. Roger of Howden said that Henry II in 1189 left a treasure worth more than one hundred thousand marks, a figure which compares startlingly with J. H. Ramsay's calculations from the Pipe Rolls of annual royal revenue of £22,336 14s 7d (1187–88), £23,648 1s 1d (1188–89), and £27,693 9s 7d (1189–90). Henry II's treasure, of course, would have included proceeds from sources other than the Saladin tithe, notably the 1187 tallage, the 1186 tallage on the Jews, and ordinary exchequer receipts.[114] The chroniclers probably overstated their case for Henry's rapacity and wealth; the evidence of the Salisbury depository suggests a rapid turnover, with money not lying idle.

Henry, however, saw the tax's potential. In 1188 William of Scotland offered Henry four thousand marks (£2,666) in return for some disputed castles, but the English king replied that it would be better (i.e., more profitable for Henry) if Scotland paid the crusade tithe. His judgement was confirmed in 1189 when Richard I settled for ten thousand marks (£6,666) for the same castles.[115] With the high level of inflation in the years around 1200, it is dangerous to draw comparisons between the 1188 tax and later levies, but it may be worth noting that the thirteenth of 1207 realised more than £57,000, which places Roger of Howden's estimate of Henry II's 1189 fortune at least within sight of credibility. The precise yield of the Saladin tithe is impossible to estimate, but the tax was evidently a success on a scale perhaps not seen since the massive gelds of the early eleventh century. The inspiration might have been foreign, eastern, or even Italian, but the application and exploitation were characteristic of the English government of the late twelfth century.[116]

Whether or not the tithe money collected in 1188–89 had been dissipated in the renewed wars in France, and whatever the size of the royal treasure in 1189, on his accession Richard I felt the need for more, and he set about raising it in spectacular fashion. As Roger of Howden saw it, "He put up for sale all he had, offices, lordships, earldoms, sheriffdoms, castles, towns, lands, everything."[117] Sheriffs were sacked and fined, and new sheriffs were appointed at a price; towns were required to pay for new charters; forest rights were sold; important officials such as Geoffrey FitzPeter paid to be relieved of their crusade vows. The justiciar Rannulf Glanvill was dismissed and fined heavily (£15,000 was fancifully mentioned by some). Bishop Hugh du Puiset of Durham paid six hundred marks for the manor of Sadberge, two thousand marks for the earldom of Northumberland, and a further one thousand marks for release from his crusade vow and a half share in the justiciarship; the transaction prompted the king to quip that he had made a young earl out of an old bishop. Hugh could afford such fees only by using the considerable treasure he had already raised for the crusade in his palatinate of Durham, probably from the Saladin tithe.[118] Chance had also bequeathed Richard a number of rich vacant sees. His father had habitually kept such sees untenanted for long periods to enjoy the revenues, but Richard, needing ready cash, sold them to men he could trust in government, such as Richard FitzNeal (London) and William Longchamp (Ely), to the pious disapproval of many chroniclers. The king was prepared to sell his demesne quite freely; famously, he was widely reported as having told his friends that he would have sold London itself if he could have found a buyer.[119] Adept at maximising his good fortune, Richard also secured the reversion of property of the Jews massacred in the attacks of Lent 1190.[120]

An experienced general, Richard recognised, as had his father, that there was probably no limit to the treasure needed to finance a crusade. The Pipe Roll of 1190 shows that, so far from being profligate, he was making prudent provision. The cost of the crusade was enormous. Henry of Cornhill rendered account for £5,023 6s 8d spent on buying ships, repairing them, paying the wages of steersmen and crew, and satisfying administrative costs. A year's pay for 790 soldiers on thirty-three ships from the Cinque Ports alone came to £2,402 18s 4d, and the full wages bill in Henry of Cornhill's account reached £3,338 2s 6d for forty-five ships' companies. The average price per ship to the government, which usually acquired them at two-thirds of full price, was £50, although one obtained for the Hospitallers cost one hundred marks (£66 13s 4d).[121] The commitment to pay sailors' wages (two pence a day for sailors, four pence for steersmen) for a full year in advance was a heavy burden even if it made strategic sense. The variable size of ships' companies recorded in the Pipe Roll (ranging from twenty-two to sixty-one crew members) compare closely with Richard of Devizes's description of the numbers of crew per ship in the crusade fleet (between thirty and sixty). Devizes's figures may represent the official formula worked out at the Winchester treasury in order to calculate the crusade budget, information about which Richard, as a monk of nearby St. Swithun's, might reasonably have had knowledge.[122] On Devizes's figures, the annual wage bill for the crews in the 1190 royal fleet of, he claimed, one hundred ships and fourteen busses (with twice the normal complement of men) would have been about £8,700. In corroboration it could be noted that Devizes's figure for the size of the fleet is in line with Roger of Howden's estimate of a hundred and six ships. If the £50 average cost of commissioning each ship (from Henry of Cornhill's account) was typical, the boats themselves could have cost (again on Devizes's figures for the size of the fleet) as much as £5,700. Expenditure on men and equipment for just one part of the crusading force, not counting the cost of any later repairs, equipment, and food, would have been about £14,000. To this would have to be added the wages and maintenance of the troops of the royal household and the crews of the ships hired at Marseilles and elsewhere in the Mediterranean. It is small wonder that Richard was eager to extract as much money as he could from Tancred of Lecce when he arrived in Sicily. It is perhaps of greater surprise that at no time does Richard's war chest seem to have run dry, despite subsidies to Philip II and payments to more or less the whole crusading army once Acre was reached.[123]

Finance may have exerted an important influence on the prior strategic planning of the crusade. The fleet which sailed in spring 1190 was assigned certain rendezvous points for its journey through the Straits of Gibraltar and into the Mediterranean: at the mouth of the Tagus, then with the king at Marseilles (which the fleet missed by only a few days), and finally at Messina.[124] Although accused of sluggish progress, Richard had to wait for his fleet; they arrived at Messina almost simultaneously. However, by early 1191 he was facing a self-imposed deadline which, in contrast to his leisurely journey of 1190, now encouraged haste. He had budgeted and was probably carrying crews' wages for one year, which at the latest expired in June 1191 and possibly ran out at Easter, 6 April. Richard probably aimed to reach the Holy Land within or as near as possible to that time-limit; he may have intended to all along. Indeed, only the storm which scattered his fleet and led him to capture Cyprus in May 1191 spoilt his calculations.[125] Richard's dilatoriness in the winter of 1190–91 is explicable, even without the complications at Messina of Sicilian and French hostility. He needed to reequip and overhaul his fleet, and he had already paid his crews for the time in which to do it.

Crewmen and ships were not the sum of official concern. According to Richard of Devizes each ship, in addition to the crew, carried forty expensive warhorses, equipment for forty knights (but not apparently the knights themselves, who were perhaps expected either to accompany the king or to pay for their own passage with the fleet), forty footsoldiers, and food for men and horses, the busses again receiving a double complement. These figures are in outline confirmed by the Pipe Rolls. It may appear strange that the Crown should take upon itself to supply horses and equipment as well as transport, but the massive purchases of horseshoes (at least sixty thousand in 1190), arrows, and crossbow bolts leave little room for doubt. The Pipe Rolls do not explicitly mention horses for the crusade or their origins. But palfries and packhorses were being sent to the king in Normandy, even if they were not the destriers of Richard of Devizes's account.[126] The king may have raised horses through "voluntary" donations; there is a reference to horses being given to the king by "the sheriffs and abbots of England," although these too were destined for Richard's contingent in northern France.[127]

The element of public as well as private enterprise is notable. It may be imagined that some, perhaps many of the soldiers with the fleet were crucesignati who equipped themselves and contributed to the cost of hiring the ships (possibly the outstanding one-third not paid by the king). But the king provided the means of transport. For example, to the Hospitallers (who were hardly destitute) he donated a whole ship. The king's fleet also carried equipment for his own knights, possibly for as many as 4,000 of them. He supplied food for all, which royal officials bought in large quantities: cheeses from Essex, beans from Kent and Cambridgeshire, and over 14,000 cured pigs' carcasses from Lincolnshire, Essex, and Hampshire.[128] Although there was a balance between royal and individual responsibility, the chief dynamism and organisation was the king's.

As an example of the range of royal preparations for the crusade, Henry of Cornhill's account is complemented by that of the sheriff of Hampshire, whose return to the exchequer itemised certain payments for crusade provisions, including £57 18s 11d for bacon, 20 shillings for beans, £14 4s 5d for ten thousand horseshoes, £19 18s 1d for one hundredweight of cheese, £25 8s 4d for the preparation of eight ships, as well as £12 2s 1d for carriage and storage of supplies and treasure.[129] What treasure remained was divided up and placed in barrels in each ship to avoid financial disaster if only a few vessels foundered. Adequate provision of food and money was obviously vital to any successful military campaign, but such lavish preparations (which were supplemented in Sicily and Cyprus) could also pay political dividends. When he landed at Acre, Richard outbid Philip II for the loyalty of their nephew Henry of Champagne, with a gift to the count of four thousand measures of wheat, four thousand bacons, and £4,000 of silver.[130] War often stimulates areas of the economy, and it is hard to imagine that none of the producers of the crusade supplies took any profit. The price paid for bacon by the sheriff of Hampshire, about one shilling five pence per carcass, compares well with the price of one shilling per pig paid by crown agents in 1192–93. On the other hand, the drain of coin from the realm may explain the temporary slowing down, and for wheat and oxen the reversal, of the rise in inflation rate around this time.[131]

The Third Crusade was a triumph of Angevin organisation and was one of the most remarkable governmental achievements of the twelfth century, especially when it is considered that the plans and preparations worked more or less as intended. The failure to take Jerusalem in 1192 was political and military, not administrative. More generally, the effort required to launch Richard I's crusade involved wide areas of the community beyond the crucesignati themselves: the nuns of Swine who bought land to provide money for a crusader; the officials, priests, collectors, and jurymen who managed the Saladin tithe and the taxpayers who paid it; the pig farmers of Warwickshire; the ironworkers of the Forest of Dean; the ship owners of the Cinque Ports and elsewhere; the dairy farmers of Hampshire; the sheriffs who paid excessive amounts for their jobs. All were bound to the enterprise alongside the crusaders themselves: the great men and brave knights who won renown at Acre, Arsuf, and Jaffa; the men from Yorkshire and Lincolnshire who found their deaths beneath the walls of Acre; the ordinary foot soldiers who after the negotiated truce of 1192, by courtesy of Saladin crowded into the church of the Holy Sepulchre to fulfil their vows before returning home.[132]

Such involvement is impressive, but before it is accepted that the whole of society was gripped by the emotional and practical imperatives of the recovery of Jerusalem an important caveat should be entered. Life and politics in England were not suspended during Richard's absence, and while some Englishmen were profoundly interested in the crusade, others were not. In contrast to the vivid accounts of Roger of

Howden (a crusader himself, of course), Ralph of Diceto, or Ralph of Coggeshall, stands Gervase of Canterbury, sacrist of Christ Church, Canterbury, in whose history the crusade was never allowed to compete with his passionate, overriding concentration on the local dispute between his fellow monks and the archbishop. Gervase gave the preaching campaign of 1188 very short shrift. He interpreted Archbishop Baldwin's tour of Wales as an attempt to avoid having to defend himself against the monks, and he blamed Baldwin for the Saladin tithe. The crusade itself is described as "this unfortunate pilgrimage," and the course of the campaigns in the Mediterranean and Syria in 1190–92 are covered in a few bare lines, in marked contrast to the pages and pages of detailed exposition of the Canterbury dispute. This parochialism has been criticised by modern historians; nevertheless it cannot have been unique.[133] By force of circumstances Gervase was immersed in his own narrow world, which, like that of Jocelin of Brakelond at Bury St. Edmunds, who also found almost nothing to say about the crusade, fully engaged if not satisfied his interests, curiosity, and ambition. Monastic affairs were Gervase's career and his life, into which the crusade scarcely intruded. That must have been common enough. Richard of Devizes found it extremely difficult to integrate news of the crusade into his description of English politics; for the years 1190 and 1191 his accounts of the two theatres of action were physically separated. Even Roger of Howden's interest in events in the East palpably waned once he had left the crusader army in August 1191.[134] The view from Acre or the exchequer should also be seen from the perspective of Canterbury or Bury St. Edmunds.

The impact of the Third Crusade should not, therefore, be exaggerated. Arguably, the most immediate domestic consequence was the massacre of the Jews, although there were long-term implications in the departure of so many crusaders. While it is surely myopic not to ascribe the severe political unrest of 1191–92 to Richard's absence and to his less-than-prescient arrangements in 1190, it is also true that the administration of government continued amidst the difficulties. The Third Crusade produced no permanent administrative innovation, even if it did provide a useful fiscal model. However large the sums collected through the Saladin tithe or Richard's expedients of 1189–90, there is no firm evidence of resulting financial exhaustion; four years later Angevin officials raised, in less than a year, one hundred thousand marks primarily from England, for Richard's ransom. The loss of continental land to Philip II in 1193–94, moreover, can be attributed more to Richard's subsequent captivity in Germany than to his crusade.[135] Thus, the effects of the Third Crusade on England are not to be found in immediate social disruption, financial debility, political feuding, or even in novel techniques of government.

The Third Crusade did, however, leave its imprint on the future. Until 1188 crusading was not in any sense a mass movement in England; after 1188, and for at least another century, wider sympathy with the ideals of crusading was converted into action, and a habit was established which touched even some of the lowest free and propertied classes. After the Third Crusade the high tide of crusade enthusiasm took a long time to ebb. In the definition of crusade privileges and methods of funding, the ordinances and techniques of 1188–90 marked a significant stage. Militarily, Richard I had shown the problems and indicated the solutions to the question of the recapture of Jerusalem; it was on his foundations at Ascalon that his nephew Richard of Cornwall began building in 1241. More people now had direct experience of crusading, and firsthand accounts of Richard's crusade spread widely by word of mouth or through the efforts of chroniclers such as Abbot Ralph of Coggeshall or the Augustinian canon Richard of Holy Trinity. An English Order of St. Thomas had been founded at Acre, where there was soon to be an English quarter. Above all, perhaps, the semi-legendary exploits of Richard himself, whether in Richard of Holy Trinity's *Itinerarium Richard Regis* (written between 1213 and 1226) or in murals decorating the palaces of Henry III, kept a particular image of crusading alive. Later English authors took especial pride in the legends of Richard I. The ambassador from Bohemund VI of Antioch in 1255, who flattered Henry III that he was Richard's heir not only by hereditary right but in virtue, would have struck a chord with him; a few years earlier, in his first enthusiasm after taking the cross, Henry had festooned his palaces with heroic images of Richard's combat with Saladin and was proud to dine beneath his uncle's shield. It was into Richard's shoes that the Lord Edward stepped after he had trod Richard's footsteps in the Holy Land in 1271. "Behold he shines like a new Richard" was one enthusiastic contemporary comment. The Richard I of legend inhabited a world of chivalric verities, central to which was the duty to recapture Jerusalem. His posthumous fame demonstrated and guaranteed that for the knightly classes and for those who emulated them, the crusade retained not simply its traditional respectability but, no less important, its glamour.[136]

4

Crusades and Crusaders,

1192–1250

In the thirteenth century crusading enjoyed a level of popularity not seen before the Third Crusade. Beginning with the reign of Innocent III (1198–1215), the papacy used the crusade against a wider variety of targets, including heretics and political enemies of the church. The institution was given intellectual coherence and canonical respectability by academics now unafraid to face the implications of a positive doctrine of holy war. At an administrative level, a greater degree of passive participation was allowed as crucesignati were permitted to redeem their vows for cash. By the 1230s crusade privileges, particularly the indulgence, were effectively being offered for sale. At the same time, preaching the cross was lent a fresh populist, if not popular, dimension by the new mendicant orders of friars, the Franciscans and the Dominicans. Finance, following the precedents of the previous century, was increasingly centralised, initially in the hands of the papacy, which controlled ecclesiastical taxation and the funds derived from crusade legacies, vow redemptions, and donations. In time political and logistic circumstances persuaded popes to hand control of crusade money to secular rulers.

Despite the greater bureaucracy and intellectual rigidity, the sharp edge of crusading remained military. In Syria, the Frankish principalities survived in attenuated form centred upon Antioch (which fell to the Moslems in 1268), Tripoli (lost in 1289), and Acre (held until 1291). They were harassed externally by the Ayyubid rulers of Damascus and Cairo and from 1250 by the Ayyubids' more aggressive Mamluk successors in Egypt. They were divided internally by inheritance disputes and the conflicting interests of local barons, the military orders, foreign absentee rulers, and the Italian maritime cities. Regular crusades from the West attempted to reestablish a kingdom of Jerusalem, the remnant of which was now almost entirely dependent for its survival on the commercial wealth of Acre. Despite the lack of success and the gradual, and finally rapid, decline, there was a greater number of substantial expeditions from the West in the thirteenth century than in the twelfth. Twice, during the Fifth Crusade (1217–21) and the first crusade of Louis IX of France (1248–54), the Egyptian port of Damietta was briefly occupied. Other crusades, directed more locally at improving the precarious Frankish hold on the littoral of the Levant, were led by the Emperor Frederick II (1228–29), Theobald, count of Champagne (1239–40), Richard, earl of Cornwall (1240–41), and the future Edward I (1270–72). Outside these campaigns a constant stream of men and money reached the East, although never in sufficient quantities to make a revival more than a dream. In addition, the estates of the military orders in the West provided revenues to support their vital defensive role in Syria. Defence was of the essence. The main achievements of Frederick II, the count of Champagne, and the earl of Cornwall were to have secured truces with the Moslems. After being decisively defeated in Egypt in 1250, Louis of France spent the next four years in Palestine reinforcing Christian strongholds. Throughout the later years of Christian rule military confraternities, some of them founded and funded by western rulers, became increasingly important in Acre itself.

On the other hand, the scope of crusading, so far from contracting, expanded in the geographic spread of crucesignati and the military application of the institution of the crusade. With some regularity popes gave crusading status to wars against the Slavs in the Baltic, until from the reign of Alexander IV (1254–61) the crusade in the Baltic was delegated more or less permanently to the Teutonic Knights. The Reconquista in Spain remained chiefly in the hands of the Iberian monarchs. In the East, the conquest of Constantinople by the Fourth Crusade (1204) opened a new field for conquest and settlement in Greece and the islands of the Aegean, although soon Romania, as it was known, itself needed defending from Byzantine counterattack. Even the Moslem targets varied more than in the twelfth century. Egypt was now seen in the West, as well as in Syria, as the key to restoring Jerusalem and, in 1270, Louis IX led his last, ill-fated crusade to Tunis in North Africa, ostensibly in preparation for an attack on the Mamluks of Egypt.

Inherent in the idea of a holy war authorised by the pope for the defence of Christendom was warfare against heretics. This idea received its fullest expression after 1208 when Innocent III instituted a crusade against the Albigensian heretics in southern France; it was the beginning of a series of campaigns by crucesignati over the following twenty years, which resulted in the extirpation of heresy and the annexation of Languedoc by the kings of France. By the same token, popes could justify wars against their political opponents as crusades. This they did with increasing frequency in their battles for political independence and control of Italy, beginning in the 1230s and 1240s with crusades against Frederick II. Crusades followed against Frederick's Hohenstaufen successors in the 1250s and 1260s and against the Aragonese in the 1280s. By that time many internecine Italian feuds, often only loosely connected with the wider papal-Hohenstaufen conflict, were characterised as crusades. The ripples of these papal crusades reached as far as England; in the mid-1250s Henry III became deeply and disastrously involved in Alexander IV's attempts to oust the Hohenstaufen from southern Italy and Sicily.

Thus in terms of the amount of action seen by crucesignati, the theatres of conflict to which the crusade was applied, as well as the number of noncombatants who could enjoy crusade privileges, the thirteenth century was the golden age of crusading. However, as the nature of the movement changed, so responses to it altered. Crusading became more frequently prone to criticism of its management and, in some cases, direction, and reactions were increasingly partisan. There had been critics before 1200, notably after the failure of the Second Crusade. Ralph Niger had denounced the materialism behind the ideal during the Third Crusade, and there had been some conservatives who disapproved of rabble-rousing crusade demagogues like Fulk of Neuilly in the 1190s.[1] However, in England, from the civil war of 1215–17, the crusade became involved in a whole series of broader public and political controversies in England, over royal policy at home and abroad, papal authority, foreign influences, and ecclesiastical privileges.

The English crusades of the thirteenth century also bear witness to the wider impact of the expedients used to relieve the Holy Land, notably centralised control of recruitment, national taxation, coordinated ecclesiastical fundraising, preaching designed to raise money as well as men, concentration on professional armies rather than on revivalist mobs, and financial exploitation of the Jews.

Paradoxically, the system of centralised funding solved some of the problems for the private crusader but made future crusading actually less likely, as governments who increasingly held the purse strings had other priorities and fewer individuals had the capacity to organise expeditions of their own. Richard of Cornwall, one of the richest men in Europe, was an exception. Diplomatically, the English experience saw the transfer of dominance over crusading from the Hohenstaufen under Frederick II to the Capetians under Louis IX.

With the awesome difficulty of achieving a successful conjunction of men, money, strategy, and timing, active crusading could rarely be a panacea for domestic troubles or a path to individual fortune, yet it retained its appeal. In the eyes of contemporaries, not the least part of the greatness of Peter des Roches, justiciar and bishop of Winchester, Richard of Cornwall, William Longsword, or Edward I lay in their visits to Palestine. The respect in which crusading and crusaders were held had occasional direct political use as a means of appeasing domestic discontent. By taking the cross political rivals could signal and confirm their reconciliation without loss of face. For the king, assuming the cross placed him at the head of a unifying cause of unimpeachable respectability.

Militarily peripheral, their achievements in the East transient and ultimately negligible, the English crusades of the thirteenth century were important in their witness to social ambition and respectability, and in their reflection of domestic political tensions and developing techniques of war management which were applicable wherever armies fought. The focus on England reveals a texture of response and impact far richer than the simple assessment of numerical commitment or military success or failure. Nevertheless, at the core of crusading was its military purpose, and any examination of wider social, institutional, or political implications must begin with consideration of what people at the time thought a crusade should aim to achieve.

ATTITUDES

For all the crusading opportunities throughout Europe and the Mediterranean, the English consistently exhibited a marked preference for the Holy Land. A few may have joined the Teutonic Knights in their campaigns against the Prussians and Lithuanians in the Baltic, possibly including merchants in search of new markets, but it seems that only one thirteenth-century English knight who fought in the Baltic can be named, Robert of Morley (d. 1288), and his identification depends on a late fourteenth-century deposition in the Court of Chivalry. The absence of English crusaders in the Baltic stands in clear contrast to the following century.[2] Spain continued to attract some Englishmen. It is possible that Englishmen took the cross to fight the Moors in 1211 and that others were among those who captured Valencia in 1238; at Seville after its capture from the Moslems in 1248 there settled one Arnold of London, a John of London, and his son. However, a long-projected Anglo-Castillian scheme for a crusade to North Africa came to nothing.[3] With anti-Hohenstaufen crusades regularly proclaimed by popes in mid-century and even during the Sicilian embroglio in the 1250s, English money rather than men was the papal priority. The only significant English force to fight in Italy was that led by Henry of Turbeville in 1238, which   89 campaigned for Frederick II against the papally-backed Lombard cities.[4] Richard of Cornwall's later involvement in Germany, although helping to confirm the dismemberment of Hohenstaufen power, was never associated with a crusade.

As crusading became more widespread, its organisation became more localised, with appeals for crusaders and money ceasing to be general. Thus, recruitment for the Albigensian crusade was not aimed at England. English participation was minimal and fortuitous, hardly surprising as England was under a papal interdict until 1213, and then from 1214 to 1217 was rent by civil war. There was also official suspicion of the motives of the northern French crusaders and their annexation of large areas of Languedoc, traditionally an Angevin sphere of interest. It was no coincidence that after his defeat by the crusaders at Muret in 1213 the count of Toulouse fled to England; King John was his brother-in-law and his overlord for the Agenais which his wife, Joan, had brought him as her dower. English fears grew as the kings of France began increasingly to control the crusade, in the 1220s their campaigns in Languedoc being hard to distinguish from their wars further north which led to their conquest of Angevin Poitou. Official anxieties were reflected in Roger of Wendover's cynical appraisal that in the 1220s crusaders against the Albigensians were moved by fear of the king of France and the papal legate, not by justice, and the leaders by territorial greed, not concern for the faith. Any English involvement tended to be personal. The papal legate who preached a renewed anti-Cathar crusade in 1214, Robert of Courçon (i.e., Curzon), was a native of Kedleston in Derbyshire; Walter Langton and Hugh of Lacy, earl of Ulster, took part in campaigns in Languedoc between 1211 and 1219. Langton, because of his close relationship to the exiled archbishop of Canterbury, his brother Stephen, and Lacy, because of his banishment from England in 1210–11, were both distinctly but uniquely available. They became loyal and valued members of the elder Simon de Montfort's military entourage. In 1211, at the siege of Castelnaudary, they were opposed by "that son of the Devil, servant of Anti-Christ, despoiler of the church and enemy of Christ" Savaric de Mauleon, the mercenary captain of King John. Five years later, he was to appear as a favoured papal crusader in defence of the English church and king. Whereas secular political divisions could remain constant, Mauleon opposing northern French interests in Languedoc in 1211 and England in 1216, papal approbation was flexible to the point of fickleness.[5] Mauleon saw at close quarters how politics and crusading could be combined, a fact he may have remembered when he took the cross to protect the Angevin dynasty in 1216.

Crusades against the Greeks, although frequently hitched to the needs of the Holy Land, consistently failed to capture English imaginations; the preaching campaigns of 1237 and 1246 and the attempt to raise a subsidy in 1262 all flopped. In 1263, when Urban IV authorised preaching for expeditions to Greece and the Holy Land, his instructions to preachers in England mentioned only the Holy Land.[6] It was not that Englishmen disapproved of fighting to protect the Frankish settlements in Greece, or necessarily approved of the Hohenstaufen, but they were unimpressed by attempts to equate all papal and Christian warfare with the crusade to the Holy Sepulchre.

Although the papacy was selective in where it sought recruits and funds, the English evidence indicates a considerable gap between papal desires and local wishes. In 1239 Richard of Cornwall swore a special oath to reinforce his refusal to be diverted from the Holy Land to Greece or Italy. In 1247 Bishop Walter Cantelupe in similar circumstances secured a papal guarantee that no crusader should be compelled either to redeem his vow if able to fight or to campaign against anybody but Saracens; the promise was repeated by Henry III in 1251.[7] Reactions could be influenced by considerations of foreign policy or political advantage. However, there appears an underlying reluctance to follow the cross wherever the pope carried it.

The chroniclers have been the traditional guides to medieval attitudes outside the academic world of the schools. But interpretation of their witness is controversial, and never more so than when concerning one of the most vociferous commentators on contemporary opinions about crusading, the St. Alban's monk Matthew Paris (d.1259). Paris was antipapal and nationalistic; but he was not a Little Englander, and he was an enthusiast for a certain form of crusading. His criticisms concentrated on three features of the administration of the crusade: creeping papal control of the English church, the misuse of crusade funds which this made possible, and some of the destinations for crusades proposed by the papacy. He drew attention to the confusion caused in the late 1240s by the conflicting crusade objectives of the Holy Land, Romania, and Frederick II.[8] The positive side of Paris's opinions—his enthusiasm for campaigns against external enemies of Christendom, especially in the East—is evident in his obituary of the crusader Philip d'Aubigny, his praise of those who died on Richard of Cornwall's crusade, and his eulogy on the fate of William Longsword at Mansourah in 1250.[9]

As will be discussed in the next chapter, Paris was far from alone in his views. For example, the worries of the clergy of Berkshire, Lincolnshire, and Lichfield were exactly the same as his: jurisdiction, encroaching papal power, the misuse of Holy Land funds, and crusades against Christians. This unanimity is not surprising. Paris and his colleagues may have complained louder than some on the continent because they had more to complain about; and such reactions were not confined to the clergy, as shown by the barons' complaints at Amiens in 1264.[10] Judged by these responses, the papacy was being too radical in its wide application of crusade institutions and in its development of the concommitant administrative machinery. However, the papacy seems to have learnt from English opposition to the anti-Hohenstaufen crusades, as crusades later in the century, against Ghibellines or Aragonese, were not preached in England. After 1265, crusade appeals by the papacy in England concentrated on the relief of the Holy Land.

Rejection of papal crusade plans did not imply any general decline in support for the ideal. Whilst it is difficult to find examples of Englishmen who vowed to crusade elsewhere, hundreds of individuals took oaths to go to the Holy Land. Other objectives are conspicuous by their absence in the sources, but there may be a number of technical reasons for this. A crusade to the Holy Places earned a longer essoin and term of protection than other journeys, including simple pilgrimages to Jerusalem.[11] The chances of lengthy absences, loss of communication, and suspected or actual decease, all of which provoked litigation and hence records, were possibly greater with journeys to Palestine, which were also perhaps more expensive. Thus the need to sell or mortgage property fell more acutely on Holy Land crusaders, so more of their transactions may survive. Wills do not show that money was bequeathed to Spain, Italy, Greece, or the Baltic, although this may be due to traditional testamentary habits and to the existence of a diocesan structure to collect specific Holy Land legacies; also, many testators had unfulfilled Holy Land vows.[12] But such explanations do nothing to diminish the cumulative impression of the overwhelming primacy of the Holy Land as opposed to the alternatives, especially as the social range of the sources is representative: artisans, small landowners, and parish priests, to the greatest prelates and princes in the land, all sections of the community with something to be sold, mortgaged, protected, inherited, or bequeathed.

Whatever the spiritual and social dividends, active crusading constituted a heavy and risky material investment. Recognising this fact, the crucesignati themselves placed the crusade in a secular order of priorities, private and public. Peter Langtoft commented on the Scottish crisis in 1293:

> And if King Edward had gone towards Acre
> Greatly would the kingdom and royalty have been in peril,

in an argument similar to those used to dissuade Louis IX from going on crusade in the 1240s and 1260s, and Henry III, in 1270.[13] War was war, whether or not it was also holy. Thus, reactions to the crusade were influenced by factors which determined the progress of any military enterprise. The political and diplomatic circumstances had to be suitable, troops had to be organised, money raised. Finance was just as significant as faith. Typical was Hugh of Neville's preoccupation in drawing up his will at Acre in 1267 to secure payment and return fares for members of his retinue, a concern which was probably mutual.[14]

The investment which crusading entailed gave primacy to the eastern passagium; only the Holy Land offered spiritual and emotional gains and social reputation commensurate with the material outlay. The fundamental appeal of crusading had changed little; the spiritual goal was the remission of sins, attained by the penitential exercise of the pilgrimage.[15] For the active crusader the path to remission was the characteristic pilgrimage by which the crusade was distinguished from other holy or just wars; the prominence of Jerusalem and the Holy Places was inevitable.[16] The failure of attempts to divorce crusading from Jerusalem in the attitudes of laymen is explained partly by this continued potency of traditional imagery (witnessed, for example, in stone by the chapel of the Holy Sepulchre in Winchester Cathedral, which is possibly associated with the crusade of Peter des Roches) and partly by long-standing habits of patronage and spiritual investment, for instance in the military orders associated with the Holy Land.[17] The very language used to try to conceal the separation of the ideal from its original objectives was inadequate. One of the commonest euphemisms for the crusade was, fairly enough, the "business of the cross," a phrase which could be used, as in the anti-Hohenstaufen preaching of the 1250s, to give the phenomenon universal application through concentration on the transcendent image of Christ.[18] Crusade sermons, often accompanying mass, frequently emphasised general service to Christ and the mystical symbolism of the cross.[19] The cult of the Holy Cross was widespread.[20] Yet the concentration on the cross failed to distract attention away from the scene and physical reality of the Passion—possibly the reverse. It evidently left active crusaders unconvinced that the *negotium crucis* was the same as the *negotium papae*. There was thus a basic weakness in the policy of extending the crusade, although in many ways it proved useful to kings and popes alike.

The Holy Sepulchre could not be hidden in the shadow of the cross. This was implicitly recognised in papal bulls and by papal agents whose main tactic to establish the efficacy of privileges was to equate them with those granted to crusaders to the Holy Land. It was precisely the contrast between this sort of rhetoric and the reality which, so Paris maintained, undermined the preaching against Manfred of Hohenstaufen in the 1250s.[21]

In England, far removed from the passions of Languedoc and Italy, only the Holy Land inspired miraculous signs in the heavens or the literary dilemma of the crusader in love.[22] Paris extracted national pride from deeds in the East. He made William Longsword into an English martyr and added his own gloss to Wendover's account of the 1227 crusade of the bishops of Winchester and Exeter, describing it as having been "to the salvation and honour of many, especially of all Englishmen." The emotion was echoed by Gregory X in 1272 when he wrote of the glory bestowed on the English people by the Lords Edward and Edmund in Palestine.[23]

Interest in crusading was not confined to concern with affairs of the East; yet in literature the Holy Land retained its primacy. Chronicles contain letters from crusaders in the Holy Land describing events in Syria or appealing for aid, news, anecdotes, legends, rumours, and eyewitness accounts of campaigns; for example, Oliver of Paderborn's description of the Fifth Crusade was reproduced by Roger of Wendover.[24] Copies of William of Tyre's monumental *History of Deeds Done Beyond the Sea* and his now-lost compilation on Islamic history, the *Deeds of the Rulers of the East*, were obtained by Matthew Paris from Peter des Roches himself in the 1230s. The supernatural associations of the Holy Land were refreshed by the arrival in England in the first half of the thirteenth century of notable relics—the Holy Rood of Bromholm, and the Host of Blood and imprint of Christ's Foot at Westminster.[25] Other tangible reminders were provided by returning crusaders in the shape of eastern luxuries, such as the rich cloth brought back by Richard of Cornwall in 1241 which found its way into Westminster Abbey. The mendicant order of Our Lady of Mount Carmel was introduced into England in the early 1240s by followers of Richard of Cornwall's crusade.[26] There was a constant flow of ambassadors and messengers from Outremer, not least of whom was the bishop of Tortosa, an Englishman who combined a diplomatic mission with an unsuccessful attempt to trace his relatives near Reading.[27]

Generalised interest without direction risked stagnating into more or less idle curiosity. Perhaps the most significant thirteenth-century innovation in generating active crusade enthusiasm was the employment of Roman Christendom's new strike force, the friars. Their freedom of manoeuvre, demotic appeal, and didactic training suited them as recruitment officers as well as preachers and salesmen of redemptions and indulgences. From the 1230s they played a leading role in national and local preaching tours, much to the anger and jealousy of some of the more traditional cloistered clergy. Additional focus came from the institution of special prayers, masses, and processions to expiate the weight of sin to which successive disasters in the Holy Land had been ascribed, and to remind the faithful of their obligations towards the land where their Saviour had lived and died.[28]

Concentration on the dangers besetting Christendom could lead to a degree of paranoia. In 1257 there were rumours of Moslem agents with evil designs destined for England from Syria. In 1238, on the express order of Henry III, a visiting "Saracen" was kept under close arrest at Canterbury to prevent his spying. There is also a hint of excessive nervousness in the royal command of June 1259 to apprehend an Ethiopian called Bartholomew "sometime a Saracen."[29] The struggle against Islam became a touchstone of Christian faith. In 1238 the scholarly Bishop Grosseteste of Lincoln protested as evidence of his loyalty to the Holy See his willingness to preach the Gospel "in the farthest regions of the Saracens, even to death."[30] Paradoxically, the greater the awareness of the forces threatening Christendom, the less accurate the knowledge and the greater the fear. The sudden violent and alarming appearance of the Mongols in Europe led in 1241 to the institution of yet more special weekly processions, prayers, and fasting; the authorities even arranged for stories of Mongol atrocities to be published in every parish.[31] The impact of such scare mongering is hard to gauge, but it had clearly reached extravagant proportions when the 1238 collapse of the Great Yarmouth herring trade was attributed indirectly to fears of a Mongol invasion of eastern Europe.[32] There was a pessimism and sense of helplessness in the face of God's displeasure, which was seen to be manifested in the successive crusading expeditions which either failed disastrously or achieved only fragile, transitory success.[33] Nevertheless, at a time when tradition, politics, language, and geography were driving the nobilities of England and France apart, the crusade retained its force as an agent of supranational cooperation and idealism, continuing to demonstrate a tenacious, practical community of interest, affiliation, and on one famous occasion, affection. For example, in 1242, Richard of Cornwall managed to extricate his brother Henry III and his army from untenable positions at Taillebourg and Saintes because the French were grateful at his having secured the release of French nobles from Egyptian prisons during his crusade the year before.[34]

THE FIFTH CRUSADE

It was not until twenty years after the Third Crusade that there was another widespread crusade effort from England. The delay was a consequence of the collapse of the Angevin continental empire between

1193 and 1204, John's failure to win back his French lands, the papal interdict of 1207–13, and the growing conflict between John and his barons.

Meanwhile, neither the lay nor clerical establishments could, or were inclined to, ignore the crusade. Political uncertainty after the death of Richard I probably accounted for the lack of general English participation in the Fourth Crusade instigated by Innocent III in 1198. The preaching campaigns in England conducted by Abbot Eustace of St. Germer de Flay in 1200 and 1201 failed to inspire massive recruitment. A clerical fortieth for the crusade was instituted in 1199 but was collected only slowly, the proceeds being scarcely forthcoming before the Interdict of 1208 severed relations with Rome and brought a halt to papally inspired taxation. In 1201, the kings of England and France, following precedent, jointly agreed to a lay crusade fortieth, but this raised little in England.[35] Crusaders were as likely to have had the pilgrimage enjoined on them as to have voluntarily taken a vow for the sake of defending the Holy Land, reflecting not hostility or disillusionment but a lack of any concerted attempt to arouse excitement, caused by the absence of political will. It also appears that some, perhaps many, of those who did take the cross in the two decades after the Third Crusade became too poor to consider the fulfilment of their obligations.[36]

Yet the authorities were just as concerned with crucesignati who never set out as with those who did. While the secular law courts dealt with possessory and inheritance problems caused by absent and possibly deceased crusaders, in 1194 the itinerant royal justices were instructed to enquire into the nature and extent of chattels held by crusaders who had died before they could begin their pilgrimage, who held them, what they comprised, and what they were worth. On the ecclesiastical side, in 1196 Archbishop Hubert Walter was asked by the pope to compile lists of crucesignati who had failed to fulfil their vows, with a view to compelling those who had stayed at home without just cause to honour their commitment.[37] The 1194 enquiry by the justices left no trace in official records and it is difficult to see what legitimate interest the Crown had in such goods. Although it was becoming increasingly common for those who died before the performance of their vow to leave money for the crusade, it was hardly yet obligatory, and even if it had been, the church, not the state, had the formal responsibility to enforce any such rules.[38] In 1194, or at any other time, profits from dead crusaders' chattels could not have been treated simply as exchequer income. Previously, the only direct royal involvement had been in implementing the 1188 ordinances on dead crusaders' property, which applied only to those actually on campaign. Explicit legacies for the crusade were to become an integral part of a permanent crusade fund; but this too would be under ecclesiastical control. Perhaps the justices in 1194 were being asked, by a government led by a justiciar who was also the archbishop of Canterbury, to assist the church's attempt to lay claim to a portion of deceased crusaders' wealth. Alternatively, the justices might have been concerned to unravel the complicated network of privileges, protection, and claims which encumbered the property even after the owner's demise. More speculatively, the justices' enquiry might have been aimed at establishing what could be included in any assessment for royal taxation, in the context of the royal tallage levied in the autumn of 1194.[39] Whatever role was envisaged for the justices in 1194 had no future, as the church retained its prerogative over such matters. But an enquiry into Yorkshire crusaders, the reason for which is obscure, was conducted by Robert of Vieuxpont in 1206; it resulted in fines being levied on certain named crusaders, which appear on the Pipe Rolls of 1207 and 1208.[40]

Active royal or aristocratic involvement in the crusade was inevitably muted until the end of the civil war in 1217, although Richard I had maintained contacts with the kingdom of Jerusalem throughout the 1190s, and successive popes had been quick to remind all Christians of their obligations to the Holy Places.[41] Once the internal unrest had subsided, the response to papal calls was considerable.

Between 1218 and 1221 magnates from both sides of the civil war left to assist in the siege of the Egyptian port of Damietta on the Nile, including the earls of Hereford, Chester, Winchester, Arundel, and Ferrers, Brian de l'Isle, William of Harcourt, Robert FitzWalter, two bastards of King John (Oliver and Richard), John of Lacy, William and Philip d'Aubigny, and Savaric of Mauleon. Politically this was a most disparate group.[42] In contrast to the Third Crusade, there was no effective deadline or conformity of departure, reflecting the lack of royal supervision. Contingents came and went from Damietta with each biannual passagium. The earl of Chester left Damietta soon after it fell to the Christians in November 1219, whereas the earl of Winchester had arrived only a short time before. Philip d'Aubigny only reached Egypt in September 1221 after the city had been surrendered back to the Moslems, and Peter des Roches, bishop of Winchester, took the cross eleven days after Damietta's fall.[43] Beyond a few subsidies to individual crusaders, official involvement is difficult to identify, although Earl Rannulf of Chester's bailiff claimed before royal justices in Yorkshire in 1219 that "the earl is in the king's service in the land of Jerusalem." This was a hint, perhaps, that the earl was fulfilling Henry III's, or possibly King John's, crusade vow as a proxy; Rannulf had been one of John's executors charged in the king's will with "sending help to the Holy Land."[44]

Some crucesignati found the crusade a useful opportunity to avoid domestic or political embarrassment. Among less exalted crusaders were suspected murderers, felons, rapists, and defendants in civil property suits.[45] The prospect of crusading in the Holy Land was not necessarily conducive to binding up civil wounds, but on more than one occasion it proved useful to the guilty, suspect, insecure, or unfavoured. Some, at least, of the baronial diehards of 1215–17 may have welcomed the respite and protection the crusade afforded. However, piety should not be ignored; dying crusaders showed gratitude, perhaps affection, to those permanently enjoined with the crusade burden who had borne so much of the labour during the long siege of Damietta. In the camp outside the city's walls John of Harcourt and Emeric of Sacy both bequeathed land to the Templars.[46]

English involvement on the Damietta campaign was not negligible. According to one eyewitness, the earl of Chester was influential in the divided high command. He also gave fifty marks towards a fort constructed by the Templars during the siege, news of his largesse later being carried back to England.[47] The earl of Arundel was a spokesman for those who resisted the bellicose plans of the papal legate, Cardinal Pelagius, and at least one English contingent, Geoffrey of Lucy's, suffered heavy casualties. It was even reported that Peter des Roches, the irrepressibly ambitious former justiciar, had been elected in absentia bishop of Damietta.[48] Writers on the spot identified the English as a distinct group. The Barnwell annalist recorded that on the fall of Damietta in 1219, in honour of the English two mosques were dedicated to the national saints Edmund the Martyr and Thomas Becket. The newly consecrated church of St. Edmund was decorated with wall paintings depicting the martyr's passion, commissioned by an English knight, Richard of Argentan. He may probably be identified with a crusader of the same name, who in 1228 personally corroborated to the monks of St. Alban's certain information supplied by the archbishop of Armenia about eastern customs and legends.[49]

The crusaders' presence in Egypt was brief, yet the Fifth Crusade renewed an impetus begun during the Third Crusade. Future English participation in crusading endeavours was taken for granted. Some individuals never escaped the emotional grip of the Holy Land. Philip d'Aubigny, the royalist civil war commander and tutor to the young Henry III, whose father Ralph had died on the Third Crusade, arrived off Damietta on 5 September 1221 only to find the Christian evacuation in full swing. By 1228 he had taken the cross again and, in 1234–35, he completed elaborate financial arrangements for another expedition east. Accompanied by his nephew Oliver and a number of other knights, he embarked once more in June 1235 for Palestine. He died in Jerusalem the following year, being buried outside the church of the Holy Sepulchre. Philip's tomb slab still bears his arms and the inscription: "Here lies Philip d'Aubigny. May his soul rest in peace, Amen." It was a grave for which, as Matthew Paris put it, "he had long yearned in life."[50] Philip's experience and ambition exposes a persistent idealism, without which no amount of spiritual or temporal inducement could have succeeded in turning men's thoughts to the cross.

THE CRUSADE OF 1227–1229

If monastic writers are to be believed, the crusade of 1227–29 made a considerable impact in England, beginning with an apparently widely successful preaching campaign in the spring and early summer of 1227. Roger of Wendover, citing a roll of names compiled by one of the preachers, Master Hubert, put the number of recruits at forty thousand, a certain exaggeration. He also recorded the appearance, on the night of 24 June, of a vision of Christ Crucified in the skies over southern England, seen by, among others, a travelling fishmonger from Uxbridge who thereafter daily regaled his customers with the story.[51] Celestial apparitions had, of course, been a regular feature of crusade recruitment since the 1090s. A similar phenomenon was noted by Wendover as accompanying the preachings of the Fifth Crusade in the Rhineland in 1216–17.[52] Although it seems that not everyone was readily convinced by hearsay evidence of such miracles, their appearance was a usual ingredient of the occasional concerted efforts to attract crucesignati, especially when, as in 1227, they received full official support.

In 1225 the Emperor Frederick II determined to embark for the Holy Land in August 1227, and in 1226 it was arranged, with the king's approval, that Peter des Roches should accompany him to fulfil the vow the bishop had taken in 1221. With Peter went William Brewer, bishop of Exeter.[53] Peter des Roches may have found an incentive to depart in the unwelcome political dominance of the Justiciar Hubert de Burgh (and no doubt Hubert would not have been unduly distressed at the absence of this hostile schemer). Brewer perhaps had a more personal reason. His uncle and namesake, William Brewer, a veteran royal official, had been one of Richard I's ministers who had received papal permission to postpone fulfilling their crusade vows in 1189. As one of the elder Brewer's colleagues, Geoffrey FitzPeter, discovered, this release had not been intended by the pope to be permanent. The obligation remained. Bishop Brewer, according to his uncle, had taken the cross in expiation of his own and his uncle's sin, and was authorised to spend four thousand silver marks which the Templars had been holding on deposit at Acre on his uncle's behalf.[54]

The two bishops were the central figures in the 1227 crusade; des Roches was appointed by the pope to organise preaching, and both received papal permission to raise money on the income from their sees. Des Roches was also released from a number of debts to the Crown.[55] Financial rather than popular support ensured the English bishops a prominent role during their stay in the Holy Land. That is not to say that few English crucesignati went with them. Chroniclers write of thousands stranded in southern Italy by Frederick's failure to embark as promised in 1227 (an indication that the English enterprise was originally planned as dependent on the emperor). A letter from leading local and visiting clerics in the Holy Land in December 1227, including the bishops of Winchester and Exeter, described how on hearing of the emperor's delay "more than 40,000" abandoned their crusade as soon as they reached Syria. However, eight hundred knights, a considerable army, remained, including, so one of the vernacular French continuations of William of Tyre has it, "many English." Among them could have been Ralph of Rouen, who had mortgaged houses in Oxford and Northampton to pay for his crusade in 1227; Geoffrey le Flemang, a man of property from Kent; and John Gole, a proxy crusader who was rewarded with a farm at Seaborough on his return in 1229.[56]

One of the ironies of the 1227–29 crusade was underlined when an English Dominican called Walter, a preacher appointed by the pope, in protest conducted mass outside the walls of Jerusalem, after it had been restored to the Christians by the excommunicate Frederick II. Among Frederick's close advisers were the English Bishops des Roches and Brewer. This schism foreshadowed the debilitating papal-imperial conflict of the next forty years, into which most western European powers were drawn. On crusade, however, the English bishops ignored papal strictures, cooperating fully with the emperor's agent Henry of Limbourg in 1227–28 and with Frederick himself after his arrival in Palestine in 1228. They witnessed the notorious treaty with the Sultan of Cairo of 18 February 1229, which restored Jerusalem peacefully to the Christians.[57] It would be misleading to see the English bishops simply as pro-Hohenstaufen or as hostile to the emperor's enemies among the local Syrian baronage and in the military orders. In fact they identified themselves with whichever group pursued an active and constructive policy, which the pullani appeared reluctant to follow. The scope for action was admittedly limited. Most thirteenth-century crusades in the

Holy Land achieved little beyond some tactical rebuilding and refortification of important coastal sites—Caesarea and Athlith in 1217–18, Ascalon in 1240–41, Caesarea again in 1250–54, Acre in 1271–72. The crusade of 1227–29 was no exception. Attempts were made over several months to refortify Caesarea, Sidon, and Jaffa, work to which the English, especially at Sidon and Jaffa, made notable contributions; in the restoration of Jaffa Peter des Roches was apparently "second to none."[58] The bishops' money was their chief service. Brewer had access to his uncle's hoard at Acre, and des Roches may have brought with him money from the 1222 tax levied in England on behalf of the kingdom of Jerusalem, from which in May 1225 he had been assigned five hundred marks. Wherever it came from, the bishop of Winchester lavished money on building operations. According to Matthew Paris, who met the bishop after his return, des Roches directed five hundred marks of his own to the transformation into a military order of the existing hospital of St. Thomas at Acre, founded by Englishmen on the Third Crusade.[59] The activities of the two bishops were widely and proudly reported by English chroniclers, and Bishop Brewer was received "with honour" on his return to his diocese in 1229, as was his colleague in 1231.[60]

Apart from the coastal fortifications, there were two lasting consequences of the 1227–29 crusade: the reestablishment of the Order of St. Thomas of Acre as a military order, which persisted as such for over a century, and as a religious order into the sixteenth century; and the development of a close relationship with the Hohenstaufen. On crusade and in the years immediately after, Peter des Roches worked intimately with many of Frederick II's advisers, notably Hermann von Salza, the influential master of the Teutonic knights (c. 1210–39), whom the bishop had met at Acre in 1227. Within a year of their meeting des Roches had reformed the Order of St. Thomas by giving it the rule of the Teutonic Order to follow; a few years later, and quite possibly on des Roches's advice, Henry III married his sister Isabella to the emperor and began payment of an annual pension to the Teutonic Knights. This continued to be paid sporadically by his successors for two centuries, the first direct contact between England and the order whose activities were to attract so many Englishmen in the fourteenth century.[61]

THE CRUSADE OF RICHARD OF CORNWALL

The crusade of Richard of Cornwall was more renowned than that of the bishops of Winchester and Exeter, partly because of the great secular lords who joined it but also partly because Earl Richard himself made sure of its fame by handling his own publicity, both in writing and by word of mouth. The flattering account by Paris, for example, relied on Richard's own newsletters and personal reminiscences. The reality was less glamorous. In 1240 before Richard arrived in Syria a treaty had been agreed between the Latins and the sultan of Damascus, which in theory restored a considerable part of the territory lost to Saladin on the west bank of the River Jordan. Whilst the sultan of Damascus might not have been in a position to deliver all he promised, the sultan of Cairo, with whom Richard struck a deal in 1241, had no control whatever over the lands he agreed to return to Christian rule. It was only Richard's trumpeting of his own achievement and his denigration of the 1240 treaty and its ostensible maker, Theobald of Champagne, in a letter written on his return from the East in July 1241, that allowed his treaty to be regarded, by Paris and many subsequent historians, as a major diplomatic success.[62] In fact both Theobald's and Richard's diplomacy formed only one part of the wider and more significant struggle for ascendancy within the Ayyubid empire between Damascus, Cairo, and al-Nasir of Kerak, ruler of southern Palestine. The Latins had little control and limited influence over the most important political developments inside the Ayyubid dominions, upon which lasting security for the kingdom of Jerusalem ultimately depended. Of greater potential use to the kingdom was Richard's rebuilding of his uncle's fortifications at Ascalon, which, if nothing else, put pressure on Egypt to open negotiations. In the eyes of the West, however, Richard's most notable achievements were the release of French prisoners captured at the rout of Gaza in November 1239 and the burial of the remains of thirty-three nobles and five hundred other troops killed in the battle, acts which established Richard's reputation throughout western chivalry.[63] In all, however, Richard's crusade flattered to deceive; its achievements were minimal.

The crusade of 1240–41 is instructive in what it shows of the domestic social and political currents which ran beneath the raising of a crusader army. Recruitment for Earl Richard's crusade had by 1240 been going on for some years and, although based on Richard's household and associates, it had attracted crucesignati from across political divisions. For example, both the former outlaw Richard Siward and the man who had got him arrested in 1236, Simon de Montfort, took the cross. Among those who at Northampton in November 1239 swore an oath alongside Richard to reaffirm their unswerving commitment to travel to the Holy Land, rather than anywhere else, were Siward, a longstanding personal enemy of the earl; Gilbert Marshal, a leader of baronial discontent against the king and his foreign advisers; and Henry of Turbeville, one of the royalist captains who had in 1233 suppressed a

Welsh uprising in support of the Marshals' opposition to the personal rule of Henry III in 1233.[64] The affiliations of those who actually embarked in 1240 were similarly disparate. The anti-alien activists Robert Tweng and Philip Basset rubbed shoulders with their former adversary William Longsword; with royal officials such as the chief forester, John of Neville, and the steward of the king's household, Amaury of St. Amand; and with close relatives of the king, Richard himself, his illegitimate half-brother Eudo, as well as his cousin Longsword.[65] Given the investment required and the inconvenience of a prolonged and hazardous absence, the composition of this, or any, crusade could not have been entirely accidental.

For all the commotion caused by the preaching and the fundraising from 1235, the number of magnates personally involved in the 1240 crusade was small and can perhaps be analysed best in social and patronal rather than in crude political terms. The initial taking of the cross in 1236 by a group of prominent barons had been an attempt to consolidate the alliance of the Marshals and Richard of Cornwall and to reconcile dissidents with elements at court. It was an exercise in expedient and symbolic compromise, which persisted at least until the oath of Northampton. However, as embarkation neared, the internal political structure of the expedition changed, with the Marshal connection, so important earlier in the 1230s, receding in significance. Gilbert Marshal himself failed to depart, and this, coupled with the death early in 1240 of Richard's wife, Gilbert's sister Eleanor, marked the end of the influential Cornwall-Marshal alliance and the emancipation of Richard of Cornwall as an independent political force. The crusade was a turning point in Richard's career. He left, somewhat disillusioned if Paris is to be believed, a rather partisan arbiter of domestic rivalries of which his wife's family and his brother's advisers tended to be the leaders. He returned with experience of command and diplomacy and a taste for the international stage. It was a progress repeated by his nephew Edward thirty years later. Although the vows of many of the crusaders in 1240 had been sworn in the context of the political infighting of the 1230s, the crusade itself scarcely reflected this, except that Simon de Montfort may have found it opportune to absent himself from court after a fierce argument with Henry III in August 1239.

The patterns of allegiance on Earl Richard's crusade were based on the affinities and family connections of each leader, in particular on those of Richard himself. Originally there was little centralised unity, and indeed two contingents, those of Simon de Montfort in 1240 and William of Forz in 1241, appear to have been more or less independent from the main body. Richard took with him members of his own household, including his steward John FitzJohn, and of his brother's, such as Neville and St. Amand, as well as his half-brother Eudo. Families with crusading traditions were represented; there were a Stuteville and at least three Furnivals. The pattern was similar in other contingents; for example, William of Forz, whose crusading ancestry stretched back to the First Crusade and whose father had fought on the Third, was accompanied by an old associate of his, Peter of Mauley.[66] There was, however, no general baronial exodus. Compared to the Fifth Crusade, involvement was slight. Even so, a number of chroniclers, possibly relying on the same source, assert that Richard was also accompanied by many of the "mediocrium" or "menu peuple," the common people.[67] Magnates were surrounded by substantial retinues, but the extent of independent "popular" involvement must be conjectural; it is difficult to corroborate even the level of participation by lesser aristocrats and knights unattached to the households of the greater lords. The surviving evidence indicates that suggestions that Richard's and Simon de Montfort's forces together might have included as many as eight hundred knights and, consequently, might have numbered some thousands in all, are extravagant.

Of Richard's treasure there is more certainty. One French continuation of William of Tyre emphasises the earl's personal riches, and another variant talks of the "great wealth" Richard brought to the East. English sources tell the same story of "pecuniam innumerabilem," in the words of Thomas Wykes, a personal friend of the earl.[68] Cash was required for the refortification of strongholds like Ascalon and for the more basic task of keeping the army in being. Paris records that three days after landing at Acre, Richard had it proclaimed through the city that he was willing to take any crusader into his pay, so that none of them need return home for lack of funds.[69]

Individual crusaders in 1240 acquired cash in traditional ways. Simon de Montfort raised one thousand pounds from the sale of his wood at Leicester, although a quarter of a century later he complained that he had been financially disadvantaged at the time by the king, and thus had been forced to alienate his property.[70] Without positive subventions from external sources or a measure of active relief from outstanding financial commitments, Simon could not afford to crusade without diminishing his estates. The king's role could be central. Henry III provided loans; one thousand pounds was lent to Richard's "chief of staff," the prior of the English Hospitallers, Thierry of Nussa. Some royal officials who had taken the cross obtained advances against their salaries, Robert of Sabloil receiving as much as two hundred marks. Others, like the king's steward Amaury of St. Amand, enjoyed outright gifts from the king, in his case fifty marks.[71] The Crown was also involved in the transfer of property caused by crusaders' cash requirements, William of Mastac mortgaging his English estates to the king for 180 marks. Most such transactions, however, probably occurred without direct royal connection, as when Ralph of Ringstone, a Northamptonshire land-owner, sold a carucate of land to his brother for one hundred marks. The king was not the only paymaster or source of cash.[72]

Although exceedingly wealthy, Richard nevertheless had the largest military establishment to maintain and the leadership of the enterprise to support; therefore, central funds were important. In 1237 Richard had been allowed by the king to receive three thousand marks from the Jews for his crusade, and in 1238 Pope Gregory IX had granted him legacies bequeathed to the Holy Land and cash redemptions of crusade vows, money which was to be paid to the earl when he reached the Holy Land.[73] Taxation of English Jewry had been associated with cru-sade finance at least since Henry II's tallage of 1188, but the exploita-tion of vow redemptions was relatively novel, marking a new stage of central ecclesiastical funding of crusade expeditions. A prominent and, for some, distasteful feature of the preaching in the second half of the 1230s was a deliberate concentration on raising money as opposed to men, primarily through the purchase of indulgences through the re-demption of crusade vows. As recently as the late 1220s diocesan con-stitutions had limited to the sick or the disabled the facility to avoid fulfilment of the crusade vow. But by 1236 full indulgences were offered for material help for the cause, regardless whether the donor had taken the cross or not or even whether he was fit to carry out his vow in person. In February 1240 the papal legate Otho was authorized to insist that those unable to fight (no explicit definition of inability was in-cluded) must redeem their vows by material donations.[74] The profits from these payments were to be stored centrally by the local churches under the legate's control. These arrangements aroused insular, conser-vative suspicions of papal power and avarice. The subsequent granting of the sums raised to the leader of the crusade signalled another fresh departure. Earlier in the century, crusade taxes (of which, de facto, pur-chased vow redemptions were a form) had been allocated to individual needy crusaders. However, the logistics of seaborne passagia and mili-tary finance increasingly determined that disposal of such funds should be placed in the hands of the commanders. This development was clearly established in the preparations for the 1248–50 crusade, but was evi-dent in Gregory IX's grant to Richard of Cornwall.[75] The older tradition was not immediately, or ever, swept aside entirely. As late as 1247 Henry III met papal resistance when he, a noncrusader, tried to gain control of the proceeds of legacies and redemptions in order to organise a new crusade.[76] It is possible that in 1237–38 Gregory IX saw Richard of Cornwall, technically at least, as merely an individual, if special, crusader in need of money, rather than as what in fact he was, as the pope must have known, the commander and paymaster of a small army.

Administratively, the new system was cumbersome. The money was raised by papal agents but stored under diocesan authority. As it came, it may be assumed, largely from individual laymen, the process required at least the tacit approval of the king; this it received. However, collection of the grant to Richard of Cornwall dragged on for almost twenty years and attracted vociferous criticism, especially as it was evident that little of it had been collected in time to be of much material assistance to Richard's actual crusade.[77] Nevertheless, it was potentially lucrative; in 1247, when Innocent IV renewed efforts to collect what was due to the earl, one archdeaconry was alleged to have raised six hundred pounds. The grant to Richard provided a precedent; one of his companions in 1240, William Longsword, after taking the cross for a second time seven years later, obtained a similar allocation of funds from the pope to the amount of two thousand marks.[78]

Richard of Cornwall's crusade also exposed the problems set by the complexities of papal politics. In the theory being established at this time, papal authority was the key qualification for a crusade, distinguishing wars fought for the cross from other forms of holy war. Therefore the attitude of the pope to any scheme to relieve the Holy Land was of some significance, both theoretically and, in view of the church's increasing capacity to raise money, practical.[79] However consistent it may have seemed to the Curia, papal policy in the late 1230s appeared confusing, if not downright perverse, to those, including Earl Richard, who shared the ambition of their ancestors to visit Jerusalem and relieve the Holy Land. Richard had taken the cross in 1236, in response to a preaching campaign instituted by Gregory IX, who was concerned to ensure protection for the Holy Land on the expiry of the 1229 truce arranged by Frederick II, which the pope now chose to see as being de facto legitimate. By the spring of 1238, however, Gregory IX, apparently afraid for English domestic stability, was advising Richard and Simon de Montfort to remain in England and urging King Henry to prevent a massive exodus of barons. At the same time, Frederick II was also suggesting delaying departure until 1239.[80] In November 1238 Gregory changed tack and tried to persuade Richard to commute his vow and to contribute the papal grant of money to a planned expedition to help the beleaguered Latin Empire of Constantinople whose emperor, Baldwin II, had visited England earlier in the year and had been given presents valued variously at seven hundred and five hundred marks.[81] The diversion to Constantinople held no appeal for Richard, and he persisted in his preparations for the Holy Land, obtaining for himself and his family the widest possible set of papal privileges and insurance.[82]

After the renewed papal excommunication of Frederick II in the spring of 1239, a move which split English opinion, neither pope nor emperor were enthusiastic about a large Anglo-French crusade to the Holy Land, although both were eager for allies.[83] Even though he did not seem to have been concerned to coordinate his plans with Theobald of Champagne, who embarked for the East in 1239, Richard set his face against diversion or undue delay. On 12 November 1239 at Northampton he and other crucesignati swore an oath reaffirming their intention to relieve the Holy Land "lest," so Paris recorded, "their honest vow be hindered by the objections of the Roman Church and diverted to shedding Christian blood in Greece or in Italy."[84] Further papal pressure to prevent the crusaders' departure and an attempt by some bishops to persuade Richard to stay in England both failed, but it hardly presented the crucesignati with a totally encouraging environment for their preparations. It was surely no coincidence that when Frederick II as a tactic in his propaganda war altered his stance to one of tentative encouragement of assistance for the Holy Land, he soon gained Richard's adherence, to their mutual advantage. The rapprochement with the Hohenstaufen was important. Although papal disapproval of Richard's crusade persisted, Gregory was in no position to forbid it. His previous actions made it difficult for him to prevent Richard from cooperating with the emperor. At Richard's side at the oath of Northampton was Henry of Turbeville, fresh from fighting beside Frederick in Italy. In 1240 on his way to Marseilles, Richard opened direct contacts by sending the renowned antipapalist Robert Tweng to inform the emperor of the crusade's progress.[85] By luck and determination, Richard managed to arrive in Palestine backed both by papal subsidies and, it seems, by some sort of accreditation as representative of the emperor, who was claiming sovereignty over Jerusalem on behalf of his son Conrad. This dual support was, in the circumstances of the imperial-papal feud, quite an achievement.

The imperial connection provided Richard with an authority in the kingdom of Jerusalem, to complement his troops and money, which impressed even those elements in Palestine disaffected with distant imperial overlordship or the nearer presence of the emperor's baillie. Richard's position allowed him to behave with considerable freedom, in negotiating with Frederick's erstwhile ally Egypt or in appointing Frederick's baillie as governor of Ascalon in the emperor's name. In a sense, Richard had in theory resolved—and would have done in practice if local hostility to the Hohenstaufen had not run so high and been fuelled by so many powerful competing interests—the problem familiar since the 1140s of crusaders visiting the Holy Land who lacked official status among the local magnates. Indeed, a figure of Richard's importance, independence, and international favour may have been attractive to certain factions in Jerusalem; in 1241 the commune of Acre petitioned the emperor to appoint one of the earl's companions, Simon de Montfort, as their governor.[86] On his return to the West in the summer of 1241, Richard, although committed to none, was a hero to the French, effectively a pensioner of the pope, and a valuable and fêted friend of the emperor. This achievement perhaps excuses his exaggerated claims for his own success.

The German dimension of the crusades of Peter des Roches and Richard of Cornwall was obviously a direct result of Hohenstaufen power in the West and interest in the Holy Land, which had been expressed through Frederick II's marriage in 1225 to Yolanda, heiress to the throne of Jerusalem. However, it was also a function of anti-Capetian foreign policy. For thirty years, until the late 1250s, a consistent theme of Henry III's ambition was the attempt to regain his ancestral lands of Anjou and Normandy (lost in 1203–4 by his father) and especially Poitou, lost to the Capetians in Henry's own reign. Relations with Louis IX, although dynastically close (their wives were sisters) were bound to be equivocal, with Angevin interests dictating alliances elsewhere. Both in the East and the West, English support and cooperation with Frederick II in the 1220s and 1240s held the prospect for both parties of substantial political dividends. In this context the apparent contradiction of more or less faithful alliance with the papacy and close ties with the Hohenstaufen is explicable.

THE CRUSADE OF WILLIAM LONGSWORD

The years after Richard of Cornwall's return witnessed the decline of the Hohenstaufen connection and the final confirmation of the Capetian conquest of Poitou, in the disastrous English campaign of 1242. With the death of Frederick's English wife Isabella and Frederick's increasing absorption in fighting papal anti-Hohenstaufen crusaders in Italy, the emperor became less useful as a counterbalance to Capetian aggrandizement. Nevertheless, suspicion of Louis IX remained to colour the nature of official English responses to the new crisis that faced Outremer after the defeat of the battle of La Forbie and the final loss of Jerusalem in 1244. These disasters aroused the conscience of the West, leading to the lavishly and carefully prepared French *magnum passagium* of 1248–50, which seemed to offer in its size, organisation, and leadership the best hope for a generation of restoring the kingdom of Jerusalem. Yet the king of England held aloof from his brother-in-law's scheme. In 1245 Henry III apparently cited his suspicion of the motives of the French king as one reason for preventing the preaching tour of the bishop of Beirut. In 1247 this hostility may have lain behind Henry's successful petition to the pope to allow English crusaders to depart a year after the French. Relations between English and French crusaders were sour even after the fall of Damietta to the Christians in 1249, and there is evidence that Henry III entertained hopes of bartering support for Louis in the East for the restoration of Angevin possessions in France.[87] Henry's attitude can only be understood in the light of this distrust of the French and his more urgent dynastic responsibility to recapture his patrimony.

Royal fears and vacillations did not, however, altogether prevent English involvement in this new adventure. Although Henry resisted ecclesiastical taxation for Louis's crusade, he did finally permit preaching. There were numerous individual gestures of support. Richard of Cornwall sent one thousand pounds to the East via the Hospitallers. A number of magnates took the cross between 1247 and 1249, including the veterans of the 1240 crusade William Longsword and Simon de Montfort, Geoffrey of Lucy, Robert de Vere, Alexander Giffard, Bishop Walter Cantelupe of Worcester and the king's half-brother Guy of Lusignan. The familiar patronal pattern of recruitment was sustained, being centred upon the followers of Longsword, Guy of Lusignan, whose entourage received direct financial assistance from the king, and Montfort, who was joined in his crusade vow by his wife and household.[88]

When finally an English contingent embarked in 1249 it was led by Longsword, Montfort having by that time been diverted to rule Gascony on the king's behalf. With Longsword were his standard-bearer de Vere and another two hundred knights, if Paris is to be believed. The year before Longsword had pleaded poverty and, following Richard of Cornwall's example, had obtained a papal grant of two thousand marks from crusade legacies and vow redemptions. Costs were probably high, especially as, like Louis IX himself, Longsword is said to have retained a number of paid knights and serjeants in addition to those companions who paid for themselves.[89] In the event the crusade in Egypt in 1249–50 was a catastrophe. There were arguments between the English, who arrived at Damietta months after its capture, and the French, which provoked Longsword's temporary withdrawal to Acre, although he returned in time to join the illfated march on Cairo in November 1249.

At the battle of Mansourah in February 1250 and during the subsequent encirclement and surrender of the Christian army, the English force was annihilated; Longsword and de Vere were both killed, and only one of their followers, Alexander Giffard, is reported as having escaped with his life. Another crusader from England, Guy of Lusignan, who had probably remained at Damietta, also survived the general crusading debacle, although by the time he reached England again he was destitute. Militarily, the significance of the English contribution to Louis IX's crusade was not great, and only English writers afforded it much recognition. Yet for them it provided, in the heroic William Longsword, cut down by Mamluk troops while rashly charging into the narrow streets of Mansourah, a "manifest martyr," a figure of present renown and future legend.[90] News of the defeat reached Richard of Cornwall on 1 August, when he was sitting in the exchequer; the shock was profound and widespread.[91] After the optimistic reports of the previous autumn, many more crucesignati had begun preparations to join the crusade; Henry III himself had taken the cross in March. Paradoxically this gesture, so far from inaugurating substantial aid for the chastened Louis of France, now resident at Acre, was instrumental in preventing any English military assistance to the East for almost a generation.[92]

5

A Problem of Priorities: Henry III and the Lord Edward

The attitude of the government was the crucial element in any crusade enterprise, positive royal support making the difference between the regular but militarily insignificant passagia of private groups of crucesignati and an effective, substantial, and well-funded public contribution to the defence of Christendom. This was a common European experience. England was uncommon, not so much in having a king like John who was prevented by civil war from even attempting to fulfil his tardy vow of 1215, but in having one like Henry III who, although a crucesignatus thrice over and reigning for over half a century (much of the time in peace and political security) and although bequeathing money and his crusader's cross to the Holy Land in his will of 1253, never in person redeemed his vow by action.[1] Henry's behaviour set him apart from his contemporaries, the kings of France, Norway, Germany, Aragon, and Castille. Like the manoeuvres of his grandfather Henry II, the conduct of Henry III poses a number of questions. Was his failure to redeem his vow accidental or calculated, a sign of incompetence, lack of interest, or bad luck?

Henry III's attitude to the crusade has aroused controversy ever since the mid-thirteenth century. He took the cross three times: immediately after his coronation in 1216, in 1250, and in 1271. The first and last occasions present the historian with few problems. The new boy-king was obediently renewing the ecclesiastical protection enjoyed by his father, at a moment when it must have seemed to be one of the last defences of his throne in the face of rebellion and foreign invasion. Fifty-five years later, the old king was sick, mindful of his soul and perhaps of his long unfulfilled commitment. The 1250 vow is, and was, less easy to explain. Matthew Paris was consistently sceptical and often downright hostile to royal motives, and was rarely afraid to elevate rumour into fact and prejudice into analysis. However, while noting that some thought the king was in it for the money, he had to confess that reasonable observers suspended judgement; he concluded lamely, "and who except God knows the thoughts of men?"[2] Henry seems to have had this confusing effect on people. Paris's mystification was probably shared by his contemporaries, as within a few weeks of taking the cross himself the king was preventing other crucesignati from fulfilling their vows. Within a few years it would have been hard even for a skilled diplomat to determine whether Henry intended to fight for the cross in Palestine, Italy, Africa, or not at all. Henry's motives, timing, and actions are all open to doubt. Above all stand the charges that by his vacillation Henry prevented a more significant English contribution to the major expedition led by Louis IX in 1248, and thereafter, by involvement in the papal crusade in Italy, caused a growth of popular cynicism towards the practice of crusading.

The first problem concerns the occasion of Henry's assumption of the cross. Prior to 1250 his behaviour had been conventional—providing individual crusaders with funds, licences to mortgage property, and royal protection, generally supporting papal directives, and taking an interest in the affairs of the Holy Land. Henry was a patron of the military orders, in 1235 adding the Teutonic Knights to the list of royal pensioners, and like his early protector William Marshal, granting the Templars the right to bury his body. Like most rulers in the West he was welcoming to a string of visitors from Outremer and the Latin Empire of Byzantium.[3] Yet until 1249 his only positive action had been to petition Innocent IV (in 1247) for a share in the profits from crusade legacies and vow redemptions. He had not taken the cross after Jerusalem was finally lost to Khorezmian raiders in 1244; he had refused to allow the bishop of Beirut to preach the cross in England in 1245; and he had delayed the departure of the crusading force led by his cousin William Longsword until 1249. Despite being surrounded by relatives and courtiers preparing to go on crusade, from his half-brother Guy of Lusignan to the royal serjeant Gervase de Meyni Froger, Henry had held personally aloof.[4] Indeed, it appears as if he regarded Guy of Lusignan's expedition as being in some sense official, conducted with royal approval and royal cash. Why, then, did Henry change his stance and assume the cross in March 1250?

Henry could not have been reacting directly to any crusade disaster. When he took the cross, news from Louis IX's campaign in Egypt was encouraging; word of the disaster after the battle of Mansourah only reached England the following August.[5] One traditional interpretation, originally derived from Matthew Paris, suggests Henry's motives in 1250 were primarily mercenary, that he wanted his share of ecclesiastical tithes and never intended to help the Holy Land, later being only too glad to divert his crusade effort towards ostensibly more lucrative and diplomatically advantageous adventures in Italy and even North Africa. This view has some plausibility. Much of Henry's energy was directed towards securing money from the church, and with papal support he did try to prevent crusaders departing in 1250. Only in April 1252 did he fix 1256 as the date for his own departure; by then, his attention was already being distracted by serious problems in Gascony. By early 1254 proposals had surfaced in diplomatic exchanges to commute his vow either to Africa or to Sicily, and by 1255 Henry had secured papal approval for reassignment of the crusade tithes to the papal enterprise to capture southern Italy and Sicily from the Hohenstaufen heirs of Frederick II.[6] According to Matthew Paris, suspicion of the king's motives surfaced at a meeting at Westminster in April 1252, attended by many Londoners, at which Henry published the date for his departure. Apparently, despite vigorous exhortation from three important prelates, only a few members of the king's own household took the cross, their gestures, it may be suspected, lacking spontaneity at such an important and carefully stage-managed ceremony. Most of the Londoners and others held back, so Paris alleges, because of the threat of papal extortion of money through redemptions or taxation (a consideration which probably weighed more heavily on the St. Alban's Benedictine monk than on London merchants) and because of private fears, based on a new papal triennial tax, that Henry was inspired by greed, not piety. Such suspicions persisted despite Henry's renewal of his oath and would hardly have been dispelled when Henry, angered that so few had taken the cross, lost his temper at Westminster and called the Londoners common money-grubbers. The Westminster meeting was a public relations disaster.[7]

Viewed from St. Alban's the evidence against Henry was black, but Paris's views were coloured by evident prejudice and bias, and he should not be taken as an objective or accurate guide. Nevertheless, his mudslinging should not be dismissed, for some of his views were shared by other monastic writers. The Tewkesbury annalist recorded how in 1250 Pope Innocent IV had prevented the departure of crusaders at Henry's request; a chronicler at St. Benet Holme in Norfolk commented upon the king's vacillation between adopting the cross and deciding when to embark; and an observer from Burton explained the friendship between the king and the pope in terms of their shared love of money.[8] Discontent at Henry's behaviour may not have been confined to the clergy.[9] There seems to be a prima facie case against Henry on the charge of harbouring mercenary intentions, even though the testimony is that of hostile witnesses.

Not all the evidence is so damning. Despite rumours to the contrary, Henry never actually commuted his personal 1250 vow either to Africa or Sicily.[10] Furthermore, the very antagonism of some writers demonstrates that it was no simple matter for the king to raise, let alone misappropriate, crusade taxes with impunity. If the pope connived at diversion, as he did in the 1250s, the local clergy would object fiercely. If the pope refused to countenance any diversion, then he too would have condemned royal action. Either way, the propaganda advantage gained by assuming the cross would be reduced. As events in the 1250s showed, any perceived royal attack on English wealth, lay or clerical, in association with the papacy and its agents, provoked strong opposition from those already disposed to distrust the king and his "foreign" entourage. That Henry was suspected of fraud in his handling of the crusade money is no proof of his guilt, more a demonstration of the difficulties he would have faced if indeed he had tried to deceive his subjects.

While it is demonstrable that the church money first granted to Henry for the Holy Land was spent in Gascony from 1253 and Italy after 1255, that does not mean that the king had planned it that way in 1250 or even 1252. Nevertheless, the problem of the timing and intention of the 1250 vow remain. The solutions may lie in domestic rather than foreign policy. Henry had displayed consistent equanimity, even generosity, to crucesignati from his household and the upper reaches of the nobility, but by 1250 the number of aspiring crusaders may have begun to present difficulties. Paris bandied the figure of five hundred knights who had taken the cross up to late April 1250, and he claimed that many others were reluctant to broadcast their crusading intentions but were nonetheless keen.[11] Henry may have felt that the situation was getting out of control. The considerable numbers who had taken the cross in 1247–50 had meant widespread alienation of secular lands, some of it held directly of the crown, much of it to religious houses. These arrangements, designed by crusaders to raise the necessary cash for the journey, probably lay behind the hostility to Henry's prohibition on departure in 1250. The cash had already been raised by many crusaders and their lands already mortgaged, leased, or sold; any delay would obviously place their preparations in jeopardy.[12] This transfer of property, some of it permanent, over which the Crown had technical but probably little effective control (it would have been difficult to refuse a crusader's application for permission to raise money), potentially diminished the king's expectation of feudal incidents, profitable reversions to the Crown, and the general taxable assets of the laity. The problems of alienation in general, and mortmain (i.e., alienation to the church) in particular, were familiar to the landowning classes of the thirteenth century and led to pressure for royal action to control them, culminating in the legislation of Edward I. Henry III himself was evidently concerned; in 1256 he tried to forbid tenants-in-chief alienating land without licence because of the potential loss of profit to the Crown.[13] Politically, too, the king might have been uneasy about potential problems with some of those taking the cross, especially difficult vassals like Humphrey of Bohun, earl of Hereford, and perhaps others implicated in the strongly voiced criticism of the king at the 1248 parliament.[14] Nor at a time of tense relations with some barons was it convenient for the crusade to remove many of Henry's powerful councillors.

Henry's solution was to place himself, rather late, at the head of the movement, backed by those of his *familia* who took the cross with him in March 1250—"a special adviser" of Henry, Paulin Peiure, the seneschal Ralph FitzNicholas, William of Valence, John Mansel, Philip Lovel and other members of the household (*aulici*).[15] Such men constituted a royal faction which balanced and could hope to control any extra-household group, who in the absence of the king or his brother Richard might have assumed leadership of the crusade. At stake, apart from reputation, was access to ecclesiastical tithes, legacies, and vow redemptions. Of course Henry could have continued without taking the cross, refused to grant licences to mortgage, lease, or alienate land or to appoint attorneys and insisted on the crusaders staying in England, as he had in 1247. But such a policy would have run into serious political and propaganda difficulties, especially as enthusiasm for the crusade had spread to Henry's own intimate circle. Pressure on him was mounting, not least, one suspects, as he saw his vassals gaining papal grants from the central crusade fund and ecclesiastical taxation.[16] By taking the cross Henry could hope to control both the political and financial aspects of the operation and expect papal support in both. The vows of important household officials in 1250 and again in 1252 signalled his intention to supervise preparations closely.

The pope soon granted Henry funds from taxes and redemptions, and his new status allowed him greater authority when he once more insisted on delaying crusaders' departures in 1250 and when he attempted to bind individual enterprises to royal plans.[17] There may have been another side to Henry's decision, although one that would hardly account for the timing of his vow. Henry may have wished to emulate his domineering, wealthy, and internationally renowned and respected brother, Richard, who was, in fact, out of England when Henry took the cross and who on his return did not follow the king's example, a rather noticeable exception.[18]

Henry was notoriously pious and, whatever the temporal considerations, it would have been surprising if the spiritual importance of his vow was lost upon him. The timing of his vow may have been determined by secular reasons; his subsequent enthusiasm was not. For over two years after March 1250 Henry exhibited, in public and in private, every sign that he was taking his vow seriously. He quickly secured the agreement of the church to a grant of a crusade tithe to be paid for two years before his departure.[19] The king also looked to his own finances. According to Matthew Paris, at Christmas 1250 the king, mindful of the cost of crusading, deliberately reduced the festive expenses and household extravagance, the nearest he came to promulgating the sumptuary laws traditionally instituted by departing crusaders. The Dunstable annalist records that nine months before, when he took the cross, Henry had reduced the size of the royal household, especially the queen's chamber. Again according to Paris, Henry also began to collect gold, specifically in order to be able to pay troops in the currency dominant in the Holy Land; apparently, petitioners at the court soon learnt to pay in gold rather than silver.[20] Paris's statements are corroborated by the accounts of Peter Chaceporc, keeper of the Wardrobe. From these it appears that deposits to the king's gold treasure, which he had amassed since 1243, increased significantly after October 1250 to an annual rate equivalent to 5,880 marks of silver, mainly thanks to contributions by laymen buying liberties, just as Paris said. The precise role of this golden hoard is unclear. Crusaders like Hugh of Neville in the next decade do seem to have thought of using gold to pay for men and services once in Palestine, and there are grounds for believing that Henry's treasure, at least immediately after he took the cross, was intended to subsidise his crusade. In the event it was spent, to some effect, on the king's campaign of 1253–54 in Gascony.[21]

Early in 1252 the financial outlook for the crusade was bright, and Henry pushed forward with detailed preparations, as well as promising some crusaders financial assistance, granting licences, recognising crusaders' privileges, and seeking papal protection. Midsummer 1256 was set as the date for departure. The military orders were asked to provide transport ships and suitable quarters in the Holy Land for the English advance guard; the financial and administrative arrangements for preaching the cross were determined; experts from Marseilles were consulted; plans were laid to send royal agents to Mediterranean ports and the Holy Land "to make necessary preparations for the execution of his [i.e., Henry's] vow"; finally, in May 1253 Henry sought information on the numbers of Irish crucesignati so that he could prepare enough ships to transport them on the passagium.[22] Something of Henry's planned strategy can be learnt from this activity. The intention appears to have been to create a depot for arms, equipment, and supplies in the Levant prior to the arrival of the main army, similar to that established in Cyprus by Louis IX in 1248. From a contract drawn up in April 1253 to furnish the king's brother-in-law Peter of Savoy with money, equipment, a ship, and horses, it seems that Marseilles had been chosen as the main port of embarkation, for it was there that Peter was to receive his grant of ten thousand marks.[23] Although the precise destination of Henry's crusade is obscure, it is possible that he envisaged continuing Louis IX's work in refortifying the remaining Latin strongholds in Syria, perhaps as a prelude for an assault on Jerusalem. It may be that the comparatively distant date for departure was chosen because by then Louis was expected to have returned from his long stay at Acre (1250–54).[24]

Recruits were encouraged by a well-planned publicity campaign and by direct royal subsidies for some close associates.[25] Propaganda was extended even into the king's private apartments. In 1251–52 a number of decorative schemes in royal palaces took their inspiration from crusade legends. The siege of Antioch of 1098, as glamourised by the *Chanson d'Antioche* cycle of poems, a copy of which was borrowed from the master of the Temple by Queen Eleanor herself in May 1250, was depicted in the queen's own Antioch Chamber at Westminster, at Clarendon, and in the Camera Rosamundae at Winchester Castle. At the same time the legendary duel between Richard I and Saladin was depicted in the king's chamber at Clarendon, at Winchester Castle, at the Tower of London, and at Nottingham. Tiles portraying Richard also appeared at Westminster and Chertsey.[26] However, the taste for crusading iconography was short-lived, apparently confined to 1251–52. Thereafter the Holy Land crusade became entangled with and finally choked by domestic and European problems.

From the spring of 1252 Henry's crusade plans were deflected, first by Gascony, then by Castille and Sicily. Although as late as May 1253 Henry still talked of meeting the 1256 deadline, even before that time limit had been fixed (in April 1252), he had become involved in a damaging enquiry into Simon de Montfort's conduct in Gascony. In June 1252 he announced a royal expedition to Gascony for the following year.[27] It may have been this distraction that prompted Henry to summon the illtempered Westminster assembly of April 1252 to allay fears of his abandoning the crusade. Yet by August 1252 plans for royal intervention in the duchy were sufficiently advanced to cast the sincerity of the concurrent crusade negotiations of 1252–53 into doubt; the Gascon enterprise inevitably placed in jeopardy the crusade's timetable, finance, and manpower. On 6 August a number of crucesignati, including William of Valence, Peter of Savoy, and Stephen Longsword, were summoned to join the Gascon expedition the following October. Although Henry did not actually embark for Gascony until August 1253, such preparations cast a shadow on the seriousness, even honesty, of both his public diplomacy and his contracts with individual crusaders such as Peter of Savoy (April 1253) (although these crusaders were presumably well aware of the Gascon dimension).[28]

The only way such a sequence of activity can be reconciled with a sincere intention by Henry to fulfil his 1250 vow is to suppose, with F. M. Powicke, that a settlement of Gascony's problems was seen as a prelude to a crusade. However, the chances of the crusade starting became increasingly slim. In April 1254 part of the crusade tax was diverted to cover the costs of the Gascon expedition, by which time Henry had also begun to dissipate his gold reserves.[29] But it was not only sudden political crises which sapped Henry's crusading zeal. In March 1254 Henry declared his wish to see Westminster Abbey rededicated, on St. Edward's Day, 13 October 1255, before he embarked for the Holy Land. He authorised a further three thousand marks to be spent on the work, hardly the most prudent way to rebuild an exhausted war fund. Thus the fate of the crusade depended on the solution of domestic problems and the fulfilment of private ambitions, both of which demanded expenditure of time, effort, and money and sharply reduced prospects for the crusade's departure; it was a vicious circle familiar to all English kings from Henry II to Edward III.[30]

After 1252 prospects for a campaign to the Holy Land soon faded, particularly after Henry early in 1254 openly committed himself to wrest the Sicilian crown from the Hohenstaufen, on behalf of his second son Edmund. This decision had been reached over the previous year, since the pope had first broached the idea. It was not the only foreign adventure Henry was contemplating. It may be a fallacy that plans of rulers, medieval or modern, inevitably possess coherence, but Henry III's diplomacy in the mid-1250s appears breathtakingly contradictory. In February 1254 Henry promised the king of Castille that he would seek papal permission to divert his crusade to Africa, yet a few days later he sent an embassy to the pope requesting a commutation of his vow to Sicily.[31] Both initiatives by themselves were understandable. Agreement to join an African crusade was an integral part of a treaty being negotiated with the king of Castille, who was otherwise threatening to assert claims to the overlordship of Gascony. An English conquest of Sicily and establishment of the young Edmund as king could have opened up almost limitless vistas of international power for the Angevins in the Mediterranean, including, it should be mentioned, the chance to aid the Holy Land. However, running the two schemes simultaneously was fraught with difficulty and risk. Some contemporaries simply assumed that Henry had in fact commuted his Holy Land vow to the Sicilian business. This assumption obviously damaged Henry's relations with Castille; in January 1256 he had to instruct his ambassadors to reassure the king of Castille that his Holy Land vow remained unaltered and therefore still available for diversion to Africa.[32] Such subterfuge was hardly edifying, and whatever problems his diplomats faced in making Henry's policies appear credible, they had only the king to blame.

Whether Henry's foreign policy was subtle, deceitful, or merely confused, it met with only mixed success. A treaty was achieved with Castille in April 1254 which secured Angevin control of Gascony, but Sicily proved a financial and political disaster, and Henry's Holy Land vow, despite being touted around, remained intact but unredeemed for twenty years.[33] The success of the Castille treaty should not be minimised. Though a decade later Henry was still having to fend off demands by Alfonso X that he fulfil his promise to join an African crusade, Angevin Gascony had been secured. This was important for the internal stability of the duchy and gave Henry a stronger hand when negotiating Gascony's status with the king of France later in the decade. The failure of the Sicily scheme was, on the other hand, complete. If intended as part of a policy to supplant the Hohenstaufen in Germany and Italy, and thus linked to the control gained in 1246 over certain Alpine passes and to the manoeuvres leading to the election of Richard of Cornwall as king of Germany in 1257, the Sicilian involvement merely served to demonstrate Angevin impotence. Indeed, the abortive deflection of English crusade effort from 1254 towards Sicily led directly to the abandonment of Henry's claims to Normandy, Anjou, and Poitou and left the Capetians dominant in France and in a position themselves to devour the Hohenstaufen inheritance in Italy. It was his Sicilian obligation that prompted Henry in May 1257 to begin formal peace negotiations with France.[34] The gestation of this new policy and the role played by successive flirtations with the crusade are obscure, but until 1254 the crusade was probably seen as a useful resource against Capetian power. In that year, the Castille treaty, the agreement to the papal offer of Sicily, and the tentative rapprochment with Louis IX at the first personal conference between the two kings (December 1254)

marked a definite shift in Henry's foreign policy, a reversal of the endeavours of the previous quarter of a century to regain the lost Angevin
territories in France.

But the new policy was scarcely easier to conduct than the old. There
was an inherent contradiction in Henry's position. The price of keeping
Alfonso X believing in future English help in north Africa—a belief in
any case compromised after 1257 when Alfonso and Richard of Cornwall became rivals for the crown of Germany—was that Henry could
not openly commute his crusade vow to Sicily. In May 1254 Henry had
pressed for such a commutation, and Innocent IV had advised against
it on the grounds that the recent death of the legitimate Hohenstaufen
ruler, Conrad IV, opened up the possibility of an easier papal annexation
of Sicily. But when the new pope, Alexander IV, called on Henry to
divert his vow in 1255 the roles were reversed; this time the king refused, presumably out of concern for Castillian feelings or fear of domestic opposition. Thereafter, diplomatic confusion intensified. In 1255
papal envoys were empowered to commute Henry's vow toward Sicily,
yet a year later the pope was ordering a new date for Henry's departure
to the Holy Land, while in 1256 and 1258 the king himself was still
protesting his willingness to join an African crusade. Henry doggedly
clung to all three strands of his crusade policy. He was still discussing
prospects for crusading in Africa in 1262, in Sicily in 1263, and in the
Holy Land in 1264, although by then, ironically, only the last destination elicited the interest of the papacy.[35] The end of the Sicilian entan-
glement was especially protracted. Alexander IV had effectively
abandoned the English alliance in 1258. Yet under the terms of the
Treaty of Paris between Henry and Louis IX in 1259, Henry secured a
subsidy for five hundred knights, probably with Sicily in mind. He persisted in describing his son Edmund as king of Sicily, until Urban IV
had to ask Edmund specifically to renounce his rights in July 1263, by
which time the pope had chosen a new champion, the Capetian Charles
of Anjou. By 1264 most of the money assigned under the Treaty of Paris
had been spent on combating domestic troubles. The exceptions were
two thousand marks allocated to the Holy Land in May 1264, on the
day before the surprising defeat of the royalists by Simon de Montfort's
rebels at Lewes, and a residue, which the victorious barons feared would
be used to subsidise a proroyalist French invasion.[36] If Henry ever had
a Grand Design incorporating his aspirations in Gascony, Germany,
north Africa, Sicily, and the Holy Land, his implementation of it was
distinctly Micawberish: optimistic, precarious, and ultimately profitless.

The king's antics did not go unremarked by his subjects, the Sicilian
dimension proving especially controversial. For the first time in England the crusade had openly been attached to an issue of temporal

foreign policy, for despite papal apologetics, the Hohenstaufen posed a secular, not spiritual, threat to the Roman Church.[37] Papal priorities were clear. A commission in 1265 empowered the legate Cardinal Ottobuono to commute all vows, including those for Jerusalem but excluding those for Sicily; not all Christians approved.[38] Paris claimed that in 1251 he was told by King Haacon of Norway that the king was always willing to fight the enemies of the church, but not all the enemies of the pope.[39] Some historians would like to dismiss such comments as figments of Paris's biased imagination, yet whether or not Haacon ever said these words, the sentiment they expressed is echoed outside the pages of Matthew Paris. The diversions of the crusade, its money, its privileges, its organisation, and its manpower to fight the Hohenstaufen provoked vocal and significant opposition in England. King Haacon's distinction between the interests of the church and the interests of the pope was not original. When the rectors of Berkshire replied to demands for a papal tax to pay for war against Frederick II in 1240, they pointed out that churches within the universal church held their own patrimonies, originally derived from the gifts of secular rulers and in no way subject to Rome; therefore they should not be ordered to contribute. They also denied the legitimacy of the papal claim to ecclesiastical taxation on the grounds of Frederick's attack on the papal states, claiming that the church should only employ the secular arm against heretics and that Frederick had not been condemned as one by the church. In 1256 clergy in the archdeaconry of Lincoln opposed the diversion of the crusade tax to Sicily, and the clergy of the diocese of Lichfield protested even more bluntly at paying a subsidy for the war in Sicily because, they said, the new cause was "not pious."[40] In 1247 Bishop Cantelupe of Worcester had successfully petitioned Innocent IV not to allow able-bodied crusaders to be compelled to redeem their vows for cash or forced to fight against anyone except Saracens.[41]

Behind these clerical complaints, and others later in the century (at the Council of Lyons in 1274, for example), lay a series of anxieties over church government, the exercise of authority, and the rights of local churches. The papal legate Rostand, empowered in 1255 to divert all crusade funds to the Sicilian campaign, to commute crusade vows, and to offer identical indulgences for helping Sicily as for aiding the Holy Land, was resented and resisted in some lay, as well as ecclesiastical, circles. Alexander IV's equation of the Sicilian business with the problems of Jerusalem did not persuade the reforming barons at Amiens in 1264:

> Again, the lord king took the cross in aid of the Holy Land
> and many of his nobles and other subjects were induced

to do likewise on the same pretext, but at length his vow and that of his entire people was unreasonably converted, against all hope and expectation, from a crusade against the Saracens who are the foes of Christ's cross into an attack on fellow-subjects of the same Christian religion. And to the greater confusion of the kingdom, a tenth of all ecclesiastical revenues was granted to him for five years for their overthrow, while churches, by payment of these tenths, and the whole land by enforced redemption of the vows, were impoverished, many thousands of marks having been collected in spoils of this kind, with enormous harm to the churches and the whole community, only to be thrown away in vain. In the end it all came to nothing, so that neither did the Holy Land, to whose aid all had manfully girded themselves up, gain anything thereby, nor did the absurd cancellation of the crusade to the Holy Land, in favour of an expedition to Sicily, in any way assist that project.[42]

Here was clear agreement with the complaints of the clergy in 1240 and 1255.

Despite the widely publicised papal authorisation of 1255, Rostand's credentials were challenged at a clerical assembly in London in January 1256.[43] Some recalcitrant opponents to the diverted crusade tithe, like the monks of St. Alban's, suffered excommunication. Nevertheless, with royal help, Rostand did manage to collect some money, assisted perhaps by signs that the king was beginning active preparations, as in September 1255 when he instructed crucesignati to improve their bowmanship.[44] In December 1255 the king was putting pressure on the prior of Westminster to hand over four thousand l.tournois of the crusade tax for Sicily; another four thousand marks came from the bishop of Hereford the following February.[45] However, rather typically of Henry's crusade plans, the sums raised never approached the required English contribution to the conquest of Hohenstaufen Sicily, and the whole enterprise ended in papal recriminations and royal humiliation.

By 1259 when Louis IX promised to pay for knights to campaign for Henry "in the service of God or of the church or for the benefit of the kingdom of England," a possible hint at a Sicilian destination, the plan had already collapsed. But it bequeathed various legacies.[46] One was the exacerbation of English clerical suspicion of papal motives, which remained a feature of Anglo-papal relations. Another was the provision of a blueprint for future royal appropriation of crusade taxation, which was so effectively exploited by Edward I and his successors. A third was perhaps accidental. The Sicilian crusade had no successors; unlike the kings of France, English rulers were never again as closely allied to the papacy and did not regularly seek papal permission to convert adventures of foreign policy into crusades. There are hints of crusading overtones in the propaganda of Edward I and Edward III in their wars with Scotland and France, but not until the crusade of Bishop Despenser and the Castillian campaign of John of Gaunt in the mid-1380s were crusade privileges again overtly advertised in what was de facto a secular cause.[47]

Disagreement, bewilderment, and suspicion accompanied discussion of Henry III's second crusade vow more or less from the moment it was sworn. The one central fact is that the vow remained unfulfilled. Perhaps it was guilt which prompted Henry, on the eve of the battle of Lewes in May 1264, to send two thousand marks "to keep in the Holy Land as many knights yearly as can be maintained by it and this in part ransom of the king's vow if by any unexpected chance he cannot go in person to the Holy Land."[48] A late middle-aged man facing the hazards of battle may well have found the burden of his omission weighing heavily. It was not as if he lacked encouragement or advice; even as late as 1263 Henry was still a principal target for appeals from increasingly beleaguered Outremer.[49] Yet not a few eyebrows might have been raised at the comparison between Henry and Richard I made by Bohemund VI of Antioch's ambassador in 1255.[50] Undeniably, English help for Louis IX in 1248 would have been greater but for Henry's behaviour. But where Henry most differed from his crusader uncle Richard was not in personal enthusiasm, for his behaviour in the 1250s if anything displays an almost overeager willingness to flaunt his interest in the business of the cross. This was perhaps his chief failing; as a crucesignatus he was a show off, too ready to fall in with the Papal Curia in regarding the crusade as an almost indefinitely flexible weapon in an essentially papal conception of the battle for the integrity of Christendom. It is hard to see that his interests as king or crusader were best served by this policy. Henry may not have compromised his personal obligation, and he may not have been confused by his many-faceted marketing of that commitment, but he certainly confused others and made it appear that he had compromised his vow. Whatever his private sincerity, Henry's actions aroused widespread suspicion, not least because, even if he did not commute his vow, some of those working on his behalf did.[51] In politics, public perception is almost everything. Where Henry III differed most from Richard I was in his ability to project an acceptable image and to cope with public relations; these Henry handled with astonishing incompetence.

THE CRUSADE OF THE LORD EDWARD

Henry's eldest son conformed much more to the Ricardian model when he led a crusade from England in 1270.[52] Most of the running for the crusade had been made by Edward himself. He proposed himself as leader of the expedition as early as 1267, although the legate Ottobuono and Pope Clement IV initially preferred his younger brother Edmund. In January 1268 Clement firmly rejected Edward's request for financial assistance, and in April the legate was empowered to absolve the king from his 1250 vow provided the Lord Edmund went to the Holy Land in his place. However, Edward's determination proved irresistible, and by June 1268 he had persuaded both king and legate to allow him to take the cross. This he did at Northampton in June in the company of leading members of the royal family, as well as Gilbert of Clare, earl of Gloucester, who had been the chief dissident of 1265–67, and a large number of others—120 according to the well-informed Thomas Wykes, although, less credibly, a local Cluniac recorded 700.[53] King Henry oscillated between willingness to see one of his sons depart in his stead and open eagerness to fulfil his vow. As late as May 1270 he insisted that he would crusade in person, although this may have been a ploy to secure lay and clerical assent to taxation or to retain control over his sons.[54]

Meanwhile Edward had proceeded with his own plans. He had been negotiating with Louis IX, who had again taken the cross in 1267. It was inevitable that any English arrangements should take account of French intentions, demonstrating the profound shift in English foreign policy during the previous twenty years. In August 1269 he agreed to integrate his force with that of Louis. Although approved by Henry, this plan was not dependent on his active participation, as the repayment of the loan offered by the French king was to come from Edward's revenues as duke of Gascony, not from England.[55] Ignoring uncertain domestic political circumstances and accepting overoptimistic financial forecasts, Edward assumed full control of the English enterprise in the summer of 1270, after his father had finally been persuaded of the folly of both the king and his heir leaving the realm at the same time.[56]

Realistically, Henry III's flirtation with the crusade should have ended here, with his vow redeemed at last by his sons. But during a serious illness early in 1271 Henry not only took the cross again, but on his recovery instituted a series of household and financial reforms designed to prepare the way for his own departure to the East. This third crusade vow cannot be dismissed simply as a predictable reaction to sickness;

to the end, Henry's attachment to the crusade was, like his personality, obstinate rather than sentimental.[57]

Edward's experience of crusading fell into two parts: the first, with the foreign French expedition to north Africa, which he joined only as it was being withdrawn from Tunis after the death of King Louis in August 1270; the second, when after wintering with the French force in Sicily, he refused to abandon his vow and sailed to Acre with only his English followers and a few French nobles such as Erard de Valéry and Otho de Grandson. Edward arrived in the Holy Land on 9 May 1271. The decision to continue to Palestine, while asserting his independence and establishing his international reputation, did little to alleviate the problem of Outremer. Once in Syria, Edward's options were extremely limited, not least by the size of his army. English records survive to provide a fuller list of crusaders for 1270 than for any previous expedition since the Third Crusade, including the names of well over two hundred individual crucesignati. Yet Edward's fleet, which arrived off Tunis in November 1270, comprised only thirteen ships. The army that reached Acre, despite having been reinforced by the Lord Edmund in Sicily early in 1271, was probably only about a thousand strong, far too small to attempt any decisive aggression against the Mamluk rulers of Egypt or the other Moslem rulers in Syria.[58] In consequence, Edward's crusade followed a predictable course. After some desultory campaigning, he was forced by local pressure to accept a truce which the local baronage had made with Baibars, the sultan of Egypt. Edward's only lasting contributions were to establish a small garrison of *stipendiarii* at Acre and to build a tower at the northeast angle of the city walls; in 1278 he entrusted the tower to the care of an English confraternity of St. Edward.[59] Even before Edward's own departure from Acre in October 1272, the English force had begun to dissolve, with Edmund leaving in May. Despite his enthusiasm, Edward had contributed almost nothing towards a political, military, or diplomatic settlement favourable to the Christians of Outremer.

Perhaps it was too late for such a settlement. Without massive military intervention from the West the Christians retained their strongholds on the mainland of the Levant almost on sufferance, as the experience of one of Edward's own companions demonstrated. Hamo l'Estrange, a marcher lord who had done well out of the civil war of 1264–67, had assigned his extensive English estates to his brothers and sister for the duration of his crusade or if, he failed to return, permanently. After Edward left Acre, Hamo stayed on to marry the heiress to the lordship of Beirut. He died soon after, but before his death he placed his wife and her city under the protection of Sultan Baibars, presumably as a means of forestalling a Mamluk attack on Beirut. Despite attempts by the titular king of Jerusalem, Hugh III of Cyprus, to annex Beirut himself, Hamo's arrangement, with Templar support, was upheld.[60] This episode encapsulates the crusading paradox of pragmatism versus conviction. Hamo exchanged secure wealth and position in the West for enhanced status but precarious, if glamorous, lordship in the East. Even if his decision was based on religious zeal, he was not prevented from putting his wife in the safe-keeping of the same infidel who months before had arranged for the attempted murder of Hamo's erstwhile lord, Edward. Hamo may not have seen any contradiction; conviction identified the problem—the liberation of the Holy Land—but pragmatism provided the answers.

Ephemeral in its consequences, the Lord Edward's crusade nonetheless had demanded a considerable administrative effort, and its preparation had by no means always been smooth. Before the pacification of the realm in the summer of 1267, after the Baron's War, Cardinal Ottobuono's preaching, although carefully organised, had met with mixed success. In 1266 the pope voiced unhappiness with the vigour of the preaching, and in February 1267 the assembled clergy and laity of the kingdom expressed downright opposition to any suggestion of denuding England of native warriors; their view was shared by the remaining rebels.[61] Predictably in the uncertain political situation, responses were sluggish until leading members of the royal family and nobility set an example by taking the cross in June 1268. However, reluctance to contribute lay or ecclesiastical subsidies persisted, final agreement not being reached until 1270. This meant that the proceeds had little chance of being collected in full by the time Edward sailed in August of that year.

In common with the practice since the 1230s, the main thrust of the preaching was to raise money through redemptions, swelling the more or less permanent fund of legacies and redemptions to which crusaders could apply for assistance and from which Clement IV hoped in 1265–66 to pay for five hundred crossbowmen for the Holy Land. The size of the fund obviously varied, but even when redemptions were few and outgoings high, legacies could bring in large sums, such as the eight thousand marks bequeathed by Richard of Cornwall in 1272.[62] It was not only leaders like Earl Richard, Simon de Montfort (who was promised four thousand marks in 1248), or William Longsword who needed subsidising. In 1266 Hugh of Neville, a former Montfortian who had suffered badly from the peace settlement, managed to obtain a papal grant of five hundred marks from the crusade fund. Unfortunately for

Hugh, although the legate agreed to release the money, the increased competition for such funds meant that little of the grant was actually forthcoming.[63] It must have been apparent to crusade leaders by the late 1260s that a more stable source of income for the crusade was required, less at the mercy of expensive pleading at the Papal Curia or of the vagaries of the preaching campaign. Reliance on redemptions and legacies exposed a paradox: if crusade preaching was successful, not only would there be more redemptions but there would also be more crusaders seeking subsidies. The chosen royal remedy was a tax of a twentieth levied on lay and clerical tenants; this took almost three years to gain acceptance, with pockets of clerical resistance persisting into 1271.[64] The proceeds of this levy, collected centrally at the exchequer or the Temple, were firmly in the hands of the Crown.

There were financial and political reasons why centrally administered national taxation was appropriate. A number of Disinherited, who after the civil war had been allowed to redeem their lands under the terms of the Dictum of Kenilworth (1266), and who, like Hugh of Neville, had taken the cross, were saddled with crushing debts arising from redemption fines. One of Edward's close companions on crusade, John of Vescy, a prominent Montfortian who submitted in 1267, was burdened with a fine of 3,700 marks. Another former rebel, William of Munchensy, was obliged, if he did not go on crusade himself, to pay William of Valence, the king's half-brother, one thousand marks for the latter's crusade expenses; the arrangement probably was part of Munchensy's redemption of his estates.[65] On the other hand, loyalists sometimes failed to realise their profits from redemptions owing to them.[66] Without a massive and efficiently directed subvention, no crusade would have been possible.

The twentieth raised some thirty thousand pounds, described by Henry III as desperately needed, but even this was insufficient. Other expedients had to be adopted. In March 1270 a tallage was levied on the Jews; but generations of fiscal exploitation had taken their toll, and soon rumours reached the government of the inability of the Jewish community to pay adequate amounts; this was a foretaste of the fiscal redundancy that led to the expulsion of the Jews in 1290.[67] An important source of immediate income came from the deal Edward struck with Louis IX in August 1269. Under this, in return for a loan of seventy thousand l.tournois, forty-five thousand livres of which was for horses, victuals, ships, and transport, and the rest for a projected Gascon contingent, Edward promised to arrive at the French muster at Aigues Mortes in August 1270 and to serve Louis "as one of his barons" (which, of course, as duke of Gascony, he was). This gave the French king the authority he had lacked when dealing with the English troops under Longsword in 1249–50, but allowed Edward to begin preparations in France independent of his father, before the proceeds of the twentieth or the Jewish tallage had begun to arrive in London.[68]

The 1269 contract with Louis also provided Edward with the pattern for the organisation of his own contingent. In July 1270 eighteen crucesignati contracted to accompany Edward and remain in his service for a year, each with a stipulated number of knights, in return for an annual payment at a rate of one hundred marks per knight to cover all expenses. Henry of Almain, Edward's first cousin and son of Richard of Cornwall, received fifteen hundred marks; William of Valence two thousand; the Lord Edmund ten thousand; and Adam of Jesmond, Payn of Chaworth and Robert Tiptoft, three whose actual contracts as well as the exchequer record survive, six hundred marks each. The total sum disbursed on 26 July 1270 was 22,500 marks. It is possible that Edward's Gascon vassals were recruited in similar fashion.[69] Like his French overlord, Edward was prepared to offer lavish inducements in return for support. In the arbitration between Edward and the unruly earl of Gloucester, the earl was to receive two thousand marks if he led an independent force in the Holy Land, but eight thousand if he agreed to enter Edward's service (in the event he did neither).[70] It is difficult to be certain how far such payments represented an investment in discipline and loyalty, an inducement to overcome reluctance, or a pragmatic assessment of projected expenditure. Royal liability was great and would have increased as the contracted term of one year was exceeded (Edward was absent on crusade for more than two years). Equally the money paid to the leading crusaders in July 1270 represented neither their full costs nor their sole source of funds.

Hamo l'Estrange received twelve hundred marks from the Crown for himself and, presumably, eleven other knights, but he also enfeoffed his brother with his lands, probably in return for cash; he had to raise an additional 375 marks once in the Holy Land, although this may have been in connection with his exotic marriage in 1271. The Lord Edmund was assigned considerable sums above the contracted ten thousand marks. Payn of Chaworth and Robert Tiptoft, on top of the contract fees, had money allocated to them from vow redemptions and other crusade obventions which, like the hapless Hugh of Neville, they failed to receive. Roger of Leyburn was more fortunate, benefiting to the tune of two thousand marks from the same source. Such additional grants were not necessarily realised easily or quickly; over half of a subsidy to the Lord Edmund of twenty-six hundred marks was still outstanding in 1286.[71]

Active royal intervention bound the crusaders more closely to their leader. It did not save them from financial difficulties, and it condemned the Crown, and Edward in particular, to massive indebtedness. In spite of a remittance of ten thousand livres in 1279, the French loan, repayment for which fell on the customs of Bordeaux and was due to have been completed by 1281, was only paid off in November 1289; this breach of contract provided the French with a useful diplomatic weapon and deprived Edward I of revenue from Gascony.[72] Edward had also received perhaps as much as £52,000 from clerical and lay subsidies, four thousand marks from the Jews, and in 1271 the proceeds of wardships and escheats, but he still dismally failed to cover expenses. During the crusade itself Edward had to borrow huge amounts, by the summer of 1272 having run up debts including three thousand marks to creditors in Acre and almost seven thousand l.tournois to a number of Italian merchants. A year later he paid two thousand marks to the under-treasurer of the Templars in Paris towards a debt of 28,189 livres, 8 sous, 4 deniers tournois.[73]

Such expenses presented the authorities in England with considerable problems. In answer to Edward's appeals, and in addition to using the 1270 twentieth, they pressed the Welsh leader Llewelyn ap Gruffydd in December 1272 to honour a treaty obligation to pay three thousand marks, on the grounds that Edward (now king, on the death of his father the month before) was "bound to divers creditors in a great sum of money for the discharge incurred by him in the service of God in the Holy Land."[74] As early as July 1272 Edward's former companion at Acre, Archdeacon Tedald Visconti, now Pope Gregory X, recognised the problem by requesting a supplementary subsidy for Edward's crusade from the English clergy, which realised twenty-two thousand marks.[75]

The financial lesson of the 1270 crusade was not ignored by its leader on his later campaigns in the West, when the precedent of tapping lay and ecclesiastical wealth specifically to assist extraordinary military expenditure was pursued with vigour. In the financing of Edward's crusade, the common experience of thirteenth-century crusaders was writ large. More widely, such problems presaged the future impotence of western rulers to raise adequate funds to fight the infidel in the Levant. In contrast to Louis IX's efficient financing of the 1248–50 expedition, Edward's expedients had brought in too little money too late.

The financial dispositions of 1269–70 helped establish centralised authority within the English contingent beyond customary patronal links. The reconciliation of royalists and dissidents may have been one intention behind the preaching of 1266–68, but in fact the 1270 crusade was dominated by associates of leading members of the royal family.

Gilbert of Clare was not the only dissident to take the cross but not embark. The contingents that did set out in 1270–71 were grouped around the households of Edward, his wife Eleanor, and his brother Edmund, and included important knights, magnates, and clerics like Anthony Bek, a future crusader-legate, down to Edward's groom and his wife's tailor. The king and queen also contributed a group of household knights and serjeants, as well as the queen's surgeon. Some of the greater magnates, such as Henry of Almain, William of Valence, and even Thomas of Clare, travelled with their own entourages, but the whole was bound together by an intricate web of contracts.[76] Edward had contracted to serve Louis IX as one of his barons, thereby reinforcing the existing feudal bond; so Edward's own leading followers entered his service in July 1270. Some in turn retained their followers by written contracts, which bear all the signs of what later developed into the system of indentured retainers familiar to the armies of the fourteenth century. Neither the household basis nor the contractual element of Edward's army was novel. Raising troops from a lord's *comitatus* was a method centuries old in the Germanic West and had long ago reached a degree of sophistication which, from the Third Crusade at least, had been augmented and strengthened by additional sources of finance and the retaining of troops for fixed periods at set rates of pay.[77] The experiences of Richard of Cornwall, Simon de Montfort, and Longsword confirmed these developments, which were common among French crusaders as well.[78]

Edward's contracts with other crucesignati were possibly prompted by the final withdrawal of Henry III. Edward, as the heir not the sovereign, could not automatically rely on the established bonds of loyalty and vassalage, any more than his uncle could thirty years earlier. Whereas for Richard of Cornwall in 1240, Louis IX at Cyprus in 1248, or Richard I at Acre in 1191, hiring retainers from the ranks of crusading knights appeared as an emergency expedient during the campaign, in 1270 written contracts of service drawn up before departure as a premeditated policy removed a potential structural and financial weakness in the army's coherence. The identification of the 1270 crusade with a royal campaign was close. Some of the letters of protection granted to those embarking for the Holy Land restricted the legal immunities of crusaders, exempting them from all pleas "except dower, novel disseisin and darrein presentment"; the restriction brought the crusader's protection into line with that customarily given to those soldiers or diplomats travelling abroad in the king's service.[79] The nature of the arrangements for the 1270 crusade, although following the precedents of the previous century, had implications for the future. Based on national lay and ecclesiastical taxation, a centralised command structure, and an army raised in the first instance by magnates, who were themselves retained by the commander through written contract and who retained their own troops in the same way, the 1270 crusade conformed to a model which came to dominate English military organisation over the next two hundred years.[80]

If the crusade in 1270 had been designed to ease tension in England, it signally failed. Suspicion between Gilbert of Clare and the government continued, despite the attempts to draw him into the crusade. Even among royalists, disputes over shares in the peace settlement after 1267 were still liable to erupt into violence. In 1270 Earl Warenne fatally assaulted Alan la Zuche in Westminster Hall and came near to launching a private war against Henry of Lacy. Throughout the last months of Henry III's reign, provincial unrest stirred almost beyond royal control in England. In Ireland John of Verdun's estates were devastated during his absence in the Holy Land.[81] Edward's absence was, to say the least, risky. Henry III was sixty-three; Henry's brother Richard, on whose guidance in the affairs of state at home Edward may have pinned some hopes, and to whom he entrusted his children, was sixty-one and in fact predeceased the king in April 1272. Of Edward's two surviving male children, John was four and Henry two. It is worth speculating on the repercussions if the assassination attempt on Edward at Acre in June 1272 had succeeded. In such a situation it is unlikely that the oaths of loyalty to Edward extracted before his departure would have held malcontents and opportunists in check.[82]

Edward pursued his crusading ambition with ruthless self-determination or courageous consistency, depending on the view taken of Edward's personality. He refused to be deflected by Clement IV, by his own father, by the huge expense, or by domestic unrest. He insisted on continuing his journey to Palestine even after the Tunis disaster; if necessary, so the story went, with only his groom Fowin for company. This gesture, though grandly romantic, prevented Edward from exploiting the psychological trauma that the Tunis disaster had inflicted upon the decimated French court. The risks Edward took at Acre were apparent both from his campaigns in Palestine, when his troops succumbed to climate and diet rather than the infidel, and from the attempt on his life. Yet in spite of all this and the mounting financial damage he was inflicting on himself, Edward remained impervious to pleas for his return to the West. The decision to depart from Acre in October 1272 was Edward's alone, uninfluenced by news of his father's death, which only reached him on his arrival in Sicily in December. Pleased, no doubt, to be playing a role of such unimpeachable merit, Edward behaved with insensitivity and obstinancy or, as some would say, strength of character; all were family traits. His crusade earned Edward the plaudits of contemporaries and later myth-makers, but it is hard to accept that the chances he took mark him as a statesman of sober judgement.[83] If the crusade taught Edward much about international diplomacy, war, finance, and military organisation, it did nothing to temper his boldness and imperious regard for his own interests, which as king brought him his greatest triumphs and his most severe difficulties. If Edward's smooth accession in 1272 while still far from home excites surprise, so should his absence in the first place.

6

Political Crusades

THE CIVIL WAR OF 1215–1217

Not all crusades were conducted against infidels or heretics on far-distant battlefields. Twice in the thirteenth century crucesignati fought in England itself. As early as the 1090s Urban II had equated certain campaigns in the West with the armed pilgrimage to Jerusalem, and the defence of Christendom could be interpreted in many ways. For rulers, the crusade provided a readily adaptable ideology of legitimate warfare which went beyond traditional forms: the enemy on a crusade was outside the law, and the wars could be financed by levies on church wealth. Recruits could be attracted by unique spiritual and temporal advantages which benefitted the living, not merely, as under older theories, those who died in battle; a crucesignatus could turn his quasi-religious status to private advantage at law or in politics.[1] The impetus for the application of crusading to domestic political crises came from the pope. In 1199 Innocent III extended crusading institutions—vow, cross, privileges—to a campaign planned against Markward of Anweiler, leader of opposition to papal policy in southern Italy and Sicily; he did so again in 1208 with the expedition to punish Count Raymond VI of Toulouse for abetting the Cathar heretics in Languedoc.[2] As a result of Innocent III's personal enthusiasm, the way was opened for a rapid penetration of crusading language and institutions into secular public affairs.

Within a generation, chroniclers had become so familiar with the extensive use of the crusade that they could be rather free in assuming its employment. For example, the St. Alban's writer Roger of Wendover, writing some years after the event, described in crusading terms the Franco-papal plans for an invasion of England in 1212. Not only was Philip II to "undertake the task for the remission of all his sins," but Innocent III was said to have appealed

133

to all the magnates, knights and other warriors of diverse nations to take the Cross to overthrow the English King and, by following the French king as their leader in this expedition, strive to avenge the injury done to the Universal Church. He ordered, furthermore, that all those who gave money or aid towards overthrowing this contumacious king should, like pilgrims to the Holy Sepulchre, rest secure in the peace of the Church, both temporally and spiritually.[3]

Wendover stretched the evidence. The most that contemporary French or papal sources allow is that Philip, whose invasion plans were independent of papal encouragement, portrayed himself as acting from pious motives, a champion of the church but not explicitly a crusader.[4] Nevertheless, Wendover was not alone in suggesting that John, under the Interdict and before submitting to the pope in May 1213, was faced by the threat of a papally inspired holy war. Wendover may have been reflecting current rumours, the wishful thinking of dissidents, or the perspective of events of 1215–17, when England did suffer a French invasion in which the images and institutions of the crusade played a significant role.

King John's submission to the papacy opened England to fiscal and preaching campaigns for the Fifth Crusade and created an atmosphere that John, after the collapse of his schemes to regain his lost lands in France in 1214, was careful to exploit.[5] He informed Innocent III that the truce agreed with Philip Augustus had been made "in order that relief may be brought more quickly to the Holy Land." This was a conventional enough formula in Angevin and papal diplomacy. John did more; faced with mounting baronial opposition and civil unrest, he took the cross with some of his supporters and household officials in London on Ash Wednesday, 4 March 1215, adopting the white crosses of Richard I's forces on the Third Crusade. In the words of one modern scholar this act was "a master stroke of diplomacy."[6] The king's motives were almost entirely secular. As a crucesignatus he could hope to enjoy active papal support against barons who now stood in danger of excommunication if they persisted in hindering John's alleged crusading purpose. His vow also won him access to the temporal as well as spiritual privileges of a crucesignatus; these could prove extremely useful to a king at bay.

With his enemies criticising John's illegal actions and flagrant disregard for "good custom," whatever that was, the king probably intended to hide behind his cross, to claim the customary crusader's delay in answering the baronial charges, to which he had promised an answer by Easter.[7] The use of a crusader vow to secure such protection was not novel. The bishop of Durham had taken the cross in 1203 as a tactical manoeuvre in his dispute with the archbishop of York, and in 1201 the persistent Gerald of Wales, according to Innocent III, "was obliged to take the sign of the cross again so that he could conduct more freely the case in which he was engaged for the church of St. David's."[8] If John had hoped to cow his enemies into political or military withdrawal or to prevent discussion of their demands, he was to be disappointed. If anything, the baronial faction took his assumption of the cross as further provocation, and their leaders immediately retaliated by calling themselves "marshals of the army of God."[9] It is unlikely that many were deceived by the king. The most reliable baronial source, the so-called Barnwell annalist, records that some interpreted John's action as motivated not by piety or love of God but by desire to perpetrate a deliberate fraud to deflect the opposition.[10]

Something of John's intention may have survived in three clauses of Magna Carta (52, 53, and 57). These dealt with outstanding disputes arising from judgements of Henry II and Richard I on seisin, forest laws, and wardship.[11] Like many of his subjects John successfully pleaded his crusader's privilege, and was allowed to delay settlement of cases for the usual crusader's term of three years, but only on issues for which he could reasonably claim no personal responsibility or those which had arisen after he had taken the cross. That this was acceptable to his opponents was perhaps because many of them were also crucesignati, destined to join the Fifth Crusade, and they and their followers were, in their private lives, frequently claiming precisely the same immunity.

John's crusader status failed to prevent civil war. Nevertheless, throughout the remaining eighteen months of his life he persisted in relying on it almost as if it had become his surest defence. Certainly, his decision to take the cross won for him his most vociferous and active ally in the pope. Even if John had taken the cross, as Wendover alleged, from fear, not devotion, he was to have reason to be thankful he had.[12] More than once between 1215 and 1217 the survival of the Angevin dynasty on the throne of England depended on the status of John and his son Henry as papal vassals and crucesignati.

All crusading rulers could expect the special protection of the Roman church. In December 1191, citing his responsibilities to protect a crusader's kingdom, Celestine III authorized the excommunication of supporters of Count John who were opposing the chancellor, William Longchamp, giving as a compounding reason the harm such dissent caused the Holy Land. Two years later Celestine threatened to anathematize Philip II unless he ceased his invasion of Normandy, during

Richard's captivity on returning from Palestine.[13] In 1191 Celestine had envisaged purely spiritual penalties, notably the deprivation of sacraments. In July 1215 Innocent III went further. Aware from his experience of John's own sang froid in the face of the Interdict that spiritual punishments alone had limited effect, Innocent called for physical sanctions. Accusing John's opponents of trying to destroy the crusade and of being "worse than Saracens, for they are trying to depose a king who, would succour the Holy Land," he excommunicated the rebels. He placed their lands under an interdict and instructed the justiciar, Peter des Roches, and his loyal colleagues "to order all the king's vassals as they hope to have their sins remitted, to give the king timely counsel and support against these evildoers." Innocent saw opposition to John as an affront to the Holy See, and insisted, rather boldly in the circumstances, that "even if the king were slack or lukewarm about the crusade, we would not leave such wickedness unrebuked, for by God's grace we know how to punish, and we are able to punish such shameless presumption."[14]

Innocent's indictment was threefold. The rebels had broken their oaths of fealty, rejected papal authority, and flouted the crusader's privilege of protection. In failing to protect papal policy, the English church hierarchy was also included in the papal condemnation. On such grounds did Innocent annul Magna Carta in August 1215.[15] Entirely partisan in his interpretation of events in England, in January 1216 Innocent encouraged the bishop of Bourges to raise troops for John:

> enjoining it on them, as from us, for the remission of their sins, to furnish immediate help and support to the king, loving and fearing the eternal King more than anything temporal, and shewing clearly by this action how valiantly for Christ's name they would range themselves against the Saracens and risk their persons and wealth if confronted by them in battle: for they have as neighbours men who in this respect are worse than Saracens, because, having taken the sign of the Cross, they now seem renegades working to fulfil the pagans' hopes by hindering such a magnificent Crusade.[16]

The reference to rebels having taken the cross themselves lent spice to the rhetoric and was probably no more than the truth.

The preaching during 1213 and 1214 had met with some success. One exchequer official, Warin FitzGerold, who defected to the rebels in the spring of 1216, was already a crucesignatus in 1214; a number of the rebels excommunicated by name in December 1215 who later went on the Fifth Crusade may already have taken the cross. They included

Robert FitzWalter, Saer of Quincy, earl of Winchester, Henry of Bohun, earl of Hereford, John of Lacy, constable of Chester, and William d'Aubigny.[17] That both sides were led by crucesignati added piquancy to the conflict and may explain the facile recourse to the nomenclature of holy war—"soldiers of Christ" versus the "army of God."[18] The practical implications of Innocent's policy for royalist recruitment were noted, with disapproval, by Abbot Ralph of Coggeshall. He described Hugh de Boves raising mercenaries for the king in Flanders and Brabant during the summer of 1215 armed "with papal letters" promising remission of sins to those who enlisted for the war in England. Ralph was sceptical of the authenticity of these and other papal letters hostile to the baronial cause, and he regarded the method of recruitment as deceitful. He therefore derived some pleasure at what he interpreted as God's judgement, when a storm sank many of the ships carrying the mercenaries to England, Hugh himself being among the drowned.[19]

The invasion of Louis of France in May 1216 and the hemorrhaging of allegiance from the Angevin to the Capetian cause drew a robust response from the papacy. F. M. Powicke's comment that the war in defence of the Angevin cause in 1216 "was a holy war, with the prestige of a crusade," was less than the truth. There can be little doubt that sometime in 1216 or early 1217 formal crusading was authorised against the antiroyalist forces in England. Vows were sworn explicitly for a war, as the Waverley annals put it, to expel Louis and the French from England, the crusaders "not wishing to have a foreigner as king of England."[20] In September 1216 indulgences were again offered to recruits for the royalist cause by the new pope, Honorius III.[21] On 7 October he announced that he had extended protection to the royalist mercenary captain Savaric de Mauleon "who has taken the cross for the defence of England."[22] In the same month the legate in England, Gualo, persuaded the new nine-year-old king, Henry III, to adopt the cross (presumably as protection) soon after his coronation on 28 October, having already prevailed upon William Marshal to assume the regency as a sacred duty for the remission of his sins.[23] The royalist cause was thereafter closely associated with a crusade both in official sources and by chroniclers, especially during the crisis of the civil war in the early months of 1217.

The death of King John in October 1216 removed a major obstacle to reconciliation, but the royalists still had to win back the renegades. The crusade association was used to rally supporters and encourage defections from the rebels. In January 1217 Honorius III confirmed the legate's authority to suspend Holy Land vows of crucesignati faithful to the king or wishing to return to obedience so they could help the royalist cause and earn "glory among men and merit before God."[24]

Already three crucesignati, the brothers Nicholas, Walter, and Peter of Lettes, had sworn on the Gospels not to leave England without royal permission before the general departure of the crusade.[25] In the same month royalists in Kent were encouraged to make contact with Philip d'Aubigny, organiser of local royalist resistance, "to the honour of God, the Holy Church, our [i.e., Henry III's] realm and our person."[26] With the temporary absence of Prince Louis in February 1217, the government stepped up its campaign. D'Aubigny was now described as "commander of the militia of God," and the loyalist garrison at Rye was promised the aid of "a great many crusaders" (multitudine crucesignatorum).[27] The Barnwell annalist recounts how the earl of Salisbury and others were lured back to the king's side by Gualo's offer of remission of sins if they fought for Henry and the church and how "they signed themselves on the breast with the cross as if they were to fight the infidels." The legate, exercising plenipotentiary powers confirmed by the pope in January, continued to allow those already committed to the Jerusalem crusade to commute or postpone their vows provided they fought for the king.[28] Like the abbot of Coggeshall when faced with indulgences to mercenaries, the Barnwell writer was unimpressed, implying that papal support for such tactics was the result of bribery and greed.[29]

The picture painted by the Barnwell and the Waverley annalists is essentially accurate. The crusade was being used openly in the battle for allegiance. In March 1217 Roger of Horn and his men were restored to royal favour provided they swore fealty to the king and took the cross "to defend the king's lands against the enemies of God and the church." In April royal partisans in Kent, Robert of Dean and William of Kenshaw (nicknamed Willikin of the Weald), were instructed to place under their protection the archbishop of Canterbury's men from the manor of Malling, once they had returned to fealty and had taken the cross "to help God, the Holy Church, and us [i.e., the king]."[30] This offer was open to loyalists as well. When the earl of Chester agreed to delay his crusade to the Holy Land in 1217, prompted by the legate he assumed "the cross on his breast to pursue the enemies of God and the church, the opponents of his lord, the king of England." It is probable that Savaric de Mauleon, another bound for the Holy Land, had undergone a similar swopping of vow and objective in 1216.[31] To help the royalists further, Honorius III in the summer of 1217 was prepared to authorise an ecclesiastical tax in their favour, in direct imitation of crusade funding.[32]

Royalist propaganda and policy, aided by events, gradually had its effect. Even the probaronial Barnwell annalist commented on the transformation of the baronial "army of God," defenders of the liberties of church and realm, into the sons of Belial and fomentors of disorder on a level with infidels.[33] The crusading overtones in the accounts of the two decisive battles of 1217 are unmistakable. Even if they reflect immediately subsequent interpretation, the variety of witness indicates that what was described happened. The Dunstable Annals says the royalists who routed the rebels at the battle of Lincoln in May 1217 wore the white crosses of the Angevins and received absolution from the bishop of Winchester, Peter des Roches.[34] A contemporary poem on the battle is explicit. The royalists "raised together the standard of the cross and ranged themselves round the new king, and the white cross decorating the bearers of the cross fixed the unstable troops in the foundation of faith."[35] Off Sandwich in August, the French relief fleet under the notorious buccaneer Eustace the Monk was defeated by a royalist fleet under Hubert de Burgh. The loss of the reinforcements off Sandwich forced Prince Louis to negotiate peace in September 1217. The royalists had received the absolution and blessing of the bishop of Salisbury before putting to sea, and on their victorious return to port they were greeted by bishops in full pontificals, and by soldiers and others carrying crosses and banners. The victory itself was remembered as a miracle. The later accounts of Wendover and Paris are shot through with crusade imagery; Paris's own drawing of the battle of Lincoln shows a royalist archer wearing a cross on his surcoat.[36]

The crusade made a definite, though not precisely definable, contribution to the royalist victory. It was probably more important than the patriotism emphasised by many contemporary writers. The nationalism which later grew from suspicion of foreign favourites and foreign influence in church and state under Henry III was only vaguely foreshadowed at this time. Opponents of John cited in Magna Carta the baneful influence of the king's foreign cronies, and patriotism was voiced in 1217 as Louis's position began to weaken.[37] However, John and later William Marshal in practice were more occupied with Englishmen only too willing to cast off national allegiance for a French pretender; until the winter of 1216–17 loyalty to country was a remote consideration on either side. The sour and aged Gerald of Wales was not the only one who looked for a transfer of dynasty; those very critics of John's alien associates in 1215 a year later swore fealty to Louis of France.[38] In the early thirteenth century no king of England could be presented as a symbol of nationality. The young Henry III simply represented one option of legitimacy which influential men found increasingly appealing. Xenophobia and traditionalism both contributed to support for Henry, but it is notable that royalist propaganda tended to characterise rebels

139

not as foreigners (which many were not) but as enemies of God and the church. The crusade was for the defence of God, the church, and the church's vassal Henry III, and only by extension for Henry's kingdom. Even the rebel sympathiser at Barnwell, while arguing that John had been deserted because of his reliance on aliens, nevertheless attributed Louis's defeat to his disobedience to the papacy.[39]

The unifying hatred of foreigners was of the future. In a war conducted by a French prince and English barons on one side and an ageing European adventurer and an Italian papal legate on the other, both assisted by continental mercenaries, xenophobia had little place or meaning. Such cosmopolitan company was more susceptible to the supranational language of crusading, which supplied a cohesive focus and a cause in theory every bit as emotionally charged, compelling, and unifying as later patriotism. It is a truism that crusading flourished in a period before the development of effective national ideologies. Its use by royalists in 1215–17—and its more allusive exploitation by the rebels in "the army of God"—testifies to a lack of any overt patriotic ideology beyond the customary rallying cries of battlefield commanders.[40] After all, both sides claimed to be fighting for freedom of the church and people.

The war in England in 1216–17 was more than a battle of words. The crusade lent practical assistance beyond a general aura of just or holy war. With the incentives of spiritual and temporal privileges and the implicit threat of uncompromising mortal combat, crusading was a stimulus to good morale and provided a clear and precise bond of mutual loyalty guaranteed by oath and by the church. The crusade could reinforce other ties of allegiance; through it loyal liegemen of the Angevins were transformed into the soldiers of Christ with a new and perhaps more intense sense of communal identity. It was as if traditional fealty to the king was thought insufficiently strong and required the support of this additional oath. This may have been Gualo's intention, for the creation of the community of loyal Angevin crusaders was solely a clerical invention, owing little to secular precedent but everything to curial ideology. Although lay leaders such as William Marshal and Rannulf of Chester openly took the cross for the sake of the king, it is remarkable that secular appeals for reconciliation in late 1216 bear no trace of crusade language.[41] Nevertheless, these leaders quickly acquiesced in the legate's policy with its obvious advantages for their cause.

The acceptance of the crusade in the context of the English civil war has a significance beyond the history of England. One of Innocent III's most potent legacies was the consolidation and extension of previous assumptions and attitudes to holy war. Abandoning reliance on anathema and interdict for the crusade was symptomatic of a new papal stridency when the rights of the Apostolic See were at stake. However, the crusade was only accepted in England because it was helpful. It knit together relations within the royalist camp; perhaps it frightened the enemy; and it supplied a means of detaching rebels from Prince Louis and binding them to the king's service by additional potent but intelligible oaths. The battles and campaigns of 1217 displayed moments of characteristic crusading savagery, yet the impact of the crusade on morale and the symbolic importance of the oath were just as important.

There were local peculiarities in the English enterprise. The English crusade of 1216–17 appears to have been portrayed differently from other crusades. These, whether against the Moors in Spain, the Slavs in the Baltic, the Albigensians, or the followers of Markward of Anweiler, had tended to be associated in their attached privileges with the expedition to the Holy Land. Apart from Innocent III's assertion that the English rebels were worse than Saracens and some other vague references to infidels, many traditional crusading phrases were absent, the rebels being described more narrowly as opponents of the Roman church, rebels, traitors, excommunicates, and sowers of discord, harmful to the Holy Land. They were not accused of being themselves infidels or even heretics; their crimes were accepted by their accusers as political, not spiritual.

Another distinctive feature was that crusaders in defence of Henry III wore the cross on their chests and not, like those bound for the Holy Land, on their shoulders.[42] In this sense, perhaps, the white Angevin crosses at Lincoln, as redolent of secular as of religious loyalties, were in the nature of being royalist uniforms. This would have been doubly appropriate. In civil wars, the devices carried by either side are likely to be difficult to distinguish in the heat of battle, as relatives contend against one another. Civil war is characterised by the collapse of justice; the common law is weakened. After peace has been restored, violent crimes committed "in time of war" are hardly to be punished in the normal way.[43] The crusader was provided with theoretical protection from civil or criminal injuries and a justification for crimes he may have committed himself in dangerous times. The crusade provided a new source of discipline, symbolised in the wearing of white crosses as witness to the new community created around the king, outside feudalism, and above the common law.

One more peculiarity of this crusade was the operation of the vow. The Barnwell chronicler reports that existing crucesignati could commute or defer their vows for the sake of this new crusade; but when

Earl Rannulf of Chester was persuaded to postpone his crusade to Jerusalem he had to take a fresh vow to fight for the king and assume a new cross, worn in a different place from the old one. This was not commutation or satisfaction of the earlier vow; it was substitution of one crusade for another in line with Honorius III's plan of January 1217 whereby the Holy Land vows would not be replaced, merely suspended.[44] The English crusade, therefore, had a second-class status, and Rannulf of Chester, with others who adopted the cross to fight for their king, later resumed his obligation to fight in the East.

There is a final problem of definition. Despite the symbols, ceremonies, and language, no specific papal bull authorising the English crusade has survived. As men clearly fought as crucesignati, this may not be thought to matter very much. However, the extension of the crusade to new theatres of conflict had considerable repercussions for the movement and for Europe in general. The process depended upon the pope as the only authority theoretically capable of promulgating a canonically legitimate crusade and instituting the necessary conditions and privileges. Therefore the papal attitude to the status of the royal campaign must be of interest. The absence of a papal bull may, of course, be deceptive, an accident of survival or a failure of research. It is indisputable that both Innocent III and Honorius III employed language evocative of crusading and allowed indulgences to be offered to supporters of the Angevins. Alone, however, indulgences did not constitute a crusade. Innocent appeared to have in mind a limited exercise to protect papal prerogative, in the shapes of his vassal King John and plans for a new crusade in the Holy Land, especially important in the context of the pope's intervention elsewhere in Europe and the summoning of the Fourth Lateran Council. Such a task was, in papal eyes, entirely meritorious and deserving of spiritual reward. But although the English rebels were repeatedly anathematized, excommunicates elsewhere did not all have crusades launched against them.

Who started the idea of inviting vows and handing out crosses for the defence of the church and the English king, and when was the decision taken to do it? The earliest evidence is the letter of Honorius III of 7 October 1216 (before the death of John and the accession of a vulnerable minor), mentioning the vow of Savaric de Mauleon; the other references are concentrated in 1217. An extension of the ecclesiastical commitment to the royalists could well have come as a reaction to military escalation of the war following the landing of Louis of France in May 1216, especially as the English rebels and their foreign patron freely publicised the religiosity of their own cause. In the previous few years papal crusaders had been unleashed against enemies of the Ap-

ostolic See in Languedoc, an issue that figured prominently at the Fourth
Lateran Council, which also excommunicated the English dissidents.
It is unsurprising, therefore, that the papacy should have been tempted
to protect John and Henry III in a similar way. However, some features
of the English crusade suggest less direct authorisation. From Honorius's letter it seems that Savaric de Mauleon made his vow sometime
before October 1216 without prior papal instigation. The pope's letter
of January 1217 shows him content to allow Legate Gualo almost complete discretion in tackling the crisis in England, including the power
to excommunicate and to divert crusaders to the protection of the king.[45]
The papacy had no doubts in extending the use of the crusade; at this
exact period Honorius III also transferred Holy Land vows to crusaders
in the Baltic.[46] England, however, presented especial difficulties after
the invasion of Louis of France because the pope needed to keep the
Capetians sweet to help the crusade in Languedoc. Philip Augustus
could not be condemned overtly for his admittedly rather lukewarm
support for his heir. Any measures against Louis and his partisans had,
perforce, to be restricted. Hence there could be no general crusade against
the abetter of Louis (and it is doubtful whether one would have attracted much support outside England in any case). The papacy had to
tread carefully if its policies in southern France, Germany, Italy, and
the Holy Land were not to unravel, caught on the point of the inconvenient crisis in England. On the other hand, it is unlikely that the
crusade in England was devised as well as executed on the sole initiative of Gualo; at every stage he received the strong support of Honorius
III. The problem was that the legate's policy had to be conducted at one
stage removed from the pope himself. Wishing the English rebels defeated, the pope could not afford a hostile France or a distraction from
the preparations elsewhere in Europe for the Fifth Crusade; therefore
authority to legitimise the English crusade was delegated to Gualo.

The English crusade was not the first campaign of the cross restricted in recruitment to one part of Europe. However, its objectives
and methods were hardly traditional, and they taught lessons for the
future. From the Papal Curia the enterprise must have seemed a great
success, demonstrating that papal pretensions could be made effective.
This practical vindication of the aggressive use of the crusade in a secular political context could only have encouraged later popes to employ
similar expedients when faced with other threats to their interests. The
phrases of 1215–17—rebels as excommunicates, enemies of the church,
worse than Saracens, hinderers of the restoration of the Holy Land—
were to be repeated more widely, more vigorously, and more frequently
against the Hohenstaufen, the precedent of England being as favourable

as that of Markward of Anweiler had been discouraging. Domestically, the use of the crusade to shore up the Angevins formed part of the establishment of a new level of papal influence in England and demonstrated how the institutions of the crusade could become engaged in political conflicts. Ironically, the crusader privileges and protection claimed so vociferously by King John and his son's guardians came, in later years, to be most loudly proclaimed by enemies of the Crown, not least by Simon de Montfort, who in the 1260s considerably developed the imprecise appeal of FitzWalter and the other rebels of 1215 in "the army of God."[47]

THE CRUSADES OF REBELS AND ROYALISTS, 1263–1265

The baronial challenge to royal authority between 1258 and 1267 again found protaganists seeking the inspiration and protection of the cross. The evidence is much less equivocal than for the civil war of 1215–17. After the failure of mediation attempts in the autumn of 1263, Pope Urban IV, responding to an appeal from Henry III, appointed Cardinal Gui Foulquois as legate in England with instructions to secure peace, if necessary by preaching a crusade against the king's enemies and excommunicating them and their allies. To those who assisted this crusade, the legate was to grant the same indulgences as had been prescribed by the 1245 Council of Lyons for those who gave succour to the Holy Land. The parallel with 1215–17 was obvious and conscious. In a letter to the barons of 26 July 1264 Foulquois himself recalled Gualo's commission and his "liberation" of England from Prince Louis; this time, however, the royalists had the support of the Capetians.[48]

The implications of the legate's appointment were readily appreciated in England. A royalist tract written after his commission but possibly before the king's defeat at Lewes (May 1264) warned the king's opponents of the consequences of the legate's imminent arrival, armed as he was with powers to revoke the Provisions of Oxford, excommunicate the rebels, confiscate their lands, and commandeer the secular arm, in the guise of the French, to punish the fomenters of revolt.[49] In fact these loyal hopes and threats were disappointed, as Foulquois arrived at the Channel only after the king had been captured at Lewes by the triumphant Simon de Montfort. The legate was refused entry to England. Although in October 1264 Foulquois excommunicated the rebels, he returned to Italy soon after on his election as Pope Clement IV, and there is no evidence that under his commission the cross was ever actually preached against the rebels.

As pope the former frustrated legate tried again. In May 1265 he appointed a successor as legate to England, Cardinal Ottobuono, who was ordered to preach the cross against the Montfortians throughout specified parts of northwest Europe, carefully avoiding the areas of recruitment in southern Europe for Charles of Anjou's campaigns for the throne of Sicily. Ottobuono's brief implied the raising of an invasion force. In July Pope Clement empowered the legate to raise a biennial ecclesiastical tenth in England to support those who helped the royalist cause, specifically mentioning the possibility of involving the Capetians. There is some indication that Ottobuono did begin to collect troops on the continent.[50] Once again, events in England anticipated foreign intervention, news of the royalist triumph at Evesham on 4 August 1265 and the death of Simon de Montfort reaching the legate before he had arrived at the Channel. Despite the cardinal's conciliatory tone in a letter to a Montfortian partisan, the threat of a crusade against any remaining rebels continued in Ottobuono's armoury, on papal orders of September or October 1265. In 1266 Clement empowered his legate in France to excommunicate Montfort's widow and son if they persisted in rebellion, and Ottobuono himself excommunicated the recalcitrant garrison at Kenilworth.[51]

Despite the lack of active preaching before or after Evesham, the instructions to Foulquois and Ottobuono were unambiguous statements of policy from popes whose interests were touched at a number of points. Alexander IV and Urban IV had both absolved Henry III from his oath to uphold the 1258 baronial settlement which Earl Simon persisted in trying to enforce; in March 1264 Urban had agreed to Louis IX's decision at Amiens to annul the Provisions of Oxford. Henry III was a papal vassal and England, by virtue of the 1213 surrender, a papal fief, both demanding especial papal protection; in his commission to Foulquois, Urban emphasised his particular paternal affection for King Henry as well as the papacy's general mission as a peacemaker. Once the legate had been appointed, any resistance or obstruction would, as Foulquois himself put it, compromise the maintenance of the honour of the Holy See.[52]

The most obvious papal interest being endangered by civil conflict was the new crusade to the Holy Land promulgated by Urban IV in 1263. This new effort in England helped publicise the crusade but, as fifty years earlier, had unexpected repercussions. In July 1263 Urban IV had instructed the bishop of Worcester, Walter Cantelupe, a veteran of crusade preaching and fundraising in the late 1240s, to gather men and money to relieve the Holy Land. The following October, only a few weeks before Foulquois's legatine commission against the rebels (who, ironically, included Cantelupe), the pope issued detailed authorisation for the bishop to offer the customary privileges and to collect a quinquennial hundredth on all ecclesiastical revenues.[53] The two crusade initiatives, Cantelupe's for the Holy Land and Foulquois's for the suppression of dissent, clashed. Foulquois was given power to commute all vows, including the *vota Hierosolymitana*, in favour of the royalist cause, perhaps necessary as there were a considerable number of English crucesignati with unfulfilled vows, some of long standing; the king's dated from 1250, Simon de Montfort's from 1248, and Bishop Cantelupe's own from 1247.[54] However, Cantelupe's authority was not specifically suspended, indeed his commission for the Holy Land crusade was the excuse and context for the draconian powers given to Foulquois. As it turned out, the civil war of 1264–65, like that of 1215–17, was led on both sides by crucesignati, although there is little sign that Henry III himself appealed for papal protection by virtue of his crusader status. Given all that had passed between the pope and the king over his 1250 vow, it would have been rather a bold stroke. However, the simultaneous pursuit of two crusading objectives combined unexpectedly, since the rebel leadership deliberately appealed to crusading ideology as a justification of disobedience to the Crown, in what could almost be called a countercrusade.

On 11 December 1263, Simon de Montfort, with a small army, found himself trapped outside London at Southwark, on the south bank of the Thames. Through collusion between the king and some rich citizens, the gates of London were shut to him and the royalist forces were threateningly near. According to the Dunstable annals, in this crisis in his affairs Simon and his followers armed themselves "and in the name of God he had himself and others signed with the cross, front and back, then, confessing their sins, they all ate the Body of Christ ready for the attack of their enemies and, for the sake of truth, to fight them."[55] In the event the royal plan misfired, and Simon was admitted to the city before battle was joined. If this description is to be believed, the incident demonstrates how politicians in extremis could turn to the crusade for encouragement. The earl's gesture was possibly premeditated. According to the chronicle of St. Benet Holme in Norfolk, when Simon returned to England in April 1263 in answer to the barons' summons, "he said he was a *crucesignatus* and was very gladly willing to die fighting wicked Christians for the liberty of England and the Holy Church as against pagans." It may have been this self-conscious posturing that prompted Montfort's troops, before launching an attack on the bishop of Hereford (April–May, 1263), to have themselves tonsured.[56] The images of holy war were everywhere.

The flaw in Simon's argument was, of course, that although crusades had been launched before against such enemies, like the Hohenstaufen, to equate tyrannical Christians with pagans as legitimate targets for crusades was the prerogative of the papacy which, in this instance, was implacably opposed to the earl and a strong supporter of the king. Nevertheless, the earl was a crucesignatus, and he persisted in portraying himself as a holy warrior and employing papal theories against papal protegés—an ironic, but not necessarily coincidental fate for the son of the scourge of the Albigensians.

Throughout the subsequent months leading to his death at Evesham, Montfort is portrayed by sympathetic writers as flaunting the language and symbols of a just cause and a holy war in the service of truth and nation. To what extent this image depended on hindsight is unclear. The antibaronial account of Thomas Wykes, for example, must act as a deterrent to easy acceptance of what is, in essence, probaronial, or at least antiroyalist, mythologising on the part of many contemporary observers.[57] Nevertheless, Earl Simon did seek to elevate his struggle with the king into one of principle, and the tone of the chronicle accounts is mirrored in the *Song of Lewes*, a Latin poem composed during Montfort's ascendancy in 1264–65, celebrating the baronial victory. It is full of high-flown religious symbolism, allegory and imagery—at one point Simon is compared to Christ the Redeemer—and the earl's cause is unequivocally identified with God's. The victory at Lewes was God-given, and the royalists were "the enemy of the English and of the whole realm . . . perchance too of the church, therefore also of God."[58] The *Song of Lewes* is a protracted apologia for resistance to royal power which relies heavily on equating the baronial interests with Divine Justice and the rebels with the Israelites of the Old Testament; it is a propagandist context into which Simon's appropriation of crusading formulae fitted neatly.

The literary association of Montfort's resistance with a holy war is unambiguous in treatments of the battle of Lewes itself. Writer after writer sympathetic to Montfort insisted on the language of Christian warfare. The earl and his followers were fighting "God's battle"; they confessed their sins and appealed to divine aid; they put on the "belt of holy knighthood," unafraid to die "pro patria" and "pro veritate."[59] Some commentators were more specific. The Furness chronicle reported that Earl Simon's troops, barons, and their retinues wore crosses on their chests and backs ("ante et retro crucesignantes") while the author of the *Flores historiarum*, a monk from St. Alban's, wrote of their wearing crosses on their shoulders and breasts ("super humeros et pectora crucizarunt se"; later at Evesham the Montfortians apparently wore crosses on the front and back of their right shoulders).[60] A later source, William Rishanger's *De Bellis*, adds plausible detail. The night before the battle Bishop Cantelupe, "that soldier of Christ," a strong supporter of the rebels, absolved the baronial soldiers of their sins, promising them remission. The following morning Earl Simon himself instructed his forces to wear white crosses over their armour, front and back, "to distinguish each other from the enemy and to demonstrate that they were fighting for justice."[61]

As at Southwark in December, so at Lewes in May, Montfort was apparently facing disaster. Confident of victory, the royalists had rejected the earl's peace overtures and had raised the Dragon Banner, a warning that no quarter was to be given, a move which alone might have provoked the rebels into similarly extreme gestures.[62] From Rishanger's description it appears that the bishop of Worcester, in common with army chaplains down the centuries, encouraged staunchness with the blandishments of the church. In the battle itself, the use of the cross as a uniform was obviously prudent, with family or patronal distinguishing signs, banners, and surcoats likely to be found in both camps.[63] The need for distinctive clothing was soon recognised by the royalists. At Evesham fifteen months later they wore red crosses on their arms to distinguish friends from foes who were again bearing white crosses. Two royalists who failed to wear the insignia of the red cross went unrecognised and were killed by men of their own side.[64]

The white crosses worn by the baronial troops at Lewes and Evesham would have been more than distinguishing marks or even generalised signs of virtue. The significance of the white cross of Angevin crusaders was unlikely to have been lost on Earl Simon, still less on Henry III, with whose cause as a child it had been so firmly associated. Henry had not been allowed by the baronial proctors at Amiens a few months before to forget his unfulfilled vow of 1250 and the illfated consequences of his delay.[65] By appropriating the white cross for himself, Simon, whose own second crusade vow was unsatisfied, had stolen a march on his enemies. What makes his gesture more intriguing is that Cantelupe—and indeed the royalists—although they knew of the approach of the legate Foulquois and the general tenor of his commission, were still in ignorance of the precise crusading terms of the new legatine powers, news of which only reached England a fortnight after the battle.[66]

Although no evidence survives of Cantelupe's actually carrying out his papal instructions of the previous year, at Lewes the bishop was probably still regarded as in possession of those papally granted powers. This fact constituted a considerable inconvenience for the royalists and a distinct boon for the rebels, which their leaders may not have been slow to exploit. Cantelupe's approval would have diminished any apparent impropriety in the rebel's use of the Angevin cross.

At the battle of Evesham the Montfortians were in no doubt where the papacy stood. But by this time the white cross had become a factional badge, its universal appeal demonstrably weakened by the royalist adoption of red crosses; two could fight holy wars. Paradoxically, by using the white cross Simon de Montfort may have contributed significantly to the secularisation of the cross as a symbol in battle and the emergence of an English royal uniform. For it was the red cross worn by royalists at Evesham that became the characteristic emblem of English troops in the later Middle Ages and beyond. Its use by the Lord Edward and his troops in 1263, and possibly again by him as king during his wars against Scotland, presaged its adoption by Edward III and its association by him with a national cult of St. George.[67] (Red crosses were, however, also to remain standard for crusaders as well.) Whether the royalists at Evesham were crucesignati under the terms of Ottobuono's brief is unclear; the extant sources describe the red crosses solely in terms of uniforms. But the symbolism would have been self-evident.

In the accounts of the battle of Evesham, Simon de Montfort and his cause found their literary apotheosis; Simon was a martyr, a "miles Christi," his slain followers "blessed souls" in Paradise.[68] Such epithets form a fitting conclusion to a conflict which, in description and probably in action, resounded to religious rhetoric. It is by no means uncommon for partisans in bitter political conflicts to assume a mantle of moral or spiritual purity. In the thirteenth century, thanks partly to the experience of the campaigns in the East and partly to papal and canonist definitions and justifications, this tendency took the guise of crusading. It is difficult to be sure how contemporaries reacted to the appropriation of crusade symbols, either by the papacy or by Simon de Montfort. On the one hand, some articulate observers were suspicious of the extension of the ideal and were aware of distinctions between fighting heretics, tyrants, and infidels, regardless of papal sophistry. Conversely, it is also apparent that the elaboration of the ideal gained wide currency; the principle that crusading could be applied to domestic political problems, provided they were proclaimed as involving church interests (rarely a difficult task), was accepted by Urban IV and Simon de Montfort alike.

Although the element of the crusade in the baronial wars of Henry III's reign may have been largely rhetorical, there was a practical dimension. In the 1260s the precedent of a papal crusade against rebels was a perceived threat to the critics of the king. Equally, the passion and tenacity with which the rebels pursued their cause in 1263–64 could only have been sustained by some sort of identification with a holy war. Politics and propaganda met in the crusade, as a symbol and a theory of legitimate resistance to a tyrannical regime or, antithetically, of the extirpation of contumacious political dissent; the former's use by Simon de Montfort was a strikingly novel tactical use of a by then well-understood convention. Superficially, Simon's actions point to a crusade ideology with an existence apart from papal authority, and it was always true that papal control of preaching and the granting of the cross was at times tenuous. However, the presence of Cantelupe suggests that the formal papal connection had not been severed, at least at Lewes, even if the pope would have objected strongly to his erstwhile representative's behaviour. Just as in the twelfth century the papacy had some difficulty imposing its theoretical authority over the crusade movement, especially where it affected private crusades outside the general passagia, so in the thirteenth century, having once established theoretical control, the papacy had problems retaining it in practice. The events of the 1260s are a good illustration of this. Simon de Montfort even copied an attendant institution of crusading when, during his period in power in 1264–65, he imposed a clerical tithe to subsidise his cause.[69]

The crusade against tyrants may have been a case of any weapon being useful in a crisis, and it had little future as a tool of dissent. Nevertheless, the use of the crusade in English politics delineates contours of a wider phenomenon. Crusade ideology had penetrated deeply into the way contemporaries approached and sought to solve political, diplomatic, and even legal problems. As a result they had fashioned it to their own image. Some historians have argued that the crusade was a mechanism used by the papacy to bring peace and reconciliation to warring factions within Christendom: unite for the sake of the Holy Land and become brothers as crucesignati in the army of God.[70] It could act in this way. However, in England in 1215–17 and 1263–65, the crusade was the reverse of this. It was deliberately employed as a means of aggression, by the papacy to suppress opposition and by Montfort to resist his legitimate overlord. Both usages may have raised the tone of the propaganda but hardly enhanced the ideal itself. Nor did they exert much effect on the course of the crisis, except to render the divisions more bitter and unbridgeable and the violence more self-righteous and thus more unrelenting and more brutal. When in 1267 the obstinate rebels of the Isle of Ely accused Cardinal Ottobuono of encouraging the continuance of war by openly throwing his authority behind the king, they were describing a papal policy only selectively committed to peace and were telling no more than the truth. The civil wars in England show that crusading ideals, like any other, reflected temporal and immediate human aspirations and fears. Therefore they were flexible, contradictory, alternately or simultaneously noble, squalid, misunderstood, or misused. In its time the crusade was probably all of these. The link between the soldiers who stormed Jerusalem in 1099 and Montfort's retainers at Lewes a century and a half later is indeed thin; yet it is there.

7

Preaching and Recruitment

PREACHING

In theory voluntary, crusading was rarely spontaneous. The ceremonial adoption of the cross usually came at the conclusion of an almost predictable sequence of events, beginning with the identification of a new casus belli and ending with a formal sermon preceding the liturgical rite of taking the cross. Alternatively, outside the context of the general or larger passagia and regardless of papal theory, individuals could seek out priests qualified to give them the cross.[1]

With changing military priorities and circumstances, by the middle of the thirteenth century crusade preaching, which was almost invariably associated with the substantial, papally authorised expeditions, had become highly systematised. The shift of purpose from the recruitment of men to the raising of money caused the setpiece sermon, although still prominent, to be supplemented, in places supplanted, by bureaucratic procedures designed to achieve cash donations or vow redemptions. Late in the thirteenth century, for example, preaching by the friars organised in the northern ecclesiastical province of England was complementary to the separate and permanent efforts of regular diocesan administrators to raise crusade money.[2]

Nevertheless, the central image of crusade recruitment, the sermon followed by the adoption of the cross, remains an accurate description of what actually occurred in England into the fifteenth century, if with decreasing regularity after 1300. At times, preaching appears almost as mechanical aping of earlier models, increasingly so as novelty became more dangerous after the appearance of Lollardy in the late fourteenth century. Yet the formal descriptions and the conventional content of such sermons did not detract from their perceived centrality to any crusade initiative. English crusading, no less than continental, is decorated by a succession of these occasions. As the pivotal mechanism which combined raising men and money for war with the spiritual exercise of granting absolution and the remission of sins, preaching was as important to the plans of Bishop Despenser in 1383, Cardinal Beaufort in 1428, or Pius II in 1463, as it was for the popes and crusading princes of the twelfth and thirteenth centuries.[3]

The importance of preaching the cross is reflected in the strenuous and largely successful efforts of the papacy to control the system through specially appointed agents, like the abbot of St. Bénigne in 1096 or St. Bernard in 1146–47, specially designated local prelates, and papal legates. Papal delegation grew in complexity, with preachers being vested by the pope with powers to organise teams of subordinates to carry the message further through the community, a task increasingly undertaken by the friars from the 1230s. Centralised control imposed an explicit uniformity in propagandising what the author of the *Itinerarium Ricardi Regis* described as the "unica causa."[4] Experience of independent preachers—such as Peter the Hermit during the First Crusade; the Cistercian Rudolph who, against papal wishes, excited the support of Rhinelanders for the Second Crusade; or Fulk of Neuilly in the 1190s— had been unhappy for the papacy. Such demagogues raised expectations, made extravagant offers and claims that ran ahead of, if not actually in a different direction from, official policy. Papal control was, therefore, extended beyond the appointment of suitable deputies and establishing an administrative framework for local endeavours to the manipulation of what was actually preached. Although individual speakers were permitted, indeed expected, to perform in as attractive fashion as they were able, the central message was ideally preordained by the papacy in the bulls authorising the crusade. In January 1181, in one of the regularly abortive attempts to rouse the West against Saladin, Alexander III instructed the clergy when preaching the cross to publicise papal letters which explained the need for a new crusade and the proffered indulgences.[5] In arranging preaching for the Fifth Crusade, Innocent III, typically, was even more insistent and precise. Writing general instructions to the teams of provincial preachers, he argued that they "must pass on with great care and attention to detail exactly what is contained in the encyclical [viz., *Quia Maior*, the great bull of 1213 launching the new expedition], transmitting carefully and effectively everything you will see has been included in that letter for the aid of the Holy Land."[6] Papal letters supplied the preacher with his authority and an authorised text presenting the casus belli in a correct theological and canonical frame with the privileges precisely outlined. In this way preachers were the main vehicles for the mass communication of the ideas and instructions of the ruling and planning elite. It is likely, for example, that Archbishop Baldwin's tour of Wales in 1188 publicised

Henry II's crusade ordinances as well as Gregory VIII's bull *Audita tremendi.*[7]

Papal control did not guarantee effective preaching. The proposed crusade of 1181 got nowhere, and even the strenuous labours of Innocent III's agents were not universally successful after 1213, the French being conspicuous by their relative lack of support for the Fifth Crusade. The career of Henry II amply illustrated how papal bulls did not necessarily translate into action. Much, if not all, depended on the attitude of the local secular ruler; in England, monarchs, although perennially sympathetic to crusading, did not invariably welcome crusade preachers. In 1245 Henry III was unimpressed by the credentials that the bishop of Beirut bore from the Holy Land and the Papal Curia; without royal assistance no preaching campaign could proceed.[8] Similarly, recruitment and donations depended on a number of external factors—financial, political, and social—not covered by papal formulae. The importance of crusade preaching in this context lay less in what it revealed of papal policy or curial attitudes to the theology of holy war than in its ability to secure recruits and donors at provincial and local levels.

The first major preaching and recruiting effort in England that is adequately documented was that of 1188. Although Englishmen had regularly taken the cross, direct evidence for the organisation of earlier concerted preaching campaigns has not survived. In 1096, the abbot of St. Bénigne, although possibly empowered by Urban II to preach in the Anglo-Norman lands, came to England primarily to negotiate the mortgage for Curthose. He may, however, have spread details of the Clermont decrees and crusade preparations beyond the court to other clerics, including, perhaps, his fellow Benedictines at Cerne.[9] Information from England on the reputedly popular fundraising and recruiting visit of Hugh de Payens in 1128 is restricted more or less to the one vague entry in the *Anglo-Saxon Chronicle.*[10] Before the Second Crusade some preaching is likely to have occurred to produce the significant contingents of crusaders from East Anglia and the south. On the other hand, all the areas mentioned as having sent men on crusade were in touch with the continent, and news of the crusade could have been disseminated by laymen like the Viels, merchants of Rouen and Southampton who themselves took the cross. The eyewitness who recorded the deeds of the English crusaders made no mention of any preaching before the embarkation from Dartmouth, an unusual omission in any account of a crusade, especially as the author was clearly familiar with the genre.[11] St. Bernard, in a letter of 1147 addressed to the English among others, admitted that he would have preferred to preach the cross in England "by word of mouth had I but the strength to come to you as I desire."

Nevertheless, his written exhortation, which reads like a sermon, may have provided a stimulus and blueprint for preaching by the clergy, particularly, perhaps, Bernard's fellow Cistercians.[12] The close involvement of the Cistercians, including Bernard and Pope Eugenius III, in the process whereby William the Fat, earl of Aumale, redeemed his crusade vow in 1150, may indicate that in England, as elsewhere, they played a prominent role in organising the initial recruitment. Similarly, it was a Cistercian monastery that the earl of Worcester, Waleran of Meulan, thought of founding in France in gratitude for being saved from shipwreck on his return from the Holy Land in 1149.[13] However, in 1146 as in 1096, political circumstances were hardly conducive to unequivocal royal or baronial support.

Between the Second and Third Crusades, despite the best endeavours of the papacy, there was only one occasion on which the cross was proclaimed in England with any publicity, the visit of Patriarch Heraclius in 1185. At his first meeting with the king at Reading the patriarch's address, according to Ralph of Diceto, reduced his audience to tears, almost a sine qua non for successful crusade sermons. Thereafter Heraclius had little opportunity to excite an audience, as the king and his councillors took firm control of proceedings at Reading and later at Clerkenwell.[14] Heraclius's Reading speech falls into a familiar category of crusade address. It had a specific political purpose and formed part of an almost ritualised form of diplomatic exchange. The public display was powerful, professionally executed, and designed to make the greatest symbolic impact possible. The work of persuading the king or others to adopt the cross would be conducted in smaller briefings and lobbyings behind the scenes. In the event Heraclius did manage to recruit a few crucesignati from Henry's court, although only with the king's express permission.[15]

Such conventional presentations could be found wherever and whenever formal gatherings were held to discuss or promote the crusade. In such circumstances responses were unlikely to be entirely spontaneous, although sometimes they were unrehearsed. When Henry III summoned Londoners to Westminster in April 1252 to affirm his intention of going on crusade in person, no less than three sermons were provided to encourage their participation; a number of curial officials were on hand, presumably by prior arrangement, to set an example to the citizens by taking the cross. Unfortunately, the audience was unimpressed, and few followed the courtiers' lead, much to the king's fury. The evidence is circumstantial but it is likely that this occasion had been carefully staged; it was, therefore, especially galling for the royal impresario that the Londoners failed to take up their cue.[16]

155

In 1188, thanks to the alliance of church and state, crusade preaching went far beyond such quasi-ceremonial court assemblies and confirmed that, even in the localities, effective recruitment depended upon careful planning, the manipulation of political circumstances, and the skilled use of rhetorical and theatrical artifice. In Gerald of Wales's invaluable if self-glorifying personal account of the preaching tour in Wales he undertook with Archbishop Baldwin in Lent 1188, these characteristics feature prominently.[17] Some of the political aspects have already been discussed. Significant here are the details Gerald provides of the techniques and stage management of the operation. The most striking impression is of meticulous organisation, notably of the itinerary designed to achieve political and ecclesiastical as well as recruitment objectives. Local magnates and bishops were visited in turn and, given the number of times the archbishop was met by local leaders immediately on entering their territory, almost certainly by prearrangement. Gruffydd ap Cynan of Gwynedd apologised for being late at Towyn. When Owain Cyfeiliog, "alone of all the Welsh princes," failed to present himself at all he was excommunicated.[18] In the attempt to impose the authority of Canterbury, Gerald himself was exploited by Angevin officials. Gerald was a passionate advocate of St. David's independent metropolitan status and a disappointed candidate for the see in 1176; his presence beside the archbishop and the complaisant Bishop Peter of St. David's at the mass Baldwin celebrated in St. David's cathedral demonstrated his defeat.[19] By involving the rulers of Wales in the crusade, the king may have hoped to restrict their ability to cause trouble. Here, too, Gerald was useful in neutralising dissent, by acting as a channel of communication to the local aristocracy, many of whom were Gerald's close relatives.[20] However, despite the political implications, the religious aspects of the tour were not ignored and, indeed, were crucial to the success of the secular objectives. Once the Welsh princes were crucesignati they became obliged to support Henry II's crusade.

Crusade preaching differed from other forms, success demanding that the audience be moved not to tears and repentance alone but to physical action. This required the stage management of an Elmer Gantry. Gerald of Wales described what happened at Radnor after the opening sermon of the tour by the archbishop:

> I myself who have written these words, was the first to stand up. I threw myself at the holy man's feet and devoutly took the sign of the Cross. It was the urgent admonition given some time before by the King which inspired me to give this example to the others, and the persuasion and oft-repeated promises of the Archbishop

and the Chief Justiciar, who never tired of repeating the King's words. I acted of my own free will, after anxiously talking the matter over time and time again, in view of the insult and injury being done at this moment to the Cross of Christ. In doing so I gave strong encouragement to the others and an added incentive to what they had just been told.[21]

Crowd psychology was important, and it was necessary to have somebody come forward promptly. Gerald in his report had to stress the voluntary nature of his act, which otherwise would have been invalid, but later he was to confess that he had been persuaded in part by the king's promise to finance his crusade. In his autobiography this equivocation remained; he explained that he had been "moved not less by [my] own devotion than by the exhortation of such great men."[22] Either way, the gesture was premeditated and had nothing to do with the quality of the sermon.

On occasion the actual sermon could be of secondary importance. Gerald gave very little information as to what was actually preached and implied that it mattered less what was said than how and by whom it was spoken. For example, Gerald had, by his own account, his greatest popular success at Haverfordwest, when over two hundred took the cross; yet he preached in French and Latin which many in his audience could not understand. Smugly, Gerald compared the effect with the response to St. Bernard's preaching in French to German congregations before the Second Crusade, which may have been the point of his story. In his description of the sermon it is the force of delivery not the content that is emphasised. Baldwin's Haverfordwest sermon had flopped badly; in general he does not seem to have been an inspiring preacher. Then the portable cross, which constituted the speaker's main prop, was handed to Gerald who recalled his technical virtuosity with pride:

> Now the Archdeacon [i.e., Gerald himself] had divided his sermon into three parts and reserved his strong power of persuasion for the close of each of these. Wherefore thrice there was such a throng of those who came and eagerly seized a Cross, that the Archbishop could hardly be protected from the crowd of those who pressed upon him and on each of these occasions the Archdeacon was forced to be silent in mid-speech and pause by reason of the tumult.[23]

Many, if not most in this enthusiastic crowd, would not have understood a word he had said.

Gerald's vanity also led him to record more articulate reactions to his oratory:

> often on that journey the Archbishop would say that he had never seen so many tears as on that day at Haverford. Now, as Jerome says in a book of his letters, the tears of the people are the glories of the preacher.

Gerald, so he later claimed, also overheard his skill likened to witchcraft; without his "soft words" and "simple looks," protested a wife of one of the crucesignati, her husband and the rest "would have got clear off, as far as the preaching of the others was concerned."[24] Such theatrical effects were not always sufficient, and elsewhere, as at the opening sermon at Radnor in front of Rhys ap Gruffydd, prince of south Wales, the message itself was important. For these occasions a Welsh interpreter was used; from Usk, the archbishop's party was accompanied by their own, Alexander, archdeacon of Bangor.[25]

If the spoken word was at times incomprehensible, the religious context was made as clear as possible. On one level, the preaching was a general call to repentance. In *Audita tremendi* Gregory VIII explained the disaster in the Holy Land as a consequence of sin. He called on the faithful "to consider not only the sins of the inhabitants [of the Holy Land] but also our own and those of the whole Christian people," to repent and to amend "in ourselves what we have done wrong and then turn our attention to the treachery and malice of the enemy"; only contrition and humility would earn reward and bring military success.[26] It is almost certain that Baldwin's team of preachers, which included a number of local prelates as well as Gerald, would have taken *Audita tremendi* as the basis for their speeches. Their penitential purpose was reinforced by the timing of the tour, which coincided with Lent, and the usual placement of the crusade sermon immediately after the celebration of mass. The elements of confession and penance are prominent in Gerald's description. In the absence of a mass, the archbishop's sermon on Anglesey was preceded by confession alone; for some recruits, such as the criminals of Usk, adoption of the cross was likened to a conversion.[27] An aura of sanctity attended the expedition: the spot at which Baldwin had given out crosses at Haverfordwest restored sight to an old blind man, and at Cardigan a commemorative chapel, built in the field where the archbishop had preached, attracted pilgrims who witnessed many miracles of healing.[28] Gerald himself was keen to stud his narrative with semimiraculous and uplifting anecdotes. Like other contemporary preachers, he no doubt enlivened his sermons with moral tales or *exempla*, such as the story of the mother who overlay and smothered her beloved little son as God's punishment for trying to prevent her husband joining the crusade.[29]

Gerald's experiences in Wales in 1188 were paralleled throughout twelfth- and thirteenth-century Europe. Timing was always important; Lent was a popular time for preaching and for taking the cross (as King John did on Ash Wednesday 1215). Urban II's appeal at Clermont in 1095 was made just before, and Innocent III's crusade decrees of 1215 were promulgated just after, the beginning of the penitential season of Advent, and Eugenius III's crusade bull of 1146 was published during Lent. Their timing may not have been coincidental, as all three were premeditated, and unlike Gregory VIII's bull in 1187, owed nothing to sudden news of disaster.[30] Certain individual days outside the penitential seasons could also be popular, especially 14 September, the Feast of the Exaltation of the Cross. This became a sort of crusaders' festival day, exploited by preachers from the Third Crusade or earlier.[31] In 1291 the friars and other clerics appointed to preach the cross in the see of York were all instructed to deliver their sermons on 14 September, testimony to the importance of the symbolism and cult of the cross within the sermons themselves and within the surrounding network of devotional habits upon which the institution of the crusade depended.[32] For the same reasons Easter, the day of St. Bernard's famous Vezelay address in 1146, could concentrate the minds of an audience. In 1188 Archbishop Baldwin's sermon at Chester on Easter Day marked the climax of the Welsh part of his preaching tour.[33]

The celebration of mass, with its liturgical concentration on confession and the figure of Christ Crucified, was an exactly appropriate preparation for the receipt of a call to take the cross. The association of the crusade and the mass was close. In the statutes of the bishop of Worcester in 1229, reference is made to a bell being rung during mass for the Holy Land at which point the Lord's Prayer was to be recited. A crusade sermon could as well form part of the service as be an appendix to it. The bishop of Oporto's sermon to the crusaders in 1147 was integrated into a celebration of the eucharist, and an English crusade-preaching manual of the early thirteenth century includes an extended meditation on Christ's presence in the mass.[34] On the 1188 Welsh tour, sermons were preached after the completion of the mass, not as part of it, perhaps for ease of administration, although other sermons on the tour are described with no indication of a connected mass. The ceremony of taking the cross was itself brief and could be accommodated to suit more or less any situation. An increasingly common feature of crusading in the thirteenth century was the institution of regular special prayers, processions, and celebrations of the eucharist specifically designed to inspire penitence and aid the cause of the Holy Land. These observances were first prescribed in detail in Innocent III's bull *Quia maior*, and show how the crusade formed part of the habitual round of the religious life of ordinary Christians in the West.[35]

Apart from liturgical support, crusade preachers had techniques and props of their own like any other public performers. Outside the walls of Lisbon the preacher carried what he claimed to be a piece of the True Cross and, in symbolic representation of the same, the preachers in Wales in 1188 held a portable cross when they spoke.[36] This habit probably dated back to the 1090s. It could backfire. According to the Winchester annals, at the time of the First Crusade a French abbot made his own cross and tried to pass it off as having been made by God; as a punishment he contracted cancer.[37] Evidence of direct divine interest was, in fact, another weapon in the preacher's armoury. Determinedly revivalist, sermons aroused emotions which were manifested in and stimulated by stories of miracles which, whatever their popular acceptance, were studiously preserved by chroniclers and preachers alike in didactic exempla. Preachers either performed miracles themselves or talked of miracles; perhaps occasionally the distinction became blurred. Preaching manuals such as the English *Ordinatio* of 1216 or the later *Speculum Laicorum*, like the continental collections of preachers such as Jacques de Vitry, are full of exempla designed to show how God's disfavour would strike those who hindered crusade recruitment. Chroniclers like Roger of Howden and Roger of Wendover preserved the miracles surrounding the preaching of charismatic figures such as Eustace of Flay in 1200 and 1201, or Roger of Lewes, an early Franciscan who cured a paralytic at Clare (Suffolk) in 1235; they also described the more general signs of divine favour—often celestial visions—which traditionally accompanied such exercises.[38]

Symbolism, the associated miracle stories, and exempla assisted the central function of crusade preaching, which was to secure recruits or money. Despite the passion of Gerald of Wales that communicated an emotion beyond words, interpreters were often important, especially as leading preachers were frequently international celebrities addressing foreign audiences. In 1147 the bishop of Oporto needed a team of interpreters to transmit his plea to the polyglot crusaders to join the attack on Lisbon. At Lincoln in 1267 Cardinal Ottobuono employed the dean of Lincoln and some friars.[39] The language of preaching can be indicative of its prospective constituency. In England there is evidence from chroniclers and the few extant sermons that the preaching was conducted in Latin and French. There may be a presumption that English was used as well, but despite the enthusiasm of thirteenth-century bishops for the vernacular there is little sign that it was commonly employed until the fourteenth century. Whereas some French vernacular exempla have survived, none have in English, which might suggest that in the twelfth and thirteenth centuries crusade recruiting agents were particularly concerned with the aristocratic and French-speaking elements in English society. Alternatively, the linguistic evidence reflects the habits of the illustrious, not the common, and may therefore distort reality; it is, in any case, meagre.

Once the message was delivered, some record of who had taken the cross was essential. The secular organisers needed to know numbers for military preparations, as well as the names of those exempt from taxation or, as in 1201, of those in line to receive payments from crusade subsidies. The local civil and ecclesiastical authorities required the same information in order to uphold crusaders' privileges and prevent backsliding. According to Roger of Wendover, Master Hubert, a papal preacher for the 1227 crusade, kept a roll of crucesignati. Earlier preachers may not have been so efficient.[40] In the late 1190s the archbishop of Canterbury had no lists of crucesignati available to him in order to discover who had failed to fulfil their vows and had to launch an inquiry to make new lists. In 1188 Gerald of Wales could only calculate roughly ("about three thousand") how many had been recruited from Wales.[41] Even if at the time of writing Gerald did not have access to a record of those who had received the cross, his figure is more credible than the supposed tally of 40,000 names on Master Hubert's roll. It is therefore likely that some sort of list had been kept on the Welsh tour. This would have been useful for secular authorities as well as for determining those exempt from the Saladin tithe.

The impression that crusade preaching became more centrally organised in the thirteenth century may not be strictly accurate in the case of England. From the beginning Crown and episcopacy kept tight rein on recruitment, as in the cooperation between William Rufus and Archbishop Anselm during the First Crusade to prevent the departure of the monks of Cerne.[42] No foreign preacher was allowed in England without the approval of the secular arm; the earliest possible extensive crusade preaching, the visit to England in 1128 of Hugh de Payens, was only conducted with express royal permission.[43] The preaching for the Third Crusade was organised by the king's council at Geddington in February 1188 and, when not pursued by roving agents of the Crown like Archbishop Baldwin or his deputy Bishop Gilbert of Rochester, it was entrusted to local bishops like Bishop Reinier of St. Asaph's, who preached the cross in the Welsh marches before the arrival of Baldwin's party.[44] This pattern of mobile expert preachers operating in conjunction with local clergy, which typified the Welsh tour of 1188, became standard in the thirteenth century, even though it could still be the parish priest who actually heard the vow and dispensed the cross. From the 1230s the system devolved onto a coalition of papal legates, local bishops, diocesan clergy, and authorised friars. The only apparently freelance preacher to receive much contemporary attention before this was Eustace of Flay, but it is likely that he, too, had authority derived at one remove from the papacy. As a colleague of Fulk of Neuilly, he was probably one of those Innocent III had empowered Fulk to appoint as preaching assistants in 1198. It is inconceivable that Eustace would have been allowed such free range on his visits to England in 1200 and 1201, with his potentially disruptive brand of sabbatarianism and moral reform, without official permission.[45]

Eustace stirred up considerable if ephemeral popular enthusiasm, but was untypical of English experience, in which there is little to compare with the accounts of public reaction to the sermons of Peter the Hermit, St. Bernard, or Fulk of Neuilly. In England, recruitment for general passagia was deliberate, ordered, and, within the confines of limited techniques of crowd manipulation and control of mass responses, orderly. Nevertheless, Abbot Eustace's intervention presaged the advent of the friars, first used as crusade preachers in England in 1235; they soon came to dominate the métier. The appeal of the friars, like that of Eustace of Flay and others of the poverty movement of the twelfth century, lay, initially at any rate, in their closeness to the people. Ironically, their introduction was not intended to extend recruitment but to raise more money through the systematic sale of vow redemptions. This was the aspect of their work that Matthew Paris repeatedly emphasised from his account of their appearance in 1235 onwards, scarcely ever concealing his distaste at this development. He was not alone. As discussed earlier, the bishop of Worcester petitioned the pope in 1247 to allow crusaders not to redeem their vows, and in 1251 Henry III had to proclaim, in response to rumours of his subjects' fears of official rapacity, that no crusader should be forced to redeem his vow for more than he had promised. The new, overtly mercenary element, while profitable and efficient for the organisers, thus had some clear disadvantages. The arrival of the friars marked a greater administrative systemisation and a definite shift of policy from men to money. Coincidentally, the message of the friars was refined by the academic influences of the schools and new universities, in which both the Dominicans and Franciscans were soon heavily involved.[46]

The friars, in contrast to St. Bernard, Gerald of Wales, or even Urban II, directed their message at sections of the community unable by themselves to afford to crusade in person, even if prosperous enough to buy redemptions. Unlike the preachers of 1188, who had aimed their message at audiences with an aristocratic nucleus, the friars were directed towards a process of penitence centred upon a financial transaction, which itself was a symptom of much wider changes in society and the economy. In 1200–1, Eustace of Flay had also been concerned to raise alms from his audiences. The friars' purpose was subtly different from that of their predecessors. However important the friars were in increasing or maintaining public awareness of the issues of crusading in the thirteenth century, recruiting sermons delivered to audiences comprising men liable to go in person still tended to be delivered by members of the traditional hierarchy; the friars were assigned elsewhere. They did not revolutionise crusade preaching or recruitment so much as crusade finance.

One of the more elusive aspects of crusade preaching is the actual content of the sermons. Twelfth and thirteenth-century survivals from England are extremely rare. No doubt the central elements, such as calls to repentance and sumptuary instructions, were common across Europe. Papal bulls or letters from the Holy Land provided the moral tone and specific casus belli, individual preachers elaborating and decorating the theme to gain effect and response; thus was Gerald of Wales successful at Haverfordwest after Baldwin had failed. Propaganda needed topicality and suitability to the audience. This could come from the top, as when in 1266 Clement IV ordered Ottobuono to preach specifically on the recent loss of Ashdod, Caesarea, and Saphet, but not necessarily so.[47] Local circumstances were often more immediately important. The bishop of Oporto in 1147 had to persuade the crusaders of the urgency of restoring the "fallen and prostrate church of Spain" before the relief of the Holy Land and, later, at the siege of Lisbon itself, the unnamed preacher had to concentrate on the crusader's immediate frontline duties and prospects of reward.[48] In a very different context, Peter of Blois, a prominent and active figure in the fertile circle of literary administrators in and around Henry II's court, carefully had to modulate his literary appeals for a crusade according to his audience and events: in the case of Archbishop Baldwin in 1187–88, the fall of Jerusalem; with Henry II in 1189, the internecine wranglings among crucesignati which had prevented any immediate crusade from embarking.[49]

Artifice could be as crucial for the content as for the delivery. In an Anglo-Norman collection of materials for crusade preaching dating perhaps from around 1216, known as the *Ordinatio de predicatione Sancti Crucis in Angliae*, there is a definition of the purpose of exempla in sermons: they should attract the listener's attention, prevent boredom, inspire contrition, and encourage the rejection of earthly vanities.[50] In the *Ordinatio* the material for the sermons themselves comprises a series of meditations on the allegorical significance and exigesis of a series of themes centred upon the figure of Christ on the cross. Complicated theology is to be expounded through simple metaphors and reference to familiar cults like those of the Virgin. Various sections deal with the Crucifixion and the paradox of life through death, the Eucharist, the spiritual rewards of assuming the cross, and the fatal delights of the flesh; they contain much standard, if slightly academic, interpretation and exposition, clear but hardly rabble-rousing. The final section of the *Ordinatio*, "The call of men to the cross," reads much more like an actual sermon addressed to a lay audience.[51] It contains a series of exempla drawn from the edifying exploits of previous crusaders, with some of the punch lines in the French vernacular (the rest is in Latin). The structure of the sermon is that of a speech with one single, simple message which is repeated in a variety of similar but different ways. It is frequently punctuated by the traditional crusading refrain "Arise, therefore, take up my [sic] cross and follow me," a phrase prominent in crusade *excitatoria* since the 1090s.[52] Gerald of Wales effectively used repeated climaxes at Haverfordwest. In the *Ordinatio*, the refrain is modified and extended to fit the rhetoric developing from the basic formula: "Arise therefore and follow the precepts of the Lord and assume the sign of God, namely the cross." The refrain echoed the theme of each individual exemplum it followed. "Arise therefore bravely and take up the cross" comes after an account of the heroic deaths, comforted by the promise of salvation, of three brothers on the Albigensian crusade. "Arise therefore you who wish to return your soul to Christ" concludes the story of a crusader wounded in four places, who returned to the fray seeking a fifth wound in memory of Christ's wounds on the cross. "Arise therefore and be a martyr of Christ" occurs after an exemplum in which a crusader eagerly rides to his death and eternal life. Finally, the dreadful pun in Hugh of Beauchamp's last words on the field of Hattin, "Although my name is Beauchamp, I was never in *beau champ* until today," is glossed with "Arise so that you may come to the *beau champ*." Each anecdote and each refrain builds cumulatively upon the central theme and the emotions of the audience, in a manner familiar to evangelical preachers of the twentieth century, who, like Martin Luther King, Jr., in his famous Washington, D.C., speech in August 1963, use repetition to induce an almost trancelike enthusiasm in large congregations, precisely the effect achieved by Gerald of Wales at Haverfordwest.

Behind the theatrical artifice the *Ordinatio*'s exempla reveal a severely practical awareness of the tastes of the audience. The cross is portrayed as confirming salvation "as if by charter," just like any land deal with which the crusader would be familiar, only the estate in this case was "the inheritance of Christ." The material in the *Ordinatio* goes beyond general calls for moral and spiritual reform and addresses itself specifically to the interests and aspirations of the warriors on whom crusading relied. Their fighting, courage, loyalty, piety, and faith were all lauded, as crusading was held up as the highest knightly function, the ideal of the chivalrous classes. The parallels with contemporary crusade poems are striking. An Anglo-Norman poet at the time of the Third Crusade stressed precisely the same points concerning the Christian obligations of the *preudome*, (i.e., roughly speaking, gentleman), which were the need to renounce fleshly pleasures and wealth, and the uplifting powers of the cross: "He who leaves his riches for the sake of God will in truth gain Paradise."[53]

The message in the *Ordinatio* was lent added force in that some of the crusaders portrayed in the exempla were recent historical figures well-known to English audiences: Jacques d'Avesnes, leader of the Flemish crusaders who sailed to the Holy Land in 1189 and who fell heroically at the battle of Arsuf two years later; the Englishman Hugh of Beauchamp who was killed at Hattin; and Enguerrand de Boves, a veteran of three crusades who left the Fourth Crusade at Zara bound for the Holy Land.[54] Superficially this encouragement to the crusading classes exposes a tension within the *Ordinatio* and perhaps in crusade preaching in general. In the *Ordinatio*'s meditation on the sins of the flesh, the rich are likened to large fish who get caught in the Devil's nets; it is assumed that, unlike the poor, the rich will be troubled by crusade teaching and will not take the cross. Yet the knights to whom the exempla were directed were, almost by definition, wealthy.[55] However, it would be a mistake to accept at face value standard attacks on riches to be found throughout crusading literature at this period; the preachers are less concerned with material indigence than with spiritual simplicity and humility, and less with the capacity to pay crusade expenses than with the dangers of luxury and carnality.

It would be dangerous to extrapolate any precise conclusions on the general nature of sermons from the English *Ordinatio*, especially as those which aimed at raising money probably did not need the same explicit concentration on the holy warrior but could dwell more on the value of crusading to the soul and on the internal spiritual health of the believer. Nevertheless, the prominent features of the *Ordinatio* are mirrored in continental sources, as well as in the sermons in the anonymous account of the sack of Lisbon. Indeed, the exegesis of the symbolism of the cross dominated crusade preaching into the fourteenth century, lending an almost formal repetitiveness to many surviving sermons.[56] In many aspects of the crusade traditional formulae bind the long history of the movement together; nowhere is this more evident than in its preaching and propaganda.

At first glance, the response to preaching, in terms of recruits, appears to have been extremely favourable. Large numbers from England took the cross for the Third and Fifth Crusades, and in the next half-century not a decade passed without widespread preaching producing a stream of individual commitments. However, three caveats should be entered. The sources describing this process are rarely objective; just as criticism tended to become stereotyped, so did descriptions of the successes of crusade preaching. It should already be clear from earlier chapters that there is no easy correlation between the crusade sermon and the assumption of the cross. Crucesignati were influenced by a range of motives apart from enthusiasm including loyalty, ambition, and fear; ties of allegiance, blood, money, and geography at times were as influential as single-minded devotion to the cause. Furthermore, despite a general acceptance of crusading as an ideal, not all preachers met with universal approval or success. Papal attempts to arouse western Europe between 1149 and 1187 failed to achieve the level of response required. The anti-Hohenstaufen preaching under Henry III met with political and institutional opposition. Once the Albigensian crusade became a limb of Capetian aggrandizement in the 1220s, at least one English observer cast aspersions on the sincerity of the preaching and of the reactions to it. In 1245 Henry III refused to accept the credentials of the bishop of Beirut, and in 1252, as has been noted, Londoners were seemingly unimpressed by the combined preaching skills of the bishops of Worcester and Chichester and the abbot of Westminster.[57]

Since the beginning of the movement, voices had been raised against the departure of rulers and other leading members of society. The obligation to fight for the cross conflicted with the responsibility to protect and support family, vassals, subjects, or lords. On his return from Wales in 1188 Archdeacon Gerald found himself attacked by the future King John, at the time owner of extensive Welsh estates, who "assailed him with bitter words in the presence of many, because by his preaching he had emptied his land of all the strength of men that was his defence against the Welsh."[58] Similarly in 1267, at a council at Bury St. Edmund's, the suggestion of Cardinal Ottobuono that crusade preaching should be accelerated was met by arguments that a crusade would denude England of natives and leave the country defenceless against foreigners.[59]

Some people expressed deeper fears. Ralph Niger condemned the whole purpose, direction, and content of the preaching of the Third Crusade; his admittedly was an eccentric view. More typical, perhaps, were the reactions to the populist preaching of Fulk of Neuilly recorded by the Winchester annalist: "Some regard him as good and a disciple of Christ, others disagree, accusing him of seducing the masses and of being the forerunner of the Anti-Christ." This second opinion was reflected in a Worcester writer's record of the unpopularity of Eustace of Flay's mission.[60] Just as the friars after them, preachers who taught the virtues of poverty and strict religious discipline could easily attract the suspicion of entrenched established clerical interests, fearful equally of the spiritual and social effects of popular excitement. Popular or not, preaching remained at the heart of crusade organisation, the sermon and the ceremonial assumption of the cross being the central and characteristic acts in the process of spiritual rededication to God and temporal commitment to join or to fund the *negotium dei*.

RECRUITMENT

Inevitably, the process of preaching says something about the audience the preachers hoped to influence and therefore illustrates certain features of what might be called the sociology of crusading. Simply put, crusading was an activity of the social elite. The sermons of Gerald of Wales and the *Ordinatio* were directed at an aristocratic audience, men who could fight. This capacity was not restricted to knights alone. In his letter to the English in 1147, St. Bernard identified two groups for whom the crusade was attractive, the "mighty men of valour" and merchants. Even if Bernard was being metaphorical in calling on mercantile interests, these were precisely the groups represented at the siege of Lisbon; knights like Hervey de Glanvill and merchants like the Viels of Southampton were hardly the *pauperes* to whom Henry of Huntingdon chose to ascribe the victory. The chronicler, like the preacher, may have been using the term figuratively, meaning the poor at heart, or merely pointing out a moral contrast, the less rich succeeding where the very rich, the kings, had failed.[61] Recruitment for the Third and subsequent crusades confirms the aristocratic and monied social origins of crusaders.

It may be argued that the surviving evidence is biased. The chroniclers concentrate on the great, and the records of justice, administration, and the land market obviously concern a socially restricted echelon, artisans, small landowners, and parish priests to the greatest prelates and princes in the land. However, the social sample is almost certainly representative; the vast majority of active English crucesignati either possessed disposable property or were employed by those who did. It was essential, both for recruitment and funding, that preaching be aimed at these sections of the community, embracing more than just the knightly classes. From the earliest years of the twelfth century, merchants like Godric of Finchale or the Viels and burgesses like Harding of Oxford were involved.[62] Prominent among the crusaders at Lisbon were men from London, Southampton, Dover, and Ipswich. In general, recruitment was based upon three principal areas—the extended households of magnates, the royal court, and towns. To great lords, knights, and burgesses were attached, often as servants, men and women from lower social strata. The social and financial exclusivity was confirmed in the pattern of preaching.

Outside aristocratic households, the crowds taking the cross tended to be urban crowds, or at least crowds in market places. Administratively this was inevitable if preachers were to attract the maximum audience for the minimum repetition of the campaign address. In 1188 the Welsh sermons were all delivered at centres of population or of secular and ecclesiastical power. Eustace of Flay directed his preaching, for reasons both sabbatarian and crusading, to places with markets. It may be significant that in 1226 the guardians of the most famous English relic of the True Cross at Bromholm in Norfolk were granted royal permission to hold a fair on 13–15 September; the dates included the Feast of the Exaltation of the Cross, a day especially attractive to pilgrims of the Holy Cross and crusade preachers alike. The introduction of the friars in itself suggests an urban dimension to crusade preaching, and indeed their first effective campaign in England in 1235 seems to have been aimed at monasteries and towns.[63] Further evidence is plentiful. In 1255 Henry III instructed his sheriffs to ensure that all crucesignati practised with the crossbow and to publish these orders to crusaders in "cities, boroughs, and market places." In 1291 the friars preaching the cross under the auspices of the archbishop of York were instructed to deliver their sermons in listed and named towns and villages such as Nottingham, Newark, Doncaster, Leeds, Scarborough, Pontefract, Rotherham, Wakefield, Pocklington, Bridlington, and Whitby, some places having been selected "where there is" or "where there is believed to be" a significant congregation, as at Preston in Lancashire.[64] The abiding interest of Londoners underlines the urban aspect of recruitment. Some urban crusaders were of considerable wealth, like Richer of Lincoln, a crusader in the 1190s, for the inheritance of whose property in the city his nephew paid one hundred pounds.[65]

Further light on the social and economic status of crucesignati is shed by a group of sources compiled within a decade or so of each other around 1200: two lists of amerced (i.e., fined) crusaders on the Pipe Rolls of 1207 and 1208, and two extant returns from an archiepiscopal inquiry into unredeemed crusade vows from the late 1190s or early 1200s. On the Pipe Rolls for 1207 and 1208, under entries from Yorkshire, there are listed as being amerced by the royal agent Robert de Vieuxpont, in sums varying from one shilling eight pence to one hundred marks eighty, named individual *cruisiati* (i.e., crusaders) and one whole vill, Beningborough near York, fined half a mark on the 1208 roll.[66] The reasons for the fines are obscure, for it is difficult to see what locus the royal officials had. Perhaps those fined had taken the cross without permission, but it is hard to see all those listed as being direct tenants or vassals of the Crown, nor is it easy to explain the huge discrepancies in levels of amercement. Perhaps the crusaders were paying a fine in lieu of paying the 1207 tax of a thirteenth on moveables, from which as crusaders they could possibly have technically been exempt; but Vieuxpont's inquiry seems to have predated the tax.[67] This explanation in any case does nothing to explain the communal crusading and fine on Beningborough or the absence of such crusader amercements anywhere else in England or, indeed, on any other Pipe Roll of the time. The oddity is that these Yorkshiremen are not crusaders who happen to have been fined but are being fined as crusaders. The royal involvement is baffling. John was not yet a crucesignatus himself. Even if, in the absence of an archbishop of Canterbury (Hubert Walter having died in 1205), John had taken upon himself the collection of vow redemptions, the uniqueness of the entries presents problems. Furthermore, the sums involved were rather high for redemptions. In Yorkshire seventy years later errant priests and laymen commonly paid five shillings; in 1286 a citizen of Worcester, James Aubyn, enjoyed the privileges of a crusader for the promise of half a mark which, although the most frequent fine on the 1207–8 rolls, at the earlier date carried a far greater value than at the end of the century. Alternatively, the inclusion in the 1208 list of the vill of Beningborough could indicate that the amercements were in some way connected with the 1201 crusade fortieth, for which the collectors had itemised by name the demesne vills on which the taxpayers, both lords and free tenants, had based their assessments.[68] Aside from these obscurities the mystery is deepened further by the statement at the head of the 1207 list that the names of the crusaders appear in "the preceding rolls" (i.e., those of 1206 incorporating the returns deposited at the exchequer by Vieuxpont and his colleagues); they do not.

Whatever the reasons for the fines, the list of crusaders exposes something of their social status through surname, occupation, and level of amercement. Among those fined were Simon the dyer, Thomas the squire, Godfrey the chaplain, William the deacon, Ralph the provost, Gilbert the serjeant, Robert the crossbowman, and Gubert the butcher. Their fines in ascending order of magnitude were five shillings for the serjeant, half a mark for the squire, chaplain, and provost, one mark for the dyer and the butcher, forty shillings for the crossbowman, and fifteen marks for the deacon. As it is unknown for what they were being amerced, it would be dangerous to assume that these sums delineate relative wealth, although it is not unlikely. From the sizes of the fines it is evident that these men belonged to a rural elite deriving some, at least, of its wealth from war, trade, and the church. Some on the list were figures of substance with previous experience of dealings with royal agents, over scutage payments and other amercements. These included Richard FitzHenry, Gilbert of Notton, William FitzHugh, Ralph FitzSimon, Robert FitzRalph, Ingelot of Easingwold, and Adam of Cleasby, some of whom held knight's fees (or part of one knight's fee) directly from the king, and all of whom were members of what could loosely be described as the knightly class, even if by no means reaching baronial status.[69] As a whole, this Yorkshire group is reminiscent of Roger of Howden's list of casualties at Acre from south Yorkshire and north Lincolnshire, men of local prominence in church and in the service or kindred of the aristocracy.[70]

The cruisiati of 1207 and 1208, whose vows could have dated from any period in the previous decade and a half, were hardly poor. The most frequent amercement, accounting for fifty of the eighty personal fines, was half a mark, (six shillings eight pence); the lowest was one shilling eight pence and the highest one hundred marks, with the deacon's fifteen marks the next highest. A comparison of these sums with figures from this period for the wages of King John's footsoldiers and the bishop of Winchester's carpenters leads to the conclusion that half a mark represented something like forty days skilled labour. Such men were not *pauperes* even if some of them could be called *rustici*.[71] On the face of it, the inclusion of Beningborough points to crusaders of humbler standing and may record an outburst of mass hysteria, perhaps caused by the preaching in that area in 1201 by Eustace of Flay.[72] Equally, however, the Beningborough entry could be the result of some arcane bookkeeping convention now lost to us.

At first sight, involvement in crusading by the lowest reaches of society is indicated by Hubert Walter's surveys of crucesignati in Cornwall and Lincolnshire who had failed to fulfil their vows. The lists were compiled in response either to Celestine III's instructions of 1196 to force inactive crucesignati to perform their unfulfilled vows or, if incapable, to send proxies instead; or to Innocent III's commands of 1200 and 1201 that the archbishop offer poor or enfeebled crusaders redemption of their vows, while compelling the rest of the backsliders to honour their obligations, on pain of excommunication.[73] The report from the inquiry in the archdeaconry of Cornwall is simply a list of forty-seven names, some distinguished by occupation or sex.[74] There are at least four and possibly five women crucesignatae, as well as two skinners or tanners, a blacksmith, a miller, a tailor, a merchant, a cobbler, a gamekeeper, and two chaplains or priests, much the same sort of social spread as the Yorkshire crusaders on the Pipe Rolls.

The list from Lincolnshire is more explicit and makes sober reading.[75] The inquiry from the deanery of Holland in south Lincolnshire includes the names of twenty-nine crucesignati, among whom were a tanner, a potter, a butcher, a blacksmith, a vintner, and a ditch cutter. The high tide of enthusiasm during the Third Crusade had ebbed leaving many stranded. In twenty cases the excuse for the nonfulfilment of the vow was poverty, the crucesignati being described variously as *minus sufficiens, pauperrimus, fere mendicus, pauperrimus mendicus*—poor, very poor, beggars. Some had got married since their vows and had produced numbers of children; possibly they hoped that the expense and responsibilities of fatherhood would both excuse and explain their inertia to the archiepiscopal inquisitors. Others had taken the cross many years before and were already middle aged, old, or enfeebled. Of the twenty-nine listed, one, Odo, son of Aulac of Boston, was actually on crusade at the time of the inquiry, and only one other, Roger Stoile of Moulton, was sufficiently young and capable (financially as well as physically it may be assumed) of undertaking the journey east in the future. Another, Ralph Haranc of Pinchebeck, denied he was a crucesignatus at all, although both the priest who had given him the cross and his neighbours swore that he had assumed the cross eight years earlier. Six had, at various times in the past, actually set out; one was still absent, two had returned with papal licences, one had turned back in Lombardy because he had been robbed, and two had come back with their vows unfulfilled, probably through lack of funds, as one of them is described as *minus sufficiens* and the other as *pauperrimus*. A seventh, Richard, son of Thurstan, a *pauperrimus* with five children (possibly cause and effect), insisted that he had been to Jerusalem and fulfilled his vow, but as the inquiry record laconically put it, "he had no witnesses."

Some of these crucesignati may have taken the cross in an unthinking or frenzied moment. Many, no doubt, had forgotten all about it until the long arm of Archbishop-Justiciar Hubert Walter reached out to them.

Their experiences reveal some of the material difficulties that separated the vow from its satisfaction. The crusade was not the preserve of princes alone; in Lincolnshire in the 1190s it was the burden of paupers. However, and this is the central point, paupers did not, could not become active crusaders even if, as here, crucesignati could become paupers. The Lincolnshire crusaders who set out evidently paid for themselves; that is why they got into difficulties. Those who could not afford it stayed at home, vow or no vow. Hubert, son of Wido of Surfleet, had taken the cross five years before the inquiry but had only got as far as Lombardy when he was robbed and forced to return home; a similar fate was suffered by the Bishop of Norwich in 1190.[76] For Andrew of Gosberton, a married clerk in minor holy orders with two children, who had taken the cross before Hattin, crusading was entirely dependent upon his material fortunes, which had been insufficient to allow his departure. Crusading required money or patronage or both, and many of the Lincolnshire crucesignati had neither. Their plight was not unique; numerous papal letters admitted that poverty was a problem for crusaders throughout Europe. It could only be remedied through direct financial assistance from funds derived from taxation and donations or, as Innocent III appreciated, through commutation and redemption. Before Innocent the importance of adequate funding suggested, not least to Urban II, that the cross should not be given to the destitute; this sentiment was strongly echoed by Ralph Niger before the Third Crusade. Indeed, as Roger of Howden observed, it was the richer people who had flocked to take the cross in 1188.[77]

That complicated military expeditions could be sustained by zealous poor peasants is inherently unlikely. The Third Crusade demonstrated how crusaders could become impoverished en route. Such losses of wealth are a cliché of crusading history from the First Crusade onward, but there is little reason to suppose that many of those taking the cross were poor to start with. Even the famous Peasants' Crusade of 1096 was dominated by knights and burgesses and led by not-inconsiderable nobles. It displayed characteristics of composition, organisation, and conduct almost identical to those of the princes' contingents.[78] Crusades by the genuinely poor, the Children's Crusade of 1212 or the Shepherds' Crusades of 1251, 1309, and 1320, never got beyond the northern shore of the Mediterranean; they ran out of money and had nobody to bail them out. English involvement in popular crusades like that of 1309 was probably more limited than some chronicle accounts suggest. Most English ports were too well controlled to allow any exodus of such humble crusaders without the approval of the secular authorities. References to English popular crusades are imprecise, the descriptions possibly referring to unauthorised crusaders rather than to crusaders drawn from the lowest social orders.[79] In 1251, the authorities expected that the French Shepherds' Crusade movement might spread across the Channel to England and instructed all sheriffs and the warden of the Cinque Ports to insist that any "band of shepherds" (pastorum congregati, the poorest agricultural wage labourers) wishing to go to the Holy Land were to leave the kingdom immediately; failing this the bands were to be arrested and dispersed. These orders are not evidence that there were any such crusading "shepherds" but only that if any had appeared they would have been prevented from hanging around ports awaiting berths.[80] The topos of the divinely aided (or condemned) crusading pauper found in chronicles and sermons corresponded to no firm reality unless interpreted as referring to the spiritually humble or the materially unrich. Even where crusade preaching was aimed at the poorer elements in society, recruitment was not.

Against this could be cited the smallness of many crusaders' holdings as revealed in land charters and legal records, sometimes amounting to a few acres with rents of a few pence. Do these not suggest the adherence of poor peasants? Possibly, but caution should be exercised. Surviving records do not necessarily or even usually reveal the full extent of a crusader's fundraising activities or of his property. It may be that these apparently poor peasants possessed widely fragmented holdings. The financial imperative remained. No individual undertook a crusade on a few shillings; if that was all he could raise, he needed assistance from a richer relative or landlord. The less his wealth, the greater the pressure on a crusader to seek assistance. The poor peasant crusader is something of a myth. In real life the poor do not inherit the earth, and in the Middle Ages paupers did not go on crusade. Non-nobles who subsidised their own crusades were characteristically men like the master carpenter at Chichester Cathedral in the 1220s or the mason who was the butt of a cautionary exemplum in a later preaching manual, men of property.[81] English crusaders faced peculiar problems of transport imposed by the need to cross the Channel, which may explain the consistently less substantial active English contribution when compared to that of the French. Nevertheless, the sociology of English crusades is replicated elsewhere in Europe.[82]

Apart from his need for money, the crusader also had to possess a degree of freedom. A servile crucesignatus was a legal contradiction. At the same time English landlords and lawyers were insisting with greater precision on the definition of the unfree status of villeinage and were prohibiting villeins the right to plead or seek protection in free (i.e., royal) courts, the legal and civil immunities of the crusader were becoming firmly established features of those very courts. This was not a question of economic but of legal status. On 7 January 1219, royal justices at Lincoln pardoned two crusaders found to be in the wrong in separate cases of disseisin, on the grounds of poverty; but both of them had had the right to plead in royal courts as freemen and to enjoy crusade privileges.[83] Economic status was no guide to legal conditions; in 1214 a fine imposed on Hugo Hareng of Dorset for illegal possession of land was pardoned on the grounds of his poverty and crusader's status. Yet although Hugo could not afford the fine, when he had taken the cross he had, or thought he had, property.[84] An unfree villein, on the other hand, had no entitlement to any such legal sympathy or protection, since English law, borrowing from Roman precepts, equated him almost with chattels. The villein owed his service and his all to his lord. He could not even pretend to be able to take the cross voluntarily without his lord's express permission; by taking the cross, the villein would have, in a sense, alienated his lord's property. The villein, according to early thirteenth-century lawyers, technically had no possessions with which to raise money for the journey, unless his lord provided for him. Villeins, and indeed other less servile peasants, had little right to leave their lords' lands without permission. However much villeins provided towards the crusade indirectly, through bearing the burden of taxation or having the product of their labour diverted towards their lords' crusade expenses, unless they were attached to a lord's military entourage they did not contribute directly. It is not simply that as villeins, they do not appear in records but, as villeins, they did not become crucesignati. This may help explain the unease of the aristocracy at peasant crusades on the continent, for if unfree men were leaving their lords' estates in large numbers and acting as independent and free men, that was indeed revolutionary. At least one English observer, the Franciscan Adam Marsh, regarded the French Shepherds' Crusade of 1251 as a plot against the clergy and a provocation to God.[85] This is not to say that rural workers were immune from crusading enthusiasm. The events of 1212, 1251, 1309, and 1320 demonstrate otherwise, but the formal process of crusading was not for villeins, except insofar as they could afford or were allowed to buy indulgences or give alms.

Formal recruitment from the lowest orders in society, those without free tenancies or legal freedom, was confined to raising troops. Not all troops necessarily had to be crucesignati, although it was obviously prudential and materially as well as spiritually beneficial for footsloggers to take the cross once hired or ordered to join a crusade. For them to do this, however, still logically implied their freedom before both common and canon law; the unfree could not enjoy the temporal privileges of a crusader, and equally the crusader's confession, vow, and repentance had to be voluntary to be valid. In 1188 *rustici* who took the cross without permission were, notwithstanding, to pay the Saladin tithe. Interpretation as to whom precisely the term *rusticus* was applied raises problems. It is sometimes argued that by 1188 it implied servility; then direct taxation of the unfree was something of a novelty. But as the word was juxtaposed in the ordinance with *burgenses* it could be thought to mean simply a countryman who, even if free, still required permission from his local priest and probably his landlord as well. If *rusticus* described a serf then licence to depart must have implied manumission, for the 1188 ordinances gave all crucesignati the right freely to mortgage their property.[86] Crusaders had to be freeman; if not, then the crusade set them free. Thus in the early thirteenth century William of Staunton manumitted Hugh Travers, who was about to go to the Holy Land as William's proxy, presumably so that Hugh could enjoy crusader immunities. It is noteworthy that on his return Hugh's lands were released from servile tenure. Also, only by setting Hugh free could William ensure that the substitution was adequate.[87] Whatever else, the crucesignati of Yorkshire, Lincolnshire, and Cornwall were free.

Assembly of crusading armies and journeys of individual crusaders came at the end of an often lengthy chain of permission. Urban II had envisaged each crucesignatus receiving clerical approval to depart—from the parish priests for laymen, from bishops and abbots for the clergy. Any crusader wishing to mortgage lands to raise money for the expedition must first have gained the consent of his relatives and his lord.[88] A vassal or tenant could not absent himself without his lord's consent. Grants of royal licences to tenants-in-chief to mortgage land held in chief and to appoint attorneys, and royal safe-conducts litter government records from the twelfth century. In 1188 Geoffrey Hose from Wiltshire paid one hundred pounds for the right of royal protection of his property and for permission to give custody of his land to whomsoever he pleased during his crusade. In 1188–89 Robert Cauchois received Henry II's permission or licence (*licentia*) to take the cross as well as to commit his lands in Normandy for three years to his nephew and heir.[89] The 1188 ordinances stipulated that burgesses sought permission to take the cross in order to enjoy immunity from the Saladin tithe.[90] Numerous charters demonstrate that the provisions of Eugenius III's *Quantum praedecessores* were followed, with mortgages and other grants being witnessed by overlords and relatives. In 1147 Philip Basset's grant of a marsh to the abbey of St. Benet Holme was witnessed before the bishop of Norwich by Philip's brothers and his

175

wife; in 1188–89 Robert the Constable's grant of Tharlesthorpe to the abbey of Meaux was formally ratified at Lambeth with the explicit consent of William of Mandeville, Robert's overlord, and Robert's surviving brother.[91] Behind such apparently smooth transactions lay a morass of complicated and often acrimonious negotiations and family disputes; these will be the subject of the next chapter. The chain of permission was pervasive. Parish priests had to ensure that their duties were performed in their absence on crusade by suitable substitutes. Even the carpenter at Chichester Cathedral had to seek the approval of the dean and chapter before embarking on crusade in the 1220s. The carpenter's problem was different from the landowner's, for he was under contract to the chapter and in order to accomplish his vow he had to provide a replacement. Unfortunately, the dean was not one to take decisions unilaterally, and so the carpenter had to present himself to the bishop to obtain official blessing for his enterprise.[92]

Crusading required organisation; for small private crusades, little more than pilgrimages with only a possibility of military action, as for the great passagia. Armies do not assemble by random coincidence, nor, once assembled, do they hold together by chance. One account of the muster of the Third Crusade describes crusaders travelling "with their households, relatives and friends"; from study of the recruitment of the Third Crusade it is evident that beyond simple enthusiasm, a number of different cohesive forces operated, in particular lordship, kinship, geography, and sworn association. Behind all of these lay the imperatives of logistics and finance.[93]

With escalating costs and the consequent centralisation of military funding onto those with access to the largest incomes, it became inevitable that the role of great lords, especially the king, would become more prominent in crusade planning. Whereas the profits from the earliest effective crusade taxation, collections of redemptions, and other obventions had been intended for individual local crusaders, by the mid-thirteenth century both sources of finance were organised centrally, with crusade leaders the chief beneficiaries.[94]

This structure reflected long practice in the organisation of crusades. The driving force behind all crusade efforts had always been lordship, as witnessed in one of the earliest of all crusader chronicles, the *Gesta Francorum*, whose writer describes clearly the strength of the affinity surrounding Bohemund of Taranto.[95] Recruitment and service on the Third Crusade revolved around great men and their dependents, from the kings downwards. Men took the cross for fear of Henry II or in the hope of being subsidised by him. Richard I not only paid for a large fleet and land army to get to the Holy Land, but once there he extended his control by offers of money; this precedent was followed by his nephew Richard of Cornwall in 1240–41 and his great-nephew Louis IX in 1248–49. The structure of all crusading armies was determined by a network of dependent relationships. Some such networks were of modest size, like Ivo of Vieuxpont's band of ten followers in 1190; others were much larger, like Richard I's *familiares* to whom he distributed command of the ships he had hired for the crusade, or like the interlaced households of the royal family on Lord Edward's crusade in 1270.[96] It is hard to read the pages of Matthew Paris without being struck by the concentration on the household as the basic unit of crusade organisation. The companions of Richard of Cornwall, some of them of individual distinction and importance, were described as being of his *familia*, an extended military household either gathered especially or possessing links over a number of years. Simon de Montfort and his wife were followed in 1248 in taking the cross by knights "and many others of their household" (*familia*). Those who became crucesignati in 1250 with Henry III included his brother, the seneschal of his household, his "special councillor" and many more "magnates and courtiers" (*aulici*, literally "house people") including civil servants such as John Mansel and Philip Lovel. Two years later the only enthusiasm for assuming the cross at the Westminster assembly was shown by three more *curiales*.[97]

Crusading was based on preexistent employment and patronage, a combination of loyalty and cash. In the Lord Edward's crusade it is possible to observe the written contractual arrangements that underpinned such relationships.[98] By the early fourteenth century a stipulation to serve on crusade was even included in some indentures, unconnected with any immediate or specific crusading enterprise. In the indenture between Batholomew of Enfield and the earl of Hereford in February 1307, Batholomew was committed to going to the Holy Land if the earl went there. In the contract by which the earl of Pembroke retained John Darcy for life in April 1310 the latter was pledged to serve Pembroke in peace and war, at home and abroad, and in the Holy Land.[99] Although actual contracts only survive from 1270, the relationships delineated in them existed long before. The system of one noble retaining another for specified service in return for material payment in land, rents, cash, or even board and lodging, arose naturally from the exigencies of war and aristocratic society, in which freelance fighting was by 1200 becoming prohibitively expensive. Any lord would have to reckon on paying his retinue's costs, even though formally the normal obligations of vassalage service did not operate between crusaders, except on the Albigensian crusade. Consequently, even the closest ties of loyalty were expressed in material and financial terms, allegiance having to be reaffirmed specifically for the crusade and rewards expressly stated. Also, because of the often disparate origins of crusaders, central control was sometimes only possible through material subsidy. Thus at Rugia in northern Syria in the winter of 1098–99 Raymond of Toulouse tried to buy the support of his colleagues, who were offered sums possibly calculated on the relative sizes of their contingents.[100] At Acre in 1191, apart from competing with Philip II over the rewards for dismantling the city's walls, Richard I advanced the duke of Burgundy five thousand marks to pay the remaining French troops, thereby establishing an uncontested field dominance over the crusader army as it moved south towards Jerusalem.[101]

Paying crusaders, even those of knightly status, in cash or in kind was as old as the movement itself. The ordinances agreed by the crusaders at Dartmouth in 1147 stipulated that "no one retain a sailor or serjeant (or servant, *servientem?*) of another in his employ."[102] Retaining troops on campaign was probably commonplace long before the 1270 contracts, as a method of hiring mercenaries and of binding other nobles, knights, and members of an extended military household more securely to the lord's service. At Damietta in 1220, Cardinal Pelagius offered French and German crusaders money for a fixed period of service.

The clearest chronicle account of the process appears in Jean de Joinville's memoirs of Louis IX's crusade of 1248. Joinville had taken with him nine knights and two knight bannerets who were already his men and whose expenses he, as their lord, was expected to bear; by the time they reached Cyprus Joinville had only 240 l.tournois left. "On that account some of my knights told me that unless I provided myself with funds they would leave me."[103] Fortunately for Joinville, King Louis bailed him out by taking him into royal service with a gift of 800 l.tournois, in essence retaining Joinville. English evidence points to similar arrangements. In the 1270 indentures the period of the retainer is one year, the same term as for the salaries paid by Richard I. That some crusaders in 1188 expected to be paid can be inferred from Gerald of Wales's later excuse for seeking absolution from his vow. It is self-evident that crusaders travelled with their households, members of which expected to be funded by their lords; it was for them as for Joinville's knights a sine qua non of their participation.[104]

The Third Crusade demonstrated that ties of lordship were a prime factor in recruitment and action, from recruitment in Wales to the arrival at Acre of the retinues of men like Ivo of Vieuxpont or the "fair company" of Warin FitzGerold. Richard I's plans depended wholly on his capacity to "retain" (Howden's word) a fleet as well as an army.

This structure of the crusade is illustrated in the testamentary arrangements of Archbishop Baldwin at Acre, recorded by Ralph of Diceto. Surrounded by his familia, followers and servants (*familiaribus et domesticis*) Baldwin appointed Hubert Walter executor of his bequests, which included payments for twenty knights and fifty serjeants. The ability to support troops was crucial; a German witness noted especially Richard I's preeminence in this.[105] What was true for knights was probably true for clerics like Peter of Blois, who travelled with Archbishop Baldwin to Acre in 1190. It was also true for humbler crusaders such as the six servants of the Warwickshire crusaders Hugh Agulun and Robert *de Furmo*, who were covered by their masters' essoin of court as crucesignati in 1275.[106] Whatever individuals raised for themselves, the ties of loyalty reinforced by cash formed a basic cohesive element in crusade armies, at all levels. Without it, disintegration threatened. Two men who buried their master, Lincolnshire crusader Adam of Croxby, in the Holy Land sometime before 1219, abandoned his widow when she failed to provide for them on their return thereby depriving her of their vital evidence of their master's decease.[107] Sentiment was not enough, although it should not be disregarded. The troops for whom Richard I arranged transport from Marseilles to Sicily almost certainly comprised his military household, for whose passage he paid; but they included men who were or became intimate with the king, like the ten who with Richard were surprised in the king's tent by the Turks outside Jaffa on the night of 5 August 1192.[108]

The power of paymasters determined the structure and course of each crusade from the moment the decision to depart was made. At Acre in 1240 Richard of Cornwall offered to take any crusader into his paid service for the term of the crusade; like Louis IX eight years later, he thereby extended his familia, which already formed the backbone of his army. In 1249, according to Matthew Paris, William Longsword retained knights and serjeants ("militibus et servientibus quos secum retinuerat stipendiariis").[109] The dependence of crusaders on the financial resources of their leader is exposed in detail by Hugh of Neville's will drawn up at Acre in 1267. Provision was made for the travelling expenses of Hugh's servants and for rewards for his priests. The arrival of more money was anticipated, with which Hugh intended to fund "his following . . . for one year in the Holy Land against the enemies of Jesus Christ." More specifically, he willed that the five hundred marks granted him by the pope from central crusade funds in England should be used to maintain soldiers in Palestine for as long as the money lasted.[110] The retainers supported in these ways were of course further bound together by their shared status as crucesignati and shared experience as fellow combatants. Although in the surviving agreements of 1270 there is no explicit instruction or commitment to the cross, those who entered into contractual relationships with the Lord Edward did become, or were already, crucesignati; in later such indentures this may not have been the case.[111] The two obligations were complementary, although it was probably legally correct not to impose a contractual obligation on a retainer to take the cross, since it had to be a voluntary act. There was no conflict in the less precise later formulae of imposing service in the Holy Land.

Lordship did not operate in isolation. Although, as the exempla in Gerald of Wales's description of the Welsh preaching tour illustrate, family pressure, especially from wives, could work against the assumption of the cross, ties of blood were often significant positive influences. Joinville went on crusade in a business partnership with his cousin, and he was not unique. Crusading ran in families. This fact might help explain the inconsistent enthusiasm displayed by the English nobility, not all families displaying equal interest. Three consecutive generations of the English royal family saw action in Palestine between 1191 and 1272, an impressive record matched by many other families. Gerard of Furnival was one of Richard I's close companions on the Third Crusade; his son, another Gerard, died in the Holy Land in 1219 during the Fifth Crusade; two, possibly three, of his grandsons went with Richard of Cornwall's crusade, on which one of them died.[112] Other families with crusading lineage reaching back into the twelfth century were also represented on Earl Richard's expedition, such as the Stutevilles and the Beauchamps. The dynastic connections of William, earl of Aumale, another casualty of 1241, demonstrates the complexity and fullness of crusading traditions. William's maternal great-grandfather had fought on the First Crusade; his maternal grandfather, William the Fat, had taken the cross before 1150, probably at the time of the Second Crusade; his father, his mother's second husband, was one of the commanders of the royal crusade fleet of 1190; his mother's first husband, William of Mandeville, had also been a crucesignatus.[113] Families like the Bohuns could boast crucesignati in the male line from the Fifth Crusade to the 1360s. Perhaps the finest family traditions, the longest and the most consistent, were those of the Beauchamps and the Percies. The former's stretched from the twelfth to the fifteenth centuries, much to their obvious pride; it was enshrined in the Beauchamp family histories by John Rous in the late fifteenth century. The latter's record began with William Percy on the First Crusade and only ended three centuries later with Hotspur in the Baltic.[114] One practical expression of the sense of family obligation was the habit, which emerged from around 1200, of relatives of crusaders who had failed to fulfil their vows to make good the default, in person, by proxy, or through a financial obvention.

Family tradition was matched by family cooperation. It was natural for kinsmen to crusade together; on the First Crusade Godfrey de Bouillon travelled with his two brothers and his cousin, while Bohemund was accompanied by his nephew Tancred and two cousins, Richard and Ralph. Dynastic economics, pride, trust, convenience, acquaintance, even personal sentiment combined to send families together to war, such as the Viels on the Second Crusade, and on the Third, the Glanvills (Rannulf, Roger, and nephew Hubert Walter), the de la Mares (Robert and Alan and possibly William and Osbert), the Stutevilles, and the "many Cornborough brothers and relations."[115] Such kindred groupings could be integrated within larger lordship units; thus on Richard of Cornwall's crusade, and mentioned as belonging to his household, were the three Furnivals.[116] Nevertheless, kinship was evidently important—Richard of Cornwall, his half-brother, and his brother-in-law Simon de Montfort in 1240, the Lords Edward and Edmund and their first cousin Henry of Almain in 1270—and it continued to form a basis for crusade recruitment throughout the fourteenth century. Examples of crusaders linked by blood abound from all expeditions.

Both lordship and blood may be regarded as part of the wider social and cultural pressure behind crusade recruitments; so too may geography. Where obvious ties of vassalage or kindred were lacking, men often grouped themselves with men from their own localities. It was surely no coincidence that Roger, parson of Howden, witnessed a charter at Acre for a local Yorkshire landowner, John of Hessle, and recorded names of casualties from the same region of south Yorkshire and north Lincolnshire; nor that John of Hessle himself had connections with another Yorkshire crusading family represented at Acre, the Stutevilles.[117] The evidence from the Second Crusade appears even more explicit. Each of the regional groups from within England seems to have had a degree of autonomous organisation under its own leaders. The Londoners on the Third Crusade acted in a similarly distinct and corporate manner.[118] Ties of locality could exert an even greater influence, contributing to the group pressure on individuals to take the cross, to which lordship and kinship also contributed. As Gerald of Wales's account of preaching in 1188 implies, if everyone else in a crowd assumed the cross the pressure to follow suit could become irresistible, not necessarily through the agency of mass hysteria, but rather through the more lasting force of conformity and comradeship, as potent in 1190 as in 1914. In Wales in 1188 "a certain rather forceful young man" unavailingly resisted the very strong pressure of his many friends who had adopted the cross; at Abergavenny, another nobleman, when offered the cross replied that he could not take such a step without consulting his friends.[119] Loyalty to peer group was just as effective a recruiting officer as loyalty to lord or kinsmen. For the crusader, once recruited and surrounded by friends and neighbours, locality could provide a separate or complementary reassuring group mentality to that of the household, military unit or kin-group. Shared locality could also provide the basis for pooling resources; in 1190 the bands of young crucesignati who massacred and plundered the Jews in King's Lynn were probably locals, as were those who wrought even greater atrocities in York a few days later. The 1270 lists of crusaders who signed up for the Lord Edward's crusade almost certainly conceal provincial as well as tenurial or dynastic relationships.[120]

In the process by which crusade armies were forged, the influences of lordship, kindred, and locality were complementary and mutually supportive. However, some crusader groups initially lacked any formal or informal structure of organisation or discipline either because all the individual crusaders had in common was geography or because the group comprised a number of distinct yet equal authorities. Yet without structure or organisation they would have had little chance of reaching their destination. For them the solution was to band together in voluntary sworn associations, communes, a method of social and political organisation disliked by contemporary academics and rulers, yet widely practiced and well-suited to the crusaders' economic and logistic needs. In 1147, the polyglot gathering of crusaders at Dartmouth not only chose leaders from each local group but imposed upon themselves "the finest pledges of peace and friendship" in order to agree on a strict code of conduct and discipline. They were in fact creating a commune, which bound the leaders at least by oath and which proved to be at least partially effective. When the Viels, some Normans, and the men of Bristol and Southampton threatened to withdraw from the siege of Lisbon, they were accused of violating the sworn association ("coniurateque societatu"). It was to the obligations imposed by this commune that Hervey of Glanvill appealed in his ultimately successful efforts to heal the split in crusader ranks: "For now that so great a diversity of peoples is bound with us under the law of a sworn association, and considering that we find nothing in its dealings which can justly be made a subject of accusation or disparagement, each of us ought to do his utmost in order that in the future no stain of disgrace shall adhere to us who are members of the same stock and blood." The details of the ordinances point to the commune's severely practical purpose: justice was to be harshly retributive; regulations were promulgated for clothing, women, religious observances, separate weekly meetings of clergy and laity. The appointment of judges who, in addition to their judicial functions, were to have authority to distribute money implies that, as with the Third Crusade, there was to be a central common fund, another manifestation of communal administration.[121] Such provisions were essential in order to keep the expedition from chaos and disintegration; the establishment of a sworn commune provided the only possible guarantee of their implementation. It might be added that elsewhere during the Second Crusade a sworn association was used. When royal authority collapsed on the French march across Anatolia in the winter of 1147–48, a form of communal organisation retrieved the situation; the crusaders formed a fraternity with the Templars, whose commands they swore to obey.[122] The 1147 Dartmouth commune was not only effective; it was long remembered. Over a century and a half later, Peter Langtoft eulogised the Lisbon expedition "Of poor people [sic] without number, who are by alliance/Sworn among themselves and are not retained"; in this context, a significant contrast.[123]

The 1147 commune was imitated in the summer of 1189 when another crusader fleet gathered at Dartmouth and, in the words of Ralph of Diceto, by common or communal consent (communi consilio) agreed their date of embarkation. It is possible that the bands of young crusaders who terrorised the Jews of England in Lent 1190 were similarly associated; at least one source describes them as "coniurati," men bound together by oath.[124] The main armies of the Third Crusade were, of course, led by kings and princes and therefore had no need of communes, although Richard I, like the crusaders of 1147, seems to have appreciated the need for strict discipline, severe punishment, and agreed and accepted judicial authority in his crusade fleets.[125] Smaller elements within the fleet of 1190 may have adopted communal organisation; for example, the ship carrying the Londoners was apparently commanded, not by royal officials, but by London citizens William FitzOsbert and Geoffrey the Goldsmith, who acted very much on their own initiative. It is perhaps significant that a few years later FitzOsbert was the leading figure of a popular communal movement in London itself, which aimed at breaking the power of the London oligarchy, itself a commune.[126]

The need to pool authority, no less than resources, and to find some formal method of binding equals together, was a problem for the great as well. When the leaders of the Fourth Crusade appointed ambassadors to arrange transport from Italian ports they sealed charters which bound all of them to accept whatever treaty their envoys negotiated. The cohesion which this agreement imposed constituted perhaps one of the main elements sustaining the unity of the crusade leadership, in the face of repeated later challenges to its policy.[127] In the absence of bonds of financial, tenurial, or dynastic dependence, it would always be difficult to maintain unity without some formal alliance. In 1239 the oath taken by the crusaders at Northampton to resist attempts to divert their expedition from the Holy Land may have served to provide this wider bond. According to Matthew Paris, they swore to set out for the Holy Land within a year. That this implied a firm corporate commitment is clear from Gilbert Marshal's insertion of the proviso that, in his case, departure depended on his making peace with the king. The need for such an oath is indicated by Paris's list of those involved: Richard of Cornwall, Gilbert Marshal, Richard Siward, and Henry of Turbeville, none of whom had strong formal dependent ties with each other.[128] At the very least, such an oath confirmed a solidarity already established by their shared status as crucesignati. Interestingly, twice previously such English crusaders had bound themselves together as coniurati or confoederati, in 1227 and 1233, even though on those occasions a domestic political motive could also be suggested for their actions.[129]

In such ways did the realities of crusading warfare and of contemporary society determine patterns of recruitment. Crusading may have been widely supported but it was not, in England at least, by nature or design a popular movement, any more than other twelfth or thirteenth-century armies were popular armies. Participants on the general passagia were soldiers, men skilled in arms who paid for themselves or who were employed by others. Those on individual, private crusades were freemen of town and country who could afford the journey. From England at least the genuinely poor crusader, even if free and able to take the cross, played no effective role in the enterprise. It was partly because of this exclusion of so many faithful from the benefits of the crusade that the institution was modified in the thirteenth century, to embrace a wider community than that comprising active crusaders alone. The crusade evolved in tune with the techniques of funding and organising warfare that developed in this period. In consequence, the pattern of preaching and recruitment changed between 1100 and 1300. By the end of the thirteenth century both theory and practice pointed to the need for centrally funded professional armies in which the power of lordship provided the coherence and material necessities, even if faith supplied the energy; thus did Hugh of Neville and his retinue wait expectantly, if not confidently, at Acre in 1267 for the arrival of money from the central crusade coffers in England.[130]

The theoretical solution to the military problems of crusading, proposed in the thirteenth and early fourteenth century, deliberately combined centralised authority and spiritual enthusiasm in an institutional structure. As early as the 1240s Matthew Paris argued for the creation of a single new military order. The idea frequently was reiterated by local English clergy (notably in 1291–92), international church councils, and writers of propaganda and advice. The order would have the resources of extensive estates, church taxes, redemptions, and other obventions. It would have the expertise and discipline to conduct a successful crusade and to organise subsequent colonisation; ideally it would be led by a prince with royal blood, perhaps even a king.[131] In such debates, however, the English contribution was hardly original and scarcely influential. One result of the divorce of preaching from military enlistment implied in such schemes, and reflected in contemporary practice, may have been that from the late thirteenth century proportionately fewer people took the cross, even though the number of crusade enterprises hardly diminished. Increasingly, preaching campaigns aimed to sell indulgences, without even the intermediate stage of taking and then redeeming the crusade vow. Neither the popularity of such indulgences nor the declining numbers across Europe who took the cross when the opportunity was presented indicates, however, any commensurate decline in crusade enthusiasm.

In conclusion, it should be stressed that a personal commitment to the crusade was neither necessarily nor wholly the consequence of the physical and organisational forces described in this chapter. It should not be forgotten that the religious and secular mentality of the period, shared by great nobles and humbler freemen alike, assured a welcome for the preacher's message which, for all its topicality and sensitivity to the secular ethics of the audience, was essentially a call to repentance and an offer of salvation. The way in which this message was couched assisted its reception but did not disguise its meaning, which was understood by many. A king like Henry III, a prince like the young Henry, or a noble like John Fitzalan of Arundel could bequeath his crusader cross to the Holy Land, as, later, men donated their hearts. The hope presumably was that the cloth cross, which had been blessed during its ceremonial adoption, would be taken east in a partial and symbolic posthumous satisfaction of the vow. When, in their land charters, thirteenth-century English knights about to embark on crusade talked of their journeys as "my urgent necessity" or "my great business," they should be understood to be referring to their spiritual and not merely material needs.[132] The crusade mattered to people on a number of different planes—as an outlet for chivalrous idealism, a channel of self-advancement, an opportunity to gain social esteem, a means of self-expression, a secular and religious obligation, and a path to eternal glory. Its apparently religious aspects had secular dimensions and vice versa. The cause, however unique, was inseparable from its immediate context, the shape of the crusade being that of contemporary cultural attitudes, religious aspirations, and social organisation. In its importance for people at that time lies its significance for historians today.

8

The Home Front

In a famous passage Jean de Joinville recalled the pain of his departure for the crusade in the early summer of 1248: "I never once looked back towards Joinville for fear my heart would be moved because of the beautiful castle I was leaving and my two children."[1] Such farewells must have been emotional, highly charged experiences. According to contemporary poets, crusaders may have hoped to gain paradise, wordly honour, and, for those who came home, the pick of the most beautiful women, but the *iter sanctum* demanded the sacrifice of comfort, ease, wealth, and loved ones. It was this last prospect that persuaded one crucesignatus, Henry of Lacy, earl of Lincoln, in an imaginary dialogue with the crusade veteran Walter Biblesworth, to argue for the abandonment of his vow. Outside of the code of courtly love the material losses may have weighed more heavily, not least with those left behind.[2] The communities left by crusaders were not held in suspended animation until the crusaders' return. The home front could be a place of strain and even confrontation, where the wider domestic audience of crusading—overlords, dependents, relatives, friends, and neighbours—was directly touched by the repercussions of a crusader's ambition.

Crusading cut into normal social activities, taking husbands from their wives, fathers from their children, priests from their parishes, landlords from their estates, businessmen from their countinghouses, vassals from their lords, artisans from their masters, and bureaucrats from their offices. The crusade disrupted the normal procedures of social relationships; it was a dislocating and, for some, fatal intrusion into the accustomed pattern of life. At its least dramatic, the crusade was inconvenient. In 1221 the absence of John le Lockier prevented the completion of a case of mort d'ancestor, because he was needed to witness the judgement; two years earlier a similar case was also halted, because a material witness was on crusade.[3] Absence and unexpected return could cause embarrassment, the sudden reappearance of the earl of Arundel in the 1150s allegedly throwing his replacement as royal butler into confusion.[4] Disruption could be more profound, with destructive financial and legal consequences. In its expressions of faith, techniques of fundraising, institutions of spiritual benefit, temporal protection, and military organisation, crusading cannot be separated from the domestic experience of western Europe. Instead, firmly rooted in surrounding contemporary circumstances, it was, as F. M. Powicke noted, "a political and economic function of society." The domestic impact had three dimensions: the effect of a crusader's financial requirements, the consequences of his absence, and the implications of his temporal privileges, enjoyed from the moment the crucesignatus publicly confirmed his vow by taking the cross.[5] They shall be examined in turn.

FINANCE: PUBLIC SOURCES

Any departing crusader would have been wise to follow the example of William Longsword, who set out in 1249 with his saddlebags full of cash.[6] The *via crucis* was massively and, for many like the impoverished knights at Acre in 1190 or Guy of Lusignan in 1250, ruinously expensive. At a conservative estimate Richard I spent as much as 20,000 pounds on preparations alone in 1189–90, or seventy percent of his annual revenue. In 1270 the going rate for crusading knights in government contracts was one hundred marks for one year's service, in addition to whatever the individual could raise for himself. Even so, for one wealthy crusader, Hamo l'Estrange, the combined capital sum was inadequate to cover his expenses.[7] For some, the crusader's privilege of exemption from usury and repayment of the principal of debts during a crusade was more than an incentive, it was essential; they needed all the money they could get. Without Richard of Cornwall's "pecuniam innumerabilem," his crusade would have collapsed as soon as it reached Syria. Money was needed for wages, transport, swords, spears, bows, arrows, armour, horses, clothing, food, tolls, bribes, relics, and brothels. It was not only the great who travelled with ready cash; recovered with the bodies of a group of crusaders drowned when the bridge at Ferrybridge (Yorkshire) collapsed in 1228 were £17 18s 10d. Contrary to the 1194 ordinance, the sum was spent not on the crusade but on the repair of the bridge.[8]

Crusading represented a severe and immediate drain on individual capital resources. In 1214 Richard of Fremingham (Surrey) was prepared to raise thirty marks or four hundred shillings on his lands for his crusade.[9] This was the equivalent of the scutage on ten whole fees levied on the fiercely opposed 1214 rate. A generation earlier, when prices were much lower (the daily wage of a knight being eight pence before 1173, and one shilling afterwards, instead of two and three shillings in John's reign) Roger of Mowbray felt the need to raise 120 marks (i.e., 1,600 shillings) for his crusade in the 1170s. At about the same time, Jocelin of Louvain received one hundred pounds for his crusade expenses as part of a land transaction with the nuns of Sixle, and this was not the only such deal in which he engaged in order to meet the costs of his journey.[10] Such large sums can be matched even earlier; in the 1150s, for example, Henry of Octon raised sixty marks.[11] By the end of the thirteenth century costs for those without extensive estates were becoming prohibitive. As a proportion of annual income rather than capital value, crusade expenses appear even greater, often the equivalent of many years' rent on the lands being demised. Calculations cannot be more precise because, as the case of Jocelin of Louvain warns, it is unlikely that any one crusader's complete detailed financial transactions survive.

There are, however, a few indications of what individual crusaders raised in toto. In 1201, it was reported to royal justices that Robert of Marsh had received from his father, for the crusade he was undertaking as his parent's proxy, twenty marks, twenty-two besants, one gold ring, one horse, one helmet, one sword, and a cloak of scarlet.[12] Robert's money was partly derived from tithes levied on his father's lands, rather than through sale or mortgage. To take gold and silver was a useful provision, as the currency of the East was still mainly gold as opposed to the silver of the West. As late as 1267 Hugh of Neville seems to have paid his own staff at Acre in silver but local tradesmen in gold. Indeed, the need for gold may help explain the role of crusading goldsmiths from twelfth-century London. Robert of Marsh had his own gold; others presumably relied on goldsmiths at home, bankers such as the Templars who had established themselves in this role by the end of Henry II's reign, or local moneychangers in the East. Personal funding of a crusade was a complicated and substantial operation, yet it is clear that crusaders regularly, perhaps invariably, underestimated the true cost of their journeys.[13]

Although the crusade was originally and essentially a private commitment, individuals were often subsumed into larger units for which the greater lords were expected to pay. Crusading was also the public business of Christendom. The establishment of Christian principalities in the East imposed a responsibility on the West to support them, which prompted the introduction of public crusade taxes. The 1166 income tax promulgated at Le Mans was for "the defence and assistance of the church and land of the east," a form of alms giving which earned the taxpayer remission of a third of enjoined penance.[14] This tax, like the subsequent levies in 1185 and 1222, was not associated directly with any general passagium; the proceeds were designed to be sent east rather than to subsidise the preparations of western crusaders. The earliest royal subsidy for a specific expedition was raised by Louis VII in 1146–47, probably only from his own vassals and the church.[15] The first national levy for a particular crusade in England was the Saladin tithe of 1188, which like the 1166 tax fell on clergy and laity alike and set a fiscal precedent copied by church and state; it was the ancestor of papal and parliamentary taxation. The Saladin tithe was designed to swell the coffers of the king and to support local crusaders, who were allowed to keep the tithes collected from their noncrusading tenants. It succeeded in providing the main incentive for men like the East Anglian Robert of Cokefield to take the cross. Payment by noncrusaders was mandatory. Thereafter, by contrast, direct taxation, with the exception of the voluntary levy of 1201, tended to be more centralised.[16]

From the late 1190s a regular sequence of voluntary, and later compulsory, taxes was imposed by the papacy on the church, until after 1215 mandatory ecclesiastical tenths for varying lengths of time became the inevitable accompaniments to general calls to arms. Secular taxation followed a less regular form. In 1201 John levied a fortieth from his own and his vassals' revenues for the Fourth Crusade; in 1222 the regency government failed to make a compulsory poll tax stick but managed to raise some voluntary contributions; in 1269–70 a twentieth was collected for the Lord Edward's crusade. On each occasion collection and distribution were administered centrally. Although financially efficient, direct taxation was politically sensitive. The howls of clerical rage at the increased demands of papal taxation have rung down the centuries; the reluctance of the laity to accept precedents for royal taxation, even to benefit the crusade, had the immediate result of making it a rarity. The social impact of these levies seems ephemeral, when compared to the effects of the much larger and more regular ecclesiastical and lay taxes from Edward I's reign onwards. Clerical taxes, however, undoubtedly contributed to a vociferous and widespread suspicion of the motives of the papacy and of foreign clerics, which played a part in undermining confidence in Henry III's regime. As late as 1267 Cardinal Ottobuono was accused of plotting to denude England of Englishmen in the interests of foreign domination.[17] In spite of what successive English delegates to general church councils in the thirteenth century maintained, it was less a matter of the English church being unable to afford to pay crusade taxes, more an expression of desire for local self-determination. There were far fewer murmurs of disapproval in the fourteenth and fifteenth centuries, when ecclesiastical taxation was more persistent but under royal control.

How much clerical and lay taxes contributed to cover the expenses of any specific crusade is hard to judge. Some hostile observers plausibly accused Henry II of squandering the Saladin tithe on his war with Philip II and Richard in 1188–89, although the tax's collection was unlikely to have been completed in time for it all to have been used within eighteen months of its promulgation.[18] The fate of the 1201 fortieth is obscure, but it seems that the provision for crusaders to have their contributions returned to them may have been carried out, if the receipt by the two Cornishmen Richard of Marsh and Walter of Dunstanville of proceeds from taxes on family lands can be dated to the same year. Otherwise money was collected and accounted for at the exchequer, although the sums that appear are extremely meagre. John subsidised his nephew Louis, count of Blois, one of the leaders of the Fourth Crusade, to the tune of one thousand marks, perhaps from the proceeds of this tax.[19] The subsidy to help John of Brienne, king of Jerusalem, in 1222 was raised on a sliding scale of minimum payments: earls, three marks; barons, one mark; knights, twelve pence; free tenants, one penny. The yield is impossible now to estimate, and, given the concern of the government to investigate the collectors' accounts in 1230, it might not have been too easy at the time either. There is no firm evidence that John of Brienne or Jerusalem received any of it, although Peter des Roches may have taken some of the proceeds east in 1227, and the Crown derived some financial advantage, in 1225 receiving two payments from the collectors totalling seven hundred marks.[20] The only other lay crusade tax for a specific expedition, in 1269–70, was apparently a considerable success, despite early problems in gaining the consent of parliament; it raised thirty thousand pounds. Even so, within two years Edward's crusade had run up massive debts. With papal taxation, it is difficult to draw a direct link between taxes paid and crusaders fighting, but it is undeniable that the papacy received large sums during the thirteenth century and that, in turn, popes spent heavily on a variety of crusading ventures. With ecclesiastical taxes being assigned directly to the king after 1250, the temptation is to assume that they were diverted to noncrusading uses. All that need be said here is that when in 1270 an English crusade did embark, 22,000 pounds of church taxes were raised towards it, and the government did not stint itself in its generosity and its efforts to collect further funds for what to Henry III and his sons was a matter of prestige as well as faith.[21]

There was one other source of crusade revenue from central taxation—the Jews. Gervase of Canterbury implied that Henry II raised 60,000 pounds from English Jewry for the crusade at the same time as the Saladin tithe, although, as was suggested earlier, this is almost certainly a mistake. Gervase confused the tallage imposed at Guildford in December 1186 with one of ten thousand marks levied probably in 1188, on which there were still unpaid arrears in 1191. On top of the ten-thousand-mark levy, Richard I mulcted another two thousand marks before his departure on crusade in 1190.[22] The connection between taxation of the Jews and the crusade was emotional as well as financial. Attacks on Jews and their property had been a feature of continental crusading since the Rhineland massacres of 1096, which were repeated half a century later. The size of the English Jewish community was still small in 1144, when anti-Semitic feeling erupted over the alleged ritual murder by Jews of William, a young Norwich boy. At the time of the Second Crusade, King Stephen apparently had to protect Jews in England from attack, thereby earning for himself the praise of the contemporary chronicler Rabbi Ephraim of Bonn. The king's motives may not have been philanthropic; already the Jews had proved their value as a source of income for the Crown.[23]

In the late twelfth century, the size and prosperity of the Jewish communities in England grew. Their role in the economy expanded with a growth in the need for credit. Thus they became increasingly valuable to their lay protector and, at the same time, became increasingly disliked. By 1190, any extraordinary royal expenditure was likely to provoke a tallage on the Jews. A crusade made such an expedient seem even more appropriate. The young crusaders who attacked the Jews at Stamford early in Lent 1190 cannot have been alone in their indignation that the enemies of Christ living there owned so much while the crusaders had so little.[24] Jews were bound to be more vulnerable when crusade preachers emphasised the Passion, the Crucifixion, and the Cross. The desire to avenge the Crucifixion was a popularly expressed emotion among crusaders, one which fuelled the jealousies and anxieties of crusaders in the midst of their attempts to raise money, an activity itself closely identified with the Jews. Kings took a different view; for them Jewry remained a useful source of income, and needed protection. In response to the failure of that protection in 1190, firmer measures were taken that succeeded in preventing a repetition of the bloodshed, except during the baronial wars under Henry III when royal control broke down.[25] In the post-1190 context, taxation paid by the Jews for imminent crusades could be seen as protection money; for if the Jews were abandoned by the king they faced the prospect of sharing the fate of their correligionists in 1190.

English monarchs, however, were not sympathetic to Jewry, and once the Jewish milch-cow had been exhausted, it was disposed of without compunction. Nevertheless, it may be thought that the financial ruin imposed by royal demands on Aaron of York in the thirteenth century was less abhorrent—to him as well as to us—than the carnage of 1190.[26] Jewish wealth was too convenient a source of revenue to be left unprotected; conversely, it was especially exploited whenever the Crown took the prospect of crusading seriously. In 1237, three thousand marks were levied on the Jews for Richard of Cornwall's crusade. One reason advanced for the collection of ten thousand marks in 1251 was Henry III's crusade commitment of the previous year. In 1269–70 six thousand marks were commandeered from the Jews for the Lord Edward's expedition, of which four thousand marks were certainly paid. The royal attitude was perhaps summarized by Henry III in May 1269 when, in return for one thousand pounds, he promised not to tallage the Jews for three years unless he or his son should go to the Holy Land.[27] Given that preparations for a crusade were already in hand, the pledge was wholly disingenuous. The final expulsion in 1290 may also have been associated with Edward I's renewed crusade plans.[28]

However, the Jews were taxed to meet any extraordinary royal expenditure. Thus the 1255 attempts to raise eight thousand marks and the successful mortgaging of control of the Jews to Richard of Cornwall for six thousand marks were not linked solely to the needs of the Sicilian crusade, in isolation from the king's general financial problems. The amounts raised for crusading by Jewish tallages were meagre compared to total royal expenditure on crusades. The 1188–90 levies covered a fraction of Richard I's costs, and in 1270 the proposed six thousand mark subsidy compares feebly with the thirty thousand pounds from the twentieth, the twenty-two thousand pounds from the ecclesiastical tenth, or the 22,500 marks paid out to contracted knights. Crusade tallages were only part of a far greater fiscal jeopardy for the Jews; for crusaders, the public mulct of Jewish wealth contributed only marginally to pay their expenses.

While the Crown benefitted from public taxation, individual crusaders turned to the permanent, ecclesiastically administered fund of crusade legacies, donations, and vow redemptions. Regular opportunities to redeem vows existed from the 1220s, but there is little evidence of what happened to the money so collected until 1238, when the pope granted Richard of Cornwall the fruits of redemptions and legacies.[29] Previously, collection had been in the hands either of local bishops or individually commissioned papal agents. For Earl Richard, proceeds were gathered centrally at the New Temple in London.[30] Thereafter, the existence of a fund for the Holy Land, held or at least accounted locally by church authorities, was taken for granted by crusaders. It became big business. Richard of Cornwall was alleged to have received "infinite" sums from this source, and he pursued his subsidy tenaciously for two decades after the original grant. In 1247 and 1251 fears were expressed lest the amount charged for redemption become excessive. In theory, redemption could be bought for the equivalent of what the crucesignatus could afford for his journey to the Holy Land, following a principle established by Innocent III at the Fourth Lateran Council. In practice redemptions could be purchased for as little as half a mark (six shillings eight pence) five shillings, or even two shillings.[31] The system could be inefficient. Not all redemptions or legacies were promptly paid; in one case a bequest to the Holy Land of £11 18s, deposited at Barnwell priory in 1250, remained unused and uncollected for twenty-five years.[32]

From 1247 the proceeds of legacies, redemptions, and gifts were regularly collected for each crusade and were directed more systematically towards individual crusaders. The process became an intrinsic feature of crusade finance, proving an effective method of translating money given by the faithful into action. In the late 1240s grantees from the fund included Geoffrey of Lucy (£132 14s), William of Valence (2,200 marks, of which he received at least £900), William of Cantelupe (over £472), Simon de Montfort (4,000 marks) and William Longsword, who actually petitioned the pope in person (2,000 marks). In the 1250s the king repeatedly and unsuccessfully tried to corner this market. By the 1260s, competition was open and fierce. Hawissa of Neville wrote to her crusader son at Acre about his grant of five hundred marks: "Dear Son, I pray you that you trust not too much to the moneys of the crusade. For many great lords of England will go on crusade, by what they say, and they will carry away whatever shall be raised from the crusade [fund] by what certain friends make me know." She also remarked that the legate would allow Neville to have the promised funds, "but little have we ever found except that they are in the hands of such as themselves would go to the Holy Land."[33] It is likely that for a major expedition there was not enough to go round; thus on the death of William of Cantelupe his grant was immediately assigned to William of Valence.[34] The disbursement of funds could be complicated; the instructions of the pope or the legate who authorised the grant were not always consonant with what was feasible, in terms of what had been collected in the local depots. William Longsword's original grant of one thousand pounds from redemptions in the diocese of Lincoln came to nothing, and a new assignment had to be made from funds collected anywhere in the realm.[35] Apart from the inevitable difficulties of administration and communication between pope, legate, local fundraisers, collectors, and individual depositories, some grants had to be carefully hedged about for fear of infringing rights of property and lordship. In 1247 Robert *de Kenci* was assigned redemptions, legacies, and donations not only from his own lands, but also from those of the earl of Winchester and of the earl's son-in-law William of Ferrers, provided that neither of them nor their vassals were crusaders.[36]

The significance of this fund is demonstrated by the preparations for the 1270 crusade. For the central organisers, proceeds could be used to hire troops, as in 1268 when it was hoped to raise five hundred crossbowmen, to be sent as an advance guard to the Holy Land. The fund was just as important to individuals. The Lord Edmund was to be subsidised from it at the legate's discretion; one thousand marks were given to Roger of Leyburn; it is likely that most of Edward's companions, and others like Hugh of Neville, were encouraged as well as assisted to go east by the legate's grants of cash.[37] The system could be exploited— Roger of Leyburn, for example, never set out—but the fund lent any crusade legate useful additional powers of persuasion. However, money from this source formed only part of what were often extensive fundraising expedients. The close friends Payn of Chaworth and Robert Tiptoft, for instance, received twelve hundred marks between them from the Crown and six hundred marks apiece from redemptions and obventions. More generally, subventions from public sources supplemented rather than replaced private efforts.[38]

FINANCE: PRIVATE SOURCES

Despite the increasing importance of central funding, the basis of crusade finance rested on what the individual crusader could raise from his own property and assets. The problem was to capitalize land, rents, and rights of jurisdiction into bullion or war materials; the solution was sale, lease, or mortgage. At its most extreme, as Ambroise put it, "And none to sell his heritage/Delayed the holy pilgrimage."[39] In 1177 Count Adalbert V of La Marche sold all his rights in the county to Henry II for the "paltry sum" of six thousand marks and a string of pack animals, just as almost a century later Robert Charles sold all his lands in order to accompany the Lord Edward.[40] For those who stopped short of selling up entirely, the material commitment was still great. Under the year 1250 Matthew Paris describes how an English baron, Roger of Montaut, took the cross and to provide for his journey enfeoffed the prior and convent of Coventry with woods and rents in the area in return for "a great sum of money," and how in addition Roger sold many things and irrevocably alienated much land "just as other nobles on both sides of the Channel."[41] Matthew's account is amply confirmed in land charters, legal records consequent on such transactions going wrong or being disputed, and royal archives. What survives is plentiful, but even so, it is likely to be only a fraction of the true extent of such arrangements.

A crusader's need for cash forced involvement in the process of crusading of his family, dependents, tenants, and the wider community beyond. The nuns of Swine (Yorkshire) contributed to the Third Crusade through both taxation and the giving of five marks to Walter the Black towards his crusade expenses, in return for two bovates of land in Skirlington.[42] The extent of property— a few acres—involved in this transaction suggests that even those with little to support their ambitions were held tightly in the grasp of the crusade.

The domestic effect of fundraising was recognised by church authorities from the 1090s. A crusader wishing to dispose of property in any way had first to gain the consent of relatives or his overlord, in addition to the consent he required to take the cross in the first place.[43] The lord stood to lose service, and relatives income, pro tem or permanently, as crucesignati sought to realise sums amounting in some cases to many times the annual revenue of the assets pledged or sold. In 1147 Philip Basset's deal, witnessed by his brothers, raised for his crusade a lump sum three times the annual rental of the land he had "donated" to the abbey of St. Benet Holme; a century later John of Arundel raised eight marks on property in Chichester, which was over seventy times its annual rental of one shilling six pence.[44] The crusader's problems were exacerbated by the very privilege which allowed him to dispose of property, for it imposed restrictions on how it was to be done. Under the provisions of *Quantum praedecessores* in 1146 crusaders could only pledge lands or other possessions to "churches or churchmen or others of the faithful." Thus the Jews, a major source of credit in the twelfth century, were theoretically excluded. The provision safeguarding the interests of the crusader's overlord could also lead to problems. In the 1270s Hamo L'Estrange's unaccountable omission in not obtaining royal licences for his elaborate land transactions prior to his crusade caused his family considerable difficulties when they tried to prove seisin after Hamo's death in the East; litigation with the Crown rumbled on until 1278.[45]

A crusader's credit was also undermined by the 1146 exemption from payment of usury (i.e., interest) on past loans. The bull *Audita tremendi* in 1187 and the 1188 crusade ordinances went a stage further and allowed not only a moratorium on repayment of debts while the crusader was signed with the cross, but also exemption from any interest on debts incurred while a crucesignatus. Superficially attractive, these provisions risked reducing a crusader's credit to nothing.[46] These decrees of 1146 and 1187–88 represent either the height of naivety or, in view of the church's role as the main source of ready cash, the depth of disingenuousness, an attempt to consolidate a near monopoly. In neither case were the interests of the crusader best served, and in the later thirteenth century, in order to facilitate borrowing, some crusaders were prepared to renounce this privilege. Most, however, with the connivance of the creditor, resorted to the simple legal fiction of mutual gifts. This had the combined advantage of avoiding prohibitions on interest and suiting the holy nature of the enterprise, which in any circumstances might have provoked charitable donations on both sides.[47] The required avoidance of open usury encouraged crusaders to seek alienation or long leasing arrangements rather than short-term loans. The device of mutual gifts was often undisguised: Walter the Black had *given* his land to the nuns of Swine "for five marks which they accordingly *gave* to me to make my pilgrimage to Jerusalem."[48]

Despite the legal niceties, such "gifts" often concealed the taking of large profits. When Philip Basset gave the abbey of St. Benet Holme his marsh and a flock of three hundred sheep the monks promised to give Philip fifteen marks immediately and to pay an annual rent of five marks, of which seven years were to be remitted from the departure of the crusade. Even assuming that the rent of five marks was economic, which may be unlikely, the abbey was to enjoy seven free years in return for fifteen marks, being effectively quit of thirty-five marks. The hidden profit was twenty marks over and above the annual profits on land and sheep during the seven years or the net surplus after paying the rent thereafter. On the lowest calculation of the remitted rent (thirty-five marks) vis à vis the fifteen marks paid out to Philip, the abbey was making a profit over its investment of one hundred thirty-three percent spread over seven years—not a bad return for an age and an institution which frowned upon usury and for a deal with a man supposedly immune from it.[49]

The explicit avoidance of the terminology and procedures of normal credit and interest may have affected mortgages too. Even where the term and loan are specified in crusader mortgage contracts, repayment of the principal advanced is not mentioned. It may be assumed that this occurred, but there are no extant suits claiming repayment from an errant excrusader. It seems, therefore, that both the interest (or profit) and the principal remained concealed behind the myth that the mortgagee or creditor gave money to the crusader. The same is true for fixed-

197

term leases. It is likely that the income from the mortgaged lands was deemed to cover both interest and principal. Alternatively, separate repayment of the principal was expected, and its invisibility is accidental. Certainly, many continental charters specify repayment of the principal, and if Orderic Vitalis is to be believed, Robert Curthose was expecting to have to repay the ten thousand marks loaned him by Rufus, despite the latter's enjoyment of ducal revenues from Normandy for five years.[50]

Anything could be sold or mortgaged or leased—land, rents, grazing rights, and wardships. From 1188 even religious benefices could be pledged.[51] In return, crusaders received a variety of grants—chiefly money, but equipment and horses as well.[52] The implications of the system were profound. For the crusader's family, the drain on immediate and future resources could be severe. For the community, the consequences could be considerable, with substantial amounts of property being placed on the market remarkably openly. In the growing freedom of competition for land in the twelfth and thirteenth centuries, the financial requirements of crusaders played a significant part.

A limited number of choices were available to the would-be crusader who owned land but was trying to raise cash, even though the fragmentation of tenancies in the twelfth century increased the number of potential buyers and mortgagees. Expediency, often shortsighted, dictated the technique chosen. Obviously it was in the crusader's long-term dynastic interests not to alienate land permanently, but this was often unavoidable. The church was both a convenient and appropriate recipient for alienation, it often being impossible to separate charity from a more strictly business arrangement. The motive behind many gifts by crusaders to religious houses was expressly pious. William of Warenne before the Second Crusade gave land to St. Pancras Priory, Lewes, "in free alms . . . for the welfare of my soul and of my father William and of all our relations." A generation later Byland Abbey (Yorkshire) received an acre of meadow from Hugh of Flamville "in pure and perpetual alms for the good of my soul and those of my father, my mother and all my ancestors and heirs." Also in the mid-twelfth century William Fossard gave land to the nuns of Watton "especially for the journey I am going to make to Jerusalem and for the remission of my sins and those of all my relatives, living and dead."[53] Such piety could find physical expression; Fulk of Rufford confirmed a grant of rent by ceremonially offering the specified twelve pence on the altar of St. Leonard's, York.[54] The verbal formulae and ceremonial gestures are identical to other grants to monasteries, unrelated to crusading. Although in these quoted instances there is no direct evidence of reciprocal financial subsidies by the religious house, it is likely that they existed. An impending crusade provided a religious context. Walter of Scoteny mentioned that his gifts to Drax Priory were made "on the point of the journey to Jerusalem," an occasion for charity as well as barter.[55]

Some gifts and enfeoffments to monasteries may indeed have been solely charitable; others, perhaps most, possessed a combination of spiritual and financial benefit. In 1174–75, The charter of Roger of Mowbray assigning rights in Nidderdale to the abbey of Fountains was placed on the altar of York Minster, like Fulk of Rufford's charter at St. Leonard's down the road. For Mowbray the return was evident; he was to receive from Fountains 120 marks "to assist his journey to Jerusalem." The monks also paid his sons Nigel and Robert ten marks and one mark respectively for their assent to the deal, providing an instructive insight into the methods necessary to obtain the consent of interested relatives.[56] In a deal between Southwark Priory and a Cambridgeshire crucesignatus, Theobald of Scalers, sometime between the Second and Third Crusades, the procedure was similar, Theobald confirming his grant of a virgate of land by offering it (perhaps the charter or another symbol) on the priory's altar; in return "the canons gave to him *in charity* three silver marks and one palfrey worth twenty shillings."[57]

The church may for spiritual reasons have been an attractive source of cash, but grants to it were liable to be irrevocable and to be upheld fiercely by the benefitting institution. The most common alternative was the crusader's own family. Sale, lease, or mortgage within the family, although no guarantee against subsequent legal complication, was convenient and less damaging to dynastic interests. The evidence of numerous lawsuits heard before royal justices suggests that relatives of crusaders were eager to advance themselves by the acquisition of their kinsmen's property, even if only for the crusader's short mortgage term of three years, as stipulated in the 1188 ordinances. Arrangements within families might have been easier to organise, especially as there existed family sentiment, if not towards the crusader then towards ancestral property and rights; hence the compensation to Mowbray's sons for the loss of family rights to Fountains Abbey. Even where grants were smaller or merely picturesque, as in the case of the pair of gilt spurs to be given annually to the heirs of Philip of Blakespaine, the urgency of the need to soothe the family loss is evident, where property left the kin.[58] Careful legal drafting, public witnessing, and secure filing were signs of the need of recipients of crusaders' lands to protect themselves against the challenges of disappointed relatives. In general kinsmen appeared eager to prevent strangers intruding onto family estates. Something of this may have been present behind events in the early thirteenth century, when, after Hasulf of Soligny in preparation for his crusade had granted a tenement in Kilmersdon (Somerset) outside the family for a fixed term, one of his sons got the beneficiary of the contract to demise the property to him; equally he may have been trying to steal a march on his brother.[59]

Family attachment to a crusader or to his land should not be exaggerated, as appearances could deceive. In 1240 Hugh of Ringstone borrowed heavily and at high interest in order to provide his crusader brother with one hundred marks, in return for the family property at Clopton (Northamptonshire); but soon after, Hugh sold the land at a profit, outside the family.[60] Nevertheless, in various ways families could and did help crusading kinsmen finance their enterprises by raising money for them or by providing them with assets which they themselves could translate into capital. Around 1230 Rose Marnet raised ten shillings by leasing out land to Carisbrooke Priory (Isle of Wight), which she gave to her son Andrew for his journey to Jerusalem. A decade later Isabelle of Bashley realised four marks on a grant to the same house, which the prior delivered directly to her son Geoffrey Hacard for his crusade. A Worcestershire crusader, Peter of Erdington, was given land by his father Thomas, which he used to raise money for his crusade sometime before 1237. In 1247–48 Nicholas and Leticia Pacche transferred some land and rents in Oxford to their son "to help him perform his journey to the Holy Land."[61] However, even with a supportive family, the crusader's search for funds was often complicated and sometimes painful. Property was a currency of prestige and power, as well as of wealth.

Deeds from the twelfth and thirteenth centuries exhibit numerous contractual permutations in sales, leases, and mortgages. Property could be leased or mortgaged for the crusader's term, for a longer period, or forever; land could be alienated only if the crusader failed to return; the crusader could retain a life interest in the property but promise the reversion to the mortgagee or, conversely, the beneficiary could be enfeoffed with only a life interest; land could be alienated in part, with the residue returning after a fixed term; property could be sold outright and unconditionally, or it could be returned to the crusader's overlord.[62] It is difficult to be certain where the balance of bargaining power lay. The crusader obviously needed the money, which he could only attract by offering some profit to prospective buyers, mortgagees, or lessees; but the crusader could not afford to underprice his land. On the other side, there was fierce competition for land, especially as the thirteenth century progressed, making it a seller's market.[63]

Of course not all crusaders relied on property transactions. Besides the public sources of finance, individual circumstances allowed different private sources to be tapped. In 1282 William of Beauchamp insisted that in the event of his departure for the Holy Land Hugh Despenser would have to complete the repayment of a debt of sixteen hundred marks. Eight years later Otho de Grandson, as part of a financial package as diverse as any in the period, was assigned, at the discretion of the archbishop of York, the first fruits of the archdeaconry of Richmond. Three quarters of a century earlier the bishop of Exeter was allowed access to his uncle's fund deposited at Acre. Trade in wardships was also available; for the Fifth Crusade Oliver FitzRoy, King John's bastard, raised one hundred marks on a wardship given him by his father, even though in this case the Crown later appeared concerned lest its rights had been infringed.[64]

WINNERS AND LOSERS

Such an eclectic and prudential system of private fundraising inevitably produced winners and losers. The winners were those with access to cash and the ability to frame a legally watertight property conveyance. They could be almost anybody—relatives, religious houses, local clergy, laymen, and laywomen like Gundreda of York, who obtained property in Mickelgate from the crusader John of Herdislawe for twelve marks and an annual rent of two pence, or Edith of Navenby (Lincolnshire) and Agnes of Vescy who, at different ends of the thirteenth century, helped their crusading sons in return for temporary possession of family land.[65] Sometimes money could come from unexpected directions. In 1190 William FitzAldelin, seneschal of the king's household, in an interesting reversal of social roles, gave some lands in Yorkshire to his serjeant, Durand, son of Drew, "for his homage and service and on account of the ten marks which the aforesaid Durand gave to me for my journey to Jerusalem."[66] Less unexpected is the involvement of merchants. When embarking on his second crusade in the 1170s, Roger of Mowbray enfeoffed William of Tickhill, a wealthy York merchant described by Roger as "my friend," with the manor, town, and church advowson of Askham Richard, in return for annual rent of one mark. William of Tickhill had evidently helped Mowbray with his expenses as an opportunity to put some of his capital into land, indulging in a pastime with a long and respected future.[67]

The layman with the most cash was the king. The Crown lent actively to crusaders in return for their lands, temporarily or permanently, 201 advanced fees and wages to royal servants about to embark on crusade, and provided unconditional gifts. Kings also made money from the grant of licences giving vassals permission to crusade, to appoint attorneys, or to mortgage land; each licence was paid for by the grantee, with an additional fee payable if he wished to have the licence enrolled in the royal archives as a further guarantee. In 1214 Richard of Fremingham paid six shillings eight pence for his deal with his brother to be placed on the Pipe Roll.[68] Everywhere the Crown revealed its characteristic stance towards crusaders—sympathy and self-interest. Helping members of the king's household and affinity pay their crusade expenses was part of the elaborate and vital function of royal patronage which was the cement of politics. Recipients varied, from men like Amaury of St. Amand, seneschal of Henry III's household, to much less exalted royal dependents such as a crossbowman, a serjeant, or a yeoman.[69] Those who supported John and the regency in 1215—17 were similarly rewarded; Rannulf of Chester was quit of exchequer debts, and Herebert *de Montibus* was provided with twenty marks in 1219 because of services he had rendered to the late king.[70]

Permanent royal devotion to the cause of the crusade was shown in the patronage of military orders: the 1178 exemption of the orders from taxes and fines, except those concerning justice of life and limb; the 1235 annual pension to the Teutonic Knights; the protection of the free export of Hospitaller responsions (annual payments from Hospitaller estates in the West to the headquarters in the East); the employment of individual members of military orders as bankers, ambassadors, almoners, and, in the case of Prior John Chauncey in 1273, treasurer; and the support of those who wished to join the orders. Peter of Burton, on becoming a Templar in 1237, received a royal grant of three marks to buy a robe, and the exchequer paid an annual pension to the master of the Temple in England to maintain one knight in the Holy Land.[71] As the history of grants to the Templar and Teutonic Knights and the Hospitaller responsions indicate, such generosity was not always easy within the context of precarious government finance. However, the advantage of this sort of investment was not financial but political and spiritual.

More material gains were available to the king when he chose to exploit his position as overlord or to enter the mortgage and credit markets; royal loans to crusaders dated back at least to the Third Crusade. Many royal grants were not outright gifts but advances in pay.[72] The business of royal licences gave the king financial profit and political control, by forcing recognition of the role of royal justice and protection as well as by exerting a measure of direction over subjects' freedom of movement and disposal or export of wealth. Although on occasion representing only an ordered ideal, royal licences to crusaders were popular as a perceived guarantee of an absent crusader's interests. It says much for the success of royal intervention in the process of local affairs that a rich and powerful corporation like the abbey of Abingdon in 1247–48 sought "with great labour and expense at court" a royal licence to confirm its purchase of a crusader's estate as security against local competitors.[73] As always, political and legal authority held the prospect of financial return. Except when the monarch shared the financial penalties of active crusading, as in 1190, 1240, and 1270, it is hard to see the king as a net loser from his subjects' crusades, especially once direct access to crusade taxation became available after 1250.

From a different perspective, it could also be suggested that on those occasions when the king was directly concerned with a crusade, wider economic advantages could follow, not to the king as sponsor or crusader, still less to the average crucesignatus, but to the suppliers of the crusade and those involved in servicing it. When, for example, Richard I spent huge sums raising and provisioning his fleet in 1190, his demands for arrows, horseshoes, bacon, cheese, and other provisions quite conceivably stimulated production, to the general economic advantage of such suppliers as the pig and dairy farmers and the iron smelters of southern England.[74] Equally, the export of large quantities of coin to pay for Richard's army probably contributed to the temporary slowing of the growth of the inflation rate, an effect compounded by the huge king's ransom of 1193–94.

If the Crown can be considered to be a corporate source of lay finance for the private crusader, so too can the Jews. For legal and sentimental reasons already described, individual Jewish moneylenders were far less in evidence in private arrangements to raise money for crusading than in other credit transactions. But indirectly, by funding those who funded the crusaders, Jews played a role. Ralph of Ringstone's money for the 1240 crusade, provided by his brother Hugh, came from a loan to Hugh by the wealthy Aaron of York, who has been described as a "Croesus of thirteenth century England."[75] Occasionally convenience outweighed the strictures of conscience or *Quantum praedecessores*. By March 1197 Humfry of Earlham in Norfolk had decided to go on crusade, for which he raised one hundred shillings as part of a land settlement; but less than six months earlier he had agreed to mortgage all his land in Earlham to Isaac the Jew and to Isaac's wife and mother. This mortgage led to extended litigation. It is not impossible that the mortgage to Isaac had also been to help finance Humfry's crusade, and that Humfry then tried to raise money on the same property twice, perhaps in consequence of the mortgage with Isaac falling through because its interest clause conflicted with Humfry's status as a crucesignatus.[76] Firmer evidence is supplied by a case heard before justices in Kent in 1227, in which the jurors attested that one William of Eure before departing on crusade had, with his brothers' consent, leased land which they held in gavelkind (i.e., in common) to a certain Aaron, clearly a Jew, for the crusader's term of three years; after that time the land was to revert to the common ownership of the brothers. Here it is possible that the common ownership of the land leased out enabled William to conceal his status and the evident purpose of the transaction.[77] Nevertheless, in spite of odd cases, Jews were almost ipso facto kept out of, or at one remove from, private crusade fundraising. On the other hand, Christian perception of their role could overlook the subtleties; Matthew Paris, for instance, talked of the snares of Jewish and Cahorsin moneylenders trapping crusaders in 1250.[78]

General Jewish financial dealings with landowners who then took the cross may have deepened the anti-Semitic feelings aroused during preparations for the Third Crusade. In Stamford and King's Lynn, the crucesignati who led the violence appeared content to rifle Jewish possessions to subsidise their journeys. Some of the leaders of the worst massacre, at York, went on the subsequent crusade; it may have been no coincidence that, after slaughtering the survivors of the mass suicide at York Castle, they went to the Minster to destroy Jewish bonds of credit held there. Even if they had not borrowed money from the Jews for the crusade, they or members of their families previously had done so for other purposes, and their own crusader's immunity would not last forever. One voiced reason for the obscene outrages of Lent 1190 was the endebtedness of landowners. Resentment at Jewish creditors, inevitable at a time of inflation, was exacerbated by the requirements of the crusade, for which so many families had to dispose of goods. The attacks on the Jews thus had both criminal and religious origins.[79] Mulcted by kings, debarred from a profitable credit market, and persecuted by the participants, the Jews derived no advantage and sustained hideous losses from the crusades. Alone of those with access to large deposits of liquid capital, the Jews were losers.

The overwhelming beneficiary of the crusaders' need of money was the church, particularly the religious houses. The church had the cash, and alienating land to it may have made the loss more bearable to the crusader, such endowment being good for his soul as well as his crusade budget. Indeed, much of the land dealing over the crusade should be seen as an aspect of a Europe-wide resurgence in the patronage of religious houses in the twelfth century.[80] The link between charity and crusade finance has already been discussed, but it is worth noting that in more general ways the church benefitted from crusade enthusiasm. Relics from the East, such as the Holy Rood of Bromholm, could transform the material fortunes of a local church or religious house. From an early date interest in the crusading ideal prompted patronage not only of the military orders but also of other religious orders associated with the Holy Land, such as the Augustinian canons of the Temple of the Lord in the twelfth century, or the Carmelite friars in the thirteenth.[81]

More direct investment, unattached to any reciprocal financial deals, could accrue from the personal expectations and experiences of individual crusaders. Before departing on the First Crusade, William Percy might have increased the territorial endowment of Whitby Abbey without receiving a financial benefit in return. More humbly, sometime in the thirteenth century William of Moyun gave a mill to Bruton Priory (Somerset) for God, the "the health of his soul," and the endowment of a regular feast for the canons "on the day of his death on pilgrimage to Jerusalem." The pious atmosphere and spirit of religious devotion surrounding the provisions of Godwin Gilbert's grant to Ramsey Abbey, mentioned in the first chapter, cannot have been unusual; the crusade was, or was supposed to be, before and after all a religious exercise.[82]

Donations were also common resulting from the gratitude of campaigning or returning crusaders or their relatives. Two wills drawn up at the siege of Damietta during the Fifth Crusade contained legacies that suited the circumstances of the dying men; John of Harcourt bequeathed land in Leicestershire to the Templars, and Emeric of Sacy, property in Selbourne and Portsmouth to the Templars and Hospitallers respectively.[83] On his return from the East in 1109 Robert of Baskerville gave a hide of land to St. Peter's (Gloucester). The abbey of La Valasse was founded by Waleran of Meulan, earl of Worcester, in thanksgiving for surviving shipwreck on his return from the Second Crusade.[84] Stephen of Mandeville was not as lucky as the earl, being killed, probably during the Second Crusade, "on the road to Jerusalem," perhaps in Asia Minor. His son Roger, for the good of his and his father's souls, gave two mills to the Cluniac priory of Montacute.[85] In 1192 Haughmond Abbey was left Uffington, under Robert de la Mare's will drawn up at Brindisi on his return from the Third Crusade.[86] Behind some patronage lay family tragedy. In 1242–43 Nigel of Amundeville gave half a bovate of land at Carlton-le-Moorland (Lincolnshire) to the Brethren of St. Lazarus of Jerusalem at Burton Lazars, because of the order's kindness to him on his journey to the Holy Land. It appears that leprosy ran in Nigel's family; he himself was probably a sufferer. In 1180 his father, Ralph, had given land to lepers at Carlton, the rents from which were to be employed, presumably on the lepers' behalf, by the Brethren of St. Lazarus; in 1194–95 Nigel's own brother Elias had provided the leper hospital of Burton Lazars with a carucate of land in Carlton, to support his daughter whom he was sending there because she too had leprosy.[87]

For the average lay crusader the transfer of land to the church had the attraction that, if alienation were unavoidable, patterns of lay landholding, and hence local lay power structures, would not be disrupted by enlarging another family's holdings. This factor may also have made such deals more acceptable to neighbours, landlords, jealous relatives, and local rivals. However, the habit did not go unchallenged, and as the thirteenth century progressed there were louder murmurs against the excessive endowment of the church. Alienation by crusaders of fiefs and subfiefs to the church, or to other laymen, played a part in producing pressure from landlords for legislation to restrict such alienations, which reached fruition in some of the statutes of Edward I, notably *Quia Emptores* and *Mortmain*.[88] Notwithstanding such anxieties, certainly in the century and a half before 1250 monasteries, to some extent *faute de mieux*, occupied a central position in private crusade finance, to their undoubted material advantage. They rapidly emerged as major institutions of capitalist enterprise, acting as bankers and financiers as well as territorial empire builders. Some monasteries, like those owning the great Cistercian sheep ranches of the north of England, could raise cash by selling produce; elsewhere cruder methods, including melting down or pawning ornaments, may have been used, as they were on the continent. Either way, money was made available, and it was probably not coincidental that ordinances regulating ecclesiastical taxation for the crusade excluded from assessment the plate and metal ornaments of religious houses.[89]

The crusade finance market was a potentially lucrative, if occasional, adjunct to more habitual monastic money spinners. Monks actively went in search of clients and touted for trade. There are signs of this in the way Adam of Fountains engineered the redemption of William the Fat's crusade vow in 1150 in return for the foundation of Meaux Abbey; Adam, St. Bernard, and Eugenius III behaving as entrepreneurs for Cistercian endowment.[90] In the case of Theobald of Scalers the evidence is more precise. According to the witnesses at Longstowe in Cambridgeshire, at the time Theobald took the cross one Canon Godfrey of Southwark Priory appeared on the scene and "had much talk with Theobald so that Theobald went to Southwark Priory and there offered the virgate of land [at Longstowe] upon the altar of St. Mary and confirmed the grant by his charter. . . . and the canons gave to him in charity three silver marks and one palfrey worth twenty shillings."

Canon Godfrey had evidently concluded a successful deal, to the mutual satisfaction of both parties and the certain advantage of the priory. Whether Theobald would have given his virgate to Southwark without Godfrey's fortuitous arrival is impossible to say—Cambridgeshire and Southwark are scarcely adjacent.[91] Persuasive Canon Godfrey may be a sign of growing competition among religious houses in the twelfth century for a share in an increasingly profitable market. Such activities were the material context for the more elevated intellectual and spiritual aspects of twelfth-century monasticism. As has been said of the 1147 contract between Philip Basset and St. Benet Holme, "apparently the business side of the deal was more in . . . mind than the encouragement of crusaders."[92]

Sometimes religious houses adopted rather aggressive tactics towards crucesignati. St. Benet Holme, for example, persuaded the archbishop of Canterbury in the 1150s to instruct William of Oby to return land he leased from the abbey before setting out for Jerusalem, lest the monks suffer any losses. Presumably the monastic overlords were anxious lest the land be disparaged in William's absence or nervous that he would burden the land with a mortgage; alternatively they were putting pressure on William to enter into some arrangement with them.[93] In similar vein, the monks of Lilleshall in 1195 insisted that one of their life tenancies should revert to the abbey if the tenant went on crusade.[94] Overlords were clearly worried at the consequences of their tenants going on crusade, especially as in most instances it would have been difficult to refuse a crusader's request to raise money in order to perform his vow. On the other hand, as creditors, not landlords, monks were as tenacious as anybody else in giving effect to land deals struck with crucesignati. In the 1150s the canons of Nostell complained that Henry of Lacy, a patron of the Templars and twice a crusader, had reneged on an agreement to give the seisin of some land and rents to the priory before setting out for Jerusalem; with the assistance of the archbishop of York, the canons got their way and their property.[95] Further south, after the Third Crusade the monks of Ramsey were even prepared to defend with armed force one estate gained indirectly from a crusader.[96]

The stimulus to monastic profits inherent in this system is obvious. More generally, however, the financial needs of departing crusaders could stimulate as well as confuse the local land market. This factor became of increasing significance in the thirteenth century as competition for land became almost literally cutthroat, as its value as a commodity of wealth and power increased in relation to its scarcity. One bizarre example illustrates the potential impact of one crusader's departure on the politics, as well as finances, of his locality. In 1247, the monks of Abingdon heard that an oppressive and widely hated local landowner, Hugh FitzHenry, had taken the cross and proposed to take an irrevocable step further and become a Templar. In realisation of this ambition Hugh put up for sale his extensive lands in and around Abingdon. Rumours of this reached court, much to the concern of the monks of Abingdon, who were determined to prevent a courtier, especially the king's brother Richard of Cornwall, from obtaining the land before they did. Despite their lack of ready cash, the monks immediately closed a deal with Hugh, which stipulated a price of one thousand marks plus a chaplain paid for by the monks to pray for Hugh's soul. The first instalment of three hundred marks was to be handed over at Michaelmas 1247, with Hugh to hold a vill belonging to the abbey as surety for the final payment of seven hundred marks at Easter 1248. When Michaelmas arrived, however, Hugh had changed his mind. He avoided receiving the Abingdon delegation by holding a feast on that day for "many knights and magnates," hoping to frustrate the whole deal. In the event the monastery's agent, Nicholas of Headington, outmanoeuvred the reluctant vendor, and after some slick counterploys, all ended happily for the monks. Hugh had probably been holding out, perhaps hoping to conduct an auction among his lay associates for a better price, in a sort of thirteenth-century gazumping.[97] The significance of the story is that Hugh's land was desirable not simply as a piece of land but in the local politics of the Thames valley, with the monks competing vigorously against lay rivals whom the monks clearly regarded as threatening their position in the area. The conduct of all parties may reveal more about English society in the thirteenth century than about the crusade. But the interplay between the requirements of a crusader and his domestic, communal environment demonstrates that the crusades were important in an English context, as much as in that of the Near East or other theatres of crusading endeavour. A variety of sources confirm the tenacity and ferocity with which land released by crusaders onto the market was pursued by anyone with an interest, claim, or money.

The competition over crusaders' lands inevitably imposed a consequent loss of expectations, for Hugh FitzHenry and many like him had heirs who were disinherited by such transactions. As notable in this process as the winners, therefore, were the losers.

DOMESTIC REPERCUSSIONS

Healthy landowners with heirs did not normally sell off their estates, causing disinheritance; to do so was a peculiarity of crusaders. Of course, not all crusaders alienated their land, but mortgages and leases could also make relatives and heirs materially worse off. The landowner's absence, even if his estates had been retained, could expose his family to a variety of physical and legal dangers. Comparing the evidence of land charters and litigation with the abundant chronicle references to financial hardship and ruin experienced by crusaders on campaign, it is hard to avoid the conclusion that the crusader, as vendor, donor, lessor, mortgagor, or absentee landlord, was imposing on himself, his family, and his heirs a medium-term or permanent diminution of estates and future profits, in return for a very short-term financial advantage, soon dissipated. Financially and economically, crusaders and their families were habitual losers. This may say something about the element of faith, devotion, and self-sacrifice in crusader motives, but the sacrifice was frequently communal. The crusader was not an island. In Joinville's emotions when he could not bring himself to look back at his castle, homesickness could have competed with anxiety and guilt; his family's emotions are not recorded.

Obviously, it was the crusader's nearest kin who stood to lose most, in particular his wife. One common problem was that of dower lands, land set aside to support the wife after her husband's death. Crusaders' mortgages frequently contained clauses protecting dower lands so that, for example, if the husband died on crusade, the mortgagee would, at the expiry of the mortgage term, remit the dower to the widow. However, such provisions did not always work smoothly, the widow sometimes having to go to law to prove her title.[98] Defence cases varied; in 1223 Roger of Lenham resisted the claim of the wife of Adam of London by denying that Adam was dead; in 1234–35 Gunnora of Bendinge's dower was placed in jeopardy by accusations that she had not been married legally to the late crusader John FitzHugh.[99] Force was not unknown. Nicholas of Greywell (Hampshire) had leased his wife Mabille's dower lands, for the crusaders term only, to one Richard Cumin. But upon Nicholas's death his overlord Gilbert of Aquilla seized all his property, which in turn found its way by royal grant into the capacious grasp of Henry III's minister Peter des Rivaux. It was probably only Peter's fall from power in 1234 that gave Mabille's heiress, her daughter Edith, a chance to recover the dower, which she achieved in a royal judgement in September of that year.[100] Such litigation, even when it ultimately upheld the protection of dowries, was expensive and fraught with uncertainties; many were less successful than the daughter of Mabille of Greywell.

In a sale of property, pressure from the crusader to raise money was probably hard for his wife to resist. In 1186 Phillippa of Trailly made a grant from her dower lands to St. Neot's "because my lord Hugh of Beauchamp has undertaken the journey to Jerusalem"; elsewhere crusaders like Jocelin of Neville on the Third Crusade and Alexander Luterel in 1270 themselves sold or donated their wives' dowries, although with the ladies' consent.[101] Agreement by spouses to alienate dower lands, although possibly signalling conjugal harmony, could prove foolish. Christian, wife of Walter the Tailor, was left destitute in 1249, after her crusader husband sold her dower in Salisbury; in 1268 Margaret, widow of crusader Thomas of Dreuton, was left insufficient property to meet Thomas's outstanding debts to Joceus of York; before joining the Fifth Crusade John de Mares sold off all his and his wife's moveables and chattels, leaving his wife defenceless against his creditors.[102] Even where adequate provision had been made, arrangements did not always stick. In Lincolnshire in 1228 Christian, wife of the absent crusader Jordan Wren, had to appear in court to defend her rights against Hugo Perun.[103] Commonly the threat came from near relations or neighbours of the departed landowner, like Thomas of Stouston in Suffolk, who was accused in 1202 of disseising John of Stouston's wife in John's absence on crusade. The courts usually tried to protect wives' interests, as in 1233 when William of Arden's land was restored to his wife Avicia. But justice could take time, especially if the crusader had died on campaign.[104] Roger le Pole, one of Hubert Walter's knights, died at Acre in the winter of 1190–91. He had left his wife Alice in possession of a third of his property, but after his death she found herself ejected from it by the earl of Salisbury and the future king John; Alice was still waging her legal battle to reclaim the land in 1199.[105] Temporary financial hardship for those left behind cannot have been exceptional. In a rare example of exchequer generosity, the sheriff of Gloucestershire's account for 1192 contained payments, made on royal authority, of 100 shillings to Emma, wife of Robert, and 130 shillings to Cecily, wife of William, to support them during their husbands' absences on crusade.[106]

Even if a family was not financially harmed by a crusade—and it should be said that many families could absorb and sustain the loss of income and property—the absence of the head of the household in itself left the wife and family vulnerable to a range of unpleasant fates. In 1252 Henry III was recognising a real problem when he made a special point of obtaining Innocent IV's confirmation of papal protection for crusaders' wives left behind against any who molested them.[107] Six weeks after William Trussel left on crusade in 1190, his wife was murdered by William's illegitimate half-brother and William's *armiger*, and her body was flung into a nearby marl pit.[108] Property, rather than passion or psychopathic homicide, was likely to have been the motive behind such a crime. A generation later, at the time of the Fifth Crusade, Simon of Duffield was hanged for strangling Hawissa, wife of Peter of Duffield who was away on crusade. From the evidence presented at Simon's trial it is clear that the attack had been long premeditated by Simon and a number of accomplices. The motive was, however, uncertain, as was Simon's relationship with Peter and Hawissa; since theft was involved, land may not have been a motive.[109] In these cases, the inadequacy of protection afforded wives was cruelly exposed.

Less dramatic than murder and less extreme than disseisin, but nevertheless posing a serious threat to patrimonies as well as to widows and daughters, was the possibility of disparagement, the forced marriage of an heiress to a suitor, usually of humbler origins, unwelcome to her or her kin. The St. Alban's chroniclers tell the story of how in 1226 Ella, countess of Salisbury, resisted the blandishments of Raymond, nephew of Justiciar Hubert de Burgh, who tried to marry her on rumours that her husband William had died on crusade.[110] However romantically tinged, this story was matched in real life. At about the same time, William Luvel adulterously and bigamously married one Cecilia while her husband was still alive in the Holy Land, with property again being the likely motive.[111] Daughters were also at risk of disparagement. In the 1220s Ralph Hodeng returned to Essex from crusade to find his daughter and heiress married (willingly or not, the court record does not say) to one of his own villeins. Ralph, needless to say, was "iratus," the implications of such an event for the future of the crusader's estates could be profound.[112]

More remarkable than arrangements that accidentally failed to protect property or family are deals struck by crusaders that consciously admit the prospect of dynastic impoverishment and plain disinheritance. From the earliest crusades, some mortgages had resulted in alienation; in this way Ivo of Grandmesnil's patrimony, in the words of Orderic Vitalis, "passed into other hands."[113] Some of the first crusaders practised straightforward alienation, like Godfrey de Bouillon; English legal and tenurial records are littered with similar arrangements made by his later imitators. Thus John de Mares sold all his and his wife's possessions for the Fifth Crusade, and Robert Charles apparently sold his entire estates in 1270, even though he intended to return.[114] The frequency of legal challenges to crusader's alienations by disappointed relatives identifies this expedient as a common source of social irritation, especially when property left the family. This could happen in the initial contract; but it also happened in cases where land was originally transferred within the family, but where pressures of finance quickly forced the land out of the kinsman's grasp in a series of secondary transactions. Either way the sale of crusaders' lands inevitably opened up the land market, to the almost invariable detriment of the crusaders' families. The process could be complicated. In the 1240s in Northamptonshire, the Hotot family gained land at Clopton as a result of paying Hugh of Ringstone 170 marks for it. As already noted, Hugh needed the money because he had borrowed 100 marks from Aaron of York at an interest rate of fifty percent (i.e., Hugh had to repay 150 marks or £100); Hugh needed the 100 marks because he had bought the Clopton land from his brother Ralph who, in turn, had required the money to pay for his crusade with Richard of Cornwall. Thus, the net result of Ralph of Ringstone's crusading ambition was that his family lost his estate at Clopton, his brother made an overall cash profit of something over £13 and a nominal annual rent, Aaron of York made 50 marks, and the Hotots gained that most precious and scarce thirteenth-century commodity, land.[115]

The consequences of alienation could be brutal and direct. In 1229 Robert Godbaud of Writtle (Essex) tried to secure the return of his crusader father's land from the son of the man to whom his father had sold it. Robert's case was heard in the Curia Regis; he lost and was liable to twenty shillings damages, despite being described in the court roll as "pauper est"; the father's crusade had ruined the son.[116] An even more startling case concerned a tenement at Bruton (Somerset) that Henry of Carevill had given to his son-in-law as a marriage portion. The son-in-law, to pay for his crusade, sold the land to Roger of Ford. Roger then died, and Henry of Carevill seized the property back, only to be ejected from it by Roger's son Walter. Henry sued, the case coming to court in 1225, but lost. Thus, thanks to his son-in-law's crusade, Henry had to accept, against his will, another family in legal possession of what had once been his own tenement.[117]

Despite clear theoretical guidance in the formulae of writs and legal textbooks, no framework of justice could prevent crusaders' dispositions leading to litigation, often fought with tigerish ferocity and leaving many severely disadvantaged. The number of disputes suggests the weakness of an as yet imperfect code of land law, a paucity of competent legal drafting, and a failure of relatives fully to grasp the implications of what their crusading kinsmen were doing. It was plainly important for the beneficiary of any transaction to receive the explicit consent of other interested parties; the canons of Brinkburne appreciated this point when they preserved a charter containing William of Framlington's confirmation of a grant to the priory of two acres by his crusading brother Robert. Others, like Geoffrey of Fremingham in 1214, looked to the Crown to guarantee contracts. Still others offered douceurs; for his consent to the transfer of his uncle's land on the Isle of Wight to God's House, Southampton (c. 1195–98) William FitzRalph de la More received a gold ring mounted with a sapphire.[118]

Sometimes the crusader himself suffered, despite stipulations, such as that made by Richard of Fremingham, to prevent the instant alienation of property in the crusader's absence. The majority of crusaders intended to return, therefore it mattered to them what happened to their property, their families, and their own interests while they were away. What actually occurred was not always to their liking. In 1250 William of Appleford tried to get a tenant and former servant, Geoffrey of Fercles, declared an outlaw during Geoffrey's absence on crusade, on the strength of a charge of theft brought by William himself after Geoffrey's departure. William overdid it by claiming the escheat of Geoffrey's land, arousing the suspicions of the sheriff of Cambridgeshire that his motive was greed, not justice. Geoffrey was reasonably fortunate; in 1276 a Nottinghamshire crusader actually was outlawed in his absence for robberies which he did not commit.[119] Other crusaders, like John des Roches early in the thirteenth century, would have been able to read their own obituaries.[120] When Reginald of Sugestaple and his wife returned from the Holy Land in 1208 they found that the land their son Lawrence had mortgaged for their expenses which he and they believed could be bought back on their reappearance, was being held by the purchaser, who claimed Lawrence had sold the land to him outright in return for an annual rent.[121] Perhaps more common was the experience of Robert the Small of Retford, who discovered that in his absence his inheritance had been seized by an intruder.[122] In addition, of course, the excrusader had to share the long-term repercussions of his consumption of irredeemable and often irreplaceable assets.

Occasionally, more was consumed than the crusader had planned. It was a frequent practice of crusaders to leave their seals at home, presumably to safeguard those left behind from bogus instructions from abroad or from instructions that contravened the powers granted to the crusaders' *custos* or attorney. The exception to this rule points to another danger; Richard I's seal was lost overboard with its keeper, off Cyprus in 1191. Nevertheless, the risks of leaving a seal behind were equally obvious in a period when attribution by seal was increasingly common and important. In 1246 Thomas of Hoggeshagh sued Ralph of Bolebec for failure to comply with a contract drawn up prior to Ralph's crusade. By the terms of the contract, Thomas, to whom Ralph had mortgaged property, was on Ralph's return to receive some land and rents. Ralph denied the authenticity of Thomas' documents, claiming that on departing for the East he had deposited his seal with the prior of Meauton, and that "if anyone put his seal to the said writing, it was . . . after he had set out for the Holy Land." In the end, Ralph settled out of court, so his defence may have been less than honest, but it does suggest the fertile possibilities for fraud.[123]

Even if such cases were not necessarily the norm, when their consequences are taken with the repercussions of land sales, it is hard not to level a charge of selfishness against the many crusaders who freely emasculated their inheritance and put their families' livelihoods at risk. That all active crusaders, even those whose financial arrangements and legal guarantees led to no disputes, risked imposing a material loss on themselves and their families is indisputable. Landlords had good reason to be nervous at their crusading tenants' dealings; they stood to lose as well. Thus in Yorkshire in the late 1150s the crucesignatus William Fossard, when endowing the nunnery of Watton had to pay compensation to his overlord, Roger FitzRoger, and to Roger's heir, William FitzGerald.[124] It is a commonly held view that medieval landholders cared passionately for the enhancement of their dynasty and the integrity of their estates. If so, many crusaders behaved with extreme and eccentric irresponsibility to their dynastic commitments, especially as crusading itself, almost sui generis, was materially unprofitable for those who fought in them, the only tangible benefits usually taking the form of relics or luxury goods such as William Marshal's silken shroud. Of course, reputations could be enhanced, and royal favour was won by many on the crusades of Richard I, Louis IX, and Edward I. Some material compensation may have been derived from the legal and financial immunities granted the crusader, although these are impossible to quantify. Nevertheless, a crusader's financial balance sheet must almost invariably have shown a loss. Small wonder crusade recruiters, poets, and propagandists tended to emphasise the intangible benefits of salvation, renown, prestige, and the promise of an enhanced sex life. For those crusaders who paid their own way there was little that was straightforwardly mercenary in a decision to take the cross. The evidence so far adduced in this chapter suggests a certain strength of faith in the breasts of the soldiers of the cross, to match the sign on their shoulders. But that faith was harsh and unsentimental, materially awkward and potentially devastating for the crusader and his family alike. In itself, some contemporaries argued, it conflicted with the Christian duty of a husband or ruler to succour family or people.[125] Crusaders may have anticipated adventure or grace; they could not expect profit.

On the other hand, a family's loss was someone else's gain. The crusade crushed some, but for others it was a vehicle of social mobility. Proxy crusaders were a case in point. It is difficult to gauge benefits to the large numbers of unspecified proxies designated by crucesignati, usually in wills, some did well, and it is likely that many were rewarded with more than the simple cost of their passage, travelling expenses, and wages. Before 1204 Brian of Buterle was given land in order to help him carry Geoffrey Foiliot's cross to Jerusalem. Around 1200 Roger the Poitevin gave his brother Hugh, "for his homage and service and for the journey that he was undertaking to Jerusalem in my place" all his land in Normanton (Yorkshire).[126] Villeins could also benefit from this system, for it cannot have been uncommon for a crusader seeking a proxy to choose one of his unfree (i.e., easily persuadable) tenants, as in the case of Hugh Travers, who was manumitted by William of Staunton on Hugh's going to Jerusalem in William's place in the early thirteenth century. On return, Hugh was released from all servile dues and granted in free tenure land that had been held by Hugh's father in servile tenure. Manumitted Hugh's descendents, released from servility, increased their holdings and, as a family of free tenants, survived in growing prosperity to the end of the fourteenth century; the crusade gave the Travers family a head start in the competitive agrarian society.[127] The material advantages to purchasers, recipients, mortgagees, and lessees, whether religious houses or laymen, could be considerable. Religious institutions could benefit from crusaders' charity; so too could laymen, as landlords were sometimes moved to generosity when embarking on crusade. In 1201–2 Wido of Creon manumitted Hubert, son of Reginald, with the proviso that if Wido failed to return from his crusade, Hubert's tenancy would become free and heritable. Apparently Wido was moved to this generosity partly by his crusade and partly by the services rendered to him by Hubert's wife, Dionisia. What those services were is not revealed.[128] The crusade could be a source of profit and a motor for social advancement, as well as a vehicle for tenurial impoverishment and a lawyer's paradise.

PROTECTION AND INSURANCE

Crucesignati were not unaware of the risks they ran and the need to find some sort of reliable security. The search for protection, especially where the only heir was a daughter, was a major theme of many a departing crusader's arrangements. The need for extrinsic guarantees was self-evident; dangers threatened from all sides. Robert the Small's property at Retford was seized by an outlaw, Walter Wallis. John of Wroxham's land, especially his woods and peat supply, was ravaged by a neighbour (or possibly a relative), Alexander of Wroxham, despite John having left a *custos* to guard his interests.[129] The case of Gilbert

Pecche exposes even greater complexities. He went on the Third Crusade, mortgaging land in Lincolnshire to his brother Geoffrey. In his absence Geoffrey, thinking his brother dead, promised the land to the abbey of Ramsey after his own death. However, Gilbert returned and it was Geoffrey who died, but, while Gilbert was reestablishing his title by doing homage to the king, the abbot of Ramsey moved in troops to defend the monks' claim to the property. Litigation continued for half a century, a final compromise only being agreed to in 1237, whereby Gilbert's son Hamo and his heirs were to hold the land from the abbey in perpetuity. It is striking testimony to the appeal of crusading that within a few years Hamo himself went on crusade with Richard of Cornwall, on which expedition he died; but at least he made more secure tenurial arrangements beforehand than his father had.[130]

One solution to the legal problems was to obtain public royal guarantees, although this cost money. As early as 1130 John *de Oburvilla* paid three marks to the exchequer for recognition of his custody of his crusading uncle's land. Later in Henry II's reign, Dionisia, daughter of Robert de Tracy, was recorded for many years as owing the exchequer twenty shillings, to have recognition of her having been granted seisin of her father's land on his departure for Jerusalem.[131] To ensure the smooth inheritance of his lands in the event of anything happening to him on crusade, in 1227 Geoffrey le Flemang appeared before the royal justices at Canterbury to declare his daughter Mary as his heir.[132]

Distant royal authority, despite the involvement of the local sheriff, could not prevent the intrusions of a Walter Wallis or an Alexander of Wroxham, even if it could later punish them.[133] More effective prevention could be afforded by the cooperation of locals. In 1240 William of Cley, about to embark for the Holy Land, leased out some land for three years in return for six marks for his crusade expenses. He was very worried about the security of his land, enjoining the lessee to hold the land intact against all comers (a provision Gilbert Pecche could have done with fifty years earlier). He also included a clause in the charter of conveyance exhorting the "prelates of the church" to honour his status and the terms of the lease "that they may protect the said land and agreement *contra malingnantes*" (against evil-doers). As a further guarantee, William stipulated that if the lessee spent any of his own money in maintaining the property, William or his heirs would reimburse him, thus avoiding the possibility that the lessee might be tempted to allow the estate to deteriorate. Finally, the charter was witnessed by at least fifteen local clergy and laymen, and a copy was deposited in the archives of Norwich Cathderal Priory (the bishop was William's overlord). It is difficult to see what more William could have done.[134]

Alternatively, crucesignati could protect themselves and their dependents by taking out various types of insurance with those who were buying, mortgaging, or leasing their property. At its simplest this took the form of writing a reversion clause into any mortgage or lease, sometimes with a term of the grantor's life or a specified period of anything up to fifteen years or more. A version of this was the stipulation that whatever financial return the grantor received, such as rent, should be paid to the grantor's heirs after his death.[135] Some crusaders made explicit provision for their dependents during their projected absence. As part of their contract with Reginald of St. Valéry (c. 1166), the canons of St. Frideswide's, Oxford, promised to give one mark to his wife. Sixty-five years later Walter Haringer, also of Oxford, arranged with the Hospital of St. John the Baptist that he should have on his return a life interest in the property demised to the hospital, and that for the duration of his absence his wife should be allowed to rent from the hospital a house near Oxford Castle, protected for life.[136] In some places provisions for the future appear distinctly meagre. Geoffrey Hachard arranged with Carisbrooke Priory to receive free food, a new tunic and an undertunic each year, but the contract concerned only a few acres.[137] Other deals could be considerably more elaborate. At the time of the Third Crusade the canons of Easby promised Ralph of Chall that if he failed to return within three years they would render his wife her dower and hold the remainder of the property he had demised to them to maintain his only daughter, either until he did get home or until his daughter received the land in her own right. Meanwhile the canons were to supply Ralph's wife, as rent for the land, with three household loaves a day and a stated quantity of flour per year. The care Ralph took to protect his family and avoid any legal doubts relating to his death is striking; unfortunately it is not known if the arrangements actually worked.[138] Elsewhere the stakes may have been larger but they were never higher; the future livelihood of a family possessed an importance unrelated to the family's economic status in the community.

PRIVILEGES

Such individual attempts to mitigate the domestic disadvantages of crusading did not stand alone. It was to intimate material concerns that the crusader's temporal privileges were addressed: protection for the crucesignatus, his family, and property; accelerated litigation before his departure; essoin of court (i.e., permission not to answer summonses) after his departure; freedom to sell, lease, or mortgage property with the consent of the interested parties; moratorium on debts; exemption from interest; and immunity from taxation. The privileges were effective the moment the cross was adopted and were designed both to encourage and to support the fulfilment of the vow. It took about a century for the full panoply of temporal privileges to be constructed; but the basic principle, whereby the crusader like the pilgrim was withdrawn from a purely secular condition and was placed under the protection and authority of the church, as if he had taken the holy orders, was established at the Council of Clermont itself in 1095, as were many of the prescriptions for protection and fundraising. The purpose of the privileges, as of the whole enterprise, was neatly summed up by a Somerset crucesignatus, Robert of Newburgh, who was a plaintiff in a novel disseisin case in 1220. The defendant pleaded Robert's crusader immunity as a reason for the case not being heard, on the grounds that if Robert need not answer, nor should anyone else involved. An exasperated Robert riposted that the suit should proceed, otherwise his interests would be harmed, and "the crusade [crussignatio] ought to improve my condition not damage it."[139]

The perceived efficacy of crusader privileges was witnessed both by their popularity and their abuse. A wide variety of suspected criminals or men facing civil suits—murderers, rapists, felons, and those accused of disseisin—availed themselves of the privileges, as well as the excuse taking the cross gave them to make themselves scarce. Even some plaintiffs decided to absent themselves rather than to pursue potentially difficult or embarrassing cases; such was the Yorkshire woman who had accused a man of raping her but left before her suit was heard.[140] The system could be manipulated by clerics, like the bishop of Durham who took the cross to assist his law suit against the archbishop of York, and laymen. In the early years of the thirteenth century, William, son of Robert, facing a suit for illegal possession of land, took the cross and pretended to set out on crusade in order to avoid having to answer the charges. It was later established that William had gone only as far as the dean of Lincoln, to whom he had given "money so that the cross was removed from him."[141] For William, the crusade with its immunities was one way out of a tight corner, but clearly the system worked, otherwise he would not have tried to exploit it. William's expectations were based on the acceptance of the crusade privileges by the secular power and its cooperation with the ecclesiastical authorities under whose jurisdiction crucesignati were theoretically placed. Essoins had to be tested in royal courts, the Crown had to recognise crusaders' attorneys, tax collectors had to be instructed to exempt the property of crucesignati, and sheriffs and justices needed vigilance in securing protection of crusaders' possessions and families. Only thus could the privileges be effective.

Of the theoretical acceptance of crusade privileges by the common law there can be no doubt. Even before the Third Crusade, the survey of English laws attributed to Rannulf Glanvill recorded special legal immunities of pilgrims to Jerusalem, including a unique variant of the writ of mort d'ancestor, a sign of the popularity of the crusade-pilgrimage to Jerusalem in the mid-twelfth century. By the thirteenth century a crusade to the Holy Places earned a longer essoin and term of protection than other journeys, including simple pilgrimages to Jerusalem. In pseudo-Bracton's *De Legibus* the legal expedients by which crusaders alienated their land were recognised, as were the inheritance problems caused by uncertainty about news of crusaders' deaths and the difficulties experienced by widows seeking their dowries.[142] The influence was not all one way, however; the secular authorities exerted an influence in the practical implementation of the privileges. The crusaders' term, specified in 1188 as three years, was seen by pseudo-Bracton as indefinite (i.e., as long as the crusader was alive abroad) as regards the essoin, and royal licences from the 1220s to the 1270s on a number of occasions extended a crusader's term to as much as five years.[143]

The scope of legal immunity was also subject to secular modification. In a case heard in 1219, Robert of Mandeville pleaded the crusaders' term of exemption in a land suit, but as the writ concerned possession by entry (i.e., novel disseisin) not by right (e.g., mort d'ancestor) the justices forced Robert to appear, notwithstanding his status as a crucesignatus. As already mentioned in a previous chapter, in 1270, in line with essoins for those abroad on royal service established by 1229, crusaders with the Lord Edward in effect limited their own legal protection by excepting from it writs of dower, novel disseisin, and *darrein presentment*.[144] The potential clash between secular and canon law was recognised by Innocent IV in 1245, when he expressly denied that crusaders should automatically be exempt from the customs of the realm.[145] It was also open to crusaders to forego their privileges; this usually occurred in contracts concerning land or loan repayments.[146] In general, however, secular pressure was reconciled with ecclesiastical precept to the theoretical benefit of the crusader, and there is overwhelming evidence that royal officials were willing to respect the protected status of the crucesignatus.[147]

Ideally, the procedure was for the ecclesiastical authorities to publish the church's extension of protection and the other privileges to individual named crusaders, thereby confirming the obligation, providing corroborative evidence for the status, and acknowledging the church's primary role in recruitment and the granting of the privileges.[148] By itself, however, ecclesiastical protection was liable to be inadequate. Enforcement depended on secular cooperation, so the next stage for the active crusader was to obtain royal licences confirming his privileges. These seem to have been given freely, if not for free. In 1250 Henry III provided an open grant of immunity from usury to any crucesignatus, which he repeated two years later coupled with an instruction that crusaders were entitled to quick justice. Alternatively, licences in support of privileges could be given on behalf of named individuals, like the men of Thierry the German in 1221 or Ralph "the Penniless" in 1203.[149] However, unlike licences to mortgage lands and appoint attorneys, or safe-conducts, licences in support of the legal privileges before they had been challenged were less common. It was more usual for royal justices to grant essoin of court or for the Crown to intervene during individual trials after the protection had been endangered. Thus the Justiciar Geoffrey FitzPeter intervened to halt a case of mort d'ancestor in March 1204 because the defendent "was a crusader."[150] The strength of the system was forged in the frequent contests in which crusader privileges were pleaded. Throughout the period the king's position was clear: provided the right to the status was proven, the privilege, with the technical exceptions already noted, was upheld. This principle extended even to sentencing, in both civil and criminal cases. A number of unsuccessful thirteenth-century litigants were pardoned fines because they were crucesignati. On the same grounds, Walter of Follifoot was pardoned for wrongful accusation at York in 1218–19, and at Worcester in 1221 Robert Wastefile and Robert William Cole had a fine of half a mark for illegally selling wine remitted because, the justices declared, they were crucesignati.[151]

At times crusader privileges could be distinctly inconvenient, if not embarrassing, to those in positions of authority. Justiciar Hubert de Burgh received a complaint that his coadjutor, the papal legate Pandulph, had infringed crusader immunity by seizing lands belonging to a former chaplain of King John. In 1219 de Burgh himself had to put into reverse the sequestration and regranting of Geoffrey of Lucy's land at Hayles, after Archbishop Langton insisted on Geoffrey's protected status as a crucesignatus.[152] This fusion of secular administration and ecclesiastical law found its clearest expression in the crusade ordinances of 1188. When in 1191 the Chancellor William Longchamp forbad the ejection of William of St. Mère l'Eglise from a benefice at Eynsford, it was on the grounds that the expulsion would contravene "the assize granted to crusaders," presumably the 1188 ordinances.[153] Despite exceptions, crusade privileges were closely integrated into the common law and administered by a usually sympathetic government.

The privileges could also be used positively by the authorities in both lay and church courts in sentencing criminals. The crusade became the successor to the penitential pilgrimage, always an inherent potential of the institution. By imposing the obligation of the crusade, the courts rendered criminals immune from other penalties whilst at the same time insisting on heavy material punishment, in some cases the equivalent of exile. This procedure had an obvious relation to the increasingly common, though controversial, practice of alms being imposed as fines, notably for breach of contract. Unfortunately it is difficult to generalise on why some felons went to the gallows and others to the Holy Land; perhaps mitigating circumstances were advanced or suspected. By the late thirteenth century some crimes, such as striking or injuring a priest, were regularly punished by an imposed penitential crusade vow, which would sometimes but not invariably be redeemed by payment of what amounted to a fine. On numerous occasions the king's pardon for homicide was granted on condition the culprit went on crusade to the Holy Land.[154] The range of serious offences punished by crusade is remarkable, including murder, assault, rape, kidnapping, robbery, and defamation. Many so condemned were given no option but to depart or face the more usual consequences. Often the crimes involved ecclesiastical persons or privileges, but not always, and it is difficult to determine in most of these cases how, if at all, the punishment fitted the crime, or whether it merely fitted the criminal.[155]

POINTS OF CONFLICT

Any picture of harmony in the operation of crusade vows and privileges should not ignore legal difficulties arising from individual circumstances. In 1225 royal justices had to decide whether William of Hokespur should enjoy essoin of court when his wife had gone to the Holy Land but he himself had received absolution from his vow.[156] More simply, it was often up to the court to decide which litigant to believe when the fact or the extent of the privileges was contested. Despite his victory in 1219, Geoffrey of Lucy's claim to crusader immunity in 1221 was challenged because the crusader's term had expired; his assertion that he had received an additional eighteen months' grace from the pope was not accepted without an official inquiry.[157] Inevitably, such claims and counterclaims led to delays in the process of justice while the truth was being discovered. Further complications could be caused by the need to determine the passage of time since the vow and whether or not the term had expired. Claims occasionally failed.[158] A Berkshire vicar pleaded protection in an ecclesiastical court in 1292, but his claim was rejected because he had taken the cross on condition that he send proxies to fulfil his vow, rather than perform it himself.[159]

Privileges did not always work, even when uncontested. Absolute protection was impossible; it is hard to see how anything could have been done to protect William Gernun, an Oxfordshire crucesignatus, from having his cow, worth 6 shillings, and 3 shillings in cash stolen in 1244.[160] Privileges sometimes perforce could only operate retrospectively, as a basis for compensation or retribution. Occasionally the pope had to intervene on behalf of a crucesignatus denied his rights, not always successfully. In 1230 Gregory IX complained that his instructions to arrange for the repayment of a loan made by Peter Mulectus, a crucesignatus, to Fawkes de Breauté had consistently been ignored by English ecclesiastical authorities. This case highlighted the inability of the distant pope to enforce canon law without local cooperation; the cause of the failure was suggested by Peter Mulectus himself, who said that in the realm of England no one dared do him justice.[161] The enforcement of privileges was prey to the caprice of local officials. In 1237 Master Robert of Gloucester complained to the pope that the archbishop of Canterbury had through personal malice refused to protect him and his brothers, crusaders all, from excessive interest demanded from them by certain Jewish moneylenders.[162]

Where personal or political interests were engaged, the rights of crusaders could occasionally be compromised. A notable example may be found in the administration of the crusader's immunity from tolls and taxes. Evidence that this privilege was upheld is plentiful, from the 1188 ordinance for the Saladin tithe onwards. Richard I prohibited the tolls customarily levied on passing crusaders by the citizens of Rochester, in the teeth of local opinion which still had to be assuaged by financial compensation almost fifty years later; not everybody felt charitable toward crusaders.[163] The practice elsewhere appears to have continued long after the Third Crusade, provoking Honorius III in 1224 to call on Henry III to ban the collection of tolls from crucesignati bound for the Holy Land.[164] Tangentially, the military orders had enjoyed financial and legal immunities similar to those of crucesignati at least since 1178. In 1207 the Hospitallers were pardoned their breaches of the Forest Laws in keeping greyhounds and a hind illicitly at Blakesley Park (Rutland); a Templar claimed immunity from a forest fine relating to Cannock Chase in 1199. Both orders retained their fiscal exemptions, the Hospitallers from the thirteenth of 1207, for example, although from a papal protest of 1247 it appears that some Templars were forced to pay ecclesiastical tithes.[165] Lay crucesignati were also granted immunity from royal taxation. As was described earlier, in 1190 crucesignati were excused payment of the Wales scutage, and this privilege was extended, at least to some active crusaders, for the scutage of 1201.[166]

Later in the thirteenth century the Crown was generous in consistently exempting crusaders from royal demesnal levies such as urban tallages, although in 1227 the privilege was expressly denied those who had no intention of going in person or who were sending a proxy.[167] Among those liable to the 1224–25 carucage, exchequer returns itemised numerous crucesignati who were exempt from payment although not from assessment; the privilege was presented in terms of defaulters being quit their debt, rather than the 1188 blanket exemption. The difference, of course, was that whereas the Saladin tithe had been a crusade tax, the carucage was not.[168]

The government's reluctance to surrender the principle of obligation to lay taxation is apparent and was powerfully confirmed by the policy adopted towards the fifteenth of 1225 for the war in Gascony. The barons' consent had been given in return for a reissue of Magna Carta. This reissue provided the government with a lever with which to extract payment from crucesignati—probably quite a large number—on the grounds of civic duty. Royal justices in Kent were instructed to

> prevail diligently upon those who have assumed the cross, except those magnates who have already made voluntary submission, that they give the fifteenth of their moveables, which has been determined upon for the tranquillity and security of our realm and the general advantage and defence of all. Make it quite clear to them that so many as withhold this gift, and their heirs, will have no share in the liberty granted to our worthy men by our charters.[169]

The obvious threat was based upon pragmatism, the need to maximise revenue, and political theory: could crusaders opt out of all social, financial, and legal responsibilities? Just as clerical independence from royal jurisdiction had been fiercely resisted, so the immunities of these "quasi ecclesiastics" could not go entirely unchallenged. On similar grounds, in 1219 crusader immunity from repayment of royal debts aroused the lively concern of prominent members of the regency administration.[170]

Conflicts between a crusader's privileges and his responsibilities as a subject tended to be resolved by compromise, not confrontation; Innocent IV openly endorsed this policy in 1245. In part, compromise was favoured because attacks on the generally admired crusade ideal could hardly enhance a ruler's reputation. In part, too, compromise resulted because of the central role played by secular authorities in the organisation of crusading expeditions and finance and in the guarantee of the temporal privileges. At the time of the Third Crusade it appeared that the Angevin government was abrogating ecclesiastical primacy in crusade administration over, for example, the destiny of the chattels of crucesignati who failed to fulfil their vows. The responsibility was given to royal agents, implicitly in the 1188 ordinances and explicitly in the instructions to the justices in 1194. In 1192 proceeds from crusaders' chattels were received at the exchequer, and over a decade later royal justices at Shrewsbury were inquiring into the whereabouts of the goods of one Robert de Boulers of Church Stretton, a crucesignatus who had died before beginning his journey.[171] The king's position as judge, overlord, tax collector, and, increasingly, paymaster, made the fusion of lay and ecclesiastical functions unavoidable. Almost inevitably, conflicts of interest arose. But if the Crown acted selfishly on occasion, to the detriment of crusaders' privileges or the church's authority, the privileges themselves could, conversely, be exploited by crucesignati against the king.

PRIVILEGES AND POLITICS

Involvement with the crusade operated at various levels. There were those who actually fought or intended to fight; there were those who redeemed their vows, bought indulgences, or despatched proxies, their numbers proportionately increasing in the thirteenth century; and there were those who took the cross primarily or partially in order to secure the privileges and protection of the crusader's status. Although both diocesan officials and royal agents were vigilant in chasing up slothful crucesignati, the methods of recruitment and fundraising after the Third Crusade increased the number of crucesignati who never left England. As the privileges were effective from the moment of taking the cross, and enjoyment of them was not dependent on immediate departure— or in practice, on any very urgent or extensive preparations—at any one time there could be hundreds of crucesignati in the community, all able to claim the whole range of immunities. The temptation to become a crucesignatus as a tactical ploy to achieve a general or specific legal, financial, or political advantage is self-evident. The tactic was hardly respectable, but was itself a result of the very success of the protection afforded by the crusade privileges. In the face of more and more resident crucesignati, official sympathy was not boundless when privileges were used as weapons of legal subterfuge or political resistance; the latter was especially sensitive for ruler and subject alike. At times the problem was expressed in terms of generalised anxiety, as in 1219 when the regency government was concerned about the immunities of opponents, who might have taken the cross to fight the Albigensians.[172]

Elsewhere the political use of crusade privileges was direct and explicit. In 1224, a halfhearted rebellion by King John's former henchman Fawkes de Breauté was crushed when royal forces captured his castle at Bedford, hanging his brother and all the other defenders, except three who were spared on condition they joined the Templars to fight in the Holy Land. In a subsequent letter to Pope Honorius III, Fawkes, who had taken the cross in 1221, expressed his outrage at the royalists' violation of the rights of crucesignati, a point he claimed his brother had made unavailingly to the besiegers at Bedford. Fawkes argued that he, his garrison, his castle and all his possessions, by virtue of his status, should have been under papal protection, and that the garrison had only surrendered because they had believed this. Fawkes's plea did him some limited good. He was allowed to leave England to go to Rome, according to the Dunstable annalist, "because he was a crusader"; Roger of Wendover reported that Fawkes avoided imprisonment in France by his former adversary in the civil war, now Louis VIII, similarly because of his status.[173] In his protest to the pope, hardly an unbiased statement, Fawkes made great play of the infringement of papal rights. This put Honorius on the spot, awkwardly placed between his vassal Henry III, himself a crucesignatus, and the need to defend his own prerogatives. In the end Honorius, rather tamely, did take up the cudgels on Fawkes's behalf, although it led to no compensation or rehabilitation for the rebel. By itself, therefore, Fawkes's crusader immunity had failed to secure adequate protection for him or his accomplices, undermined as it was by his own contumacy and a determined government. Yet his appeal to the pope was not idle special pleading; royal authority could be swayed by respect for crusaders' rights. The crucial factor in 1224 was the vigilant hostility of Archbishop Langton, who had not only excommunicated Fawkes but might also have offered indulgences to those who attacked Bedford Castle. When supported by the local ecclesiastical authorities, the crusader had a fairer chance of seeing his privileges respected, as when Langton himself intervened on Geoffrey of Lucy's behalf in 1219 or in 1238 when a crucesignatus called William Goscelin was let out of the Tower on the king's command. Goscelin had been incarcerated for attacking the papal legate at Oxford, but it was the legate himself who had requested his release.[174]

Even in the face of powerful secular resolve, ecclesiastical authority was not ignored. In July 1232, as a result of a palace coup, Justiciar Hubert de Burgh, who had captured Bedford eight years earlier, was dismissed and disgraced. Within a matter of weeks his titles, offices, and castles were stripped from him, and he faced trial. Hearing of the king's command that nobody, not even his son, was permitted to continue in allegiance to him, Hubert, states the Tewkesbury annalist, "on the 27 August took upon himself the cross of Christ, which he had taken long ago."[175] Only a few months earlier the archbishop of Canterbury had accused him of failing to fulfil an earlier vow, but Hubert had correctly pointed out that he had been absolved of the obligation by the Legate Pandulph. Why, then, did he resume the cross?[176] It may have been in self-defence. When the following month Hubert was run to earth in a chapel at Brentwood (Essex), he faced his captors bearing the Host in one hand and a cross in the other, perhaps symbolising the dual protection of sanctuary and the crusader's immunity. Initially this gesture of defiance did Hubert little good, as he was summarily dragged off to the Tower of London. But the bishop of London then protested at the violation of sanctuary, and ecclesiastical pressure persuaded the king to restore Hubert to the chapel at Brentwood, if only temporarily. A year later Pope Gregory IX himself was pleading with Henry III and Peter des Roches, the architect of the justiciar's fall, for Hubert's release on the grounds that he was a crucesignatus, prepared to go to the Holy Land; the argument was identical to Langton's over Lucy's land in 1219.[177] Hubert's fate was ultimately determined by politics, not canonical propriety; nevertheless, at the moment of supreme danger, he appears to have seen in a crusader vow a means of delaying, if not escaping, his fate.

The defence of the cross was not always so flimsy, even for opponents of the Crown. Richard Siward was a partisan of a group of barons hostile to the growing Poitevin influence at court in the 1230s and to the centralising policies of Peter des Roches and his son Peter des Rivaux after the fall of Hubert de Burgh. In the early 1230s Siward engaged in a sort of high-class banditry, guerilla warfare aimed at supporters of the king. In 1233 he joined other *confoederati* against the king, including the earl Marshal and Gilbert Basset, and in October that year he helped rescue Hubert de Burgh from Devizes Castle. For this he was briefly outlawed. Thereafter in and out of royal favour, in 1236 Siward was first banished, then arrested and imprisoned at Gloucester. However, a short while before, he had taken the cross. Whatever his pious intentions, this proved a wise insurance. His status provoked calls for his immediate release from prison by church leaders including Siward's spiritual adviser Bishop Grosseteste of Lincoln, who in a very donnish and acerbic letter to the king argued for a scrupulous interpretation of canon law. Siward, the bishop argued, was a crucesignatus under the protection of the pope and his diocesan bishop, in this case Grosseteste himself, who had also been the one from whom Siward had accepted the cross in the first place. Therefore, the bishop continued, unless

Siward had been charged with profanity (which the bishop must have known was not the case), he must be released for, Henry was reminded, crucesignati "devote and sanctify themselves to defend the Christian faith and fight unbelief even to the shedding of blood and death." With the archbishop of Canterbury also playing a part, Siward was released, so the Dunstable annalist explained, "because he was a crusader."[178] Any such claim was bound to place both king and pope in difficulties. The papacy consistently condemned English rebels but equally vigorously insisted upon papal prerogatives; on the other hand, the king, as he himself recalled in 1253, had enjoyed just such papal protection as a crucesignatus at the beginning of his reign, and for all his brusqueness towards opponents, Henry preferred to preserve good relations with the papacy.[179] Wide acceptance of the importance of crusader privileges is attested in Grosseteste's letter about Siward; the bishop was no friend of undue papal influence over the English church, but he based his demand for Siward's release on the power delegated to diocesans by the pope. At the very least a crusader's status could not lightly be ignored, a fact that may itself have aided recruitment. It may be noted that Siward was not the only active opponent of the king to take the cross in the 1230s; others included Gilbert Marshal, Philip Basset, and Robert Tweng, leader of a terrorist campaign against foreign ecclesiastics in 1231–32. Their crusade immunity was potentially useful, if their opposition were to lead to attempts to confiscate their property or to arrest them.[180]

The government was not unaware of the political dangers of crusader privileges; when the Gascon lord Guillaume Sequin confirmed his loyalty to the king in 1254 he had explicitly to renounce all crusader privileges.[181] It should be added that the status of crucesignatus could fulfil contradictory purposes, on the one hand extending succour to dissidents, on the other preserving an opportunity for reconciliation. In 1236 Siward had become a crucesignatus perhaps to insure against political persecution, but he had taken the cross with Richard of Cornwall, with whom he had had a long feud, and who apparently had been responsible for Siward's banishment. The crusader vow was indeed serviceable. Yet although it could be manipulated for the advantage of a party or faction, the spirit itself remained nonpartisan in its appeal. The incidence of crusading and crusade vows, even where associated with political crises, cannot be linked to any particular or exclusive social, political, or philosophical attitude. Royalists and rebels fought side by side on the Nile during the Fifth Crusade. Hubert de Burgh and the man who tried to destroy him, Peter des Roches, were fellow crucesignati in 1221. Henry III took the cross three times, Simon de Montfort twice.

Clearly not every decision to become a crusader was prompted by religious idealism alone, but the catholic appeal of the *negotium crucis,* as a part of habitual contemporary spirituality as much as an expression of any special religious intensity, argues for motives beyond the narrowly functional or self-interested—quite apart from the likelihood of material loss for those who actively attempted to fulfil their vows. Independent of external considerations, the crusade provided opportunities for the ambitious to play a role universally respected, and for the pious to seek redemption; they could be the same person. The taking of the cross was an event of considerable importance for the crusader and for the community around him. Whatever its role in relations between Orient and Occident, Christian and infidel or heretic, the crusade was embedded in the daily operation of English society, its significance reaching far beyond the immediate despatch of armies and the quest for martial glory. In the many ways described in this chapter, the crusade was a prominent, influential, and characteristic feature of medieval England, the concern alike of the hugely wealthy and of men who keenly felt the loss of a few shillings. For both, as for William of Muntford from Hampshire, it was their "great business"; a unique cause indeed.[182]

9

Missed Opportunities or The End of An Era?

1272–1337

The period between Edward I's return to Europe in 1272 and the outbreak of the Hundred Years War in 1337 possesses a unity in the history of the crusades often unrecognised by modern historians. Until the late 1330s veterans of Christian Syria, from the days before its loss in 1291, still haunted the courts of Europe. Between 1274 and 1333 the papacy imposed four mandatory income taxes on the English church solely for crusading (in 1274, 1291, 1312, and 1333), and a number of others linked in part to the needs of the Holy Land, but none thereafter. Edward I and Edward II both took the cross, but although the young Edward III briefly contemplated doing the same, no subsequent reigning English monarch or heir to the throne became a crucesignatus. The 1330s was possibly the last decade in which the Holy Land and its Mamluk conquerors could be regarded in the West as the primary military target for an eastern expedition. The advance of the Turkish warbands in the Aegean and the subsequent rise of the Ottomans and collapse of Byzantium sharply altered strategic, although not emotional, perceptions. The Hundred Years War was encouraged by church and state and promised material profits of an order not associated with the reality of crusading. It provided a respectable local outlet for martial endeavour unavailable to earlier generations and diverted the energy behind the popularity of holy war to national and dynastic conflicts in western Europe. The crusade was relegated to an occupation of truces or a device of diplomacy. Expectations changed with circumstances; after 1336–37 few could seriously anticipate an imminent crusade, whereas for the previous sixty-five years it had seemed a distinct possibility.

These years witnessed problems of political priorities and misuse of crusade funds, as the institution was increasingly manipulated by rulers to further their secular, noncrusading ends. Such occurrences have prompted some historians to see a decline in enthusiasm for the ideal. It used to be suggested that commitment to the crusade became at best an unrealistic, sentimental anachronism, or at worst a thinly disguised hypocritical deceit, a symptom, in fact, of the "waning of the middle ages," although recently the pendulum of opinion has swung against this view.[1] The policies and behaviour of the first three Edwards confront this crux of crusade historiography: the need, the professed enthusiasm, and the funds for the crusade all existed, yet no general passagium to the East was launched.

The only significant, internationally preached expedition to the East in this period was the crusade controlled by the Hospitallers in 1308–10. Although causing quite a stir in the West, in the East it resulted neither in the defence of Christian Armenia and Cyprus nor the recovery of bases in the Holy Land, but only in the consolidation of the conquest of the island of Rhodes from the Christian Byzantines.[2] Yet there were major appeals for a new general passagium by Gregory X at the Council of Lyons in 1274, by Nicholas IV in 1291, by Clement V at the Council of Vienne in 1311–12, and by John XXII in 1333. On each occasion ecclesiastical tithes and full crusade privileges were granted. Many western monarchs promised to undertake the expedition, and not a few actually took the cross, including, apart from Edward I and Edward II, James I of Aragon, and Philip IV of France, his three sons, Louis X, Philip V, and Charles IV, and his nephew Philip VI.[3] Where monarchs led, their courtiers and some of their subjects followed. Viewed from the royal, papal, and episcopal chanceries, which continued to produce indulgences, privileges, authorisations for preaching, protections, and safe-conducts, the year 1291, when the last Christian strongholds in mainland Syria were finally lost, marked no immediate turning point, any more than 1250 or 1272. For individuals taking the cross, purchasing indulgences, or donating or bequeathing funds for the Holy Land, the machinery of crusading continued to function apparently unimpaired.[4] However, by themselves the presence of crucesignati and substantial deposits of money had never produced a general passagium unless harnessed by royal and ecclesiastical endorsement, encouragement, and leadership. For that to happen political circumstances had to be favourable; they never were under the first three Edwards.

EDWARD I

A possibly fictitious description of a fit of royal temper in 1300, recorded a century after the event, alleges that Edward I swore at the archbishop of Canterbury, who was making a halfhearted attempt to persuade the king to cease his war in Scotland: "By God's Blood! For Zion's sake I will not be silent, and for Jerusalem's sake I will not be at rest, but with all my strength I will defend my right that is known to all the world."[5]

True or not, this anecdote expresses Edward's consistent position. As king he never went to war except to defend his self-proclaimed and frequently challenged rights, in Wales, Gascony, or Scotland. Conversely, Edward never gave up announcing publicly his intention to support the crusade in person or by proxy. Throughout his reign, and in common with many of his contemporary rulers, he placed his actions in the context of the needs of the Holy Land.[6] Even at the very end of the reign, at the knighting of his son in 1306, Edward swore that once he had defeated Robert Bruce in Scotland he would not bear arms again, except on crusade in the Holy Land.[7] The crusade was always the next task but one, pushed into the future by domestic crises, but not forgotten.

Edward certainly had much to occupy him closer to home. In the 1270s and 1280s he completed the conquest of Wales. From 1285 until 1288 he played a leading role in negotiating peace between Aragon and Naples and the release from Aragonese captivity of Charles II of Naples, for which Edward himself pledged twenty thousand silver marks. When seeking a subsidy from his subjects to pay off this debt in 1291, Edward explained with some justice that Charles's liberation was in the interests of the Holy Land.[8] Even after the tentative reconciliation of Naples and Aragon, the situation in the rest of western Europe was hardly conducive to the peace regarded as necessary for a new general passagium. After 1290, the Scottish succession crisis and French pressure on Gascony demanded Edward's attention, in his view, more urgently than the crusade.[9] Up to a point, the king was quite frank about this; in the 1280s he admitted to Pope Nicholas III that he was too busy to contemplate going on crusade in person. He repeated this claim more than once.[10] Some of his explanations were, however, disingenuous. In 1283 he justified appropriation of crusade taxes by claiming that he was protecting the money from criminals; in fact, he needed it for his campaign in Wales. The excuse was rightly dismissed by Martin IV as "frivolous."[11] That Edward placed domestic above crusade duty, even after he took the cross again in 1287, is neither surprising nor shocking. Ever since the 1090s such priorities had been recognised. Edward took his responsibilities as king seriously, elaborating a high conception of royal authority and rights and, hence, duties, which made it more likely that he would not allow the crusade to force him to desert these God-given tasks.[12]

231

Edward's insistence that the crusade had to take second place, despite persistent papal pressure on him to take the cross and embark, was neither devious nor novel and met with the approval of some contemporaries.[13] All agreed that peace was necessary before a crusade could succeed, and probably no ruler in Europe worked harder for such a peace than Edward I in the years 1285 to 1290, when he tried to reconcile Aragon, France, and Naples. Like most politicians, Edward identified his own interests with the greater good and contended that only through achievement of his rights could peace be achieved. It was a view endorsed by Peter Langtoft who, eulogising Edward's Scottish triumph in 1295, declared:

> Henceforward there is nothing to do but provide his
>   expedition
> Against the king of France to conquer his inheritance
> And then bear the cross where Jesus Christ was born.[14]

Unfortunately both Scotland and France proved more intractable than Langtoft anticipated. The possibility of anybody other than the king, such as his brother Edmund, leading a substantial crusade was precluded by Edward's massively expensive and politically debilitating wars. Once Edward was committed to fighting after 1294 on at least two fronts, in Scotland and France, any prospect of imminent English help for Outremer vanished. However, before this the costs of the Welsh campaigns, the building over many years of the great castles in the principality, and the pledge for Charles of Naples's release denied Edward any spare cash.[15] One sign of his worsening financial position was the expulsion of the Jews and the confiscation of their goods, which removed a traditional, but now feeble, prop of crusade finance. Another was the lack of direct financial support for the crusaders who set out from England for the Holy Land in 1290, led by the veteran of the 1270 crusade, Otho of Grandson.[16] After having borrowed, plundered, and finally legitimately received funds from the 1274 and 1291 crusade tithes, and having exploited all sources of secular revenue, Edward still could not pay for his wars.[17] In the light of Edward's own estimation that his honour lay in asserting his rights in the British Isles and France, his prevarication is not unduly disingenuous.

Edward I undoubtedly possessed more than a rhetorical interest in the Holy Land. Apart from inevitable and frequent diplomatic contacts with Outremer, Edward continued his father's close links with the military orders. His wife, Eleanor, did business with a merchant from Syria, Roger of Acre, from whom she bought a miscellany of goods: jewels,

Venetian glassware, Damascus metalwork, amber, silks, and camelhair from Tripoli.[18] In 1272 Edward had left a paid garrison behind at Acre, and six years later he gave control of the tower he had built there to the Order of St. Edward. After a quarter of a century of prevarication, in 1302 he could still write to the illfated last master of the Templars, Jacques de Molay, that only his wars had prevented him from "going to Jerusalem as he had vowed . . . upon which journey he has fixed his whole heart." This emotion was confirmed by his vow of 1306 and by his will of 1307, in which, like a number of his contemporaries, he bequeathed his heart to the Holy Land with a hundred paid knights to serve the cross of Christ for a year.[19] When the opportunity arose, Edward did more than talk.

Between 1287 and 1290, and perhaps as late as 1294, serious preparations were in hand, creating firm expectations. Public activity was to some extent forced upon Edward, as successive popes made access to crusade taxes, redemption fines, donations, and legacies dependent on the adoption of the cross or, after 1287, definite preparations.[20] Not that Edward was reluctant to keep the crusade at the forefront of politics. Even between 1274 and 1287, he seemed to regard himself as committed to the relief of the Holy Land. This self-imposed personal obligation perhaps supplied part of the psychological and political incentive for him to conduct the reform of royal administration that marked the decade after his return from the East; his uncle, Louis IX, had behaved similarly between his two crusades of 1254 and 1270. More obviously, Edward's reputation, inclination, and experience as a crusader gave him a useful weapon in his dealings with the French and the Scots, both of whom could be branded as hindrances to his crusade plans. Edward had to work to maintain his position as arbiter of the West, hence the judicious, almost monotonous larding of his diplomatic correspondence with references to the plight of Outremer, his own devotion to the Holy Land, and his intended expedition there.

The king's commitment is shown by his acquiescence to the appointment of Antony Bek, bishop of Durham, to the by then honorific title of patriarch of Jerusalem in February 1306. Bek, a veteran of the 1270 crusade, had been a close adviser of the king, although they latterly had quarrelled. Sometime before 5 June 1305, with a number of his clerks, Bek had again taken the cross, and it seems that Clement V, who appointed him patriarch, expected him to visit the Levant, as later fourteenth-century patriarchs were to do. Instead, Bek returned to England where, briefly reconciled with the king, he played a prominent part in the ceremonial knighting of Prince Edward in May 1306, at which the king reaffirmed his crusade intentions.[21] Although scarcely a supporter of papal patronage and influence over his bishops, Edward may have considered it politic not to spurn an English patriarch of Jerusalem at a time when Philip IV of France was trying to wrest leadership of the crusade from Edward and restore it to the Capetians; an attempt that succeeded only after Edward's death. The importance of the patriciate to the plans of crusade leaders was amply demonstrated in the symbolic and propagandist use made of Bek's successors by the French kings over the following twenty-five years.[22]

Bek probably owed his appointment to his famed wealth (or, as a St. Alban's chronicler put it more politely, "his generosity and magnificence of heart"), which was surprisingly underestimated by some contemporaries at five thousand marks income per annum. Excluding profits from regalian liberties, Bek's Durham estates alone realised five thousand pounds in 1306–7. Clement V may have been more impressed by Bek's typically extravagant offer to pay for three hundred knights to fight in the East for three years than by his piety.[23] The net results of Bek's entrepreneurial instincts were the patriciate, papal favour, and an eminent position within the English church at a time when the archbishop of Canterbury lay under suspension.[24] Bek benefitted financially from his new office; at his death in 1311, apart from his own bequest to the Holy Land of one thousand marks, he controlled John of Vesci's crusade legacy of one thousand marks and four thousand marks of crusade money assigned him by the pope.[25] That the king tolerated this pluralist magnifico may appear surprising, but it was neither coincidental nor inappropriate that the only Englishman to become patriarch of Jerusalem was a subject of Edward I.

After the Treaty of Rhuddlan in 1284 freed him from domestic entanglements, Edward I fixed his attention on the crusade and the need for peace in Europe. Diplomatic problems of western Christendom had worsened dramatically during the war between Aragon and France, Naples, and the papacy, following the Sicilian Vespers of 1282 and the subsequent Aragonese annexation of Sicily and expulsion of the papally backed Angevin rulers of Naples from the island. Some relief came in 1285 with the deaths of most of the protagonists—Martin IV, Peter II of Aragon, Charles of Anjou, and Philip III of France—but the problem of the captivity in Aragon of Charles II of Naples remained. Edward's diplomacy to solve this dispute was conducted with the crusade explicitly in mind. In contrast to his earlier prevarication, by May 1284 he had announced to the pope his decision to join the crusade in person.[26] This promise helped assuage papal anger at the king's seizure of crusade funds in 1283 and allowed Edward to negotiate for control of crusade money outside the realm. However, further action was required both to encourage more papal grants and to secure Edward's diplomatic role between Aragon and Naples. After agreement with Pope Honorius IV in 1286, Edward took the cross, probably in June and certainly before October of 1287, in Gascony, perhaps at Blanquefort. Because Honorius IV had in the meantime died and no successor had been elected, the nuncio who gave Edward the cross lacked unequivocal authority under canon law to perform the ceremony and, oddly, it took nearly four years for his action officially to be ratified. Contemporary English chroniclers are strangely vague as to the time and place of the ceremony, in marked contrast to accounts of similar occasions in 1188, 1215, 1250, 1268, and 1313.[27] Despite this, Edward's renewed status as a crucesignatus stimulated serious planning and focussed the aspirations of others upon him.

An indication of the practical international prestige available to a royal crucesignatus can be found in the appeals of two Aragonese noblemen in 1293 to be taken into Edward's pay. They reminded Edward of their offers to serve him on crusade, one with a hundred knights, the other with two or three hundred; significantly one of them, Philip de Castro, proffered service even in the event of there being no crusade.[28] But Edward was not a crusader simply for European political and diplomatic benefits. In 1287 he announced to ambassadors from the Mongol ruler of Persia, the Il-Khan, "I have the sign of the cross on my body; this affair is my chief concern."[29] One immediate consequence, according to observers at St. Alban's with admittedly shaky chronology, was the expulsion of the Jews from Edward's French lands "an enemies of the cross." This move had more than symbolic significance, for the proceeds of the expulsions from Gascony in 1288 and England in 1290 perhaps marginally eased Edward's financial problems.[30] The release of Charles of Naples in 1289 enabled Edward to begin planning in earnest. In 1290 he negotiated with the pope for the receipt of substantial grants of ecclesiastical taxation and crusade obventions, and his departure was set for the summer of 1293. The Il-Khan of Persia was sent falcons and jewels, as a prospective ally in the Levant who had promised to supply Edward with horses and equipment. Andrew, king of Hungary, offered to pay for a thousand knights and mounted archers for a year if Edward travelled east overland, but, according to the king's reply in the summer of 1292, it had already been decided that the crusade would go by sea; the Hungarian monarch was encouraged to send his contingent nonetheless.[31] By this time preaching had begun, and people were taking the cross. Edward himself had already despatched a force to the Holy Land under Otho of Grandson and had toyed with the idea of a preliminary campaign of his own in Greece.[32]

However, Edward's luck ran out. The autumn of 1290 saw the deaths of his much cherished wife, Eleanor, and of the young Queen Margaret of Scotland, the "Maid of Norway." The ensuing arbitration by Edward on the succession to the Scottish throne lasted until November 1292, by which time the deadline for departure, midsummer 1293, was bound to be missed, and with it the chance of uncontested access to crusade money. The fall of Acre and the last Christian strongholds on the mainland of Syria to the Mamluks in 1291 was a serious strategic blow, depriving the crusade of vital land bases and ports. It did not immediately deflect Edward's purpose; perhaps the reverse, as the propaganda war could now be spiced with scaremongering and accounts of Moslem atrocities. A supposed letter from the conqueror of Acre, Sultan Khalil, was circulated to diocesans and recorded by chroniclers such as Bartholomew Cotton, a monk of Norwich, with clear propagandist intent. The letter gave an arrogant description of the massacre of members of the military orders, the sale of Christian women into slavery, and the imprisonment of lay nobles, ending with a threat of further Islamic conquests in the West.[33] In the short term, more obstructive than the fall of Acre was the papal vacancy from April 1292 to July 1294. By the time the cardinals elected the ill-suited Celestine V the diplomatic situation in Europe had changed, with Edward facing war with France over the confiscation of Gascony. In June 1294 Edward wrote to Florent of Hainault, prince of Achaea in Frankish Greece, of his anger that rapid changes in circumstances had rendered the crusade impossible.[34] Within a year Edward's problems were compounded by a Welsh rebellion and the Franco-Scottish alliance of 1295. However, as early as June 1294 royal officials had been instructed to secure for general purposes the proceeds of the 1291 sexennial crusade tithe.[35] Edward's crusade had been overtaken by events.

The expedition of Otho of Grandson to the East was the most tangible assistance that Edward gave the Holy Land after his second assumption of the cross. By 1290 a number of Englishmen, including Edward's chief adviser Robert Burnell, had taken the cross.[36] At a ceremony in June or July 1290 Archbishop Pecham preached the cross, which was received by "many magnates," including the earl of Gloucester (even though his 1268 vow remained unfulfilled), the earl's new wife, Princess Joan (Edward's daughter, born at Acre in 1272), Thomas Bek, bishop of St. David's, elder brother of the future patriarch of Jerusalem, Sir Robert of Thateshales and his son, and Otho of Grandson; a curial group who, with Gloucester, symbolised political unity and royal resolve.[37]

Only Otho can be shown to have accomplished his vow. Preparations for his expedition were afoot by May 1290. He received the customary royal protection and licence to appoint attorneys in June. The Patent Rolls identify fifteen others who obtained similar privileges between

3 June and 20 July. Some were explicitly associated with Otho's expedition, including two of his nephews. The list also included two king's yeomen. Travelling with them was the Hospitaller prior of England, William of Henley, and his entourage.[38] Direct royal funding was not lavish. The king remitted some of Otho's debts, negotiated a loan of three thousand marks to Otho from Italian bankers, and presented lengths of worsted worth 28 shillings 8 pence to William of Henley. Otherwise Otho seems to have had to rely on assigning away his property, and on receiving a grant of the first fruits from the archdeaconry of Richmond (Yorkshire), subsidies from the Channel Islands (whose warden he was), and a retrospective allocation of two thousand pounds from the 1291 crusade tax.[39] Some contemporaries thought Otho carried English treasure to Acre. If so, he must have lost it in the fall of the city, for when he found himself in Cyprus after the evacuation of the mainland he needed assistance from England that included clothing and a horse.[40]

Otho's mission was closely related to Edward's general crusade strategy, although it must be doubted whether his role was primarily military. When he left England there was a truce between the Franks of Syria and the Egyptian sultan. William of Henley was described as an ambassador, and Otho himself met the pope at Orvieto on his journey south. The supposed hoard of English royal treasure for the relief of Acre may have comprised little more than the expenses of Otho's *équipe*. Almost all English expeditions to the Holy Land attracted stories of vast treasure, in 1227, 1240, and 1290 no less than under Henry II; some of the stories contained more wishful thinking than truth. Otho's purpose was probably to discover the nature of the problems at Acre, rather than to solve them immediately. In the event Otho and his colleagues were engulfed in the final catastrophe and had to fight for their lives. In the last defence Otho was prominent, perhaps because of his position as Edward's representative. Having made good his escape to Cyprus (some alleged by disreputable means) and apparently destitute, Otho remained in the East visiting Armenia, making the acquaintance of several local nobles, and mediating in disputes between the Venetians and the Genoese. It was not until 1294 that he returned to the West.

It was probably in Cyprus after the fall of Acre in May 1291 that Otho heard of the death of Queen Eleanor. The news prompted him to return to the Syrian mainland, this time as a pilgrim. While Christian captives from Acre were glutting the local slave markets, Otho visited the Holy Places; his journey was later commemorated in a painting on Queen Eleanor's tomb at Westminster. It is entirely possible that Eleanor had taken the cross with her husband in 1287, as she had in 1268 (and as her daughter-in-law was to do in 1313), and that Otho visited the Holy Sepulchre to fulfil her vow as well as his own.[41] There may also have been a practical motive behind Otho's visit to Jerusalem; as Egyptian sultans later discovered, a palmer's walking staff might actually be supporting a spy.[42]

Otho's travels, like those of many other Westerners in the East, may not have been purely devotional, recreational, or adventurous. In his journeys to Armenia and Jerusalem he would have had ample opportunity to accumulate information useful for a crusade to the Holy Land. For many years Otho has been regarded by some historians as the probable author of a memorandum composed between 1289 and 1307 containing a plan to launch a new crusade.[43] The evidence for Otho's authorship is circumstantial and inconclusive; however, that Otho or someone like him composed such a manual is entirely credible. Many of the paper plans for the recovery of the Holy Land written in the two centuries following the fall of Acre were by men who had travelled in the Near East, some with the express intention of gathering information. At least until the mid-fifteenth century the despatch of agents to reconnoitre both friend and foe in the East was a regular feature of western crusade preparations. Such an exercise may well have formed part of Otho's brief in 1290. The advice attributed to him argues that Armenia should provide the initial target and base for any new passagium. This matches Otho's experience as a visitor to Armenia, a friend of Armenian princes (one of whom, Prince Hayton, also wrote a plan for a new crusade in 1307), and a witness to the internecine feuding. However, such a correlation of personal experience and theoretical advice was by no means unusual.[44]

Otho's personal interest in crusading persisted. He was appointed to discuss the matter with Clement V in 1305; two years later he was cited as a referee by Prince Hayton at the papal court at Poitiers. He took the cross for a third time, probably in 1307, being released from his vow on the grounds of age and infirmity only in 1319, for a payment of ten thousand gold florins. He was at the time about eighty, although he still had nine years to live.[45]

Otho's reputation was not unsullied by rumour, innuendo, and slander. Like some other survivors of the fall of Acre, he was criticised. As the 1975 fall of Saigon demonstrated, no sudden evacuation of a capital city by a whole community of soldiers and civilians, including clerics, women, merchants, and children, in the face of an invading army, is anything but messy. In the panic of the moment and the subsequent trauma of defeat, few even of the bravest escape opprobrium, survival itself becoming grounds for suspicion. With the fall of Acre this was especially so, as it was widely and plausibly rumoured that fortunes had been made and presumably lost on that chaotic quayside, as ship space was sold to the highest bidders. Yet even if he paid heavily to escape, most accounts suggest that Otho fought valiantly until almost the end. Despite the attempts to blacken his name, he may be thought more fortunate than many, including one English squire at Acre who burnt to death inside his armour like, one witness recalled, "a burning tar-barrel."[46]

At home, crusade activity remained centred upon the royal court, whence other sections of the community, particularly the church, could be mobilised through propaganda, publicity, and the dissemination of the usually bad news from the East, which was only alleviated by the widespread false rumours that a Christian Mongol Il-Khan of Persia, Ghazan, had captured Jerusalem and liberated the Holy Land in 1300.[47] The fall of Acre demanded a reappraisal of Edward's plans. Otho's journey proved to be the last crusade sponsored by an English king which saw action in the Holy Land. Although the numbers taking or redeeming crusade vows remained more or less constant, numbers actually departing for the East seem, from the evidence of royal licences, temporarily to have dried up once the news of the Acre catastrophe reached the West in the late summer of 1291. The new situation called for fresh initiatives.

In response to a papal request for advice after the fall of Acre, a number of local church assemblies discussed how best to recover the Holy Land. This remained topical as the preaching and fundraising instituted in 1290 continued despite the news from the Levant. English replies to the papal questionnaire came from at least three dioceses, and a provincial council was held by Archbishop Pecham in London in February 1292. The suggestions collated in the archbishop's reply to the pope were typical of contemporary theories. They included calls for the training of experts in eastern languages; a new western emperor to impose discipline on Christendom; the establishment of peace in the West; a unified crusade leadership; the concentration of funds on whatever expedition embarked; the union of the military orders (a suggestion previously made at the Council of Lyons in 1274 and by Nicholas IV in 1291); and the harnessing of the orders' wealth to the cause (an idea at least half a century old). There were, however, local features that distinguished the English advice from the almost identical opinions voiced at similar assemblies on the continent. Primarily, the clergy's fear of

239

unchecked papal power was clearly expressed, as it had been at Lyons in 1274, when the English proctors had gone so far as to oppose any crusade taxes on the English church.[48]

The widespread debate on strategy and organisation conducted in 1291–92 came to nothing, the death of Nicholas IV (1292), the long papal vacancy (1292–94), the disastrous interlude of Celestine V (1294), and the outbreak of war in Scotland and Gascony (1294) effectively quashing any chance of a new passagium. In diplomacy and in the sponsorship of Otho de Grandson's crusade, Edward I had showed himself willing to consider a new crusade; that political problems prevented him, or any of his major vassals, from pursuing this ambition after 1294 hardly reflects upon the earlier commitment. It might be added that in attempts to play a positive role in the recovery of the Holy Land, no other European monarch was any more successful.

EDWARD II

After the death of Edward I in 1307 prospects for English involvement in, let alone leadership of, a crusade diminished further. The Capetians were quick to assume control of the enterprise. Their coup was signalled by the attack on the Templars (1307–14) and the initially related plans of 1308–13 for a French-led crusade, to be preceded by a Hospitaller campaign and a general council of the church. Edward I died in July 1307, and the following September Philip IV of France issued his orders for the arrest of the Templars, which were carried out the following month. Philip deliberately placed this act in the context of his and his nation's special mission to recover the Holy Land. It is hard to conceive how Philip, not as yet a crucesignatus, could have adopted such a position if Edward had still lived. Whatever the pretensions of the French, Edward had remained the senior statesman and crusader in Europe, retaining to the end a primacy of respect.[49] In 1306 the Norman lawyer Pierre Dubois dedicated the second part of his massive book of crusade advice, *The Recovery of the Holy Land*, to Philip IV; but the longer and more grandiose first part he addressed to King Edward.[50] By contrast, after 1307 most of the running for the recovery of the Holy Land was made by Philip IV and his successors and none of it by Edward II, a consequence of the Capetian's deliberate association of the crusade with his general political aspirations at home and abroad, and of the series of debilitating political crises in England which lasted until the fall of Edward II's immediate successors in power, Queen Isabella and Roger Mortimer, in 1330.[51]

This does not mean that England withdrew into isolation. The king remained a target for appeals from the East, and his subjects still took, or expected to take, the cross. In 1308 there was a rumour that a contingent of five hundred English knights were ready to crusade at their own expense. Magnates included provisions for service in the Holy Land in their indentures, and some looked to Edward to fulfil his father's ambition.[52] It may be significant of Edward I's legacy that his son refused to accept the French accusations against the Templars of blasphemy, idolatry, and sodomy, only moving against them on papal instructions. Even then, the English hearings were not conducted with anything like the repulsive persecutory zeal of the Capetian proceedings, showing rather, it has been observed, "the general failure to make the charges stick except with the aid of torture."[53] By the time the order was suppressed at the Council of Vienne in 1312, however, the crusade had become almost a French monopoly, and Edward II had other things on his mind.

While Edward II's reign conforms to the established pattern in which the crusade provided one of the moves in the diplomatic game, the king did as little to hinder departing crusaders as he did to encourage them. In 1308 Pope Clement V promulgated a new issue of crusade privileges for those who assisted the Hospitaller expedition to the East designed to relieve Armenia and Cyprus, preparatory to a general passagium.[54] Although Edward II ruled out personal aid to Armenia, a number of his subjects were more enthusiastic. Before preaching began, a crusading yeoman of the king received royal letters addressed on his behalf to the king of Cyprus and the master of the Hospital. In August 1308, despite a ban on the export of bullion, permission was granted to another crusader, Payn of Turbeville, to take three hundred marks with him, although Payn appears to have delayed his departure until after preaching had begun.[55] Some continental sources suggest that a number of Englishmen set out without adequate funding or leadership and were forced to turn back before reaching the Mediterranean; other sources hint that they were actually rejected by the Hospitallers, who were intent on raising a professional force to the exclusion of the independent amateur.[56] In England, there was a profitable trade in indulgences to help the Hospitaller crusade; in two years the archbishop of York received nearly £500 for the expedition, mainly from indulgences, although only £25 14s 8d from commuted vows.[57] The process of the redemption of vows had increasingly been replaced by a system in which the swearing of the vow before money changed hands was no longer necessary for the enjoyment of the indulgences.

Not everybody was content to contribute with cash alone. Between December 1308 and July 1310, ten royal licences were issued to people departing for the East, including the wealthy Turbeville, Francis of Vilers, "a knight of the king's household," William of Chesney, "the king's cousin and yeoman," and a woman, Alice, wife of Robert FitzWalter.[58] Some of these were crusaders and not simply pilgrims, although the official warrants merely refer to the Holy Land as their destination and are silent on their status. Chesney and his unnamed companion were recommended to the master of the Hospital; Francis of Vilers was bound for Jerusalem "on the service of God," and many years later his widow, Alice, described his great services to Edward I and II "in the Holy Land, Gascony, Wales, Scotland, Flanders and England," an equation that does not suggest a purely pacific purpose for his pilgrimage.[59] The term of these protections and licences to appoint attorneys, between three and five years, were traditional for crusaders. It would be foolish to suppose that those described as travelling "on pilgrimage to Jerusalem" before 1291 tended to be crusaders and that those after were pilgrims. The distinction in the fourteenth century, no less than in the twelfth century, is false. Both before and after 1291 Jerusalem and the Holy Land stood for Outremer in general, and were often the ultimate, if not the immediate, objective. Payn of Turbeville's three hundred marks suggests he was travelling expensively, with a significant retinue. Twenty-five years later, a financially and militarily hard-pressed Edward III was determined to ensure that one Richard of Averenges who was "about to set out on pilgrimage to the Holy Land" took with him "no destriers or armour . . . nor any vessels of gold or silver, in silver plate or sterling"—hardly the equipment normally associated with humble palmers.[60] From the 1308–10 list the intentions of Geoffrey of Saleby, "surgeon," or Alice FitzWalter may be conjectured, but, in the fourteenth century as earlier, the pilgrim could be equipped to fight, and the crusader, like Otho de Grandson or even the followers of Richard I in 1192, prepared to be a pilgrim. The fusion of the two practices reflected both habit and canon law.

Over Edward II's adoption of the cross there is less difficulty. Once Clement V had announced a new crusade with full traditional privileges at the Council of Vienne (1311–12), it was imperative for rulers wishing to benefit from crusade taxes and obventions to assume the cross. For Edward there were other advantages. He received the cross in Paris in June 1313 with his wife, Isabella, her father, Philip IV, her brothers, and most of the great vassals of the French king; it was very much a Capetian family affair. In return for this gesture of open support for Philip IV's crusading preeminence, Edward secured charters of remission for various fines and debts imposed by the French king on his

Gascon subjects. The charters explicitly referred to Edward's taking the cross, an act which provided the douceur for this temporary easing of Capetian judicial pressure on the English king's vulnerable subjects in southwest France.[61]

The link between the crusade and the issues of Anglo-French conflict was not new. Since the early 1290s the crusade had been entwined in the affairs of Gascony and Scotland, making it impossible for Edward II to remain neutral or disinterested. In 1295 the Franco-Scottish alliance had included a clause stipulating that the king of Scotland would depart on crusade—Edward I's crusade—only with French agreement.[62] From 1306 the kings of England and Scotland proclaimed themselves willing to go on crusade once their dispute was resolved. As compromise was impossible, such gestures were somewhat empty but important, as the crusade was part of the propaganda of both sides. In the Declaration of Arbroath (1320), the Scots asserted that English avowals of interest in a new passagium were bogus, whereas their own King Robert was eager to go to the Holy Land once the English ceased their harassment. These arguments precisely mirrored English diplomacy, which strove to brand the Scots as hindering the crusade. This sort of tit for tat was a feature of the generation before the Hundred Years War.[63] In 1317 an English embassy at Avignon was ordered to extract from the new pope, John XXII, the same crusade terms as the French, while insisting that English cooperation in a passagium depended on the cessation of the war with Scotland. To achieve peace the envoys were to suggest that Robert Bruce be excommunicated and Scotland placed under an interdict.[64] The years 1313–23 were a dress rehearsal for the 1330s. All parties—England, France, and Scotland—proclaimed devotion to the crusade, as a necessary preliminary to hurling accusations of bad faith at their enemies in the hope of gaining material and spiritual support from the papacy. The French also tried to employ this tactic against Flanders, with equally frustrating results.[65] It could be argued that this refraction of the crusade into diverse areas of secular politics indicates a decline in its hold and purity. Alternatively, lip service paid to the recovery of the Holy Land reflected an habitual acceptance of crusading as a respectable political and moral objective. The association of the needs of Outremer with the resolution of domestic problems was traditional and was typical of crusading from its origins. In the readiness of Edward II, no less than Henry II, to place his policies in a crusade frame lay one strength of the institution, integrated with secular affairs rather than separated from them.

This is not to say that Edward II had any serious intention of going on crusade, but he had to play the game according to long-established rules. To safeguard his French interests he shadowed the efforts of the

French kings in securing preferential treatment from the papacy by virtue of their status as crucesignati and their willingness to plan and launch crusading expeditions. French kings of the early fourteenth century were, within the confines of political reality and expediency, sincere in their eagerness to do something for the Holy Land, to which end they invested time, men, and money.[66] Their neighbours, however, saw in French policy the threat of being branded as obstructive to the *sanctum negotium* and the danger of disparagement of their own sources of ecclesiastical revenue, in French attempts, for example by Charles IV in 1323, to secure church taxes from countries outside the borders of France. This ploy had been essayed a generation earlier by Edward I in not-dissimilar circumstances.[67] As Edward II's position was especially vulnerable because of relentless Capetian pressure on Gascony and Franco-papal refusals to abandon Bruce, his need to join in French crusade plans was more urgent. This was one of the motives behind Edward's taking the cross in 1313, as well as the 1317 Avignon conference, and, as shall be discussed below, English involvement in French plans for crusades to Spain in 1329–31 and to the Holy Land between 1331 and 1336. French crusade schemes directly threatened the English king's sovereignty in Gascony, as successive kings of France deliberately tried to entice Gascon nobles into joining the crusade as vassals of the French crown. By becoming a crucesignatus himself Edward could hope to limit the damage done to his authority by such Capetian poaching. Such considerations only demanded formal participation, and in any case, for most of his reign Edward was hardly in a position to render any more positive assistance. Successive failures in Scotland, chronic financial problems, worsening relations with sections of the baronage culminating in civil war in 1321–22, the war of St. Sardos with France itself in 1323 and the subsequent wrangle over homage for Gascony, and the coup d'état of 1326–27, stifled any close commitment to the crusade by the last English king to take the cross as monarch.

The use of the crusade in diplomacy depended on the survival of interest in the ideal in royal circles and beyond. Formally, the king shared this concern. Despite a characteristic royal reluctance to allow unlimited free passage out of his realm for knights, squires, men-at-arms, and even some pilgrims, on occasion Edward encouraged those bound for Palestine.[68] In 1317 Sir Edmund of Kendale, the king's bachelor, in order to fulfil a vow to go to Jerusalem taken "when he was in peril in Scotland," was quit six years' rent to the exchequer on a manor in Rutland, which he was allowed to lease out for the same period.[69] In 1313 and 1320 royal letters smoothed the path for groups of Franciscans and Dominicans bound for the Holy Land on preaching missions to convert the infidel.[70] Another friar, the Carmelite John of Bouhkil, was described in 1312 as "going on the king's behalf on a pilgrimage to the land of Jerusalem," the king requesting the prior of the Carmelites in England to provide Brother John with a companion and permission to depart on his journey. John had, so Edward's letter declared, "vowed to go the Holy Land for the welfare [or salvation? (*salus*)] of the king and his subjects"; a romantic gesture indeed, especially as it was made before Edward had taken the cross, reflecting, perhaps, royal anxiety that his reign had begun so inauspiciously.[71] Had God, who so obviously had been on the side of Edward I, abandoned his son?

Perhaps a similar mood inspired one of the more bizarre exchanges in Edward II's reign. Sometime between 1316 and 1320 the king privately sought papal advice on whether he should be reanointed with a mysterious oil, said to have been given by the Virgin Mary to the exiled Thomas Becket with the promise that if the fifth king in succession to Henry II (i.e., Edward II) received this unction he would recover the Holy Land. Verisimilitude was lent this legend by the involvement of the duke of Brabant and his sister, the countess of Luxembourg. The duke was supposed to have brought the oil to Edward's coronation in 1308, when its use was rejected by the king and his council. Subsequently, the countess provided authentication of the oil's supernatural properties through having a bad wound healed by it.

It is clear from John XXII's reply to Edward's letter that the king, at a low point in his fortunes, was clutching at straws. The pope, hardly surprisingly, was cautious: if Edward believed in the oil and would receive it in a faithful frame of mind and with a determination to crusade against the infidel, then no harm would come of it, and it would in no way compromise the king's previous anointing at his coronation. But John ducked the central issue and refused to advise Edward on whether he should believe in the oil or be anointed with it, merely commenting that if the king decided to be reanointed he should do it in secret to avoid scandal, a suggestion that would have robbed the act of any propaganda value, even if it might still have stiffened Edward's morale. What the king did is unknown, but the mysterious oil reappears in Thomas Walsingham's account of the coronation in 1399 of Henry IV, a king who had better cause than Edward II to doubt the legitimacy of his position; anointed with the Virgin's gift to Becket, Henry would be the "champion of the church."[72]

If this obscure episode in Edward II's reign had been reported by a chronicler, it would most probably have been dismissed as idle invention, but the sole evidence for it comes from a product of the papal chancery, a place not noted for indulgent romanticism. The story reveals the existence, only slightly below the surface of public business, of a world of superstition, imagination, and magic which fed on images and stories of crusading and which in turn provided the source for much of the excitement of crusaders themselves. The legend of the holy oil is not, after all, so very far from the spurious charges levelled against the Templars or the rumours circulated in 1320 that Jews, Moslems, and lepers had conspired together to poison the water supply of Christendom both of which were widely, if conveniently, believed.[73] More generally, the legend of the oil is a reminder that material prosperity, spiritual salvation, and the fate of the Holy Land were still closely linked in the minds of many influential fourteenth-century Europeans.

Edward had more direct contact with Palestine. Sometime before 1315 he commanded one of the yeomen of his chamber, John of Bosham, to visit the Holy Sepulchre. Unfortunately, John's chaperone, a Hospitaller from Rhodes, turned out to be a scoundrel who robbed the Englishman of 150 gold florins, reparation for which the king extracted from the Hospitallers in England.[74] What John was to do in the Holy Land is not clear. Was he a simple pilgrim, or was he a spy as well? Perhaps Edward thought it prudent to have firsthand knowledge of what remained a central issue for debate and diplomacy, rather than having to rely on the rarely objective opinions of the French and papal courts. If so, any scheme Edward might have formed came to nothing. But the evidence of royal contact with pilgrims and other travellers to the East from his own household, slight though it is, suggests that the responsibilities of a crucesignatus could not be and were not entirely ignored. Edward II may never have actively begun to prepare for a crusade, but after his deposition and death a Hospitaller, Adam of Cokerham, "out of the affection that he bore the said king," set off for the Holy Land "to fulfil the vow that he made for the salvation (*salus*) of the late king." It looks as if Edward's debt, outstanding since 1313, was posthumously honoured.[75]

EDWARD III

With Edward III's seizure of power in 1330 from his mother and her lover, the pulse of crusade expectation quickened. Yet for all Edward's youthful ambition and martial enthusiasm he was in no position to give a lead even if he had wished to, and despite his carefully fostered chivalric reputation, there is little sign that he was ever particularly eager to crusade, in Spain, Prussia, or the Levant. In the first decade of his rule the determinant factors of his foreign policy were Scotland and Gascony; on both he risked such large amounts of political and financial capital that he had none to invest in the crusade. Edward III was the first English king since Stephen not to take the cross. He was unusual in this even among his own contemporaries, as a large number of noble families, including Edward's own and those of his closest associates, boasted active crusaders during his reign.[76] Like his grandfather, Edward concentrated on local wars of personal and national importance. Even so, for reasons similar to those that had persuaded his father to take the cross, Edward III could not escape the crusade entirely.

Even before Edward assumed power, the French had tried to recruit English support for a crusading expedition against the Moors of Granada in southern Spain. Nothing came of this, but the diplomacy surrounding the enterprise exposed how crusading could be exploited for political advantage, in this instance by Philip VI.[77] Despite Edward's having paid homage to Philip at Amiens in 1329 for his French lands, the precise nature of the obligation remained uncertain. The French pressed for full liege-homage, to be explicitly recognised in writing and by a new ceremony. At the same time, May 1330, the English agreed to negotiate with the king of Aragon over prospects for an allied campaign against the Moors, and a year later Edward formally agreed to participate in the campaign.[78] His gesture was far from spontaneous. By 1331 Philip VI had recruited for the Spanish crusade the hitherto pro-English count of Hainault and a number of Edward's own vassals from Gascony, notably the influential lords of Craon, Albret, Isle Jourdain, and Armagnac. This demonstration of loyalty to the Valois put pressure on Edward to resolve the issue of homage, especially as the lord of Craon, once seneschal of Gascony, had been given by King Philip the responsibility of confiscating the duchy if Edward refused to comply with the French homage demands. By suggesting that Edward join the Spanish crusade, Philip was emphasizing Edward's subservience but was also offering him a respectable and palatable way of demonstrating it. Edward's agreement to participate was simultaneous with his furtive trip to France in April 1331 to perform the required full liege-homage, for which the quid pro quo was a settlement of outstanding problems of the status of Gascony. The homage and the stated willingness to follow Philip to Spain marked a nadir of English prestige, not so much in the content of the agreement as in the manner in which Edward had been forced to submit. The progress of the subsequent negotiations at Agen over mutual territorial disputes (1331–34) could not have filled Edward with any optimism over French intentions.[79]

Such was the diplomatic background to the French invitation to Edward in the autumn of 1331 to join a crusade to the Holy Land. Initially Edward considered the proposal seriously; it gave him a role on the international stage, and no advantage could be gained by allowing Philip a monopoly on crusade funds or prestige. As long as the crusade looked a real possibility, Edward went along with the French plans, to protect his own interests. The crusade could work to Edward's benefit, by distracting Philip's attention from potential areas of dispute in Scotland and Gascony and by imposing on him responsibilities, as crusade commander, to strive for peace in western Europe, without which the pope would be reluctant to allow either the expedition or the collection of ecclesiastical taxes. Provided the diplomatic smokescreen could be maintained, English ambitions nearer home need not be compromised; nor were they. Edward agreed in principle to accompany Philip, and in March 1332 parliament, while proposing a later date for departure than the one suggested by the French and insisting that the kings should embark together, gave general approval. However, there was no active preparation by the English beyond frequent exchanges of ambassadors with France to discuss the crusade in the context of possible marriage alliances and the wider issues of disagreement.[80] Instead, the summer of 1332 found Edward giving tacit approval to an attempt by some of his nobles, led by Edward Balliol and Henry of Beaumont, to topple the Bruce regime in Scotland. After initial success Balliol was thrown out of Scotland in December 1332, prompting Edward to transfer the exchequer and the court of Common Pleas to York and to issue writs for the raising of troops, in a clear demonstration of royal priorities that remained unshakable.[81]

Edward's involvement in Scotland led directly to the abandonment of the French crusade and the outbreak of the Hundred Years War. In 1333, publicly for the first time, Edward made his participation in the French passagium conditional on receiving satisfaction over Gascony. Once it became evident to the French in the winter of 1333–34 that Edward's crushing victory over the Bruce party at Halidon Hill the previous summer had failed to destroy support for the Bruce cause, they threw their weight behind Scottish resistance to the English. Where Edward was offering to join the crusade if left a free hand in Scotland, in the spring of 1334 Philip VI countered by insisting that the problems of Scotland and Gascony were inseparable, and that the French-Scottish alliance of 1295 remained operative. Soon the young David Bruce took refuge in France, and Philip was covertly threatening direct action against England. Thus within a year of John XXII's launching a new crusade in July 1333, England and France had entrenched themselves into almost irreconcilably hostile positions.[82]

Much of the responsibility for this lies with Edward III. It must have seemed a risk worth taking. Despite various rumours and scares of a

French invasion or direct French military help for the Scots, Philip VI was hamstrung by his role as commander of the crusade.[83] When he wrote to Edward that as captain of the passagium it was his duty to arrange a peaceful solution to the Anglo-Scottish conflict, he was telling no more than the truth.[84] Neither the suspicious John XXII nor, still less, his serious-minded Cistercian successor, Benedict XII, would allow money to be raised without some overt attempt by Philip VI to engineer peace. In 1333–35 Philip could neither morally nor financially afford open military opposition to Edward. Thus the English king was a beneficiary of the conventional restraints imposed on serious crusaders for, unlike Edward, Philip appears to have been genuine in his desire to recover the Holy Land and to support words with deeds.[85] Edward, on the other hand, was all talk. At a parliament in September 1334 the crusade was again discussed inconclusively, the official deadline for embarkation of July 1336 being totally ignored, while at the same assembly money was agreed for the Scottish wars. But the talk persisted. In December 1335 Edward promised to help Armenia, and over the following months he received offers of Genoese galleys for his sanctum passagium. Negotiations with the French and the pope continued. Even as late as November 1337, with all prospects of a crusade long vanished, Edward was declaring himself willing to supply one thousand men-at-arms for a crusade.[86]

Nothing was actually done. Edward was more concerned to pursue his aggressive policies in Scotland and then France, and beyond paying the normal courtesies to visiting Levantine diplomats, the question of Outremer was set aside. Edward appears to have been a brazen hypocrite when he commiserated with King Leo of Armenia in 1343 over renewed Mamluk attacks, saying that he would have helped had it not been for his "great war."[87] Perhaps such extremes of duplicity should be ascribed to self-deception, but Edward probably knew what he was about, and it is significant that, unlike others, he did not commit himself too far by taking the cross. Although having little intention of honouring his crusade promises, Edward found the crusade useful. Initially it was mutually important for Edward and Philip to cooperate; English participation reduced French fears of a stab in the back, and in 1331–33 at least, the crusade offered Edward an opportunity to gain prestige, international recognition, and influence. Despite the deepening rifts over Scotland and Gascony, each side still needed the other's acquiescence. Appointed captain of the crusade in 1333, Philip needed peaceful conditions in which to leave his kingdom, and he had to be seen as a peacemaker to retain papal confidence. When Benedict XII lost confidence that peace was imminent, he cancelled the crusade in March 1336.[88]

Edward, to protect himself from possible papal penalties, had had to persist in declaring his enthusiasm. In his own account of Anglo-French relations in the 1330s, circulated throughout the kingdom in 1337 as part of a propaganda campaign aimed at persuading the king's subjects of the justice of his cause, Edward revealed his fears. He asserted that he had offered to accompany Philip on crusade, provided he received his rightful lands in France beforehand "so that no hindrance of the crusade could be alleged against him," and that later in the face of French intransigence he had proposed restitution of land he claimed in France after the crusade's return "to stop the malice of the king of France, who was striving to blame the prevention of the said crusade on the king of England."[89] This was the rub. Those who hindered the crusade were vulnerable to papal censure, even papally authorised military retribution; thus had the English sought Robert Bruce's excommunication, and the Capetians, anathema against the Flemish. As numerous rebels and opponents of the papacy in the thirteenth and fourteenth centuries could testify, such threats were not always idle.[90] In the mid-1330s Edward III was wary lest Philip VI try the same tactic. His anxiety was witnessed by a copy, made by English officials about 1337–39, of a 1252 bull of Innocent IV which outlined papal protection for crusaders. On the back of the copy, salient details of Innocent's bull were compared with the clauses in the 1333 crusade bulls of John XXII which appointed Philip VI captain of the crusade and which prescribed excommunication to all who troubled, invaded, or disturbed Philip's lands, rights, or property.[91] The cap fitted Edward III only too obviously. The charge that the English king had prevented the *saint voiage* supplied a major plank of French propaganda in the early years of the Hundred Years War. Memories of English perfidy and betrayal lingered in French court circles for half a century.[92]

Edward was fortunate that Benedict XII was not a pawn of France and had a genuine desire to reconcile warring interests in Christendom, without partiality.[93] Ironically Benedict's pacific intentions, which led him to postpone the crusade indefinitely in 1336, pushed England and France nearer the open war the pope was endeavouring to avoid. Neither side had any further interest in the restraint the crusade had imposed. Within months of the postponement, Philip despatched his crusade fleet from Marseilles to the Channel, and Edward began to prepare for war by seizing crusade funds.[94] The pope cancelled the crusade tithe in December 1336, finally removing the need for pretence. By the following summer the Hundred Years War had begun, irrevocably altering the course of crusading history.

The collapse of Philip VI's passagium was perhaps inevitable, as the plan provided for a degree of French control impossible for any English king to tolerate, still less one striving to regain territory within France and to assert independence of action over one of France's traditional allies. Much of Edward III's policy in the 1330s was aimed at reducing the effect of the liege-homage of 1331, sworn at a time of uncertainty and weakness. After Halidon Hill Edward was determined to succeed where his father and grandfather had failed, both in Scotland and Gascony. Philip VI, intransigent over Gascony and proprietary toward Scotland, was complacent, patronising, and high-handed, consistently and disastrously underestimating his second cousin. However, disintegration of the political equilibrium was neither expected nor desired; Edward's initial willingness to assist schemes for the recovery of the Holy Land in 1331–32 assumed no such breakdown. Despite the turmoil of Edward II's reign, many still looked to the day when a crusade would embark. Their expectations constituted part of the pressure on European rulers to take the issue seriously. Thus in 1328 John of Hampton from Oxfordshire left six marks each to certain people who would go to the Holy Land "when the king went there."[95]

Edward III attracted his share of such expectations. Early in his reign he received a book of advice and information on the crusade to the East called *Li charboclois d'armes du conquest precious de la terre sainte de promission*, written by a veteran Hospitaller, Roger of Stanegrave, who had returned from the Levant some years before after a long period spent in an Egyptian prison.[96] The book describes in detail the geography, material strengths, and social structure of Mamluk Egypt in a manner not dissimilar to other contemporary works by crusade theorists, such as the Venetian Marino Sanudo.[97] Stanegrave also included, by way of establishing his credentials, a certain amount of autobiographical information. Like Sanudo, his experience of the East stretched back before 1291, probably to the reign of Hugh III of Cyprus-Jerusalem, who died in 1284. It is likely that Roger, in common with a number of other Englishmen, was captured in 1291. If so, he spent more than two decades in Mamluk confinement, long enough for him to have become knowledgeable and refreshingly accurate in his information on Islam.[98] His release came sometime after the Hospitallers occupied Rhodes. To repay his heavy ransom, twelve thousand gold florins, he travelled, as he had promised the Sultan, to England to raise the money from his friends. He reached home in the winter of 1318–19, accompanied by a Jew called Isaac who had to obtain a royal safe-conduct before they could proceed to Yorkshire, where Roger had relatives.[99]

Stanegrave's book, given its optimistic spirit and the likely age of the author, should probably be dated soon after Edward's declared interest in the Holy Land crusade late in 1331, when according to the Parliament Rolls, the king was recognised as having a strong desire to join the passagium. Despite its improbably romantic background, it conformed to the general pattern of crusade literature in the early fourteenth century. It combined powerful religious exhortation, practical information about the Near East, and detailed advice on strategy and tactics, including, interestingly enough from a Hospitaller, the suggestion that the military orders be united, with a wealth of supporting evidence derived from personal experience, the classics (including Aristotle's pseudonymous letter to Alexander the Great), crusade history, and medieval epic and romance, notably the stories of Charlemagne and Lancelot.[100] Here, at least, Stanegrave would have touched a chord in his dedicatee, Edward "of Windsor," as he insisted on calling him in an arch literary vein, as the young king was conspicuous in his devotion to chivalry; "the flower of Christian knighthood" in 1331 had even jousted dressed up as a Tartar.[101]

The Christianization of the western European warrior's military values found no clearer expression than the crusade, and few more revealing commentators than Roger of Stanegrave. In a society still dominated by the requirements and compulsions of war, such legitimization continued to be both important and, as the *Charboclois* testifies, acceptable. This in itself put pressure on a monarch like Edward III to take the crusade seriously.

THE USE OF CRUSADE MONEY

When Adam of Murimuth commented that from the discussion of the crusade at the parliament of 1334 "nothing was afterwards done," he was echoing the sentiment of a generation.[102] Earlier, the far-from-flattering contemporary biographer of Edward II had observed that the new crusade and fundraising campaign launched at the Council of Vienne "profited the Holy Land nothing at all."[103] The stir caused by successive promulgation of new general passagia in 1274, 1291, 1312, and 1333 was not followed by any significant military response. Yet on each occasion the financial machinery was put into operation, and just as surely, in 1283, 1294, 1314, and 1336, the kings of England had seized the money raised.[104] A distinction should be drawn between church taxes and the other sources of crusade money—legacies, redemptions, donations, indulgence fees, and payments made for the Holy Land in cases of breach of contract. Although the latter category was as vulnerable to royal seizure as the former, and even though each new crusade proposal was accompanied by efforts to sell indulgences and collect redemptions, the short duration of some of the fundraising campaigns, notably after 1313 and 1333, probably precluded much income from that source.

Furthermore, such income tended to remain under ecclesiastical control. W. E. Lunt commented that "the major portion of the sum yielded by the legacies and obventions given or promised for the Holy Land during the reign of Edward I found its way into the papal camera." This may have been more accident than design, but it is certain that the proceeds of the well-publicised indulgences of 1308–9, unlike the concurrent taxes, were paid to the Hospitallers.[105] In practice, therefore, the issue of misappropriation largely concerns ecclesiastical taxation.

The repeated sequestration of crusade taxes provides the chief indictment of the crusading sincerity of later medieval monarchs, and of their subjects who tolerated their behaviour. It is therefore important to establish the case in its proper perspective. As a feature of the later Middle Ages as a whole, the phenomenon of kings diverting crusade taxes to secular ends was temporary, as no new mandatory crusade taxes were levied by the papacy in England after 1336. Equally, seizure by kings was not new; it is probable that Henry II spent part of the Saladin tithe on his wars in France in the last months of his life.[106] The opportunity to rifle crusade treasure was, if anything, greater in the early thirteenth century, when collection was less regularized and centralized, and accounting less meticulous.[107] Nicholas IV could have discovered with fair accuracy how much Edward I had confiscated of the 1274 grant; his predecessors Clement III or Innocent III would have had much less idea about the fate of the 1188, 1199, or 1215 levies. The main reason historians have pounced on sequestration as evidence of the supposed declining popularity of the crusading ideal is that it corresponds chronologically to a lack of action. But just as twelfth-century misuse does not suggest any new "decline" in crusade idealism, so the excuses and reasons given by the rulers in the fourteenth century for their failure to use the crusade money in action were as old as the movement itself, and they should be treated the same as those of earlier centuries.

Nevertheless, the charge needs to be taken seriously, for it could be argued that what has been taken in this chapter as evidence of continued interest in crusading in fact was little more than a series of disingenuous attempts to secure licitly the profits of ecclesiastical taxation. On this line of reasoning, Edward's proposal that his brother Edmund act as his substitute for the crusade during the Welsh wars of the 1280s was intended simply to unfreeze the money collected from the 1274 tithe, rather than to save the Holy Land or even to help his brother's career.[108] Similarly, Edward I's and Edward II's assumptions of the cross in 1287 and 1313, the former's 1290 pledge to depart in 1293, and Edward III's adherence to Philip VI's plans could be interpreted as tactical manoeuvres in the quest for grants from the accumulating crusade treasure stored in English monasteries and cathedrals. While it would be perverse and naive to deny the existence of an element of calculation, of financial as well as political advantage, in the crusade policies of successive English kings stretching back to Henry II, the evidence of what actually happened to the crusade money does not reveal the period between the last concerted international crusade of 1270–72 and the opening of the Hundred Years War as particularly aberrant, or English rulers of the time as any more deceitful, corrupt, insincere, or dishonest than their predecessors.

A hostile impression of events has largely been derived from the chronicle sources, written by monks, canons, and friars who were more or less united in their disapproval of what seemed to them novel and excessive taxation of the church (i.e., themselves). The English clergy were consistent in their reluctance to pay papal crusade taxes, as they voiced at Lyons in 1274 and again at the diocesan assemblies in 1292. Occasionally kings could exploit this reluctance; in 1274 Edward I posed as the protector of the native church against papal despoliation. However, the church was suspicious of royal motives, and the clergy were alert to the dangers of royal no less than papal misuse of taxes.[109] Furthermore, despite individual and collective grumblings at Roman greed and the valuations on which the taxes were based, the English church was not protestant. Once a tax had been imposed, many diocesans saw it as their duty to abide by the provisions of the papal grant and, therefore, to oppose unauthorised lay appropriation.[110] More often than not the king and the pope cooperated, to their own advantage rather than that of the English church. In practice this meant dividing the spoils of taxation between them, to the anger of the local church. In consequence, the king stood to receive as bad a press as the pope. But none of this is evidence that either king or pope intended any diversion when the tax was first granted. Only in the hindsight of contemporaries like Murimuth or of modern historians was a new crusade in this period impossible, and therefore the raising of money for it inherently duplicitous.

From the middle of the thirteenth century income from ecclesiastical crusade taxes had been offered with increasing frequency to monarchs who took the cross, but only on certain conditions. The 1274 grant to Edward I was dependent on his assumption of the cross and the near-completion of his preparations for departure; that of 1291, on Edward embarking in 1293; and the assignments of 1312 and 1333, on the crusade actually taking place. On each occasion secular crises interposed, but the ultimate intended destination of the grants—secular rulers and crusaders—was never in doubt. Faced with mounting costs of secular war and government, growing crusade deposits, and diminishing prospects for a crusade, the English kings were obviously tempted by arbitrary confiscation; yet that is precisely what did not happen.

The process of transferring crusade funds from the control of the ecclesiastical collectors to the king was elaborate, legalistic, even, on occasion, forceful, but never covert.[111] The brusque seizure of March 1283 was short-lived, a temporary measure to tide Edward over an expensive campaign season in Wales; by the end of November the money (40,000 pounds) had been restored to the church's depositories.[112] The Welsh emergency over, Edward reopened crusade negotiations with the papacy. These dragged on for many years, but in the end Edward did fulfil one of the stipulations of 1274 by taking the cross in 1287. The delay in finalizing terms was caused more by the deaths of Martin IV (1285) and Honorius IV (1287) than by any prevarication on Edward's part. Meanwhile, in 1285 and 1286, with the approval of the papal tax collector in England, the king was allowed access to over £18,500 of crusade money on sureties from a consortium of Italian bankers, the Hospitallers, and fourteen monasteries.[113] This use of crusade funds as a general source of credit became something of a habit. In 1293 ten thousand pounds was loaned to the king's brother, Edmund Crouchback, from the yield of the 1291 tithe, and Bishop Antony Bek borrowed at least five thousand pounds from the same source.[114] In 1291, however, Nicholas IV granted Edward one hundred thousand marks outright from the 1274 tithe, probably over half the total yield, and instituted another sexennial tithe to be paid to Edward on his departure. In 1294, the deadline having passed, the pressure of war once again prompted the king to seize the tithe money already collected, some thirty-three thousand pounds of it. This met with considerable resistance from local clergy. Edward also extracted money from other clerical sources, but it was soon restored. In the event the 1291 tithe was collected for four years, not six years as planned, and long negotiations culminated in a settlement in 1301, whereby the king kept what he had taken in 1294 as well as being quit of the loan for Edmund Crouchback. Boniface VIII, normally belligerent but now facing a growing crisis in his dealings with France, needed Edward as an ally and so refrained from pushing the sequestration issue to confrontation. As in 1291, Edward in the end received more than half the tithe proceeds.[115]

By 1300 it seems that the papacy had become reconciled to secular rulers expropriating clerical taxes provided they obtained papal approval. Boniface VIII himself connived in this development. In 1301 part of a triennial tenth was assigned to Edward unconditionally. A series of tithes granted by Clement V between 1305 and 1309 were ostensibly for "the needs of the Holy Land," but from the start the king of England and his near relatives were the stated beneficiaries, to the Crown's ultimate profit of one hundred thousand pounds.[116] John XXII extended this policy by providing Edward II with tithes to help pay his debts (1317), his expenses in the Scottish wars (1319), and the defence of the realm (1319 and 1322), by which time John was freely using clerical taxation to support his allies or buy favours from potential foes.[117] The policy obviously suited Edward I and Edward II, but it had been inspired by the papacy and, despite the rhetoric, had only a tangential relevance to the crusade. It is significant that the Hospitaller crusade of 1308 was planned to be funded not by clerical taxation but by the sale of indulgences, and that the net proceeds of that sale were paid over to the order.[118] In all this, royal duplicity is less than self-evident. The impression is reinforced by the fate of the sexennial crusade tithe imposed by the Council of Vienne in 1312. It had only been levied for one year when Clement V's death in 1314 suspended collection; it was cancelled by the new pope, John XXII, in 1316. On Clement's death Edward II seized the money already gathered, but secured the agreement of the English bishops. In return the king promised to indemnify them against any future papal reprisals and to allow them to reimburse themselves from any subsequent clerical subsidy. On his accession John XXII permitted Edward to retain the money as a loan, in order to pay off inherited debts and solve domestic problems, both necessary prerequisites for a crusade. Here was realism, not hypocrisy.[119]

Edward II had taken a significant step when he began to use his own clergy to validate his handling of papally authorised taxes; the trend to greater institutional nationalism became a prominent feature of the later medieval English church. In 1336 Edward III followed his father's lead. The fate of the 1333 tax was similar to that of 1312; the pope who initiated it died soon afterwards, and after a couple of years his successor cancelled it, in December 1336. By then the king, pressed in Scotland and threatened by France, had ordered some of the crusade money to be paid to the Italian bankers, the Bardi, in payment of a royal debt, while other sums he took for war expenses. Again there was some clerical opposition, but the order to transfer funds to the Bardi had come from the archbishop of Canterbury himself. By the time a papal instruction arrived to the effect that, as no crusade was to take place, all the money collected should be returned to the taxpayers, the convocations of Canterbury and York had already agreed that in case of a papal revocation of the tithe, the proceeds should instead go to the king.[120] Once more, there was no disguise, even if there was misuse.

How much did the English kings benefit from this trade in church taxes? W. E. Lunt has calculated that Edward I made £66,666 from the 1274 grant and £44,000 from the 1291 tax. The Vienne tithe yielded between £17,235 and £18,500 for Edward II, a sum probably similar to the amount Edward III received in 1336.[121] These were useful additions to royal income, especially in time of war, but they did not make the difference between solvency and bankruptcy. Between 1271 and 1304 the cost of building castles in Wales was over £78,000, and M. C. Prestwich has suggested that between 1294 and 1298 alone overall military expenditure perhaps reached as much as £750,000.[122] The scale of benefit relative to the costs of war, coupled with the risks of diplomatic opprobrium and excommunication attendant on any illicit misappropriation, render it unlikely, the 1333 tax possibly excepted, that English kings adopted the misuse of crusade money as a deliberate policy from the moment each new tax was proposed. The kings could not have concealed their peculation even if they had wanted to, as the accounts of what was raised were kept meticulously by papal agents.[123] In fact, there is little sign that kings even attempted to conceal their use of crusade money. It was the papacy that diverted the taxes to secular national affairs, with no provision for recouping the money for the crusade.

There is a final point. It is impossible to know what would have happened if and when a general passagium had actually occurred; would the king have acknowledged his financial obligation? Possibly not, but the situation never arose, not because the crusade's funds were stolen, but because the political problems that confronted the first three Edwards relegated the crusade to a less immediate concern and consequently provided the circumstances in which crusade funds were liable to be plundered. Money was needed for war; if that war had been in the Levant, it is likely that, as in 1270, money would have been found. The history of misappropriated crusade funds follows the contours of the domestic politics of this period, not vice versa.

The years between 1272 and 1337 demonstrate that the major weakness in the West's response to the challenge of rescuing the Holy Land was not emotional or financial but administrative. The whole process of agreeing papal grants, launching preaching campaigns, collecting taxes and obventions, raising troops, and establishing political security at home was infinitely cumbersome and liable to prolonged delay. For example, John XXII's crusade bulls of July 1333 authorising taxation, indulgences, and collection of obventions for an expedition to embark in 1336 were only published by the archbishop of Canterbury in May 1335 and were only received by his suffragans between June and September. In the northern province collecting chests were only commissioned in May 1336, and the chapter at York only received copies of the 1333 bulls the following December. This was hardly rapid, even allowing for the intervening change of pope.[124] It was a pattern familiar elsewhere in Europe, and indeed, even optimistic theorists of the time assumed a delay of several years between the call to arms and the departure. The remorselessly slow timetables of 1290, 1312, and 1333 by themselves invited failure.

10

Crusades in "Hethenesse"

1337–1410

POPULARITY AND CRITICISM

In the late 1380s the veteran knight Sir Maurice de Bruyn listed the familiar battlegrounds of his lifetime: Scotland, France, Gascony, Brittany, Normandy, Spain, "beyond the Great Sea" (i.e., the Mediterranean), and Prussia. The last three involved crusading. Sir Maurice's inclusion of them in evidence he presented to the Court of Chivalry was no more than an accurate description of where Englishmen fought and died in the fourteenth century. During the very case in which he was a witness, that between Richard le Scrope and Sir Robert Grosvenor over the right to bear the traditional Scrope arms (*azur a bend or*), at least fourteen individual crusaders either testified or were mentioned, their exploits of the previous twenty-five years stretching from Egypt to Lithuania.[1] Crusading in fourteenth-century England was as habitual as it had been in the thirteenth; an indenture between John of Gaunt and John Neville of Raby in 1370 included the special terms under which Neville, if the occasion arose, would serve Gaunt against "les enemys Dieux."[2] Motives were traditional too: strategic—the Holy Land remained in Moslem hands, and by the 1360s the threat of the Ottomans to eastern Europe was apparent to all; religious—the "saving of the soul" and the "aid of the faithful" against the Turks, mentioned in the royal and papal licences for John de la Ryvere's journey towards the Holy Land in 1346; and secular.[3] When the Black Prince asked the Lord d'Albret for two hundred lances for his Spanish campaign of 1366–67, instead of the one thousand originally agreed upon, d'Albret was furious, as this meant that eight hundred knights and squires had needlessly been prevented from earning profit and honour elsewhere. Some of them had been wishing to pass the sea to Jerusalem, Constantinople, or Prussia, "as every knight and squire who wishes to advance himself does."[4]

In fact, with the notorious exception of the sack of Alexandria in 1365, there was little material profit to be gained from crusading; but as a result there was commensurately greater honour to be won, as witnessed in the deeds of Chaucer's imaginary knight in the *Canterbury Tales* or those of Chaucer's own patrons and audience at the very real court of Richard II.[5] The obituary of young Sir John Paveley in the *Westminster Chronicle* particularly noted that he had distinguished himself by his conduct in pagan lands.[6] Of course, honour and reputation could bring tangible rewards, perhaps even an earldom, as in the case of John Beaufort in 1397 or, if the poets Gower, Chaucer, and Guillaume de Machaut are to be believed, a lady's love.[7]

The appeal of crusading was not limited to rich knights. The Picard crusader and propagandist Philippe de Mézières, a veteran of the Smyrna and Alexandria campaigns (1344 and 1363), envisaged a new crusading order, the Order of the Passion, comprising three divisions: kings and princes; common people (i.e., infantry); and an intermediate group composed of "knights, squires, barons, nobles, *bourgeois* [i.e., townspeople], merchants, and men of honour of middling rank ['gens d'onneur de moien estat']."[8] The great were accompanied on crusade by large retinues, some travelling in style, like Henry Bolingbroke on his trip to fight the Lithuanians.[9] The less exalted also displayed interest in crusading; in 1347 John of Bron, a tanner from Beverley, left the residue of his estate to provide for one man to accompany the next passagium to the Holy Land, perhaps in fulfilment of a crusade vow. Whilst the crusade legacy of Sir Roger de Beauchamp of Bletsoe in 1379 was worth two hundred marks, thirty years earlier Agnes le Horir, the widow of a Southampton burgess, left just three pence for the Holy Land.[10] This wide social embrace is confirmed by the accounts of papal collectors in England between 1317 and 1378. They show a continuing trickle of Holy Land legacies and a few vow redemptions, although numbers and amounts declined towards the end of the period. A high proportion of obventions came from clerics, bishops, rectors, vicars, canons, archdeacons, and cathedral officials of varying financial standing. Among lay donors were knights of substantial means, such as John de Beauchamp who redeemed a vow for £23 7s 6d, but also those of humbler means, like the poor woman from the diocese of Winchester who gave four pence. Geographically as well as socially the spread of testators was wide, from the north of England to London to the west country.[11]

Devotion to the Holy Land remained part of the mentality of the period. A number of fourteenth-century gilds—pious, charitable, and commercial—provided special funds for pilgrims, especially those bound for Jerusalem, and prayed regularly for the patriarch of Jerusalem. Two such gilds were founded in Norfolk in 1384, the Fraternities of St. Christopher in Norwich and of the Assumption of the Blessed Virgin Mary at Wiggenhall on the Ouse. Each began meetings with prayers for the recovery of the Holy Land: at St. Christopher's at Norwich, "for ye holy londe and ye holy crosse, yat Godd for his myght and his mercy bryng it oute of hethen power into reule of holy chirche"; and at Wiggenhall, "also we shal be-seke for ye holy lond yat Jhesu crist, for is mekul mercy, brynge it in to criste powere."[12]

Higher up the social scale the households of the nobility were decorated with tapestries illustrating crusade legends. The bellicose fourth son of Edward III, Thomas of Woodstock, earl of Gloucester, whose own crusade to Prussia was frustrated by bad weather, and his wife, Eleanor, herself the daughter of a crusader of the 1360s, Humphrey de Bohun, earl of Hereford, possessed copies of the romances of Godfrey de Bouillon, and their country residence, Pleshey Castle, contained fifteen tapestries on the same subject.[13] Relics of crusading were still cherished. In 1376 Mary, countess of Pembroke, left to Westminster Abbey "a cross with a foot of gold and emeralds" which her long-dead father-in-law, William of Valence (d. 1296) had brought back from the Holy Land in 1273. It is possible that the mail coat with an attached brass cross that Eleanor of Gloucester left to her son in 1399 had been made for her husband's, or possibly even her father's, crusade.[14]

On the other hand there were, as always, critics, mainly of the practice rather than the ideal. Concerned with politics and religion, the crusade was bound to be controversial as long as it remained a live issue. Common targets of criticism were crusades against Christians and misdemeanours of knights, either because they fought for the wrong reasons or because they failed to fight at all. To the moralists of the age, crusading presented opportunities for vainglory as well as for spiritual regeneration.[15] Public opinion is hard to gauge, even with the elaborate techniques of the late twentieth century, and any assessment of fourteenth-century attitudes can only veer between the partial, the anecdotal, and the impressionist. Especially in the later fourteenth century, the absence of frequent papal offers of crusade indulgences makes it impossible to use surviving collectors' accounts to assess precise levels of popularity. Although individuals demonstrated the persistent popularity of the ideal, there were points of unease. The Hundred Years War highlighted the ugly and grasping, as well as the glamorous, aspects of the warrior code. Some observers, like the Frenchman Honoré Bonet (fl. 1368–1405), saw national discipline as the solution to unchecked violence; others, like Pope Urban V (1362–70), Gregory XI (1370–78), or Philippe de Mézières, still looked to the crusade. Few vocally dismissed the entire concept of the crusade. However, the pacificism and the abhorrence at slaying infidels expressed in John Gower's *Confessio Amantis* (c. 1390), although to be seen in a literary context rather than at face value, suggests that arguments over the legitimacy of violence were in circulation. Some of the Italian crusades, Despenser's expedition in particular, as well as the clergy's love of war in general, drew sharp criticism from a variety of observers—from the heretical divine John Wyclif to the radical but orthodox poet William Langland. Not all accepted the papal view of the theoretical, rather than political, justification for crusades against Christians. Even the conservative and orthodox Thomas Walsingham turned against the wars of the Teutonic Knights, once the Lithuanians became Christian.[16] Against this, Despenser's crusade against the Flemish in 1383 attracted large numbers of recruits and was only widely criticised in hindsight. Few, however, could have been under many illusions at the combination of national war, crusade indulgence, and pay; when the trick was repeated in 1386 it failed.

E. Siberry has argued that even the well-known Lollard attacks on the crusading ethic were limited. While William Swinderby and a few others, such as the authors of the twelve propositions displayed at Westminster in 1395, were outright pacifists, Wyclif himself was concentrating his fire on Despenser's crusade, not the movement in general. Furthermore, some Lollard knights—John Montagu, John Clanvow, William Neville, and Lewis Clifford—actively volunteered for crusades. However, to observe that some Lollards were not pacifists and that Wyclif nowhere explicitly condemned fighting the infidel misses the fundamental force of the Lollards' attack on the foundations of crusading, implicit in their views on the papacy, the church, and salvation. As a religious exercise the crusade depended on acceptance of a doctrine of remission of sin mediated through indulgences prescribed by the church and authorised by the pope; without the indulgence the crusade as such could not exist, as it would become a war like any other, just or not. The Lollards rejected the authority of the church, dismissed the papacy as a corruption of the Devil, and specifically denied the church's power to grant indulgences; that denial was inevitable in a system of thought infused with the theory of predestination.[17] Thus all crusade indulgences were per se invalid.

What then of the Lollard knights, whose interest in fighting in the East has been taken to indicate a lack of fundamental opposition to crusading? Lollardy, though not an instantly cohesive doctrine and containing latitude of belief amongst sympathisers, was coherently admin-

262

istered, through the organisation of preaching and the dissemination of the main Lollard texts. If Lollards at all, these knights would have been in touch with the orthodoxies of the sect. However, even within Lollard belief, such knights could have disowned indulgences and the precepts of the church, whilst still condoning the traditional, honourable, and even Wycliffite acceptance of fighting for the love of God, which was not a product of the corrupt church but was supported by reference to patristic texts of which the heresiarch approved.[18] Furthermore, Lollardy, until Sir John Oldcastle's revolt of 1414, was not necessarily incompatible with existing social mores, provided that spiritual attitudes were purified.

The precise balance of motives behind active support for crusading, collective or individual, is impossible to reconstruct with precision. Froissart argued that the crusade plans of the 1330s were especially popular among warlike knights, who at the time had nothing better to do.[19] The appeal of a good fight, in all senses, is apparent in the fourteenth century, when warriors, mercenaries, and others hardened by the campaigns in France and elsewhere were available in abundance and often eager to employ their skills. This violent and opportunist quality can be illustrated in the career of John Holland, earl of Huntingdon, half-brother to Richard II. Holland was a proven murderer who redeemed his reputation as a vigorous captain on Gaunt's crusade to Spain in 1386. An intimate of his brother the king, he went to Hungary in 1394 to negotiate with King Sigismund for possible Anglo-French assistance against the Ottomans; he himself was prepared to join any immediate action against the infidel. According to Richard II in January 1394, he travelled "for military honour and in the zeal of faith," armed with papal indulgences, his destination Hungary and Jerusalem.[20] On this occasion Holland's restlessness went unsatisfied. In 1395, he was given an abridged version of Philippe de Mézières's scheme for a new crusading order. As Holland soon became a patron of this order, his concern with the crusade was certainly more than casual; it appealed to his spirit of adventure, as well as to his sense of Christian duty and knightly responsibility.[21] The enthusiastic crusader and warrior was not exclusive in his choice of campaign; in 1397 he again essayed a crusade, this time in answer to a papal appeal for a campaign in Italy against the new Avignon pope, Benedict XIII. Holland and his followers were to receive full Holy Land crusade indulgences, and a crusade tax was announced, modelled on the tithe ordered at the Council of Vienne. In his Italian enterprise Holland was following the precedent of Henry of Beaumont and Bishop Despenser of Norwich, who had fought in the Italian papal crusades of John XXIII and Urban V; Walsingham equated

263

this scheme with the papal crusades of Despenser and Gaunt.[22] Although instructions to implement the 1397 plan were sent to England, nothing came of it, the earl being spared to pursue the vicious politiking of the last years of Richard II and to end his own career at the hands of an executioner in 1400. A magnate of ambition, proximate to power, energetic, and violent, who three times flirted with the idea of a crusade, Holland is perhaps more typical of fourteenth-century English crusaders than is Chaucer's Knight. From Holland's case it is easy to believe that the holy war satisfied baser as well as nobler human instincts; therein lay part of its tenacity.

Yet beside the restless and ruthless earl of Huntingdon in the entourage of Richard II were a number of crusaders of very different stamp. It is a commonplace that particular spiritual attitudes are revealed in certain religious exercises, the eager patrons of monasteries in the twelfth century, the serious-minded pious layman of the fourteenth and fifteenth founding chantries, or the godly of the sixteenth establishing schools or lectureships. In general terms, crusading conformed to a pattern of doing the right thing for the community in the cause of personal salvation. As a military expression of this spiritual function, the crusade from its inception appealed to military men or those who aspired to belong to that increasingly separate elite of knights who could afford to fight. Some crusaders were, no doubt, unthinking or secular-minded, accepting their pay and food, if they could get it, and pleased with the social cachet of being a holy warrior; but there was another side.

Sir John Clanvow, with his friend and fellow Lollard William Neville, wished to join the Tunis crusade in 1390 and he died in 1391 near Constantinople. He was a courtier and a soldier whose spiritual life, revealed in his remarkable religious tract *The Two Ways*, was dominated by a sense of his own unworthiness, the sinful nature of the world, and the difficulty of attaining eternal life. In particular Clanvow castigated the warrior class and the worldly respect earned by men who "destroyen and winned many lands and wasten and given much good to them that have enough and that dispenden outrageously ... and living in ease, sloth and many other sins." He noted, too, that those who lived in patient, unworldly simplicity were abused as "lollers and losels, fools and shameful wretches." However, Clanvow pointed out, "the world scorned Christ and held him a fool ... and therefore follow we his traces and suffer we patiently the scornes of the world as he did." The treatise is significant precisely because the ideas expressed in it are, for a Lollard, unexceptional.[23] The acute sense of the degradation of the soul by the weakness and wickedness of the flesh was shared by Lewis Clifford, another Lollard knight and a member of Mézières's Order of the Passion, whose will spoke of his corpse as "stinking carrion" and himself as "unworthy" and "God's traitor."[24] For such men the crusade could offer relief, if not release, in subjecting the body to the will of God in, to use a phrase common to Clanvow and countless crusade preachers, following the footsteps of Christ; on this journey the spiritual and the physical could in theory meet without disgust. Only thus could Clifford espouse the cause of the recovery of Jerusalem, within the Order of the Passion, which gave no emphasis in its statutes to unacceptable (for Clifford) indulgences. Nevertheless, the inherent tension between crusading and Lollard doctrine remained. Clanvow, Clifford, and the rest may have been able to rationalise their acts in terms of fighting God's war, regardless of the company they kept or the corrupt trappings of the enterprise. Alternatively they were simply unable or unwilling to reconcile their spiritual and social lives. Their crusading does not mean they were not Lollards, any more than their Lollardy implies Wycliffite approval of the institution of the crusade; but their actions, although typical of their knightly class, nonetheless grate against their apparent beliefs. It was not only heretics who shared similar contradictions. The same sense of physical distaste, expressed rather more equivocally, permeates another, nonheretical crusader's religious tract, the *Livre de Seyntz Medicines*, a meditation on the state of his soul by Henry of Grosmont, earl of Lancaster and father-in-law of Chaucer's patron John of Gaunt. Such personal documents, composed by laymen, give for the first time a direct glimpse of the thoughts of those who fought for the cross, freed from the interpretation of churchmen. They reveal that holy warfare could be a religious exercise for serious, pious, even puritanical men, through which the unquiet soul as well as the restless body sought comfort.[25]

There was nothing intrinsically new in such complexity of motive. However, the period from the outbreak of the Hundred Years War to the defeat of the Teutonic Knights at the battle of Tannenberg in 1410 displays certain other new and distinct characteristics. The localisation of crusading persisted, with crusades within or on the fringes of Europe led by local rulers with or without international assistance: Alfonso XI of Castille at Algeciras (1343); the king of Cyprus at Satalia (1361) and Alexandria (1365); papal crusades in Italy; local wars in the Balkans; and the Teutonic Knights' everlasting war against the Slavs in the Baltic. Lack of regular opportunities in the eastern Mediterranean led English crusaders to seek fulfilment elsewhere, primarily in the Baltic, even though there was little left to conquer in the region that the Teutonic Knights could reasonably expect to hold. The Baltic episode came to an end only after the defeat of the German order at Tannenberg by the newly Christian Polish-Lithuanian kingdom. After 1410 practical outlets for active crusading were extremely rare, while the alternative fields for honour, glory, preferment, and profit were reopened by Henry V in France. Earlier the Hundred Years War had exerted a profound influence on the timing of the crusades through a tightening of royal control, chiefly through wartime prohibitions on the export of money and war materials and the refusal to grant licences to departing crusaders.[26] Such measures effectively reduced crusading to periods of truce in the Anglo-French war, notably after the pauses in hostilities in 1360 and 1389.

With war liable to recur at any time, crusaders took to campaigns of one season only, winter or summer, lasting months rather than the years an expedition to the Levant could occupy. Fighting in the Baltic, Italy, or Spain was less expensive and, with the famously generous hospitality of the Teutonic Knights or a grateful Spanish king, possibly more congenial. It would be wrong, however, to separate too clearly the various crusading goals; although the Holy Land retained its primacy of respect and ambition, contemporaries looked on all expeditions against the infidel as equivalent in some informal fashion. The list of Chaucer's knight's campaigns "in hethenesse" included Algeciras, Alexandria, Satalia, Russia, Prussia, and Granada, in no particular order of merit or distinction. This catholic approach reflected life. Henry of Grosmont fought the Moors of Spain and the Slavs of the Baltic. His grandson Henry Bolingbroke planned to join a French crusade to Tunis in 1390 but, baulked of that, immediately found his way to Prussia, and in 1392, being unable to fight in Prussia, he went to the Holy Land as a pilgrim. Bolingbroke's half-brother, John Beaufort, actually reached Tunis; he fought in Prussia and possibly also against the Turks in eastern Europe. The less-exalted William Scrope of Bolton saw service in both the Mediterranean and the Baltic in the 1360s, as did the Suffolk knight Richard Waldegrave. Many other English nobles and gentlemen also had experience of both northern and eastern crusades.[27] To John Capgrave, writing in the 1440s, all battlefields on Christendom's frontiers with the pagans, Turks, and Saracens were of equal merit for, whether in Prussia, the East, or Granada, the enemy all held Christ and his cross in contempt; this view mirrored the reality of three-quarters of a century earlier. In 1365, when Pope Urban V heard that Thomas Beauchamp, earl of Warwick, had taken the cross, he congratulated him on his devotion, whether he was going to the Holy Land or to Prussia.[28]

PRUSSIA

Crusading in the Baltic was first authorised by Bernard of Clairvaux in 1147 in the context of the Second Crusade. Over the following two centuries the political and territorial expansionism of Germans, Danes, and Swedes, in Prussia, Finland, Livonia, Estonia, Lithuania, and Russia, received the blessing of the Roman Church. By the fourteenth century, with the exception of the Swedish interest in Finland and Russia, the conduct of warfare against the remaining non-Christian Baltic power of Lithuania had devolved onto the order of the Teutonic Knights, despite unsuccessful attempts by the papacy to exert greater direct control. Originally based in the Holy Land, the order had since 1229 become dominant in the conquest and suppression of the pagans of Prussia, Livonia, and Estonia. After the loss of their Palestinian bases in 1291, the Knights, like the Templars and Hospitallers, drifted somewhat aimlessly until, in 1309, in reaction to the fate of the Templars, and at the same time as the Hospitallers were securing their own future in Rhodes, the order moved its headquarters from Venice to Marienburg in Prussia. Thereafter all their energies and resources were concentrated in the Baltic.

In the thirteenth century, open papal injunctions to fight the Baltic pagans together with the order's authority to remit sins, attracted a stream of reinforcements, primarily from Germany and central Europe.[29] English participation was minimal. There were a few individual exceptions; Robert de Morley died, perhaps on crusade in Prussia in 1288, and Bishop Thomas, an Englishman, attempted to convert part of Finland in 1230. Only commercial links between England and Scandinavia expanded in the thirteenth century.[30] Fourteenth-century contacts were more than economic. The incentive to fight in the Baltic in the fourteenth century was partly determined by external factors: the loss of the Holy Land, the war with France, or even perhaps the outbreaks of plague in 1348–49. Campaigning in Prussia was a unique chivalric experience, because the Teutonic Knights had developed a knightly package tour, complete with feasting, hunting, military action, and even a system of prizes to appeal to the most restless and vainglorious noblemen. This service was possible only because the war with the Lithuanians had reached stalemate. Campaigns were conducted, often in winter, when the rivers and marshes were frozen and passable on horseback, across increasingly familiar terrain—a devastated no-man's-land known as the Wilderness, that offered little prospect of decisive battles but many opportunities for tactical raids known as reysas. Foreign knights arrived in the Baltic, campaigned, and were feasted and fêted before returning home with honour, reputation, and spiritual reward, all in a matter of weeks. It may not have been as impressive as a passagium to the Holy Land, but it compared well with alternative military enterprises.

From 1329 English knights were to be found on summer or winter reysas at regular intervals for the rest of the century. The periods of greatest activity followed the truces and peaces of the Hundred Years War, notably in the years 1347–52, 1362–68, and 1390–98.[31] In particular, the years 1362–68 witnessed an almost annual exodus of knights and their retinues to Prussia. The Patent Rolls recorded a climax of activity between November 1367 and February 1368, when royal licences to depart were granted to fourteen individuals and their followers, a total of ninety-seven men, ranging from the three sons of the earl of Warwick, who travelled with nine esquires, twenty yeomen, thirty horses, and one thousand marks for expenses, to William Dalleson, esquire, accompanied by a solitary yeoman, two hacks, and thirty marks.[32] For some the expedition to Prussia became a habit. Thomas Ufford, son of Robert, earl of Suffolk, fought with the Teutonic Knights in 1348, 1362, 1365, and possibly 1352. Sir Thomas Boynton first campaigned in Prussia as a teenager in 1362 and returned in the winter of 1367–68; at the same time Hugh Despenser received his first licence to go to the Baltic, which was repeated in 1383.[33]

The traceable crusaders of the 1360s came from all parts of gentle society and all regions of England. They included the earl of Warwick in 1365 and his sons in 1367–68; the earl of Hereford in 1363; substantial provincial noblemen such as Geoffrey Scrope of Masham in Yorkshire, killed on campaign in Lithuania in 1362; his companion in arms, Richard Waldegrave of Bures in Suffolk, who travelled with the earl of Hereford to the Vistula in 1363; humbler squires such as Dalleson in 1367 and Geoffrey Scrope's own squire, John Ryther; and the yeomen and other members of the retinues of the great.[34] Crusading in the Baltic, as elsewhere, ran in families. M. H. Keen has demonstrated the lively and persistent interest in crusading of a number of noble families, including the Beauchamps, Uffords, Bohuns, Percies, Despensers, FitzWalters, Beaumonts, Scropes, Courtenays, and Montagues. To the Baltic went not only Thomas Beauchamp, earl of Warwick, and his three sons but also, probably in the first decade of the fifteenth century, his grandson Richard. Three Courtenay brothers journeyed to Prussia together in 1368. Henry Percy, the famous Hotspur, was in the Baltic in 1383, and his uncle was there nine years later. Extended family ties were evident and probably influenced recruitment; in the second half of the fourteenth century the Beauchamps, Uffords, Cliffords, and Ferrers of Groby, all closely interrelated by marriage, all produced Baltic crusaders (in the Ferrers' case the representative was illegitimate).[35]

Problems of recruitment and finance also influenced how such expeditions came to be organised. The first wave of popularity, roughly between 1347 and 1368, displayed signs of private enterprise, which the public wars of Edward I and Edward II had made look somewhat old-fashioned and inefficient. Groups of crusaders did not necessarily form or coalesce into one retinue, although inevitably great men such as Henry of Grosmont in 1351–52, the earl of Warwick in 1365, or his sons two years later, had considerable personal followings.[36] By contrast, in 1362 with the illfated Geoffrey Scrope were a number of other knights of independent means and standing who, a quarter of a century later, bore witness to those distant events on the bleak Lithuanian frontier. Their evidence does not indicate whether the knights had planned their conjunction or had acted in concert only for immediate convenience.[37] A clearer pattern of association can be identified in January 1363 when a group of four knights joined with Humphrey de Bohun, earl of Hereford, in raising 2,600 *écus* (c. £470) from merchants at Thorn on the Vistula. One of the knights, Richard Waldegrave, had been in the earl's company two years earlier at the capture of Satalia in southern Turkey by the king of Cyprus, and another, Miles de Stapleton, also appears to have been with the earl in the eastern Mediterranean. Yet these knights appear as the earl's equals in agreeing to the terms of the loan.[38] Such an association of knights with a magnate or a magnate's son was common; in 1362 Robert Howard, a man of some material standing, travelled with Thomas Ufford. The ten royal licences granted between 8 and 28 November 1367 point in the same direction; the sons of the earl of Warwick with their substantial *équipe* and treasure provided leadership for a party of others with lesser means, who nevertheless were not retainers but paid for themselves and their smaller, autonomous retinues.[39] The problem with such informal associations was less of command, which was supplied on campaign by the master or the marshal of the Teutonic Knights, than of transport and finance.[40]

Pressures grew for Baltic crusaders to combine before they embarked from England or Calais. Politically, royal approval and licences were not always willingly granted.[41] Careful planning was an advantage when strict conditions were liable to be laid on departure. In November 1367, for instance, Richard Mauleverer had to provide surety that he would depart within a month of the licence being issued and would return by the following Midsummer, the king being especially concerned lest any French hostages should accompany him.[42] Financial problems elicited traditional remedies. Early in Edward III's reign William of Hastings (d. 1349) raised money on his manor of Speen-by-Newbury for his journey to "Frontier and Spruz"; he was absent for forty weeks before his return and resumption of his land. In 1390 another crusader bound for Lithuania borrowed twenty pounds from the chapter of Lichfield, forcing the canons to pawn a chalice to raise the cash.[43] But the Prussian expedition differed from crusading to the East in that no subsidies from taxation, redemptions, or other obventions were available. As with other crusades, some participants were unprepared for the expenses involved. When the earl of Hereford and his companions secured their loan in 1363 (probably on their return journey), they had to have new seals made before they could attest the contract.[44] Others were better equipped. In 1367 Hugh Despenser took with him letters sealed by his brother Lord Despenser, "for receiving a certain sum in parts beyond the seas," and early the following year the Courtenay brothers arranged with a Lombard banker for £130 to await them on their arrival at Calais.[45] Such tactics to some degree circumvented the ordinances prohibiting the export of bullion, but may not have guaranteed the financial viability of a campaign.

There was little material profit to be made in the Baltic. The land over which the reysas were conducted was by the mid-fourteenth century largely deserted or uncultivated, and with any conquered territory being placed under the strict control of the Teutonic Knights, crusaders had no scope for the profiteering familiar to veterans of the French wars. Victorious crusaders would be fêted, but little else. According to an eyewitness, probably a herald, of Henry Bolingbroke's reysa of 1390, all the earl received for his labours was "copious thanks."[46]

Although the renown of Prussia as a field of chivalry grew as the century progressed, such material constraints reduced its attraction for self-supporting independent gentlemen like Stapleton, Waldegrave, or FitzHenry. It was a rich man's game, and increasingly knights sought the direct protection of a great magnate rather than independent association. Crusading remained popular with nobles on the make; the future earls of Somerset (John Beaufort), Salisbury (John Montagu), and Worcester (Thomas Percy), all of whose titles were new creations of Richard II, saw service in the Baltic in the 1390s, as Richard's new earl of Wiltshire, William Scrope, had in the 1360s. However, expeditions in the 1390s appear to have been fewer, larger, and dominated more by barons than by knights. Knights did not stop going to Prussia, but they went in someone else's retinue.

According to the Patent Rolls, the fifty-strong retinue of Thomas, Lord Despenser, in 1391 was considerably larger than any of those of the 1360s. His colleagues on campaign were peers—the Lords Clifford, FitzWalter, Beaumont, and Bourgchier—who may be expected to have had entourages of similar size.[47] Greater centralisation may have disguised greater popularity, more individuals going to Prussia but in larger single groups. The most famous example perhaps was the expedition of Bolingbroke in 1390, but his retinue, although larger than anything seen in the 1360s, was much smaller than contemporary estimates of three hundred. The earl's own accounts put at seventy-one the total of retained knights, esquires, other soldiers, and domestic staff, including minstrels, paid during the weeks of the actual reysa. Retinues of the knights themselves may have added to this number; some knights used their own pay to provide archers. A herald estimated Bolingbroke's warband at fifty lances and sixty bowmen, probably including the Frenchmen who had joined the expedition as well as those engaged locally.[48] Among Bolingbroke's knights were retainers who later provided administrative support for the successful establishment of the usurping Lancastrian dynasty; Hugh Waterton, John Norbury, and Thomas Erpingham all became royal councillors. They were the heirs of the knightly companions of Geoffrey Scrope or the earl of Hereford, but now serving a greater lord for pay. There was nothing new in crusaders accepting wages, but the two shillings a day received by Erpingham and his colleagues may illustrate a disadvantageous shift in the material equation that lay behind any individual decision to go on crusade. One of Bolingbroke's knights, by contrast, did maintain a more independent position; John Loudeham was loaned fifty pounds for the campaign. Unfortunately his fate, like his independence, recall the days of Geoffrey Scrope; Loudeham was killed on the reysa to Vilna aged twenty-five (Scrope had been about twenty-two), and his body was brought back to Konigsberg for burial in the Marienkirche, which by 1390 had become a mausoleum and a monument to the international appeal of the Baltic crusade.[49]

There were cracks in the glamorous image. The flow of Englishmen joining the reysas dried up in the late 1390s, and after Tannenberg (1410) it vanished altogether, as a result of political unrest in England, renewed tension with France, and the ebbing of international support for the Teutonic Knights since the Lithuanians began to convert to Christianity after 1386. The report of Bolingbroke's campaign of 1390, which reached England and was copied by historians at Westminster and St. Alban's, still referred with pride to the conversion of captured Lithuanians. But the fiction could not last and a reaction against the order soon set in, culminating in its battle for survival at the Council of Constance (1414–18).[50] After 1423 even German crusaders abandoned the enterprise, as the order subsided into the role of local tyrant. Even before Tannenberg and Constance, the wider disputes of the Great Schism had interfered with the smooth operation of the knights' campaigns. Religious divisions followed political and led to incidents such as the 1391 affray between the Scottish William Douglas and the English Lord Clifford in which Douglas and two other Scotsmen perished. International cooperation was still possible, as the French recruits in Bolingbroke's 1390 army showed, but it only needed an incident such as Douglas's being refused the sacrament, or an outbreak of the long-standing dispute between English crusaders and the Teutonic Knights over the right to bear the banner of St. George, to disrupt the reysas.[51]

Wounded pride was inescapable in a society where the chivalric code of honour, loyalty, and prowess was elevated almost to a spiritual dimension. Indeed, the author of one of the most influential syntheses of this period, Jan Huizinga, two generations ago dismissed the whole Baltic episode on precisely such grounds: warfare was distorted by romantic chivalrous notions, and the crusaders engaged in it "lighthearted-edly," as it was merely "a question of going to kill a handful of heathen peasants."[52] The end of the Baltic crusade, therefore, prompts questions on its nature and its appeal to the English. Was Huizinga's contempt justified? Alternatively, was Lucy Toulmin-Smith, the editor of Boling-broke's accounts, correct about his or any other Baltic campaign when she wrote: "It is hardly to be called a crusade; it was a military expedition in aid of a friendly power brought about by political necessities"?[53]

Materially, as has been suggested, it is difficult to see where Baltic crusaders could have expected to reap the normal rewards of war. Even ransoms may have been denied them. In 1390 the marshal of the Teutonic Order seems to have taken all the Lithuanian prisoners into the order's control, while leaving Bolingbroke to try all by himself to ransom men from his own contingent captured by the enemy.[54] Expenses were consistently high; in 1390–91 Bolingbroke spent £4,438 8s 3 1/2d, and the order did little to lessen his financial burden. The earl, it must be said, lived luxuriously, having the richest man in England, his father John of Gaunt, to pay most of the bill. It was only the order which gained from such recruits, especially if they behaved like Bolingbroke, who indulged in lavish display far overshadowing overtly spiritual gestures: £69 went in gambling expenses in 1390–91 compared to only £12 in alms.[55] There was another side, equally devoid of material profit; in 1349 a group of English knights proposed to build a castle and chapel in the Wilderness between Lithuania and Prussia, as a refuge for Christians escaping the pagans and as a centre for converts.[56]

Not all parts of the Baltic were as remote and unfriendly as the devastated frontier in Samogitia. Close links between England and Scandinavia existed long before the advent of English crusaders in the region and survived after their deeds had become distant memories. Paradoxically, throughout the period of greatest English participation in the crusades, commercial relations were strained. English merchants attempted to infiltrate the Baltic in the face of the jealous protectionism of the Hanseatic League and the Teutonic Knights, English seamen regularly molesting Hanse fishing fleets in the North Sea. It was more than a question of trade in fish, furs, and wood. In 1373 a York bowyer, John Swerd, received royal approval for a scheme to establish a bowmaking factory in Prussia, and a year later Walter Brown of Norwich was given permission to ship fourteen tuns of Spanish wine from Yarmouth to Prussia that because of "its weakness and age . . . may not advantageously be sold in England."[57] The dumping of vinegar on the Prussian market, however, was not the most serious issue at stake. By 1390 English merchants had settled in Danzig and Konigsberg; many English sailors no doubt shared with Chaucer's Shipman a knowledge of the harbours of Gotland; and at least one noble, Lord Bourgchier, owned a house in Danzig.[58] As the century drew to a close, relations deteriorated, with repeated Prussian demands for compensation for damages to their shipping inflicted by the English. Treaties attempting to resolve outstanding disputes were agreed in 1388 and 1409, when two instalments of damages were paid by the English exchequer amounting to £3,555 13s 4d.[59]

Superficially, the crusade had no connection with this trade war. Despite the commercial conflicts, kings and nobles apparently maintained good relations with the Teutonic Knights; Henry IV, in the midst of combative trade negotiations, repeatedly expressed his personal devotion to the order.[60] Nevertheless, it was difficult for crusaders not to become concerned with local disputes, as Bolingbroke himself did in a case implicating some English herring traders in 1391. Such involvement, however, conflicted with the policy of the Knights to exclude new principalities, foreign staples, or privileged trading stations from the order's sphere of influence. The less visiting nobles interfered with local affairs and commerce, the better.[61]

As the order was dependent on international favour for grants of land and money, and for regular reinforcements, this was a delicate policy to pursue. The presence of great English princes of the blood with large retinues and fat treasuries may have made the order nervous. In 1352 and 1392 the two Henries of Lancaster, grandfather and grandson, saw no action in spite of their lavish preparations. This may have been deliberate on the order's part. Even if campaigning was on both occasions inconvenient, the Knights had been known to arrange short expeditions more or less on demand to satisfy other foreign customers.[62] The failure to do the same in 1352 and 1392 suggests a reluctance to allow these visitors a chance to stay for any length of time in Prussia.

Occasionally the diplomatic, and by extension commercial, implications of crusading were explicit. When the duke of Gloucester embarked for Prussia in September 1391 he was empowered to negotiate "on certain matters" with the grand master of the Teutonic Knights on behalf of Richard II. The business was almost certainly the failure of the 1388 treaty. In the event Gloucester got no further than Scotland because of atrocious weather in the North Sea. With his diplomatic credentials Gloucester carried jewels and cloth; the former perhaps as insurance against escalating costs, or as a douceur for the grand master, but the latter could have been for trade.[63] The French war had disturbed Anglo-French and Anglo-Flemish trade, provoking a search for new markets in a manner not dissimilar to its effect on the opportunities for crusading—the Baltic was a new area of enterprise for merchants and knights alike.

But knights were not merchants, and it would be misleading to portray the Baltic crusade as an essay in economic imperialism. Rather it displayed the characteristic contrasts of its age. On the one hand were the glitter of chivalric adventure, the trappings of noble living, the fighting, the feasting, the exotic hunting, the extravagant presents, and the good living spiced with danger. On the other hand were knights slogging through the frozen or boggy wastes with no prospect of material profit, and Englishmen building their lonely outpost of Christendom on the frontiers of "hethenesse." Beside the glorious deaths of young knights like Geoffrey Scrope and John Loudeham, cut off in the flower of youth, were the sober futures of William Scrope, later earl of Wiltshire and Richard II's treasurer; Richard Waldegrave, speaker of the House of Commons in 1381; the bureaucrats Waterton and Norbury; the professional soldiers Henry Ferrers and Nicholas Sabraham, veterans of campaigns throughout the known world; and that most effective and ruthless of political opportunists, Henry Bolingbroke. Between the gambling and entertaining, men fought and died in conditions that speak of anything but lightheartedness.

Geoffrey Scrope and John Loudeham died for a cause respected not simply because it was noble and adventurous—so was the war in France—but because it was holy.[64] The enemy were infidels, their lands "hethenesse," and the object of the campaign was the extension of Christendom. The king of Poland was a "dangerous adversary to Christians," and the report of the 1390 reysa that reached England carefully stressed that the Christian army had captured heathens who would be converted.[65] The Christian element in the ethic of chivalry is easily obscured by the exhuberant display of aristocratic and martial self-confidence; but without it, how were the knights on either side of the Samogitian Wilderness to be distinguished? Without an appreciation of the piety of the crusaders, the Baltic crusade would appear bewildering, at once squalid, cynical, self-seeking and self-deceiving. But the men who fought, like Henry of Grosmont, had a subtler creed.[66] The paradox of arrogant and humble knighthood, even if impervious to entirely rational explanation, was a mark of crusaders, who were also pilgrims to Jerusalem and elsewhere, like Bolingbroke and many others. Both sword and staff were weapons of the Christian knight, and there can be little doubt that the warriors who travelled to the Baltic accepted the righteousness of their deeds.

With their contradictions and secular trappings, can the Baltic wars properly be called crusades? In the absence of many features commonly linked with crusading, there may be some doubt. There were no preaching campaigns in England for the Baltic crusade in the fourteenth century, very few specific papal bulls, little evidence of the ceremonial adoption of the cross and none of the customary local ecclesiastical administration; here the contrast with the schism crusades of 1383 and 1386 is striking. To those who wish to impose a tightly canonistic definition of what constituted a crusade, the Baltic wars leave something to be desired. Contemporaries had fewer doubts. Unsurprisingly, the chroniclers and apologists associated with the Teutonic Knights are clearest in their identification of the reysa with the crusade. Wigand of Marburg almost invariably called visiting knights "pilgrims." Henry of Hervod referred to Henry of Grosmont's journey in 1352 as a pilgrimage to fight the pagans, to expand Christianity, and to glorify Jesus Christ. An early fifteenth-century writer described those killed at Tannenberg as "cruceferi," bearers of the cross, crusaders. The Knights and their allies often appear protected by the banners of St. George and the Virgin Mary. At the Council of Constance, in defence of the legitimacy of the Teutonic Knights' role, Peter Wormditt, the grand master's proctor, had no doubts as to the holy nature of the order's struggle, and despite the rebuttal and counterattack by the Polish delegation, the general equation of the Baltic wars with crusades elsewhere was widely accepted.[67] English writers echo the theme. For Henry Knighton, Henry of Grosmont's expedition was a "pilgrimage against the enemies of Christ." Half a century later Capgrave had no doubts that Bolingbroke had gone to Prussia "against the enemies of Christ's cross" to "avenge the Crucified."[68] In 1395 a Lollard critic of the Baltic campaigns attacked those knights who rushed off "into hethenesse," arguing they won no divine favour but "bad grace" instead; the point would have lost its force had the knights in question not believed that they would earn divine grace, or indulgences, by their actions.[69]

Some campaigners did take the cross, like the earl of Warwick, whose vow was regarded by the pope as interchangeable between Prussia and Palestine. Bolingbroke's preparations in 1390 were originally intended

275

for Tunis as much as Prussia. Others equally certainly received indulgences; in 1390 Bolingbroke received the plenary remission of sins granted by Boniface IX for all who visited and gave alms to four churches in Danzig, the earl's journey there being called a pilgrimage in his accounts.[70] If war and pilgrimage are seen as central, distinctive, and associated features of crusading, then it must be seen that the Teutonic Knights and the papacy provided both in Prussia. Objections may revolve around a lack of specific papal authorisation, of a kind familiar in papal bulls for other crusades. The explanation goes back to the thirteenth century, when a combination of papal authority and resignation, coupled with the order's efficiency and organisation, established what was in effect an autonomous crusading enterprise, run by and for a military order with original papal approval and, as regards foreign recruits, continued encouragement. Urban V repeated his predecessors' support for campaigns against Lithuania.[71] The religious context of decisions to join a reysa is apparent. The earl of Gloucester showered Westminster Abbey with gifts on the eve of his departure in 1391, and Henry of Grosmont received from the pope and the king a variety of privileges closely associated with crusading.[72] In order to receive royal licences it is probable that those going to Prussia had to have made some open commitment such as a vow, if they did not actually take the cross. While not conforming to any textbook model of a crusade, the Baltic wars displayed so many of the formal and informal features of crusading that no other contemporary category of warfare could adequately describe them to those who fought in them. Even if viewed as sui generis, the Baltic wars can only be explained in the context of a crusading enterprise, with an appeal that was secular and religious, social and devotional. Thus, the reason for the decline becomes obvious; by 1410 the enemy were no longer infidels. As Walsingham put it, because of the king of Poland-Lithuania's conversion, "it was now necessary to stop."[73]

SPAIN AND NORTH AFRICA

In contrast to the Baltic crusades, the crusades launched against the Moors of Spain and North Africa were peripheral to the experience of English nobles in the fourteenth century. This was partly because the crusades in the western Mediterranean had increasingly become the preserve of Iberian rulers or, in the case of North Africa, of Italian commercial interests, and partly because of the war with France. Anglo-Iberian diplomacy and commerce, both of long standing, provided the frame for English military contributions to the *reconquista*, as in the twelfth century. The Hundred Years War lent Anglo-Iberian relations a new significance, as English and French protagonists competed for influence and alliances, and especially, in the early years of the war, for the support of the powerful Castillian fleet. Other episodes in this Anglo-French competition were the Black Prince's intervention into the Castillian succession in 1367, Trivet's campaign in Navarre in 1378–79, the earl of Cambridge's presence in Portugal in 1381, and Gaunt's campaign of 1386. Even interest in the projected crusade of 1330–31 was largely a function of Anglo-French relations. Vice versa, there was an attempt to characterise the 1367 campaign that culminated in the victory of Najera as a crusading venture, Walsingham reporting that the Black Prince's enemies included Saracens. This may have been induced by the explicitly crusading propaganda of the French, who associated England's ally Peter the Cruel with the Moors of Granada and North Africa.[74]

The wider conflict in northern Europe, febrile dynasticism in the peninsula, disputed successions, and civil wars ensured that the Moors, in their mountainous redoubt of Granada, from mid-century had little to fear. The one major English intervention was characteristic. In the early 1340s Alfonso XI of Castille (1312–50) had succeeded in gathering land and sea forces from Aragon and Portugal as well as from his own kingdom, in an attempt to clear the Moors from the ports nearest the African coast, Algeciras and Gibraltar. In October 1340 the allies achieved a major victory at the river Salado, and in 1344 Algeciras fell after a siege lasting two years, which attracted substantial support from north of the Pyrenees including, in May 1343, a contingent led by Henry of Grosmont, then earl of Derby, and William Montague, earl of Salisbury. Their presence was not accidental, the siege coinciding with a period of Anglo-French truce. Knights from France, including Philip VI's cousin Philip of Navarre and the count of Foix, also joined the operation. Northern rivalries persisted in the Christian camp; recruits from German allies of England combined with the earl of Derby against the northern and southern French under Foix. Behind this conflict lay serious diplomacy. Derby and Salisbury had instructions to negotiate with Alfonso XI, and they vied with Foix to gain the king's favour and the prize of an alliance that would settle on which side the Castillian fleet would be deployed. An English presence at Alfonso's camp was, therefore, more or less mandatory, regardless of any crusading motives.[75] Initially, English bargaining was more persuasive; Foix had a serious row with Alfonso, whereas the English impressed him by their gallantry. The English earls joined Castillian galleys in an attack on a Moorish fleet off Ceuta (opposite Gibralter), after which the Castillian admiral, the Genoese Egidio Boccanegra, offered his ships and crews for service under Edward III.[76] In the event, however, the Castillian fleet fought for the Valois.

Nevertheless, the earls' retinues greatly exceeded those required by simple ambassadors. At one point in the siege, Alfonso, to frighten some Moorish envoys, showed them round the English camp, which must have been large enough to impress. Accounts of the siege mention the important military contribution of the English; Derby acted as a leader around whom men from England's allies rallied.[77] The earls had come to fight as well as talk. In the words of a contemporary Castillian writer, they had come "for the salvation of their souls . . . besides to see and get to know the king." Officially, Derby had gone to Spain to fight "the enemies of God and the Christian." It would be wrong to belittle the crusading aspects of an expedition that fits well with Henry of Grosmont's later career in the Baltic. His deeds at Algeciras were to form part of the litany of praise bestowed on his memory by John Capgrave a century later.[78]

The siege of Algeciras caused little stir amongst English chroniclers at the time, hardly rating a footnote to Grosmont's more illustrious career north of the Pyrenees. Even though it was the only English expedition to the Iberian peninsula in the fourteenth century directed openly against the infidel, its impact at home was minimal. The same is true of another example of Englishmen fighting against the Moors mentioned by observers in England. Walsingham noted that in 1415 Englishmen (in one version he called them merchants) fought under the king of Portugal and, as at Algeciras, in company with Germans at the capture of Ceuta, on which campaign English ships and equipment were also used.[79] However, this involvement was more a result of the close and friendly diplomatic relations between the English and Portuguese courts, which had been fostered in no small measure by the marriage in 1386 of James I of Portugal to John of Gaunt's daughter Philippa, granddaughter of Henry of Grosmont.[80] Despite, or perhaps because of, intimate and at times intense political relations between England and the Iberian peninsula, the Spanish crusade against the Moors was of little importance in fourteenth-century England, in contrast to France.

The Genoese-sponsored attack on Tunis in 1390, led by Louis II, duke of Bourbon, drew a more substantial English response. After the Anglo-French truce of 1389, English and French courtiers celebrated with lavish tournaments at Smithfield in London and St. Inglevert near Calais. The social contacts there established encouraged English knights to join Bourbon's expedition, which was an explicitly aristocratic affair.

Limited to fifteen thousand, the recruits had to be knights, squires, or others qualified by gentle birth who could pay for themselves. This requirement (which, presumably, did not apply to the archers) arose out of financial prudence as much as snobbery, for there was no central fund on which crusaders could draw. Once in North Africa, the lack of financial control cost the expedition dearly, as the Genoese and almost all other contingents outside Duke Louis's own household including the English broke ranks in the face of Moslem peace terms and, against Bourbon's wishes, forced the abandonment of the siege of al-Mahdiya after only a few wasted summer months.[81]

The need for private funding restricted recruitment to the affinities of the great. Originally, the wealthy Henry Bolingbroke was to have led an English force, and the troops, notably archers, were to have been paid by him, although raised by men like William Willoughby, Thomas Swinford, and William Bagot, all closely linked to the Lancastrian house. In the same way a group led by Henry's illegitimate half-brother, John Beaufort, offered the duke of Bourbon a retinue of twenty-five knights and a hundred archers. Bolingbroke's army gathered at Calais bound for "Barbarie" during May 1390, the month of the jousts at nearby St. Inglevert that also attracted a number of other Tunis recruits.[82] At Calais, wages were disbursed by Bolingbroke's officials for about 120 men—knights, squires, and at least forty-one archers. Unfortunately, despite the Anglo-French rapprochement in 1389, Bolingbroke's request for a safe-conduct through France to join Bourbon at Marseilles was refused, and in June he disbanded his army at Calais, returning to England to prepare for his alternative scheme of campaigning in Prussia.

The reasons for the prevention of Bolingbroke's African crusade are obscure. Possibly the French were wary of allowing so distinguished a prince of the Blood to cross their land at the head of an army. Possibly Richard II himself was reluctant to permit a former Lord Appellant, who had threatened his deposition only a couple of years previously, to play such a glamorous international role and covertly influenced the French decision. Such speculation is supported by the safe-conducts issued by the French to other English lords bound for Africa, including John Beaufort. Alternatively, the French refusal might have had more to do with the size of Bolingbroke's retinue and the severe shortage of space in the Genoese fleet.

Although weakened, the English force at al-Mahdiya was not negligible and included a number of distinguished knights apart from Beaufort: John Russell, Henry Scrope, John Clanvow, William Neville, a Courtenay (possibly the earl of Devon himself), John Clinton, John Cornwall, and a squire, William Fotheringay.[83] The presence of intimate members of the royal household such as Clanvow and Neville suggests that in general English involvement met with the king's approval and again indicates royal interference in Bolingbroke's plans. At al-Mahdiya the English and their archers played a praiseworthy part, and their leaders were prominent among Bourbon's military advisers. Casualties were probably light, although Fotheringay was killed, and another twelve Englishmen died of disease at Genoa on the return journey.[84]

The Tunis crusade had no importance in the fight against Islam. Yet the adventure made some impression on English sources close to the court, and Froissart claimed that processions and prayers for the crusaders' victory were conducted in England.[85] However, unlike the crusades of 1383 and 1386 no sermons or offers of indulgences were authorised by the pope in England. The affair was deliberately restricted to courtiers and their retinues, because the Genoese wanted professional allies to assist an exercise of commercial aggrandizement rather than a general crusade. The Tunis campaign also had a posthumous importance; it returned crusading against Islam to the agenda of practical politics after a generation's absence and demonstrated that diplomatic reconciliation between England and France could be turned to a noble military purpose. The precedent was not lost on either court in the following years when ideas began to circulate for a new passagium to the East, a prospect before which Spain and even North Africa paled.

THE IMAGE OF THE HOLY LAND AND PILGRIMAGES

Although warfare against infidels, wherever they were to be found, drew on a ready supply of recruits, as a focus of idealism and a goal of ambition the Holy Land was unrivalled. Few in the fourteenth century would have cavilled at the insistence of the English bishops at the Council of Vienne (1311–12) that any new general passagium and ecclesiastical levy should be directed at the recovery of Jerusalem, rather than at any intermediate target such as Tunis. Certainly the gild members in Norfolk who prayed for the Holy Land and the patriarch of Jerusalem would not have objected, nor would have those with a taste for literature.[86]

One of the most popular books of the later Middle Ages was the mid–fourteenth century compilation known as the *Travels of Sir John Mandeville*, of which about two hundred and fifty manuscripts survive. Originally written in French, it was translated into English more than once before 1400. An exotic mixture of travelogue, itinerary, and storybook, the purpose of the *Travels* was stated in the Prologue: "For als moche as it is long tyme passed that ther was no generalle passage . . .

and many men desiren for to here speke of the Holy Land and han thereof great solace and comfort." Christians were called on to remember the Life and Passion of Christ, through which the Holy Land was "behighte [i.e., promised] us in heritage." "Wherfore euery gode Christene man that is of powere and hath whereof scholde peynen him with alle his strengthe for to conquere oure right heritage and chacen out alle the mysbeleeuynge men."[87] This was a common theme of contemporary writers. For example, Philippe de Mézières's *Epistre* of 1395 to Richard II described the Holy Land as the king's own inheritance ("propre heritage") purchased by Christ's Passion.[88]

There was a substantial market for works on the Holy Land other than romances, throughout the princely and comital courts of Europe. The fourteenth-century manuscript that preserves the memoir of Roger of Stanegrave also contains extracts from William of Tyre, Marco Polo, and the thirteenth-century encyclopaedist Vincent of Beauvais on the Tartars, as well as Hayton's *Flowers of the History of the East* (1307), a tract *On the Condition of the Holy Land* by Amerigo Monaco de Corbizzi, patriarch of Jerusalem from 1194 to 1202, and two descriptions of the Holy Places, one of them by Fretellus, a mid–twelfth century archdeacon of Antioch.[89] Such works filled the libraries of the nobility, part of a literary tradition and cultural atmosphere that guaranteed a hearing for propaganda designed to inform and exhort through lengthy discussions of crusade history, contemporary politics, and the military and geographical logistics of campaigning in the Levant, often couched, as in Mézières's *Songe du Vieil Pèlerin* (1389), in the imaginative language of chivalric allegory. In the world of "Mandeville" and the nobility of fourteenth-century England, Jerusalem had lost little of its power.

Political circumstances in Europe and the Mediterranean—the Hundred Years War, the rivalries in Romania, Naples, and Cyprus, and between Venice and Genoa, and, later, the papal schism—largely frustrated any effective united western action in the Levant. The expeditions that did embark, such as the Holy Leagues of 1334 and 1343–44, and the crusades of Humbert, dauphin of Vienne (1345–47) and Count Amadeus of Savoy (1366), were dominated by French and papal interests which were regarded in England with suspicion, if not outright hostility. John of Reading, a monk of Westminster and a good source of contemporary gossip, imputed the motives of John II of France and those who took the cross with him at Avignon in 1363 to a desire "for their own profit and honour not for the love of Christ."[90] English contributions to these campaigns were restricted to individuals. Sir John Garin from the diocese of St. Asaph possibly joined Humbert of Vienne's crusade in 1345. Nicholas Sabraham met up with Amadeus of Savoy's expedition after the sack of Alexandria, and Richard Musard carried the count's standard in the final assault on Gallipoli in August 1366. With them on Amadeus's crusade were some English mercenaries who had hired themselves to the count.[91] Until the Anglo-French truce of 1389, there was active English participation only where the control of the crusade was clearly not in the hands of the Franco-papal alliance, as in Peter I of Cyprus's campaigns at Satalia (1361) and Alexandria (1365). Even so, the sum total of English crusading in the eastern Mediterranean was numerically unimpressive.[92]

Fourteenth-century concern for the Holy Land was neither entirely impotent nor tangential to the active lives of Englishmen. Many individuals, often those who campaigned in Lithuania and North Africa or planned to throw back the Ottomans, visited Jerusalem. In the later Middle Ages pilgrimage to the Holy Land, for long overshadowed by its martial offspring, returned *faute de mieux* into prominence, its popularity suggesting a sympathetic audience for plans to recover Outremer. Conversely, the determination of so many knights to visit the Holy Places as pilgrims makes it possible to modify any excessive emphasis that "the glamour of martial glory and social esteem" was the mainspring of crusade motivation. Crusaders may have sought "worldly honour through an activity recognised in its terms as glamorous, not salvation," as M. H. Keen has argued, but their manner of seeking it is inexplicable if the abiding element of pilgrimage is ignored.[93]

Pilgrims to the Holy Land were interested in more than social esteem. The Tunis campaigners earned indulgences (even if some Romanists may have been uneasy at Clementist privileges) and no end of esteem, but some of them saw Tunis as a mere staging post. Froissart records that after the withdrawal from al-Mahdiya many struck bargains with Genoese captains to ship them "to Naples . . . to Sicily, Cyprus or Rhodes there to perform a pilgrimage to Jerusalem."[94] On one of these pilgrimages, the deaths of Sir John Clanvow and Sir William Neville caused a greater stir than their exploits in Africa.[95]

Crusading and pilgrimages were intimately associated but separable. The licences and safe-conducts given to John de la Ryvere by Edward III and Clement VI in 1346 and the papal privileges bestowed on Bartholomew Burghersh clearly distinguished the military and pilgrimage aspects of their intended crusades.[96] The same distinction is evident with some Baltic crusaders. In 1391 Lord Clifford—perhaps in penance for his part in the slaying of William Douglas—and in 1393 Henry Bolingbroke followed their visits to Prussia with pilgrimages to the Holy Places.[97] These pilgrimages might have been favoured by serious and pious knights and therefore have constituted a minority interest, but they show that somewhere in the background of plans to recover the Holy Land lay a practical spirituality concerned with the benefits of pilgrimage, notably, as Ryvere's licence put it, "the saving of his soul." Thus, to an otherwise brief, factual account of his master's pilgrimage to Jerusalem in 1392–93, Thomas Brygg appended a full note on the spiritual privileges to be gained: seven years and 280 days indulgence for all the Holy Sites, except those where the Cross had been, which earned the penitent and confessed pilgrim plenary remission of sins.[98]

The social origins of fourteenth-century pilgrims to the Holy Land were identical to those of crusaders: magnates, barons, knights, squires, donsels, burgesses, civil servants, monks, secular priests, and women. Elizabeth of Asheton set out from Dover in March 1348 with a chaplain and two yeomen. Elizabeth of Keynes embarked with some of her Dorset neighbours, perhaps foolhardily, in Christmas Week 1373. Thirteen years later five women were organising funds for their trip to Palestine. The best-known woman pilgrim was the Norfolk mystic Margery Kempe, who visited Jerusalem in 1414. As Chaucer's Wife of Bath "thryes hadde she ben at Jerusalem," these women cannot have been alone.[99] Among men there were representatives (sometimes more than one) of important families such as Stafford, Faucomberge, Burghersh, Umfraville, Neville, Courtenay, Roos, Percy, Mowbray, Beauchamp, and Lancaster, many of which also boasted active crusaders in the fourteenth century.[100]

Piety was not the exclusive inspiration. The earl of Stafford, who died at Rhodes in 1386, may have left distressed at the unpunished murder of his eldest son by John Holland the year before. Two years later the earl of Arundel's intended visit to Jerusalem probably owed much to his political difficulties at home.[101] In 1343 the king's secretary, William Kildesby, combined diplomacy with pilgrimage, being accredited to all the leading Christian powers in the region. A nervous Edward III may have wanted information of the true intentions of the Holy League formed by Clement VI, and he certainly used Kildesby in an attempt to counter any propaganda advantage gained by the French because of their involvement in the League.[102] A more down-to-earth motive may be ascribed to Thomas Lamb of Aply (Lincolnshire) who was suspected of stealing thirteen rafters from a local cleric before he left for the East.[103]

The pilgrim trade remained big business for Italian shippers; pilgrims needed both money and stamina. Many died: Stafford (1386), Clanvow, Neville and Clifford (1391), Lord Roos (1393), Sir John Clifton, a landowner in Essex and Lincolnshire, at Rhodes (1388), Roger le Wright of Northamptonshire (1347), Richard Stok of Leicestershire

(1357), and Elizabeth of Keynes.[104] Some, like the Londoner Thomas of Burton in the late 1360s, or a chaplain from Bangor in 1412, faced hostility and imprisonment from the Mamluk authorities.[105] Others fell foul of authorities nearer home; in 1345 three English pilgrims were incarcerated at Pisa. More, perhaps, suffered at the hands of nature. A monk from Malmesbury, Richard Chastellayn, found himself caught in a severe earthquake at Rhodes in April 1364, and John of Holdernesse from Essex was so impressed by a storm he encountered on pilgrimage in 1367 that he vowed to visit all saints' shrines in the whole of England if he were spared.[106] The material implications of pilgrimages, like crusades, could be distinctly disadvantageous. Despite royal protection, John Marmion returned from Palestine in 1331 to find his deer had been poached. The attorneys of Edmund of Morteyn feared that his lands and possessions were about to be plundered in his absence in 1366. When John FitzHenry of Northumberland died, probably at Rhodes in the summer of 1345, he left his lands precariously in the hands of his eighteen-month-old son.[107] The exiled and disgraced duke of Norfolk, Thomas Mowbray, returned from Palestine in 1399 heavily in debt and broken in spirit, to die in Venice.[108]

The consequence of mishap could be grave. When news of Thomas of Burton's imprisonment reached his wife in 1369, she sold all her disposable property to raise a ransom, only to be arrested at Gravesend for trying to export money without a licence; fortunately the government heeded requests for restitution to this devoted wife. The financial problems facing pilgrims were exacerbated by the need to pay for a royal licence to export cash or bullion, and because of the war all pilgrims required a licence simply to leave the country.[109] This system of licencing had its origins in the permissions granted crusaders by twelfth-century kings, but in the fourteenth century control of passage and export was enforced with greater stringency.

Some idea of the nature and scale of expeditions less extravagant than Bolingbroke's may be gleaned from Thomas Brygg's list of expenses on Thomas Swinburne's pilgrimage, incurred between Venice and Beirut from September to January 1392–93 (he and Bolingbroke missing each other in Jerusalem by little over a month). Apart from the cost of transport across the Mediterranean (sixteen ducats each, perhaps four marks) and board and lodging, there were customs duties, tolls on rivers and entry to cities, payments for safe-conducts from local authorities, and, in Egypt and Palestine, boats, camels, and mules, and wages for camel and mule drivers. The all-important interpreters and guides, the *dragomani*, appear to have charged four ducats (one mark) per head of pilgrim, although the *dragomanus* who took Swinburne's party from Alexandria to Cairo charged six ducats (one pound); more had to be hired at each subsequent stage, two for the journey across Sinai to Gaza and yet more in Syria. Swinburne's total expenditure is impossible to gauge, since the size of his retinue is unknown, as are incidental expenses of food, drink, and alms. But it has been calculated that if his retinue was a mere ten strong, the three month period covered by Brygg's account might have cost in the region of eighty pounds.[110]

The prudent arranged credit with Italian bankers, as did a group of eight pilgrims in London in 1386, or, more riskily, carried sufficient cash, royal licence permitting. In 1368 William of Birmingham and five others were allowed forty pounds, as was William atte Lee, esquire, and his yeoman in 1390; in 1414 Margery Kempe set out with twenty pounds.[111] The king does not appear to have played much of a role in funding pilgrims, beyond the issuing of licences, although in 1353 a veteran wardrobe official who had worked for Edward I received two marks from the exchequer for his journey to Jerusalem and Mt. Sinai, and in 1398–99 it was on Richard II's personal recommendation that the senate of Venice allowed Thomas Mowbray to hire a galley. However, the duke had to pay for the galley himself.[112]

The need for money was recognised by some of the charitable gilds. In Hull a member of the Gild of the Virgin Mary (founded 1357) wishing to go on pilgrimage to the Holy Land was exempted from annual gild payments "in order that all the gild may share in his pilgrimage." At Lincoln members of the Gild of Tailors (founded 1328) had to donate one penny to a "brother or sister" bound for Jerusalem (one half-penny to those going to Compostella or Rome), and members of the Gild of the Resurrection (founded 1374), one-half penny. Here and elsewhere the gild ensured that the pilgrim was given a grand send-off and welcome on his return.[113] Such provisions highlight the social kudos as well as the expense of pilgrimages. Some pilgrims relied wholly on charity, like William of Nesham, who returned from the Holy Land in 1334 supported by "the alms of the faithful" and a year later began collecting for a second visit, although he could not have been completely destitute as he was able to afford to pay for his royal licence to be enrolled.[114] Sometimes economies of scale may have been possible for the rich, like Bartholomew Burghersh the elder (1348) and Sir Hugh Neville (1349), with retinues of fifty and thirty respectively, or the Franciscans Andrew Chesham and John Pouher, who travelled with thirty companions to augment their order's presence in the Holy Land in 1362.[115] On a humbler level, it was common practice for pilgrims to associate with each other from the start, perhaps for company as much as for protection or economy, like Elizabeth of Keynes and her neighbours (1373) or Walter Yonge and his seven companions (1386). Of course, knights and gentlemen would never travel alone. Ultimately, most pilgrims joined up with large companies on the regular pilgrim sailings from the ports of southern Europe. Swinburne travelled with German and Bohemian pilgrims in 1392, and the chaplain from Bangor arrived in Palestine in a polyglot party of five hundred in 1412. The pilgrim would probably only have been solitary at his own front door.[116]

A number of those who received royal or papal licences to visit the Holy Land swore associated vows to combat the infidel. Among these were John de Faucomberge (1343), John de la Ryvere (1346), and the elder Burghersh (1349; he never fulfilled either the pilgrimage or the vow).[117] Some carried with them the instruments of war. In 1357 Robert Umfraville and Roger Percy were given permission to take horses, armour, and military equipment. Both Hugh Neville in 1348, with thirty companions, and Bolingbroke in 1392–93, with perhaps forty or fifty followers, had the capacity to lend military assistance to local Christians if required. When Venice supplied Bolingbroke with a galley, the earl was expected "to arm" it himself, and it may be noted that the knights who accompanied him to Jerusalem continued to draw wages. Less extravagantly, in 1390 Sir William de Botreaux embarked from Dover with five serjeants, horses, and equipment.[118] Many aristocratic pilgrimages were organised much like military campaigns, complete with paid, armed troops. Knights, serjeants, yeomen, horses, and military equipment were the common accompaniments to the pilgrimages of the nobility.[119]

Many visits to the Holy Places were brief. The earl of Warwick spent just ten days in Palestine in 1393. Bolingbroke's trip from Venice to Jerusalem and back took only twelve and a half weeks. From Venice, Swinburne reached Beirut after the full tour of the Holy Sites via Alexandria, Cairo, Mt. Sinai, Jerusalem, and Damascus, in almost exactly four months.[120] The Mamluk authorities would have in any case encouraged visits to be as short as possible. With many English pilgrims calling at Rhodes, the opportunity to fight alongside the Hospitallers was always available, and at least one English knight in the fourteenth century, Sir Hugh Hastings, took advantage of it.[121] Pilgrimages, like Baltic crusades, were more frequent during lulls in the Hundred Years War, especially in the late 1340s, the 1360s, and the early 1390s.[122]

It is difficult to determine whether pilgrims for whom no specific military vow survives had any intention to fight if the opportunity arose. In the thirteenth century, a simple pilgrimage to the Holy Land earned an essoin of one year; a crusade was supposed to take longer.[123] Thirteen of the twenty-six pilgrims whose licences specify a time limit between 1320 and 1390 had a term of one year; one, a term of less than a year because he was in mid-journey; four, a term of two years; six, a term of three years; and two, a term of four years. There are a further four licences to appoint attorneys without any specified time limit, as well as six other safe-conducts. To draw conclusions from such statistics is difficult. The base is very narrow, not all licences were enrolled, and enrollment was no guarantee of departure. Some well-known pilgrims are absent from the Patent Rolls—Thomas Swinburne for one. Nevertheless, some tentative comments may be possible. For one thing, the figures for 1320–90 are in marked contrast to those of 1308–20, when only two out of fourteen licences issued had a term of one year, but three had a term of three years; two, a term of four years; and four, a term of five or more years. The longer terms, for example in 1309, perhaps indicated putative crusaders. From the 1320–90 list, the liccences of Robert Umfraville and Roger Percy in 1357 and Walter Paveley in 1354 had no time limit, allowing presumably for the possibility of an extended absence on campaign.[124] In 1270 the crusaders' term had, de facto, most commonly been of four years.[125] With the longer or indefinite terms in the fourteenth century there must be a presumption of diversification, either of business or itinerary, in particular because of the usual brevity of pilgrim tours in Egypt and Palestine.

Whether or not pilgrims intended to fight, the coincidence of social and family groupings with those of crusaders shows how influential figures continued to express devotion to the Holy Land. Crusaders and pilgrims helped keep Englishmen informed of events in the East: Richard Chastellayn's travellers' tales, given to a fellow monk at Malmesbury; the Bangor chaplain's information to the chronicler Adam of Usk of his unpleasant experiences at the hands of the Mamluks; written accounts of pilgrimages, like Brygg's description of Swinburne's journey in 1392; or newsletters, such as the one on which the Westminster chronicler based his account of the deaths of Clanvow and Neville in 1391. The death of Lord Roos at Paphos, on his return from Jerusalem in 1393, was commemorated in even more striking fashion, by a painted mural, still surviving on the north wall of the nave of Bradfield Combust church in Suffolk. The mural depicts the slaying of the dragon by St. George, whose own armour and horse's armour are decorated with crosses and whose helm bears the peacock feathers of the Roos heraldic crest—a significantly martial epitaph for a pilgrim.[126]

Although interest in the Holy Land suffused society, of more immediate relevance to any potential crusade planning was that many pilgrims had close connections with the royal court: most obviously earls like Bolingbroke or Warwick and barons like the elder Burghersh, who had risen through royal service, but also second-rank royal agents and courtiers. John Clanvow and William Neville were close to Richard II; Thomas Swinburne was captain of Guines and a future mayor of Bordeaux; and William de Lisle was "from the king's chamber."[127] At court the context for crusading action was not generalised but immediate.

THE RECOVERY OF THE HOLY LAND

If Englishmen had not forgotten Jerusalem, what did they do about its recovery? Once again the historian confronts the paradox of enthusiasm matched by inaction. Crusading emotions were channelled to the Baltic, to national wars, and to the pilgrimage, but were baulked of the satisfaction of the most attractive prize. Some reasons for this have already been advanced, in particular western political rivalries. Twice in the fourteenth century, however, it appeared that genuine opportunities existed for a general international passagium to repulse the Turks and reconquer Palestine. On both occasions the role of England and Englishmen was pivotal, as only with Anglo-French peace and cooperation could any international enterprise be contemplated. Unfortunately for those who dreamt of a new Christian kingdom of Jerusalem, these opportunities led merely to the occupation of part of the port of Alexandria by an unruly allied force under Peter I of Cyprus, for less than a week in October 1365, and to the disastrous defeat and massacre of a largely French crusading army by the Ottomans at Nicopolis on the Danube in September 1396.

Huizinga suggested that the failures were the result of the flawed psychology of chivalry, which insisted on treating the war against the Turks as secondary to the traditional aim of reconquering Jerusalem and thereby prevented adequate and essential intelligence work, planning, and preparations.[128] More recently, Terry Jones has turned the argument on its head: Chivalry was not decadent but a sham, which concealed not the lighthearted *ingénus* of Huizinga's waning Middle Ages but cynical, greedy, and vicious *routiers* who betrayed whatever higher aspirations their leaders affected.[129] Huizinga believed that crusading was a symptom of hollow but largely unconscious role-playing; Jones believes that most contemporaries saw the practice of crusading as being as despicable as he does.

Neither was the case. Opposition to crusading was by no means widespread, and criticism of the ideal was even rarer. The crusade remained a practical and far-from-amateurish concern throughout the century. There was no shortage of serious technical and logistical advice or of experience of campaigning in the East. For example, Philippe de Mézières, the most prolific crusade propagandist of the second half of the century, had been a councillor of Peter of Cyprus and a crusader himself. He later helped the Cypriot king organise the abortive crusade of 1365. Philippe's leading publicist, Robert "the Hermit," was a Norman knight who had travelled to Palestine. Nearer home, in the 1340s John de la Ryvere fought against the Turks and Mamluks and used his experience and his visit to the Holy Places to become expert in Moslem military strength. The crusaders themselves were men of sober military and political experience. Every court in Europe had men with direct acquaintance with the realities of war in the eastern Mediterranean, in the local representatives of the Order of St. John—veteran knights like Roger of Stanegrave or prominent Hospitaller dignitaries like Robert Hales, a commander at Alexandria and later illfated treasurer of England.[130]

Huizinga, Jones, and other modern critics of crusading, such as Sir Steven Runciman, have been mislead into imagining a greater homogeneity of motive, action, and reaction in fourteenth-century crusading than actually existed. The attitudes of a man like Richard Waldegrave, crusader in the Levant and the Baltic and Speaker of the House of Commons, cannot be reconstructed from the formalised raillery of Gower or Chaucer, even less from the vituperation of Lollards, without taking account of his actions. It is unwarranted to assume an identity of purpose between a man like Robert Woodhouse, a member of the mercenary English company at Pisa who wished to join the 1365 crusade, and Humphrey de Bohun, earl of Hereford, who probably led the English at Alexandria; or to assume the reverse. The crusader Nicholas Sabraham spent a whole career in arms from the 1330s, but his status as a more-or-less professional soldier does not mean that his crusading was a cynical deceit, any more than Bohun's was a romantic one.[131] Salvation, honour, wealth, and a good fight were complementary incentives, not mutually exclusive. The combination and fusion of motives makes a great deal of psychological and historical sense. Most contemporaries, at least those who actually became crusaders, would have had difficulty in seeing much contradiction among them.

In the 1360s there were three elements in English involvement in the eastern Mediterranean: the court, individual nobles and knights, and the English Free Companies, which were organised, autonomous bands of mercenaries left without employment by the 1360 Treaty of Brétigny between England and France. The treaty released knights not only to Prussia but also to the Mediterranean. Peter of Cyprus launched attacks on Turkish and Mamluk ports partly as a result of this pool of western knights seeking adventure, even before his recruiting tour of the West in 1363–64. Among Englishmen at Peter's capture of Satalia in southern Turkey in 1361 were the earl of Hereford, Sir William Scrope, and Richard Waldegrave.[132] Some of the knights were very young: Waldegrave was twenty-three, Hereford nineteen, and Scrope possibly even younger; if John Godard was at Satalia, which is possible, he would only have been about fifteen. These men were winning their spurs in a fashion common throughout western Europe; Mézières, a generation earlier, had fought in Italy and at the capture of Smyrna, and had visited Jerusalem by the time he was nineteen.[133]

The presence of Hereford and his compatriots in the Levant in the early 1360s may have prompted King Peter to suppose that he could call upon greater support from north of the Alps in 1363–64 than was forthcoming. For two years the king, accompanied by an exotic oriental troupe as well as by officials such as Mézières, now his chancellor, visited the leading monarchs of the West to drum up recruits for a new general passagium. He reached England at the turn of the year 1363–64. His arrival had been anticipated at a tournament held at Smithfield in 1362 that attracted knights from Cyprus and Armenia as well as from France and Spain. Throughout his reign Edward III had been kept informed of the deteriorating position of the Christian outposts in the East. Now, in the winter of 1363–64, London became the scene of a crusade conference involving the kings of England, France, Scotland, and Cyprus.[134] Despite Peter's advocacy and strong papal pressures, Edward declined to take the cross, although he allowed his subjects to enlist in the Cypriot crusade on a personal basis. Indeed, according to an unsympathetic French source, Edward was almost mocking. Once at dinner he suggested that if King Peter successfully recovered Jerusalem, Cyprus "which my ancestor Richard entrusted to your predecessor to keep" should be restored to him. Peter pretended not to hear, but left the English court soon afterwards.[135] The story is probably apocryphal, but Edward III was consistent in refusing to become involved in crusade plans. Without his active participation, little help could be expected from either the Scots, nervous of their frontiers, or the French, whose king, John II, although having taken the cross in 1363, was a captive in England and in no position to influence events in France.

Edward probably regarded the official leadership of crusades as a cosy preserve of the French kings, regularly granted them by a succession of indulgent or optimistic popes. Edward had little inclination or political need to emulate his grandfather and usurp this, by mid-century, almost honorific position. At home there was less pressure, as the English nobility consistently invested less in the eastern crusade than the French did. Edward may also have noticed the conflicting motives of the crusade organisers. The Cypriots saw the Anglo-French peace of 1360 as a chance to capitalize on the existing policy of seizing Moslem ports and to effect major conquests on the Asian mainland. The French and the pope were almost certainly more concerned to use the crusade as a means of ridding Italy and France of the now-unemployed, but still voracious, Free Companies, which posed greater threats to France and Italy than to England.

In the face of Peter's failure to secure the support of Edward or Regent Charles of France, Urban V became a military entrepreneur. In April 1364, after negotiations with Robert Woodhouse of the English Free Company based in Pisa under the command of Albert Stertz, Urban promised the mercenaries full indulgences and money from a subsidy to be raised from the Italian church, provided that they took the cross and joined the Cypriot crusade. Urban hoped they would set an example to the other Free Companies in Italy. At the same time, he tried to interest the English Company in an association with two English crusaders, Thomas Ufford, son of the earl of Suffolk, and William de la Pole of Castle Ashby, a substantial landowner in the Midlands and East Anglia. Ufford and Pole were to persuade their compatriots to embark on crusade and to arrange for their provisions and passage through Italy.[136] No direct evidence has revealed the reaction of Stertz and company to this attempt to insinuate a leadership congenial to the crusade organisers. However, Peter of Cyprus did retain English troops for a year, possibly from the mercenaries stationed at Pisa, who in the actual attack on Alexandria fought under the command of a leader of distinguished lineage, perhaps the young earl of Hereford.[137]

The recruitment of European mercenaries made for disunity on campaign. At Alexandria the bulk of the army Peter had raised insisted against the king's wishes on evacuating the city once it had been sacked. The main culprits were identified by Mézières, who was there, as English knights. The circumstances of the failure of the Alexandrian crusade prompted adverse comment from interested contemporaries, including Mézières and the poet Guillaume de Machaut. These have been amplified by Terry Jones: "The debacle at Alexandria was seen as a text book example of the danger in relying on such mercenary riff-raff and the need for troops with some commitment or loyalties beyond the acquisition of hard cash."[138] In fact, the behaviour and the construction of the crusader army were more typical of earlier crusades than Jones here allows. Like crusade commanders since at least the Third Crusade, King Peter had to pay for recruits. The 1364–65 contracts of service for one year compare with the preparations of Richard I in 1190, William

Longsword in 1249, and the Lord Edward in 1270. The lack of cohesion was not new either. All crusader camps echoed to heated debates among the leaders over tactics, and it was usually only when moral authority was supported by control of the purse strings that decisions could be imposed. Responsibility for the failure to exploit the initial advantage at Alexandria is difficult to apportion, but breakdown of discipline is not a natural consequence of hiring paid troops; rather, the reverse. The weakness lay in the nature of a polyglot alliance of Cypriot vassals, European recruits, and the Hospitallers from Rhodes, brought together under an inadequate command structure that gave too much responsibility to individual units and their captains, like the young and possibly impressionable earl of Hereford. Much the same, however, could be said of earlier crusades, such as the siege of Damascus in 1148.

Apart from de la Pole (who may have died during the campaign), Ufford, and Hereford, there were a number of other English recruits for the Cypriot crusade whose names have survived: the earl of Warwick, who reached Italy, although he probably diverted his crusade to Prussia; Sir Stephen Scrope, knighted at Alexandria by King Peter himself; Nicholas Sabraham; and the English Hospitallers including Robert Hales, whose reputation was made by the expedition, and William Middleton.[139] There was possibly even an Englishman on the Moslem side, a former Hospitaller who had been captured by the Mamluks many years before and who had pretended to apostatize. He encountered a foraging party outside Alexandria and warned the crusaders, in English, to evacuate the city, as they stood no chance against the advancing Egyptian army.[140] This picturesque story may have been devised to explain both the sudden retreat and the English role in it, but the details are not so entirely fantastic when the experiences of Roger of Stanegrave are recalled. A renegade Hospitaller could have been welcome to the Mamluks, nervous of the Hospitaller presence at Rhodes.

The credentials of the English crusaders underline the reality behind the glitter of chivalric reputation. Hereford, still only twenty-three, had already fought at Satalia and in the Baltic and was still campaigning in the East in 1367.[141] Stephen Scrope, also in his twenties, was the younger brother of Geoffrey, who had died in Prussia. Sabraham, a veteran of Crecy, campaigned in Scotland, France, Spain, Prussia, Hungary, Greece, and Turkey, as well as in Egypt, in his long and distinguished career. After the retreat from Alexandria he joined Amadeus of Savoy's crusade to the Dardanelles and the Black Sea in 1366, on which, in addition to more English mercenaries, Sabraham possibly had for company another unnamed member of the Scrope family.[142] Youth, a semiprofessional dependence on warfare, and temporary closures of the French theatre of action impelled these crusade recruits. Their rewards were usually intangible; it was Hereford's fame that preceded his return to London in 1366.[143]

The sack of Alexandria did have material repercussions. Walsingham noted that the price of spices rose as a result of the attack on the chief entrepôt for the East-West spice trade. Also "many Englishmen and Gascons" brought back from Egypt "cloth of gold, silks and splendid exotic jewels in witness of such a victory achieved there."[144] Terry Jones may not be proud of the sack of Alexandria, with some justice, but it was admired by Walsingham and his contemporaries including Chaucer, who twenty years later gave evidence in the Scrope-Grosvenor case alongside veterans of 1365, whose renown he borrowed for his knight in the *Canterbury Tales*.

The Alexandria crusade also confirmed that Edward III was unusually impervious to the lure of the crusade. He permitted his subjects to spend time and money on adventure, but he invested his own revenues in political advantage near home. There were no royal handouts to the crusaders of 1364–65. In the absence of the crusade funds characteristic of the thirteenth century, crusaders had to find their own money; William de la Pole, for instance, raised money in the City of London.[145] Edward III enjoyed extravagance and was famous as a paragon of chivalrous virtue, but he saw largesse and heroism as useful weapons of monarchy, not as ends in themselves. Once war with France recommenced in 1369, he quickly reharnessed the excess military energy of his nobles towards national ends, with men like the earl of Hereford soon pressed into service. The king's attitude was shared by his eldest son, the Black Prince, and possibly by his youngest son, Thomas of Gloucester, who responded with hostility to arguments presented in 1390 in favour of peace with France in the interests of a crusade against Islam, although personally he planned to fight in the Baltic a few months later.

Such responses contrast sharply with those of fourteenth-century French kings and nobles, who commonly encouraged with financial assistance and leadership individual crusaders as well as substantial campaigns. The enthusiasm of the Valois dukes of Burgundy and the house of Bourbon was matched by the usually parsimonious Charles V, who lent Bertand de Guesclin 300,000 gold francs for an expedition against Granada.[146]

The lack of English royal support for Peter of Cyprus, which if given could have put pressure on Regent Charles to join a Holy Alliance, was perhaps fatal. The failure of the Cypriot crusade was certainly traced to England by Philippe de Mézières, who twenty-five years later blamed Edward for sabotaging the efforts to recover the Holy Land of both Philip VI and John II.[147]

The nationalist and publicly anti-papal policies of Edward III complicated English response to the crusade and might have contributed to a decline in the numbers and amounts of Holy Land legacies and donations finding their way into the coffers of papal tax collectors. In the face of royal propaganda, it might no longer have appeared quite loyal or respectable to hand money to agents of what was paraded as a hostile power. The surviving papal collectors' accounts from 1317–78 show diminishing returns: for 1317–23, over 500 marks; 1329–32, £82 13s; for 1335–43, £59 7s 8d was declared by Collector Bernard de Sistre (although his detailed account shows returns of £90). He laid the blame for the lack of income on Benedict XII, who after the cancellation of the crusade in 1336 told Bernard not to bother collecting legacies and vow redemptions any more. For 1349–58, nearly £90 was received; 1358–63, £31 10s, or possibly slightly more; for 1364–66, only £10; and nothing at all in the 1370s.[148] An annual average of £10 or less from mid-century suggests that, although income had never been massive, the papal system of collection had collapsed, reflecting growing royal control over the administration of the English church. As the crusade was particularly a concern of the pope, the widespread suspicion of papal motives among those sections of the laity most likely to be interested in crusading—the classes and groups that were also represented in parliament and pressed for antipapal legislation—could only have been dispelled by a show of royal enthusiasm which was not forthcoming until the peculiar circumstances of 1382–83. Those who could afford it still went on crusade when the opportunity presented itself, and people continued to remember the Holy Land in their wills, but without royal initiative such efforts never rose above the spasmodic and the ineffectual.

That a sympathetic royal policy could transform prospects for a general passagium was shown after the Anglo-French truce of 1389 when, as J. J. N. Palmer has demonstrated, the courts of the young kings Richard II and Charles VI seriously contemplated plans to repel the Ottomans and recover the Holy Land.[149] The mood of both courts in this period forced even the most reluctant supporter of the rapprochement with France, Thomas of Woodstock, not only to listen to detailed crusade proposals but to lend his name as patron to the new crusading order of one of the central figures in the exchanges between the two monarchs, Philippe de Mézières.

Mézières's Order of the Passion, which had existed on paper and in its founder's conversation for a generation, tried to organise the existing commitment to the crusading ideal. Between 1390 and 1395 a number of courtiers promised to become members or agreed to act as patrons and supply the order with funds. None of them were called upon to do more than give a verbal pledge, and no formal assembly of the order ever seems to have been held, even though Mézières had composed details of organisation and had designed robes for the various categories of membership. Consequently, it is impossible to be certain of the motives of the participants, especially as one of the chief critics of the whole crusade policy, Thomas of Gloucester, was also a patron. The cohesion and enthusiasm of the order may only have existed in Mézières's mind. Nevertheless, a number of the twenty-five ordinary members and three patrons, listed in the abridged version of the order's ordinances presented by Mézières to the earl of Huntingdon in 1395, had or were to acquire suitable credentials. The Earl Marshal and Ralph Percy both visited the Holy Land; Lord Despenser and Sir Hugh Despenser had campaigned in the Baltic; of the patrons (the dukes of Lancaster and Gloucester, and the earl of Huntingdon) John of Gaunt was, with the dukes of Burgundy and Orleans, one of the prime movers in the 1390s crusade policy; and Huntingdon was, as has been noted, closely involved in negotiations with Sigismund of Hungary.[150]

If membership of an order of chivalry implied certain attitudes, the crusade plans of 1392–96 had a wide basis of courtier support. Recruitment had been pursued as an adjunct of diplomacy. The personal envoy to the English of Charles VI and Philippe de Mézières was the same man, Robert the Hermit. He played a double role. On the one hand he conveyed messages between the kings, including letters drafted by Mézières; on the other, he acted as one of Mézières's four "evangelists" of his order, carrying letters from the founder to prospective members. Robert was not alone in this dual function. A number of the order's members, in addition to Huntingdon, were engaged both in the peace and crusade negotiations.[151] The rather fragile Anglo-French alliance was being cemented by the crusade policy, and an attempt was being made to bind those most nearly concerned into a form of freemasonry. The message and the techniques of propaganda were well adapted to Richard II's nobles; they elsewhere displayed a taste for books, personal religious devotion, and hermits, precisely the elements assembled by Mézières.[152]

The tenacity of the crusade planners was remarkable in view of the obstacles in the crusade's path, which included the precarious health of Charles VI; the increasing tension between Philip of Burgundy and the king's brother, Louis of Orleans; the unrest in Gascony; the financial difficulties of both governments; the lukewarm attitude of the Teutonic Knights when aid was proposed for them; the continued mutual suspicion of former adversaries; the open antagonism to peace, and hence the crusade, expressed by opponents of Richard II like the earl of Arundel; and the papal schism.

The connection between Anglo-French peace and the crusade might first have been drawn in the winter of 1385–86, when the exiled King Leo VI of Armenia visited England. Although some observers were cynical about Leo's motives, Walsingham seeing him as a mercenary wanderer "happier in flight in foreign lands than ruling peacefully in his own" (rather an unfair jibe as his country had been occupied by the Mamluks) and the Westminster chronicler describing him as calculating, the Armenian king played a central role as an arbiter between England and France and must share some of the credit for the truce of 1389.[153] Diplomacy was personal and tough, especially when dealing with aggressive personalities like Thomas of Woodstock. However, the fourteenth-century ambassador had ample opportunities to influence the thinking of his interlocutor, and it was through such personal contacts that the idea of the crusade crystallised. After the assassination of Peter of Cyprus in 1369, Mézières had found his way to the French court, where he became a royal councillor and tutor to the young Charles VI. While in Paris, Mézières made the acquaintance of Leo of Armenia, and by the time Leo visited England in 1385 Mézières had begun to assemble his "evangelists": Robert the Hermit; Jean de Blaisy, a Burgundian lord and chamberlain at the French court; Louis de Giac from the Limousin; and Otto de Granson from Savoy, of renowned crusader lineage and "knight of honour" of Richard II and John of Gaunt.[154]

Granson supplies a direct link between the Holy Land pilgrimages of the early 1390s and the crusade plans. A paid retainer of Lancaster and his son, Granson accompanied Bolingbroke on his journey to Jerusalem in 1392–93, and with the English prior of the Hospital, John Redington, on the return journey led a delegation on Bolingbroke's behalf to the king of Cyprus. It may be that Granson stayed in Cyprus to negotiate on his own (i.e., the crusade's) account, as it seems that he left Bolingbroke's party at this point.[155] There is considerable circumstantial evidence connecting individual pilgrims to the circles closest to Richard and to John of Gaunt, who had adopted the idea of the crusade at the latest by the summer of 1392.[156] Even if neither spies nor ambassadors, Clanvow, Neville, Swinburne, and Roos are witnesses to the prevailing attitudes at court upon which Mézières and his associates played with some success.

By 1393 Robert the Hermit had met and had been interrogated by the leading politicians at both the English and French courts, and had begun to be accorded a semiofficial position in negotiations. Soon a small Anglo-French force was sent to help Sigismund of Hungary, and by 1395 the lobbying and talking bore fruit in a plan that shows unmistakable signs of Mézières's influence. Both popes issued crusading bulls. A preliminary crusade under the dukes of Burgundy, Lancaster, and Orleans would clear eastern Europe of the Ottomans, preparatory to a general crusade to recover the Holy Land led by the kings of England and France.[157]

The plan of 1395 had a severely practical objective, the defeat of Islam, but an extravagantly emotional incentive, the recovery of the Holy Land. Its political appeal depended on the prospect of solutions to a range of major problems in international and domestic affairs. Mézières's crusade predicated a united and peaceful Christendom, joint action by the kings of France and England to end the schism, and lasting peace between the two kingdoms. Mézières was sensitive to his audience. His letter of 1395 to Richard II, for example, showed a marked softening of tone from his massive *Songe du Vieil Pèlerin* six years earlier, in which the English, although not their king, were berated as warmongers, and the resolution of the schism was envisaged in terms of a victory for Clement VII. By contrast, the *Epistre* of 1395 is diplomatic in its studied generalities, all details being declared negotiable, preferably through envoys like Robert the Hermit. The letter's vagueness made it more appealing. By emphasising the nobility and urgency of peace and unity for the crusade, the kings could skirt entrenched positions on the war settlement and the schism and bypass diehards like Gloucester and Arundel, whose opposition to anything resembling a withdrawal from at least the Brétigny terms could hardly be sustained in the face of a concerted publicity campaign for a crusade.

For Richard II the dividends from such propaganda were plain. Peace and the healing of the schism would allow him greater freedom to secure his position within his kingdom without any loss of face; indeed, the reverse. He appears to have seized the opportunity enthusiastically. J. J. N. Palmer convincingly argued that the Wilton Diptych, that most luminously beautiful painting from the court of Richard II, should be associated with the crusade plans of 1395 in date and iconography.[158] If so, the picture eloquently reflects the advantages available to Richard as patron of a crusade. The king is depicted as a beautiful youth supported by saints and martyrs, including two canonised English kings, Edward the Martyr and Edmund of East Anglia, whose cults had sustained crusaders of earlier centuries. The king is being presented to the

---

On the following pages, the Wilton Diptych. Reproduced by courtesy of the Trustees, the National Gallery, London.

Virgin and to the Child, who appears to be blessing a crusade banner. The iconography of the cross and the symbols of the Passion are strongly reminiscent of the manuscripts of Mézières's *Epistre* and the abridged ordinances of the Order of the Passion presented to the earl of Huntingdon, both of 1395. The youthful king and the angels who surround the Virgin and Child are shown wearing the liveries of both Richard and Charles VI, the White Hart and the Broom-pods. The panel is powerful political propaganda in support of an exalted image of monarchy and is a testament to the use Richard could have hoped to make of his patronage of a new crusade.

Significant changes in political direction usually owe as much to atmosphere as to detailed policy. The mood that allowed the continued Anglo-French peace in the 1390s was in part created by the talk of a crusade. Did it contribute to action? C. L. Tipton has argued, in relation to the expedition that ended in the disaster at Nicopolis in 1396, that "the English government was in no way officially involved in the crusade," and that there were no English troops at Nicopolis beyond some English Hospitallers from Rhodes. Palmer has refuted many of these arguments in detail. It is evident that in 1394–95 there was joint diplomatic action towards preparing the way for a crusader. A plan was agreed in outline by both governments, and money may have been allocated to the enterprise.[159]

However, the crusade that set out in 1396 bore little relation to the one envisaged. It was almost exclusively Burgundian and French in leadership and personnel. Commanded by John of Nevers, not his father, the duke of Burgundy, it was more limited than had been planned a year before. Palmer has suggested that there was an English contingent of perhaps one thousand men, under John Beaufort, Gaunt's eldest illegitimate son, including Ralph Percy, one of Mézières's recruits for the Order of the Passion. It is by no means improbable that some Englishmen accompanied Nevers's force, as testified to by many contemporaries on the continent, although significantly not in England. But the detailed evidence is weak. English writers are remarkably reticent, and there does not appear to be evidence that ransoms were demanded for any English nobles captured by the Ottoman sultan at Nicopolis. When John Beaufort was created earl of Somerset in 1397 on his return to England, reference was made in parliament to his deeds ("journees et travaulx") "in many kingdoms and lands overseas" ("d'outremer"). This could have meant Gascony as much as anywhere further east; if Hungary had been in mind, "outremer" is an unusual way of describing it.[160]

Although Palmer identifies the English troops at Nicopolis as those fifteen hundred soldiers who crossed to Gascony with Gaunt and Beaufort in the autumn of 1394, it is more likely that these troops went to put down the Gascon revolt rather than to join the crusade, especially as details of the crusade had not been finalised by the autumn of 1394. Few commanders would have relished trying to keep an army together indefinitely. Ralph Percy does appear to have gone abroad in the early summer of 1396, but the Evesham chronicler is probably wrong in saying that he was killed at Nicopolis, as royal inquiry established his death as occurring a year after the battle.[161] Therefore, even though individual participation is quite possible, it is exceedingly unlikely that any official English contingent of the sort discussed in the negotiations of 1394–95 fought at Nicopolis. Once again, the crusade had had a greater impact on England than vice versa.

The good intentions of 1395 were overtaken by events, especially trouble in Gascony, almost before they had time to reach fruition. The army of 1396 only partly fulfilled the hopes of the planners, and prospects for a subsequent general passagium were not high even before the news of catastrophe reached the West. The opportunity for unity and peace soon vanished. With hindsight, the battle of Nicopolis appears as a decisive moment. The force cut to pieces beside the Danube was the last great western European army to take the offensive against the Ottomans for over five hundred years. Its failure sealed the fate of eastern Europe, not because the Ottomans were invincible—the Mongols in 1402, the Hospitallers in 1480, and the Hungarians in 1456 demonstrated they were not—but because international cooperation in the West became more difficult, and political difficulties within and between states conspired to prevent any concerted action. Nicopolis had shown how hard the task was. Schemes for crusades continued to be devised, and spies continued to gather information, but the elaborate plans of fourteenth-century publicists were tempered by recent and inglorious experience. As a result, the western response to the eastern problem in general and to the crusade in particular assumed a different character. Resistance to Islam had, perforce, to become almost the exclusive responsibility of those in the front line.

The Fifteenth Century and Beyond: A Continuing Tradition

In the course of a conversation with the German ambassador on 2 May 1484, Richard III learnt of a Hungarian victory over the Ottomans the previous autumn and exclaimed delightedly: "I wish that my kingdom lay upon the confines of Turkey; with my own people alone and without the help of other princes I should like to drive away not only the Turks but all my foes."[1]

This exclamation captures many of the nuances of western responses to the crusade in the fifteenth century. They included concern at the advance of the Turks; impotence allied to ambition; the attenuation of enthusiasm; the monopoly over action of rulers on the frontiers of Christendom, in Hungary, Cyprus, Rhodes, and the Aegean; the enervating jealousies of nationalism; the eclipse of the Holy Land as the main focus of practical attention by the Ottomans; and the ordering of the crusade within wider, but nearer, political priorities. With the contraction of crusading opportunities after Tannenberg, the resolution of the schism, the effective abandonment of papal Italian crusades thereafter, and the reduction of the temporal power of the papacy to an Italian dimension, the eastern problem dominated crusade prospects, with the exceptions of the Iberian peninsula and Bohemia. As a result, the gulf between western aspirations and crusade endeavour became almost unbridgeable.

Any direct military role was abdicated to distant princes or to the Knights of St. John, involvement with the fight against Islam becoming mainly diplomatic and, sporadically, financial. This shift provoked a modification in attitudes and perhaps greater realism. The German Dominican Felix Faber remarked after his second pilgrimage to Jerusalem in 1484 that pilgrims to the Holy Places had ceased to anticipate or expect the recovery of the Holy Land "unless it should please God to work some miracle to that end."[2] A century earlier men had talked of armies and ships. However, the ideal of crusading in the fifteenth century was neither anachronistic or decadent; rather, it ran in different channels.

In the winter of 1446–47, John Capgrave, prior of the Augustinian friary at King's Lynn, composed a work of unoriginal sycophancy, *The Book of Famous Henries*, for dedication to the friary's new patron, Henry VI. One of these, Henry of Grosmont, Henry VI's great-great-grandfather, was described by Capgrave as a father of knights, whose success and reputation were explained by his early career. In youth Grosmont had, according to Capgrave, sought all the battlefields against the pagans and Turks—Prussia, Rhodes, Cyprus, the Levant, Granada, and Spain. Men had flocked to his banner as a result of his deeds against those "who held the Cross of Christ and Christ himself in contempt." In the same work, Capgrave made considerable play with the Jerusalem pilgrimage and Baltic campaign of Henry IV and with the crusading deeds of Henry de Bohun, earl of Hereford (d. 1220) and Henry of Champagne, ruler of the restored kingdom of Jerusalem after the Third Crusade, who as Richard I's nephew was counted as an honorary Englishman.[3] Although literature is a notoriously controversial witness to contemporary attitudes, the testimony of the fifteenth century suggests that Capgrave, far from indulging in an isolated bout of nostalgia for a glorious crusading past, was in tune with his audience.

Enguerrand de Monstrelet had a story that depicted Henry V insisting, with more or less his dying breath, that he had hoped to lead a crusade to Jerusalem.[4] Certainly, the crusade was familiar at the Lancastrian court. Henry's father, grandfather, and great-grandfather had all fought for the cross. After the treaty of Troyes in 1420 Henry himself, with his ally Philip the Good, duke of Burgundy, commissioned a Burgundian nobleman, Ghillebert de Lannoy, to conduct a spying mission in the East, preparatory to a new passagium. Lannoy later consigned the results of his inquiry to a book. Henry V was not noted for impractical romanticism, but the commitment to Lannoy was sufficiently strong to persuade the financially hard-pressed regency council in 1423, after Henry's death, to pay all Lannoy's expenses and to throw in a gift of one hundred pounds.[5] Henry's interest was not merely public. His aunt Joan Beaufort had lent him *Les Cronikels de Jerusalem et de Viage de Godfray de Boylion*; it is refreshing to learn that this monarch, who at times seems almost too good to be true, failed to return it, his aunt having to petition the council in 1424 to retrieve it from the royal library.[6]

Similar networks of interest, revealed by the possession or manufacture of books, are replicated in less-exalted although still wealthy circles. William Worcestre, amanuensis of Sir John Fastolf, one of those captains who made a fortune out of the French wars in the generation after Agincourt, was a notable antiquary. In his *Itinerary* of 1480 he recorded miscellaneous items to be found in Bristol, such as the board hanging in the Temple Church there explaining the foundation of the Hospitallers and an account of a pilgrimage to Jerusalem in 1446 by a Bristol merchant, Robert Sturmy. In 1478, Worcestre compiled a list of the islands of the Greek Sea "lying between Venice and Rhodes towards Jerusalem" from a book by one Christopher Baldemont that had belonged to Fastolf himself.[7] There are other examples of Fastolf's interest in the East. In 1460 shortly after Fastolf's death, another member of his household, John Bussard, wrote, or more likely copied, probably from an original in Fastolf's library, "a cronekyl off Jerusalem" which he then sent to Worcestre.[8] Fastolf had sophisticated literary tastes; he also had more than a literary concern with the crusade. In 1435, pleading before the Anglo-Burgundian Parlement in Paris, Fastolf rebutted charges of cowardice levelled at him by a former servant by claiming that "from a young age he had applied himself to the service of the king in arms in England, Ireland and the journey [*voyage*] to Jerusalem."[9]

Admiring references to crusading were made in a context of sustained practical interest. At the end of Thomas Malory's *Morte d'Arthur*, Sir Bors, Sir Blamore, Sir Ector, and Sir Bleoberis finish their careers fighting "miscreants and Turks" in the Holy Land, in an anachronism which may indicate the influence of the poet's relative Robert Malory, an active Hospitaller who fought in the Levant and became prior of the Hospital in England (1433–40).[10] There was a market for accounts of contemporary battles against the Turks, such as those by Jean de Waurin which the author presented to Edward IV. The dedication to the king suggests the authenticity of Waurin's comment that in 1463–64 Edward offered to send archers on the crusade organised by Philip of Burgundy and Pope Pius II.[11] Crusade chronicles maintained their popularity; in the 1470s John Paston II possessed a chronicle, apparently in English, about Richard the Lionheart.[12]

Such works could be put to some practical use. At Coventry in 1459, a papal legate, to persuade Henry VI of the dangers of Christian dissension in the face of the Turkish menace, produced "various writings and histories," in particular by "the author of the history of the Jerusalemites."[13] Very probably this was William of Tyre or one of his French translators and continuators. By the fifteenth century, William's long description of the First Crusade had often been extracted to form a separate book, which in its French translation served as a popular romance, *Godfrey de Bouillon or the Siege and Conquest of Jerusalem*. It was under this title that William Caxton translated and printed it between March and November 1481, dedicating it to Edward IV.[14] It was probably the work Joan Beaufort had lent her dilatory nephew sixty years earlier. The French redaction had been familiar in the libraries of Europe since the thirteenth century, crusading literature featuring prominently in contemporary inventories. However, Caxton's edition was the first translation into English.[15] It matches in chivalric nature many of his early editions, such as the *Order of Chivalry* by the thirteenth and early fourteenth-century Catalan mystic and crusade propagandist Ramon Lull, its production presumably reflecting the printer's perception of his market.[16]

Caxton was not alone in making this business assessment. Enthusiasm across Europe for news of the fight against Islam was demonstrated at the same time as Caxton's *Godfrey de Bouillon* by the sales and editions of Guilluame de Caoursin's eyewitness printed account of the unsuccessful 1480 siege of Rhodes by the Turks. With its vivid woodcut illustrations, it became an immediate best seller; between 1481 and 1489, editions were published in Venice, Ulm, Salamanca, Paris, Bruges, and London. The English translation, probably printed before 1484, was made for Edward IV by the Poet Laureate, John Kay.[17] Similarly, before 1500 two printed editions of *Mandeville's Travels* were produced, by Richard Pynson (1496) and Wynkyn de Worde (1499). Such tastes survived well into the following century. In the 1520s a new English translation of Hayton's *Flowers of the History of the East*, an early fourteenth-century work of crusade propaganda, was published by Pynson.[18]

These printers were feeding a rich and literate market, centred at court but reaching out through and beyond it to merchants like Caxton himself, families of lesser nobles, and administrators in contact with or dependent upon courtiers. Thomas Leventhorpe (1424–98) of Bedfordshire, from a family that had been employed by the Lancastrians as administrators for generations, bequeathed to his son Caxton's edition of *Godfrey de Bouillon*.[19] This does not, of course, imply that Bedfordshire gentry were all itching to go on crusade, nor even that Leventhorpe himself ever actually read the book; he could have obtained it as a gift from court or as the latest fashionable *curio*. However, there is little doubt that printing facilitated the circulation of books, and it is notable that works of crusading history were among the earliest to be produced by the new technology. Caxton, for one, was clearly pleased with his contribution and recalled it with pride perhaps indicating a successful venture, in the introduction to his edition of Malory's *Morte d'Arthur* in 1485.[20]

Caxton's stated purpose in publishing *Godfrey de Bouillon* is striking. His tone is that of Mandeville and Froissart. He argues that memories of noble deeds inspire readers to avoid evil and to remind them of the responsibilities of princes and nobles, the first of which is "the recuperation of the Holy Land, whiche our blessyd lord Ihesu Criste hath halowed" and the relief of eastern Christians. The relevance of Godfrey de Bouillon's deeds to contemporary problems was Caxton's declared rationale for translating his history, "in whiche I fynde very causes, as me semeth, moche, semblable and lyke unto suche as we have nowe dayly tofore us, by the mescreantes and turkes emprysed agenst Cristendom." Caxton's early and formative career as a mercer and printer in the Low Countries had brought him into close contact with the Burgundian court, a centre of serious crusade planning. Now, he insisted, the Turkish threat was worse than it had been four hundred years before; Constantinople had fallen and in "this sayd yere" (1480–81) Rhodes had been assailed, yet few princes were doing anything about it. Caxton hoped to use "this noble hystorye whiche is no fable ne fayned thynge, but alle that is therein trewe" to persuade "alle Cristen prynces, lordes, barons, knyghtes, gentilmen, marchauntes and all the comyn peple" to follow Godfrey's example, fight the Turk, and recover the Holy Land. In particular Caxton wished that Edward IV or "some noble capytayn of his subgettes," perhaps one of his sons, would undertake the struggle, confident as he was that "every man wyll put hand to in theyr propre persones and in theyr meuable goodes." To this end he called on people to read his book to learn the methods of crusading and, no less important, how "to deserve laude and honour . . . that their name and renomme may encreace and remayne perpetuel."[21]

Such rhetoric may be regarded as a formal sales technique, and the works themselves as little more than familiar sensational adventure stories. However, the issues Caxton raised went deeper than that. Alongside his prologue, and its use of history to instruct and inspire modern crusaders, can be set the "small book of instruction" sent by the king of Portugal to Henry VII in 1505 with a view to persuading him to join a crusade "against the infidels . . . who hold and occupy the Holy Land."[22] Englishmen had been made aware of the victories of the Turks, especially the fall of Constantinople in 1453 and the siege of Rhodes in 1480, primarily through news carried by pilgrims, papal appeals for subsidies, and offers of indulgences to finance the defence of Christendom. Indulgences proved a profitable line for all the earliest printers in England, Caxton included; the indulgence forms they produced did not lie unused.[23] Ottoman atrocities were a byword for evil. Edward IV accused Henry VI's henchmen of "such cruelness as has not been heard done among Sarcens or Turks to christen men." When Pius II was elected pope in 1458, with a reputation as a crusade enthusiast, the University of Oxford congratulated him in the hope and expectation that he would give the lead in combatting the depredations of the Turks. In the late 1440s Henry VI himself received a tract, *De Regimine Principium*, that urged reconciliation between England and France so that the recovery of the Holy Land could be put in hand.[24]

The mentality of the fifteenth century was separated by no great divide from the outlook of earlier generations. It may be noted that Christopher Columbus's will of 1498 made provision for a fund to be established at Genoa for the recovery of Jerusalem.[25] At Edington in Wiltshire, the college of Augustinian Bonneshommes constructed their own replica of the Holy Sepulchre to house ornaments, hangings, and relics brought back from the Holy Land in 1462 by one of their associates, William Wey, formerly fellow of Exeter College, Oxford, and Eton College.[26] In midcentury Sir Thomas Cooke, a draper and alderman of London, was reported to have paid a massive eight hundred pounds for a piece of arras very reminiscent of the Gloucester hangings at Pleshy in the 1390s, "wrought in most richest wise with gold of the whole story of the siege of Jerusalem." His refusal to sell the arras to the dowager duchess of Bedford, mother-in-law of Edward IV, at a price of her choice apparently lay behind a charge of treason brought against him in 1468; such was the duchess's desire to own it. She may have been aroused more by the material splendour than by the scenes depicted, but the latter were clearly in vogue at Edward's court.[27]

Such evidence derives from ephemera; to demonstrate that crusading retained a more signal place in contemporary attitudes it is necessary to test Caxton's assumption of a general willingness to help the cause. One thing is clear—the ceremony for becoming a crucesignatus was still available. The liturgical formula continued to appear in pontificals and manuals such as those of Innocent VIII (1484–92) and in the widely used late fifteenth-century Salisbury Missal, and it was used.[28] In December 1462, the penitentiaries of Christ Church, Canterbury, signed one Robert Almer with the cross. Almer had come to them, after having vowed to visit Rome and the Holy Land, in search of the cross and the customary ecclesiastical blessing for his journey.[29] On 2 February 1479, Richard Walshall, sub-*custos* of the chapel of St. Andrew at St. Alban's, after hearing their confession and giving them the sacrament, signed John Saynton and William Atwood with the cross. They proposed to fight "the enemies of Christ." As Walshall judged their intentions pious and meritorious, he provided them with open testimonials validated by his and the abbot's seals and called on Christians to aid their journey with alms. Walshall recorded that they had received iron crosses (*cruce ferrea*) "as is the custom." The allusion to the custom is intriguing, and the mention of iron, baffling, perhaps a copyist's misreading. Walshall declared he derived his authority from the abbot, which makes it unlikely that the ceremony was part of a general preaching campaign.[30]

Preaching was envisaged for England by Eugenius IV in 1444–45 and by Pius II in 1460 and 1463. Pius authorised the assumption of the cross, with crucesignati being expected to fight for a specified minimum period or to send equivalent material assistance, in return for the same indulgences granted by previous popes "in subsidium terrae sanctae." In 1428–29 ceremonies at which the cross was taken formed part of Cardinal Beaufort's preparations for a crusade against the heretical Hussites of Bohemia.[31]

Whether or not Almer, Saynton, and Atwood took the cross in response to papal directive, the men who gave them the cross emphasised the customary nature of the ceremony; such traditional responses persisted to the end of the century and beyond. In 1499 John Ocle and John Davy of Norwich, probably worsted weavers, vowed to fight God's enemies in the Holy Land; they sought the customary protection of the king, and their vows were supervised by their local parish priest, the mayor of Norwich, two sheriffs, and two aldermen of the city. Almost certainly they published and confirmed these vows by taking the cross.[32] The same emotions prompted Henry Still (or Style); according to his testimonials to Ferdinand of Aragon from Henry VII and Queen Elizabeth, "although small of body," he was held "in good reputation among strong and vigorous knights" and wished "to fight the enemies of the Christian faith," in the shape of the infidel of North Africa.[33]

The crusading habit did not invariably meet with royal approbation. In the winter of 1471–72, Edward IV's brother-in-law, Lord Rivers, planned an expedition to Portugal against the "Saracens" and hoped to persuade John Paston III to accompany him. But the scheme aroused the monarch's scorn. Edward was reported as saying that whenever there was much to be done Rivers would immediately ask permission to leave the kingdom, which the king provocatively ascribed to "kowardyness."[34] Such conflicts could be resolved with less acrimony. Thomas Montagu, earl of Salisbury (d. 1428) fell ill upon returning from his first visit to Jerusalem and vowed that if he recovered he would revisit the Holy Sepulchre; he later repeated the vow in the heat of battle. Twice his attempts to fulfil this second vow were thwarted by the refusal of royal permission; on his third attempt, the regency council in France, where Salisbury was a key military commander in the 1420s, reminded him of his oaths of fealty to Henry VI, from whose service he could not absent himself without permission. The council then obtained the pope's authorisation for the archbishop of Rouen to commute Salisbury's "votum ultramarinum" to other works of piety.[35] Although there is no direct evidence that Salisbury intended to fight in the East he had earlier signalled his support for the armed struggle against Islam by helping to subsidise the construction of the Hospitaller castle at Bodrum in southern Turkey.[36]

The intentions of others are plainer. Fastolf claimed to have served "in arms" in the East early in the century; perhaps he was with the raids on the mainland of the Levant led by the Frenchman Marshal Boucicaut in 1403, although he would have been very young at the time. In 1443–44 an English archer led a landing near the Dardanelles. At about the same time a Welshman, Hugh John, was campaigning in the eastern Mediterranean "against Moors and Saracens on the sea with intent to obtain plenary remissions of all his sins." One Englishman, Stephen Ward, was in midcentury master of the Arsenal at Rhodes; during the great siege of 1480 another, in the service of the grand master of the Hospital, led a group of swimmers to cut adrift a strategic Turkish pontoon threatening the city's defences.[37] The fall of Constantinople provoked at least two bands of Scotsmen to fight the Turks in the later 1450s, and in 1458 three Englishmen, Robert and Thomas Garnet and Robert Allerton, called *domicelli* (donsels, young nobles, or gentlemen with reputations to make), proposed "to fight the Turks in accordance with vows taken in England."[38] Such men were the equivalent in fact and probably in status of crucesignati of earlier centuries, but there were not many of them. There are no stories from the fifteenth century of great numbers taking the cross.

Nevertheless, pilgrimages to Jerusalem continued to be popular. With the famous exception of Margery Kempe, the mystic daughter of a former member of parliament for King's Lynn, most of the pilgrims whose names have survived were, as in the fourteenth century, established clerics and noblemen: Walter Metford, a clerk from London (1421); Nicholas Bildeston, an archdeacon of Winchester a decade later; donsels like John Credi (1409) or John Cressewelle (1413); gentlemen like Roger Wood from Norfolk (1520); great prelates like Bishop Beaufort of Winchester (1417); nobles like Robert de Willoughby; and men from families with proud experience of the East, like John Scrope of Masham and his son-in-law Henry in 1435. Pilgrimages continued to feature in wills; Robert Baxter, former mayor of Norwich, left forty pounds in 1429 for a local hermit to travel to Jerusalem for the good of Baxter's soul.[39]

Some pilgrims left accounts of their journey: William Wey visited the Holy Land in 1458 and 1462; Richard Torkington, a protegé of Sir Thomas Boleyn, the father of Anne Boleyn, travelled in 1516–17; and the chaplain of Sir Richard Guildford wrote about his master's pilgrimage to Jerusalem in 1506 with the prior of Guisborough. Guildford was well-connected; his father had been comptroller of Edward IV's household, and he himself was a privy councillor of Henry VII, master of the Ordnance, and a knight of the Garter. His chaplain's account of his pilgrimage was printed by Richard Pynson in 1511.[40] What these descriptions share is an almost stereotyped devotion to the Holy Shrines and the associated spiritual privileges, barely distinguishable from Brygg's in the late fourteenth century. The accounts of Guildford's chaplain and Torkington are in places actually identical, Torkington evidently having taken the printed report of Guildford's journey as the basis of his own record. The extensive plagiarism is particularly evident in the descriptions of the Holy Sites, where Torkington lifted passages from the earlier work wholesale, although in places pruning the original or adding the odd point where his experiences differed from his predecessor's. In describing the entry to the Holy Sepulchre, the 1507 "we were admytted by the lordes Mamolukes of the Cytie" was amended by Torkington in the light of the intervening Ottoman conquest of Palestine to "the lordes Turkes and Mamolukes."[41] There are some differences of emphasis in the three descriptions. Wey was interested in provisions and rates of exchange, whereas Guildford's chaplain was struck by local legends and colour, noting that the Holy Sepulchre reminded him of the Temple Church in London. Torkington, where original, was most impressed by relics, although this was common to all three. There is considerable homogeneity between these descriptions and earlier accounts. Wey's list of motives and incentives for a pilgrim to the Holy Land—the events and scenes of Christ's life and Resurrection; the requirement to follow in his footsteps; the exhortations of the church fathers; the indulgences; the need to strengthen personal faith; relics; holy geography; and the pervasive imperative of the remission of sins through a good and active deed—could have been composed at almost any time between the twelfth and sixteenth centuries.[42] Torkington's otherwise surprising plagiarism reinforces the impression of overwhelming traditionalism.

Pilgrims were not blind to the political realities of the eastern Mediterranean. Wey was haunted by rumours of Turkish victories, defeats, and impending attacks. A description of a pilgrimage in the 1480s describes in detail the cannon, spears, lances, shields, catapults, bows, and missiles carried by pilgrim ships for protection.[43] In 1517, Torkington's ship carried a contingent of Hospitallers armed with handguns, although in the event they were employed only in foraging.[44]

Guildford's party a decade earlier had to dodge Turkish shipping and had difficulty in finding a Christian port in which to resupply after a storm. Torkington's own ship in 1516 deliberately avoided Rhodes on the outward trip, so as not to antagonise the new Ottoman authorities in Palestine who regarded any association with the Hospitallers as a hostile act.[45]

Pilgrimages were still hazardous. Guildford and the prior of Guisborough both died in Jerusalem in 1506, and their ship almost foundered. In 1446 the ship of Richard Sturmy of Bristol was less fortunate, the wreck claiming thirty-seven lives. On Torkington's pilgrimage, a priest and a London pewterer succumbed.[46] These published descriptions conveyed to their readers in England, probably, it is true, not a very large circle, fear of the Moslems, a keen desire to avoid provocation, and some implied outrage.

There was one haven of peace. In October 1506 Guildford's chaplain and his companions put in at Rhodes on their return journey and were richly entertained by the English knights of St. John on duty there. Torkington had a similar welcome a decade later although, with a stunning lack of originality, he again filched the exact words of his predecessor to describe the occasion, adding only the name of John Booth to those of Thomas Newport and William Weston (the future prior of England, 1527–40) as the most prominent of his hosts.[47] Such conviviality "in the jaws of the Turks," as a contemporary phrase had it, exposes the nature of active fifteenth-century crusading.[48] Pilgrims demonstrated that the Holy Places continued to hold strong attraction and to arouse lively sympathy, but westerners prosecuted the crusade against Islam by proxy. In some ways this was a logical extension of practices introduced since the late twelfth century. The relationship of most people with the crusade had become financial rather than military, and hopes of a Christian counterattack concentrated on well-funded professional armies or military orders. By design and default, the faithful in the fifteenth century paid for indulgences and vow redemptions, or donated money to support either papal efforts to organise crusades or the knights of St. John at Rhodes. The Hospitallers, in turn, were also supported by recruits into the order, never in very large numbers, and a few western adventurers; they were subsidised by annual levies (responsions) on their extensive estates in the West and by occasional specific sales of indulgences on their behalf, as in 1480–81.[49]

After Nicopolis, indirect involvement was probably the only effective option available to Westerners, as demonstrated by reactions to Byzantine appeals for help. The failure of the 1396 crusade confirmed the isolation and vulnerability of the Greek empire. Emperor Manuel II Palaeologus, now a client of the Ottoman sultan, sought aid from the West, reinforcing his demands with a personal mendicant tour of the courts of Italy, France, and England.[50] In 1398 Boniface IX instituted a new issue of crusade indulgences on Manuel's behalf; it was an important lead, as western attitudes to the Greeks were by no means friendly.[51] Apart from the small expeditions of the count of Savoy in 1366 and Marshal Boucicaut in 1399, and attempts by publicists like Mézières to get Byzantium accepted as part of Christendom and therefore worth defending, the West persisted in regarding the Greeks with suspicion as schismatics. As late as 1413 a papal nuncio was collecting money on behalf of John XXIII to aid the Holy Land "against Saracens, Turks, Greeks and other infidels and heretics and rebels of the Roman Church."[52] All too easily the image of perfidious Byzantium, ingrained in western attitudes by centuries of crusading myths and by the tangled history of Frankish Romania, could be revived.

In 1398 Richard II arranged for "voluntary" contributions for Byzantium, over and above money collected from indulgences in parish collecting boxes. One member of his council was instructed by the king to pay forty marks; the two archbishops, the bishop of Winchester, the earls of Northumberland, Worcester, Gloucester, Salisbury, and Westmorland, Thomas Percy, and Lord Lovell contributed one hundred marks each; the bishops of London, Salisbury, Exeter, and Ely forty pounds each; the bishop of Chichester twenty pounds; and the bishop of St. Davids ten pounds.[53] These donations, combined with other gifts received by the exchequer, produced almost fifteen hundred pounds. In addition, Richard II himself had granted two thousand pounds in the form of an advance, to be recouped by the Crown from the proceeds of indulgences, the sale of which was in the hands of papal agents led by the Greek bishop of Chalcedon. Significant sums were raised by local depositories, presumably from indulgences; the churches in Lincolnshire and Leicestershire alone raised £325 11s 10d.[54] Manuel himself was royally entertained at Christmas 1400 by Henry IV, who conspicuously tried to honour his predecessor's commitments, and the emperor's expenses of four hundred pounds incurred during his two-month stay at Calais were paid by the exchequer.[55]

Although the proceeds from indulgences probably tailed off after 1399, money was collected throughout the kingdom, English generosity being noted in a number of contemporary chronicles. In general, the effort to prop up Byzantium in this way was accepted as worthwhile. Walsingham pointed out that although Manuel was a schismatic he was nevertheless a Christian, and Adam of Usk even referred to a mythical common ancestry of the Greeks and the British through Constantine.[56] Even so, by 1401 the bishop of Chalcedon had received on Manuel's behalf only £158 11s 3d. Although Henry IV paid over the two thousand pounds promised by Richard II, which had mysteriously got mislaid in transit, and donations were still being chased as late as 1426, it is clear that much of the subsidy stayed in England, with the exchequer perhaps realising a profit of some two thousand pounds.[57] After the initial enthusiasm and despite the continued approval of the new Lancastrian regime, the fundraising ran into the sands, probably for administrative reasons. The whole operation was extremely complicated, with the ecclesiastical collectors and the exchequer acting as separate foci of organisation, despite some attempt to integrate them. As so often, the shortfall between promises and income was only bridged by the use of bankers and credit facilities, which opened wide prospects for peculation, incompetence, and delay, as shown by the fate of Richard II's initial grant, which the king's Genoese agent seems simply to have lost. In the diocese of Chichester in 1400 it was suspected that one of the local indulgence collectors, the Dominican John of Strasbourg, had absconded with some of the proceeds.[58]

Nevertheless, the effort was, initially at least, by no means negligible, and it may have attuned some Englishmen to look with greater sympathy on the plight of Byzantium. Later in the century, apart from general indulgence campaigns in favour of the stricken eastern Christians in 1439 and 1455, money was raised for individuals suffering at the hands of the Turks. In 1427 Paul, count of Valache "from Greece," received an annual exchequer pension of forty marks from the regency council, because he had been left destitute by the Ottoman advance. After the fall of Constantinople itself, bishops offered indulgences to all who contributed to the relief of individual, named Greeks badly affected by the conquest.[59] Such sponsorship was, from the English point of view, convenient and cheap and, even if it did little to mitigate Byzantine suffering, it signified that not everybody had turned his back on the misfortunes of eastern Christendom.

The Byzantine subsidy of 1398–1401 also set the pattern for material English contributions to crusading in the fifteenth century. Only the Hussite crusade of 1428–29 led to any significant or centrally organised recruitment; for the rest it was a matter of raising money through the sale of indulgences or taxation of the clergy. Occasionally these efforts were very specific, such as the offer of indulgences between 1409 and 1414 to provide money to build the Hospitaller fortress at Bodrum in southern Asia Minor. For some time the Hospitallers had sought to augment their annual revenues from responsions by offering partial indulgences to the faithful, the sales techniques of their pardoners causing considerable resentment among parish clergy in the 1360s and 1370s.[60] In the early years of the fifteenth century, the Knights, having lost their stronghold at Smyrna to Timur the Lame in 1402, were establishing a new base at Bodrum, the site of ancient Halicarnassus and its famous Mausoleum, stone from which was used in the construction of the Christian fortress dedicated to St. Peter. This fortress was to act not simply as a military post, but also as a refuge for fugitive Christians from the Ottoman Empire. According to Pope Alexander V in 1409, over the two previous years the Hospitallers had spent 700,000 florins on building the castle and on general defensive measures against the Turks. To those who contributed to the order, the pope offered the right to appoint a confessor who could grant plenary remission of sins at the hour of death; the offer was to last for five years. Precedents for such fundraising for crusader fortifications stretched back at least to the early thirteenth century. Alexander's bull circulated slowly through England, only being published by the bishop of Durham, for example, in 1413. Each diocesan, as further immediate incentive, added forty days remission of enjoined penance to contributors. To further the campaign the grand master of the Hospitallers, Philibert de Naillac, visited the order's English headquarters at Clerkenwell in 1410.[61]

Already in the autumn of 1409 one English nobleman, Henry FitzHugh, was exporting bows, arrows, bowstrings, and a "steyne cloth" bought by him in the City of London "for furnishing the castle of Saint Peter."[62] The papal indulgence, although published by the local bishops and ecclesiastical authorities, was administered by the Hospitallers themselves through proctors like John Seyvill, a knight of the order, two of whose confessional letters have survived. The English evidence is slim, the three extant letters confirming confession, contribution, and privilege all dating from 1413–14. These letters reveal that among those who purchased the indulgence were John and Agnes Groby and their three children, and Sir William FitzHugh and his wife Margery. The FitzHughs were conforming to family tradition. The Henry FitzHugh who sent equipment to Bodrum in 1409 was probably William's father, later chamberlain of Henry V and guardian of the infant Henry VI; William's son, another Henry, received a licence to visit Jerusalem in 1468. As previously, crusade interest ran in families.[63]

The castle of St. Peter itself provides more striking witness to English participation. Over the gateway to one of its towers, known as the English Tower, twenty-six coats of arms were set up in stone, including those of Henry IV, the Prince of Wales, the dukes of Clarence, Bedford, and Gloucester (the king's sons), the duke of York, and the families of Grey, Zouche, de la Pole, Neville, Percy, Holland, Beauchamp, Burleigh, Strange, Arundel, Montague, Stafford, de Vere, Courtenay, FitzHugh, Cresson, Woolfe, and Fairfax, many of whom could boast of both long and recent crusading traditions.[64] It is an eclectic parade, one unlikely to have been erected from any roll of arms without some specific reason. It is probable, therefore, that these shields signify the magnates who had contributed to the Bodrum appeal, some of whom might have been lobbied by the grand master himself on his visit to England. The link between Bodrum and England was not to be solely financial. At least two prominent Hospitallers, William Dawney in 1448 and John Langstrother a decade later, did tours of duty as captains of the castle of St. Peter.[65]

The 1409 appeal, like the 1479–82 appeals for Rhodes and Bodrum, was unusual in being designed for such a precise purpose and administered by other than papal or diocesan agents.[66] The fate of the more usual indulgence can, however, offer the historian an insight into both the subjects brought to the attention of the faithful and their response to them.[67] The fact that the papacy persisted in the indulgence as a method of fundraising itself suggests a continuing popularity of this form of investment. Between 1444 and 1502 there were twelve sales campaigns in England to raise money for a crusade against the Turks. In addition there were fundraising exercises for crusades against Ladislaus of Naples in 1411 and the Hussites in 1427. Money was also sought outside the general campaigns; thus, from 1442, three-quarters of the proceeds of the plenary indulgences offered to those who visited Henry VI's foundation at Eton was to be spent on resistance to the Turks.[68] Evidence of yields is incomplete, although there are signs of a relative decline in profitability from about 1455. Even so, the 1476–78 indulgences realised at least £1,500, with those of 1487–93 bringing in over £890. Polydore Vergil claimed that Jasper Ponce's indulgences mission in 1501 raised "great sums of money." He also noted that, in order that "the people might aid more freely," Pope Alexander VI had strengthened the offer of Jubilee indulgences by announcing "for the first time to undertake a war against the Turks; thus much money was brought together." The implication is that, in the pope's view at least, indulgences could be profitable, but crusade indulgences especially so.[69]

The precise rates of payment for the indulgences were usually left to the discretion of the papal commissioners. Assessment was increasingly related on fixed scales to wealth. This was both prudentially fairer and easier to calculate than the traditional formula of estimating the cost to the recipient of performing a crusade in person or sending a proxy. In addition to granting indulgences, Ponce in 1501 was empowered to pardon a wide range of criminals and usurers and to create doctors of civil and canon law "as well as if they were created in any university," always provided the beneficiary came up with adequate cash.

A list of charges survives from Ponce's mission. The scale of assessment for laymen was as follows:

Annual income from lands, tenements, rents £s	Payment to gain indulgences		
	£	s	d
2,000+	3	6	8
1,000+	2	0	0
400+	1	6	8
200+		13	4
100+		6	8
40+		2	6
20+		1	4

Value of moveables (i.e., income from sources other than property) £s			
	£	s	d
1,000+	2	0	0
400+		6	8
200+		2	6
20+		1	0

If purchasers' moveables were worth less than £20, they were to contribute "as it shall please them of their devotion." The money collected in this way was declared to be "for the relief and defence of our faith against the most cruel and most bitter enemy of the same, the Turk."[70] It may be thought that those at all levels were buying remission on distinctly favourable terms.

From the 1470s indulgences commissioners had the benefit of the new technology of printing, which must have eased the bureaucratic burden considerably. Printers such as Caxton, Lettou, Wynkyn de Worde, and Pynson printed batches of indulgence forms, leaving blank spaces for the recipient's name to be filled in at the time and place of sale. The use of these printed forms may even have expanded the market. A number survive, including the 18 April 1481 sale, at Oxford, to John and Katherine Frisden of indulgences for the relief of Rhodes. The indulgence letter issued to Henry and Katherine Langley of London on 13 December 1476 may be the earliest surviving example of English printing.[71]

An indulgence purchase might not have been a sign of enthusiasm for the crusade, despite Polydore Vergil's remarks. However, the repeated sales do signify a tenacious papal concern with the problem of the East that ensured the retention of the crusade as a feature of public religion and politics in the fifteenth century. Doubts as to that cause's popularity have been widely voiced by modern historians. G. A. Holmes, writing of a legacy of ten marks given to the Hussite crusade in 1429 by a Yorkshireman, John Pigot, commented that he "may have been an eccentric enthusiast for crusade since he also left 40s for the defence of Rhodes."[72] Holmes overstates the case, for Pigot was not alone in his anxiety or in seeing pious bequests and donations as a path to salvation. In 1457 the new bishop of Durham, Lawrence Booth, gave three hundred pounds to help arm a fleet against the Turks. Twenty years later Thomas Belasyse of Hewknolle received indulgences from the abbot of Abingdon in return for confession and "a suitable quantity" of subsidy to equip and maintain ships to oppose the Turks. In 1507 Henry Sharpe, a Norwich rector, left six shillings eight pence "to the Christian wars against the unfaithful Turks." Popular interest in the fight with Islam, expressed through financial payments, was assumed by critics of Edward IV in 1469, when Warwick and Clarence, in a manifesto aimed at rallying opposition to the king, accused Edward of spending "the goods of our Holy Father [i.e., the pope] the which were given him for the defence of the Christian faith of many goodly disposed people of this land without repayment of our said Holy Father." The reference was either to the 1464 crusade tax on the church or to the 1463–66 sale of indulgences—probably the latter, as the chronicler's own words imply ("many goodly disposed people"). There is evidence that some of the 1464 church subsidy actually reached the papal treasury, whereas there is no sign that any of the indulgence money did.[73]

Apart from indulgences and private gifts, traditional financial support of the crusade was through clerical taxation. However, royal policy was consistent in denying direct papal authority to levy mandatory crusade subsidies on the English church. Both king and church were united in their insistence on the voluntary nature of any grants, each of which required royal approval and authority. Since the end of the last mandatory papal tax in 1336 the church had paid subsidies to the Crown instead. In 1388 the position was formalised by parliament; it was reinforced by royal action against the collection of a papal twentieth the following year. In fact, in the forty years before the schism of 1378, popes had generally avoided taxing the English church. After the end of the schism in 1417 they continued to be reluctant to call upon the clergy for any direct subsidy, mandatory or voluntary, except for the crusade. Even here, the delicate triangular relationship of king, pope and local clergy, together with the French wars and the domestic feuding around the throne, prevented much effective fundraising. In 1428–29, despite the apparent agreement of convocation, a voluntary clerical subsidy for the Hussite campaign planned by Cardinal Beaufort was blocked by the royal council. In 1481–82, Sixtus IV's request for a subsidy after the siege of Rhodes and the Ottoman capture of Otranto was talked out by an ecclesiastical commission. Even when the response had been more positive, in 1444–46 and 1463–64, instead of a mandatory or voluntary papal levy being raised, the clergy were invited to make a grant to the king, who promised then to donate the proceeds to the pope. However, on each occasion the royal grant was designed to raise considerably less than the full ecclesiastical tenth demanded by the pope—a quarter of a tenth in 1464 and an eighteenth of one in 1446.[74] The most successful negotiations in terms of raising money were those of 1501–3, which resulted in a clerical tax to the king for the crusade; the tax collected over twelve thousand pounds, none of which Henry VII kept for himself.[75]

By 1501, the chronic weakness of the Crown's finances had been ameliorated, and there was no apparent immediate crisis. Henry VI and Edward IV could not have afforded to be so generous with ecclesiastical funds, which had provided an important source of Crown income. Yet official attitudes were not purely mercenary. For one thing, each papal demand called into question the extent of independence won by the English church in the concordat with Martin V after the end of the schism. For another, kings and ministers were not untouched by an appreciation of the object of crusade levies; the complaints against Edward in 1469 suggest that any overt hostility to them would have proved bad politics. Indeed, in 1464 Edward himself had pressed for a higher rate of tax than the church authorities were initially disposed to grant, and at the same time he may have been toying with the idea of sending archers to join the papal-Burgundian "blessed viage."[76] Richard III's concern has already been mentioned. The status of crusade money, once gathered, still prohibited easy diversion into royal coffers, the more so in the later Middle Ages because the Crown had much freer direct access to other church taxes and so had less need to risk obloquy over crusade money. It is also notable that successive regimes, although tempted by the wealth sent out of England each year by the Hospitallers, resisted pressure from the Commons to appropriate the annual responsions in the interests of the realm.[77]

When action against the Turks appeared imminent, with evidence of concrete plans instead of discrete schemes and pious hopes, English kings tended to be sympathetic. Thus Edward IV only agreed to authorise a crusade grant when Pius II actually announced the papal alliance with Burgundy and Venice and the muster of an army at Ancona. In 1502–3 Henry VII sent money directly to the front line, the Emperor Maximilian and the pope, at a time when plans for attacks on Islam in

Central Europe and the Mediterranean held some prospect of fruition. English governments had no wish to subsidise the papacy but were prepared occasionally to help the crusade against the Turks. The reaction to other crusading targets was, on the other hand, rather more equivocal; in 1428–29, for instance, the regency council was content merely to act as a broker rather than as an investor in Beaufort's crusade.[78]

The sums of money involved in crusade taxes or indulgences were meagre, even when compared to the cumulative contributions of the Hospitallers in England, let alone to regular domestic taxation. The highest fifteenth-century yields—such as over £4,000 from indulgences in 1455 that was probably sent by the pope to Rhodes, around £4,000 raised in 1464, or the £12,000 subsidy of 1502—compare feebly with parliamentary or convocation grants which, combined, averaged £17,000 a year between 1461 and 1470. Crusade subventions contrast even more with the levels of domestic expenditure, Edward IV's in the 1460s being estimated at £50,000 per year, with royal income in the 1470s running at £65,000 to £70,000 a year. The 1446 crusade levy of £1,000 was trifling when set against exchequer receipts of 1445–46 of between £90,000 and £105,000.[79] On this basis, material involvement by the community in the crusade may appear largely symbolic.

That is not the whole story. For several reasons, events prevented Englishmen from forgetting the crusades. The papacy continued to use the crusade in support of its own temporal and ecclesiastical interests, for example against Ladislaus of Naples in 1411 and the Hussites of Bohemia in the 1420s. Popular reaction in England to these crusades, both of which offered privileges explicitly associated with the Holy Land, even though equally explicitly concerned with European politics, was minimal in the first instance and obscure in the other. Beaufort's preaching and fundraising for a crusade against the Hussites was well-organised, from the grand ceremonial processions at St. Paul's to the parochial collecting chests labelled for the "croyserie." Some at least of the more than £7,000 paid to Beaufort for crusade expenses must have come from the sale of indulgences, although what proportion is impossible to know. Money alone had been sought for the Neapolitan crusade, but Beaufort managed to gather some sort of army large enough to require fifteen hundred horses. The recruits would presumably have qualified for the status and privileges of crucesignati, even though ultimately they were diverted to combat the Valois resurgence in France. Beaufort clearly anticipated that recruits would adopt the cross; he provided detailed instructions for the ceremonial giving of the cross, in this instance a red cross of silk or woollen cloth.[80]

Interest in crusading relied on more than papal bulls and fundraising. The crusade constituted almost the last active demonstration of the practical unity of Christendom under nominal papal leadership. More particularly, it was significant as one means of protection against the Turkish threat, the seriousness of which could no longer be regarded as distant. By the 1460s the Ottomans were on the Danube and the Adriatic; in 1480 they were in Italy. In October 1463, in almost Churchillian vein, Pius II spoke with more than rhetorical significance of the Ottoman seizure of noble provinces from the Black Sea to Hungary, from the Aegean shore to the Danube: "Christianity has been restricted to an angle of the world."[81]

As the papal legate pointed out to Henry VI at Coventry in 1459, the growing Ottoman pressure on the Danube presented a potential danger to the Rhine and, hence, directly to English interests.[82] The advance of Islam in central Europe was alarming enough, but the growing Ottoman naval presence in the Mediterranean from midcentury was noticed by a wider audience than nervous pilgrims, as it began to affect trade. England had been used to importing yew for bowstaves from the Black Sea through Venice, but from the 1470s this traffic was seriously interrupted. Supplies ran short and prices rose rapidly, to the vocal consternation of the Commons, although members were inclined to believe a Lombard plot was behind the dislocation. In 1472 an act was passed insisting that Venetian importers carry four bowstaves per ton of cargo; in the next decade the tariff per butt of Malmsey or Tyre wine was placed at ten bowstaves, and the price per stave was fixed at three shillings four pence. More general fears of a Turkish trade embargo continued to be expressed openly into the sixteenth century, as some English eyes remained focussed on the East.[83]

Papal bulls were not the only source for news of events in the East. In 1457, a so-called priest from Hungary toured England publicising three letters. One purported to be from the sultan of Egypt to the pope, Calixtus III, another was the supposed papal reply, and the third, allegedly by a Dominican, outlined the scale of the Turkish threat to Hungary and contained an account of how the Hungarian regent, Hunyardi, had repulsed the Turks from Belgrade in 1456. The purpose of the letters was to arouse or heighten anti-Turkish feeling and to encourage greater participation in the specific appeals for money. The first two letters set the tone and context, the third gave, in colourful language, some focus of fact. When the Hungarian priest reached the abbey of St. Alban's he had an interview with the abbot, whom he told of Hunyardi's successful defence of Belgrade and the need for more Christian aid in the East. The abbot had the last letter copied into the abbey's register, in order to keep the memory of the Hungarian victory and the Turkish menace fresh forever.[84] The first two, purely fictional, letters he did not preserve.

Political preoccupations ensured very muted responses. The fate of the papal appeals of the 1450s and 1460s, at a time when prospects for a papal-Burgundian crusade were promising and English kings sympathetic, illustrates the difficulties. From the 1440s the debacle in France, economic and financial disasters, and civil and political unrest precluded public action. For a generation after 1450 no English government could seriously contemplate even the most modest of foreign adventures beyond France. Crusading was also complicated by diplomatic rivalries. In the 1450s, for reasons connected with the tortuous politics of the Sicilian succession, the pope was reluctant to support the English faction led by Margaret of Anjou, Henry VI's aggressive wife. More pertinently, Burgundy, the pope's ally in crusade plans, supported the increasingly restive Yorkish party. The bias of both crusade protagonists, therefore, was hardly designed to elicit a favourable response from the beleaguered Lancastrian regime. As Pius II himself noted in 1460, "England holds out no hope."[85]

The outbreak of civil war in that year confirmed his pessimism. In 1459 Pius had sent Francesco Coppini, bishop of Terni, to England in an attempt to reconcile the factions, preach the crusade, and offer indulgences; only in the last did Coppini have any success, and that was very small.[86] In part, this was his own fault. Far from trying to mediate, Coppini became a rabid Yorkist partisan, perhaps unsurprisingly in view of papal-Burgundian sympathy for the duke of York. Before the battle of Northampton in July 1460 the papal "mediator" excommunicated the Lancastrians, offered the Yorkists absolution and plenary remission of sins, and forbade the burial of any Lancastrian dead, in a startling, but not unprecedented, diversion of his original commission. Coppini and the pope perhaps reckoned that a strong Yorkist regime with a puppet Henry VI to maintain legitimacy (a solution canvassed at the time) would be the best means to secure English help for the crusade. Two things spoilt the plan: the failure of the Yorkists to deliver a conclusive military verdict in 1460; and, after the decisive Yorkist victory at Towton in March 1461, the death of Charles VII of France four months later, which opened the way for the new French king, Louis XI, to begin to undermine the dukes of Burgundy, in which cause he allied himself to the dispossessed Margaret of Anjou. To achieve the reconciliation of France and Burgundy, a prerequisite for any new crusade, the pope now had to soften his anti-Lancastrian line, at least on the continent. Yet even if the diplomatic circle could have been squared, the precarious finances of the politically still-vulnerable Edward IV forbade foreign adventures. Thus, at the moment when there was greatest political will in Europe for a new crusade, an overeclectic and perhaps overambitious papal policy conspired with the circumstances to prevent any effective English response. Papal policy was so far the slave of the moment that in 1462 Pius II, eager to ingratiate himself with the French, repudiated the hapless Coppini, who found himself incarcerated inside a papal prison when his only crimes had been to be excessively zealous in the pope's cause and to be overtaken by events. Pius II's crusade plans, thwarted by circumstances, died with him at Ancona in 1464.

This confused and ultimately frustrating scenario was replicated in a variety of ways throughout the century and all over Europe, and it would be wrong to attribute such failures to organise crusades to accident alone. The political disequilibrium that hamstrung the plans of midcentury, and the instability of the English Crown in its volatile relations with the nobility and its chronic financial weakness, were due as much to wider structural changes in the economy and society as to the chance of battle or the accession of infants and weaklings. The inability of the papacy to provide consistently effective leadership was the consequence of forces that had their roots less in the alleged corruption of institutions or individuals than in changing spiritual patterns of observance and belief on the one side, and an emergent autonomy of national legal and political systems on the other. So, too, it could be argued, the advance of the Ottomans and the collapse of parts of the eastern defences of Christendom owed more to the long-term disturbance of traditional commercial, cultural, and administrative structures than to the skill of Mohammed the Conqueror or the fanaticism of the janissaries. Thus any counterfactual model of the fifteenth century that removed the accidental hindrances would still not necessarily admit the crusade as a practical option. Equally, however, any picture of fifteenth-century Europe would be incomplete without a place for the crusading habit as a secular mentality and a religious exercise.

Although political and logistic obstacles to English crusading may have been insurmountable, the attitudes and aspirations of the aristocracy embraced not only the still-cherished ambition of conquests in France but also the grander dream of the defence of Christendom. Many of those more accustomed to the battlefields of the Midlands did not forget those of the Middle East. Interest in crusading literature and indulgences was by no means decadent, even in the face of practical disappointment and national outlets for the energy and emotions traditionally associated with crusading, notably the French wars and nascent patriotism. Although primarily appearing as a characteristic of the aristocratic mentality, the cause of the crusade was not unknown in lower ranks of society. Crusading remained an issue, regularly drawn to popular as well as noble attention. As the familiar framework for solving what was perceived by many as the most urgent problem facing Europe, the crusade still provided a focus for debate, planning, and hope, not least in the period of respite in Ottoman western advances in the forty years following the siege of Rhodes in 1480. In the sixteenth century, in addition to its role in the fight against Islam, the crusade also supplied a customary weapon for a church under attack from within. Thus, the crusade continued to address some of the most prominent and contentious political issues of the day.

National Crusades?

The question of the decline of the crusade still exercises historians. In the fourteenth century any decline was concealed by fragmentation, as the papacy summoned crusades with the same, if not greater, frequency as before. In the fifteenth century the change was unmistakable. There were fewer crusades and fewer crucesignati, as practical crusading opportunities contracted in the two centuries after 1300, in the Mediterranean, Spain, and ultimately Prussia and Italy. Changing social and cultural habits within the fighting classes found new means of chivalric expression. By 1400 international crusading had to compete as never before with national wars as alternative fields for noble deeds and martial endeavour. Some of this change is reflected in the evidence adduced in the last two chapters, where the emphasis is increasingly on what people thought and aspired to rather than what they did. But the crusade did not vanish; the ideal remained very much alive. Traditional forms and ideology persisted in their own right, available and understood by Richard III as much as they had been by Edward I, even though not used. Exclusive concentration on formal crusading cannot avoid leaving the impression of decline. The crusade was not dead in 1500, but it had lost its centrality in political debate, military planning, and religious observance.

However, concentration on formal crusading misses the protean quality of the crusade, which had always given it its importance and now ensured its survival in forms other than itself. If formal crusading declined under pressure of events, crusading ideology and emotions did not. Rather they infected other sorts of warfare in a process from which emerged the sanctified patriotism distinctive of late medieval and early modern Europe. This contribution was largely literary and emotional, but occasionally tangible, and rarely unconscious. What happened was a fusion of the religious and the secular, centred on the figure of the ruler and the perception of nationality. Arguably the fusion was less the result of new concepts or ideologies than of altered circumstances. Nevertheless, the crusade's part in the process marks it as a formative influence on the development of the modern world.[1]

The fourteenth and fifteenth centuries saw changes in the practical nature of warfare evident in the thirteenth reach fruition. The costs of war, the extensive range of patronage, and, particularly in England, the extraordinary taxation at the disposal of princes, coupled with social, linguistic, and political developments, consolidated the power of central authority—the monarchy in England, and later in France and Spain, and the local dynasts in Germany and, briefly in the fifteenth century, the Low Countries. Private war could no longer be sustained legally or financially, and in England as in the rest of Europe, nobles and rulers had to resort to mutual support. Edward III obtained his generals and his taxes, and in return his nobles received titles, estates, lucrative military commands, and the profits of war. This view may at first sight seem eccentric, as between 1300 and 1500 four English kings were deposed and murdered, another briefly forced into exile, another killed fighting rebels. Almost all had serious trouble with prominent nobles at some stage in their reigns. Yet the internecine conflicts of the reigns of Edward II, Richard II, and the Lancastrian and Yorkist kings reflected a mutual dependence between magnate and ruler; they were fights for shares in wealth and power that only the monarch could provide.

The concentration on the ruler affected the role and perception of the monarchy. A "religion of monarchy" was developed, most notably by Philip IV of France and his ministers in the early fourteenth century.[2] A roughly similar process occured in England and was manifested in Edward I's elaboration of the Roman Law concepts of treason and lèse majesté, in the legal separation of the public institution of the Crown from the private person of the king, and in the almost obsessive recitation by Edward I, Edward III, and his eldest son, the Black Prince, of the supreme need to defend the royal honour, in Scotland or France.[3] If in England the "religion of monarchy" never reached the sophistication of its French counterpart, under a Richard II or a Henry V it could approach it. In such developments the Hundred Years War played an important part as a sounding board for royal publicists and a motor for changing attitudes, as the issue of dynastic and legal sovereignty merged into a wider contest for Right, Justice and Honour, causes which were identified with the nation, not just the king.

Just as in France hatred of the invading English hardened over the decades into a form of patriotism, so English fear of French or Scottish attack became the obverse of national pride. The successful warrior kings Edward I, Edward III, and Henry V took great pains to aid the process by informing their subjects of the progress of the war, always with a suitably religious and patriotic gloss. Much of this constituted short-term political prudence, as England could only sustain her war effort by unprecedented levels of taxation requiring a measure of public consent. It was therefore essential for successive monarchs to identify their interests with those of their subjects. Announcing the victorious outcome of the Agincourt campaign to parliament in 1415, the chancellor, Henry Beaufort, bishop of Winchester, proclaimed that it had brought "the greatest honour and profit to the realm of England." The sentiment was endorsed by the Commons when, in gratitude it seems, they immediately granted the king additional subsidies; Agincourt had not only exalted Henry V's crown and fame but had been a "singular comfort to his loyal lieges" and a "perpetual profit to all his realm."[4]

The merging of royal and national identity opened new avenues for respectable military employment, especially when both sides in the Hundred Years War proclaimed their confidence that God and their patron saints succoured and sustained their causes. To serve one's lord had always been honourable; to serve him in a just cause which, being national, embraced one's own interests as well as his, and which received the support of divine favour, was even more so. In 1351, Bartholomew Burghersh, at Edward III's request, received a papal dispensation to defer his crusade vow for three years, during which time he was forbidden to fight Christians *except* in defence of himself or the king within England. Increasingly, from Edward I's campaigns in Wales and Scotland to the French wars, royal battles were characterised as conflicts involving the welfare of the subject. They attracted an aura of sanctity in consequence; this was public war, not private war writ large. That at least was the royal theory, although Edward I failed to convince all his vassals of the difference in the 1290s.

Public war pleasing to God had clear connotations. A poem on the Scottish wars composed in the late 1290s not only praises Edward I as "entirely devoted to Christ" and deserving of God's favour, but extends the king's deserts to his subject: "May the Governor of the universe whom we address as God, who protected the Hebrew people through many difficulties, give the English victory over their enemies." This identification of the English with the Israelites was expressed even more plainly by the bishop of St David's, Adam Houghton, when he addressed parliament as chancellor in January 1377: "God would never have honoured this land in the same way as he did Israel through great victories over their enemies, if it were not that he had chosen it as his heritage."[5]

The biblical association was one commonly ascribed to crusaders, often by themselves. As military aristocrats had always been attracted to crusading partly by the "glamour of martial glory and social esteem," this sanctified national cause suited their aspirations.[6] Like the crusade, a holy national war was the public business of the Chosen People of God and therefore a field in which the highest renown could be won. Governments and war theorists were not slow to appreciate this. The intellectual and propagandist debate on warfare led in the fifteenth century to the emergence of what has been called "national chivalries": a new, systematised focus for traditional pursuits that embraced the shifting realities of military and social organisation, as well as the arguments of influential theorists such as the Frenchman Honoré Bonet or the carefully manicured propaganda of the English chancery.[7]

During the Hundred Years War the liturgy itself was pressed into service, with special prayers and processions, as well as sermons, devoted to the royal and national cause. Prayers for the king were, of course, a venerable tradition, and prayers specifically for royal success in battle can be seen in eleventh century *laudes regiae*. The immediate precedents for Edward III's use of prayers and processions were, however, to be found during his grandfather's wars of the 1290s. In 1294 the king requested prayers to be said by the clergy in support of his war with France over Gascony, and in 1298 processions as well as prayers were authorised prior to a campaign in Scotland; such measures were repeated by Edward II in 1312. Public religious displays of loyalty, whatever their effect in harnessing divine approbation, were clearly useful in propagandising the king's cause as just and holy, in defence of the church as well as the realm. The institutional debt to the crusade is obvious. By assuming for themselves and their followers the mantle of divinely sanctioned patriotism, monarchs appropriated some of the rhetoric, much of the emotion, and ultimately, in the sixteenth century and beyond, most of the traditional appeal of crusading. Only the full crusade indulgence was impossible to transfer without papal sanction. National wars could thus fill the vacuum left by the lack of opportunities to fight for the cross. The red cross displayed at Evesham became the emblem of English fighting forces in France and Spain and was even adopted by some of the peasants in revolt in 1381. At the same time, it remained the sign borne by crusaders in Prussia, on Despenser's Crusade (1383), and later, in Bohemia.[8]

The fusion of crusade and national war helps explain the gradual submergence of the crusade, at least in the fifteenth century. The process was less one of decline than of translation, although the rise of nationally focussed holy war did not necessarily preclude traditional crusading when the opportunity arose. These developments may be seen as the culmination of the transformation of attitudes to just and holy war outlined in the first chapter. Specifically, crusade ideology had never detached itself from older and concurrent traditions of legitimate violence. Since the 1090s the two traditions had cross-fertilised; theories of holy war had provided intellectual substance to the armed pilgrimage, but thereafter the latter had consistently infected the former. The process involved more than warriors simply claiming, like William the Conqueror at Hastings or both sides at the battle of Lincoln (1141), that God was on their side. The exhortations before the attack on Lisbon (1147) and the battle of the Standard (1138), the one overtly crusading, the other not, referred alike to honour, glory, reputation, defence of home, country, and comrades, and the will of God, in support of the forthcoming action, promising salvation to those who died in God's cause. On both occasions religious banners were used to concentrate and externalise divine approval.[9] This identity of war in defence of the patria and the crusade was inherent in much papal crusade propaganda in the twelfth century. It is illustrated forcefully in the speech of the "saintly" archbishop Dubricius in Geoffrey of Monmouth's *Historia Regum Britanniae*, where the symbols and privileges of the crusade, the cross and the plenary absolution, are used in defence of the fatherland.[10] There may be argument over the precise legal status and the canonical implications of such privileges being offered to warriors in secular conflicts in the twelfth century, but the general inference is obvious: long before national wars subsumed it, crusading, in a literary form, had attached itself to the idea of patriotic warfare. In turn this may have contributed to the way in which the later national wars came to be perceived. The genesis of "national chivalry" was a long one.

Certain features of the extension of crusade institutions to secular disputes in the thirteenth century are also relevant. In some accounts of the crusade against the rebels in 1216–17 and of the crusading posturing of Simon de Montfort in 1263–65, crusaders are described as fighting "pro patria." The Waverley annalist attributes the desire of royalists to expel Prince Louis in 1217 to their wish to have a native rather than a foreigner as king. The royal partisan who wrote the poem on the battle of Lincoln (1217) characterised the royalists with their white crosses as "the strength of England" pitted against "the French fury."[11] These accounts have led to speculation that the crusade of 1216–17 was "the first example of a type of national crusade which was to recur in the Hundred Years War."[12] But, as suggested, the patriotic gloss to events is largely an accretion of later xenophobia.[13] Similarly, references to Montfortians being prepared to die at Lewes "pro patria" owe more to hagiography than fact. The weight of contemporary evidence suggests that Earl Simon, a Frenchman, on the contrary saw as the central issue liberty of the church and people from royal, as much as foreign, tyranny.[14] Circumstances hardly allowed for a clear-cut patriotic crusade on either side. The crisis was domestic, not patriotic.[15] It is hard to see either 1216–17 or 1263–65 as witnessing any national crusade, even if strands of anti-alien feeling were exploited by those people who were also associating their actions with a crusade.

Nevertheless, national self-consciousness was evident. The 1188 crusade ordinances had recognised feudal, rather than national, divisions in providing for vassals of the kings of France and England and the count of Flanders to wear crosses of different colours. But national divisions can be observed on the Third Crusade in the export to Palestine of the cult of Thomas Becket by Londoners and others in 1190 and in the foundation of the Order of St. Thomas of Acre. In the same way, some sort of German identity lay behind the establishment in Syria a few years later of the Teutonic Knights. During the Fifth Crusade national groups were recognised in the allocation of mosques at Damietta in 1219. However, recognition of local cults and local solidarity on crusade are very early stages in the development of national self-awareness. Dislike or fear of foreigners are insufficient of themselves to forge patriotism into a positive military or political force, or to produce conditions in which national self-interest could acquire a prestige and appeal equivalent to that of the crusade.

The key to the growth of a sense of specifically national identity was royal policy and the changing material circumstances of war and warrior society apparent in the wars of Edward I and Edward II. Clerical xenophobia, literary conventions, and the extension of crusading helped prepare the ground; so too did certain aspects of the administration of English law and the heightened claims of the king. In 1216–17 a crusade was fought for the king, but it cannot be described as national. By 1300 the distinctions were beginning to blur, as Edward I's assertion of his sovereignty was supported by a nobility generally eager to share the fruits of victory and the patronage of the subsequent peace, and was sustained by the advice and consent to national taxation of the commons in parliament. The unity of purpose was not perfect and almost collapsed in 1297–98. But cooperation and mutual involvement became integral to the smooth working of the state. Legally, the king's service, including military service, had long held a superior status, his servants being, with pilgrims and crusaders, automatically entitled to essoin of court. A merging of crusader privileges with those enjoyed by royal servants was effected at the time of the 1270 crusade.[16] However, none of these elements by themselves could have led to royal campaigns being regarded or planned as crusades in all but name; only the pressure of events could do that.

In the 1280s and 1290s Edward I's campaigns against the Welsh and the Scots were presented by church and state as struggles for the church and orthodoxy as much as for royal rights and the protection of the realm. Archbishop Pecham excommunicated the Welsh for rumoured atrocities and condemned them for their unorthodox religious observances. His successor Winchelsey saw the war with the Scots as a defence of the church. With the institution of prayers and processions, the causes of religious faith and secular loyalty were deliberately combined in royal propaganda. Again this was not entirely novel; in 1138 the Scots had been, like the Welsh in the 1280s, likened to heathen. However, Edward I gave such emotions a clearer public and national focus.

Against Scotland in the 1290s Edward I exploited not simply his overlordship but also his leadership of the crusade. When he tried to extract crusade tithe money from the Scottish church, refusal to pay invited the traditional penalty of excommunication.[17] Nonpayment became a symbol of Scottish independence, and with the outbreak of war between the English and Scots in 1296, some Scottish churchmen argued, like Simon de Montfort in 1263, that resisting Edward I was more justified than fighting Saracens.[18] They were opposing fire with fire, as Edward's insistence on the perfidy of the Scots rarely lacked a religious tinge. In 1299 Edward described the Scottish rebels as sacrilegious. A year later he apparently went a stage further.[19]

According to a St. Alban's account of the summer campaigns of 1300 to Annandale and Carlaverock, when Edward moved into Scottish territory he "signed himself with the banner of the Lord's Cross" and, covered by its protection, "he sewed [it] on front and back with all the rest of his fellow soldiers."[20] This is an isolated reference on which, perhaps, too much should not be based; yet the contemporary writer may have distilled current propaganda into a psychologically striking, and possibly factually accurate, image. The grounds for a crusade or pseudocrusade against Scotland could have been twofold. Edward was a crucesignatus, and the Scottish rebellion prevented the fulfilment of his vow, to his and Christendom's detriment. The fomentors of discord had to be extirpated as a preliminary to the general passagium, although, unlike 1216–17, there was no overt papal blessing; rather the reverse, as Boniface VIII tried to bring peace to the north by being even-handed and by refusing to accept Edward's claims outright. The crosses in Annandale may, of course, have been the chronicler's blunder; he may, for example, have mistaken for crusade devices the black crosses of St. Cuthbert worn by the substantial contingent from Durham under Bishop Bek.[21] Alternatively, if Edward did adopt the cross, he may have been reviving the royalist crusader badges of 1265, in what he was labouring to portray as a similar circumstance of sovereign versus contumacious rebels, in which case the incident belongs more properly to the history of English military uniforms. Wherever the truth lies, the image was potent. English policy continued to display signs of what could be called quasi crusading. It was encouraged by continued talk of a new passagium; by traditional elements of hostility to the Scots, which had assumed an aura of divine protection before; and by Scottish counterpropaganda, especially by Bruce, which attempted to turn a calculated factional coup to seize the Scottish crown in 1306 into a holy war of national resistance to English aggression.[22]

In 1306, after Robert Bruce had murdered his rival claimant John Comyn and had had himself crowned king of Scotland, Edward I complained that some of Bruce's clerical partisans were preaching that his supporters would earn as much merit by fighting for the rebellion as if they had gone in service of God to the Holy Land. This line of exhortation does appear to have formed part of Bruce's early propaganda.[23] At the knighting of Prince Edward at Whitsun 1306, the king swore a public vow—one account says he made it "to the sign of the cross"—to avenge Bruce's murder of Comyn and to expel him for "his contemptible attack on God and the church," as a final deed of arms before departing to fight in the Holy Land.[24] The new Scottish crisis was placed squarely in the context of the crusade and disobedience to the church. This theme was pursued early in the next reign, when Clement V confirmed Bruce's excommunication for contumacious disobedience to his liege lord Edward II and for the murder of Comyn on consecrated ground, acts which manifestly injured the prospects of the "negotium Terrae Sanctae."[25] The attempt to put Bruce beyond the ecclesiastical pale, and therefore make him legitimate prey to revolt from his subjects and attack from his "sovereign," was pursued for some years. As the Scots themselves observed in the Declaration of Arbroath (1320), the English charge that the Scots were hindering the crusade was loudly proclaimed.[26]

Although aimed at diplomatic advantage, such policies reflected attitudes to public war which presaged the developments of the Hundred Years War. For more than a century the popes had used the crusade against political foes; it is hardly surprising that secular rulers followed suit.[27] English efforts to launch a crusade against Scotland were unsuccessful, but they marked a step in the attempt to reconcile royal, and by more than implication, national, interests with a holy and righteous cause.

Similar ideas had been apparent before when the Scots attacked northern England. Ecclesiastical figures such as the bishop of Durham and the archbishop of York (Archbishop Thurstan in 1138, Zouche in 1346, and Bowet in 1417) played conspicuous parts in raising troops and organising local resistance. Rannulf Higden saw the defeat of the Scots at Neville's Cross in 1346 as primarily the work of monks and priests; this point was also emphasised in a contemporary poem celebrating the victory as both divinely and patriotically inspired. Almost half a century later Henry Knighton, a canon of Leicester, drew a graphic picture of the English at Neville's Cross preparing to live or die "for the salvation of the kingdom," confident in the justice of their cause and God's favour, marching to battle with prayers of comfort ringing in their ears and the "sign of the cross" borne before them as one of their banners.[28] Although there was no papally constituted crusade, the 1346 Scottish episode consistently attracted literary parallels with crusading. The Scottish wars were not national crusades, but they became patriotic wars with deliberate crusade associations; Brian de Jay, master of the Temple in England, died fighting not the infidel but the Scots, on behalf of his liege lord Edward I at the battle of Falkirk in 1298.[29]

When Edward III launched his French campaigns the tools of propaganda and publicity that were to sustain the English war effort for the next century already existed. The French wars accelerated and consolidated the image of the king's war as holy and just—a secular crusade at a time when prospects for a traditional general passagium were remote. Edward openly used the church, including the friars, to publicise his cause. The identification of his French war with a sort of national crusade was soon evident. A poem criticising the truce of 1347 explained God's protection of the English as a consequence of both the justice of Edward's case and the Christian virtues of his troops. Although not borne out in reality or always in contemporary observations, such as the so-called *Prophecies of John of Bridlington*, divine protection of warriors fighting a just war was an almost universal feature of English panegyrics.

By the 1390s, propaganda on occasion went beyond simply regarding God as being naturally, if not an Englishman, then at least an ally of the new Israelites. Knighton's retrospective on the war, written probably between 1390 and 1395, contains some revealing passages. Edward III's departure for France in 1355 is prefaced by celestial visions. The troops of the Black Prince, preparing to meet the enemy at Poitiers in

1356, "sign themselves with the sign of the Holy Cross." A popular verse on this battle, included by Knighton, asserts that the pope had become French, but Jesus had become English. English archbishops and bishops are described as offering "grandes indulgentias" in 1360 to all who joined the war in France, each recruit also being allowed the privilege of choosing his own confessor, a right commonly granted to crusaders. The clergy themselves were, in this account, to provide proxies or supply funds for others to fight.[30] Although formally inaccurate, except as regards to Despenser's crusade of 1383, such attributions to a wholly secular royal expedition were not accidental.

Whether or not English troops were offered spiritual privileges to fight the French, temporal privileges had already been requested for men serving in the royal armies and fleets in the 1340s, including essoin of court, exemption from taxation, temporary moratorium on debts, and pardon from crimes—the privileges of the crucesignatus.[31] It is immaterial whether the crusader's privileges and these secular privileges grew up simultaneously, or whether one imitated the other, and if so, which came first. What is important is that the soldier of the king might expect to share certain material benefits with the soldier of Christ. In itself this may have helped establish the popularity of national holy war.

However, Knighton touched on the profound difference between the French war and the crusade when he talked of spiritual privileges. Only during the Great Schism was the full armoury of crusading privileges trained on the enemy, and warfare pursued, as one Carmelite friar put it in 1386, "principally in two ways, in battle and in indulgences."[32] National wars may have supplied a respectable alternative to crusading, in the process pilfering many of its trappings, but they were not direct substitutes. Technically, the first national crusades carrying full papal authority were those conducted by the bishop of Norwich and the duke of Lancaster in the 1380s. Yet the ideologies of crusade and the national holy war are scarcely distinguishable.

The crusades against Flanders (1383) and Castille (1386) arose out of a temporary coalition of mutual self-interest between the Roman pope, Urban VI, and certain influential leaders in the English government, and led to the merging of the papal schism and the Anglo-French war.[33] In the early years of the schism that had begun in 1378 between Urban VI and the Avignon pope, Clement VII, both sides contemplated a military solution, the so-called *voie de fait*. According to Jean Froissart, the prolific chronicler and intimate of both the French and English courts, the crusade bulls offered to the English in 1382 by Urban matched similar incitements to crusade issued by his rival Clement to the French.

Three years later at the battle of Aljubarrota in Portugal each side, invading Castillian Clementists and defending English-backed Urbanist Portuguese, were promised crusade indulgences by their priests.[34]

As early as 1379 bulls of Urban VI for a general crusade against the Clementists were circulated in England, and in March 1381 Urban placed the direction of this crusade in England in the hands of the colourful and controversial Henry Despenser, bishop of Norwich, a veteran of papal wars in Italy who enjoyed donning armour for a good fight.

General injunctions to attack the Clementists had earlier held little appeal for the English government, whose ambassadors tried to persuade the pope to specify France, Spain (i.e., Castille), and Scotland as the targets for such an enterprise.[35] The motives of the pope, Bishop Despenser, and the English government were, therefore, at variance and only briefly conjoined. Urban's concern was to establish his undisputed power in Christendom. The bishop was ambitious, warlike, and used to independent action, clearly fancying himself in the role of a military general and papal legate who would destroy the French by battle, not diplomacy. In the English government different factions pressed for different policies. A group of younger earls, including Buckingham and Arundel, were eager to pursue the war with France. John of Gaunt, duke of Lancaster, the most powerful man in the kingdom, preferred that resources be directed towards securing his claim, through his wife, to the throne of Castille. The young Richard II himself, on the other hand, whose influence had grown since the Peasants' Revolt of 1381, was already surrounding himself with advisers who sought a settlement with France rather than escalating hostilities.[36] The maverick Despenser fitted none of these court factions. In 1382 he rejected the king's caution and argued for a campaign in Flanders, contrary to Gaunt's wishes; he later disdained to have Arundel with him as secular lieutenant-general. The crusade, when it came in 1383, was founded on shifting sands.

The unity necessary for acceptance of Despenser's crusade plan was fragile. Early in 1382 the king and his council wanted direct papal financial support for any such military enterprise, hoping, misguidedly as it turned out, that the crusade would pay for itself. After the Peasant's Revolt and the collapse of the expedient of the poll tax, any new fiscal demands had to be handled with particular delicacy.[37] Renewal of hostilities with France became more likely as a revolt by Ghent against the Francophile count of Flanders created severe instability in England's main trading partner. In October 1382 the government presented parliament with the options for a crusade. One alternative was a crusade to Spain in support of John of Gaunt's claim; the other was a "croiserye general" to be led by the bishop of Norwich. Although the decision, after considerable haggling, was left to the king and council, the Commons had no doubts that the most cost-effective campaign would be one in Flanders, and their opinion soon gained the strength of political necessity when in November the French defeated the Ghent rebels at the battle of Roosebeke. In retaliation for English support for the Ghentois, English goods in Flanders were confiscated and trade severed.[38] National interests were now directly at stake, and by the end of December the king had authorised his subjects to join Despenser's crusade. The papal bulls were published, and administrative machinery put into action.[39]

The papal privileges were customary: crucesignati were to enjoy the full Holy Land indulgences, which could also be purchased, in full or in part, by gifts. Although the operation was sluggish in producing soldiers, many laymen and clerics took the cross, and considerable sums were apparently raised. Froissart estimated twenty-five thousand francs, and the heresiarch John Wyclif, a vehement opponent of the whole business, put the figure at some thousands of pounds. Most chroniclers agree on the powerful impact of the sale of indulgences.[40] Exact totals cannot be ascertained, but it was clearly a profitable enough exercise to encourage imposters to ply a lucrative trade.[41] Despite a few vitriolic attacks on the venture by Wyclif and others, the element of the crusade indulgence added to the popularity of the enterprise.[42]

The effect of the indulgences on military recruitment remains uncertain. As Froissart observed, "Men at arms cannot live on pardons, nor do they pay much attention to them except at the point of death." Despenser recognised this by offering to pay yearly wages to those who joined his expedition.[43] Many who accompanied Despenser to Flanders in the summer of 1383 were, according to their royal warrants, specifically "in the king's service" and, presumably, his pay. Thomas Walsingham at St. Alban's reported that among those Despenser hired were two knights: William Beauchamp, who received five hundred marks which he in fact kept for himself without joining the crusade; and Thomas Trivet, who did embark but was later accused of treachery.[44] Pay rather than faith alone was mainly responsible for recruitment. In return for a parliamentary fifteenth, in February 1383 Despenser agreed to provide twenty-five hundred men-at-arms and twenty-five hundred archers for a year and a suitably armed and manned fleet. For this purpose he ultimately received from the exchequer £37,475 7s 6d which, despite the fact that he broke his contract as regards both length of time served and number of troops recruited, he was in the end allowed to keep.[45] The nucleus of Despenser's army was paid out of these central funds controlled by the bishop and his treasurers; the government itself saw to the amassing of bows and arrows.[46] Muster was fixed for Sandwich on 27 April, although many were late and some never reached the anticipated destination.[47] There were probably some volunteers as well, but they appear from the Westminster chronicle to have been less than welcome. In June 1383 at the siege of Ypres, Despenser ordered that "all who were not in receipt of official wages should return to England."[48] Walsingham confirms that these volunteers were ill-disciplined, having only joined up at the prospect of booty. Even so, some privately funded recruits were shipped across the Channel by Sir John Philpot, a London merchant who acted as the expedition's banker and, with Despenser's treasurer Robert Foulmere, had charge of its finances.[49] Paid for by the exchequer, raised by what look like a series of indentures, with a commander approved by king, council, and parliament, Despenser's crusade, for all its canonical propriety, was the Hundred Years War thinly disguised.

Some contemporaries noticed. Froissart, admittedly a hostile witness, was struck by the hypocrisy of the crusade, and it is hard not to agree with him.[50] Walsingham used full-blown conventional crusade rhetoric to describe the crusaders' attack on Gravelines:

> Our men . . . having the banner of the Holy Cross before them . . . thought that victory in this cause was glory but death reward . . . those who suffered death would be martyrs . . . and thus the blessing of the cross was achieved, and the *crucesignati* gloriously captured the town and there destroyed the enemies of the cross so that not one of them remained alive.

In fact, these "enemies of the cross" were Urbanists.[51] Only one of Despenser's commanders, Sir Hugh Calverley, made any attempt to find schismatic Clementists to fight. Otherwise, the Urbanist crusaders progressed through Urbanist territory, withdrawing from the siege of Ypres and ultimately the whole campaign, before they ever engaged the army of the king of France.[52] Of course, English chroniclers did not report it that way, nor, perhaps, did many contemporaries see it like that either. It could be argued that they appreciated the essence of the operation: an English campaign to restore their interests in Flanders, which in the normal course of things could have merited quasi-religious status. The criticisms of the crusade voiced by chroniclers, and, indeed, by members of the government and parliament, tended to concentrate not on the expedition's hypocrisy but on its failure and the faults of its leader.

During the crusade itself official pronouncements stressed the insep-arability of national and religious objectives, while effectively implying the secondary nature of the latter. In October 1382 the bishop of Here-ford emphasised that the alternative crusade schemes concerned "the salvation of the realm."[53] Despenser himself agreed that if the Clem-entists were converted to the Roman allegiance he would merely swop the "banner of the crusade" for that of the king, and his instructions to crusade preachers urged them to organise processions and prayers to God "in salvation of the state of Holy Church, the kingdom, the expe-dition and the crusaders."[54] In March 1383 officials were calling the campaign "a crusade for the defence of the Holy Church and the realm of England," and in April Despenser was described as being "about to sail overseas on the king's service."[55] In the same month Archbishop Courtenay pointed out that the French, in addition to being the worst schismatics, were "the chief enemies of the king and the kingdom of England," and that Despenser was moved to secure "the peace of the church no less than the safety and defence of the realm out of the bond of nature." The peace of church and kingdom were inextricably linked, and of course, there was more merit and propriety in fighting for God and the faith.[56]

Military failure soon blew away the religious panoply. There is some evidence that the new chancellor, Michael de la Pole, tried to stop the expedition even before it embarked, and he certainly deserted the bishop at the soonest opportunity thereafter.[57] The earlier vociferous enthusi-asm of the Commons for Despenser's crusade can probably be attrib-uted more to their distrust of Gaunt than to their crusading ardour. Even those chroniclers favourable to the enterprise—and not all were—identified, perhaps with hindsight, greed as the motive of those who volunteered to fight in Flanders.[58] The crusade of 1383 was primarily an episode in the war against France and in the newly self-conscious nationalism which that conflict helped develop. Apart from the rheto-ric, the privileges, and the indulgences, the Flemish *chevauchée* had in practice little to do with crusading as a means of defending the church or Christendom, especially as Flemish Urbanists suffered more than the supposed Clementist targets. A suitably equivocal symbol for the operation was provided by the apprentices of London who, hearing of the crusaders' victory at Gravelines in May, left their work and rushed to join the crusade wearing white hats, red scabbards, and red crosses—signs of the crusader, the patriot, or St. George? Perhaps all three.[59]

Despenser's crusade was a fiasco. A military disaster, its leaders dis-graced and its investment wasted, it merely served to highlight political fissures at the top of the English government. Despenser was hounded from his temporalities, and his treasurer Foulmere and five leading commanders (excluding Calverley) were imprisoned and fined a total of 14,600 gold francs, which they allegedly had received in bribes from the French to cease hostilities.[60] However, it is easy to see the initial attraction of the scheme, especially once intervention in Flanders became almost imperative after Roosebeke. From the 1330s the English had feared a Francophile pope promulgating a crusade against them. The schism provided an opportunity to reverse the weapon. The pope himself would give little trouble provided the expedition was a success. With the expected profits from the sale of indulgences, the campaign could be run comparatively cheaply, which would help persuade the Commons to grant a subsidy. What was more, the church could be involved in raising money, inspiring enthusiasm, and imposing discipline by threats of excommunication.[61] To create such an apparent wave of popular support for government action, only two years after the Peasant's Revolt, was an achievement. There were of course dangers in using the church in this way. The ceremonies where Despenser formally adopted the cross and the crusade banner, and the sermons, masses, processions, and confessions, could stimulate popular commitment; but away from the crowds and the collecting boxes, some peers voiced serious misgivings at allowing a cleric like Despenser so much authority.[62] Citing the example of the pope's attempt to control Naples after its conquest in 1381 by a similar papal champion, they argued that "the rights of the king of England . . . in France . . . might easily be extinguished . . . if the bishop, in ostensible consequence of having taken the cross, were to subdue France by military action, especially as he would seem to have made his conquests in the church's cause rather than the king's."[63] To meet this problem, an attempt was made, which Despenser ignored, to impose on him a royal lieutenant to safeguard the king's legitimate interests. More generally, the propaganda already discussed, equating royal and ecclesiastical objectives, may have been designed to minimise any potential conflict.[64] As a reflection of the development of patriotic sacred warfare and of the adaptability of the crusade, therefore, Despenser's expedition is significant. As evidence of the vigour of the pristine crusade ideal, however, it has little to offer the historian.

Another perspective on Despenser's crusade is opened up by that of John of Gaunt. Even though its stated context was also the strategic welfare of England, this was in practice more a personal enterprise. The comparative lack of chronicle attention suggests it made much less of an impact in England than Despenser's crusade, despite many similar characteristics. Gaunt's crusade depended on a complementary parliamentary grant, obtained late in 1385, as well as papal bulls originally

338

issued in 1383 but republished in February 1386, specifying indulgences the same as those offered by Innocent III in the decree *Ad liberandum* in 1215.[65] An ecclesiastical administration was organised, preaching undertaken, and an additional range of dispensations offered (for example, from pilgrimages and for marriages within the prohibited degrees of consanguinity). There is no firm evidence of widespread popularity of these devices, although conceivably John Holland joined Gaunt in Spain in part expiation for the murder of Ralph Stafford.[66] The authorities seemed to lack the confidence of 1383 and were nervous even of minor critics such as John Elys of Stowmarket in Suffolk, who was ordered to be arrested and hauled before the king's council for preaching that, in spite of Urban VI's bulls, Gaunt's crusade was "suspicious and not true"; hardly very radical criticism, especially when compared to the tirades of Wyclif and his followers in condemnation of Despenser's campaign.[67] This sensitivity was a general feature of the regime at the time. In May 1383 a Norfolk man, Thomas Depham, was imprisoned for doubting in public the presumably official news bulletins on the progress of Despenser's crusade.[68] Nevertheless, the number of troops recruited (by what means is unclear, although it is unlikely that many were enlisted by crusade preaching) was adequate. Gaunt soon gave up his crusade, on entering into an agreement with Castille in 1387 of a sort he had solemnly promised a year earlier never to undertake. The Westminster chronicler's comment on this volte-face, even if not intended to be sarcastic, exposes the problem of credibility: "If the king of Spain refused to agree to these terms, the duke [of Lancaster] was of course free to take vigorous military action against him to destroy him and his people, as being in the truest sense enemies of Christ's cross."[69] In any case, Gaunt's sale of crusade indulgences does not seem to have amounted to much, a fact attributed by Walsingham to indulgences having been offered so often that, at any rate in the short term, they had become cheapened and debased.[70]

Whatever the public or the government view of these crusades and the efforts to raise money for them, the irascible Urban VI took them seriously, and it was with some disgust that he rescinded Gaunt's privileges in January 1389.[71] Increasingly the *voie de fait* had proved a dead end for both popes and was not universally popular within the church. The *Eulogium historiarum* laments the loss of monks who fled their monasteries under the pretext of going to fight the antipope.[72] Walsingham commented on a similar exodus from St. Alban's in 1383.[73] In 1386 preachers offered papal chaplaincies for sale, attracting the youthful, the restless, and even potential heretics. An Augustinian canon who availed himself of the opportunity ended his career a Lollard; at

least, that is Walsingham's story.[74] The history of one young Benedictine is eloquent of how the exigencies of the crusade still had the power
to destroy traditional expectations and to transform the life of a humble, provincial monk. Walsingham names among those who joined Despenser's crusade one William Shepey, who returned to St. Alban's at
the end of the crusade, but evidently, having seen the world outside,
wanderlust had gripped him. Three years later he bought one of the
proffered papal chaplaincies and was off again, although not quite for
good. In 1421–22, thirty-five years later, Shepey sought readmission to
his old abbey and, fortunately for the reputation of St. Alban's, he was
allowed to return.[75]

The expeditions of Despenser and Gaunt saw the crusade manipulated, with varying degrees of success, for national and personal advantage. What marked these campaigns out from other English wars was
that, in the unique circumstances of the schism, the pope connived at
the association. Despite their critics, then and now, the popes did not
commonly allow such diversions in the fourteenth century where their
immediate interests were not threatened. The crusades in Flanders and
Spain were approved as extreme measures in an unprecedented church
crisis. It was not until the sixteenth century that any part of the Anglo-
French conflict was once more so openly identified by the pope with a
crusade, not a fact until Henry VIII's invasion of France in 1512.[76] By
then English monarchs had less need of additional spiritual privileges
to gild their war machine, for in the years after 1386 the rhetoric of
national war and the skilful elaboration of the religion of monarchy, in
the context of the war with France, had reached new heights of
sophistication.

It hardly mattered whether Henry Knighton or his contemporaries
in the 1390s really conceived of English warriors in 1346, 1356, or 1360
as crusaders, which technically they were not—the merging of symbols
and objectives was almost complete. Over the previous two hundred
years the idiom of holy, as opposed to just, war had largely, although
not exclusively, been that of the crusade and its recognised targets—
infidels, heretics, and fomentors of schism. Now the emphasis shifted.
It would be misleading to describe the shift as a secularisation of the
crusade, because the religious justification for the English cause remained strong, as demonstrated in Knighton, in Chancellor Haugh-
ton's speech to parliament in 1377, in Archbishop Courtenay's letters
of 1383, and in the round of special prayers for the king's wars. Nor did
these wars become legally or canonically identical to crusades; they
could not, for example, automatically attract papal indulgences. The

fusion was instead one of emotion and ambition, which reached its apogee in the propaganda surrounding the campaigns of Henry V.

One account of the battle of Agincourt in 1415 has King Henry commanding each soldier before the battle to make a cross on the earth and then to kiss it "in remembrance that God died on the cross for us . . . and in tokening that we will rather die on this earth than flee." It is a neat juxtaposition that goes some way to explain why field commanders were fond of such high symbols; they were good for morale.[77] An even clearer report of how Henry V appropriated the images of the holy warrior is by one of his own army chaplains at Agincourt. He described how, on the eve of the battle, every English soldier made confession and "put on the armour of penitence," and how in the original "Agincourt speech" Henry referred to his troops as "God's people" and cited for their encouragement the example of Judas Maccabeus, the familiar crusader prototype.[78] During the battle the chaplain and his fellow priests prayed hard and reminded the deity that the king's devotion was aimed "to the worship of God, the extension of the church and the peace of kingdoms"; truly Henry was, the chaplain later described him, God's own soldier as well as the Lord's anointed.[79]

Away from court there may have been diminishing enthusiasm for the sanctity of the royal cause in France, witnessed by a falling off of the number of special prayers for the war experienced in the diocese of Lincoln in the early fifteenth century, a sign perhaps of disillusion or just boredom. On the other hand, where the government controlled events, extravagant applause could be expected in recognition of the holiness of the French war.[80] The apotheosis of Henry V as a holy warrior, no less worthy of fame, respect, and divine favour than any crusading hero of the past, came with the king's entry into London a month after the victory at Agincourt. The capital was bedecked with statues, flags, coats-of-arms, puppets, human tableaux, and choirs, all designed in praise of blessed England, its patron saints, holy kings, and present hero.[81] In such extravagant and carefully orchestrated explosions of religiously buttressed patriotism, it may be thought that the crusade had become redundant, replaced by a new secular martial cult no less emotionally satisfying than the old. This indeed was the experience of England in the sixteenth and seventeenth centuries. However, there were many who found room beside the new national religion for the crusade: traditionalists, and those who were afraid of heresy, felt threatened by infidels, were in love with adventure, or were doubtful of the absolute sanctity of killing Christians—even Henry V's chaplain worried about that. For all Henry V's noble deeds in his holy cause in France, the chivalrous contemporary chronicler Monstrelet revealed a still-sensitive emotional chord when he chose to depict Henry's last thoughts on earth as being fixed on his unfulfilled quest to recover Jerusalem.[82] Even stripped of its original objective and its canonical privileges, the crusade's characteristic compound of secular ambition, emotional community, religious enthusiasm, and military idealism continued to penetrate society into the sixteenth century, sometimes in its own right and sometimes as a dynamic ingredient in the ideology of national religious warfare.

13

The Tudors, the Reformation, and the Crusade

On 22 October 1536 contingents of rebels from the northern counties of England began to gather at Pontefract in southern Yorkshire. One of the rebel groups, from the lands of the bishopric of Durham, wore a distinctive insignia, the Black Cross of St Cuthbert, and a badge showing the Five Wounds of Christ—a wounded heart in the centre with blood dripping into a chalice with two pierced feet below.[1] The castellan of Pontefract, Thomas, Lord Darcy, on seeing the badges of the Five Wounds was reminded that he had used the same device on an expedition he had led to fight the Moors of North Africa in 1511. He may not have been alone in this reminiscence, as one of the rebel leaders at Pontefract, Sir Robert Constable, and another knight who had been persuaded to join the rebellion, Sir Ralph Ellekar, had also been on that expedition.[2] Darcy remembered that somewhere in the castle there was a store of these badges left over from 1511. A search was instituted, the store was found, and the badges were promptly distributed among the rebels, Darcy himself presenting one of them to the pacific leader of the rebels, Robert Aske.

This curious moment in the Pilgrimage of Grace aroused the intense interest of the government, in particular Thomas Cromwell. Pontefract was a royal stronghold and Darcy a royal officer, yet he had surrendered the castle and given rather peculiar succour to the self-proclaimed pilgrims. Darcy's gesture was especially significant because the crisis of the rebellion seemed at hand; a royalist army had mustered a few miles down the road at Doncaster. Among the questions put to Darcy by his interrogators in 1537 were a number specifically drawn up by Cromwell, who was keen to pin prior knowledge and support of the rebellion on Darcy. After trying to elicit why Darcy had surrendered Pontefract and had, apparently voluntarily, associated himself with the rebels by taking the pilgrims' oath, the questioners continued:

Why you gave badges of the Five Wounds of Christ. Was
it not to make the soldiers believe that they should fight
in defence of the Faith? Was not that badge of Five Wounds
your badge, my Lord Darcy, when you were in Spain?
Whether those badges were new made or were the same
you gave in Spain or what remained of them? Could you
not have disposed the said badges before the insurrection?
Did you keep them for that purpose? If they were new
who made them, and where? And how long before the
insurrection? For what intent you made those new badges?
Was it not for setting forth the insurrection of Yorkshire,
encouraging the soldiers to believe their rebellion was for
defence of the Faith? If you were suddenly taken of the
commons, is it likely you had leisure to make such badges?
Did you cause your soldiers and servants within or without Pomfret Castle to wear those badges on the King's
side before you joined the rebels? Why you brought forth
those badges when you joined the rebels rather than before when you professed to stand for the King? What number there were of the said badges? Whether those who
wore them were not told they were Christ's soldiers?[3]

Although admitting that the Five Wounds badge had been used in
1511, Cromwell clearly doubted whether the Pontefract badges had
been those left over from that expedition, and if the badges were new,
Cromwell was insinuating, the rebellion could not have taken Darcy
by surprise, because such badges could not have been run up in a few
days. But even if Darcy was telling the truth, the crucial point of why
he had given them to the rebels remained. The inference drawn by
Cromwell is evident in the last question: Did the rebels think of themselves as Christ's soldiers (*milites Christi*, one of the oldest descriptions
of crusaders)? Cromwell's fears were not unique. Bishop Latimer of
Worcester took the point immediately. In a sermon delivered on 29
October 1536 at St Paul's Cross on the text "Put on all the armour of
God," Latimer declared against the rebels, "They arm themselves with
the sign of the Cross and of the Wounds and go clear contrary to him
that bore the Cross and suffered those Wounds."[4]

This episode at Pontefract reveals three strands which can be unrav-
elled from the history of Tudor England to demonstrate the continuing
influence and significance of the crusade. As shown by Darcy's 1511
foray against the Moors, there was in sixteenth-century England some
concern and interest in fighting the infidel and in the general problem

of the advancing Turks. This sixteenth-century Eastern Question was interpreted on more than one occasion by Henry VII and his successors in terms of a crusade. Further, the use by the Pilgrims of Grace in 1536 of the badge of Five Wounds, the cross, and the crucifix referred to a more general association of the symbols of the Passion with Christian warfare, not only against infidels but against heretics and tyrants as well, warfare which was still seen in the sixteenth century in the context of crusading. Christ's Blood called for revenge against all his enemies as well as for consecrating the Holy Land as "every Christian's birthright."[5] Crusades could, therefore, be threatened against Henry VIII and launched against Elizabeth I because of their alleged heresy. Domestically, rebels fighting ostensibly for the old religion could bear symbols redolent of crusading. In the 1530s in Lincolnshire, Yorkshire, and Devon, in the Western Rebellion of 1549, and even in the revolt of the Northern Earls in 1569, these signs proclaimed a legitimate form of civil disobedience. Finally, the personal commitments of some of those at Pontefract in October 1536 are equally indicative of the tenacity of crusading habits of thought and action. Darcy, Constable and Ellekar had wished to fight the Moors in 1511. They were not alone. Under Henry VII and Henry VIII many individuals and groups were eager to revive active crusading: kings, courtiers, soldiers, and, most obviously, the Order of St John of Jerusalem, the Knights Hospitaller of Rhodes and Malta whose suppression in England in 1540 was a break with a familiar and glorious crusading past.

The extent to which there was or could be a glorious crusading present in the sixteenth century must be a matter of debate. The crusade was a carefully defined weapon in the temporal and spiritual armoury of the western church, the particular prerogative of the papacy. It was not simply a matter of fighting the infidel or even waging a just war. The crusade was a canonical institution and a spiritual exercise as well as a category of violence, distinguished by the religious trappings of vows, indulgences, and other spiritual and temporal privileges which were available to a hugely greater proportion of society than that which was involved in actual fighting against the enemies of the church. The crusade was an integral part of the Catholic penitential system and possessed moral and spiritual implications; it was embedded into the religious and secular life of western Europe. With the Protestant attacks on the Catholic penitential system, in particular indulgences, and on the authority of the pope, the crusade as an ecclesiastical institution inevitably suffered. But elements of the ideal persisted, even when the formal apparatus had been abandoned in Tudor England.

THE TURKS

That Europeans continued to be exercised by the Islamic threat is hardly surprising and not in doubt. The frontier of Christendom in the sixteenth century ran up the Adriatic and across central Europe. Hungary was lost after the disaster at Mohacs in 1526. Vienna was besieged in 1529; its survival was of considerable significance to the subsequent course of events in sixteenth-century Europe. In the Mediterranean, Rhodes fell in 1522–23, and Cyprus fell in 1571, by which time the Ottomans were threatening to dominate the central narrows of the Mediterranean, and hence the Levant trade, in addition to maintaining their firm hold on the middle and lower Danube. Until the successful defence of Malta (1565) and the battle of Lepanto (1571), pessimism was rife. In 1530 an Italian observer, echoing Pius II in 1463, feared that Christendom would be reduced to a "canton of Europe," and a generation later the English martyrologist John Foxe hoped that Christ would inspire resistance "if not to recover that which is lost, yet at least to retain what little is left."[6] Foxe was not optimistic. In 1566 he reported further Ottoman advances in Transylvania and gave credence to rumours of an Ottoman invasion of Apulia.[7]

Faced with the Ottoman threat, western Europe possessed one international weapon of defence and counterattack, the crusade. Despite the equivocal policies of, for example, Francis I of France, for historians to relegate to the realms of rhetoric or hypocrisy avowals of support for the crusade and statements about the obligation of all Christian rulers to resist the Turks, made by some of the shrewdest politicians of the time (including the first three Tudors), is to ignore their cultural milieu and the persuasiveness of fear which continued to bind Christendom together in spite of the growing religious divisions. The German Protestant leader Ulrich von Hütten argued in the 1520s that the money saved by throwing off the burden of papal taxation should be used to equip a Christian army against the Turks.[8]

However, a problem lies in distinguishing general concern and specific crusading reactions. Certainly in Tudor England there existed an audience potentially receptive to appeals for Christian resistance to Islam, especially, perhaps, among men such as Henry VIII who, according to Edward Hall, "greatly delighted in feates of chivalry."[9] Indeed, the early sixteenth century has been described, rather misleadingly, as the "Indian Summer of English Chivalry." The traditional image of the Christian knight retained its lustre, notwithstanding new Erasmian and humanist interpretations and the changing social role of the knight. Stephen Hawes's *Passetyme of Pleasure*, written in 1506 but still being reprinted under Queen Mary, was a popular chivalric adventure story, not a precursor of the satire of Cervantes or the nostalgia of Spenser.[10] Lord Berners's famous translation of Froissart's *Chronicles* appeared between 1523 and 1525, printed by the king's publisher Richard Pynson, who had already published his edition of *Mandeville's Travels*.[11] As described in an earlier chapter, Caxton printed a number of popular theoretical works on chivalry, notably Christine de Pisan's *Feat of Arms and Chivalry* and Lull's *Book of the Order of Chivalry;* this latter appears to have been a dominant influence in chivalric writing at the beginning of the sixteenth century.[12] Lull's concept of an international community of Christian knights could still be taken seriously when kings were ostensibly considering united action against the Ottomans or the Moors. Pynson's translation of Hayton's *Flowers of the History of the East* contained detailed, if rather fanciful, information about the Turks, Arabs, and Mongols, a mass of topographical observations, and a serious plan for a crusade, first against those occupying Greece and Asia Minor, and second against the rulers of the Holy Land.[13] It may have been read as fiction, but it is as likely that parts, at any rate, were taken seriously. As the victories of Suleiman the Magnificent (1520–66) mounted, so did western fears and, hence, interest. Foxe included a long "History of the Turks" in his *Acts and Monuments*, full of Turkish atrocities, antipapal vitriol, moral outrage, and genuine concern for Christendom.[14]

The East held the imagination as well as fear. A prophecy of about 1531 predicted that a king would reign in England for fifty-five years, and after restoring peace in England, he would recover the Holy Cross from Jerusalem as the summit of his career: it is a story very similar to the medieval legends of the Last Emperor.[15] Fascination with the East continued to be displayed in Elizabethan plays, such as Kyd's *Solyman and Perseda* (1599) and Marlowe's *Tamburlaine* (1587). Shakespeare based his description of a battle with the Turks in *Othello* on an account of the battle of Lepanto in Knollys's *History of the Turks* (1603), although for some reason he placed the action in a period between the 1480s and the fall of Rhodes in 1523. In *Henry IV*, Part 2 he indicated knowledge of the rather revolting inheritance procedures of the Ottoman royal family.[16] Shakespeare's portrait of Henry IV as a crusader echoes with some accuracy fourteenth-century attitudes and may suggest that the crusade provided for the late sixteenth century a theme which was understood, even if some of the values, beliefs, and assumptions of crusaders were hardly taken seriously.[17]

By denying the paramount and unique role of the church, in particular the church of Rome, as mediator between man and God, Protestants condemned the whole paraphernalia of crusading penance, indulgence, and temporal privileges. In few places was the Reformation more clearly an instrument of change than in this rejection of one of the most inbred and characteristic institutions of the Christian West. An intellectual as well as diplomatic question not lost on Elizabeth I was whether the Catholic Philip II or the Moslem sultan was more of a threat to Christianity.[18] Such dialectical problems were not wasted on John Foxe, either; his critique of the crusading movement well illustrates the Protestant stance. He too found it difficult to decide whether the Turks or the papacy "hath been the more bloody and pernicious adversary to Christ."[19] Foxe argued that the crusades failed and "the Turk hath prevailed mightily, not because Christ is weak, but because Christians be wicked and their doctrine impure." He explained, "We war against the Turk with our works, masses, traditions and ceremonies, but we fight not with Christ." Only when Christianity had been reformed and "Christ alone shall be received to be our justifier, all other religions, merits, traditions, images, patrons and advocates set apart" would "the sword of the Christians, with the strength of Christ, . . . soon vanquish the Turk's pride and fury." Papal corruption of pure religion, the accretion of indulgences, and the intercession of saints had prevented Christian success. Salvation had been treated as "merchandise," and Foxe acidly remarked, "He that bringeth St. George or St. Denis, as patrons, to the field against the Turk leaveth Christ, no doubt, at home."[20] The papacy had been too busy persecuting upholders of purer faith as when the Albigensians and Waldensians were attacked by the "pope's crossed soldiers." Foxe consistently blamed the church and the papacy for the famous defeats at Acre (1291), Nicopolis (1396), Varna (1444), and Mohacs (1526). Foxe even suggested that the successful defence of Vienna in 1529 was only due to the presence of good German Protestants among the defenders.[21] The corrupt practices of crusading condemned Christians to defeat which, unless they reformed, was deserved. The Turks were, in this context, the arm of God's chastisement.[22]

But abandonment of the forms of crusading removed neither the sense of fear nor the feeling of Christian duty inherent in the rejected institution. The advances of Suleiman continued to impress. Edward VI's own "political chronicle" or diary is, from 1551, peppered with references to Islamic successes.[23] Foxe retained the concept of threatened Christendom, and although seeing the Turks as agents of God's wrath, he described the war against the infidel as "the public cause," a precise echo of earlier descriptions of crusading.[24] Similarly, Edward VI and his ministers in 1552 referred to the Turks as "the old common Enemy to the Name and Religion of all Christianity" and declared to the Emperor Charles V that Edward had "the zeal to the conservation and surety of Christendom, which in a Christian Prince is duly required."[25] Here, religious divisions have not yet destroyed the image of Christendom in opposition to Islam, as they were to do under Elizabeth. Even more striking evidence that a common, nonsectarian Christian interest in combatting the Turks still was appreciated is to be found in the reaction of Londoners to the news of the great Christian victory over the Turks at Lepanto on 7 October 1571. This victory was won by a Catholic Habsburg crusader, Don John of Austria, in alliance with the papacy, Venice, and the knights of Malta, and at the head of an unequivocally crusader fleet. The Turks were putative commercial allies of England, and a year before Lepanto Elizabeth had been excommunicated by the architect of the Holy League, Pius V, who had called upon Englishmen to overthrow their monarch. Yet Raphael Holinshed recorded that when the news of Lepanto reached London in November 1571 a sermon of thanksgiving was preached at St Paul's

> to give thanks to almightie God for the victorie, which of his merciful clemence it had pleased him to grant to the Christians in the Levant seas, against the common enemies of our faith. . . . And in the evening, there were bonfires made through the citie, with banketting and great rejoicing, as good cause there was, for a victorie of so great importance unto the whole state of Christian commonwealth.

Indeed, Holinshed proceeded to advocate freedom of religious conscience for Catholic and Protestant "so that compounding their controversies among themselves, with tolerable conditions, they might emploie their forces against the common enemy, to the benefit of the whole Christian world."[26] It is sometimes argued that the sixteenth century saw the emergence of a secular concept of Europe which replaced the religious idea of Christendom. Holinshed, and indeed later writers such as Cartwright in *The Preacher's Travel* (1611), suggest that the change was neither so simple nor so rapid as some may have thought and that views from the statesman's council chamber or the divine's study are not the only ones. In the 1580s, however, Elizabeth I and her ministers distanced themselves from Catholic Europe when dealing with the Ottomans. Their arguments proclaimed a decisive break in the traditional unity of Christendom, to which even Francis I had hypocritically paid lip service, and to which Edward VI, Foxe, and Holinshed seemed to have adhered. Indeed, the English treaty with the Turks handed Catholic polemicists a ready weapon of assault. The Queen, fulminated Thomas Stapleton in his *Apologia*, had allied with "the public enemy of all Christian profession."[27]

The Spanish successes in the Netherlands and the formation of the Catholic League in France in the 1580s accelerated this process of alienation. Victories over the Turk could still be welcomed on both sides of the religious divide, but the enthusiasm was now more clearly compromised by doctrinal disagreement. The Virgilian epic on Lepanto composed in 1585 by the teenaged James VI of Scotland (later James I of England), is a barometer of the change. Although unashamed at his choice of subject, James did see the need to defend himself against those who saw the poem as "praise of a forraine Papist bastard" (i.e., Don John) and thus "far contrary to my degree and Religion." In fact, the precocious king insisted, the poem was intended as an allegory to inspire Protestant comfort and resistance to the newly formed Catholic League. Lepanto had been a "wondrous worke of God" even though the "Christian navie" had been manned by those "That beare upon their brow/That mark of Antichrist the whore." If God gave victory to false Christians "What will he more to them that in/His mercies onelie trust?" Thus the Catholic triumph over the Turk is taken not simply, as by Holinshed, as a welcome Christian success but as a sign "That God doth love his name/So well that he did them aid/That serv'd not right the same." From this, all beleaguered Protestants should derive confidence that, ipso facto, God's support for them would be even surer. King James's *Lepanto* witnesses the splitting of some of the last strands uniting the two halves of Christendom. It was a moment fatal to crusading as a universal Christian institution.[28]

Before the parting of the ways under Elizabeth, the general sense of Christian identity was expressed on occasion in obvious, specifically crusading forms. This was especially evident in diplomatic exchanges among England, Spain, Portugal, the papacy, and the Empire between the 1480s and the 1520s. Many of the treaties and leagues which bobbed ineffectually around the Italian wars had, like the League of Cambrai (1508), a new crusade as their professed objective.[29] Elsewhere, both Maximilian in Central Europe and the Iberian kings in North Africa and the Mediterranean had immediate practical interests in crusading. Almost as soon as Henry VII had established himself after the battle of Stoke in 1487, the papacy tried to involve him in moves to resist the Turks. Papal efforts to raise money and men for the European and the Mediterranean fronts were a feature of the next thirty-five years, and the kings of England often appeared sympathetic.[30] R. B. Wernham has commented that "promises to take part in crusades always sat lightly on sixteenth century princes," and it is undeniable that Henry VII and Henry VIII hedged their enthusiasm for crusading with tight conditions and empty rhetoric.[31] Henry VII was particularly suspicious of the ploys of Alexander VI, but he never dropped the subject and entered into serious discussions over possible plans of action with both Julius II and Ferdinand of Aragon. It has often been supposed that negotiations for a new crusade were conducted either fraudulently or unrealistically. Yet the king of Portugal repeatedly offered firm proposals for a campaign against the Moors of North Africa and in 1505, as already mentioned, sent Henry VII "a little book of instruction" on the subject of the recovery of Jerusalem.[32] Although this seemingly unrealistic goal remained prominent in the rhetoric of a Charles VIII or a Julius II, it should not conceal such clearheaded plans as were drawn up, for example, by Ferdinand of Aragon in 1502; he proposed that all crusade taxes should be consigned to the military orders to build a crusade fleet, to be commanded by the grand master of the Hospitallers and based at Rhodes.[33]

Henry VII did more than talk. In 1502 Maximilian received ten thousand pounds from Henry, ostensibly to fight the Turks, although the grant also had the aim of neutralising the threat of imperial support for the exiled royal claimant Edmund de la Pole. Possibly because of Ferdinand's scheme of 1502, Henry also handed over to the pope at least four thousand pounds provided from the 1502 crusade tax.[34] In 1504 Henry paid a further twenty thousand gold crowns of his own money to the pope for the crusade, apparently being the only prince in Europe to contribute personally.[35] Indeed, Henry acquired something of a reputation as a crusade enthusiast. In 1506 he was made "protector of the Order of St. John of Jerusalem at Rhodes," a hitherto unique privilege, only conferred once more on a western monarch, to Henry VIII in 1511. In 1508 Thomas Wolsey, then an obscure diplomat, reported that imperial negotiators had called Henry VII "the most suitable instrument of Christ to defeat the enemies of the Christian religion."[36]

Some of this crusade talk was the result of external factors, which convinced the generation around 1500 that there were brighter prospects for a new crusade. The successful defence of Rhodes in 1480 led to a new confidence in the ability of the knights of St. John to survive and to an increase in the number of recruits and donations to the order.[37] The defection of Djem persuaded Bayezid II (1481–1512) to suspend attacks on the West, and his successor, Selim (1512–20), concentrated on Persia and the conquest of Egypt. This forty-year respite allowed western rulers to bathe in false optimism, which was a cause of the violence of the disillusion and shock when Suleiman returned Ottoman attention to the West in the 1520s.

In the early years of his reign Henry VIII continued to talk of a new crusade. In the summer of 1511, in response to an appeal by Ferdinand of Aragon, who had already occupied Oran in 1509, Henry sent Lord Darcy to Cadiz, at Darcy's own request, with fifteen hundred archers ready to fight the Moors of North Africa alongside the Spaniards. Darcy's companions included Lord Anthony Grey, brother of the marquess of Dorset, Henry Guildford, the royal household esquires Weston, Brown, and Sydney, Sir Robert Constable, Sir Roger Hastings, Sir Ralph Ellekar, John Bartholomew, and William Symonde. Unfortunately, the English archers behaved in Cadiz rather like modern English football fans abroad. They got very drunk on local wine and smashed up the place. One Englishman was killed, as were a number of Spaniards. Ferdinand was not amused, and in a diplomatic move of lightning speed, he made a truce with the Moors and managed to ship the English home only a little over a fortnight after their arrival. Those archers still capable of it had not seen a single Moor.[38] In the next decade, the crusade remained the stated context and excuse for trying to resolve the bitter conflicts in Italy and elsewhere between Habsburg and Valois. The Anglo-French Treaty of London (1518) included clauses designed to create an international alliance against the Turks, in support of the crusade being preached at that time by Leo X.[39] Of course, much of this sort of crusade talk was pious lip service to an often impractical dream, and once an occasion for ill-natured badinage, when the resurrection of English claims to Cyprus was voiced by a number of English courtiers, including Wolsey, to various Venetian ambassadors; this was fantasy as well as rudeness and bad law.

However, at times genuine enthusiasm could erupt. In a startlingly emotional letter of August 1519, Henry VIII announced that, following the appeal of the papal legate to England, Cardinal Campeggio, "We gird ourselves for this most holy expedition, and dedicate our whole kingdom, our wealth, our authority, our goods, our prestige to it; yes our very blood and body we offer and dedicate to Christ and His Vicar."[40] Unusually, Henry mentioned precise numbers (twenty thousand fully equipped infantry, seventy ships, etc.) and his own personal involvement, if by the time the crusade began he had an heir. Henry wrote again to Leo X in eager vein in December and was still discussing the project in March 1520, after which his enthusiasm died. Nevertheless, Henry did send considerable material help to the Hospitallers in 1528 and was said to have been angry at not being consulted about the siting of the new Hospitaller base at Malta in 1530.[41] Perhaps, as J. J. Scarisbrick suggests, in 1519–20 Henry had been bored.[42] Even so, such an outlet for boredom was consonant with his father's later foreign policy and with the traditional aspirations of the European nobility.

Such traditionalism can be traced elsewhere. In his letter to Leo X of August 1519, Henry predicted that to his royal crusading army "will be added private contingents of those many gentlemen and nobles of England who will hasten to this holy expedition out of zeal for the Christian religion." Events denied these gentlemen and nobles the chance to show themselves or their zeal, but that some individuals were enthusiastic for the crusade cannot be doubted. Diminutive Henry Still was not alone in wishing to "fight the enemies of the Christian faith."[43] In Hall's account of the 1511 expedition, Lord Darcy, accepting the fait accompli of the sudden truce with the Moors, declared "but surely it is agaynste my hart, which ever hath desired to fight against God's enemys."[44] Such aspirations are mirrored by deeds of individual crusading heroism by Englishmen for the rest of the century, at Rhodes, Malta, and elsewhere. For example, in July 1551 the English Hospitaller Nicholas Upton, commander of the sea defences of Malta and evidently one of the English langue who refused to accept the dissolution of 1540, repulsed a surprise attack on the island on his own initiative. Unfortunately, a day in the saddle fighting in full armour proved too much for Upton's massive corpulence, and as soon as the fighting ended, he collapsed and died.[45] A rather more romantic and distinctly remarkable exploit was that of Thomas Stukeley, originally from Devon, a onetime soldier of fortune, mercenary, and pirate, a sort of recusant Drake who had commanded three galleys at Lepanto. In 1577–78 he was placed in charge of a papal fleet bound for Ireland to enforce the bull of 1570. Instead, Stukeley took the fleet and his troops to fight with King Sebastian of Portugal against the Moors, and he died alongside the Portuguese king at the disastrous battle of Alcazar in 1578. Despite his well-publicised and officially condemned association with papal attempts on Ireland, Stukeley's reputation for gallantry and heroism was popularly preserved in plays such as the anonymous *Captain Thomas Stukeley* and Peele's *The Battle of Alcazar*. In the latter, despite being criticised for a lack of patriotism, he is treated sympathetically, his treachery being dramatically mitigated by his bravery in the face of the infidel.[46]

Such anecdotal evidence, although proving little beyond the commitment of individuals, points to some survival of receptiveness to crusading sympathies amongst the vigorous classes. Of more general significance, perhaps, are some remarks Lord Darcy made to Archbishop Lee of York in December 1536. The archbishop, in a noisy bout of self-pity, had been proclaiming his desire to die for his faith when faced with the hostility of the Pilgrims of Grace at the archbishop's apparent withdrawal of support. Confronted by this prating insistence on martyrdom, Darcy commented that "whosoever desires such high perfection may, with the king's licence, be sped in Africa or Turkey."[47] The institution of the crusade, which traditionally promised martyrdom to those crusaders who died on campaign, was still intelligible to some at least, complete with awareness of royal insistence on licensing departing crusaders.[48]

A strand of personal commitment is stitched into much of the response to the Turkish threat. It is evident that the court milieu of Henry VIII was little different from that of his grandfather, Edward IV, or even, in some respects, from that of his famous namesake Henry V, whose glory Henry Tudor seems to have been tempted to emulate and whose reputation remained undimmed for the rest of the century. In such an atmosphere crusading attitudes and aspirations circulated naturally.

Away from court, at least one feature of the crusade institution was still popular in the early sixteenth century—the indulgence. Although the sale of indulgences, to raise money for the crusade or for the Hospitallers defending Rhodes, had become massively bureaucratised and in places appears to have become a gigantic racket, most contemporaries did not share the distaste for the system of Wyclif, Hus, or Luther. The attraction of remission of sins in return for financial contributions to the war against the infidel remained strong, as the evidence from Jasper Ponce's mission, discussed earlier, suggests. However, the system could lead to sensitive political and financial problems. The last papal indulgence collected in England was for the building of St. Peter's in Rome and was completed in 1522; it had realised £1,144 13s 11d over five years for the papacy. Henry VII was reluctant to allow even this small drain of national resources to continue without royal control. The ending of indulgences in England was not a result of popular indifference. Much of the criticism of the system had been directed not at the stated objectives of the fundraising, notably the crusade, but at the rumoured corrupt and deceitful administration of the funds. As elsewhere, a distinction must be drawn between popular support for certain ecclesiastical facilities and religious aspirations, and public disquiet, cynicism, even hostility, to the machinations of individual priests and of the church hierarchy—especially where it involved foreigners. There is no evidence that the crusade or genuine crusade indulgences were unpopular in early sixteenth-century England.[49]

THE HOSPITALLERS

Englishmen and English resources also continued to contribute directly to the front line of Christendom, through the English langue of the knights of St. John. One of Darcy's companions in 1511 was Sir Richard Weston, builder of the early English Renaissance masterpiece Sutton Place, near Guildford. Weston had a quietly successful career in government service, surviving even his son's execution in 1536 as one of Anne Boleyn's lovers. Already by 1519 Weston was being described by Hall as a "sad and ancient knight."[50] Richard Weston's family connections reveal a more unusual and somewhat neglected side of Tudor public life. The Westons came from Lincolnshire. Richard's great-uncle, two of his uncles, his brother, and his nephew were all Hospitallers. The great-uncle, William Dawnay, led an active military career in the Levant, becoming captain of Bodrum in southern Turkey (1448–49) and Turcopolier. Uncle William Weston fought at the defence of Rhodes in 1480, whilst uncle John was prior of England (1476–89). Richard's brother William was appointed prior in 1527, after Richard had asked Wolsey to intervene on his behalf, and his nephew Thomas Dingley died for his faith on the block in 1539.[51]

English Hospitallers could hold significant political or diplomatic positions. Prior John Langstrother had been treasurer during the Readeption of 1470–71, and, like his equally illfated predecessor Robert Hales in 1381, lost his head. The prior was automatically a royal councillor. He had to receive a royal licence before accepting office or assuming control of the order's English estates. The prior, although a member of a religious order, was also the premier baron of England, ranking above all lay barons and immediately after dukes, earls, and marquesses, as is well depicted in the contemporary illustration of the 1512 parliament procession, when the prior was Thomas Docwra.[52] Docwra, prior from 1501 to 1527, a diplomat of skill and a soldier whose career stretched back to the 1480 siege of Rhodes, embodied the crusade tradition. The gatehouse he built at the priory in Clerkenwell in 1504 still stands. In 1515 he deposited twenty thousand gold ducats of his own money at Rhodes for the use of the grand master in the defence of the island.[53] Here was an English peer and courtier who had spent money and risked his own life "in the jaws of the Turk."

As the prospects for a counterattack on the Ottomans improved, because of Bayezid II's weak dynastic control and Selim's concern with the East, there was a revival in Docwra's time of interest and investment in the order. It has been estimated that the number of knights from all langues resident at Rhodes rose by a third between 1476 and 1512.[54] Statistics are incomplete, but this increase was probably reflected in the English langue. Although there were many distinguished individual English knights—Docwra, the Westons, or John Kendal, hero of the 1480 siege and prior (1489–1501)—the total numbers in the English langue were not great. Following the late medieval pattern, recruiting ran in families, usually not of the highest nobility and predominantly from the north of England. At the final siege of Rhodes there were possibly twenty English knights on the island.[55] This figure obviously excludes those knights in England minding the commanderies and preceptories, as well as the serjeants, chaplains, and servants. However, by the suppression of 1540 the total number of full knights was at most somewhere in the low twenties.[56] Even so, such individuals had direct experience of fighting Islam, as they were all obliged to serve regular tours of duty at Rhodes, only being permitted three years in England at a stretch. In one sense their influence and presence might have been symbolic, but neither they nor their contemporaries thought that they were being overtaken by events, or that they or their order were anachronisms.

The chief contribution of the English langue to the fight against Islam was financial. The knights were not only warriors, they were major landowners, representatives of a large international order which held property in almost every shire of the realm. The English lands contributed about an eighth of the order's European income. Although no complete figures are available for the early Tudor period, the order's archives in Malta reveal some substantial payments. In 1495 Prior Kendal was quit of 4,990 ducats and was held still to be in arrears another 1,567 crowns; in October the same year, the commanderies of Temple Brewer and Ribeston paid a total of 1,400 ducats to the treasury at Rhodes.[57] Edward IV had been so concerned with the drain of money out of the kingdom that he had tried unsuccessfully to halt it, and then to control the order by installing his youthful brother-in-law as prior.[58] The wealth of the order was considerable. Docwra's gift to Rhodes of twenty thousand ducats compares with William Weston's payment of four thousand pounds to Henry VIII for the privilege of taking possession of the priory in 1527–28.[59] The central authorities in Rhodes were stern masters and insisted on the fullest possible extraction of profit from the order's estates, especially after the 1470s when Rhodes was in a constant state of military alert. As a result the Hospitallers were notoriously harsh landowners; but, as surviving letters from English brothers on Rhodes illustrate, they were equally concerned with good management.[60] Saddled with possibly rather inflexible management procedures, by virtue of the frequent absences of the commanders and bailiffs in the Mediterranean, the order nevertheless had a duty to maximise profits. Here, in the profits from Hospitaller lands, was the most tangible and durable link between the English countryside, villages, farms, and even mines (e.g., at Temple Sowerby) and the battlefields of the cross and the crescent in the eastern Mediterranean.[61]

Individual knights, many of whose colleagues were slaughtered at Rhodes in 1522, could play significant roles in England as landlords, warriors, politicians, and men of affairs. Taken, as they had to be, from noble stock, this is hardly surprising even for less important knights. For example, Edward Bellingham entered the order in 1523, a year after his uncle John Shelley had been killed in the final defence of Rhodes. After the dissolution of 1540, Bellingham entered royal service, becoming member of parliament for Gatton in 1545 and in 1548 Lord Deputy of Ireland. Henry VIII in his will left Bellingham two hundred marks personally.[62] Other Hospitaller members of parliament included Bellingham's cousin Richard Shelley (Gatton, 1547), Oliver Starkey (St. Albans, 1554) and Thomas Tresham (Northamptonshire, 1539, 1542, 1554, and Lancaster, 1553), although these three only became Hospitallers after their parliamentary careers were over, when Mary revived the order in 1557 (with the possible exception of Shelley, who may have been associated with the order before 1540). Starkey, a contact of Cardinal Pole, left England in 1558 and fought in the siege of Malta in 1565, when he was Latin secretary to Grand Master La Vallette.[63]

Henry VIII's attitude to the order was characteristically self-interested. Protector of the international order since 1511, after the fall of Rhodes Henry toyed with the idea of making the English langue responsible for the defence of Calais, thus, in emulation of Spanish precedents, directing the order's considerable resources to national and secular duties, giving the langue a new function, and ameliorating the king's own financial problems.[64] In one sense, Henry's plans were a logical outcome of persistent and only partially successful royal efforts over many generations to control the order. However, after strong pressure from the grand master and with the news that Charles V was to install the order on Malta, Henry reluctantly abandoned the scheme. Indeed, in 1528 he gave the order in the Mediterranean nineteen bronze cannon with 1,023 cannon balls.[65]

Yet in April 1540 Henry dissolved the order in England, as the climax of his destruction of religious houses. The grounds given in the Act of Dissolution were that the knights seditiously and contumaciously continued to acknowledge the authority of the pope. The lands were seized by the Crown and many estates sold; the knights were secularised and sixteen of them granted pensions. Bellingham's pension came in the form of an annuity from Hospitaller lands in Sussex.[66] One of Richard Weston's acquisitions to his Sutton Place estate was, ironically, the former Hospitaller manor of Temple Court in Surrey.[67] Henry's motives—greed and expedience—were unexceptional. In the 1530s the order had remained constitutionally and emotionally firmly attached to the papacy, and it was still very wealthy. Such a combination could not survive Thomas Cromwell. Moreover, some Hospitaller families were linked to known adherents of papal Christianity and potential rebels. Two of the Hospitallers pensioned off in 1540 were Edward and James Hussey, relatives of Lord Hussey, a plotter against Cromwellian and Henrician changes with Darcy and Charles V in the 1530s.[68] Three Hospitallers were executed for refusing to accept the Act of Supremacy—Adrian Fortescue and Thomas Dingley in 1539 and David Gunstone in 1541.[69] Although those knights who were in England in 1540 refused publicly to admit any errors or guilt, they went quietly, their morale broken by government hostility and internecine bickering in the langue on Malta. Prior Weston himself died on 7 May 1540, the very day the Act of Dissolution took effect. But it should be noted that the order was dissolved for openly political reasons, as Henry's ultimatum to the order in July 1539 made clear. It was for their continued adherence to papal supremacy, not for their commitment to the crusade, that the knights suffered. Yet if Henry and his contemporaries could see a distinction, the next generation could not.

The last chapter is brief. Finding parliament reluctant to reverse the Act of Dissolution, Queen Mary revived the order in England by Letters Patent of 2 April 1557.[70] New knights were created, including Thomas Tresham, who became prior. Where possible (i.e., where they were still in royal hands), the order's lands were restored. There was some continuity. George Aylmer, who was made commander of North Baddersley in 1557, had fought at the final defence of Rhodes in 1522.[71] Tresham was summoned to parliament, as his predecessors had been, in 1557 and 1558, and again in January 1559 to the parliament which constructed the Elizabethan settlement. Tresham asked for Archbishop Heath to act as his proxy in 1559 and did not attend the debates. He died on 3 March 1559, shortly before the order's lands were once more confiscated.[72] The confiscation marked the end of the Order of St. John of Jerusalem in England after more than four hundred years, although curiously the order was not formally dissolved. In theory the Letters Patent of 1557, which revived the order "in perpetuity," remained in force. But without income there was no point in continuing. England's direct contact with the crusading East was finally broken. Some loyal Catholics, such as Oliver Starkey, went to make their careers at Malta. Others merely melted into their rural gentry backgrounds. We may leave the last active English crusaders in the East, with the sad scene depicted in a list of Philip II of Spain's pensioners in the later 1560s: "Master Richard Shelley, who is called lord great prior of England. He hath not any pension but doth maintain himself by making knights of the Order of Malta."[73]

THE CRUSADE AGAINST ENGLAND

As in the thirteenth, fourteenth, and fifteenth centuries, in the sixteenth century war against the infidel was not the sole application of the crusade as a letter written on 31 May 1512 by Henry VIII to Cardinal Bainbridge makes clear: "[I am] of the opinion that, for its number, never had a finer army been seen, or one better disposed to die courageously in defence of the church and the pope, as the indulgence sent by him [the pope] has marvellously roused them against their foes, whom they consider Turks, heretics and Infidels."[74] Henry is referring to the army which had just embarked to invade France; the "Turks, heretics and Infidels" were Frenchmen. For three hundred years the crusade had been turned against internal enemies of the church, doctrinal and political, and in the sixteenth century it had lost none of its adaptability. Once Henry VIII's breach with Rome had placed the gulf of heresy between the king and the traditional church, in the eyes of many at home and abroad there was always a chance that the crusade could once more enter English domestic politics, as in the thirteenth century, either as a tool of foreign invaders or as a defence and justification for internal rebellion. In the event, although no formal crusade, either as foreign invasion or domestic revolt, was proclaimed in Henry's lifetime, a papal legate was appointed with an invasion in mind, the crusade tradition was appealed to, and crusading language and symbols were freely exploited by Henry's opponents.

In January 1536 the papal consistory finally summoned up the nerve to agree to Henry VIII's excommunication with the prospect of deposition which that implied, but they failed to publish the bull. Even if they had, the cardinals would still have been too late. Catherine of Aragon died in January, Anne Boleyn went to the block in May, and Henry and Cromwell were engaged in resurrecting the Habsburg alliance. Between 1532 and 1536 many in England, in default of papal action, had looked to the Emperor Charles V to intervene in favour of his aunt, Catherine, and her religion. There were unmistakable crusading overtones. In September 1533 Bishop Fisher of Rochester told Charles, via his ambassador in England, "the pope's weapons become very malleable when directed against the obdurate and pertinacious and, therefore, it is incumbent upon Your Majesty to interfere in this affair and undertake a work which must be as pleasing in the eyes of God as war upon the Turks."[75] A few weeks later Catherine of Aragon was expressing her hopes "of the defeat and death by the pope's hands of this second Turk," the joint invocation of papal authority and the

Turk indicating that Catherine was anticipating an anti-Henrician crusade.[76] Chapuys, Charles V's ambassador, was a busy man in these years conveying the treasonable thoughts of Englishmen to the Emperor. In September 1534 he reported to his master that Lord Darcy had promised northern support for any Habsburg invasion: "With the assistance of Your Majesty Darcy would raise the banner of the Crucifix together with yours."[77] Cromwell had been right. Darcy was a traitor long before October 1536. The crusade associations are direct. The banner of the Crucifix was a familiar crusade banner in the sixteenth century; it was used by Don John at Lepanto and by the Armada, as well as by the Pilgrimage of Grace. It may have been no coincidence if, as some accounts maintained, Thomas More carried to the scaffold a small red cross, the symbol of English crusaders since 1265.[78]

The crusade theme was taken up by Princess Mary in October 1535, the year of More's death. Commenting to Chapuys on Charles V's recent conquest of Tunis, she remarked that the conquest of England "itself will be highly acceptable in the eyes of God and no less glory will be gained by it than by the conquest of Tunis or even that of Africa."[79] These somewhat nebulous plottings were given an intellectual structure in 1536 by Reginald Pole, soon to be made cardinal and papal legate for the enterprise of England. In a rambling, splenetic, and passionate book *Pro Ecclesiasticae unitatis defensione,* commonly known as *De Unitate,* Pole systematised, as M. E. James has observed, the "images and language" of the crusade, "which had been fostered in the circle of Catherine of Aragon, Fisher and More."[80] But apart from an invasion scare in 1538–39, the hostility between Charles V and the kings of France in the 1530s and 1540s precluded any serious plan for an invasion of England under the banner of the Cross, despite occasional papal sallies and the presence at the pope's elbow of Edward IV's great-nephew Reginald Pole.

The next serious external threat of a crusade occurred some years after Elizabeth I was excommunicated in 1570. The crusading nature of the papally initiated expedition to Ireland of 1578, under the command of Thomas Stukeley, was evident. When King Sebastian of Portugal petitioned Gregory XIII for Stukeley to be allowed to divert his troops from the Irish project, he expressed the hope that the pope "might approve their going on this enterprise of Africa which likewise is against infidels."[81] Stukeley had already received a papal grant of partial indulgence in 1575 "for taking part in warfare against foes of our holy faith" with plenary remission for any who followed him and died in such a conflict. The language in which diplomats privately described the 1578 Irish expedition confirms its status: "so holy a cause," "for the glory of

God and the defence of the Catholic religion," a "scheme for the expulsion of heretics and schismatics from Ireland and the restoration of the Catholic Faith and religion in the country," "a cause in which the glory of God and the service of Christendom are exclusively concerned," a "duty most pleasing to God and very appropriate to the charge which his Holiness has of Vicar of Christ on earth."[82]

This last theme was taken up by Nicholas Sanders, an English Catholic divine appointed as the papal legate for the Irish enterprise, who with another disaffected Catholic vagrant, James FitzMaurice Fitz-Gerald, reconstructed the expedition after Stukeley's defection to Africa. The new force landed in Ireland in 1579. Trying to secure the adherence of a local gentleman, Sanders explained his mission in familiar canonical terms: "We are fighting by authority of the head of the church . . . . if it please you to join with us in this holy quarrel you shall be under the protection of the prince whom God shall put in place of this usurper [Elizabeth] and of God's Vicar."[83] However, the invasion soon foundered. FitzMaurice was killed and Sanders became a hunted fugitive, dying in destitution while still on the run.

The involvement of Sanders, a former fellow of New College, Oxford, and a leading intellectual figure among the Catholic exiles, provided a link between the theoretical apologists of resistance to a heretical ruler and the forum of practical action. His presence in Ireland was a sign of a growing convergence of the crusading romanticism of Stukeley and FitzMaurice with the casuistry of the Catholic intellectuals. In his *De Visibili monarchia* of 1571, Sanders had constructed a theory of resistance based upon the supreme spiritual and temporal authority of the papacy. However, the timing of both Sanders's ideas and his mission to Ireland was ill-judged, and the content of his message oversubtle.[84] It was only after his death, from the mid-1580s, that a simpler theory and practice of holy war against Protestants united in print and in battle. This development was prompted by the war in the Netherlands, which propagandists on both sides proclaimed a struggle for religion, a holy war. Instead of elaborating sophisticated arguments for a just war of resistance, as Sanders had, or relying on a spiritual conquest, as other Catholic missionaries did, a number of Catholic writers now fell back on the ideology of the crusade, stressing not the political challenge to illicit authority but the religious validity of the armed struggle against heretics.[85] One convert from the doctrine of spiritual regeneration to that of military force was William Allen, the leading English Catholic divine. In his *Defence of Sir William Stanley's Surrender of Deventer* (1587), ostensibly aimed at English soldiers in the Low Countries, Allen argued that to fight for or to obey a heretic was indefensible and an invitation to damnation, whereas death "for defence of true Religion and God's honour" was "plaine martyrdom"; the profession of Christian knights was the defence of the Catholic church "and to be sworne adversaries and persecutors of God's enemies; the Crosse and Cognizance [i.e., emblem] they weare protesting the same."[86] Allen was describing crusaders. Such crusading analogies were later underlined in other Catholic polemics. For example, the Jesuit Robert Persons referred to England (i.e., Catholic England that he fondly imagined lay beneath the surface of Protestant tyranny) and to the English Faithful as "the elect sons of Israel."[87]

These traditional formulae were not simply figures of speech, apt only for literary polemic. They increasingly reflected the practical militancy that followed the execution of Mary, Queen of Scots in 1587 and the ascendancy of the Guise faction in France, when the persistent although at times equivocal appeals of Pope Sixtus V were finally heeded by Philip II of Spain. Crusade indulgences were granted, and the pope permitted Philip to collect crusade taxes. On 25 April 1588 the banner of the Armada was blessed in the cathedral of Lisbon, in a scene reminiscent of a similar ceremony at Messina in 1571 before Lepanto. As the Armada banner was carried to the fleet, friars announced the papal crusader absolution and indulgence granted to the soldiers and sailors of the enterprise. On the banner were the images of the Crucified Christ and the Virgin Mary flanking the arms of Spain above the inscription "Arise, O Lord, and vindicate thy cause."[88] The bull issued by Sixtus V extended to those who bore arms against the English the benefits offered in 1585 by his predecessor, Gregory XIII, for the war against the Turks, including, for those who fought for a year, the plenary remission of sin which previous popes had been "accustomed to give . . . to those who goe to helpe to recover the holy londe." The words are from an English translation of the bull for the "crusades" that was printed with a rabidly hostile Protestant commentary in the Netherlands and London in the autumn of 1588, as part of the anti-Spanish propaganda campaign. For Englishmen that year, the Catholic crusade "against the faithlesse and heretiques, the enemies of our holy fayth and christian religion" was a menacing reality.[89] However, in 1588, and not for the first time, the crusade did not receive God's blessing, and the pope's was evidently not enough.

CRUSADE AND REBELLION

Such external threats were matched from the 1530s by the possibility of internal revolts associated with crusading justifications. The rebellions of 1536, 1549, and 1569 all displayed crusading symbols, just as they all laid claim to religious motivation. Holinshed commented on the 1569 revolt of the Northern Earls: "And to get the more credit among the favourers of the old Romish religion, they had a crosse with a banner of the five wounds borne before them."[90] However, these religious symbols meant different things to different men. On the Pilgrimage of Grace, Robert Aske saw them as pacific symbols of his peaceful pilgrimage, and he explained the adoption of the badge of the Five Wounds simply as a means of identification, a uniform.[91] But beside Aske there was a militant party led by Lords Lumley and Latimer and that putative campaigner against the Moors, Sir Robert Constable. It was this group which had first adopted the badge of the Five Wounds and had, therefore, been responsible for its wholesale adoption at Pontefract. Darcy, despite his protestations of innocence, had not only gone to fight the Moors in his youth but had also as recently as 1534 been interested in holy rebellion; it was he who persuaded Aske of the badges' usefulness.[92] If, as Darcy claimed, his conversion to the rebels' cause had been made under duress, it is astonishing that he chose to provide them with so potent a symbol of religious war. In 1569 there is little doubt that violence was in the minds of the rebels, to whom, as to some at least in 1536, the religious symbolism implied a justification for holy violence, not passive resistance.

Another strictly crusading feature of the Pilgrimage of Grace may be indicated by a monastic song in favour of the rising:

> And for the space of their trace
> Send them God speed
> With health, wealth and speed
> Of sins release
> And joy endless
> When they be dead.[93]

This is a loud echo, if not a direct reference, to the crusade indulgence, forgiveness of sins. It is possible to argue differently, of course, and to say that it refers to the pilgrim's, not the crusader's, indulgence. But pilgrims were not, as crusaders were, offered Paradise as reward for their penance.

What is equally remarkable is that, both in 1536 and 1569, commentators and the government seemed alarmed at precisely these crusading overtones. Latimer's 1536 sermon was specific: "They arm themselves with the sign of the Cross."[94] In similar vein was an anonymous *Homily against Rebellion*, first published in 1571 and almost certainly having the 1569 revolt in mind:

The rebels display and bear about engines and banners, which are acceptable unto the rude ignorant common people, great multitudes of whom by suche false pretences and shews they do deceave and drawe unto them. [There follows a description of the religious symbols carried by rebels, including the Five Wounds.] though they, little knowyng what the cross of Christe meaneth, which neither carver not paynter can make, do beare the image of the crosse paynted in a ragge against those that have the crosse of Christ painted in their hartes, yet though they paynt withal in their flagges, *Hoc signo vinces*, By this sign thou shalt get the victory, by a most fond imitation of the posie of Constantinus magnus, that noble Christian emperor, and great conqueror of God's enemies, a most unmeete ensign for rebels, the enemies of God, theyr prince and countrey: or what other manner so ever they shall beare, yet let no good subject upon any hope of victory or good successe folowe such standarde bearers of rebellion.[95]

The association of the cross with a justification for rebellion is clear enough. The reference to a classical inspiration may indicate the fading of crusading ideology, but it should also be noted that the story of Constantine and the cross was available in a still-popular thirteenth-century compilation, the *Golden Legend* of James of Voragine, and that some Catholic proponents of holy war against the Protestants cast Philip II in the role of the first Christian emperor.[96] Such allusions, therefore, may not reveal any great progress of a new classicism to oust traditional crusade ideology. In general the homilists attack on the symbols parallels Latimer's. John Foxe, writing within a few years of the homilist, repeated both the disapproval and the awareness of the significance of the symbols, when he attacked the banners of the Pilgrimage of Grace as "ensigns of hypocrisy and feigned sanctity" whereby the rebels pretended "to fight for the faith and the right of holy church."[97] Again, the military use of the symbols ("ensigns") is assumed. It appears, therefore, that Latimer, Foxe, and the homilist were all concerned to scotch any crusading support for rebellions, by attacking the ideological basis both of the institution and of its associated iconography. On a practical level, too, Protestant pamphleteers were quick to associate domestic revolt, such as that in 1569, with the foreign incursions of FitzMaurice and Sanders a decade later.[98]

Anxiety on the part of the authorities over the possible ideological justifications for disobedience employed by rebel leaders is indicated by the interrogations following the Pilgrimage of Grace and the revolt of the Northern Earls. Cromwell insisted on knowing from Darcy whether the rebel leaders had consulted academic opinion on the legitimacy of rebellion, and if so, whether they had spread seditious doctrines to their troops. Thus Cromwell asked "Was it not a double iniquity to fall into rebellion and afterwards procure matter to justify it?" Who proposed the arguments that "subjects might lawfully . . . move war against their prince?" Cromwell finally revealed his fears: "Was it not proposed that it should be determined . . . that rebels might lawfully make war against their prince in the cause of Faith?"[99] The rebels' attitudes to Henry VIII's religion were crucial, and Darcy's position cannot have been encouraging to the government. Earlier in the rebellion he had declared that he was prepared to obey the king in all things, provided Henry remained faithful to the church.[100]

The threat of papal excommunication was important; revolts of the faithful against heretics or tyrants, if fought with papal approval, could, and from the thirteenth century often did, attract crusading status. Cromwell feared that the conversion of a rebellion into a holy cause and, thus into an unofficial crusade (with the distinct possibility of papal blessing if the rebellion made progress) was providing a potent counterideology to the increasingly dominant doctrine of unquestioning obedience to the prince. Cromwell's worries were echoed in the interrogation of the earl of Northumberland after the 1569 revolt, when the authorities tried to ascertain whether the possibility that the queen was to be excommunicated had played any part in the revolt. As in 1536, they were very much interested in the intellectual arguments used by the rebels' advisers to justify rebellion. Northumberland's answers were unhelpful. The rebel leaders had consulted learned men and "their judgement was . . . we ought not to wager battaile against our anointed Prince unless they were lawfully excommunicated by the head of the church," but Northumberland stated that he had not thought that Elizabeth had been lawfully excommunicated which, indeed, in 1569 she had not.[101] Once again, however, the spectre perceived by the government was less of religious civil war than of legitimate holy rebellion.

The tradition of crusades against excommunicates, papally defined tyrants, or simply political opponents of the pope had a long history, as has been shown in earlier chapters. To harness violence to the crusade ideal was to hope to legitimize or justify that violence and to reassure the participants, for Cardinal Allen as for Simon de Montfort or William Marshal. Even where the formal apparatus of crusade vows and privileges was absent, the strong associations of the cross and the Passion with the crusade and holy war were still available to military commanders in the sixteenth century, as the supporting theory was to the propagandists. However, perceptions did not remain static. It is possible that Constable and Darcy in 1536 drew directly and consciously on formal crusading which, as displayed by the works of Foxe, from an even later generation, were by no means forgotten. Constable and Darcy certainly called upon the less legalistic but emotionally still potent popular symbols of crusade and holy war embodied in their crusading and crypto-crusading images and language. The Pilgrimage of Grace, an uprising which publicly proclaimed its religious quality, may not have been a canonically authorised crusade, but it made deliberate use of traditions of especial crusading relevance. Crusade associations provided intellectual credibility, propaganda, and morale for the troops. The symbols of the crusade could help bind the rebels of 1536 into an alternative community of the faithful, in opposition to the secular community of Cromwell and the Tudor government. Whatever Darcy's excuses, he could not have been ignorant of the power inherent in the badges he lent the insurgents at Pontefract.

In the case of the Pilgrimage of Grace, this alternative community was openly proclaimed by the Oath of Association Aske imposed on his followers. In Aske's mind the oath was primarily pacific. However, the militants, before and at Pontefract, added symbolism as redolent of holy war as of holy pilgrimage. In the 1530s it is evident, from the writings of Pole, the correspondence of the circle of Catherine of Aragon, the attitudes and actions of some 1536 rebels, and the reactions of Cromwell, that in a period which was witnessing, to use M. E. James's phrase, a moralisation of politics, some English rebels of militant persuasion, in order to escape the crushing doctrines of obedience, not only applied the traditional medieval excuse for dissent, by blaming the king's advisers rather than the monarch himself, but also grasped for the traditional prop of the righteous against the faithless, the heretic, and the tyrant—the crusade. Thus it was as succour to a doctrine of rebellion that the crusade jolted the regime of Henry VIII.

Given their experience of war, their probable education, and their literary and cultural milieu, the aristocratic leaders of the Pilgrimage of Grace could hardly have been unaware of the implications of their subcrusading posturing. In their lifetimes the crusade had been a serious subject for diplomacy, imagination, action, and gossip. The government certainly read the signals in 1536. But in 1569, outside the fevered rhetoric of opposing ideologies, the extent to which the rebels or society in general shared this awareness and understanding of crusading ideology and its implications is much less certain. Intellectuals such as Foxe, historians such as Holinshed, or writers such as Shakespeare recognised the phenomenon and perhaps glimpsed its practical uses. But the resurrection during the revolt of the Northern Earls of the religious symbols of the previous generation, for example at Durham, have the stale air of anachronism. The focus of militant ideology was now diffuse and lacked any clear structure. By 1569 the only active English crusaders were the few remaining knights of Malta of the English langue. In England, the Catholic warriors of the late sixteenth century were to be Jesuits, not crusaders. Increasingly, active crusading must have appeared, if it was thought of at all, as a limb of Spanish foreign policy, old-fashioned, alien, distant, and papist. This must have been true especially of crusades not aimed against the Turk. Homilists such as Foxe or the author of the *Homily against Rebellion* could become exercised by the trappings of crusading, but the institution no longer held any practical reality in England. The leaders of the 1569 rising had never embarked to fight the infidel, as had Darcy, Constable, Ellekar, and other courtiers of Henry VIII. The prevailing climate of religious propaganda was hostile to crusading patterns of belief. More fundamentally, the social self-image and social role of the Elizabethan knight or gentleman had changed to the diminution of his military function and, hence, of the education and mores which underpinned crusading ideology. The exemplar of a knightly education was no longer Ramon Lull's *Book of the Order of Chivalry*, but Thomas Elyot's *Boke named the Governour* which emphasised the nonmilitary, secular duties of a knight—public service rather than Christian chivalry. In Ferguson's words, "by Elizabeth's day . . . chivalry had become a memory"; and with it, the crusade.[102] Inherited memories can assume a guise of reality, but are not the same as actual experience.

PROTESTANT CRUSADES?

The events of the 1580s, when Englishmen confronted Catholic crusaders in the Channel and Catholic warriors in the Netherlands, may have temporarily revived awareness of crusading ideology. In a paradox which itself exposes a vigorous traditionalism in attitudes, the propagandists of the Protestant resistance to Catholicism appropriated the language and the emotions of their enemies in what has, perhaps misleadingly, been dubbed the "Protestant crusade."[103] The English intervention in the Netherlands from 1584 was interpreted by participants and observers as a religious war and was justified accordingly. In Stow's record of a speech to the troops by Sir Philip Sidney, the enemy were "men of false religion, enemies of God and his church"—the Anti-Christ. Sidney was also reported to describe the Protestant troops as fighting

367

for "God's cause, under whom and for whom they fought, for Her Majesty, whom they knew so well to be good unto them." Although the rhetoric had strong doses of chivalric imagery and overtones of crusade ideology, most accounts reveal that patriotism featured as prominently, if not more so, than traditional, formal religious justifications.[104]

Nevertheless, a sort of Protestant countercrusade ideology was developed in the 1580s. St. George with his emblem of the red cross was rehabilitated as a protector of Protestant soldiers. The war against Spain after 1588 was seen as a just war, and, according to Thomas Nun's *Apologia of the Portingall Voyage* (1596), to die in such a cause "is no bane," the casualties being "a great blessing to the land that they never returned"; they were martyrs.[105] The parallel with contemporary Catholic ideology is even more distinct in a tract published in September 1588 that talked of English bishops raising troops to resist the Armada, which were referred to as "milites sacri."[106] The image of the holy Protestant warrior contending against the impious and the Anti-Christ, commonly identified as the pope (and his followers) or the Turk, was powerful. Despite abandoning the theology that supported the Catholic idea of the crusade, the Protestant ideal owed much to its medieval ancestor. The author of the notorious *Vindiciae Contra Tyrannos* called for aggressive warfare for the true religion and cited the example of the crusade in support. Half a century later William George insisted that the enemies of Protestantism were not only spirits but men as well: "infidels, idolators, heretics, wordlings, all sorts of persecutors . . . and false brethren." With the theme of temporal militancy, expressed by George as complementary to the spiritual conflict espoused by many Protestant ideologues, inevitably marched the image of martyrdom and the fighting Elect. M. Walzer has even drawn an analogy between the ideology of the crusade and the revolutionary theories which sustained Oliver Cromwell's New Model Army in the 1640s.[107]

Yet although the language, the emotions, and some of the theoretical justifications for violence against religious and political foes of the True Religion bear the unmistakable imprint of crusade theories, this should be attributed more to a common western European cultural and intellectual heritage, that survived the Reformation intact, rather than to a deliberate or direct assumption of the crusade as a weapon of Protestantism, let alone revolution. There was no officially formulated Protestant doctrine of the crusade. Protestant concepts of Christian holy war were derived as much from the church fathers and the Bible as from the crusades, and in justifying religious violence or resistance, they shared with the Catholics a tradition that both pre- and postdated the crusade, the theology of which Protestants rejected utterly. When faced with the need to justify certain forms of warfare, it is perhaps unsurprising that aristocrats and intellectuals on both sides of the religious divide reached for similar models, but it would be a misuse of language for the historian to talk of Philip Sidney or Oliver Cromwell as crusaders.

As for the traditional target of crusading, the Moslem, it is harder still to identify genuine crusading enthusiasm far into the seventeenth century. The Turk became synonymous with the Anti-Christ and, as such, "Turk" could degenerate into a term of common abuse; thus Louis XIV earned himself the name of "the Christian Turk" in the 1690s.[108] The memory of crusading lingered in academic, literary, and antiquarian circles, but the resonances grew fainter. Past reality became increasingly distanced by contemporary literary adaptation of familiar themes, as in Tasso's *Gerusalemme Liberata* (1580), which was translated into English by R. Carew (1594) and Edward Fairfax (1600), the latter giving his version the evocative title *Godfrey de Bouillon*. But Jerusalem, although still an attraction for passing tourists, was no longer a focus for Christian idealism, let alone Christian militancy, in England. In poems such as *Jerusalem my happy home* (1601) it once more had become, as it was in centuries before 1095, a metaphor of heaven. The images and ideology of holy war and pilgrimage could still accurately be recalled, by dramatists or in poems like *Give me my scallop-shell of quiet*, once attributed to Sir Walter Raleigh, but they no longer lived. The surviving tangible reminders of the once intense relationship of England and the Holy Land became of interest only to antiquarians, like the Yorkshireman Abraham de la Pryme, who on 1 May 1697 came across the coat-of-arms of the kings of Jerusalem in the church of St. Mary's, Barton-on-Humber.[109]

Interest in the Turk and his "horrid tyranny," as William Burton called it in 1643, remained, both in political and apocalyptic vein. But even though alarm was felt in England at the Ottoman advance in the 1670s and early 1680s, the response had long since been compromised and complicated by realpolitik in commerce and diplomacy, by further internecine and local religious controversy, and even by some feeble stirrings of religious toleration and rational examination of religious phenomena.[110] Concern with the depredations suffered by Christendom and Christians was slow to die (if it ever has). Near the easternmost rim of England in 1661, the village of Darsham in Suffolk collected six shillings nine pence for fellow Protestants in Lithuania; in 1671 the parish raised nine pounds thirteen shillings for the redemption of Christian slaves of the Turks.[111] However, such Christian solidarity cannot be interpreted in the context of any vestigial relevance of the crusade.

The personal experience, sentiments, and religion of Thomas Darcy or William Weston or the first two Tudor monarchs were of another time and of a different mentality.

With the suppression of the Hospitallers and the collapse of the unity of western Christendom, the crusade as a living institution lost its place in patterns of thought and deed. If anywhere, the end of the story of England and the crusades is thus to be placed in the reign of Elizabeth I. A generation and a half later, in 1639, Thomas Fuller published his *History of the Holy Warre,* the first and one of the more interesting histories of the crusades written by an Englishman. The production of an historical account may itself be proof of the decease of an historical phenomenon. The reality of crusading for Englishmen had withered and died amidst the shifting spiritual, social, and political winds of the sixteenth century. The debris of a once dominant spiritual exercise still littered the stage of aristocratic society, but by the time Shakespeare's Henry IV was urging his courtiers

> . . . to the sepulchre of Christ—
> Whose soldier now, under whose blessed cross
> We are impressed and engag'd to fight[112]

the crusade was no longer a practical military ambition or a clearly defined, easily recognisable path to salvation.

Genealogies and Maps

Relationship of the Ruling Houses
of England, Flanders, and Jerusalem

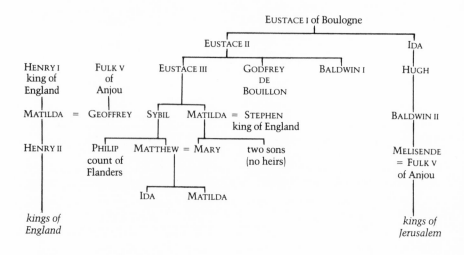

Relationship of the Ruling Houses
of England, Anjou, and Jerusalem

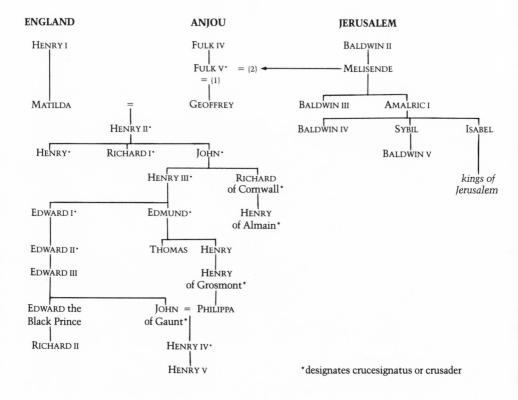

ENGLAND **ANJOU** **JERUSALEM**

HENRY I FULK IV BALDWIN II

FULK V* = (2) ◄──────────── MELISENDE
= (1)

MATILDA = GEOFFREY BALDWIN III AMALRIC I

HENRY II* BALDWIN IV SYBIL ISABEL

HENRY* RICHARD I* JOHN* BALDWIN V

HENRY III* RICHARD
of Cornwall* *kings of
Jerusalem*

EDWARD I* EDMUND* HENRY
of Almain*

EDWARD II* THOMAS HENRY

EDWARD III HENRY
of Grosmont*

EDWARD the
Black Prince JOHN = PHILIPPA
of Gaunt*

RICHARD II HENRY IV*

HENRY V *designates crucesignatus or crusader

373

SCOTLAND

England

Edinburgh

Carlaverock

Durham

Beningburgh ◆YORK
Howden
Pontefract

LINCOLN

Nottingham
HOLLAND
Kings Lynn ◆ NORWICH
Yarmouth
Stamford
Geddington ◆ Bury St. Edmunds
WALES
FOREST
OF DEAN
Evesham Northampton Ipswich
Oxford
Westminster LONDON
Reading Canterbury ◆
Bristol Dover
Salisbury ◆WINCHESTER Hastings
Southampton Lewes ◆
Portsmouth

0   25   50   75   100
MI
0   25 50 75 100
KM

Dartmouth

MAP 1

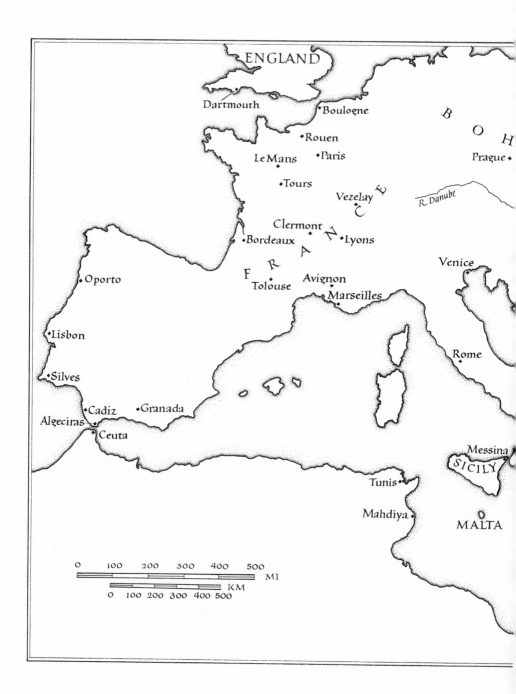

MAP 2

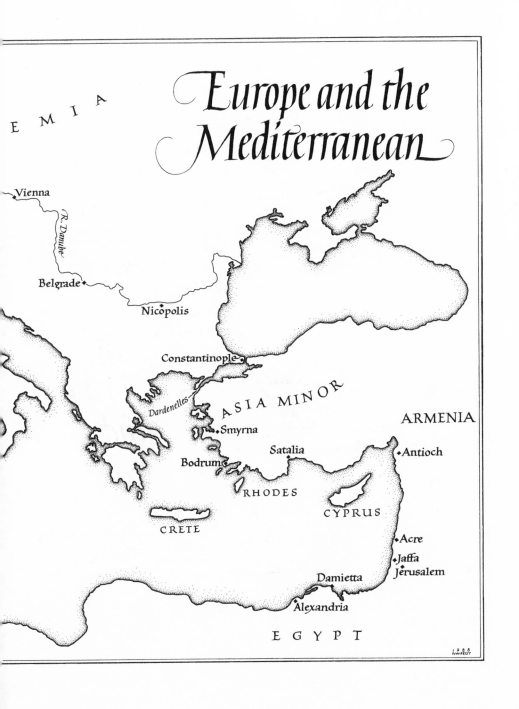

Europe and the Mediterranean

EMIA

Vienna

R. Danube

Belgrade

Nicopolis

Constantinople

Dardenelles

ASIA MINOR

ARMENIA

Smyrna

Satalia

Antioch

Bodrum

RHODES

CYPRUS

CRETE

Acre

Jaffa

Damietta

Jerusalem

Alexandria

EGYPT

Satalia

C I L I C I A N
A R M E N I A

Edessa •

•ANTIOCH

•Lattakiah

CYPRUS

•Limassol

•TRIPOLI

M E D I T E R R A N E A N   S E A

•Beirut
•Sidon
•DAMASCUS
•Tyre
ACRE• •Hattin
Lake Tiberias

Caesarea•
Arsuf•
Jaffa•
JERUSALEM•
Ascalon• •Gaza

R. Jordan

Dead Sea

ALEXANDRIA

•DAMIETTA

Mansourah

CAIRO

E G Y P T

R. Nile

S I N A I

The
Holy Land
and
Egypt

0   25   50   75   100
MI

0 25 50 75 100
KM

MAP 3

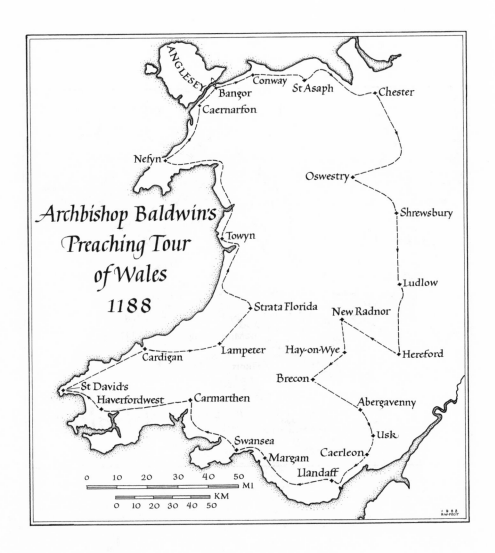

MAP 4

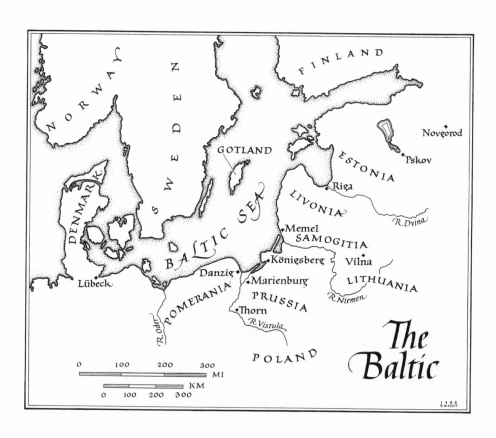

The
Baltic

MAP 5

Abbreviations

Ann.Mon.	*Annales Monastici*, ed. H. R. Luard, 5 vols., RS (London, 1864–69).
BIHR	*Bulletin of the Institute of Historical Research*.
C.C.R.	*Calendar of Close Rolls*.
C.Inq.P.M.	*Calendar of Inquisitions Post Mortem*.
C.Lib.R.	*Calendar of Liberate Rolls*.
C.M.	Matthew Paris, *Chronica Majora*, ed. H. R. Luard, RS (London, 1872–84).
Complete Peerage	*The Complete Peerage of England, Scotland, Ireland, Great Britain and the United Kingdom*, ed. G. E. Cockayne, new ed., ed. V. Gibbs, G. H. White et al., 13 vols. (London, 1910–59).
Councils and Synods	*Councils and Synods with Other Documents Relating to the English Church*, gen. ed. F. M. Powicke, vol. 1 (Oxford, 1981), and vol. 2 (Oxford, 1964).
C.P.R.	*Calendar of Patent Rolls*.
Cal.Pap.Reg.	*Calendar of Papal Registers*, ed. W. T. Bliss et al., 14 vols. (London, 1893–1960).
C.R.R.	*Curia Regis Rolls*.
D.N.B.	*Dictionary of National Biography*.
E.H.D.	*English Historical Documents*, gen. ed. D. C. Douglas, vols. 1–4 (London, 1955–75).
EHR	*English Historical Review*.
E.Y.C.	*Early Yorkshire Charters*, ed. W. Farrer and C. T. Clay, Yorkshire Archaeological Society, 12 vols. (1914–65).
Foedera	*Foedera, Conventiones, Literae, etc.*, ed. T. Rymer, 3d ed. (The Hague, 1745).
Gransden, *Historical Writing*	A. Gransden, *Historical Writing in England, c. 550 to the Early Sixteenth Century*, 2 vols. (London, 1974–82).
H.M.C.	*Historical Manuscripts, Royal Commission on*.

Lunt, *Financial Relations*	W. E. Lunt, *Financial Relations of the Papacy with England*, 2 vols. (Medieval Academy of America, Cambridge, Mass., 1939 and 1962).
Pipe Roll	*The Great Rolls of the Pipe* (Pipe Roll Society, 1884–).
P.R.O.	Public Record Office.
R.H.C.Occ.	*Recueil des historiens des croisades, Historiens Occidentaux*, 5 vols. (Paris, 1844–95).
R.H.F.	*Recueil des historiens des Gaules et de la France*, ed. M. Bouquet et al. (Paris, 1738–1876).
Rot.Parl.	*Rotuli Parliamentorum.*
Rot.Litt.Claus.	*Rotuli Litterarum Clausarum in Turri Londonensi asservati, 1204–27*, ed. T. D. Hardy, 2 vols. (London, 1833–44).
RS	*Rolls Series: The Chronicles and Memorials of Great Britain and Ireland during the Middle Ages* (London, 1858–).
S.R.P.	*Scriptores rerum Prussicarum*, ed. T. Hirsch, M. Toeppen, and E. Strehlke, 5 vols. (Leipzig, 1861–74).
TRHS	*Transactions of the Royal Historical Society.*
V.C.H.	*Victoria History of the Counties of England.*

Notes

N.B. Published translations of sources are cited in the notes; where the translation is mine, the original is cited.

INTRODUCTION

1. *The Letters of Evelyn Waugh*, ed. M. Amory (London, 1980), 103. Instead, he wrote a couple of essays some years later on the Empress Helena and on the Holy Places as he saw them after 1948, published in *The Holy Places* (London, 1952), in which (1–3) he also describes his earlier, abandoned scheme for England and the Holy Places.

CHAPTER ONE

1. Bede, *Ecclesiastical History of the English People*, ed. B. Colgrave and R. A. B. Mynors (Oxford, 1969), 214–15, 231, 240–43, 251.

2. Einhard, *Life of Charlemagne*, trans. L. Thorpe, *Two Lives of Charlemagne* (London, 1969), 61–64; J. M. Wallace-Hadrill, *The Barbarian West* (London, 1969), 96–98.

3. Aelfric, *Lives of Saints*, ed. W. W. Skeat, Early English Text Society (London, 1890), vol. 2, 115, lines 708–9.

4. J. Campbell et al., eds., *The Anglo-Saxons* (Oxford, 1982), 156, for the Abingdon sword hilt; *E.H.D.* 1:181 (883 annal; cf. 893 annal, 187); ibid. 264–76, for Asser's *Life*, esp. 272; for the date of the London incident, F. M. Stenton, *Anglo-Saxon England* (Oxford, 1943), 256.

5. *E.H.D.* 1:293–97.

6. C. Erdmann, *Die Entstehung des Kreuzzugsgedanken* (Stuttgart, 1935), trans. M. W. Baldwin and W. Goffart, under the title *The Origins of the Idea of the Crusade* (Princeton, 1977).

7. Aelfric, *Saints* 2:113, line 686.

8. For the three Lives, Aelfric, *Saints* 2:66–125 (Maccabees); 124–43 (Oswald); 324–35 (Edmund).

9. Campbell, *Anglo-Saxons*, 206; for Abbo as Aelfric's source, *Saints* 2:314–15.

10. Aelfric, *Saints* 2:66–125 (Maccabees), lines 314–15.

11. Ibid., lines 411–12; ibid., lines 638–40; ibid., line 660; ibid. (Oswald), line 167.

12. Ibid. (Maccabees), lines 385–416; ibid., lines 459–513.

13. Ibid., lines 528–29.

14. Ibid., lines 680–83.

15. Ibid. 2:144–59.

16. Ibid., lines 688–704; Gransden, *Historical Writing* 1:83.

17. *E.H.D.* 2:606; D. Wilkins, *Concilia Magnae Britannicae et Hibernicae* (London, 1733–37), vol. 1, 366; for the lack of academic support, J. Gilchrist, "The Erdmann Thesis and the Canon Law, 1083–1141," *Crusade and Settlement*, ed. P. W. Edbury (Cardiff, 1985), 37–45.

18. *E.Y.C.* 1:116, no. 126.

19. *Cartularium Monasterii de Ramesia*, ed. W. H. Hart and P. A. Lyons, RS (London, 1884–93), vol. 3, 173; Symeon of Durham, *Historia Regum, Opera Omnia*, ed. T. Arnold, vol. 2 RS (London, 1885), 174; William of Malmesbury, *Gesta Pontificum Anglorum*, ed. N. E. S. A. Hamilton, RS (London, 1870), 286; idem, *Vita Wulfstani*, ed. R. A. Darlington, Camden Society (London, 1928) 30.

20. Florence of Worcester, *Chronicon ex chronicis*, ed. B. Thorpe (London, 1848–49), vol. 1, 209–10; the Abingdon version of the Anglo-Saxon Chronicle placed Sweyn's death at Constantinople, *E.H.D.* 2:127; E. King, *Peterborough Abbey, 1086–1310* (Cambridge, 1973), 11–12.

21. In general, S. Runciman, *A History of the Crusades*, vol. 1 (Cambridge, 1951), 38–50, esp. 46–47; D. C. Douglas, *The Norman Achievement* (London, 1972), 42 and note 37; D. Bates, *Normandy before 1066* (London, 1982), 246 and note 33, for an early twelfth-century claim that the popularity of the Jerusalem pilgrimage only dated from the mid-eleventh; A. Grabois, "Anglo-Norman England and the Holy Land," *Anglo-Norman Studies* 7 (1984):132–141; C. H. Haskins, "A Canterbury Monk at Constantinople," *EHR* 25 (1910):293–95; Saewulf, *Relatio de peregrinatione Saewulfi*, ed. T. Wright et al., Palestine Pilgrims Text Society, no. 4 (London, 1896), 31–52; *Anglo-Saxon Chronicle*, s.a. 1120, in *E.H.D.* 2:187.

22. *Calendar of Documents preserved in France illustrative of the History of Great Britain and Ireland, 918–1206*, ed. J. H. Round (London, 1899), 25, nos. 87, 88; D. C. Douglas, *William the Conquerer* (London, 1969), 188.

23. Orderic Vitalis, *The Ecclesiastical History*, ed. and trans. M. Chibnall (Oxford, 1969–80), vol. 3, 216.

24. H. E. J. Cowdrey, "The Anglo-Norman Laudes Regiae," *Viator* 12 (1981):73; *Gesta Francorum et aliorum Hierosolimitanorum*, ed. R. Hill (London, 1962), 69.

25. Orderic, *History* 2:202–4; ibid. 4:17; ibid. 5:38; Anna Comnena, *The Alexiad*, trans. E. R. A. Sewter (London, 1969), 95–96; J. Godfrey, "The defeated Anglo-Saxons take Service with the eastern Emperor," *Anglo-Norman Studies* 1 (1978):63–74; K. Ciggaar, "England and Byzantium on the Eve of the Norman Conquest," *Anglo-Norman Studies* 5 (1982):78–96; J. Shepard, "The English and Byzantium," *Traditio* 24 (1973):53–92, esp. 79 note 156 for a seal; M. Biddle, ed., *Winchester in the Early Middle Ages* (Oxford, 1976), 478.

26. William of Poitiers, *Histoire de Guillaume le Conquérant*, ed. R. Foreville (Paris, 1952), 144–45; see Anselm's letter trying to dissuade one such recruit, *Opera Omnia*, ed. F. S. Schmitt (Edinburgh, 1938–61), vol. 3, 151–55, no. 117.

27. Raymond of Aguilers, *Historia Francorum qui ceperunt Iherusalem*, *R.H.C.Occ.*, vol. 3, trans. J. H. Hill and L. L. Hill (Philadelphia, 1968); Fulcher of Chartres, *Historia Hierosolymitanae*, ed. H. Hagenmeyer (Heidelberg, 1913), trans. R. Ryan and H. Fink (Knoxville, Tenn., 1969); *Gesta Francorum*.

28. *E.H.D.* 2:173; William of Malmesbury, *Gesta Regum Anglorum*, ed. W. Stubbs, vol. 2, RS (London, 1889), 431.

29. Henry of Huntingdon, *Historia Anglorum*, ed. T. Arnold, RS (London, 1879), 219; Henry borrowed the idea from Robert of Rheims.

30. *Cartularium Abbathiae de Whiteby*, ed. J. C. Atkinson (Durham, 1879–81), 2–3; C. W. David, *Robert Curthose* (Cambridge, Mass., 1920), 89–119 and appendix D, 221–29; F. Barlow, *William Rufus* (London, 1983), 361–67.

31. William of Tyre, *A History of Deeds done beyond the Sea*, R.C.C.Occ., vol. 1, trans. E. A. Babcock and A. C. Krey (New York, 1976), 177–78 and note 20.

32. Barlow, *Rufus*, 246–47, 362–65; David, *Curthose*, 91–92.

33. Orderic, *History* 5:27.

34. Barlow, *Rufus*, 259 and 363, bases his calculation of royal income in the 1090s on the figures in the Pipe Roll of 1130.

35. Orderic, *History* 5:280; however, Barlow, *Rufus*, 414–19, disputes that this was the king's intention.

36. Orderic, *History* 5:278–80.

37. E.g., ibid., 208; Florence of Worcester, *Chronicon* 2:40; William of Malmesbury, *Gesta Regum* 2:371–72.

38. Eadmer, *Historia Novorum in Anglia*, ed. M. Rule, RS (London, 1884), 74–75.

39. Florence of Worcester, *Chronicon* 2:40; William of Malmesbury, *Gesta Regum* 2:371.

40. It is likely, however, that Anselm at least had received copies of the Clermont decrees. H. E. J. Cowdrey, "Pope Urban II's Preaching of the First Crusade," *History* 55 (1970):183–84; R. Somerville, "The Council of Clermont and the First Crusade," *Studia Gratiana* 20 (1976):331; *Councils and Synods* 1:pt. 2, 648–49.

41. R. L. G. Ritchie, *The Normans in Scotland* (Edinburgh, 1954), 95; William of Malmesbury, *Gesta Regum* 2:310, 449.

42. Anselm, *Opera Omnia* 3:252–55, no. 117.

43. Ibid. 4:85–86, no. 195.

44. Ibid. 5:355, no. 410; H. E. J. Cowdrey, "Cluny and the First Crusade," *Revue Bénédictine* 83 (1973):305–9.

45. Raymond of Aguilers's account, being that of an eyewitness, is probably to be preferred as far as it goes, as it was also written the soonest after the events described. *R.H.C.Occ.* 3:290–91; David, *Curthose*, appendix E, 230–44, discusses the conflicting sources; for Daimbert's letter of April 1100, H. Hagenmeyer, *Die Kreuzzugsbriefe aus den Jahren, 1088–1100* (Innsbruck, 1902), no. 22, 177; cf. ibid., no. 27, 165–66, with Raymond's account of events 1097–98.

46. Shepard, "English and Byzantium"; see notes 25 and 41 above for Edgar's presence in Scotland and the East. Earlier the Vikings had sailed through the Straits of Gibraltar. Adam of Bremen preserved an eleventh-century *portolano* describing the journey from Denmark and Flanders to Acre via the Devonshire coast, Galicia, Lisbon, Gibraltar, Tarragona, Barcelona, Marseilles, and Messina, in *Gesta Hammaburgensis Ecclesiae Pontificum*, ed. B. Schmeidler (Hanover, 1917), 228–29; H. R. Loyn, *Anglo-Saxon England and the Norman Conquest* (London, 1962), 95–96.

47. *De Expugnatione Lyxbonensi*, ed. C. W. David (New York, 1976), 3–26, 56–57, 102–3, 160–61.

48. David, *Curthose*, 233–34; *R.H.C.Occ.* 3:649.

49. Henry of Huntingdon, *Historia*, 262–63; cf. ibid., 270–72, for the speeches before the battle of Lincoln (1141) containing appeals to God and assertions of a just cause.

50. Geoffrey of Monmouth, *Historia Regum Britanniae*, ed. A. Griscom and R. Ellis Jones (London, 1929), 437–38; ibid., trans. L. Thorpe, under the title *The History of the Kings of Britain* (London, 1966), 216, which is somewhat interpretive, but "professione insigniti" must imply, as Thorpe inferred, the sign of the cross.

51. Gransden, *Historical Writing* 1:204.

52. Orderic, *History* 5:xiii–xix, 189; Runciman, *Crusades* 1:330.

53. Orderic, *History* 5:4–190; William of Malmesbury, *Gesta Regum* 2:358, 390–463.

54. William of Malmesbury, *Gesta Regum* 2:433, 460, 461; Orderic, *History* 5:xvii–xix and notes.

55. Gaimar, *Lestoire des Engleis*, ed. T. D. Hardy and C. T. Martin, RS (London, 1888–89), vol. 1, 244–45.

56. William of Malmesbury, *Gesta Regum* 2:320–22; Orderic, *History* 5:46, 106–8.

57. Quoted by David, *Curthose*, 225–26; cf. Orderic's story (*History* 5:171) of Roger Bigod discovering a ball of the Virgin's hair in the church of the Holy Sepulchre which he later distributed to churches and monasteries in France; *Libellus de Vita et Miraculis S. Godrici Heremitae de Finchale*, ed. J. Stevenson, Surtees Society, vol. 20 (1847), 300–1, for more Jerusalem relics in England.

58. *De Expugnatione Lyxbonensi*, 156–57.

59. Henry of Huntingdon, *Historia*, 238.

60. David, *Curthose*, 179, note 17.

61. Orderic, *History* 5:98; ibid. 6:18.

62. H. W. C. Davis, "Henry of Blois and Brian FitzCount," *EHR* 25 (1910):301–3.

63. When referring to the crusaders answering Urban's call Brian appears to have confused the councils of Clermont (November 1095) and Tours (March 1096); alternatively he may have preserved a memory of the pope's preaching at Tours in March 1096 mentioned by Orderic, *History* 5:29.

64. Albert of Aix, *Liber Christianae expeditionis*, R.H.C.Occ. 4:596.

65. *Eynsham Cartulary*, ed. H. E. Salter (Oxford, 1907–8), vol. 1, 37, no. 7.

66. Landowners: *Historia Monasterii S. Petri Gloucestriae*, ed. W. H. Hart, RS (London, 1863), vol. 1, 81; Pipe Roll 31 Henry I (1130), ed. J. Hunter (London, 1833), 33; H. E. Salter, *Facsimilies of Early English Charters in Oxford Muniment Rooms* (Oxford, 1929), nos. 3, 8; *Cartularium de Rameseia* 1:252–53; J. R. West, ed., *Register of St. Benet of Holme*, Norfolk Record Society, nos. 2 and 3 (1932), vol. 1, 54, 87, nos. 92, 155; *E.Y.C.* 3:62, no. 1342; *De Expugnatione Lyxbonensi*, 54–56; Burgesses: *De Expugnatione Lyxbonensi*, 56; *Regesta Regum Anglo-Normannorum, 1066–1154*, vol. 3, *Regesta Henrici Primi, 1100–35*, ed. C. Johnson, H. A. Cronne, and H. W. C. Davis (Oxford, 1956), 240, no. 1653; Merchants: *Libellus de Vita Godrici*, 33, and *De Expugnatione Lyxbonensi*, 100–2, provide examples of merchants, demonstrating the plausibility of the legend that Thomas Becket's father, Gilbert, a merchant, like the Viels, with trans-Channel interests, went to Jerusalem; J. H. Round, *Geoffrey de Mandeville* (London, 1892), 308 note; Clergymen: for Gilbert of Hastings, *De Expugnatione Lyxbonensi*, 178–80.

67. William of Malmesbury, *Gesta Regum* 2:310.

68. *R.H.C.Occ.* 4:595–96, 631; *De Expugnatione Lyxbonensi*, 16–21 and notes; *Brut y Tywysogion*, ed. J. W. ab Ithel, RS (London, 1860), 167.

69. Orderic, *History* 6:400–2.

70. *Gesta Stephani*, ed. K. R. Potter and R. H. C. Davis (Oxford, 1976), 179, 191, 193.

71. *Select Documents of the English Lands of the Abbey of Bec*, ed. M. Chibnall, Camden Series (London, 1951), 16–17 (although the dating of the charter is obscure and the element of financial quid pro quo speculative).

72. Orderic, *History* 6:18.

73. *Annales Cambriae*, ed. J. W. ab Ithel, RS (London, 1860), 38.

74. *Libellus de Vita Godrici*, 33.

75. See note 66 above.

76. Robert of Torigni, *Chronicle*, ed. R. Howlett, *Chronicles of the Reigns of Stephen, Henry II, and Richard I*, vol. 4, RS (London, 1889), 150–51.

77. Fulcher of Chartres, *Historia*, 149.

78. *Libellus de Vita Godrici*, 33–34, 52–57. Cf. William of Newburgh's statement that Godric had gone to the Holy Sepulchre in his youth barefoot and in great poverty, *Historia rerum Anglicarum*, ed. R. Howlett, in *Chronicles of the Reigns of Stephen, Henry II, and Richard I*, vol. 1, RS (London, 1884), 149.

79. For "Gudericus Pirata," Albert of Aix, *Liber, R.H.C.Occ.* 4:595.

80. William of Malmesbury, *Gesta Regum* 2:310, 449; Albert of Aix, *Liber, R.H.C.Occ.* 4:596; Saewulf, *Pilgrimage of Saewulf to Jerusalem*, ed. J. Brownlow (London, 1892), 26–27; *De Expugnatione Lyxbonensi*, 16–21.

81. Albert of Aix, *Liber, R.H.C.Occ.* 4:631–634.

82. In 1148, despite inducements to stay in Portugal, many crusaders continued their journey to Jerusalem; see note 103 below.

83. David, *Curthose*, 224, 227, 229; cf. L. Riley-Smith and J. Riley-Smith, *The Crusades: Idea and Reality, 1095–1274* (London, 1981), 98–100; in general see G. Constable, "The Financing of the Crusades in the Twelfth Century," in *Outremer*, ed. B. Z. Kedar, H. E. Mayer, and R. C. Smail (Jerusalem, 1982), 64–88.

84. Orderic, *History* 5:280.

85. Orderic, *History* 6:18.

86. Riley-Smith, *Crusades*, 57–59, for a translation.

87. Orderic, *History* 6:18.

88. R. Röhricht, *Regesta Regni Hierosolymitani* (Innsbruck, 1893), 57, no. 226; ibid., 58, no. 229; ibid., 61, no. 242.

89. William of Tyre, *Historia, R.H.C.Occ.* 2:35–36; B. Hamilton, *The Latin Church in the Crusader States: The Secular Church* (London, 1980), 123.

90. William of Tyre, *Historia, R.H.C.Occ.* 2:162; in general on Ralph, Hamilton, *Latin Church*, 117–18, 123, 125, 130–31, 157, 164–65.

91. Hamilton, *Latin Church*, 125.

92. William of Tyre, *Historia, R.H.C.Occ.* 2:162–63.

93. J. Riley-Smith, "The Motives of the Earliest Crusaders and the Settlement of Latin Palestine," *EHR* 98 (1983):730; William of Malmesbury's reference implies that Robert arrived in the East only shortly before his death, although it describes him as being with four others "militibus comitatus" of Baldwin I; this may, but equally may not, signify formal vassalage.

94. Hagenmeyer, *Kreuzzugsbriefe*, 177.

95. William of Tyre, *Historia, R.H.C.Occ.* 1:519–20; ibid. 2:59; Orderic, *History* 6:18; Pipe Roll 31 Henry I (1130), 33.

96. *E.H.D.* 2:195; William of Tyre, *Historia, R.H.C.Occ.* 2:40.

97. Henry of Huntingdon, *Historia*, 250.

98. W. E. Wightman, *The Lacy Family in England and Normandy, 1066–1194* (Oxford, 1966), 185, 189, 207, 212–13, 259; *De Expugnatione Lyxbonensi*, 57 note 3; *Charters of the Honour of Mowbray*, ed. D. E. Greenway (London, 1972), 116, no. 155 (1146); ibid., 124, no. 170 (1138); ibid., 183–

84, no. 273; *Records of the Templars in England in the Twelfth Century*, ed. B. A. Lees (London, 1935), 24, 80, 99; for grants by King Stephen and Queen Matilda 1137–54, *Reg. Regnum Anglo-Norm.* 3:310–19; other orders in England before 1150 apart from the Hospitallers included the orders of the Holy Sepulchre, the Temple of the Lord (as opposed to the Temple of Solomon, i.e., the Knights Templar), and St. Lazarus.

99. A. Borg, "Crusader sculpture," *St. John Historical Society Newsletter* (December 1985):26; M. Gervers, "Rotundae Anglicanae," *Acts of the XXII International Congress of Art History* (Budapest, 1969). In fact the similarities are general and schematic rather than accurate and precise; also not all Templar churches were round and one supposed Holy Sepulchre model for other churches was only completed in 1149.

100. R. H. C. Davis, *King Stephen* (London, 1977), 89; J. Le Patourel, *The Norman Empire* (Oxford, 1976), 105; *Register of St. Benet Holme* 1:87; J. H. Round, *Feudal England* (London, 1895), 471; for hardships suffered by Waleran of Meulan, *Chronica Valassensa*, ed. F. Sommènil (Rouen, 1868), 8–9.

101. *Chronica Monasterii de Melsa*, ed. E. A. Bond, RS (London, 1866–68), vol. 1, 76; David, *Curthose*, 228.

102. The deaths of Warenne and Peverel were noted with admiration by John of Hexham, Symeon of Durham, *Opera* 2:319, and *Gesta Stephani*, 179. Bishop Clinton died at Antioch 16 April 1148. R. W. Eyton, *Antiquities of Shropshire*, vol. 6 (London, 1856), 319; in general, G. Constable, "The Second Crusade as seen by Contemporaries," *Traditio* 9 (1953):213ff.

103. *De Expugnatione Lyxbonensi*, 79; G. Constable, "A Note on the Route of the Anglo-Flemish Crusaders," *Speculum* 28 (1953):525–26; for a flavour of St. Bernard's preaching, Riley-Smith, *Crusades*, 95–98; *Letters of St. Bernard of Clairvaux*, trans. B. S. James (London, 1953), nos. 391–401, 408, 410.

104. *De Expugnatione Lyxbonensi*, 52–184.

105. *De Expugnatione Lyxbonensi*, 70–84, 104–110, 146–58; for the crusade and the Reconquista, R. A. Fletcher, *St. James' Catapult* (Oxford, 1984), 297–300.

106. *De Expugnatione Lyxbonensi*, 71, where the writer breaks out of the past tense used in the narrative and introduces the sermon: "Thus it begins" (*"qui sic incipit"*).

107. Philippians 1:21; *Letters of St. Bernard*, no. 391.

108. *De Expugnatione Lyxbonensi*, 158.

109. Ibid., 102, 130, 160.

110. R. W. Southern, *Medieval Humanism* (Oxford, 1970), 158.

111. R. Mortimer,"The Family of Rannulf de Glanville," *BIHR* 54 (1981):1–16, esp. 10.

CHAPTER TWO

1. Röhricht, *Regesta*, no. 397; Roger of Howden, *Gesta Regis Henrici Secundi*, ed. W. Stubbs, RS (London, 1867), vol. 1, 159, 359; ibid. 2:22 (for the attribution, see note 13 below); S. Painter, *William Marshal* (Baltimore, 1933), 54–56; *Waverly Annals*, Ann. Mon. 2:241; *Materials for the History of Thomas Becket*, ed. J. C. Robertson and J. B. Sheppard, RS (London, 1875–85), vol. 6, 76; Wightman, *Lacy Family*, 83–85; *E.Y.C.* 3:289, no. 1629; for a St. Neot's charter mentioning Beauchamp, G. H. Fowler, "The Beauchamps of Eaton," Bedfordshire Historical Record Society, vol. 2 (1914), 70; *The Thame Cartulary*, ed. H. E. Salter, vol. 1 (Oxford, 1947), 53, no. 60; D. Walker, "A letter from the Holy Land," *EHR* 72 (1957):662–65; *Charters of the Earldom of Hereford, 1095–1201*, ed. D. Walker, *Camden Miscellany* 22 (1964):56;

Storgursey Charters, ed. T. D. Tremlett and N. Blakiston, Somerset Record Society (Frome, 1949), 4, no. 3, for Richard "Jerosolimitanus"; in general, see W. L. Warren, *Henry II* (London, 1973), 604–5.

2. R. C. Smail, "Latin Syria and the West, 1149–1187," *TRHS,* 5th ser., 19 (1969):1–20.

3. *Itinerarium peregrinorum et gesta regis Ricardi,* ed. W. Stubbs, RS (London, 1864), 396; cf. the reference to the Normans at Jerusalem and Antioch borrowed from Henry of Huntingdon, in Roger of Howden, *Gesta* 1:52–53; for criticism arising from the Second Crusade, E. Siberry, *Criticism of Crusading, 1095–1274* (Oxford, 1985).

4. William of Newburgh, *Historia,* 66; cf. similarly damning comments by Gervase of Canterbury, *Historical Works,* ed. W. Stubbs, RS (London, 1879–80), vol. 1, 137–38.

5. *Letters of John of Salisbury,* ed. W. J. Millor and C. N. L. Brooke, vol. 2 (Oxford, 1979), 632, no. 287; *Cartulary of the Cluniac Priory of Montacute,* ed. Bishop Hobhouse et al., Somerset Record Society (1894), 184–85, nos. 167–68, and note.

6. Ralph Niger, *De Re Militari et Triplici Via Peregrinationis Ierosolimitano,* ed. L. Schmugge (Berlin, 1977), 186, 193; cf. Gregory VIII's bull *Audita Tremendi* launching the Third Crusade, trans. Riley-Smith, *Crusades,* 64–67.

7. Roger of Howden, *Gesta* 1:359; although the burden of insensitivity could sometimes be on Westerners, as in 1177; William of Tyre, *Historia, R.H.C.Occ.* 2:417–25; ibid., 192–95, for his identification of the Damascus siege (1148) as leading to lasting hostility between crusaders and pullani.

8. Gerald of Wales, *De Principis instructione, Opera,* ed. J. S. Brewer, RS (London, 1861–91), vol. 8, 207.

9. Smail, "Latin Syria," 20.

10. William of Tyre, *Historia, R.H.C.Occ.* 2:418.

11. E.g., *Itinerarium,* 305–6, 337; Ambroise, *The Crusade of Richard Lion-Heart,* trans. M. J. Hubert and J. L. La Monte (New York, 1976), 332; for divine portents associated with the victory of Montgisard, Gervase of Canterbury, *Works* 1:274.

12. Ralph Niger, *De Re Militari,* 186–87, 193–94.

13. Roger of Howden, *Chronica,* ed. W. Stubbs, RS (London, 1868–71); he was also the author of the *Gesta Henrici* formerly attributed to Benedict of Peterborough (D. M. Stenton, "Roger of Howden and Benedict," *EHR* 68 [1953]:574–82; D. Corner, "*The Gesta Regis Henrici Secundi* and *Chronica* of Roger Parson of Howden," *BIHR* 56 [1983]:126–44, which dispels the doubts of Gransden, *Historical Writing* 1:226–30). For the Templars and Hospitallers, Gerald of Wales, *Opera* 8:194, 255–56; Roger of Howden, *Gesta* 1:169. Henry's diplomatic links with Byzantium and Antioch have left traces on the Pipe Rolls: Pipe Roll 23 Henry II (1177), 166, 187, 192, 208; ibid., 24 Henry II (1178), 19, when the emperor was sent some dogs as a present from the king; ibid., 25 Henry II (1179), 125, and 31 Henry II (1185), 216.

14. Roger of Howden, *Gesta* 1:116; Gervase of Canterbury, *Works* 1:371–72.

15. *Letters of John of Salisbury* 2:569, no. 272.

16. Röhricht, *Regesta,* no. 497; Smail, "Latin Syria," 16.

17. Henry's awareness of their dangerous ferocity is recorded by Gervase of Canterbury, *Works* 1:325, with reference to the mission of Heraclius.

18. Warren, *Henry II.*

19. A point stressed by Ralph of Diceto, *Ymagines Historiarum, Opera Historica,* ed. W. Stubbs, RS (London, 1876), vol. 2, 33–34.

20. Roger of Howden, *Gesta* 1:289, 297–98, 338; Gerald of Wales, *Opera* 5:363; Ralph of Diceto, *Ymagines* 2:34.

21. *R.H.F.* 16:66, in a letter from Reginald of St. Valery to Louis VII.

22. *Letters of John of Salisbury* 2:568–69.

23. *Letters and Charters of Gilbert Foliot,* ed. A. Morey and C. N. L. Brooke (Cambridge, 1967), 241, no. 170.

24. Gervase of Canterbury, *Works* 1:208; *Letters of John of Salisbury* 2:632–35.

25. *Letters of John of Salisbury* 2:692–95.

26. The various texts for the Compromise of Avranches are discussed in *Councils and Synods* 1:pt. 2, 942–56.

27. *Materials for Becket* 4:163, cf. 174; Roger of Howden, *Chronica* 2:17. The murderers were, according to popular report, eventually buried outside the Temple in Jerusalem. But for a different account of the murderers' fate, F. Barlow, *Thomas Becket* (London, 1986), 258–59.

28. Gerald of Wales, *Opera* 8:170–71.

29. Ralph Niger, *Chronicles,* ed. R. Anstruther, Caxton Society (London, 1851), 94.

30. Roger of Howden, *Gesta* 1:23–24, 198–99, 276; Robert of Torigni, *Chronicle,* 249; Gerald of Wales, *Opera* 5:190, where, in the *Topographia Hibernica,* he implies Henry's frustrated interest in fighting in Spain.

31. Roger of Howden, *Gesta* 1:116.

32. Ibid., 193–94; Gervase of Canterbury, *Works* 1:272–74.

33. Roger of Howden, *Gesta* 1:275–76.

34. Gervase of Canterbury, *Works* 1:371–72.

35. Gerald of Wales, *Opera* 5:190, 304.

36. Ibid., 303; ibid. 8:207 for the quotation.

37. S. K. Mitchell, *Taxation in Medieval England* (New Haven, Conn., 1951), 114–19 and notes; W. E. Lunt, "The Text of the Ordinance of 1184," *EHR* 37 (1922):240–42; *Councils and Synods* 1:pt. 2, 1022–24; F. A. Cazel, "The Tax of 1185 in Aid of the Holy Land," *Speculum* 30 (1955):385–92; Gervase of Canterbury, *Works* 1:198–99.

38. B. Z. Kedar, "The General Tax of 1183 in the Crusading Kingdom of Jerusalem," *EHR* 89 (1974):339–45.

39. Robert of Torigni, *Chronicle,* 230; Pipe Roll 13 Henry II (1167), 194.

40. *Ex Chronico anonymi Laudunensis canonici, R.H.F.* 18:705.

41. Cazel, "Tax of 1185," 389.

42. *Chronica Monasterii de Melsa,* ed. E. A. Bond, RS (London, 1866–68), vol. 1, 200; Smail, "Latin Syria," 14.

43. Roger of Howden, *Gesta* 1:158–59.

44. Gervase of Canterbury, *Works* 1:298–300.

45. Walter Map, *De Nugis Curialium,* ed. M. R. James, revised C. N. L. Brooke and R. A. B. Mynors (Oxford, 1983), 482–85; H. E. Mayer, "Henry II of England and the Holy Land," *EHR* 97 (1982):728.

46. Mayer, "Henry II," 721–39.

47. Henry's habit of sending money on deposit to Jerusalem is mentioned in 1189 by Gerald of Wales, *Opera* 4:363; in his 1192 will, by Gervase of Canterbury, *Works* 1:298, as well as by the Palestinian writer Ernoul in the late 1190s, *R.H.C.Occ.* 2:46–47. See appendix to chapter 2.

48. Cazel, "Tax of 1185," 391–92; *R.H.F.* 18:705.

49. *Histoire de Guillaume le Maréchal,* ed. P. Meyer (Paris, 1891–94), lines 7245–58; Roger of Howden, *Chronica* 2:147–48.

50. E.g., Lucius III's letter of 1184, Roger of Howden, *Gesta* 1:332–33; William of Newburgh, *Historia*, 245–47.

51. Roger of Howden, *Gesta* 1:116, 133, 158. Henry, by virtue of descent in the male line, had a stronger claim to any regency for, or succession to, Baldwin IV.

52. William of Tyre, *Historia, R.H.C.Occ.* 2:417, 419.

53. Roger of Howden, *Gesta* 1:116.

54. Ambroise, *Crusade*, 290; *Itinerarium*, 295; cf. Richard's relations with Tancred of Lecce in Sicily in 1190–91 over the terms of William II's will and the treatment of his sister Joanna.

55. J. O. Prestwich, "Richard Coeur de Lion: Rex Bellicosus," *Accademia Nazionale dei Lincei: Problemi attuali de scienza e di cultura* 253 (1981):8, cf. 7–8 for Richard's dynastic motivation.

56. Warren, *Henry II*, 148.

57. Roger of Howden, *Gesta* 1:289, 297–98; *Histoire de Guillaume le Maréchal*, lines 6891–6911, 7233–95.

58. William of Tyre, *Historia*, in *R.H.C.Occ.* 2:491–98, also puts a rather hostile gloss on Guy's achievement.

59. Roger of Howden, *Gesta* 1:335–36; Gervase of Canterbury, *Works* 1:325; Ralph of Diceto, *Ymagines*, 2:32–34; Gerald of Wales, *Opera* 5:360–63; ibid. 8:202–12; William of Newburgh, *Historia*, 245–47, for Pope Lucius's letter the Patriarch carried.

60. Ralph of Diceto, *Ymagines* 2:32–33; Gervase of Canterbury, *Works* 1:373, on the other hand, thought that the Jerusalemites had offered Henry "the crown and sceptre of the kingdom"; but Gervase was no friend of the king.

61. Gerald of Wales, *Opera* 5:361; H. E. Mayer, "Kaiserrecht und Heiliges Land," *Aus Reichsgeschichte und Nordischen Geschichte*, Kieler Historische Studien (Stuttgart, 1972), 201–6.

62. Ralph of Diceto, *Ymagines* 2:27–28, for the king's letter written after his envoys had reached Brindisi; the papal letter given to Heraclius made no reference to royal authorisation of the mission.

63. William of Newburgh, *Historia*, 246–47; William of Tyre, *Historia, R.H.C.Occ.* 2:508; ibid., 6–8; Gervase of Canterbury, *Works* 2:83; *Chronique d'Ernoul et de Bernard le Trésorier*, ed. L. de Mas Latrie (Paris, 1871), 116–17.

64. *R.H.F.* 18:704; cf. Rigord's and Ralph Niger's accounts of Heraclius in Paris; Rigord, *Gesta Philippi Augusti*, ed. F. Delaborde, *Oeuvres de Rigord et de Guillaume le Breton*, vol. 1 (Paris, 1882), 46–48; Ralph Niger, *De Re Militari*, 187.

65. Gervase of Canterbury, *Works* 1:325; Herbert of Bosham, *Vita S. Thomae, Materials for Becket*, vol. 3, 514–17.

66. Mitchell, *Taxation*, 118; Cazel, "Tax of 1185," 387, 390; Pipe Roll 31 Henry II (1185), 45; Rigord, *Gesta*, 47–48.

67. Roger of Howden, *Gesta* 1:359; ibid. 2:22 for the fates of Mowbray and Beauchamp in 1187.

68. Ralph Niger, *Chronicles*, 94, although Gregory VIII, the former Cardinal Alberto di Morra, had died on 17 December 1187.

69. E.g., Ambroise, *Crusade*, 36–37; *Itinerarium*, 141–42.

70. *Itinerarium peregrinorum*, ed. H. E. Mayer (Stuttgart, 1962), 269; *R.H.C.Occ.* 2:88–93; for an eyewitness account, *De expugnatione Terrae Sanctae per Saladinum Libellus*, ed. J. Stevenson, RS (London, 1875), 218; for Conrad's letter, Ralph of Diceto, *Ymagines* 2:61, where the writer notes

the damaging refusal of the Templars to use their alms. However, it is difficult to distinguish between money put on deposit by Henry in an account of his own and money given by him to the military orders for their own use. One bezant equalled two shillings, according to Pipe Roll 32 Henry II (1186), 149.

71. Roger of Howden, *Gesta* 1:159; *R.H.F.* 18:705; Gervase of Canterbury, *Works* 1:325.

72. Gervase of Canterbury, *Works* 1:298, for the will; for the later tradition, Roger of Wendover, *Flores historiarum,* ed. H. G. Hewlett, vol. 1, RS (London, 1886), 128; he was followed by Matthew Paris, *Historia Anglorum,* ed. F. Madden, RS (London, 1866–69), vol. 1, 424; *Annales Cambriae,* 55 (from a thirteenth-century MS); John Capgrave, *De Illustribus Henricis,* has a fifteenth-century version, ed. F. C. Hingeston, RS (London, 1858), 79; cf. the text in Ralph of Diceto, *Ymagines* 2:10. Warren, *Henry II,* 559, makes the point that the so-called will was in fact a testament to be executed after the king's death.

73. *R.H.C.Occ.* 2: esp. 46–47, and variants, 47; possibly it was the presence of these Englishmen that dictated the flying of the Angevin standard.

74. Ralph of Diceto, *Ymagines* 2:80–81; A. J. Forey, "The Military Order of St. Thomas of Acre," *EHR* 92 (1977):481–86; Roger of Howden, *Gesta* 2:116; *Itinerarium,* 116.

75. Gerald of Wales, *Opera* 5:363; R. Bartlett, *Gerald of Wales, 1146–1223* (Oxford, 1982), 77–86.

76. Henry of Huntingdon, *Historia,* 236; A. Gransden has noted the influence of Henry's *De contemptu mundi* on Gerald in a review, *EHR* 100 (1985):160.

CHAPTER THREE

1. In general see S. Painter, "The Third Crusade: Richard the Lionhearted and Philip Augustus," *History of Crusades,* ed. Setton 2:45–85; J. Gillingham, *Richard the Lionheart* (London, 1978), 108–14, 131–216. For the flavour of contemporary enthusiasm, *Itinerarium,* 32–33.

2. *Audita tremendi* is translated in Riley-Smith, *Crusades,* 64–67.

3. See the comments of so-called Ansbert, *Historia de expeditione Friderici Imperatoris,* ed. W. Stubbs; Roger of Howden, *Chronica* 3: cxxxvii–cxxxxviii.

4. *E.H.D.* 1:219, 222, provide examples of governmental efficiency in the early eleventh century with which the effort for the Third Crusade could be compared; see also J. Campbell, "Observations on English Government from the Tenth to the Twelfth Century," *TRHS,* 5th ser., 25 (1975):39–54.

5. Ralph Niger, *De Re Militari,* 193 and note 3.

6. *Itinerarium,* 32; Gervase of Canterbury, *Works* 1:389; Gerald of Wales, *Opera* 8:244–45; William of Newburgh, *Historia,* 271.

7. Rigord, *Gesta* 1:83–84; Gervase of Canterbury, *Works* 1:406; Roger of Howden, *Gesta* 2:29–30; Ralph of Diceto, *Ymagines* 2:50; William of Newburgh, *Historia,* 272; *Itinerarium,* 140; Ambroise, *Crusade,* lines 113–54.

8. Ralph of Diceto, *Ymagines* 2:54–55. The leader of the revolt, Geoffrey de Lusignan, had reached the Holy Land by the end of the year. On the 1188–89 hostilities, Warren, *Henry II,* 616–26.

9. The treaty of Nonancourt is in Ralph of Diceto, *Ymagines* 2:73–74.

10. Gerald of Wales, *Journey through Wales*, trans. L. Thorpe (London, 1978), 184.

11. Ralph of Diceto, *Ymagines* 2:51–54.

12. On potential ambiguities and tensions in Anglo-German relations, K. J. Leyser, "Frederick Barbarossa and the Hand of St. James," *EHR* 90 (1975), 481–506.

13. Quoted by E. N. Johnson, "The Crusades of Frederick Barbarossa and Henry VI," in *History of Crusades*, ed. Setton 2:93.

14. Roger of Howden, *Gesta* 2:30–33; Gervase of Canterbury, *Works* 1:409–10; Gerald of Wales, *Journey*, esp. 30–36 for a conjectural itinerary; Pipe Roll 34 Henry II (1188), 11, 106, 216; cf. Rigord, *Gesta* 1:84–85, and below note 107.

15. Ralph of Diceto, *Ymagines* 2:51; *Itinerarium* 140–41.

16. *Councils and Synods* 1: pt. 2, 1025–29, for a recently collated text.

17. William of Newburgh, *Historia*, 273–74.

18. Robert Cauchois of Normandy received Henry II's permission (*licentia*) to take the cross in 1188–89, *Chartes de prieuré de Longueville*, ed. P. le Cacheux, *Société de l'histoire de Normandie* 89 (1934):53–54. Apparently Rannulf Glanvill needed permission from Richard I to go to Jerusalem in 1189, Roger of Howden, *Gesta* 2:87.

19. For instance, the discrepancy of ideal and practice formed a central theme of Ralph Niger's *De Re Militari*.

20. Pipe Roll 2 Richard I (1190), 3; *Itinerarium*, 197–98.

21. Ralph Niger, *De Re Militari*, 198; Ambroise's *Estoire de la Guerre Sainte* gives a vivid picture of camp life during the crusade.

22. Roger of Howden, *Gesta* 2:130–31; idem, *Chronica* 3:59.

23. Ambroise, *Crusade*, lines 5678–80, for quotation.

24. Ibid., lines 5695–98.

25. Ibid., lines 12237–41.

26. Roger of Howden, *Gesta*, 110–11. The crusaders with the fleet had to swear to abide by the terms of these assizes.

27. Odo of Deuil, *Du Profectione Ludovici VII in orientem*, ed. V. G. Berry (New York, 1948), esp. 20, 66, 74, 124–26.

28. Roger of Howden, *Gesta* 2:119–20, when, at Lisbon, to restore order, Richard of Camville and Robert de Sablé, two of the justiciars of the fleet, insisted that the crusaders renew their oaths to obey the assizes; cf. the punishments meted out to thieves by Richard I's justiciars at Messina, Richard of Devizes, *Chronicle*, ed. J. T. Appleby (London, 1963), 16.

29. Ralph of Diceto, *Ymagines* 2:88.

30. Roger of Howden, *Gesta* 2:129–30.

31. *Itinerarium*, 218–19, cf. 134–50; Ambroise, *Crusade*, lines 4413–62.

32. At Acre the princes as well as the common fund provided seige engines, Ambroise, *Crusade*, lines 4743–4840. The fate of the goods of deceased crucesignati, especially if they had failed to fulfil their vows, remained of concern to planners and commanders; cf. the instructions in 1194 to itinerant justices in England to ascertain the nature, extent, and ownership of dead crusaders' possessions, Roger of Howden, *Chronica* 3:264.

33. This according to the semi-official court chronicles, Rigord, *Gesta* 1:85–91.

34. Roger of Howden, *Gesta* 1:336–37; ibid. 2:32; idem, *Chronica* 2:302, named Archbishop Baldwin, the archbishop of Rouen, Rannulf Glan-

vill, and Bishop Hugh of Le Puiset of Durham as having taken the cross in 1185.

35. *Itinerarium*, 141; William of Newburgh, *Historia*, 275; Gerald of Wales, *De Principis Instructione*, in *Opera* 8:251; C. R. Cheney, *Innocent III and England* (Stuttgart, 1976), 255; cf. for one mercenary crusader, Robert of Cokefield, *C.R.R.* 1:430.

36. Richard of Devizes, *Chronicle*, 10–11, 15, 27–28.

37. Jocelin of Brakelond, *Chronicle*, ed. H. E. Butler (London, 1949), 39–40, 53–54.

38. Roger of Howden, *Chronica* 3:17; Richard of Devizes, *Chronicle*, 6, 7.

39. Richard of Devizes, *Chronicle*, 27–28; cf. Roger of Howden, *Gesta* 2:158; Ralph of Diceto, *Ymagines* 2:90–91. In fact, the king needed the archbishop to bring peace to England.

40. William of Newburgh, *Historia*, ed. H. C. Hamilton (London, 1856), vol. 2, 144 (other references to William of Newburgh, *Historia*, unless otherwise stated, are to the Rolls Series edition by R. Howlett); Roger of Howden, *Gesta* 2:90–91.

41. Gerald of Wales, *Opera* 1:84–85; Corner, "Roger of Howden," 126–40.

42. Richard of Devizes, *Chronicle*, 28.

43. *Itinerarium*, 33, 139. The first book of this compilation (5–137) is derived from the *Itinerarium peregrinorum* of 1191–92; see H. E. Mayer's edition, 96–102; the rest is either from Ambroise or Ambroise's source, 1195–96. Ralph of Coggeshall, *Chronicon Anglicanum*, ed. J. Stevenson, RS (London, 1875), 45, for Neville's report; *Chronica Monasterii de Melsa* 1:lxxviii; cf. Gransden, *Historical Writing* 1:239–40, 324.

44. Richard of Devizes, *Chronicle*, 15, talks of one hundred ships capable of carrying thirty sailors and forty infantry, and fourteen busses with double that complement; Roger of Howden, *Gesta* 2:117, although he later increased the number on board the Londoners' ship to one hundred; idem, *Chronica* 3:43.

45. Roger of Howden, *Gesta* 2:112, 115, figures based on the assumption that the complement of fighting men on a galley was similar to that on a buss; cf. the Moslem galley with eighty men on board in 1190; *Itinerarium*, 104; cf. Gillingham, *Richard*, 146–47.

46. *Itinerarium*, 93–104.

47. Gillingham, *Richard*, 142–47; Richard of Devizes, *Chronicle*, 28; cf. *Chronica Monasterii de Melsa* 1:252.

48. Roger of Howden, *Gesta* 2:89–90; Ralph of Diceto, *Ymagines* 2:65–66; *Itinerarium*, 64.

49. Gerald of Wales, *Journey*, 20.

50. Ibid.; Ambroise, *Crusade*, lines 1–160, 3521–3770, 4179–4202; *Itinerarium*, 97–109, 138–39.

51. Gerald of Wales, *Journey*, 75; see below.

52. Gerald of Wales, *Opera* 1:75 (in his autobiography *De Rebus et Gestis*); idem, *Journey*, 75–76; Rhys ap Gruffyd, the prime catch at Radnor, was Gerald's cousin.

53. Gerald of Wales, *Journey*, 75–76, 164, 202, 31–36.

54. Names appear throughout the narrative sources, local charters, and the Pipe Rolls; e.g., Pipe Roll 2 Richard I, 9; *E.Y.C.*, refs. at note 64 below; Roger of Howden, *Gesta* 2: 110, 144, 147–50; idem, *Chronica* 3:87–90; L. Landon, *Itinerary of King Richard I* (London, 1935).

55. Landon, *Itinerary*, 44, 173–80; *Itinerarium*, 184; on the crusade chancery, J. Sayers, "English charters from the Third Crusade," in *Tradition and Change: Essays in Honour of Marjorie Chibnall*, ed. D. Greenway, C. Holdsworth, J. Sayers (Cambridge, 1985), 195–200.

56. *Epistolae Cantuariensis: Chronicles and Memorials of Richard I*, ed. W. Stubbs, vol. 2, RS (London, 1865), no. 375; Roger of Howden, *Chronica* 3:129–33; Gervase of Canterbury, *Works* 1:493–94, 509–10; cf. the despatch of the archbishop of Rouen to England from Sicily, and for embassies from England to Richard, Pipe Roll 4 Richard I (1192), 201–2, and *Itinerarium*, 333; for the possible lengths of time involved in such contacts, Landon, *Itinerary*, 184–88 (and 60, for news of Longchamps's deposition reaching the king in January 1192).

57. *Epistolae Cantuariensis*, nos. 345 and 346; Ralph of Diceto, *Ymagines* 2:84, 88–89; *Itinerarium*, 93; Roger of Howden, *Gesta* 2:115, 142–45; Ambroise, *Crusade*, lines 4203–4526, for conditions before Acre in the winter of 1190–91; Gerald of Wales, *Journey*, 205–8, for a by-no-means dispassionate view of Baldwin.

58. *Itinerarium*, 120–23; Conrad's letter to Archbishop Baldwin 20 September 1188, in Ralph of Diceto, *Ymagines* 2:60–62.

59. Roger of Howden, *Gesta* 2:144, 150; idem, *Chronica* 3:xxviii, note 2; Richard of Devizes, *Chronicle*, 5–7.

60. *Itinerarium*, 242, 345–46, 372, 432, 437–38; Ambroise, *Crusade*, lines 11881–84, 12101–93.

61. *Itinerarium*, 413–24; Ralph of Coggeshall, *Chronicon*, 45; Ambroise, *Crusade*, lines 11410–38, for the list of Richard's ten companions in a desperate engagement near Jaffa, August 1192; for Philip of Poitiers, Landon, *Itinerary*, 49, 60, 70. For Neville's obituary, *C.M.* 3:71.

62. Gerald of Wales, *Journey*, 114, 140, 204.

63. Gerald of Wales, *Opera* 1:75.

64. J. T. Appleby, *England without Richard* (London, 1965), 167; for the Yorkshire crusaders, *E.Y.C.* 1:434–35; ibid. 3:79, 116, 298–99, 375–76, 405; ibid. 6:167–68.

65. *Rotuli Curiae Regis*, ed. F. Palgrave (London, 1835), vol. 1, 54 for a crusader "in the service of the king"; *Rolls of the Fifteenth (1225) and the Fortieth (1232)*, ed. F. A. Cazel and A. P. Cazel (London, 1983), 54, 66, 99, 106; J. A. Brundage, *Medieval Canon Law and the Crusader* (Madison, Wis., 1969), 184, and below chapter 8.

66. Pipe Roll 2 Richard I (1190), 18, 35, 73, 109–10, 117; ibid., 3 Richard I (1191), 28, 43–44, 58, 115, 121, 152; ibid., 4 Richard I (1192), 200, 261, 262, 308.

67. Pipe Roll 3 Richard I (1191), 43–44.

68. Ibid., 121, and Roger of Howden, *Gesta* 2:149 (Pole); Pipe Roll 2 Richard I (1190), 110, and *Itinerarium*, 218 (Malet); Pipe Roll 4 Richard I (1192), 200, Roger of Howden, *Gesta* 2:149, and *C.R.R.* 3:259 (Odell).

69. Pipe Roll 3 Richard I (1191), 33; ibid., 4 Richard I (1192), 179; Roger of Howden, *Gesta* 2:149.

70. Pipe Roll 34 Henry II (1188), 141; ibid., 5 Richard I (1193), 80.

71. Pipe Roll 4 Richard I (1192), 285.

72. *C.R.R.* 1:85; Gerald of Wales, *Journey*, 172, and *Opera* 1:75, 77–78, for hostile wives.

73. Pipe Roll 2 Richard I (1190), 110; ibid., 3 Richard I (1191), 44; *Itinerarium*, 217–18; Roger of Howden, *Gesta* 2:150.

74. William of Newburgh, *Historia*, 308–24.

75. Ralph of Diceto, *Ymagines* 2:65.

76. E.g., *E.Y.C.* 3:116.

77. William of Newburgh, *Historia*, 310–11.

78. Stenton, "Roger of Howden," 576–77; Roger of Howden, *Gesta* 2:149.

79. Ambroise, *Crusade*, lines 3381–87, 3563–82, 3819–37, 3971–86, 4203–24, 4061–66, 4989–5024.

80. Ibid., lines 4257–59; cf. ibid., lines 4451–58, for the social mix of the indigent.

81. Ibid., lines 4575–88. Philip offered three bezants a month, Richard four; cf. the story of Richard offering first two, then three, then four bezants to anybody bringing him a stone from the walls of Acre (lines 4948–55) and his offer to pay for two hundred knights and two thousand serjeants to stay in the East in 1192 (lines 8591–94).

82. Gerald of Wales, *Opera* 1:85; the evidence from land charters will be discussed more fully in chapter 8.

83. E.g., for a slightly later case of a servile proxy, F. M. Stenton, "Early Manumissions at Staunton," *EHR* 26 (1911): 95–96: P. R. Hyams, *Kings, Lords, and Peasants* (Oxford, 1980), 32, note 37, for the date.

84. See above chapter 2; *De Expugnatione Lyxbonensi*, 56 and note 2; Pipe Roll 15 Henry II (1169), 172, recorded Hachard's debt of one hundred shillings, still unpaid in 1175, and his journey to Jerusalem.

85. Roger of Howden, *Gesta* 2:89–90, 116–18; *Chronica Monasterii de Melsa* 1:252 has the same story but says that the Londoners filled ten ships, one of which sank in the storm, and that all three saints appeared in visions dressed in full pontificals. It is likely that this Meaux version is a garbled derivative of Howden.

86. Ralph of Diceto, *Ymagines* 2:80–81; *Itinerarium*, 91 for the archdeacon's presence by July 1190.

87. *The London Eyre of 1244*, ed. H. A. Chew and M. Weinbaum, London Record Society (London, 1970), 120, no. 295; for FitzOsbert's sticky end, Roger of Howden, *Chronica* 4:5–6; Ralph of Diceto, *Ymagines* 2:143–44.

88. *Chronica Monasterii de Melsa* 1:252–53; *Itinerarium*, 403.

89. Roger of Howden, *Gesta* 2:147–50; Pipe Roll 1 Richard I (1189), 20; Ralph of Diceto, *Ymagines* 2:80–81; *Curia Regis Rolls, 1194–95*, ed. F. W. Maitland (London, 1891), 113; *Select Cases for the Ecclesiastical Courts of the Province of Canterbury c. 1200–1301*, ed. N. Adams and C. Donahue, Selden Society (London, 1981), 45; Ralph of Coggeshall, *Chronicon*, 54.

90. *Itinerarium*, 116.

91. Ambroise, *Crusade*, lines 1607–16; *Itinerarium*, 192–93.

92. Ralph of Diceto, *Ymagines* 2:84; *Itinerarium*, 91–93; Roger of Howden, *Gesta* 2:142, 147; A. Morey and C. N. L. Brooke, *Gilbert Foliot and his Letters* (Cambridge, 1965), 274.

93. Prestwich, "Richard Coeur de Lion," 12.

94. Pipe Roll 34 Henry II; Mitchell, *Taxation*, 121.

95. *Epistolae Cantuarienses*, nos. 158, 167; the law suit concerned Baldwin's foundation of a college of secular canons at Haskington, which the monks of Canterbury saw as a direct threat to their rights and privileges; cf. Gervase of Canterbury, *Works* 1:394 et seq.

96. Rigord, *Gesta* 1:85 described the crusade tithe granted at Paris in March 1188 as "que dicta sunt decima Salahadini," which incidentally demonstrates a more accurate transliteration of Arabic than many later medieval writers.

97. Roger of Howden, *Gesta* 2:30–32; Mitchell, Taxation, 12–14, 119–23, 169–71.

98. Roger of Howden, *Gesta* 2:33.

99. Pipe Roll 34 Henry II, 11, 216.

100. Roger of Howden, *Gesta* 2:33.

101. Gervase of Canterbury, *Works* 1:199.

102. But see William of Newburgh, *Historia*, 273, who has the current harvest (1187 or 1188?) excluded and the subsequent one (1188 or 1189?) taxed.

103. Gervase of Canterbury, *Works* 1:409–10, although 422–23 implies immediate royal pressure on taxpayers by Easter 1188; William of Newburgh, *Historia*, 273–75, also omits mention of any deadline.

104. Rigord, *Gesta* 1:88; the Le Mans and Geddington decrees refer to no such exemption, but the Waverly Annals, *Ann. Mon.* 2:245, imply that the initiative for the Saladin tithe came from the papacy and that the Cistercians were generally exempt; this may be a later gloss.

105. Roger of Howden, *Gesta* 2:33; for a resumé of the criticism, Mitchell, *Taxation*, 121–22.

106. Ralph of Coggeshall, *Chronicon*, 25; *Chronica Monasterii de Melsa* 1:239; Gervase of Canterbury, *Works* 1:422–23 (hardly unbiased).

107. *Recueil des actes de Philippe Auguste*, ed. H. F. Delaborde, vol. 1 (Paris, 1916), 305–6, no. 252; cf. J. W. Baldwin, "La décennie décisive: les années 1190–1203," *Revue historique* 266 (1981):311–37.

108. Roger of Howden, *Gesta* 2:44–45.

109. *Epistolae Cantuariensis*, no. 325; for the troubles in the southern Angevin lands, Warren, *Henry II*, 608–26; Gillingham, *Richard*, 131, is perhaps too sanguine about contributions from Aquitaine.

110. Pipe Roll 34 Henry II, 14; ibid., 1 Richard I, 105–6, 178; ibid., 5 Richard I, 120; Mitchell, *Taxation*, 12–14; for other Pipe Roll references to the tithe, 34 Henry II, 11, 216; ibid., 1 Richard I, 5, 12; ibid., 4 Richard I, 305.

111. *C.R.R.* 1:430; for references to the dispute and Robert's career, including his time as the abbey's strong-arm agent, Jocelin of Brakelond, *Chronicle*, 51, 123, 138–39; for the 1201 tax, Roger of Howden, *Chronica* 4:188–89.

112. Roger of Howden, *Gesta* 2:47–48.

113. Pipe Roll 1 Richard I, 5, 178; cf. Appleby, *England without Richard*, 6.

114. Gervase of Canterbury, *Works* 1:422–23; Roger of Howden, *Chronica* 3:8; J. H. Ramsay, *A History of the Revenues of the Kings of England, 1066–1399* (Oxford, 1925), vol. 1, 179–91, 227; for the Jewish tallage, Roger of Howden, *Gesta* 2:33; Pipe Roll 1 Richard I, 230; H. G. Richardson, *The English Jewry under the Angevin Kings* (London, 1960), 162–64.

115. Roger of Howden, *Gesta* 2:44, 98.

116. Mitchell, *Taxation*, 31; cf. Ramsay, *Revenues* 1:179 for the estimate for a fifteenth in 1214, and 194 for the 1162 Danegeld yield.

117. Roger of Howden, *Gesta* 2:90; Gillingham, *Richard*, 125–42; Appleby, *England without Richard*, 4–24.

118. William of Newburgh, *Historia* (Hamilton ed.) 2:11, 144; Richard of Devizes, *Chronicle*, 6; Roger of Howden, *Chronica* 3; 13–15; G. V. Scammell, *Hugh du Puiset* (Cambridge, 1956), 50 and notes 2, 4; for his lavish crusade preparations, ibid., 106, 135.

119. William of Newburgh, *Historia* (Hamilton ed.) 2:121; Richard of Devizes, *Chronicle*, 9.

120. Pipe Roll 2 Richard I, 1.

121. Ibid., 8–9.

122. Richard of Devizes, *Chronicle,* 15.

123. On the role of finance see Prestwich, "Richard Coeur de Lion," 11–12.

124. Roger of Howden, *Gesta* 2:110–26; idem, *Chronica* 3:35–55. These rendezvous were not accidental.

125. Roger of Howden, *Gesta* 2:115–16, for the English, and 110–11, for the continental fleets' departures; Hubert Walter's letter from Acre, in Ralph of Diceto, *Ymagines* 2:88–89, could be taken to imply that he was expecting Richard by Easter 1191.

126. Richard of Devizes, *Chronicle,* 15; Pipe Roll 2 Richard I, 3, 53, 131.127.

127. Pipe Roll 2 Richard I, 3.

128. Ibid., 11, 53, 104, 112, 128, 131.

129. Ibid., 8–9, 131–32.

130. Richard of Devizes, *Chronicle,* 42.

131. E. Miller and J. Hatcher, *Rural Society and Economic Change, 1086–1348* (London, 1978), 66–67.

132. See the vivid account of this in Ambroise, *Crusade,* lines 11863–12199.

133. Gervase of Canterbury, *Works* 1: 410, 485, 489–90, 512–13; for criticisms see Gransden, *Historical Writing* 1:259, although the incident cited, Glanvill's return to England to collect troops in June 1189, must surely have been connected with Henry's troubles in France rather than with the crusade, as Gransden, but not Gervase, infers.

134. Corner, "Roger of Howden," 140.

135. For the effects of political uncertainty on Richard's crusade, Richard of Devizes, *Chronicle,* 73, on the failure of warring factions to send money east in 1191–92; Ramsay, *Revenues* 1:227; Gillingham, *Richard,* 135–36, 233–36.

136. Gransden, *Historical Writing* 1:239; H. M. Colvin et al., eds., *History of the King's Works,* vol. 1 (London, 1963), 129; E. W. Tristram, *English Medieval Wall Painting: The Thirteenth Century* (Oxford, 1950), 70–71, 132, 184–85, 215; *C.Lib.R.* 1245–51, 362; Gillingham, *Richard,* 291; *Ann. Mon.* 1:369–70; *C.M.* 5:480; *Political Songs of England,* ed. T. Wright, Camden Society (London, 1839), 128, for a poem celebrating Edward I's accession; for an unflattering comparison between the first six years of Edward I's reign and the crusading glories of Richard I's first three years, written in 1313, *Vita Edwardi Secundi,* in *Chronicles of the Reigns of Edward I and II,* ed. W. Stubbs, vol. 2, RS (London, 1883), 191.

CHAPTER FOUR

1. Siberry, *Criticism of Crusading;* Ralph Niger, *De Re Militari,* 92–98, 193–200; Winchester Annals, *Ann. Mon.* 2:67–68.

2. *Complete Peerage* 9:210 and note 4.

3. "Poésies du troubadour Gavaudan," ed. J. Jeanroy, *Romania* 34 (1905):535; *History of Crusades,* ed. Setton 3:430; A. Mackay, *Spain in the Middle Ages* (London, 1977), 69.

4. *C.M.* 3:485.

5. Peter of Vaux-de-Cernay, *Historia Albigensis,* ed. P. Guébin and E. Lyon (Paris, 1926–39), vol. 1, 247, 253–54; ibid. 2:129–32, 155; ibid. 3:86–87; *La Chanson de la croisade Albigeoise,* ed. E. Martin-Chabot (Paris, 1931–61), vol. 1, 93, 213; ibid. 2:121, 175, 293; ibid. 3:23, 75–77, 85, 93, 95, 121, 173, 175, 189, 213, 265, 293; Roger of Wendover, *Flores* 2:305; *Cal.Pap.Reg.* 1:41.

6. Lunt, *Financial Relations* 1:434–35, 436–37; Roger of Wendover, *Flores* 2:479; *Registres d'Urbain IV*, ed. L. Dorez and J. Giraud (Paris, 1899–1958), nos. 393, 397, 466–68, 472.

7. *C.M.* 3:620; *Foedera* 1:pt. 1, 163; N. Denholm-Young, *Richard of Cornwall* (Oxford, 1947), 38–42; *C.M.* 3:485.

8. Cf. the acid remarks attributed to King Haacon of Norway, in *C.M.* 3:287–88, 373–74; ibid. 4:9, 133–34; ibid. 5:67, 73–74, 201.

9. *C.M.* 3:373; ibid. 4:175; ibid. 5:150–54.

10. W. R. Lunt, *Papal Revenues in the Middle Ages* (New York, 1965), vol. 1, 41–42; *Ann. Mon.* 1:265–67, 360–63; *Documents of the Baronial Movement of Reform and Rebellion, 1258–67*, ed. R. E. Treharne and I. J. Sanders (Oxford, 1973), 278–79.

11. Glanvill, *Tractatus de legibus et consuetudinibus regni Angliae*, ed. G. D. G. Hall (London, 1965), 16–17, 151; Henry de Bracton (*sic*), *De legibus et consuetudinibus Angliae*, ed. T. Twiss, RS (London, 1882), vol. 5, 159–69; John of Longueville, *Modus Tenendi Curias, The Court Baron*, ed. F. W. Maitland and W. P. Baildon, Selden Society (London, 1891), 82 (written c. 1307). Note the last two sources draw a clear distinction between a general passagium and a simple pilgrimage to the Holy Land.

12. See at random *C.R.R.* 8:297; *C.C.R. 1247–51*, 352; ibid. *1256–59*, 485; *Register of Bishop William Ginsborough of Worcester*, ed. J. W. Willis Bund, Worcester Historical Society (Oxford, 1907), 283, 312, 388.

13. *Chronicle of Pierre de Langtoft*, ed. T. Wright, RS (London, 1866–68), vol. 2, 267. Cf. Henry III's similar sentiment in 1246 when trying to discourage recruits for Louis IX's crusade, *C.M.* 4:488–89.

14. M. S. Giuseppi, "On the Testament of Sir Hugh de Neville," *Archeologia* 56 (1889):352–54.

15. E.g., Simon de Montfort in 1248, *C.M.* 5:1; Giuseppi, "Testament," 362.

16. See in general, F. H. Russell, *The Just War in the Middle Ages* (Cambridge, 1975). The designation of the crusade as a pilgrimage was habitual in the thirteenth century.

17. Tristram, *Wall Painting*, 163–66.

18. *Ann. Mon.* 1:351–53; *Monumenta Franciscana*, ed. J. S. Brewer, RS (London, 1858), 620, for Henry III asking the Dominicans to preach the *verbum crucis* in August 1255; cf. *Ann. Mon.* 1:240; ibid 3:40, and *C.P.R. 1247–58*, 507, for the king's injunction to continental subjects to assist the collector of the crusade tax in November 1255 "for the love of the Crucified whose business is principally engaged in this behalf," although the money was already destined for Sicily.

19. *Ordinatio de predicatione S. Crucis in Angliae*, ed. R. Röhricht, *Quinti Belli Sacri Scriptores Minores, Societe de l'Orient Latin* 2 (Geneva, 1879):vii–x, 1–26 (attributed to Philip of Oxford, a preacher in England of the Fifth Crusade). The emphasis on the cross is standard in thirteenth and fourteenth-century western Europe. See also C. Morris, "Dissemination of the Crusading Ideal in the Twelfth Century," *Studies in Church History*, no. 20 (1983), 79–101.

20. *Ann. Mon.* 3:56, 97; ibid. 4:495; Roger of Wendover, *Flores* 2:274–76; *Gesta Abbatum Monasterii Sancti Albani*, ed. H. T. Riley, RS (London, 1867–69), vol. 1, 282; cf. the Holy Rood at Bromholm.

21. *C.M.* 5:519–22, 536; notice the papal attempts to concentrate on Manfred's Moslem mercenaries at Lucera, ibid., 681; *Ann. Mon.* 1:350–53.

22. E.g., during the recruitment for the Fifth Crusade and the 1227 crusade, *Ann. Mon.* 3:53; Roger of Wendover, *Flores* 2:323. Cf. *C.M.* 4:345–46 for portents of disaster, i.e., the loss of Jerusalem in 1244. For a late

thirteenth-century version of the common literary theme, "The Dialogue between Henry de Lacy and Walter Biblesworth on the Crusade," *Reliquae Antiquae,* ed. T. Wright and J. O. Halliwell (London, 1841–43), vol. 1, 134–36.

23. *C.M.* 3:127; ibid. 5:150–54; *Register of Archbishop Walter Giffard of York,* ed. W. Brown, Surtees Society (Durham, 1904), 39–41.

24. Roger of Wendover, *Flores* 2:228 et seq.

25. Ralph of Coggeshall, *Chronicon,* 201–3; *C.M.* 4:641–43; ibid. 5:29, 82, 195; Matthew Paris, *Hist. Anglorum* 1:163 and note 4, 228.

26. *C.Lib.R. 1240–45,* 205; D. Knowles, *The Religious Orders in England,* vol. 1 (Cambridge, 1948), 196–97.

27. *C.M.* 5:72; Matthew Paris, *Hist. Anglorum* 3:50–51.

28. *Councils and Synods* 2:175 (Statutes of Worcester, 1229) and 781–82 (Cardinal Ottobuono's legatine decrees, 1267).

29. *Diplomatic Documents, 1101–1272,* ed. P. Chaplais (London, 1964), no. 288; *C.C.R. 1237–42,* 136; *Foedera* 1:pt. 1, 133; *C.P.R. 1258–66,* 28.

30. Robert Grosseteste, *Epistolae,* ed. H. R. Luard, RS (London, 1861), 144.

31. *Councils and Synods* 2:338–40.

32. *C.M.* 3:488.

33. See the references collected by P. Throop, *Criticism of the Crusade* (Amsterdam, 1940), 171–80. Throop's conclusions should not, however, be followed, as he fails to distinguish between sorrow at the outcome and criticism of individually unsuccessful expeditions, and disenchantment with the ideal itself; for a recent corrective, Siberry, *Criticism of Crusading.*

34. *C.M.* 4:211–12, 218.

35. Cheney, *Innocent III,* 239–59, esp. 248 note 45; J. L. Cate, "The English Mission of Eustace of Flay," in *Etudes d'histoire dédiées a la mémoire de Henri Pirenne* (Brussells, 1937), 67–89; Roger of Howden, *Chronica* 4:123–24, 167–72.

36. C. R. Cheney, *Hubert Walter* (London, 1967), 127–28; for poor crusaders, *Rolls of Justices in Eyre in Yorkshire, 1218–19,* ed. D. M. Stenton, Selden Society (London, 1937), 259–60, no. 698; *Rolls of Justices in Eyre, Lincolnshire, 1218–19 and Worcestershire, 1221,* ed. D. M. Stenton, Selden Society (London, 1934), 108, no. 248, and 198–99, no. 427; *H.M.C., Report on Various Collections,* vol. 1 (1901), 235–36; *Cal.Pap.Reg.* 1:13; for enjoined crusades, Pipe Roll 4 John (1202), 20; Worcester Annals, *Ann. Mon.* 4:413.

37. Roger of Howden, *Chronica* 3:264, 317–19.

38. Cf. King John's own will, W. L. Warren, *King John* (London, 1961), 276; for episcopal enquiries, *Rolls and Register of Bishop Oliver Sutton,* ed. R. Hill, Lincoln Record Society, vol. 3 (Hereford, 1954), 157–59; *Registrum Ricardi de Swinfield,* ed. W. W. Capes, Canterbury and York Society (London, 1909), 78–79; *Councils and Synods* 2:805–6; Brundage, *Canon Law,* 114.

39. Pipe Roll 7 Richard I (1195), 98, 110–11, 141, 182, 215, 249–50; Brundage, *Canon Law,* 184.

40. Pipe Roll 8 John (1206), 72, 204, 205; ibid., 9 John (1207), 72–73; ibid., 10 John (1208), 150–51.

41. Roger of Howden, *Chronica* 3:233; Cheney, *Innocent III,* 240, 247.

42. See the respective *D.N.B.* entries and refs.; Dunstable Annals, *Ann. Mon.* 3:54; Worcester Annals, *Ann. Mon.* 4:411; Waverly Annals, *Ann. Mon.* 2:289, 292; *Barnwell Chronicle, Memoriali Walter de Coventria,* ed.

W. Stubbs, RS (London, 1872–73), 240–41, 246; Oliver of Paderborn, *Capture of Damietta, Christian Society and the Crusades, 1198–1229*, trans. E. Peters (Philadelphia, 1971), 69, 84; *C.R.R.* 8:326–27. For some English crusaders on the Fourth Crusade, *Rotuli Litterarum Patentium*, ed. T. D. Hardy, vol. 1 (London, 1835), 2, 11, 15, 22.

43. *C.M.* 3:67–68; Waverly Annals, *Ann. Mon.* 2:295 (19 September; Damietta was surrendered on 8 September).

44. *Extracts from a Yorkshire Assize Roll, 3 Henry III (1219)*, ed. W. T. Lancaster, *Miscellanea*, vol. 1, Yorkshire Archeological Society Record Series, no. 61 (1920), 179.

45. *Rolls of Justices, Yorkshire, 1218–19*, 3, no. 15; 275, no. 740; 355–57, no. 979; *Rolls of Justices in Eyre, Gloucestershire, Warwickshire, Staffordshire, 1221, 1222*, ed. D. M. Stenton, Selden Society (London, 1940), 39, no. 108.

46. *Rott.Litt.Claus.* 1:401, 402.

47. Oliver of Paderborn, *Damietta*, 79; Barnwell Chronicle, 246.

48. Oliver of Paderborn, *Damietta*, 103; Ralph of Coggeshall, *Chronicon*, 190; *C.R.R.* 10:240.

49. Barnwell Chronicle, 243; *C.M.* 3:164; perhaps even the same as or related to, the Templar who died defending Jerusalem in the late 1230s, Matthew Paris, *Hist. Anglorum* 2:399; Dunstable Annals, *Ann. Mon.* 3:150.

50. *C.M.* 3:67–68, 373; *C.P.R. 1216–25*, 287; ibid., *1225–32*, 175, 188; ibid., *1232–47*, 21, 74, 93, 101, 106; *Rott.Litt.Claus.* 1:511, 515; *C.Lib.R. 1226–40*, 93; ibid., *1267–72*, appendix 1, 249; C. E. Town, "From the Crusades to Clerkenwell," *St. John Historical Society Newsletter* (September 1983):14.

51. Roger of Wendover, *Flores* 2:323; cf. E. Peters, *Christian Society and the Crusades, 1198–1229* (Philadelphia, 1971), 146–47.

52. Roger of Wendover, *Flores* 2:207–8; for the Fifth Crusade itself, Roger used the eyewitness account of Oliver of Paderborn, a preacher of the crusade in the Rhineland, ibid., 228 et seq.; Matthew Paris, *Hist. Anglorum* 2:297–98.

53. For Frederick's plans and campaign, T. C. Van Cleve, *The Emperor Frederick II of Hohenstaufen* (Oxford, 1972), 158–233; idem, "The Crusade of Frederick II," in *History of Crusades*, ed. Setton 2:429–62; Roger of Wendover, *Flores* 2:323–27; *C.M.* 3:127; for des Roches, *C.P.R. 1216–25*, 318–19; *Rott.Litt.Claus.* 2:204 (3 November 1226; his crusading plans predated Henry III's declaration of his majority in January 1227; pace Powicke, *Henry III*, 76).

54. *C.P.R. 1225–32*, 90–91; Richard of Devizes, *Chronicle*, 6; Cheney, *Innocent III*, 253–55, 260.

55. *Register of St. Osmund*, ed. W. H. Rich-Jones, RS, vol. 2 (London, 1884), 77–78; *Cal.Pap.Reg.* 1:116, 117; *Rott.Litt.Claus.* 2:189–90.

56. *R.H.C.Occ.* 2:371, cf. 378, 489 for the Englishman killed defending Jerusalem in 1229; Dunstable Annals, *Ann. Mon.* 3:107, 111; Roger of Wendover, *Flores* 2: 324–27; Peters, *Christian Society,* 147–50; *C.P.R. 1225–32*, 120, 122; *C.R.R.* 13:64, no. 292; *Cartulary of Muchelney Abbey*, ed. E. H. Bates, Somerset Record Society (1899), 75.

57. Powicke, *Henry III*, 76; Roger of Wendover, *Flores* 2:373; *C.M.* 3:177.

58. Matthew Paris, *Hist. Anglorum* 2:304, 410, 412; *R.H.C.Occ.* 2:371; Dunstable Annals, *Ann. Mon.* 3:126.

59. *C.P.R. 1216–25*, 527–28; *C.M.* 3:490; Forey, "Order of St. Thomas," esp. 487–88.

60. Tewkesbury Annals, *Ann. Mon.* 1:73; Dunstable Annals, *Ann. Mon.* 3:126; *C.M.* 3:127, 489; Matthew Paris, *Hist. Anglorum* 2:298, 333.

61. Forey, "Order of St. Thomas"; Roger of Wendover, *Flores* 2:324–27; Comte Riant, "Privilèges octroyées aux Teutoniques," *Archives de l'Orient Latin* 1 (1881):418, dated 24 April 1235.

62. *C.M.* 4:43–47, 71, 144–48, 166–67, 138–44 for the letter of self-congratulation and justification sent by Richard to Baldwin de Redvers; R. Vaughan, *Matthew Paris* (Cambridge, 1958), 13. In general, Denholm-Young, *Richard of Cornwall*, 38–43; S. Painter, "The crusade of Theobald of Champagne and Richard of Cornwall," in *History of Crusades*, ed. Setton 2:463–85.

63. *C.M.* 4:107, 143–45; 211–12, 218.

64. Ibid. 3:368–69, 620.

65. Ibid. 4:44, 174–75, for those who set out. On the political background, Powicke, *Henry III*, 70–83, 123–55.

66. *C.M.* 4:44, 89 for the two parties, 174–75 for those who died, and 11 for the earl's disillusion with English politics; Denholm-Young, *Richard of Cornwall*, 41.

67. Thomas Wykes, *Chronicon, Ann. Mon.* 4: 86–87; for almost identical words to his, see the Rothelin continuation of William of Tyre, *Historia, R.H.C.Occ.* 2:527–28.

68. Painter, "Crusade of Richard of Cornwall," 483; *R.H.C.Occ.* 2:421, 555; Wykes, *Chronicon, Ann. Mon.* 4:86; for Wykes's association with Richard, Gransden, *Historical Writing* 1:464–65.

69. *C.M.* 4:71.

70. Ibid., 4:7; Dunstable Annals, *Ann. Mon.* 3:152; C. Bémont, *Simon de Monfort*, Trans. E. Jacob (Oxford, 1930), 61.

71. *C.P.R. 1232–47*, 209; Denholm-Young, *Richard of Cornwall*, 41; *C.Lib.R. 1216–40*, 378, 471, cf. 373, 379, 400, 463, 464.

72. *C.Lib.R. 1216–40*, 384.

73. *C.C.R. 1234–37*, 40; ibid., *1237–42*, 4, 197; *Registres de Grégoire IX*, ed. L. Auvray (Paris, 1890–1955), no. 4268.

74. *Councils and Synods* 2:196; *C.M.* 3:373–74, and 287–88 for a similar way of raising money in 1234; for Otho's commission, ibid. 4:6–7.

75. Lunt, *Papal Revenues* 1:76; cf. the 1215 crusade tax with those of 1245 and 1250, ibid., 86–91, 93, 94. For the finances of the 1248–50 crusade in France, W. C. Jordan, *Louis IX and the Challenge of the Crusade* (Princeton, N.J., 1979), 65–104.

76. *Registres d'Innocent IV*, ed. E. Berger (Paris, 1884–99), nos. 4054–55. The pope made no complaint at Henry's crusader half-brother, Guy of Lusignan, receiving a share.

77. *Foedera* 1:pt. 1, 137; *C.P.R. 1232–47*, 250; *Cal.Pap.Reg.* 1:240, 346 (1247 and 1257); *C.P.R. 1247–58*, 371 (1254). The original grant had been made in 1238. *C.M.* 5:188–89, complained about the collection for Richard in the early 1250s.

78. *C.M.* 4:635–36; *Cal.Pap.Reg.* 1:184–85. Paris uncharacteristically underestimated what Longsword received, *Cal.Pap.Reg.* 1:242.

79. Russell, *Just War*, 204–6.

80. Denholm-Young, *Richard of Cornwall*, 38–43; Powicke, *Henry III*, 197–200; Painter, "Crusade of Richard of Cornwall," 482–83; *Cal.Pap.Reg.* 1:167, 170, 177, 186.

81. *Reg. Grégoire IX*, nos. 4608–9; *Cal.Pap.Reg.* 1:177; *C.M.* 3:480–81.

82. *Cal.Pap.Reg.* 1:184–85.

83. *C.M.* 3:609–27.

84. Ibid., 620.

85. Ibid., 485, 620; ibid. 4:26–29, 46–47.

86. R. Röhricht, "La croisade de Prince Edouard d'Angleterre, 1270–74," *Archives de l'Orient Latin* 1 (1881): 402–3; *R.H.C.Occ.* 2:421–22, 555–56.

87. *C.M.* 4:488–89; ibid. 5:131, 134–35, 280–81; Matthew Paris, *Hist. Anglorum* 3:85; *C.P.R. 1247–58*, 157.

88. A. J. Forey, "The Crusading Vows of the English King Henry III," *Durham University Journal* 65 (1973):231–33; *C.M.* 4:415–16, 473, 521–22, 629; ibid. 5:1, 73–74, 76, 156; *Foedera* 1:pt. 1, 157; *Reg. Innocent IV*, no. 4054; *Cal.Pap.Reg.* 1:232; *C.P.R. 1247–58*, 19, 43; *C.Lib.R. 1245–51*, 48, 52, 159. For a less exalted crucesignatus, John Pacche, whose parents held land in Oxford, possibly a connection of Hamo Pecche, *Cartulary of Osney Abbey*, ed. H. E. Salter, vol. 1 (Oxford, 1929), 319, no. 363.

89. *Cal.Pap.Reg.* 1:242, 255; Matthew Paris, *Hist. Anglorum* 3:55; *C.M.* 5:76, 131; Bémont, *Simon de Montfort* (Eng. trans.), 71–72. Paris's date for the departure, July 1249, is hardly credible if Longsword sailed from Europe to Damietta, then to Acre, and then back to Damietta, all before the November march on Cairo.

90. The fullest account is in *C.M.* 5:76–77, 105–9, 116–17, 130–34, 138–44, 147–75, 201–4. For the beginnings of the Longsword legend and the visions of his mother, the abbess of Laycock, ibid., 147–49, 150–51, 153–54 (where he is called "martyr manifestus"), 173. His bones were buried at Acre, ibid., 342, and an effigy of him was placed in Salisbury Cathedral. It is possible that a book belonging to Guy, earl of Warwick (d. 1315), *La Romaunce de Williame de Loungespe*, concerned his exploits, although the title could as well refer to his father (d. 1226), M. Blaess, "L'abbaye de Bordesley et les livres de Guy de Beauchamp," *Romania* 78 (1957):511–18.

91. *C.M.* 5:147, 170–73, 254, 280–81.

92. Forey, "Crusading Vows."

CHAPTER FIVE

1. *Foedera*, ed. T. Rymer (London, 1816), vol. 1, pt. 1, 496.

2. *C.M.* 5:102; Forey, "Crusading Vows," 229–47.

3. *C.M.* 3–5 passim; Forey, "Crusading Vows," 230, and notes 9–15; for the pension to the Teutonic Knights, Riante, "Privilèges," 418; for the grant of the king's body to the Templars, *C.C.R. 1237–42*, 6 and Henry's will, *Foedera* (London, 1816 ed.) 1:pt. 1, 496.

4. *Reg. Innocent IV*, no. 4054–56; *C.Lib.R. 1245–51*, 48. Others who took the cross between 1245 and 1250 included William Longsword, Robert de Vere, Alexander Giffard, Simon de Montfort, Geoffrey de Lucy, Robert de Quincy, the earl of Hereford, and the bishops of Hereford and Worcester. *C.M.* 4:488–89, 629; ibid. 5:1, 76, 98–99, 156.

5. Ibid. 5:147.

6. *C.P.R. 1247–58*, 79; for the hostile reaction, *C.M.* 5:102–3, 134–36, 200–2; for the deadline announcement, *C.P.R. 1247–58*, 157–58; Forey, "Crusading Vows," 235–36.

7. *C.M.* 5:281–82 (Paris gets the date of departure wrong by a year, 1255 instead of 1256). Of course the failure of the April assembly may have been touched up by Paris, but opposition there certainly was. *Councils and Synods* 2:449 et seq.

8. *Ann. Mon.* 1:141, 323; *Chronica Johannis de Oxenedes*, ed. H. Ellis, RS (London, 1859), 189. In fact, this is the chronicle of St. Benet of Holme, Gransden, *Historical Writing* 1:402.

9. Cf. *C.M.* 5:102–3 and *C.C.R. 1251–53*, 436–37.

10. Forey, "Crusading Vows," is convincing on this.

11. *C.M.* 5:99, 102.

12. Ibid., 96, 103.

13. E. Miller, "The State and Landed Interests in Thirteenth-Century France and England," *TRHS*, 5th ser., 2 (1952):esp. 122–26; for an early ban on alienation to a religious house, idem, *The Abbey and Bishopric of Ely* (Cambridge, 1951), 130 note 1.

14. *C.M.* 5:5–8, 20–22, 98–99; *D.N.B.* entry for Hereford; F. M. Powicke, *Henry III and the Lord Edward* (Oxford, 1947), 290–342 for the background.

15. *C.M.* 5:101–2; cf. the further household officials who took the cross in 1252, ibid., 282.

16. *Cal.Pap.Reg.* 1:239, 263; for Henry's two half-brothers Guy and Geoffrey de Lusignan as crucesignati, *Reg. Innocent IV*, nos. 4054–55, *C.P.R. 1247–58*, 58.

17. *Cal.Pap.Reg.* 1:263–64.

18. *C.M.* 5:159. Richard was at the Papal Curia.

19. *Councils and Synods* 2:448–51, 468–72, 482–83.

20. Matthew Paris, *Hist. Anglorum* 3:98–99, 320; *Ann. Mon.* 3:184; in his will of 1253 Henry specifically asked for his gold to be sent to the Holy Land, *Foedera* (1816 London ed.) 1:pt. 1, 496.

21. I am indebted to Dr. David Carpenter for generously allowing me to see a draft of his then-unpublished paper, "The Gold Treasure of Henry III," which is in *Thirteenth Century Studies*, ed. S. Lloyd (Woodbridge, 1987); Giuseppi, "Testament of Hugh de Neville," 54.

22. *C.P.R. 1247–58*, 159; *Foedera* 1:pt. 1, 167, 170–71, 173; *C.C.R. 1251–52*, 272–77, 281.

23. *C.P.R. 1247–58*, 188–89.

24. Cf. Henry's cat-and-mouse promise to Louis at Acre of early English assistance if Louis restored the lost Angevin lands in France, *C.P.R. 1247–58*, 157.

25. *C.C.R. 1251–53*, 231, 436–37; *C.P.R. 1247–58*, 164, 168; *Cal.Pap.Reg.* 1:279–80; the unfortunate April meeting in 1252 was possibly intended to launch this new concerted effort.

26. *C.Lib.R. 1245–51*, 358, 362; Colvin, *History of the King's Works* 1:128–29; Tristram, *Wall Painting*, 16–17, 70–71, 73, 106–7, 110–11, 130–32, 184–85, 215.

27. *C.P.R. 1247–58*, 188; Bémont, *Simon de Montfort* (Eng. trans.), 97–126; Powicke, *Henry III*, 227–31.

28. Bémont, *Simon de Montfort* (Paris, 1884), 278–79, no. 12.

29. Powicke, *Henry III*, 230–31; *Councils and Synods* 2:482–83; Carpenter, "Gold Treasure."

30. *C.P.R. 1247–58*, 281.

31. Forey, "Crusading Vows," 238–39.

32. *Royal Letters of Henry III*, ed. W. W. Shirley, RS (London, 1862–66), vol. 2, 110–14, no. 506; *C.C.R. 1254–56*, 390.

33. Forey, "Crusading Vows," esp. 246–47, notes.

34. *Foedera* 1:pt. 1, 25; on the intricate diplomacy of the 1250s and Angevin aspirations, Powicke, *Henry III*, 208–58, 343–409; M. T. Clanchy, *England and its Rulers* (London, 1983), 230–40; both Powicke (246) and Clanchy (239) are wrong to say that Alexander commuted Henry's Holy Land vow in 1254.

35. *C.C.R. 1256–59*, 315; ibid., *1261–64*, 173; *Foedera* 1:pt. 1, 19, 49, 62, 65–66, 80–81; *C.P.R. 1258–59*, 317; for Bishop Cantelupe's commission to preach the Holy Land crusade, *Reg. Urbain IV*, nos. 397, 466, 468–69, 472.

36. *Reg. Urbain IV*, nos. 140–43, 297–98; *C.P.R. 1258–66*, 317; for a translation of the Treaty of Paris, *E.H.D.* 3:376–79; cf. Powicke, *Henry III*, 479.

37. The papal view was close to that of the influential Savoyard canonist Hostiensis (Henry de Susa), who had worked for Henry III in the 1230s and 1240s, Russell, *Just War*, 201–10, esp. 205.

38. *Registres de Clément IV*, ed. E. Jordan (Paris, 1893–1945), no. 56.

39. *C.M.* 5:201.

40. Burton Annals, *Ann. Mon.* 1:265–67, 360–63; *Councils and Synods* 2.

41. *Cal.Pap.Reg.* 1:234.

42. *Documents of the Baronial Movement*, 279.

43. *C.M.* 5:521–22, and on Rostand's mission in general, 519–40, 553–59, 581–84; *Foedera* 1:pt. 1, 195–96; *Councils and Synods* 2:507.

44. *C.C.R. 1254–56*, 221.

45. *C.M.* 5:383; *C.C.R. 1254–56*, 380–81, 393–94.

46. *E.H.D.* 3:377–78.

47. See below, chapter 6.

48. *C.P.R. 1258–66*, 317.

49. *List of Ancient Correspondence*, rev. ed., vol. 15 of *P.R.O. Lists and Indexes* (New York, 1968; reprint), vol. 5, no. 56, vol. 55, no. 2.

50. Burton Annals, *Ann. Mon.* 1:369–71.

51. *Cal.Pap.Reg.* 1:329.

52. R. Röhricht, "Croisade de Prince Edouard," 617–32; Powicke, *Henry III*, 597–606; B. Beebe, "The English Baronage and the Crusade of 1270," *BIHR* 48 (1975):127–48; S. Lloyd, "The Lord Edward's Crusade of 1270–72," in *War and Government in the Middle Ages*, ed. J. Gillingham and J. C. Holt (Woodbridge, 1984), 120–33; Forey, "Crusading Vows," 245–47.

53. *Reg. Clément IV*, nos. 609, 1288; *Cal.Pap.Reg.* 1:422, 439; Wykes, *Chronicon*, *Ann. Mon.* 4:217–18; H. M. Cam and E. F. Jacob, "Notes on an English Cluniac Chronicle," *EHR* 44 (1929), 104.

54. *Foedera* (1816 London ed.) 1:pt. 1, 483.

55. *Diplomatic Documents* 1:no. 419; J.-P. Traubaut-Cussac, "Le financement de la croisade anglaise de 1270," *Bibliothèque de l'école des chartes* 119 (1961):113–40.

56. *Foedera* 1:pt. 1,115.

57. Forey, "Crusading Vows," 247 and note 138; *Foedera* 1:pt. 1, 118; *C.P.R. 1266–72*, 531; cf. Henry III's will of 1253, *Foedera* (1816 London ed.) 1:pt. 1, 496.

58. *Chronicle of Walter of Guisborough*, ed. H. Rothwell, Camden Series (London, 1957), 207; Wykes, *Chronicon*, *Ann. Mon.* 4:240–243; for the lists of crusaders receiving protections, privileges, etc., *C.C.R. 1268–72*, 260, 278, 281–84, 288–90; *C.P.R. 1266–72*, 411, 424, 440–41, 443, 464–65, 479–80, 484–85, 587; Beebe, "English Baronage," 131–32, 142–48; other names can be found in legal records and land charters.

59. *C.P.R. 1272–81*, 296; William Rishanger, *Chronica*, ed. H. T. Riley, RS (London, 1865), 78, note 60; Röhricht, "Croisade de Prince Edouard," 629, note 81; J. Riley-Smith, "A Note on Confraternities in the Latin Kingdom of Jerusalem," *BIHR* 44 (1971):301–8; for the location of the English tower, see the maps of Acre by Pietro Vesconte and Paolino Veneto drawn in the 1320s, reproduced in *Outremer*, ed. Kedar et al., 209.

60. Powicke, *Henry III*, 605–6; R. Grousset, *Histoire des croisades*, vol. 3 (Paris, 1936), 665–66; H. Le Strange, *Le Strange Records* (London, 1916), 140–49.

61. *Reg. Clément IV*, nos. 1110, 1146; Wykes, *Chronicon, Ann. Mon.* 4:218; Rishanger, *Chronica*, 52–53; idem, *De Duobus Bellis*, ed. J. O. Hal-

liwell, Camden Society (London, 1840), 60–62; *Councils and Synods* 2:732, 734.

62. Wykes, *Chronicon, Ann. Mon.* 4:217–18, 227–28; *Councils and Synods* 2:797; Powicke, *Henry III*, 563–69; *Royal Letters of Henry III* 2:338; *Historical Papers and Letters from Northern Registers*, ed. J. Raine, RS (London, 1873), 23; *Cal.Pap.Reg.* 1:428, 436 (for the crossbowmen), 621 (for Earl Richard's legacy).

63. Guiseppi, "Testament of Hugh de Neville," 352–54, 358–60; Bémont, *Simon de Montfort* (Eng. trans.), 72 and note 2. For redemptions of vows imposed in 1267 as punishments by the archbishop of York, *Historical Papers from Northern Registers*, 46–49.

64. Powicke, *Henry III*, 566–68.

65. C. H. Knowles, "The Resettlement of England after the Barons' War," *TRHS*, 5th ser., 32 (1982):25–41, esp. 41; *C.C.R. 1268–72*, 241.

66. E.g., William "de Pecco," a crusader, *C.Lib.R. 1267–72*, 151.

67. *List of Ancient Correspondence* 2:no. 127; ibid. 7:no. 147; *Royal Letters of Henry III* 2:338.

68. Trabaut-Cussac, "Le financement"; *C.Lib.R. 1267–72*, 123, no. 1069, 126, no. 1100 (April and June 1270).

69. T. H. Turner, "Unpublished Notices of the Time of Edward I," *Archeological Journal* 8 (1851):46; Beebe, "English Baronage," 142; Lloyd, "Lord Edward's crusade," 126–28; Riley-Smith, *Crusades*, 153, follows H. G. Richardson and G. O. Sayles, *The Governance of Medieval England* (Edinburgh, 1963), 465, in mistranslating the number of knights accompanying Adam of Jesmond; it should be five, not four.

70. *Historical Papers from Northern Registers*, 27–30; *Reg. Archbishop W. Giffard of York*, 237–40.

71. *Le Strange Records*, esp. 141 and 146; *C.P.R. 1266–72*, 668–69; *C.C.R. 1272–79*, 182–83; *Issues of the Exchequer*, ed. F. Devon (London, 1837), 96; Lloyd, "Lord Edward's crusade," 126–27; *Cal.Pap.Reg.* 1:445; *Registres de Grégoire X*, ed. J. Guiraud (Paris, 1892–1969), 171–232.

72. Trabaut-Cussac, "Le financement," esp. 122, for the table of repayments.

73. M. C. Prestwich, *War, Politics, and Finance under Edward I* (London, 1972), 169–70; *Royal Letters of Henry III* 2:347–51; *Issues of the Exchequer*, 86; *List of Ancient Correspondence* 8:no. 28a.

74. *C.C.R. 1272–79*, 2.

75. *Cal.Pap.Reg.* 1:444; Powicke, *Henry III*, 568–69; *Reg. Archbishop W. Giffard of York*, 39–41.

76. *C.P.R. 1266–72*, 480; Rishanger, *Chronica*, 68; *Johannis de Trokelowe et Henrici de Blandeforde: Chronica et Annales*, ed. H. T. Riley, RS (London, 1866), 29; Lloyd, "Lord Edward's crusade," 126–32; Powicke, *Henry III*, 698–701.

77. See below, chapter 7. J. O. Prestwich, "The military household of the Norman Kings," *EHR* 96 (1981):1–35; for two surviving contracts, Richardson and Sayles, *Governance of Medieval England*, appendix 6, 463–65 (Adam of Jesmond), and Lloyd, "Lord Edward's crusade," 126–27 (Chaworth and Tiptoft); ibid., 129–31, for Edward's followers' contracts with their followers.

78. *C.M.* 4:71; ibid. 5:131; Jean de Joinville, *Life of St. Louis*, trans. M. R. B. Shaw (London, 1963), 198.

79. *C.C.R. 1268–72*, 571–72; *Somerset Pleas*, ed. L. Landon, Somerset Record Society (1923), 134; D. Sutherland, *The Assize of Novel Disseisin* (Oxford, 1973), 54–55.

80. For the French precedents of 1248–50 and 1268–70, *R.H.F.* 20:305–6; ibid. 21:732–34.

81. *List of Ancient Correspondence* 22:no. 51; Powicke, *Henry III*, 530, for the disturbances caused in the Midlands by Roger Godberd until 1272, and 583–96, where evidence is produced which could be interpreted as contradicting Powicke's own roseate view of stability in the realm.

82. The Lord Edmund and Thomas of Clare hastened home before Edward, and earlier, messengers had been sent from the home government, such as William de Columbariis "in haste" in March 1271, *C.Lib.R. 1267–72*, 167, no. 1491, and William Bagot in the spring of 1272, G. Wrottesley, *A History of the Bagot Family: Collections for a History of Staffordshire*, n.s. 11 (London, 1908), 131. The time for such messengers to reach Acre from London varied, but less than three months must have been exceptional. In 1260 a Templar managed it in thirteen weeks, *Flores historiarum*, ed. H. R. Luard, RS (London, 1890), vol. 3, 451–52. Such separation was clearly a major inconvenience.

83. Edward's legend was almost immediate, viz., the stories of Fowin the groom and the assassination attempt; see also an anonymous poem celebrating his accession in 1272 which likened him to Richard I, *Political Songs*, 128, and Langtoft's comments a few years later, *Chronicle of Langtoft* 2:152–60.

CHAPTER SIX

1. Riley-Smith, *Crusades*, 40; Riley-Smith, J., *What Were the Crusades?* (London, 1977), 24–28; for individual cases of using crusade privileges against authority, see below, chapter 8.

2. J. P. Migne, *Patrologia Latina* (Paris, 1855), vol. 264, cols. 779–82, esp. no. 221, and vol. 265, cols. 1246–48.

3. C. R. Cheney, "The alleged deposition of King John," *The Papacy and England* (London, 1982), vol. 12, 105.

4. Rigord, *Gesta* 1:253; ibid. 2:247–48, 255.

5. Waverly Annals, *Ann. Mon.* 2:281 (s.a. 1214); Dunstable Annals, *Ann. Mon.* 3:40 (misdated to 1212); Ralph of Coggeshall, *Chronicon*, 168.

6. The phrase is that of Cheney in "The Eve of Magna Carta," *Bulletin of the John Rylands Library* 38 (1955–56):313; *Selected Letters of Pope Innocent III*, ed. C. R. Cheney and W. H. Semple (London, 1953), 192; for the 1215 ceremony itself see the so-called *Barnwell Chronicle*, 219; for the Southwark Annals, M. Tyson, "The Annals of Southwark and Merton," *Surrey Archeological Collections* 36 (1925):49.

7. Warren, *King John*, 244–45.

8. Cheney, *Innocent III*, 254–55.

9. *Barnwell Chronicle*, 220; Ralph of Coggeshall, *Chronicon*, 171.

10. *Barnwell Chronicle*, 219.

11. Magna Carta clauses 52, 53, 57.

12. Roger of Wendover, *Flores* 2:114; *C.M.* 2:585–95, for an even later opinion that John took the cross for protection.

13. Roger of Howden, *Gesta* 2:221–22; idem, *Chronica* 3:151–52, 208.

14. *Selected Letters of Innocent III*, 207–9.

15. Ibid., 212–16; these arguments were reported by the *Barnwell Chronicle*, 226.

16. *Selected Letters of Innocent III*, 227.

17. *C.R.R.* 7:107; Waverley Annals, *Ann. Mon.* 2:292; Ralph of Coggeshall, *Chronicon*, 188; *Barnwell Chronicle*, 246; *Rolls of Justices, York-*

shire, 1218–19, 2, no. 10; respective *D.N.B.* entries for those excommunicated as rebels; *Foedera* 1:pt. 1, 70–71.

18. *Selected Letters of Innocent III*, 227; Ralph of Coggeshall, *Chronicon*, 171; *Barnwell Chronicle*, 219.

19. Ralph of Coggeshall, *Chronicon*, 174–75.

20. Powicke, *Henry III*, 5; Waverley Annals, *Ann. Mon.* 2:287; Gervase of Canterbury, *Works* 2:110.

21. *R.H.F.* 19:611–12.

22. *Cal.Pap.Reg.* 1:41.

23. Forey, "Crusading Vows," 229–230; *Chronicle Walter of Guisborough*, 158, preserved 1 November as the date Henry took the cross; Powicke, *Henry III*, 4; in 1253 Henry himself confirmed that he had taken the cross in 1216, *C.C.R. 1251–53*, 448; *Hist. Guillaume le Maréchal*, lines 15537–61; *Chronicon Petroburgense*, ed. T. Stapleton, Camden Society (London, 1849), 7.

24. *Royal Letters of Henry III* 1:appendix 5, 528.

25. *C.P.R. 1216–25*, 25; cf. the original licence nine days earlier, ibid., 21. The Fourth Lateran Council had fixed the general crusade muster for 1 June 1217.

26. *C.P.R. 1216–25*, 25; Powicke, *Henry III*, 9.

27. *C.P.R. 1216–25*, 108–9.

28. *Barnwell Chronicle*, 235.

29. Ibid., 235–36.

30. *C.P.R. 1216–25*, 34, 57.

31. *Foedera* 1:pt. 1, 73; Waverley Annals, *Ann. Mon.* 2:289, for the earl's vow; Savaric was already a crucesignatus by 21 September and later played a conspicuous role at the siege of Damietta, Oliver of Paderborn, *Damietta*, 84.

32. *Royal Letters of Henry III* 1:532.

33. *Barnwell Chronicle*, 236.

34. Dunstable Annals, *Ann. Mon.* 3:49: cf. the continuation of Gervase of Canterbury, *Works* 2:110, "many nobles and common people took the sign of the cross on their breasts to expel Louis and the French from England."

35. *Political Songs of England*, 22–23; *Hist. Guillaume le Maréchal*, lines 16225–32, for the plenary indulgences offered before Lincoln by the legate, and lines 16147–52 and 16305–6, for William Marshal's exhortation to the royalists to defend the church and thereby gain plenary indulgences.

36. *C.M.* 3:29; Worcester Annals, *Ann. Mon.* 4:408; M. R. James, "The Drawings of Matthew Paris," *Walpole Society* 14 (1935–36):no. 37; cf. ibid., no. 38.

37. Ralph of Coggeshall, *Chronicon*, 185–86; *Barnwell Chronicle*, 229, 247, 251; *C.M.* 3:18; *Hist. Guillaume le Maréchal*, lines 16139–46; Magna Carta clauses 50, 51; Waverley Annals, *Ann. Mon.* 2:287.

38. Bartlett, *Gerald of Wales*, 91–100; *Barnwell Chronicle*, 226–27.

39. *Barnwell Chronicle*, 232, 239.

40. Cf. the battle of the Standard, Henry of Huntingdon, *Historia*, 262–65, and William Marshal at Lincoln, *Hist. Guillaume le Maréchal*, lines 16139–96; but also cf. ibid., lines 16204–24 for self-conscious Norman elements in the royalist forces.

41. *Foedera* 1:pt. 1, 71, 72; perhaps the comparative failure of these secular appeals made the crusade option more attractive.

42. *Foedera* 1:pt. 1, 73; *Barnwell Chronicle*, 235; Gervase of Canterbury (i.e., his continuator), *Works* 2:110; Dunstable Annals, *Ann. Mon.* 3:49;

Waverley Annals, *Ann. Mon.* 2:287. All deliberately mention "in pectore" as if it was distinctive.

43. *Rolls of Justices, Yorkshire, 1218–19*, 353, no. 972.

44. *Barnwell Chronicle*, 235; *Foedera* 1:pt. 1, 73; *Royal Letters of Henry III* 1:528.

45. *Royal Letters of Henry III* 1:528.

46. *Regesta Pontificium Romanorum, 1198–1304*, ed. A. Potthast, vol. 1 (Berlin, 1874), 482, no. 5481.

47. See below, chapter 8.

48. *Reg. Urbain IV*, nos. 595–97, 609–10; *H.M.C., Fourteenth Report*, appendix 8 (1895), 173–74.

49. Tewkesbury Annals, *Ann. Mon.* 1:179–80. In general, Powicke, *Henry III*, 450–530.

50. *Reg. Clément IV*, nos. 56–59, 62, 121, 358.

51. R. Graham, "Letters of Cardinal Ottobuono," *EHR* 15 (1900):87–88; *Reg. Clément IV*, no. 362; *Cal.Pap.Reg.* 1:419, 434, 435; Rishanger, *De Bellis*, 57.

52. *Reg. Urbain IV*, no. 581; *H.M.C., Fourteenth Report*, appendix 8, 173–74; Powicke, *Henry III*, 420, 423, 427, 429.

53. *Reg. Urbain IV*, nos. 397, 466, 468–69, 472; *Cal.Pap.Reg.* 1:379. For Cantelupe's activities on behalf of the crusade, 1247–50, ibid., 234–35, 244, 263.

54. *Reg. Urbain IV*, no. 596; *C.M.* 4:629; ibid. 5:1.

55. Dunstable Annals, *Ann. Mon.* 3:226; Powicke, *The Thirteenth Century* (Oxford, 1962), 182.

56. *Chronica Oxenedes*, 226; *Flores historiarum* 3:256.

57. Gransden, *Historical Writing* 1:404–38, 463–70.

58. *Song of Lewes*, trans. *E.H.D.* 3:899–912.

59. Dunstable Annals, *Ann. Mon.* 3:232; *Chronica Oxenedes*, 222; *Flores historiarum* 2:495.

60. The Furness Chronicle appears as a continuation of William of Newburgh, in *Chronicles of Stephen, Henry II, and Richard I* 2:543; *Flores historiarum* 2:495.

61. Rishanger, *De Bellis*, 30–31.

62. Ibid., 32; cf. the Battle Chronicle account in Bémont, *Simon de Montfort* (French ed.), 376. N.B., the Dragon was red, possibly a royalist colour; cf. the royalist crosses at Evesham.

63. *Chronicle of Guisborough*, 200.

64. *Flores historiarum* 3:5–6; Rishanger, *De Bellis*, 46.

65. *Documents of the Baronial Movement*, 278–79.

66. Powicke, *Henry III*, 479.

67. *Annales Regis Edwardi Primis*, printed in Rishanger, *Chronica*, 439, for the wearing of crosses on the 1300 Annandale campaign, although it is not stated of what colour they were.

68. *Chronicle of Guisborough*, 201; Osney Annals, *Ann. Mon.* 4:169; Rishanger, *De Bellis*, 47.

69. Powicke, *Thirteenth Century*, 193.

70. E.g., Beebe, "English Baronage," esp. 128–30; it seems inadequate to accept at face value the papal sophistry that violent attacks on papal opponents were the same as reconciliation beneficial for the Holy Land.

CHAPTER SEVEN

1. *Libellus de Vita Godrici*, 33; J. A. Brundage, "*Cruce Signari:* The Rite of Taking the Cross in England," *Traditio* 22 (1966).

2. *Historical Papers from Northern Registers*, 46–58, 93–96; in general, Lunt, *Financial Relations* 1:esp. chapter 8.

3. See below, chapters 11 and 12.

4. *Itinerarium*, 139; for a convenient summary, see Riley-Smith's general remarks on preaching, *What were the Crusades?*, 42–45.

5. Roger of Howden, *Gesta* 1:275.

6. For a translation of Innocent's instructions, Riley-Smith, *Crusades*, 130–31; see also C. Morris, "Propaganda for War," 79–101.

7. Roger of Howden, *Gesta* 2:33; Gerald of Wales, *Journey*, 132–33, for evidence that the Saladin tithe might have been discussed.

8. *C.M.* 4:488–89.

9. H. E. J. Cowdrey, "Urban II's Preaching of the First Crusade," *History* 55 (1970):183–84.

10. *E.H.D.* 2:195.

11. *De Expugnatione Lyxbonensi*, 70–85, 146–59.

12. *Letters of St. Bernard*, no. 391.

13. *Chronica Monasterii de Melsa* 1:76; G. H. White, "The Career of Waleran, Count of Meulan," *TRHS*, 4th ser., 17 (1934):40.

14. Ralph of Diceto, *Ymagines* 2:32–33; Roger of Howden, *Gesta* 1:335–36.

15. Roger of Howden, *Gesta* 1:336–37; idem, *Chronica* 2:302.

16. *C.M.* 5:281–82.

17. *Itinerarium Kambriae*, Gerald of Wales, *Opera* 6:3–152, trans. in idem, *Journey*, 63–209.

18. Gerald of Wales, *Journey*, 202.

19. Ibid., esp. 164–69; for the bishop of St. David's with the preaching party, ibid., 75–76.

20. See above, chapter 3.

21. Gerald of Wales, *Journey*, 75.

22. Gerald of Wales, *Opera* 1:74; idem, *De Rebus a se gestis*, trans. H. E. Butler, under the title, *The Autobiography of Giraldus Cambrensis* (London, 1937), 99.

23. Gerald of Wales, *Autobiography of Giraldus*, 99–101; idem, *Opera* 1:75–76; cf. idem, *Journey*, 141.

24. Gerald of Wales, *Autobiography of Giraldus*, 100–1, 104; idem, *Opera* 1:75, 77–78.

25. Gerald of Wales, *Journey*, 75, 114, 185–86.

26. Trans. in Riley-Smith, *Crusades*, 64–67.

27. Gerald of Wales, *Journey*, 114, 185–86; idem, *Opera* 6:55 ("sunt conversi").

28. Gerald of Wales, *Journey*, 141, 172.

29. Ibid., 172.

30. Riley-Smith, *Crusades*, 37, 57–59, 124–29.

31. E.g., Alan of Lille's sermon on 14 September 1189, "Sermon de cruce domini," *Textes inedits*, ed. M. T. d'Alverny, *Etudes de philosophie mediévale* 52 (Paris, 1965):281–82.

32. *Historical Papers from Northern Registers*, 93–96.

33. Gerald of Wales, *Journey*, 200.

34. Ibid.; *Councils and Synods* 2:175; Morris, "Propaganda for War," 90; *De Expugnatione Lyxbonensi*, 84–85; *Ordinatio*, 1–26.

35. Riley-Smith, *Crusades*, 123–24; cf. for local application, *Register of Bishop John de Pontissara of Winchester*, Surrey Record Society, 191–94.

36. *De Expugnatione Lyxbonensi*, 147; Gerald of Wales, *Autobiography of Giraldus*, 100; idem, *Opera* 1:75.

37. Winchester Annals, *Ann. Mon.* 2:38.

38. Roger of Howden, *Chronica* 4:123–24, 167–72; Roger of Wendover, *Flores* 3:107–8; G. R. Owst, *Preaching in Medieval England* (Cambridge, 1926), 56–57.

39. *De Expugnatione Lyxbonensi*, 71; Barling's Chronicle, in *Chronicles of Edward I and II*, ed. W. Stubbs, RS (London, 1883), vol. 2, cxvi.

40. Roger of Wendover, *Flores* 2:323.

41. Gerald of Wales, *Journey*, 204.

42. See above, chapter 1.

43. *E.H.D.* 2:195.

44. Roger of Howden, *Gesta* 2:33; Gerald of Wales, *Journey*, 201.

45. Cate, "Mission of Eustace of Flay," 67–87, esp. 71.

46. *C.M.* 3:287–88; cf. ibid., 373–74; ibid., 4:9; ibid., 5:73–74; but cf. Vaughan, *Matthew Paris*, 122, for evidence that even Paris could moderate and change his views on the friars; *Reg. Innocent IV*, no. 2960; *Cal.Pap.Reg.* 1:234; *Foedera* 1:pt. 1,163. In general see A. G. Little, *Studies in English Franciscan History* (Manchester, 1917), 126–27 and refs., e.g., *C.C.R. 1251–53*, 219; A. Lecoy de la Marche, "Le prédiction de la croisade au treizième siècle," *Revue des questions historiques* 48 (1890):5–28.

47. *Cal.Pap.Reg.* 1:436.

48. *De Expugnatione Lyxbonensi*, 70–85, 146–59.

49. R. W. Southern, "Peter of Blois and the Third Crusade," in *Studies in Medieval History presented to R. H. C. Davis*, ed. H. Mayr-Harting and R. I. Moore (London, 1985), 207–18.

50. *Ordinatio*, 24, and, in general, 1–26.

51. Ibid., 18–26.

52. Cf. *Gesta Francorum*, 1.

53. (My italics.) "Parti de mal et a bien aturné," *Les chansons de croisade*, ed. J. Bédier and P. Auby (Paris, 1909), 67–73; for the use of objects and signs to confirm contracts, M. T. Clanchy, *From Memory to Written Record* (London, 1979), esp. 244–48 for crosses.

54. *Itinerarium*, 65, 275–77; Roger of Howden, *Gesta* 1:359; ibid. 2:22; J. Longnon, *Les compagnons de Villehardouin* (Geneva, 1978), 123–4.

55. *Ordinatio*, 17.

56. For fourteenth-century examples, see the crusade sermons of 1332–33 by Pierre Roger, the future Clement VI, or those of his contemporary, Canon Vivien de Montaut of Rodez. C. J. Tyerman, "The French and the Crusade," D.Phil. diss., Oxford (1981), 318–22, 391.

57. Roger of Wendover, *Flores* 2:305.

58. Gerald of Wales, *Autobiography of Giraldus*, 101; idem, *Opera* 1:76.

59. *Councils and Synods* 2:734.

60. Winchester Annals, *Ann. Mon.* 2:67–68; *Florence of Worcester*, ed. B. Thorpe (London, 1848–49), vol. 2, 164–65.

61. *Letters of St. Bernard*, 462; *De Expugnatione Lyxbonensi*; Henry of Huntingdon, *Historia*, 281; cf. *Chronica Monasterii de Melsa* 1:138, which also calls them *pauperes*.

62. *Libellus de Vita Godrici*, 33; *Eynsham Cartulary* 1:37.

63. Powicke, *Henry III*, 80–81, for Bromholm; *C.M.* 3:287–88, for friars.

64. *C.C.R. 1254–56*, 221; *Historical Papers from Northern Registers*, 93–96.

65. *Rotuli de Oblatis et Finibus*, ed. T. D. Hardy (London, 1835), 16, although Pipe Roll 2 John (1200), 86, mentions a relief of forty pounds.

66. Pipe Roll 9 John (1207), 72–73; ibid., 10 John (1208), 150–51.

67. *Rolls of the Fifteenth (1225) and the Fortieth (1232)*, 3, 54, 66, 99, 105, 106, for exempted crucesignati; but *C.P.R. 1216–25*, 572–73, for government insistence on some sort of payment by crusaders.

68. *Reg. Archbishop W. Giffard of York*, 277–86; *Historical Papers from Northern Registers*, 46–58; *Register of Bishop Geoffrey Giffard of Worcester*, ed. J. W. Willis Bund, Worcester History Society (Oxford, 1899–1902), 284; Roger of Howden, *Chronica* 4:188–89, for the 1201 writ.

69. Pipe Roll 8 John (1206), 74, 99, 123, 164, 200, 203.

70. Roger of Howden, *Gesta* 2:149.

71. P. D. A. Harvey, "The English Inflation of 1180–1220," *Peasants, Knights, and Heretics*, ed. R. H. Hilton (Cambridge, 1976), 67–68, 71; S. Harvey, "The Knight and the Knight's Fee in England," ibid., 158–59.

72. Roger of Howden, *Chronica* 4:169.

73. Cheney, *Hubert Walter*, 124–32; Roger of Howden, *Chronica* 3:317–19.

74. *H.M.C., Fifth Report*, Appendix (London, 1872), 462; Cheney, *Hubert Walter*, 132.

75. *H.M.C., Report on Various Collections*, vol. 1 (London, 1901), 235–36.

76. Richard of Devizes, *Chronicle*, 10–11.

77. Roger of Howden, *Gesta* 2:32; idem, *De Re Militari*, 224, 227.

78. See esp. F. Duncalf, "The Peasants' Crusade," *American Historical Review* 26 (1920–21):440–53.

79. E.g., *Annales Gandenses*, ed. H. Johnstone (London, 1951), 97.

80. *C.C.R. 1247–51*, 549.

81. W. H. Blaauw, "Letters of Ralph de Neville," *Sussex Archeological Collections*, vol. 3 (1850), 75; Owst, *Preaching in Medieval England*, 56–57.

82. B. Z. Kedar, "The Passenger List of a Crusader Ship, 1250," *Studi Medievali*, 3d ser., 13 (1972).

83. *Rolls of Justices: Lincolnshire, 1218–19, and Worcestershire, 1221*, 108, no. 248, 198–99, no. 427; cf. *Rolls of Justices, Yorkshire, 1218–19*, 259–60, no. 698; in general, Brundage, *Canon Law*, and Hyams, *Kings, Lords, and Peasants*.

84. *C.R.R.* 7:297.

85. Adam Marsh, *Epistolae*, no. 24, *Monumenta Franciscana*, ed. J. Brewer, RS (London, 1858), 109.

86. Roger of Howden, *Gesta* 2:32; Hyams, *Kings, Lords, and Peasants*, 152, 250, note 113; generally on *rustici*, A. Murray, *Reason and Society in the Middle Ages* (Oxford, 1978), 237–44. A loose definition which did not imply serfdom may also have been more likely, as the decree was a joint Angevin-Capetian ordinance rather than the work of the English chancery alone.

87. F. M. Stenton, "Early Manumissions at Staunton," *EHR* 26 (1911):95–96; cf. Hyams, *Kings, Lords, and Peasants*, 32 and note 37. It should be noted that all Frankish settlers in Outremer were, by definition, free.

88. For Urban's view, see his letter to the Bolognese, trans. in Riley-Smith, *Crusades*, 38–39; cf. also the charter of Raymond of Toulouse in 1096, *Histoire général de Languedoc*, ed. C. de Vic, J. Vaissete, and A. Molinier (Toulouse, 1872–1904), vol. 5, cols. 745, 748, and that of Nivello, trans. in Riley-Smith, *Crusades*, 99–100; cf. for Eugenius III's legislation prescribing this acquiescence, *Quantum praedecessores*, ibid., 59.

89. Pipe Roll 34 Henry II (1187–88), 141; *Chartes de prieuré de Longueville*, 53–54.

90. Roger of Howden, *Gesta* 2:32–33; Gervase of Canterbury, *Works* 1:409.

91. *Reg. St. Benet Holme* 1:54, 87, nos. 92 and 155; ibid. 2:205; *E.Y.C.* 3:79, no. 1364.

92. Blaauw, "Letters of Ralph de Neville," 75; *Reg. Bishop G. Giffard of Worcester*, 285.

93. *Itinerarium*, 147.

94. Lunt, *Papal Revenues* 1:76.

95. *Gesta Francorum*, 7–8.

96. *Itinerarium*, 104; Roger of Howden, *Chronica* 3:8; Lloyd, "Lord Edward's crusade."

97. *C.M.* 4:44; ibid. 5:1, 101, 282.

98. Lloyd, "Lord Edward's crusade," 126–27.

99. *Calendar of Documents relating to Scotland*, ed. J. Bain (London, 1881–88), vol. 1, no. 1899; *Complete Peerage* 4:55, note D.

100. *R.H.C.Occ.* 3:271; Runciman, *Crusades* 1:261.

101. *Itinerarium*, 291.

102. *De Expugnatione Lyxbonensi*, 56–57.

103. For the translation, see *Chronicles of the Crusades*, trans. M. R. B. Shaw (London, 1963), 198; for Pelagius's efforts, Oliver of Paderborn, *Damietta*, 104–5.

104. Gerald of Wales, *Opera* 3:285.

105. Pipe Roll 3 Richard I, 44; Ralph of Diceto, *Ymagines* 2:88; *Itinerarium*, 104; Ambroise, *Crusade*, 200–1; Roger of Howden, *Chronica* 3:8; for the reference to so-called Ansbert, ibid., cxxxvii–cxxxviii.

106. Southern, "Peter of Blois," 215–16; *V.C.H. Warwickshire* 2:8.

107. *Rolls of Justices: Lincolnshire, 1218–19, and Worcestershire, 1221*, 315, no. 655.

108. Roger of Howden, *Gesta* 2:112 ("conduxit" is "he hired"); *Itinerarium*, 415–16.

109. *C.M.* 4:71; ibid. 5:131.

110. Giuseppi, "Testament of Hugh de Neville," 352–54.

111. *C.P.R. 1266–72*, 411, 440, 443, 464–65, 479–80, 484–85, 587.

112. *Rott.Litt.Claus.* 1:390; *C.M.* 4:44, 175; *Itinerarium*, 415, 432.

113. Richard of Devizes, *Chronicle*, 10; *Chronica Monasterii de Melsa* 1:76; Matthew Paris, *Hist. Anglorum* 1:57, 76; David, *Curthose*, 228.

114. E. Mason, "Legends of the Beauchamps' Ancestors," *Journal of Medieval History* 10 (1984):25–40.

115. Ambroise, *Crusade*, 119–201; *Itinerarium*, 93, 217–18, 345; *Cartulary of Haughmond Abbey*, ed. V. Rees, Shropshire Archeological Society (Cardiff, 1985), 224, no. 1228; Pipe Roll 2 Richard I, 110.

116. *C.M.* 4:44.

117. Stenton, "Roger of Howden and Benedict," 576–77; Roger of Howden, *Gesta* 2:149; *E.Y.C.* 9:99, for Robert de Stuteville confirming John's grant of land in North Ferriby to the Austin Canons of the Temple of Jerusalem.

118. *De Expugnatione Lyxbonensi*, 52–57; Roger of Howden, *Gesta* 2:90, 116–17.

119. Gerald of Wales, *Journey*, 109, 201.

120. William of Newburgh, *Historia*, 309–10, 313–14; *C.P.R. 1266–72*, 411, 440, 443, 464–65, 479–80, 484–85, 587.

121. *De Expugnatione Lyxbonensi*, 56–57, 104–5; cf. *Chronica Monasterii de Melsa* 1:137 for a description of bands (*socii*) on the Second Crusade.

122. Odo of Deuil, *De Profectione Ludovici*, 124–27.

123. *Chronicle of Langtoft* 1:495.

124. Ralph of Diceto, *Ymagines* 2:65.

125. Roger of Howden, *Gesta* 2:110–11.

126. Ibid., 116; idem, *Chronica* 4:5–6.

127. Villehardouin, *Chronicles of the Crusades*, trans. M. R. B. Shaw (London, 1963), 31.

128. *C.M.* 3:620.

129. Roger of Wendover, *Flores* 2:321; ibid. 3:53–54.

130. Giuseppi, "Testament of Hugh de Neville," 352–54.

131. Cf. *C.M.* 4:291; cf. *Councils and Synods* 2:1097–1113, for the advice of English church councils of 1292; on crusade advice, A. S. Atiya, *The Crusade in the Later Middle Ages* (London, 1938), 29–154.

132. *Foedera* (1816 London ed.) 1:pt. 1, 496; *Hist. Guillaume le Maréchal*, lines 6891–6911, 7233–95; *Cartulary of Haughmond Abbey*, 157, no. 770, 200, no. 1067; *Cartulary of the Priory of St. Denys near Southampton*, ed. E. O. Blake, Southampton Record Society (Southampton, 1981), vol. 1, 26, no. 39; cf. Robert de Marsh being sent to Jerusalem with his father's cross sometime before 1201, *Pleas before the King or his Justices, 1198–1202*, ed. D. M. Stenton, Selden Society (1948–49), vol. 1, 135–36, and vol. 2, 49, no. 248.

Chapter Eight

1. Riley-Smith, *Crusades*, 160, for a translation.

2. "Parti de mal et a bien aturné," *Chansons de croisade*, 67–73; "Dialogue between Henry de Lacy and Walter Biblesworth on the Crusade," 134–36.

3. *Rolls of Justices, Gloucestershire, Warwickshire, and Staffordshire, 1221, 1222*, no. 659; *C.R.R.* 8:71–72. The witness had returned two years later, *C.R.R.* 10:76.

4. Walter Map, *De Nugis Curialium*, ed. M. R. James, C. N. L. Brooke, R. A. B. Mynors (Oxford, 1983), 492–93.

5. It is surprising that Brundage's leads into English sources in his *Canon Law* have not been pursued more fully.

6. Matthew Paris, *Hist. Anglorum* 3:55.

7. See above, chapter 5; *Le Strange Records*, 140–49.

8. *C.C.R. 1227–31*, 34–35; Roger of Howden, *Chronica* 3:264.

9. Pipe Roll 16 John (1214), 38; eighteen marks down and twelve marks forty days before Richard's departure.

10. *Charters of the Honour of Mowbray*, 83–85, nos. 111 and 112; F. M. Stenton, *Transcripts of Charters relating to Gilbertine Houses*, Lincoln Record Society, vol. 18 (1922), 6–7; *E.Y.C.* 11:68; cf. Salter, *Facsimilies of Early Charters in Oxford Muniment Rooms*, no. 38; cf. Harvey, "The Knight and Knight's Fee," 159, 169: C. W. Hollister, *The Military Organisation of Norman England* (Oxford, 1965) 157, 212–15.

11. *E.Y.C.* 2:373.

12. *Pleas before the King or his Justices, 1198–1202* 1:135–36; ibid. 2:49, no. 248.

13. Giuseppi, "Testament of Hugh de Neville," 352–54; see the papers in P. W. Edbury and D. M. Metcalf, eds., *Coinage in the Latin East* (Oxford, 1980), by Metcalf, 1–17, and P. R. Hyams, 133–35.

14. Gervase of Canterbury, *Works* 1:198–99.

15. Constable, "The Financing of the Crusades," 64–69.

16. *C.R.R.* 1:430; for taxation in general, Lunt, *Financial Relations* 1:419–60, and appendix 1, 607–9.

17. *Councils and Synods* 2:734.

18. Ralph of Coggeshall, *Chronicon*, 25; *Chronica Monasterii de Melsa* 1:239.

19. *Pleas before the King or his Justices, 1198–1202* 1:135—36; ibid., 2:49, nos. 247–48; Cheney, *Innocent III*, 248.

20. Not eight hundred marks as in Mitchell, *Taxation*, 35–36; *C.P.R. 1216–25*, 512, 527; *Rott.Litt.Claus.* 1:516, 593, 594, 630; Waverley Annals, *Ann. Mon.* 1:296.

21. Prestwich, *War, Politics, and Finance*, 169–70 and note 1.

22. Gervase of Canterbury, *Works* 1:422; C. Roth, *A History of the Jews in England* (Oxford, 1978), 17; Richardson, *English Jewry*, 163–64; cf. Pipe Roll 3 Richard I, 50 for the 1188 tallage; ibid., 1 Richard I, 230, and 3 Richard I, 139, for 1186 tallage.

23. Ephraim of Bonn, *The Book of Remembrance*, in *The Jews and the Crusades*, ed. and trans. S. Eidelberg (Madison, Wis., 1977), 119, 122–23, 131, 177; in general, see Roth, *Jews*, 1–37, esp. 8; Richardson, *English Jewry*; R. B. Dobson, *The Jews of Medieval York and the Massacre of 1190*, Borthwick Papers, no. 45 (York, 1974).

24. William of Newburgh, *Historia*, 310.

25. Roth, *Jews*, 28–30, 61–63.

26. R. B. Dobson, "The Decline and Expulsion of the Medieval Jews of York," *Miscellanies* 11, in *Transactions of the Jewish Historical Society of England* 26 (1979), 34–52, esp. 35–36.

27. *C.C.R. 1234–35*, 410; ibid., *1237–42*, 4, 197; *C.P.R. 1232–47*, 173; ibid., *1266–72*, 671; Richardson, *English Jewry*, 161–75, 214; Roth, *Jews*, 44, 46–47, 64, 67; Powicke, *Henry III*, 311 note 1.

28. See below, chapter 9.

29. Lunt, *Financial Relations* 1:esp. 419–45; in general, idem, *Papal Revenues* 1:120–25.

30. *Reg. Grégoire IX*, no. 4268.

31. *Cal.Pap.Reg.* 1:234; *Reg. Innocent IV*, no. 2963; *Foedera* (1816 London ed.) 1:461; *Reg. Bishop G. Giffard of Worcester*, 284; *Reg. Archbishop W. Giffard of York*, 277–86 (278, Henry of Rillington paid two shillings).

32. Cases cited in Lunt, *Financial Relations* 1:448, 473.

33. Ibid., 437–38; Giuseppi, "Testament of Hugh de Neville," 358–60.

34. *C.P.R. 1247–58*, 411.

35. Lunt, *Financial Relations* 1:438.

36. *Cal.Pap.Reg.* 1:239.

37. Ibid., 421, 436; *Reg. Clément IV*, no. 609; Lunt, *Financial Relations* 1:445–48.

38. *Cal.Pap.Reg.* 1:444, 445; Lloyd, "Lord Edward's Crusade," 126–27.

39. Ambroise, *Crusade*, lines 67–68.

40. Roger of Howden, *Gesta* 1:196–97; *C.P.R. 1272–81*, 170.

41. *C.M.* 5:98.

42. *E.Y.C.* 3:116, no. 1409.

43. Cf. the charter of Nivello in 1096 and Eugenius III's *Quantum Praedecessores*, trans. Riley-Smith, *Crusades*, 59, 99.

44. *Reg. St. Benet Holme* 1:54, 87, nos. 92, 155; *Chartulary of the Priory of Boxgrove*, ed. L. Fleming, Sussex Record Society 59 (1960):88, no. 152; cf. the ten shillings granted on land with three pence annual rental, *Cartulary of Carisbrooke Priory*, ed. S. F. Hockey (Isle of Wight, 1981), 85, no. 123.

45. *Le Strange Records,* 145, 148, 163, 171; cf. the 1225 case of crusader William Pollard's land held of the king, alienated without royal licence and as a result confiscated, *C.R.R.* 7:156, no. 755.

46. Gregory VIII's bull, trans. Riley-Smith, *Crusades,* 64–67; Roger of Howden, *Gesta* 2:32; Brundage, *Canon Law,* 183.

47. Brundage, *Canon Law,* 183.

48. *E.Y.C.* 3:116, no. 1409 (my italics).

49. *Reg. St. Benet Holme* 1:87, no. 155.

50. Orderic, *History* 5:278–81.

51. E.g., *Charters of the Honour of Mowbray,* 83, no. 111 (grazing rights); *Cal.Inq.P.M.* 1:235, and *C.R.R.* 9:359 (wardships); *Cal.Pap.Reg.* 2:137 (benefices); Roger of Howden, *Gesta* 32.

52. E.g., Ralph Bolebec got forty marks and a horse worth three marks from Malton Priory in the 1240s, D. M. Owen, *Church and Society in Medieval Lincolnshire* (Lincoln, 1971), 125.

53. *Chartulary of the Priory of St. Pancras of Lewes,* ed. L. F. Salzman, Sussex Record Society (Lewes, 1932), 37; *Early Yorkshire Families,* ed. C. Clay and D. E. Greenway, Yorkshire Archeological Society Record Series (1973), 111–12, no. 8; *E.Y.C.* 2:396, no. 1095.

54. *E.Y.C.* 1:434–35, no. 556.

55. Ibid. 6:167–68, no. 78.

56. *Charters of the Honour of Mowbray,* 83, no. 111.

57. British Library, MS Cotton Nero C iii, fol. 201a. I am endebted to Dr. W. J. Blair for bringing this document to my attention (my italics).

58. *Chartulary of Boxgrove Priory,* 122, no. 260.

59. *Somersetshire Pleas,* 65, no. 302.

60. *A Northamptonshire Miscellany,* ed. E. King, Northamptonshire Record Society (Northampton, 1938), 45.

61. *Cartulary of Carisbrooke Priory,* 85, no. 123, 112–14, nos. 164, 166; *C.R.R.* 16:31, no. 115; *Cartulary of Osney Abbey* 1:319, no. 363.

62. Cases of each technique appear in monastic cartularies, miscellaneous land deeds, and the records of central and itinerant royal courts.

63. Richard Hotot, who acquired a crusader's estate indirectly but as a result of crusade expenses, spent at least £534 5s 4d on buying land in the first half of the thirteenth century, *Northamptonshire Miscellany,* 32, 45.

64. *C.C.R. 1279–88,* 184; *Register of Archbishop J. le Romeyn,* ed. W. Brown, Surtees Society (Durham, 1913), vol. 1, 344–45; *C.P.R. 1225–32,* 90–91; *C.R.R.* 9:359.

65. E.g., for laymen of modest means, *E.Y.C.* 3:62; *Yorkshire Deeds,* ed. C. Clay, Yorkshire Archeological Society Record Series, 7 (1932), 83, no. 237; for clerics, *Cartulary of Carisbrooke Priory,* 85; for women, *Chartulary of the Priory of Healaugh Park,* ed. J. S. Purvis, Yorkshire Archeological Society Record Series (1936), 156; *Rolls of Justices, Lincolnshire, 1218–19, and Worcestershire, 1221* 70, no. 159; *Cal.Inq.P.M.* 2:447, no. 723.

66. *E.Y.C.* 3:298–99, no. 1641.

67. Ibid. 1:426–27, no. 547.

68. Pipe Roll 16 John, 38.

69. *Issues of the Exchequer,* 12; *C.Lib.R. 1216–40,* 217, 219; ibid., *1245–51,* 48; ibid., *1267–72,* 167; for other royal gifts to crusaders, cf. *Rott.Litt.Claus.* 1:447, 449, 457; *C.Lib.R. 1216–40,* 380, 384, 471; ibid., *1240–45,* 313; ibid., *1267–72,* 3.

70. B. E. Harris, "Rannulf III, Earl of Chester," *Journal of the Chester Archeological Society* 58 (1975):107 and note 77; *Rott.Litt.Claus.* 1:391.

71. *Dialogue of the Exchequer,* ed. C. Johnson (London, 1950), 51–52; for the 1235 pension see above, chapter 4; *C.C.R. 1247–51,* 251; *C.Lib.R.*

1216–40, 271; ibid., *1251–60*, 54, 173, 482; T. W. Parker, *The Knights Templar in England* (Tucson, Ariz., 1963), 44–45; *Handbook of British Chronology*, ed. F. M. Powicke and E. B. Fryde (London, 1961), 100.

72. For royal loans, mortgages, and advances, *Ancient Charters Prior to A.D. 1200*, ed. J. H. Round (London, 1888), 90, no. 54. (Henry of Cornhill acting here as elsewhere on behalf of the king); *C.Lib.R. 1216–40*, 81, 373, 378, 379, 384, 400, 463, 464, 471; ibid., *1240–45*, 29, 31; ibid., *1245–51*, 52, 159, 328; *C.P.R. 1232–47*, 209.

73. R. Hill, *Ecclesiastical Letter-Books of the Thirteenth Century*, Oxford B. Litt. thesis (1936), 272.

74. See above, chapter 3.

75. Dobson, "Decline and Expulsion," 36; *Northamptonshire Miscellany*, 45.

76. Richardson, *English Jewry*, 33–39.

77. *Bracton's Note Book*, ed. F. W. Maitland (London, 1887), vol. 3, 598–99, no. 1770.

78. *C.M.* 5:118.

79. The clearest evidence of such connections is given by William of Newburgh, *Historia*, 295–99, 308–24; see also, Dobson, "Jews of York."

80. Constable, "Financing the crusades," and idem, "Medieval Charters as a Source for the History of the Crusades," in *Crusade and Settlement*, ed. Edbury, 73–89.

81. A. Linder, "An Unpublished Charter of Geoffrey, Abbot of the Temple in Jerusalem," 119–29; D. Knowles, *The Religious Orders in England*, vol. 1 (Cambridge, 1948), 196–99.

82. *Cartularium de Whiteby*, 2–3 (but cf. *E.Y.C.* 2:198–201); *Cartulary of the Augustinian Priory of Bruton*, ed. Bishop Hobhouse et al., Somerset Record Society (1894), 59–60, no. 245; *Cartularium de Rameseia* 1:252–53.

83. *Rott.Litt.Claus.* 1:401, 402.

84. *Historia monasterii Sancti Petri Gloucestriae* 1:81.

85. *Cartulary of the Cluniac Priory of Montacute*, 184–85, nos. 167–68.

86. *Cartulary of Haughmond Abbey*, 224, no. 1228.

87. *E.Y.C.* 1:175; Lincolnshire Architectural and Archeological Society, *Reports and Papers*, vol. 3 (1945), 128.

88. E. Miller, "The State and Landed Interests," esp. 121–29.

89. Constable, "Financing the Crusades," 64–65, and idem, "Medieval Charters," 80; Roger of Howden, *Gesta* 2:30–31.

90. *Chronica Monasterii de Melsa* 1:76.

91. See note 57 above.

92. *Reg. St. Benet Holme* 2:205.

93. Ibid. 1:18–19.

94. Eyton, *Antiquities of Shropshire* 8:247–48.

95. *E.Y.C.* 3:194–95, no. 1503; Wightman, *The Lacy Family*, 82–84.

96. *Cartularium de Rameseia* 1:123–24.

97. Hill, *Ecclesiastical Letter-Books*, 269–72.

98. For the formal legal protection, Bracton, *De Legibus* 4:463–65.

99. *C.R.R.* 11:85, no. 452; ibid. 15:315, 346, nos. 1267, 1369.

100. *C.C.R. 1231–34*, 510–11.

101. Fowler, "The Beauchamps of Eaton," 70; *E.Y.C.* 4:pt. 2, 122, no. 215; *C.C.R. 1268–72*, 278–79.

102. *Civil Pleas of the Wiltshire Eyre, 1249*, ed. M. T. Clanchy, Wiltshire Record Society (Devizes, 1971), 141, no. 483; *C.C.R. 1264–68*, 479, 480; C.R.R. 11:262.

103. *C.R.R.* 13:206, no. 958.

104. *C.R.R.* 2:134; *C.C.R. 1231–34*, 248.

105. *C.R.R.* 1:85; for Roger's crusade and death, Pipe Rolls 3 and 4 Richard I, 121; Roger of Howden, *Gesta* 2:149.

106. Pipe Rolls 3 and 4 Richard I, 285.

107. *C.C.R. 1251–53*, 210.

108. *C.R.R.* 10:293; *Bracton's Note Book* 2:159–60, 196.

109. *Rolls of Justices, Yorkshire, 1218–19*, 298–301, no. 823.

110. *C.M.* 3:101–2; discussed by J. C. Holt, "The Heiress and the Alien," *TRHS*, 5th ser., 35 (1985):28.

111. *C.R.R.* 13:347, no. 1636.

112. Ibid., 370, no. 1760.

113. Orderic, *History* 6:19.

114. *C.R.R.* 11:262; *C.P.R. 1272–81*, 170.

115. *Northamptonshire Miscellany*, 45.

116. *C.R.R.* 13:298, no. 1371.

117. *Somerset Pleas*, 77, no. 334.

118. *Chartularium Prioratus de Brinkburne*, ed. W. Page, Surtees Society (Durham, 1893), 12; Pipe Roll 16 John, 38; *Cartulary of God's House, Southampton*, ed. J. M. Kaye, Southampton Record Series (Southampton 1976), vol. 1, 178–79.

119. *C.C.R. 1247–51*, 368; *C.P.R. 1272–81*, 169.

120. *C.P.R. 1307–13*, 131, 379; *Cal.Inq.P.M.* 5:175; *C.C.R. 1307–13*, 366.

121. *C.R.R.* 5:289.

122. *C.C.R. 1254–56*, 328.

123. *Feet of Fines for Yorkshire, 1232–46*, ed. J. Parker, Yorkshire Archeological Society Record Series (1925), 139 and note 2; see above note 52 for Ralph's other attempts to raise money; cf. similar instances, *Cal. Docs. in France* 1:226–27, no. 646 (c. 1190); *Le Strange Records*, 170 (1270).

124. *E.Y.C.* 2:396, no. 1095.

125. The principle was powerfully expressed by Archbishop Hildebert of Tours c. 1131. See R. W. Southern, *The Making of the Middle Ages* (London, 1968), 93. Cf. the similar views expressed to Louis IX by his mother in the 1240s, by Joinville in the 1260s, and by Henry III in 1270.

126. *C.R.R.* 3:197–98; *E.Y.C.* 3:248, no. 1573.

127. Stenton, "Early manumissions," 95–96; Hyams, *Kings, Lords, and Peasants*, 32, note 37.

128. *C.R.R.* 2:13–14.

129. *C.C.R. 1254–56*, 328; *C.R.R.* 16:446, no. 2234.

130. *Cartularium de Rameseia* 1:123–24; *C.C.R. 1237–42*, 394; *C.M.* 4:175.

131. Pipe Roll 31 Henry I, 33; ibid., 30 Henry II, 84; cf. ibid., 34 Henry II, 174.

132. *C.R.R.* 13:64, no. 292.

133. *C.C.R. 1227–31*, 161, for the sheriff of Hampshire being alerted to a land deal in 1229.

134. *Charters of Norwich Cathedral Priory*, ed. B. Dodwell, vol. 2 (London, 1985), 84, no. 140; for the usefulness of records, *Cal.Inq.P.M.* 2:447, no. 723.

135. *C.R.R.* 1:85; *E.Y.C.* 8:152.

136. *Cartulary of St. Frideswide's, Oxford*, ed. S. R. Wigram, vol. 2, Oxford Historical Society, vol. 31 (1896), 303, no. 1080; *Cartulary of the Hospital of St. John the Baptist*, ed. H. E. Salter, vol. 2, Oxford Historical Society, vol. 68 (1915), 134–35.

137. *Cartulary of Carisbrooke Priory*, 113–14, no. 166.

138. *E.Y.C.* 5:122, no. 215; cf. J. Sayers, "English Charters from the Third Crusade," *Tradition and Change: Essays in Honour of Marjorie Chibnall*, ed. Greenway, 201–2.

139. *C.R.R.* 8:324; in general, Brundage, *Canon Law.*

140. E.g., *Rolls of Justices, Yorkshire, 1218–19,* 3, no. 15, 263–64, no. 713, 275, no. 740, 297, no. 818, 344–45, no. 944, 353, no. 972, 255–57, no. 979; *Rolls of Justices, Gloucestershire, Warwickshire, and Staffordshire, 1221, 1222,* 39, no. 108, 520–21, no. 1188; *Rolls of Justices, Lincolnshire, 1218–19, and Worcestershire, 1221,* 87–88, no. 206, 313–15, no. 654, 593, no. 219; *Calendar of Roll of Justices, 1227 (Buckinghamshire)* 6:62, no. 692.

141. Cheney, *Innocent III,* 254; *Rolls of Justices, Lincolnshire, 1218–19, and Worcestershire, 1221,* 150, no. 324; cf. Gilbert Ken's failed attempt to plead crusader's immunity before justices at Coventry in 1221, his absence being caused by poverty not the cross, *Rolls of Justices, Gloucestershire, Warwickshire, and Staffordshire, 1221, 1222,* 275, no. 614.

142. See above, chapter 5, note 10; Bracton, *De Legibus* 1:157–59; ibid. 4:117, 463–65; ibid. 5:159.

143. *C.P.R. 1225–32,* 120, 122; ibid., *1247–58,* 75; *C.C.R. 1251–55,* 436; ibid., *1268–72,* 260, 278; most others in 1270 received a four year term, cf. *C.C.R. 1268–72,* 271–74, 288–90, and the lists on the Patent Rolls.

144. *C.R.R.* 8:23–24; *Somersetshire Pleas,* 134 (41 Henry III); *C.C.R. 1268–72,* 571–72; Sutherland, *Novel Disseisin,* 54–55.

145. *C.M.* 4:521.

146. E.g., *Durham Annals and Documents of the Thirteenth Century,* ed. F. Barlow (Durham, 1945), 181; *Vetus Liber Archidiaconi Eliensis,* ed. C. L. Feltoe and E. H. Minns (Cambridge, 1917), 169, 201.

147. For a sample, see refs. in Brundage, *Canon Law,* 160–84.

148. For a random selection, *Rotuli Hugonis de Welles Episcopi Lincolniensis,* ed. W. P. W. Phillimore, Lincoln Record Society no. 6 (Lincoln, 1912–13), vol. 1, lx; ibid. 2:196 (diocese of Lincoln, 1221); Eyton, *Antiquities of Shropshire* 10:150–51 (Shrewsbury, 1253); *V.C.H. Warwickshire* 2:8 (Warwick, 1275); Hill, *Ecclesiastical Letter-Books,* 114–15, 132 (diocese of Salisbury, 1280s); cf. papal protection of Henry III as crucesignatus in 1220, *Cal.Pap.Reg.* 1:72.

149. *C.P.R. 1247–58,* 75; *C.C.R. 1251–53,* 231; *C.P.R. 1216–25,* 301; *C.R.R.* 3:32.

150. *C.R.R.* 3:193.

151. *Rolls of Justices, Lincolnshire, 1218–19, and Worcestershire, 1221,* 641, no. 1428 (cf. 108, no. 248, 198–99, no. 427); *Rolls of Justices, Yorkshire, 1218–19,* 259–60, no. 698; cf. *C.R.R.* 7; 297.

152. *List of Ancient Correspondence* 1:no. 208; *Acta S. Langton,* ed. K. Major (London, 1950), 61, no. 45.

153. *Epistolae Cantuarienses* 2:343, no. ccclxix.

154. *Reg. Archbishop W. Giffard of York,* 277–86; for alms as penalty for breach of contract, e.g., *Letter Book of William of Hoo,* ed. A. Gransden, Suffolk Record Society (Ipswich, 1963), no. 220; N. Hurnard, *The King's Pardon for Homicide* (Oxford, 1969), 35–36, 195, 227 note 1, and refs.

155. The evidence is overwhelming and diverse, from Guy of Lusignan, the future king of Jerusalem, and the murderers of Becket, downwards (Roger of Howden, *Chronica* 1:273–74; ibid. 2:17). Many had royal or clerical connections. Here is a selection: Murder: *C.R.R.* 5:245; *C.C.R. 1227–31,* 565; *C.P.R. 1258–66,* 426–27; ibid., *1281–92,* 194; *Reg. Bishop G. Giffard of Worcester,* 277–78; *Rolls and Reg. Bishop O. Sutton* 4:13; ibid. 5:lx (Hereford, 1965), 10, 19–20; *Cal.Pap.Reg.* 1:617; Rape: *Reg. Bishop G. Giffard of*

Worcester, 279; Illicit marriage: *Cal.Pap.Reg.* 3:226; Defamation: *Letter Book of William of Hoo,* no. 208.

156. *C.R.R.* 12:12, no. 69.

157. Ibid. 10:240; for similar delays and inquiries, ibid. 14:422–23, no. 1962; *Cal.Pap.Reg.* 1:413–14; for the expiry of the term, *C.R.R.* 3:234; ibid. 4:71–72.

158. *Earliest Northamptonshire Assize Rolls,* ed. D. M. Stenton, Northamptonshire Record Society (Lincoln and London, 1930), 100, no. 631; *C.R.R.* 12:47–48, no. 268.

159. *Select Cases Ecclesiastical Court of Canterbury, 1200–1301,* 383.

160. *C.R.R.* 11:391, no. 1951.

161. *Reg Grégoire IX,* no. 85; *Cal.Pap.Reg.* 1:124; cf. the papal intervention on behalf of Hugh Wake, a companion of Richard of Cornwall in 1240, *Cal.Pap.Reg.* 1:176.

162. *Reg. Grégoire IX,* no. 3419; *Cal.Pap.Reg.* 1:159.

163. Pipe Roll 5 Richard I (1193), 166; *C.Lib.R. 1216–40,* 338.

164. *Foedera* l:pt. 1, 92.

165. *Dialogue of the Exchequer,* 51–52; Pipe Roll 9 John (1207), 138; ibid., 1 John (1199), 49; ibid., 7 John (1205), xciii; *Cal.Pap.Reg.* 1:232, 268.

166. Pipe Roll 4 John (1202), 98.

167. *Rott.Litt.Claus.* 2:188; cf. *C.C.R. 1231–34,* 408; ibid., *1234–35,* 82.

168. *Rolls of Diverse Accounts,* 24.

169. *C.P.R. 1216–25,* 572–73.

170. *List of Ancient Correspondence* 1:26.

171. *Pleas before the King or his Justices, 1198–1202,* 69, no. 670; Pipe Roll 4 Richard I, 305; Roger of Howden, *Chronica* 3:264; for ecclesiastical responsibility, *Councils and Synods* 2:196, 805–6; *Rolls and Reg. Bishop O. Sutton* 3:157–59; *Regestum Ricardi de Swinfield,* 78–79; *H.M.C., Eighth Report* (London, 1881), appendix 1, col. 1.

172. *Foedera* 1:pt. 1, 77.

173. *C.M.* 3:94, 97–98 (Wendover's text); Dunstable Annals, *Ann. Mon.* 3:86–89; for Fawkes's letter of complaint, *Barnwell Chronicle,* 259–72, and 272–74 for Honorius III's letter to Henry III.

174. *C.C.R. 1237–42,* 95.

175. *Ann. Mon.* 1:86; Roger of Wendover, *Flores* 3:36, 57.

176. *Cal.Pap.Reg.* 1:63.

177. *Reg. Grégoire IX,* nos. 1561–63; *Cal.Pap.Reg.* 1:137.

178. Dunstable Annals, *Ann. Mon.* 3:144; *C.M.* 3:368–69; Powicke, *Henry III,* 128–29, 131, 140–41; Robert Grosseteste, *Epistolae,* 114–15.

179. *C.P.R. 1251–53,* 448.

180. *C.M.* 3:123–25, 368–69; H. Mackenzie, "The Anti-Foreign Movement in England in 1231–32," *Anniversary Essays by Students of C. H. Haskins* (Boston, 1929), 183–203; Denholm-Young, *Richard of Cornwall,* 42.

181. *C.P.R. 1247–58,* 354.

182. *Cartulary of St. Denys Priory near Southampton* 1:26, no. 39: it is a phrase sometimes associated with death. *Itinerarium,* 139, for the "unica causa."

CHAPTER NINE

1. J. Huizinga, *The Waning of the Middle Ages,* trans. F. Hopman (London, 1938), 92–93; cf. the standard works on the crusades by R. Grousset (1934–36), S. Runciman (1951–54), H. Mayer (Eng. trans. 1972), and J. Prawer (1969–70), as well as Throop, *Criticism of the Crusade;* but see now Siberry, *Criticism of Crusading.*

2. Annales Paulini, *Chronicles of Edward I and II* 1:266; A. Luttrell, "The Hospitallers at Rhodes, 1306–1421," in *History of Crusades*, ed. Setton 3:282–86; *Regesta Clementis V*, ed. Monachi Ordinis S. Benedicti (Rome, 1885–92), nos. 2988, 2989.

3. For James I of Aragon, Throop, *Criticism*, 223–35; for the French, Tyerman, "French and Crusade."

4. Study of the relevant calendars of documents in the P.R.O. confirms this.

5. T. Walsingham, *Historia Anglicana*, ed. H. T. Riley, RS (London, 1863–64), vol. 1, 82.

6. See his correspondence with the papacy in *Foedera* 1:pts. 2–4, and *Cal.Pap.Reg.* 1; M. C. Prestwich, *War, Politics, and Finance*, 189–90.

7. Nicholas Trivet, *Annales*, ed. T. Hog (London, 1845), 408–9; cf. Adam Murimuth, *Continuatio Chronicarum*, ed. E. M. Thompson, RS (London, 1889), 9.

8. *C.P.R. 1281–92*, 419.

9. For general accounts, M. C. Prestwich, *War, Politics, and Finance*; idem, *The Three Edwards* (London, 1979), 1–78; Powicke, *Thirteenth Century*, esp. 234–318, 401–444, 598–617, 644–719.

10. *Historical Papers from Northern Registers*, 63; *Register of Archbishop W. Wickwane*, ed. W. Brown, Surtees Society (Durham, 1907), 185, no. 467.

11. *C.C.R. 1279–88*, 235; *Cal.Pap.Reg.* 1:476.

12. On earlier priorities, see above, chapters 1 and 2.

13. *Chronicle of Langtoft* 2:195.

14. Ibid., 266–67.

15. Prestwich, *War, Politics, and Finance*, esp. 169–76.

16. See later in this chapter.

17. For tithes, Lunt, *Financial Relations* 1:310–65.

18. *C.C.R. 1272–79*, 546, for Teutonic Knights grant; ibid., *1302–7*, 208, for a letter to the master of the Templars; cf. *List of Ancient Correspondence* 3: no. 105; ibid., no. 84; ibid. 18: nos. 134–40; ibid. 21: nos. 1–5, 100; *Records of the Wardrobe and Household 1285–86*, ed. B. F. Byerly and C. R. Byerly (London, 1977), 205, no. 209; J. C. Parsons, *The Court and Household of Eleanor of Castille in 1290*, (Toronto, 1977), 85 and note 115, and 108.

19. Rishanger, *Chronica*, 78; *C.P.R. 1272–81*, 296; *C.C.R. 1302–7*, 208; Edward's will does not survive, but is described in Trivet, *Annales*, 413–14; a contemporary lament on Edward's death also refers to his wish for his heart to be sent to Jerusalem, *Political Songs*, 243; a much later mention is by Walsingham, *Historia Anglicana* 1:115, which confirms the outlines of the instructions although differing over details; for similar clauses for subsidising crusaders in wills, cf. those of the earl of Warwick (d. 1298), *Testamenta Vetusta*, ed. N. H. Nicholas (London, 1836), 52, and the earl of Cornwall (d. 1296), in *Chronicle of Walter of Guisborough*, 348. N.B. Robert Bruce's famous bequest of his heart to the Holy Land in 1329.

20. Lunt, *Financial Relations* 1:310–65, 448–57.

21. *Cal.Pap.Reg.* 1:616; ibid. 2:5, 10 (February is wrong; it should be April), 12; *Reg. Clement IV*, nos. 305–6, 722, 821, 925–28; C. M. Fraser, *A History of Antony Bek, 1283–1311* (Oxford, 1957), 163–65, 201.

22. Tyerman, "French and Crusade"; S. Schein, "Philip IV and the Crusade," *Crusade and Settlement*, ed. Edbury, 120–26.

23. Rishanger, *Chronica*, 228; *Chronicle of Walter of Guisborough*, 348, 362; Fraser, *Bek*, 207.

24. Fraser, *Bek*, 165; J. H. Denton, *Robert Winchelsea and the Crown, 1294–1313* (Cambridge, 1980), 235.

25. *Historical Papers from Northern Registers*, 263.

26. *Cal.Pap.Reg.* 1:473–74, 477.

27. Lunt, *Financial Relations* 1:336–39, 388 note 9, for a summary of the chronicle evidence for the 1287 ceremony; *Cal.Pap.Reg.* 1:552.

28. *Foedera* 1:pt. 3, 117, 122.

29. Powicke, *Henry III*, 731.

30. Rishanger, *Chronica*, 116.

31. *Cal.Pap.Reg.* 1:527, 551–52; Lunt, *Financial Relations* 1:338–40; *C.C.R. 1288–96*, 145, 266–67.

32. *Historical Papers from Northern Registers*, 93–97; *Reg. Archbishop J. le Romeyn* 1:113, ibid. 2:8–9; Prestwich, *War, Politics, and Finance*, 190.

33. *Reg. Bishop J. de Pontissara*, 481–82; Bartholomew Cotton, *Historia Anglicana*, ed. H. R. Luard, RS (London, 1859), 215–17; cf. a similar letter, ibid., 217–19, 199–203, for Nicholas IV's bull announcing the fall of Acre. The three seem to fit together as a propaganda package.

34. Prestwich, *War, Politics, and Finance*, 190; the relevant extract is printed in E. L. G. Stones and G. G. Simpson, *Edward I and the Throne of Scotland* (Oxford, 1978), vol. 2, 297; cf. ibid. 1:10 for evidence of Edward's sincerity.

35. Lunt, *Financial Relations* 1:361–63.

36. *Cal.Pap.Reg.* 1:510; *C.P.R. 1281–92*, 297, 345, 357.

37. Cotton, *Hist. Anglicana*, 177.

38. *Reg. Archbishop J. le Romeyn* 1:344–45; *C.P.R. 1281–92*, 356, 357, 362, 364, 365, 366, 367, 368, 371, 372, 373, 374, 376, 377.

39. *C.P.R. 1281–92*, 373; Parsons, *Court of Eleanor of Castille*, 108; *Cal.Inq.P.M.* 3:47, no. 65; *Reg. Archbishop J. le Romeyn* 1:344–45; E. R. Clifford, *A Knight of Great Renown* (Chicago, 1961), 112; Lunt, *Financial Relations* 1:359; *Registres de Boniface VIII*, ed. G. Digard (Paris, 1884–1935), no. 4490.

40. *Chronicle of Walter of Guisborough*, 229; Clifford, *Knight*, 124, and for Otho's 1290–91 crusade in general, 107–33.

41. Clifford, *Knight*, 126 et seq.; Tristram, *Wall Painting*, 152–53; John of St. Victor, *Excerptae memoriali historiarum*, R.H.F. 21:657; *Registres du trésor des chartes; Inventaire analytique*, ed. R. Fawtier (Paris, 1958), no. 1970; *Cal.Pap.Reg.* 3:605. Isabella was finally absolved from her vow in January 1359.

42. Compare the spying activities in the 1330s of the pilgrim James of Verona, in *Liber Peregrinationis*, ed. R. Röhricht, *Revue de l'Orient Latin* 3 (1895).

43. C. Köhler, "Deux projects de croisade en Terre Sainte," *Revue de l'Orient Latin* 10 (1903–4):406–57; accepted by Clifford, *Knight*, 129–33.

44. For the theorists, Atiya, *Crusades*, 29–186 (62–64, for Hayton's advice); for the relationship of theory to practice, C. J. Tyerman, "Marino Sanudo Torsello and the Lost Crusade." *TRHS*, 5th ser., 32 (1982):52–73.

45. Clifford, *Knight*, 230, 246–47; John XXII, *Lettres Communes*, ed. G. Mollat (Paris, 1904–47), no. 9566.

46. Quoted by Clifford, *Knight*, 122.

47. S. Schein, "Gesta Dei per Mongolos 1300: The Genesis of a Non-Event," *EHR* 94 (1979):805–19; *Foedera* 1:pt. 4, 1–2, and, as an example of its dissemination, *Annales Regis Edwardi Primi*, William Rishanger, *Chronica*, 465–70, for a bull announcing Ghazan's conquest of the Holy Land; for Edward I seeking advice on this from Otho de Grandson, *Cal. Chancery Warrants 1244–1326*, 110–11.

48. Cotton, *Hist. Anglicana*, 199–215; *Chronica J. Oxenedes*, 284–85; Worcester Annals, *Ann. Mon.* 4:507; *Councils and Synods* 2:810–11, 814–16, 1097–1113; *C.M.* 4:291, under 1244.

49. Most recently M. Barber, *The Trial of the Templars* (Cambridge, 1978), but cf. J. Favier, *Philippe le Bel* (Paris, 1978), 426–80.

50. Pierre Dubois, *The Recovery of the Holy Land*, trans. W. I. Brandt (New York, 1956), 69–70, 197–98.

51. An early sign of the assertion of French leadership may be seen in letters sent by Philip IV to the kings of England and Scotland, inviting them to a conference to discuss the crusade in 1308, in *Annales Paulini* 1:266.

52. E. Baluze, *Vitae paparum Avenionensis*, ed. G. Mollat (Paris, 1914–27), vol. 3, 89–90; *C.C.R. 1307–13*, 24; *Cal. Chancery Warrants 1244–1326*, 292; *C.P.R. 1307–13*, 224; ibid., *1321–24*, 26; *Cal. Docs. Scotland* 1:no. 1899; *Complete Peerage* 4:55 note D. Cf. comments in a contemporary lament, *Political Songs*, esp. 244–45.

53. Barber, *Templars*, 204, and in general, 192–204.

54. Lunt, *Financial Relations* 9:458–59; for the preaching, *Annales Londoniensis, Chronicles of Edward I and II* 1:156; *Annales Paulini*, 266.

55. *Foedera* 1:pt. 4, 113 (Edward to Leo of Armenia, 3 March 1308); *Cal. Chancery Warrants 1244–1326*, 273; *C.C.R. 1308–13*, 122; *C.P.R. 1307–13*, 102.

56. *Annales Gandensis*, 97; Ptolomey of Lucca, *Vitae paparum Avenionensis* 1:34; ibid. 2:81; N. J. Housley, "Pope Clement V and the Crusades of 1309–10," *Journal of Medieval History* 8 (1982):29–43.

57. *Historical Papers from Northern Registers*, 200–1.

58. *C.P.R. 1307–13*, 96, 102, 107, 114, 115, 117, 121, 181, 224, 233, 234; *Cal. Chancery Warrants 1244–1326*, 292.

59. *Rot. Parl.* 2:381 (after 1327).

60. *C.C.R. 1333–37*, 520.

61. H. Finke *Acta Aragonensia* (Berlin and Leipzig, 1908–66), vol. 1, 459–60, no. 308; *Registres du trésor des chartes* 1:nos. 1970–72, 1975, 2002, 2006, 2009, 2011, 2020, 2024, 2026–32, 2174.

62. Henry Knighton, *Chronicon*, ed. J. R. Lumby, RS (London, 1889–95), 299.

63. *E.H.D.* 3:543; cf. the 1309 excommunication of Bruce as an obstacle to the crusade after English pressure, *Historical Papers from Northern Registers*, 189–91.

64. *Vita Edwardi Secundi*, 78–79; *Cal. Chancery Warrants 1244–1326*, 455.

65. C. J. Tyerman, "Philip V of France and the Crusade," *BIHR* 57 (1984):18–19.

66. Ibid.; C. J. Tyerman, "Philip VI and the Recovery of the Holy Land," *EHR* 100 (1985): 25–52; idem, "Sed Nihil Fecit?" *War and Government*, ed. Gillingham and Holt, 170–71.

67. *Acta Aragonensia* 1:493–94; John XXII, *Lettres secrètes et curiales relatives à la France*, ed. A. Coulon et al. (Paris, 1906–72), no. 1848.

68. *Cal. Chancery Warrants 1244–1326*, 413; cf. *C.C.R. 1308–13*, 124, for the 1308 restriction of passage.

69. *Cal. Chancery Warrants 1244–1326*, 462; *C.P.R. 1313–17*, 628.

70. *Cal. Chancery Warrants 1244–1326*, 390, 511; *C.C.R. 1318–23*, 326; *C.P.R. 1317–21*, 506.

71. *C.C.R. 1308–13*, 542; *C.P.R. 1307–13*, 481, 566.

72. *Cal.Pap.Reg.* 2:436–37; O. Raynaldus, *Annales Ecclesiastici* (Lucca, 1747–55) vol. 5, s.a. 1319, par. 20; T. Walsingham, *Ypodigma Neustriae,* ed. H. T. Riley, RS (London, 1876), 388. See now J. R. S. Phillips, "Edward II and the Prophets," *England in the Fourteenth Century,* ed. W. M. Ormond (Woodbridge, 1986).

73. On the leper scare and its credulous reception, J. M. Vidal, "La poursuite des lépreux," *Mélanges de littérature et d'histoire religieuse* (Paris, 1899), 483–518.

74. *C.P.R. 1313–17,* 277.

75. *C.C.R. 1330–33,* 315.

76. In general, M. H. Keen, "Chaucer's Knight, the English Aristocracy, and the Crusade," *English Court Culture in the Later Middle Ages,* ed. V. J. Scattergood and J. W. Sherborne (London, 1983), 45–63.

77. For what follows see Tyerman, "Philip VI," 25–52.

78. *Foedera* 2:pt. 3, 47; R. Cazelles, *Lettres closes de Philippe de Valois* (Paris, 1958), 39, no. 32.

79. G. P. Cuttino, *English Diplomatic Administration, 1259–1339* (Oxford, 1971), 100–111.

80. *Rot. Parl.* 2:64, 65; *C.C.R. 1330–33,* 533; for the diplomatic exchanges, E. Déprez, *La Papauté, la France, et l'Angleterre, 1328–42* (Paris, 1902), 83–132.

81. R. Nicholson, *Edward III and the Scots* (Oxford, 1965), 75–109, and in general, 75–138.

82. *Grandes chroniques de France,* ed. J. Viard, vol. 9 (Paris, 1937), 134; Tyerman, "Philip VI," 31–32.

83. *Grandes chroniques* 9:138; R. Cazelles, *La société politique et la crise de la royauté sous Philippe VI de Valois* (Paris, 1938), 144.

84. Canon of Bridlington, *Gesta Edwardi Tertii, Chronicles of Edward I and II* 2:124–25 (letter of July 1335).

85. Tyerman, "Philip VI."

86. Murimuth, *Continuatio Chronicarum,* 73; *Annales Paulini* 1:362; *Rot. Parl.* 2:447; *C.C.R. 1333–37,* 537; *C.C.R. 1341–43,* 371; Tyerman, "Philip VI," 47 note 8; *Chronicle of Lanercost,* trans. Sir H. Maxwell (Glasgow, 1913), 309.

87. *C.C.R. 1327–30,* 568.

88. Benedict XII, *Lettres closes et patentes intéressant des pays autres que la France,* ed. J. M. Vidal (Paris, 1913–50), no. 732; for papal policy at the time, H. Jenkins, *Papal Efforts for Peace under Benedict XII* (Philadelphia, 1933), esp. 22–25.

89. *E.H.D.* 4:62–63 for a translation of this manifesto.

90. E.g., N. J. Housley, *The Italian Crusades* (Oxford, 1982).

91. Chaplais, *Diplomatic Documents* 1:178–79, 268.

92. *Grandes chroniques* 9:199; Murimuth, *Continuatio chronicarum,* 113; Philippe de Mézières, *Le Songe du Vieil Pèlerin,* ed. G. W. Coopland (Cambridge, 1969), vol. 2, 389–99.

93. Jenkins, *Papal Efforts;* M. McKisack, *The Fourteenth Century* (Oxford, 1959), 124–25.

94. Tyerman, "Philip VI," 47 and note 4; Lunt, *Financial Relations* 2:92–93.

95. *V.C.H. Oxfordshire,* ed. A. Crossley, vol. 4 (Oxford, 1979), 72.

96. British Library, MS Otho, D V fols. 1–15; the author has generally been misnamed "Stavegni," e.g., McKisack, *Fourteenth Century,* 123, and Déprez, *Papauté,* 85; the MS contradicts their reading.

97. Tyerman, "Sanudo."

98. Cf. Godfrey de Semery, who spent nine years in an Egyptian prison after the fall of Acre, *Annales Regis Edwardi Primi*, 442–43.

99. *C.P.R. 1317–21*, 254.

100. *Rot. Parl.* 2:65.

101. *Chronica Monasterii de Melsa* 2:354; *Annales Paulini* 1:354.

102. Murimuth, *Continuatio Chronicarum*, 73; cf. the almost identical verdict on Philip IV's crusade plans from a source close to the French court, Guillaume de Nangis, *Chronique Latine avec des continuations*, ed. H. Géraud (Paris, 1843), vol. 1, 392.

103. *Vita Edwardi Secundi*, 46.

104. The most comprehensive account is in Lunt, *Financial Relations* 1:311–460 and 2:88–94.

105. Ibid. 1:456, 459–60.

106. See above, chapter 3.

107. In general, Lunt, *Papal Revenues*.

108. *Historical Papers from Northern Registers*, 63–64; *C.C.R. 1279–88*, 235–36.

109. *Councils and Synods* 2:810–11, Lunt, *Financial Relations* 1:311, 346.

110. Lunt, *Financial Relations* 1:336 note 4, 361, 363, note 8; ibid. 2:8; W. A. Morris and J. R. Strayer, *English Government at Work, 1327–36* (Cambridge, Mass., 1947), 260–61.

111. In 1283 royal officials arrived at Worcester "with horses and arms," *Ann. Mon.* 4:486–87.

112. Lunt, *Financial Relations* 1:336–37.

113. Ibid., 343.

114. Ibid., 361–62 and note 1; Fraser, *Bek*, 122.

115. Lunt, *Financial Relations* 1:346–65; cf. ibid., 346, for the division of the spoils from the 1274 tax.

116. Ibid., 366–95.

117. Ibid., 395–418.

118. Ibid., 458–60.

119. Ibid., 395–404.

120. Ibid., 2:88–94.

121. Ibid. 1:346, 365, 404; ibid. 2:93. The 1312 and 1333 taxes were levied for similar lengths of time. Cf. ibid. 1:399–400.

122. *History of the King's Works* 2:1029; Prestwich, *War, Politics, and Finance*, 175, cf. 169–76.

123. *Accounts Rendered by Papal Collectors in England, 1317–78*, ed. W. E. Lunt and E. B. Graves (Philadelphia, 1968).

124. Lunt, *Financial Relations* 2:89–90, 528–29.

CHAPTER TEN

1. *The Scrope and Grosvenor Controversy*, ed. N. H. Nicolas (London, 1832), collated by C. G. Young (Chester, 1879), vol. 1, 161.

2. *Indentures of Retinue with John of Gaunt, 1367–99*, ed. N. B. Lewis, *Camden Miscellany* 22 (London, 1964):89.

3. *C.P.R. 1345–48*, 128; *Cal.Pap.Reg.* 3:28, 33; see Aitya, *Crusade*, for a general survey; it needs updating.

4. J. Froissart, *Chronicles*, trans. J. Johnes (London, 1839), vol. 2, 356; J. Barnie, *War in Medieval Society* (London, 1974), 86.

5. G. Chaucer, *Canterbury Tales*, ed. W. Skeat (Oxford, 1894–97), General Prologue, lines 43–78.

6. *The Westminster Chronicle*, ed. L. C. Hector and B. F. Harvey (Oxford, 1982), 511.

7. *Rot. Parl.* 3:343; T. Jones, *Chaucer's Knight* (London, 1980), 38, 52, and the references there to the *Confessio Amantis*, *Dit d'ou Lion*, *le confort d'Ami*, and *The Book of the Duchess*.

8. Philippe de Mézières, *Epistre lamentable et consolatoire*, ed. Kervyn de Lettenhove, Froissart, *Chroniques*, vol. 16 (Brussels, 1872), 467–473.

9. F. R. H. du Boulay, "Henry of Derby's Expeditions to Prussia, 1390–91 and 1392," *The Reign of Richard II*, ed. F. R. H. du Boulay and C. M. Barron (London, 1971), 153–72.

10. *The Chapter Act Book of the Collegiate Church of St. John of Beverley*, ed. A. F. Leach, vol. 2, Surtees Society (Durham, 1903), 136; *Bedfordshire Wills*, ed. F. A. Page-Turner, Bedfordshire Record Society, vol. 2 (1914), 6–9; *Cartulary of the Priory of St. Denys near Southampton* 1:88, no. 61; ibid. 2:181–82, no. 36.

11. *Accounts rendered by Papal Collectors, 1317–78*, 34, 48, 49, 84.

12. T. Smith, *English Gilds*, Early English Text Society, vol. 40 (London, 1870), 11, 22, 114.

13. A. Goodman, *The Loyal Conspiracy* (London, 1971), 81–82.

14. *Testamenta Vetusta* 1:100, 148; Goodman, *Loyal Conspiracy*, 78.

15. Cf. John Bromyard's homilies, G. R. Owst, *Literature and the Pulpit* (Oxford, 1961), 158, 175, 247–48, 316, 412; see now Siberry, "Criticism of Crusading in Fourteenth-Century England," *Crusade and Settlement*, ed. Edbury.

16. Walsingham, *Historia Anglicana* 2:284–85; *St. Alban's Chronicle, 1406–20*, ed. V. H. Galbraith (Oxford, 1937), 38; see chapter 12 for Despenser's crusade.

17. For a summary, Lunt, *Financial Relations* 2:614–15; cf. *Johannis de Trokelowe and Henrici de Blandforde: Chronica et Annales* (in fact by Walsingham), 181.

18. Wyclif, John, *Tractatus de Officio Regis*, ed. A. W. Pollard and C. Sayle (London, 1887), 261–62, 272; K. B. McFarlane, *Lancastrian Kings and Lollard Knights* (Oxford, 1972), 139–292, esp. 177–78.

19. Froissart, *Chronicles* 1:39.

20. In general see *D.N.B.*; *Diplomatic Correspondence of Richard II*, ed. E. Perroy, Camden Series (London, 1933), 144–45, no. 199; *Cal.Pap.Reg.* 4:489; J. J. N. Palmer, *England, France, and Christendom, 1377–99* (London, 1972), 200, 240–42; Aitya, *Crusade*, 435–36; Froissart, *Chronicles* 2:434–36.

21. M. Clarke, *Fourteenth-Century Studies* (Oxford, 1937), 287–90; Philippe de Mézières, *Le Songe du Vieil Pèlerin* 1:4–5, for similar motives.

22. *Johannis de Trokelowe*, 201; *Cal.Pap.Reg.* 4:294–95; Lunt, *Financial Relations* 2:549; Capgrave, *De Illustribus Henricis*, 169–70.

23. A. Hudson, *Lollards and their Books* (London, 1985), 54, for Clanvow's lack of originality, evidently a demerit for a literary scholar but not for a social or religious historian; for the quotations and an analysis of the text, McFarlane, *Lancastrian Kings*, 199–206; cf. 177–78, for Clanvow and Neville on crusade or pilgrimage together.

24. *Testamenta Vetusta* 1:164.

25. K. Fowler, *The King's Lieutenant* (London, 1969), 193–96; J. Catto, "Religion and the English Nobility in the Late Fourteenth Century," *History and Imagination*, ed. H. Lloyd-Jones et al. (London, 1981), 43–55.

26. *C.C.R. 1346–49*, 403, for a general prohibition of 1347 on knights and squires leaving for Prussia because of the fragility of the truce with France.

27. Keen, "Chaucer's Knight," 45–63; on Waldegrave, J. S. Roskell, "Sir Richard Waldegrave," *Proceedings of the Suffolk Institute of Archeology* 27, pt. 3 (1957):154–75.

28. Capgrave, *De Illustribus Henricis*, 161; *Cal.Pap.Reg.* 4:19. Possibly the pope was making a virtue of necessity because Warwick, originally headed for the East, diverted his crusade to the Baltic.

29. E. Christiansen, *The Northern Crusades* (London, 1980), 80, and passim, for the best modern account in English.

30. *Archives de l'Orient Latin* 1 (1881): 418; *Complete Peerage* 9:210 and note 4; Christiansen, *Northern Crusades*, 112. The money evidence is weak.

31. See references in the following notes.

32. *C.P.R. 1367–70*, 24, 56, 57, 58, 64, 72, 127, 128.

33. *S.R.P.* 2:514, 531, 549, 551; Capgrave, *De Illustribus Henricis*, 8; *Scrope-Grosvenor* 1:117; *C.P.R. 1361–64*, 251–52; ibid., *1367–70*, 58, 65; ibid., *1381–85*, 274.

34. *Cal.Pap.Reg.* 4:19; *Chronica Johannis de Reading et Anonymi Cantuariensi*, ed. J. Tait (Manchester, 1914), 172, 338–40; *C.P.R. 1367–70*, 24, 56, 57; *Anonimalle Chronicle*, ed. V. H. Galbraith (Manchester, 1927), 170 note 51; *Scrope-Grosvenor* 1:117, 123, 144–46.

35. Keen, "Chaucer's Knight," esp. 51–56; *Complete Peerage* 5:348; ibid. 12:151, 372–82; *C.P.R. 1367–70*, 128; *S.R.P.* 2:646, 648.

36. *S.R.P.* 2:549.

37. *Scrope-Grosvenor* 1:117, 123, 188, for Boynton, FitzHenry, and Henry Ferrers; *C.P.R. 1367–70*, 128; *S.R.P.* 2:646, 648.

38. *Anonimalle Chronicle*, 51, 170 note 51; *Scrope-Grosvenor* 1:165–66.

39. *C.P.R. 1361–64*, 251–52 (Howard could afford an attorney and the enrolment of the licence), and 24, 56, 57, 58, 64, 65, 72.

40. But cf. 1352, when other visitors accepted Grosmont as leader in Prussia, *Chronique des quatre premiers Valois*, ed. S. Luce (Paris, 1862), 13–14 (under the wrong date, *S.R.P.* 3:452).

41. *C.C.R. 1346–49*, 403.

42. *C.P.R. 1367–70*, 64.

43. *Cal.Inq.P.M.* 6:229, no. 378; *V.C.H. Staffordshire* 3:153.

44. *Anonimalle Chronicle*, 170.

45. *C.P.R. 1367–70*, 58, 128.

46. *Westminster Chronicle*, 444 note 1, 447.

47. *C.P.R. 1388–92*, 413; *Westminster Chronicle* 434, 474; *S.R.P.* 2:644, 797; ibid., 3: 171–72, 457–620.

48. *Expeditions to Prussia and the Holy Land made by Henry, Earl of Derby*, ed. L. Toulmin-Smith, Camden Society (London, 1894), xliii, xlv; *Westminster Chronicle* 445.

49. *Expeditions to Prussia*, 53, 88, 142–43, 303–4; *Westminster Chronicle*, 447; Keen, "Chaucer's Knight," esp. 59.

50. *Westminster Chronicle*, 444–49; Walsingham, *Historia Anglicana* 2:197–98; Christiansen, *Northern Crusades*, 219–53; M. Burleigh, *Prussian Society and the German Order, c. 1410–66* (Cambridge, 1984).

51. For cases of disruption, *Expeditions to Prussia*, xlix; *Westminster Chronicle*, 474–79; G. L. Tipton, "The English and the Scottish Hospitallers during the Great Schism," *Catholic Historical Review* 52 (1966):240–45; cf. I. B. Cowan et al., ed., *The Knights of St. John of Jerusalem in Scotland* (Edinburgh, 1983), xxxv–xl; A. D. Macquarrie, *Scotland and the Crusades* (Edinburgh, 1985), 85–87.

52. Huizinga, *Waning of Middle Ages*, 92.
53. *Expeditions to Prussia*, xv.
54. *Westminster Chronicle*, 449; *Expeditions to Prussia*, xxxi–ii.
55. *Expeditions to Prussia*, and Du Boulay, "Expeditions," 168–70, for finance.
56. *Cal.Pap.Reg.* 3:331.
57. *C.P.R. 1370–74*, 264; *C.C.R. 1374–77*, 11.
58. *Expeditions to Prussia*, xiii; Goodman, *Loyal Conspiracy*, 57; *Canterbury Tales*, General Prologue, lines 407–8.
59. *Diplomatic Correspondence of Richard II*, 66, no. 101; cf. 67–68, no. 102; J. H. Wylie, *History of England under Henry the Fourth*, vol. 4 (London, 1898), 1–15, esp. 14.
60. Wylie, *Henry IV* 4:7–9.
61. *Expeditions to Prussia*, xxxiv.
62. Christiansen, *Northern Crusades*, 150–56.
63. *Westminster Chronicle*, 478–79, and note 2, 482–85; Goodman, *Loyal Conspiracy*, 57–58.
64. For tangible signs of special respect, M. H. Keen, *Chivalry* (New Haven, Conn., 1984), 195.
65. Walsingham, *Ypodigma Neustriae*, 361; *Westminster Chronicle*, 448–49.
66. Fowler, *King's Lieutenant*, 193–96; Catto, "Religion and Nobility."
67. *S.R.P.* 2:479, 510, 514, 523, 544, 558, 646, 648, 741; ibid. 3:452, 724; ibid. 5:617–18; Christiansen, *Northern Crusades*, 223–33.
68. Knighton, *Chronicon* 2:69–70; Capgrave, *De Illustribus Henricis*, 99.
69. *Johannis de Trokelowe*, 181; *Complete Peerage* 11:391. One Baltic crusader in 1395 was the Lollard John Montague.
70. *Expeditions to Prussia*, 117. Cf. the privileges granted by the pope in 1352 to Henry of Grosmont and those going "mainly at their own expense against the enemies of the Christian faith," *Cal.Pap.Reg.* 3:459.
71. Christiansen, *Northern Crusades*, x.
72. *Westminster Chronicle*, 478–88; *Cal.Pap.Reg.* 3:459; *C.P.R. 1350–54*, 191.
73. *St. Alban's Chronicle*, 58.
74. Walsingham, *Historia Anglicana* 1:304; Tyerman, "Philip VI," 26–27; in general, P. E. Russell, *The English Intervention in Spain and Portugal* (Oxford, 1955); for French propaganda, R. Delachenal, *Histoire de Charles V*, vol. 3 (Paris, 1916), 247–50; Cuvelier, *Chronique de Bertrand du Guesclin*, ed. E. Charrière (Paris, 1839), vol. 1, 264–402; Peter did in fact have Moslem allies.
75. *Cronica del Rey Don Alfonso el Onceno, Cronicas de los Reyes de Castilla*, ed. C. Rosell, *Biblioteca de autores españoles*, vols. 66, 68 (Madrid, 1875, 1877), vol. 1, 337–46; Russell, *Intervention*, 7–10.
76. *C.C.R. 1343–46*, 456.
77. *C.P.R. 1343–46*, 18 for licence to Thomas Cok "going to Spain there to stay in the company of . . . Henry de Lancastre."
78. *Crónica Alfonso* 1:360; Fowler, *King's Lieutenant*, 45; Capgrave, *De Illustribus Henricis*, 161.
79. Walsingham, *Historia Anglicana* 2:314; *St. Alban's Chronicle*, 98; *Foedera* 4:pt. 2, 101, the remission of 20 January 1415 for the export without customs duty of military equipment purchased on behalf of the king of Portugal, viz., armour for six men-at-arms and 350 lances.

80. Russell, *Intervention*, 526–48.

81. J. Cabaret d'Oronville, *La Chronique du bon duc Loys de Bourbon*, ed. A.-M. Chazaud (Paris, 1876), 246–50; Atiya, *Crusade*, 398–434; Froissart, *Chronicles* 2:434–449, 465–77, 481–84.

82. E.g., Sir John Russell, *Expeditions to Prussia*, xxxvii–xliii, 118–27; *Westminster Chronicle*, 432–35; Cabaret d'Oronville, *Chronique*, 222–23; Atiya, *Crusade*, 408 note 3, 519–22.

83. Ibid., 408 note 3; *Westminster Chronicle*, 432–33; Goodman, *Loyal Conspiracy*, 82.

84. Froissart, *Chronicles* 2:477; Cabaret d'Oronville, *Chronique*, 257.

85. Froissart, *Chronicles* 2:477; cf. *Westminster Chronicle*, 432–35.

86. H. Finke, *Papsttum und Untergang des Templerordens* (Münster, 1907), vol. 2, 241.

87. *Mandeville's Travels*, ed. M. C. Seymour (Oxford, 1967), 1–4. Seymour's view of the work as a "second-hand compilation" (xiv) is convincing, but others accept the attempts in the text to establish verisimilitude, e.g., J. A. W. Bennett, *The Rediscovery of Sir John Mandeville* (New York, 1954). Some contemporaries were also deceived by the circumstantial biographical information, e.g., *Chronica Monasterii de Melsa* 2:158–59.

88. Philippe de Mézières, *Letter to King Richard II*, ed. G. W. Coopland (Liverpool, 1975), 29, 102; cf. 26–27, 99–100.

89. British Library MS Cotton Otho D. V.

90. *Chronica J. Reading*, 156–57; in general, Atiya, *Crusade*; J. M. A. Delaville le Roulx, *La France en Orient au XIVe siècle* (Paris, 1885–86).

91. *Cal.Pap.Reg.* 2:18; *Scrope-Grosvenor* 1:124–25, where Sabraham recalls his deeds in the Dardanelles and Messembria in Bulgaria, both scenes of Amadeus's crusade; for Musard, Atiya, *Crusade*, 388; for the English mercenaries under "Lebron" and William, ibid., 384.

92. *Scrope-Grosvenor* 1:70, 124–25, 165–66.

93. Keen, *Chivalry*, 252–53.

94. Froissart, *Chronicles* 2:483; Cabaret d'Oronville, *Chronique*, 223; Atiya, *Crusade*, 406, for the indulgences.

95. *Westminster Chronicle*, 481.

96. *C.P.R. 1345–48*, 128; *Cal.Pap.Reg.* 3:28, 33, 353, 359, 394–95.

97. *Westminster Chronicle* 481 (Clifford died en route "deeply penitent"); *Expeditions to Prussia*, esp. lx–lxxx.

98. Thomas Brygg, *Itinerarium in Terram Sanctam domini Thomae de Swynburne*, Archives de l'Orient Latin 2 (1884): 386–87.

99. *C.C.R. 1346–49*, 501; *Cal.Inq.P.M.* 14:248, no. 234; *C.C.R. 1392–96*, 523; *The Book of Margery Kempe*, ed. B. A. Windealt (London, 1985), 96–111; *Canterbury Tales*, General Prologue, line 463. Women had gone on crusade ever since 1096, often, like Godehilde of Tosni (1096), Eleanor of Aquitaine (1147), and Eleanor of Castille (1270), with their husbands, but sometimes on their own, like Ida of Austria in 1101. Armies were also accompanied by prostitutes and concubines. While not all women on crusade took the cross, some did, like Countess Eleanor, wife of Simon de Montfort (*C.M.* 4:1). For a less-exalted French crucesignata, *Archives de l'Hôtel Dieu de Paris*, ed. L. Brièle (Paris, 1894), 87–88, no. 203.

100. *Cal.Pap.Reg.* 3:353, 359, 394–95; *C.P.R. 1354–58*, 155; ibid., *1343–45*, 6; *C.C.R. 1354–60*, 378; *Cal.Pap.Reg.* 3:269; *Westminster Chronicle*, 481.

101. Goodman, *Loyal Conspiracy*, 54.

102. *C.C.R. 1343–46*, 106, 107, 351, 361.

103. *C.P.R. 1367–70*, 229; *1370–74*, 299.

104. Clanvow, Neville, Clifford, and Stafford: see above; Roos: *Johannis de Trokelowe*, 164–65; Clifton: *Cal.Inq.P.M.* 16:258, no. 676; Wright: ibid. 12:246, no. 261; Stok: ibid. 15:64, no. 159: Keynes: ibid. 14:248, no. 234.

105. *C.C.R. 1369–74*, 27–28; Adam of Usk, *Chronicle*, ed. E. M. Thompson (London, 1904), 280–81.

106. *C.C.R. 1343–46*, 639, 646; *Eulogium Historiarum*, ed. F. S. Haydon, RS (London, 1863), vol. 3, 237–38; *C.P.R. 1364–67*, 375.

107. *C.P.R. 1327–30*, 304; ibid., *1330–34*, 202; ibid., *1364–67*, 193; *Cal.Inq.P.M.* 8:455, no. 609.

108. Goodman, *Loyal Conspiracy*, 72, 163.

109. *C.C.R. 1369–74*, 27–28; cf. the proclamation forbidding the export of bullion, *C.C.R. 1337–39*, 414, and *1343–46*, 35, for licence to depart.

110. Brygg, *Itinerarium*, 379–88; for Bolingbroke's expenses of £4,915, 5s ¾ d, *Expeditions to Prussia*, 145–292; Du Boulay, "Expeditions," 168–69.

111. *C.C.R. 1392–96*, 523; *C.P.R. 1367–70*, 129; ibid., *1338–92*, 200; *Book of Margery Kempe*, 100.

112. *Issues of the Exchequer*, 159; Comte Riant, "Pièces relatives au passage de pèlerins à Venise," *Archives de l'Orient Latin* 2:243.

113. Smith, *English Gilds*, 157, 177, 182.

114. *C.P.R. 1334–38*, 188, 343.

115. *Cal.Pap.Reg.* 3:269, 353; ibid. 4:29–30.

116. *Cal.Inq.P.M.* 14:248, no. 234; *C.C.R. 1392–96*, 523; Brygg, *Itinerarium*, 480; Adam of Usk, 280–81.

117. *C.P.R. 1354–58*, 6; *Cal.Pap.Reg.* 3:33, 394–96.

118. *C.P.R. 1354–58*, 631; *Cal.Pap.Reg.* 3:269; *Expeditions to Prussia*, l–liv, lxxxvii–xciii, 264–72; *C.P.R. 1382–92*, 324.

119. *C.P.R. 1333–37*, 520 for the prohibition on Richard de Averenges's exporting war materials.

120. *Expeditions to Prussia*, lxiv, lxxvi–lxxvii; Brygg, *Itinerarium*, 380–88.

121. Keen, "Chaucer's Knight," 50–51.

122. *C.C.R. 1343–46*, 106; William Kildersby's safe-conduct in 1343 mentioned the truce.

123. Bracton, *De Legibus* 5:159–65; the following evidence is from *C.P.R. 1307–92*; for the authenticity of "Bracton," S. E. Thorne's introduction to Bracton, *De Legibus* (Cambridge, Mass., 1977), 3:xiii–lii.

124. *C.P.R. 1354–58*, 55, 631; ibid., *1358–61*, 3.

125. E.g., ibid., *1266–72*, 411, 440, 443, 464–65, 479–80, 484; *C.C.R. 1268–72*, 260, 278, 281–84, 288–90. The term was not immutable.

126. *Eulogium Historiarum* 3:238; Adam of Usk, *Chronicle*, 280; *Westminster Chronicle* 481, note 4; for the Roos mural, N. Scarfe, *Suffolk in the Middle Ages* (Woodbridge, 1986), plates 13 and 80.

127. Brygg, *Itinerarium*, 379.

128. Huizinga, *Waning of Middle Ages*, 92; Atiya, *Crusade*, esp. 281–462; idem, *Crusade of Nicopolis* (London, 1934), and the relevant passages in vol. 3 of *History of Crusades*, ed. Setton.

129. Jones, *Chaucer's Knight*, esp. 34–63; cf. Runciman, *History of the Crusades*, 3:427–68.

130. Atiya, *Crusade*, 29–154; N. Iorga, *Philippe de Mézières et la croisade au xive siècle* (Paris, 1896); *Letters of Richard II*, xxii–xxiv; Clement VI, *Letters Closes*, no. 1605; L. H. Butler, "The Order of St. John and the Peasants' Revolt," *St. John Historical Society Pamphlets*, no. 1 (1981).

131. *Cal.Pap.Reg.* 4:8, for Woodhouse.

132. *Scrope-Grosvenor* 1:165–66; others who may have been there include William Lucy, John Godard (ibid., 77–78, 171–72: the latter saw William Scrope armed "beyond the Great Sea") and Sabraham; Sir Miles Stapleton, who was with Hereford in Prussia in 1363 and was thought to have been with him at Alexandria, was in fact already dead, *Anonimalle Chronicle*, 51, 170.

133. Philippe de Mézières, *Songe du Vieil Pèlerin*, 3–5.

134. Atiya, *Crusade*, 330–41; Walsingham, *Historia Anglicana*, 296–97; *Chronica J. Reading*, 152–53. Atiya, *Crusade*, 333 and note 6, suggests that Walsingham misdated the tournament; it is more likely, given the corroboration of John of Reading and the fact that Smithfield was a common site for royal tournaments, that there were two, one in 1362, and one to celebrate the arrival of King Peter. Other accounts of the 1363–64 summit are in *Eulogium Historiarum* 3:233, and Knighton, *Chronicon* 2:118.

135. *Chronique des quartres premiers Valois*, 128.

136. *Cal.Pap.Reg.* 4:8–9; Pole was a J.P. in Bedfordshire in 1361, *C.P.R. 1361–64*, 64; for his wealth, *C.C.R. 1360–64*, 425–27.

137. Guillaume de Machaut, *La Prise d'Alexandrie*, ed. M. L. de Mas Latrie (Geneva, 1877), lines 3378–85, and 282 note 24, for Mézières's refusal to identify the noble-born leader of the English who precipitated the withdrawal; but cf. *Anonimalle Chronicle*, 51, for Hereford's presence.

138. Jones, *Chaucer's Knight*, 48, and in general, 42–49; Guillaume de Machaut, *La Prise*, 282 note 24, for Mézières's comments in a letter written for the papal legate Pierre de Thomas.

139. *Cal.Inq.P.M.* 12:56, no. 76, for Pole's death sometime before 1 October 1366; *Cal.Pap.Reg.* 4:8–10; *Anonimalle Chronicle*, 51; *Scrope-Grosvenor* 1:124–25; Luttrell, "The Hospitallers at Rhodes, 1306–1421," 299 note 43.

140. *Anonimalle Chronicle*, 52–53.

141. Guillaume de Machaut, *La Prise*, 206, 229, and lines 6794–6804.

142. Perhaps Henry Scrope of Masham, Keen, "Chaucer's Knight," 52 note 20.

143. *Chronica J. Reading*, 172.

144. Walsingham, *Historia Anglicana* 1:301–2.

145. *C.C.R. 1364–68*, 172.

146. Froissart, *Chronicles* 2:586–88; *Mandements et actes divers de Charles V*, ed. L. Delisle (Paris, 1874), 437 no. 851. Burgundy's role in the 1390s and Louis II of Bourbon's crusade in 1390 are dealt with elsewhere in this chapter. Louis's grandfather was also a crucesignatus and a patron of crusaders, 1316–36; see Tyerman, "Philip VI" and "Philip V." For the popularity of crusading with French captains, P. Contamine, *Guerre, état et société au fin du moyen âge* (Paris, 1972), 562–93.

147. Philippe de Mézières, *Songe du Vieil Pèlerin* 1:185, 399.

148. *Accounts in England*, ed. Lunt and Graves.

149. Palmer, *England, France, and Christendom*, esp. 180–210.

150. A. Molinier, "Description de deux MSS," *Archives de l'Orient Latin* 1 (1881):353–54, and in general, 335–64; Clarke, *Fourteenth Century Studies*, 288 note 2, and 286–90; Palmer, *England, France, and Christendom*, 199–202, 240–42; Atiya, *Crusade*, 140–43; Philippe de Mézières, *Letter to Richard II*, ix–xxxiv.

151. Philippe de Mézières, *Letter to Richard II*, xxii–xxiv; Froissart, *Chronicles* 2:548–88; *Westminster Chronicle*, 375, s.a. 1388; *Diplomatic Correspondence of Richard II*, 102–3, 160, nos. 151, 219; Molinier, "Description," 362.

152. Catto, "Religion and nobility."

153. *Westminster Chronicle,* 155–57, 161 and note 5, 399; Walsingham, *Historia Anglicana* 2:142, 151; Palmer, *England, France, and Christendom,* 68, 84–85, 107, 181, 190–91, 199.

154. Palmer, *England, France, and Christendom,* 186–90; Iorga, *Philippe de Mézières;* Atiya, *Crusade,* 136–54, esp. 143 note 1; Molinier, "Description," 362.

155. *Expeditions to Prussia,* 226; cf. ibid., 264 for his wages; S. Armitage-Smith, *John of Gaunt* (London, 1904), 441.

156. Palmer, *England, France, and Christendom,* 149–50, 184–85, 198–99.

157. C. L. Tipton, "The English at Nicopolis," *Speculum* 37 (1962):536 note 65, 539; Palmer, *England, France, and Christendom,* esp. 184–85, 205; Atiya, *Crusade,* 435–36; Lunt, *Financial Relations* 2:548–49.

158. Palmer, *England, France, and Christendom,* 242–44; cf. Clarke, *Fourteenth Century Studies,* 272–92.

159. Tipton, "English at Nicopolis," 528–40; Palmer, *England, France, and Christendom,* 200–1, esp. 239–40.

160. *Rot. Parl.* 3:343.

161. Palmer, *England, France, and Christendom,* 240.

CHAPTER ELEVEN

1. C. A. J. Armstrong, *The Usurpation of Richard III* (Oxford, 1969), 137; P. Tudor-Craig, *Richard III,* National Portrait Gallery (London, 1973), no. 105, describes these remarks as "the best authenticated . . . Richard is known to have made."

2. Atiya, *Crusade,* 224.

3. Capgrave, *De Illustribus Henricis,* 98–99, 156, 161, 165–66; cf. his account of the foundation of the Templars, 157–58.

4. Enguerrand de Monstrelet, *Chroniques,* ed. J. A. C. Buchon (Paris, 1836), trans. T. Johnes (London, 1877), 530.

5. Atiya, *Crusade,* 190–97; *Proceedings of the Privy Council,* ed. H. Nicolas, vol. 3 (London, 1834), 117–18.

6. *Foedera* 4:pt. 4, 105.

7. William Worcestre, *Itineraries,* ed. J. H. Harvey (Oxford, 1969), 307, 313, 372–73.

8. *Paston Letters and Papers,* ed. N. Davis (Oxford, 1971–76), vol. 2, 201.

9. *English Suits before the Paris Parlement, 1420–36,* ed. C. T. Allmand and C. A. J. Armstrong, Camden Society (London, 1982), 263; for Fastolf's books in the stewhouse at Caister, *H.M.C., Eighth Report* (London, 1881), appendix 1, 268.

10. Thomas Malory, *La Morte d'Arthur,* ed. J. Rhys (London, n.d.), vol. 2, 400–1; P. J. C. Field, "Sir Robert Malory," *Journal of Ecclesiastical History* 28 (1977):249–64.

11. Jehan de Waurin, *Recueil des chroniques d'Angleterre,* ed. W. Hardy and E. L. C. P. Hardy, RS (London, 1881), vol. 5, 430; Gransden, *Historical Writing* 2:289–91.

12. *Paston Letters,* 516–18.

13. *Registrum Abbatiae Johannis Whethamstede,* ed. H. T. Riley, RS (London, 1872–73), vol. 1, 334–35.

14. E. G. Duff, *Fifteenth-Century English Books* (Oxford, 1917), no. 164; William Caxton, *Godeffroy de Boloyne,* ed. M. N. Colvin, Early English Text Society (London, 1893).

15. *H.M.C., Eighth Report,* 268; for continental inventories, L. Delisle, *Le Cabinet des manuscrits,* vol. 1 (Paris, 1868), 10–121.

16. Duff, *English Books,* nos. 58, 96.

17. Ibid., no. 75; L. H. Butler, *The Siege of Rhodes* (London, 1980), 22–24.

18. Duff, *English Books,* nos. 285–86; *D.N.B.* entry on Alexander Barclay, the translator of Hayton's *Flowers.*

19. Desribed as *The Seige of Jerusalem, Bedfordshire Wills,* ed. M. McGregor, Bedfordshire Record Society, vol. 58 (1979), 50; for the circulation of texts, P. R. Coss, "Cultural Diffusion in Medieval England," in *Past and Present* 108 (1985):35–79.

20. Malory, *Morte d'Arthur,* 1.

21. Caxton, *Godeffroy de Boloyne,* 1–5, for the prologue.

22. *Letters and Papers of Richard III and Henry VII,* ed. J. Gairdner, RS (London, 1861–63), 128.

23. Duff, *English Books,* 53 and nos. 204–212.

24. *C.C.R. 1461–68,* 54; *Epistolae Academicae Oxoniensis,* ed. H. Anstey, Oxford Historical Society, vol. 36 (1898), 346–47; *Tractatus de Regimine Principum,* ed. J.-P. Genet, *Four English Political Tracts of the Later Middle Ages,* Camden Series (London, 1977), 70.

25. C. Colon, *Los cuatro viages del almirante y su testamento* (Madrid, 1964), 213–14.

26. William Wey, *Itineraries,* Roxburghe Club (London, 1857), xxviii–xxx.

27. Gransden, *Historical Writing* 2:231–32.

28. M. Andrieu, *Le Pontifical Romain au Moyen Age* (Vatican, 1940), vol. 2, 27, 418–20; ibid. 3:541; J. A. Brundage, "*Cruce Signari:* The Rite of Taking the Cross in England," *Traditio* 22 (1960):289–310.

29. *Literae Cantuariensis,* ed. J. Brigstocke Sheppard, RS (London, 1887–89), vol. 3, 239, no. 1051.

30. *Registrum Whethamstede* 2:191–92; cf. perhaps, the countess of Gloucester's armour with its brass cross. The St. Alban's crosses were to be worn on the chest, not shoulder.

31. D. Wilkins, *Concilia* 3: 541–44, 587–94; Lunt, *Financial Relations* 2:125–68; ibid., 558–620, for fundraising; see note 80 below, for the 1428–29 campaign.

32. N. P. Tanner, *The Church in Late Medieval Norwich* (Toronto, 1984), 87–88; cf. J. A. Brundage, "A Note on the Attestation of Crusaders' Vows," *Catholic Historical Review* 52 (1966–67):236–39.

33. *Letters of Richard III and Henry VII* 1:111–12.

34. *Paston Letters* 1:440, 446, 566–67, 570.

35. *Cal.Pap.Reg.* 7:439–40, 468.

36. See later in this chapter.

37. See note 9 above; Waurin *Recueil* 5:39–40; *Cal.Pap.Reg.* 9:519; Butler, *Seige of Rhodes,* 2, 11.

38. *Cal.Pap.Reg.* 1:158, 173, 519, 590.

39. *C.C.R. 1419–22,* 174; *Cal.Pap.Reg.* 8:278; ibid. 6:100, 150; *Wills Proved in the Consistory Court of Norwich,* ed. M. A. Farrow, Norfolk Record Society, vol. 16 (1945), vol. 3, 403; *St. Alban's Chronicle,* 107; *Cal.Pap.Reg.* 1:93, no. 72; *C.P.R. 1436–41,* 27; *Complete Peerage* 11:543; *Foedera* 5:pt. 1, 14; Tanner, *Church in Norwich,* 62; cf. *Bedfordshire Wills* 2:42 (1429); *North Country Wills,* ed. J. W. Clay, Surtees Society (Durham, 1908), 31 (1420); *Somerset Medieval Wills,* ed. F. W. Weaver, Somerset Record Society (1901), 225–26 (1473).

40. Wey, *Itineraries; Ye Oldest Diarie of Englysshe Travell: The Pilgrimage of Sir Richard Torkyngton*, ed. W. J. Loftis (London, 1884); *The Pylgrymage of Sir Richard Guylforde to The Holy Land in 1506*, ed. Sir H. Ellis, Camden Society (London, 1851).

41. Cf. *Pylgrymage of Guylforde*, 18–19, 22–24, 27, 31–32, 35, 36, with *Oldest Diarie*, 28–29, 34–35, 38–39, 44, 46, 47.

42. Wey, *Itineraries*, 25–26; cf. the similar list of crusading motives in Humbert of Romans, *Opus Tripartium* (1274), Lecoy de la Marche, "Le prediction de la croisade," 11.

43. Atiya, *Crusade*, 221 note 1.

44. *Oldest Diarie*, 62.

45. *Pylgrymage of Guylforde*, 12, 61; *Oldest Diarie*, 21–22.

46. *Pylgrymage of Guylforde*, 40, 68–69; Worcestre, *Itineraries*, 307; *Oldest Diarie*, 56.

47. *Pylgrymage of Guylforde*, 67–68; *Oldest Diarie*, 57; while the 1506 party only stayed one night in Rhodes, Torkington, who was ill, remained there for six months.

48. Archives of Malta, MS Register of the Order of St. John, 367, fol. 201 verso; licence of William Brerton to return from Bodrum to England via a pilgrimage to Egypt and the Holy Land in 1458. A transcription of this document by Dr. L. H. Butler was kindly made available to me by his widow, Mrs. G. Butler, and the curator of the library of the Venerable Order of St. John in Clerkenwell.

49. There is no satisfactory account of the western dimension of Hospitaller operations, but for a general description of their activities, Luttrell, "The Hospitallers at Rhodes, 1306–1523," 278–339.

50. D. M. Nicol, "A Byzantine Emperor in England," *University of Birmingham Historical Journal* 12:204–25.

51. Lunt, *Financial Relations* 2:549–50.

52. *Cal.Pap.Reg.* 6:176–180.

53. Nicol, "Byzantine Emperor," 216, note 36; *Diplomatic Correspondence of Richard II*, 173–74, 241, 255–56; M. D. Legge, *Anglo-Norman Letters and Petitions* (Oxford, 1941), 152, no. 103; *C.P.R. 1396–99*, 597; A. Steel, *Receipt of the Exchequer, 1337–1485* (Cambridge, 1954), 80–81, 84; Lunt, *Financial Relations* 2:551.

54. Lunt, *Financial Relations* 2:556–57.

55. Nicol, "Byzantine Emperor," 212; *Register of Bishop Robert Rede of Chichester*, ed. C. Deedes, Sussex Record Society, vol. 1 (London, 1908), 73; *Royal and Historical Letters of Henry IV*, ed. F. C. Hingeston, RS, vol. 1 (London, 1860), 39–40, 56–57; Legge, *Anglo-Norman Letters*, 418–19, 465–66; *C.C.R. 1399–1402*, 255.

56. Lunt, *Financial Relations* 2:550–57; Walsingham, *Historia Anglicana* 2:229–30; Adam of Usk, *Chronicle*, 246, 272–73.

57. Nicol, "Byzantine Emperor"; *C.C.R. 1399–1402*, 417.

58. *Reg. Bishop R. Rede*, 73–74.

59. Lunt, *Financial Relations* 2:570–82; *Issues of the Exchequer*, 401–2; *V.C.H. Cambridgeshire* 2:161; cf. Henry IV's and Henry VI's friendly contacts with Byzantium, *C.C.R. 1402–5*, 43; *Royal Letters of Henry IV* 1:101–3, 427–28; T. Bekyngton, *Official Correspondence*, ed. G. Williams, RS (London, 1872), vol. 2, 478.

60. Wilkins, *Concilia* 3:84–85; Lunt, *Financial Relations* 2:478.

61. *Register of Thomas Langley*, ed. R. L. Storey, Surtees Society (Durham, 1956–70), nos. 197, 313; E. King and H. Luke, *The Knights of St. John in the British Realm* (London, 1967), 65–66; Lunt, *Financial Relations* 2:558–59; Wilkins, *Concilia* 3:331–32; cf. Gregory IX's indulgences for

building Montfort in Galilee in 1230, by the Teutonic Knights, E. Strehlke, *Tabalae Ordinis Teutonics* (Berlin, 1869), no. 72.

62. *C.C.R. 1409–13*, 2, 3.

63. *H.M.C., Second Report* (1871) Appendix, 93; Lunt, *Financial Relations* 2:559; King and Luke, *Knights of St. John*, 66; *Complete Peerage* 5:421–27.

64. King and Luke, *Knights of St. John*, 66–67, and note 1, 67; for a photograph of the arms, ibid., facing 56.

65. Archives of Malta, MS Register 361, fols. 301 and 369, fols. 238–238 verso (Butler transcriptions).

66. Lunt, *Financial Relations* 2:591–93.

67. For what follows see Lunt, *Financial Relations* 2: 573–620.

68. *Cal.Pap.Reg.* 8:239, 246, 271; ibid. 11: 386.

69. Lunt, *Financial Relations* 2:586–90, 595–98; Polydore Vergil, *Anglica Historia*, ed. D. Hay, Camden Society (London, 1950), 120 note; cf. Lunt's translation, *Papal Revenues* 2:477.

70. *Letters of Richard III and Henry VII* 2:93–100; cf. scale laid down by Innocent VIII in 1488, Wilkins *Concilia* 3:626–29.

71. Duff, *English Books*, no. 208, cf. nos. 204–21; Lunt, *Financial Relations* 2:589 and note 77.

72. G. A. Holmes, "Cardinal Beaufort and the Crusade against the Hussites," *EHR* 88 (1973): 743.

73. Lunt, *Financial Relations* 2:149–50, 583, 585, 588; Tanner, *Church in Norwich*, 87; *H.M.C., Report on Various Collections*, vol. 2 (1908), 19–20; J. Warkworth, *A Chronicle of the First Thirteen Years of the Reign of King Edward IV*, ed. J. O. Halliwell, Camden Society (London, 1839), 49.

74. *Rot. Parl.* 3:246–47; Lunt, *Financial Relations* 2:125–68; *Register of T. Bourgchier*, ed. F. R. H. du Boulay, Canterbury and York Society (Oxford, 1957), xxx, 116–29, 136–38, 146–50; Wilkins, *Concilia* 3:541–44, 594–96, 598.

75. Wilkins, *Concilia* 3:646; Lunt, *Financial Relations* 2: 156–60; *Letters of Richard III and Henry VII* 2:116–17, and below, chapter 13.

76. *Reg. T. Bourgchier*, 116–29; Waurin, *Recueil* 5:430.

77. *Rot.Parl.* 2:175, 217–18, 221–23; ibid. 3:179, 213, 670; ibid. 6:115.

78. Holmes, "Cardinal Beaufort"; cf. lack of support for John XXIII's crusade against Ladislaus of Naples.

79. Lunt, *Financial Relations* 2:134, 147–50, 158, 581–82; C. Ross, *Edward IV* (London, 1974), 371–72, 373, 385–86; Steel, *Receipt of Exchequer*, 222–26.

80. Holmes, "Cardinal Beaufort," esp. 743, for the funds and 741–42, for the troops; cf. Lunt, *Financial Relations* 2:562–70, and for the Naples crusade, 559–62; *Cal.Pap.Reg.* 6:170, 171–72, 183–85; *Reg. T. Langley*, nos. 794–96.

81. Wilkins, *Concilia* 3:588.

82. *Registrum Whethamstede* 1:333–34.

83. *Rot. Parl.* 6:156; *Statutes of the Realm*, 12 E. IV, c. 2; ibid., 1 Ric. III, c. ll; ibid., 3 Hen. VII, c. 13; *Cal. State Papers* (*Domestic*), Henry VIII, XIII, 1, no. 115; F. Braudel, *The Mediterranean and the Mediterranean World in the Age of Philip II*, trans. S. Reynolds (London, 1973), 801 and note 227.

84. *Registrum Whethamstede*, vol. 1, 268–79.

85. Quoted by C. Head, "Pope Pius II and the Wars of the Roses," *Archivium historiae pontificae* 8 (1970):150.

86. £160 8s according to Lunt, *Financial Relations* 2:584. For the embassy of Coppini in general, Head, "Pope Pius," 139–78.

CHAPTER TWELVE

1. See in general, P. Contamine, *Guerre, état et société;* idem, *La Guerre au moyen âge* (Paris, 1980); Keen, *Chivalry,* 238–53, for a recent survey.

2. J. R. Strayer, *The Reign of Philip the Fair* (Princeton, N.J., 1980).

3. Prestwich, *The Three Edwards;* for late medieval England in general, the best survey is still M. H. Keen, *England in the Later Middle Ages* (London, 1973).

4. *Rot. Parl.* 4:62–63.

5. *Political Songs,* 163; *Rot. Parl.* 2:362; for Burghersh, *Cal.Pap.Reg.* 3:394–95.

6. Keen, *Chivalry,* 252.

7. H. Bonet, *Tree of Battles,* trans. G. W. Coopland (Liverpool, 1949); N. A. R. Wright, "The Tree of Battles of Honoré Bouvet," *War, Literature, and Politics in the Late Middle Ages,* ed. C. T. Allmand (Liverpool, 1976), 12–31.

8. Cf. above, chapter 1; A. K. McHardy, "Liturgy and Propaganda during the Hundred Years War," *Studies in Church History,* vol. 18, ed. S. Mews (Oxford, 1982), 215–27; *Councils and Synods* 1:pt. 1, 54, 206; ibid. 2:pt. 2, 1129 note 2, 1191–92, 1195–98, 1375 note 1; for the red crosses in Prussia and at Blackheath, *Anonimalle Chronicle,* 139, 171; W. R. Jones, "The English Church and Propaganda during the Hundred Years War," *Journal of British Studies* 19 (1979):18–30.

9. Henry of Huntingdon, *Historia,* 262–63, 270–72; *De Expugnatione Lyxbonensi,* 71–85, 105–115.

10. Geoffrey of Monmouth, *Historia Regum Britanniae,* ed. A. Griscom and R. Ellis Jones (London, 1929), 437–38.

11. *Waverley Annals, Ann. Mon.* 2:287; *Flores historiarum* 2:495; *Political Songs,* 22–23.

12. N. J. Housley, "Crusades against Christians," in *Crusade and Settlement,* ed. Edbury, 31.

13. See above, chapter 6.

14. Cf. *Flores historiarum* 2:475, and Rishanger, *Chronica,* 25–26.

15. See above, chapter 6.

16. See above, chapter 5.

17. W. R. Jones, "English against the Celtic Fringe," *Cahiers d'histoire mondiale* 13 (1971):155–71; D. Douie, *Archbishop Pecham* (Oxford, 1952), 235–37, 242, 265; see note 8 above; *Historical Papers from Northern Registers,* 112–14.

18. *Chronica J. Oxenedes,* 226; A. D. Macquarrie, "The Ideal of the Holy War in Scotland, 1296–1330," *Innes Review* 32 (1981): 83–92; idem, *Scotland and the Crusades,* 71–73.

19. Rishanger, *Chronica,* 194.

20. Printed as *Annales Regis Edwardi Primi,* Fragment 1 from a MS of St. Alban's material in Rishanger, *Chronica,* 439.

21. *Siege of Carlaverock,* ed. N. H. Nicolas (London, 1828), 52–54.

22. Macquarrie, *Scotland and the Crusades,* 71–73.

23. *Documents and Records Illustrating the History of Scotland,* ed. F. Palgrave (London, 1837), 330, 347–48.

24. Trivet, *Annales,* 408–9; Murimuth, *Continuatio Chronicarum,* 9.

25. *Historical Papers from Northern Registers,* 189–91.

26. *E.H.D.* 3:543.

27. Tyerman, "Philip V," 18, 20, for a French attempt at a crusade against Flanders.

28. *Political Poems and Songs*, ed. T. Wright, RS (London, 1859–61), 41–51; R. Higden, *Polychronicon*, ed. J. R. Lumby, RS (London, 1882), vol. 8, 342; H. Knighton, *Chronicon*, 42, 45.

29. Parker, *The Knights Templars in England*, 48, note 50.

30. *C.C.R. 1346–49*, 57, for the use of Dominican preachers in 1346; *Political Poems* 1:53–58; cf. other poems and the "Bridlington Prophecy," ibid., 58–215; Knighton, *Chronicon* 2:80, 88, 94, 110; for a different approach to some of this material, Barnie, *War in Medieval Society*.

31. *List of Ancient Correspondence* 40:nos. 2, 5, 7, 9–22; cf. Sutherland, *Novel Disseisin*, 54–55.

32. *Fasculi zizaniorum Magistri Johannis Wyclif cum Tritico*, ed. W. W. Shirley, RS (London, 1858), 507.

33. E. Perroy, *L'Angleterre et le grand schisme d'Occident* (Paris, 1933); Palmer, *England, France, and Christendom*, esp. 1–87; Russell, *English Intervention in Spain*, esp. 173–525.

34. Froissart, *Chronicles* 1:756; Perroy, *L'Angleterre*, 232.

35. See also Lunt, *Financial Relations* 2:535–44.

36. In addition to Palmer, see, on the factions, Goodman, *Loyal Conspiracy*.

37. Perroy, *L'Angleterre*, 397–404.

38. *Rot. Parl.* 3:133–34, 137, 140; Perroy, *L'Angleterre*, 181.

39. *Foedera* 3:pt. 3, 145.

40. Perroy, *L'Angleterre*, 189; Lunt, *Financial Relations* 2:541, collects the references.

41. *C.P.R. 1381–85*, 261.

42. Most recently on Wyclif's criticisms, Siberry, "Criticism of Crusading in Fourteenth-Century England," 127–28. Her conclusions cannot entirely be accepted.

43. Froissart, *Chronicles* 1:756; *Westminster Chronicle*, 35; cf. *Rot. Parl.* 3:146–48.

44. *C.C.R. 1381–85*, 280, 290, 305; Walsingham, *Historia Anglicana* 2:88, 94.

45. *Rot. Parl.* 3:146–48; Lunt, *Financial Relations* 2:543; *Issues of the Exchequer*, 222–23.

46. *C.C.R. 1381–85*, 284–85.

47. Perroy, *L'Angleterre*, 189–90.

48. *Westminster Chronicle*, 45.

49. Walsingham, *Historia Anglicana* 2:95; Perroy, *L'Angleterre*, 189.

50. Froissart, *Chronicles* 1:758–65.

51. Walsingham, *Historia Anglicana* 2:88–89.

52. Perroy, *L'Angleterre*, 195.

53. *Rot. Parl.* 3:134.

54. Ibid., 147; Knighton, *Chronicon*, 201–2.

55. *C.C.R. 1381–85*, 260–61, 305.

56. Wilkins, *Concilia* 3:177–78.

57. Palmer, *England, France, and Christendom*, 47–50.

58. *Eulogium historiarum*, 357; Walsingham, *Historia Anglicana* 2:95–96; *Westminster Chronicle*, 45.

59. Walsingham, *Historia Anglicana* 2:95.

60. *Rot. Parl.* 3:153–55; *C.C.R. 1381–85*, 368–69.

61. *C.C.R. 1381–85*, 305.

62. *Westminster Chronicle*, 33, 39.

63. Ibid., 37.

64. *Rot. Parl.* 3:147–48, 153–55.

65. See in addition, Lunt, *Financial Relations* 2:544–48.

66. *Westminster Chronicle,* 161.

67. *C.P.R. 1385–89,* 319.

68. *Calendar of Select Pleas and Memoranda of the City of London, 1381–1412,* ed. A. H. Thomas (Cambridge, 1932), 36; Barnie, *War in Medieval Society,* 142–45.

69. *Westminster Chronicle,* 195.

70. Walsingham, *Historia Anglicana* 2:143; Higden, *Polychronicon* 8:474.

71. *Cal.Pap.Reg.* 4:270–71.

72. *Eulogium historiarum* 3:357.

73. *Gesta Abbatum* 2:416.

74. Ibid., 417; Walsingham, *Ypodigma Neustriae,* 348.

75. *Gesta Abbatum* 2:416–18; *Annales S. Albani a Johanne Amundesham monacho,* ed. H. T. Riley, RS (London, 1870–71), vol. 1, 86–87.

76. See below, chapter 13.

77. *The Brut,* ed. F. Brie (London, 1908), vol. 2, 378.

78. *Gesta Henrici Quinti,* ed. F. Taylor and J. S. Roskell (Oxford, 1975), 79.

79. Ibid., 87, 99.

80. McHardy, "Liturgy and Propaganda."

81. *Gesta Henrici Quinti,* 101–13.

82. Enguerrand de Monstrelet, *Chroniques* 1:483.

Chapter Thirteen

1. M. H. Dodds and R. Dodds, *The Pilgrimage of Grace and the Exeter Conspiracy* (Cambridge, 1915), 238 and refs. The Five Wounds badge, said to be that which belonged to Sir Robert Constable, is illustrated as the frontispiece to F. Rose-Troup, *The Western Rebellion of 1549* (London, 1913).

2. Dodds, *Pilgrimage of Grace,* 18–19; E. Hall, *Chronicle* (London, 1809), 520; *D.N.B.* entries for Darcy, Constable, and Ellekar.

3. *Calendar of Letters and Papers Foreign and Domestic of the Reign of Henry VIII,* ed. J. Gairdner (London, 1890), vol. 12, pt. 1, 402.

4. Dodds, *Pilgrimage of Grace,* 274; Rose-Troup, *Western Rebellion,* 413.

5. *Mandeville's Travels,* 2.

6. Braudel, *Mediterranean World* 2:665; J. Foxe, *Acts and Monuments,* ed. S. R. Cattley (London, 1837–41), vol. 4, 52; in general, K. Setton, *The Papacy and the Levant,* vols. 3 and 4 (Philadelphia, 1984).

7. Foxe, *Acts* 4:77, 93.

8. Braudel, *Mediterranean World* 2:843.

9. Hall, *Chronicles,* 520.

10. A. B. Ferguson, *The Indian Summer of English Chivalry* (Durham, N.C., 1960), 59.

11. Ibid., 8; *D.N.B.* entries for Berners and Pynson; Duff, *English Books,* nos. 285, 286.

12. Duff, *English Books,* 126, nos. 58 and 96; Ferguson, *Indian Summer.*

13. *D.N.B.* entry on Alexander Barclay, the translator; for Hayton's original, *Recueil des historiens des croisades: Documents Arméniens,* vol. 2, ed. C. Kohler (Paris, 1906), 111–363.

14. Foxe, *Acts* 4:18–123, 131–32, for Foxe's prayer for salvation from the Turks.

15. Dodds, *Pilgrimage of Grace,* 82.

16. "Not Amurath an Amurath succeeds/But Harry Harry," *Henry IV*, Part 2, act 5, sc. 2, lines 48–49; cf. *Othello*, act 1, sc. 3, lines 1–43; S. Welles, a letter in *Times Literary Supplement* (1984), 811; E. Jones, " 'Othello', Lepanto and the Cyprus Wars." *Shakespeare Survey* 21 (Cambridge, 1968):47–52; *Othello*, act 1, sc. 3, lines 20–35, suggests a modification of Jones's view, as the lines indicate Rhodes still to be in Christian hands.

17. Cf. *Henry IV*, Part 1, act 1, sc. 1, lines 18–27; on the interest in war against the Turks, L. B. Wright, *Middle Class Culture in Elizabethan England* (Chapel Hill, N.C., 1935), 543–545.

18. H. G. Rawlinson, "The Embassy of William Harborne to Constantinople, 1583–88," *TRHS*, 4th ser., 5 (1922):5–6; A. L. Horniker, "William Harborne and the Beginning of Anglo-Turkish Diplomatic and Commercial Relations," *Journal of Modern History* 14 (1942):306–315.

19. Foxe, *Acts* 4:122; cf., in general, K. R. Firth, *The Apocalyptic Tradition in Reformation Britain, 1530–1645* (Oxford, 1979); for the disputes as to the relative claims of pope and Turk as Anti-Christ, C. Hill, *Anti-Christ in Seventeenth Century England* (London, 1971), 35.

20. Foxe, *Acts* 4:19–20.

21. Ibid. 2:445–46; ibid. 4:27–28, 33–34, 38, 52, 113, 117–20.

22. Ibid. 4:19–20; cf. ibid. 5:666 and note 4, where Foxe quotes a remark of Luther, which he glosses: "He meaneth that we should specially reform our lives, which deserve the Turks to plague us." This is a standard Protestant theme. Cf. Pierre Viret (1560): "God is now punishing the Christians through the Turks . . . the Turks are . . . the rod and scourge and fury of God." Quoted by Braudel, *Mediterranean World* 2:665.

23. *Chronicle and Political Papers of Edward VI*, ed. W. K. Jordan (London, 1966), e.g., 85, 144.

24. Foxe, *Acts* 4:69; cf. Lucas de Tolentis's description of the crusade in 1473 as "la chose publique de la religion chrétienne," R. J. Walsh, "Charles the Bold and the Crusade," *Journal of Medieval History* 3 (1977):56.

25. G. Burnet, *History of the Reformation*, ed. E. Nares (London, 1830), vol. 4, 322.

26. R. Holinshed, *Chronicles of England and Ireland* (1587; reprint, 1808–9), vol. 3, 262–64.

27. Wright, *Middle Class Culture*, 544, for Cartwright's comments on the advantages to Christians of inciting war between Turkey and Persia; P. Holmes, *Resistance and Compromise: The Political Thought of the Elizabethan Catholics* (Cambridge, 1982), 143.

28. *The Poems of James VI of Scotland*, ed. J. Craigie, Scottish Text Society (Edinburgh, 1955–58), xlviii, 197–257, esp. 198 and lines 1, 292, 971–72, 994–96, 1022–24.

29. R. B. Wernham, *Before the Armada* (London, 1966), 50, 58, 79, 93–94; S. B. Chrimes, *Henry VII* (London, 1972), 288–89, 304–5; J. J. Scarisbrick *Henry VIII* (London, 1968), esp. 105–6.

30. B. André, *Vita Henrici VII, Memorials of Henry VII*, ed. J. Gairdner, RS (London, 1858), 54, 83, 112; *Letters of Richard III and Henry VII* 1:109, 116–18, 154–56, 158–61, 170, 175, 176, 287–88, 441; ibid. 2:125–32, 138–39, 146, 168–79.

31. Wernham, *Before the Armada*, 94.

32. *Letters of Richard III and Henry VII* 2:125–32. On Henry VII's role, Setton, *Papacy and Levant* 3:47–50.

33. André, *Vita Henrici VII*, 410–14. Charles VIII linked his invasion of Italy in 1494 with plans to reconquer Constantinople and recover Jerusalem. For an example of Julius II's rhetoric, *Letters of Richard III and Henry VII* 2:170–74.

34. *Letters of Richard III and Henry VII* 1:xlv; Wilkins, *Concilia* 3:646; *Letters of Richard III and Henry VII* 2:lxiii; above note 33.

35. *Letters of Richard III and Henry VII* 2:116.

36. Ibid. 1:287–88, 441; King and Luke, *Knights of St. John*, 99 and note 1.

37. Luttrell, "The Hospitallers at Rhodes, 1421–1523," esp. 333–35; Butler, *Siege of Rhodes*, 24.

38. Dodds, *Pilgrimage of Grace*, 19; Scarisbrick, *Henry VIII*, 28 and note 1; Hall, *Chronicles*, 520–22.

39. Wernham, *Before the Armada*, 93–94.

40. Scarisbrick, *Henry VIII*, 105–6; *Letters of Henry VIII* 3:432; for the claims to Cyprus made informally in 1516 and 1522, G. F. Hill, *History of Cyprus* (Cambridge, 1940–52), vol. 1, 68–69.

41. *Letters of Henry VIII* 3:537, 689; A. Mifsud, *Knights Hospitaller of the Venerable Tongue of England* (Malta, 1914), 190–91, and the illustration facing 190; King and Luke, *Knights of St. John*, 100–2.

42. Scarisbrick, *Henry VIII*, 106: Perhaps it "represented a momentary, but sincere impulse of an impetuous and maybe bored man."

43. *Letters of Richard III and Henry VII* 1:111–12; *Calendar of State Papers, Spanish* 1: (Henry VII), 212, no. 245.

44. Hall, *Chronicles*, 522.

45. King and Luke, *Knights of St. John*, 108–9.

46. *D.N.B.*; George Peele, *The Battle of Alcazar*, ed. J. Yoklavich, in *The Dramatic Works of George Peele*, ed. C. T. Prouty (New Haven, Conn., 1952–70), vol. 2, esp. 247–73, 343–45.

47. Dodds, *Pilgrimage of Grace*, 380; *Letters of Henry VIII* 11:1336.

48. See above, chapter 11.

49. Duff, *English Books*, nos. 204–21; A. W. Pollard and G. R. Redgrave, *Short-Title Catalogue, 1475–1640*, vol. 2, ed. W. A. Jackson, F. S. Ferguson, and K. F. Pantzer (London, 1976), nos. 114–33; Lunt, *Financial Relations* 2:593–620; J. J. Scarisbrick, *The English People and the Reformation* (Oxford, 1984), 57–58.

50. T. Bindoff, ed., *The House of Commons, 1509–58*, vol. 1 of *History of Parliament* (London, 1983), 590–92; *D.N.B.* entry.

51. S. Dyer, "The Weston Family and the Order of St. John," *St. John Historical Society Newsletter* (September 1983):8–9; E. Waterton, *MS Roll of English and Irish Knights Hospitaller* (1903), St. John's Gate MS, 270, 272–75, 318–20; King and Luke, *Knights of St. John*, 74–75, 90, 98–106.

52. J. E. Powell and K. Wallis, *The House of Lords in the Middle Ages* (London, 1968), plate 18, cf. plates 20 and 21.

53. Butler Papers, St. John's Gate MSS; Notes and transcriptions from Archives of Malta, Register 404, fol. 149–150v; Waterton, *Rolls*, 296; King and Luke, *Knights of St. John*, 98.

54. Butler Papers, File A.6, based on evidence from the order's registers.

55. King and Luke, *Knights of St. John*, 90–91. The full complement would have been twenty-eight; only fourteen names are recorded for the 1480 seige. Ibid., 88.

56. Ibid., 114–15.

57. Butler Papers, A.O.M. 392, fols. 104v–107; Butler Papers, file "Rhodes and England, 1450–1500."

58. King and Luke, *Knights of St. John*, 72; Ross, *Edward IV*, 96 note 3, 183 for the three hundred pounds fine on Prior Tournay and three other Hospitallers in 1471; Butler Papers, Box "England," File "Langstrother."

59. King and Luke, *Knights of St. John*, 101–2.

60. Butler Papers, file "Rhodes and England, 1501–23," A.O.M. 393, fol. 110–110v, 30 August 1501. Robert Dalausen, viceregent of the turcopolier (the head of the English langue at Rhodes) and preceptor of Temple Combe and Aulston, sent two other English brothers from Rhodes back home to investigate the running and yield of his preceptories. They were to report back to Rhodes where, Dalausen noted, most of the English preceptors were then resident. Dalausen was worried at deteriorating efficiency and diminishing returns. Cf. Butler Papers, file O.S.J. II, for a letter of 1448 by a Hospitaller in Rhodes giving detailed instructions to his bailiff on the running of his estates at Temple Brewer in Lincolnshire; E. J. King, "A Letter to his Agent," *Order of St. John of Jerusalem Historical Pamphlets* no. 4 (1930).

61. P. Willis, "Temple Sowerby," *St. John Historical Society Newsletter* (December 1983):11.

62. Bindoff, *House of Commons, 1509–58* 1:414–15.

63. Ibid. 3:308–10, 378–79, 482. Notice the typical family links of Richard Shelley, nephew and cousin of Hospitallers.

64. King and Luke, *Knights of St. John*, 99–100.

65. Mifsud, *Knights Hospitaller*, 190–91, and picture facing 190. The armaments were part of Henry's promised gift of twenty thousand crowns.

66. Bindoff, *House of Commons, 1509–58* 1:414–15.

67. Ibid., 590–92.

68. King and Luke, *Knights of St. John*, 114; *Letters of Henry VIII* 7:466–68, no. 1206.

69. King and Luke, *Knights of St. John*, 104–7, for the executions and the 1540 dissolution.

70. Translated in ibid., appendix C, 265–68.

71. Ibid., 91, 111, 114, note 1.

72. Bindoff, *House of Commons, 1509–58* 3:482; *Journals of the house of Lords* 1:536–37, 541; *Statutes of the Realm* 4:1 Eliz. I, c. 24.

73. Bindoff, *House of Commons, 1509–58* 3:308–10.

74. *Cal. State Papers, Venetian* (1509–19)2:63–64, no. 169.

75. *Cal. State Papers, Spanish* 4:pt. 2, vol. 2, 813, no. 1130.

76. Ibid., 843, no. 1145.

77. *Letters of Henry VIII* 7:466–68, no. 1206.

78. *The Genius of Venice*, catalogue of the Royal Academy of Arts exhibition, ed. J. Martineau and C. Hope (London, 1983), 401, H.19; G. Mattingly, *The Defeat of the Spanish Armada* (London, 1961), 207; Holinshed, *Chronicles* 3:800; Dodds, *Pilgrimage of Grace*, 330; R. Marius, *Thomas More* (London, 1985), 348; cf., for More's use of the image of the Great Turk in his *Dialogue of Comfort against Tribulation*, A. Fox, *Thomas More* (Oxford, 1982), 223–42.

79. *Cal. State Papers, Spanish* 5:1, 559–60, no. 218.

80. M. E. James, *English Politics and the Concept of Honour, 1485–1642, Past and Present* Supplement 3 (1978):37 and refs.

81. *Cal. State Papers, Rome* 2:208–9, 289, 290, 367, 492, 493.

82. Ibid., 208–9, 289, 290, 367, 492, 493.

83. *D.N.B.* entry for Sanders; cf. *D.N.B.* entries for Stukeley and FitzMaurice (under FitzGerald).

84. Holmes, *Resistance*, esp. 23–29, and, for the reaction against Sanders's position, 29–34.

85. Ibid., 143–46.

86. W. Allen, *Defence of Sir William Stanley's Surrender at Deventer, 1587*, ed. T. Heywood, Chetham Society (1851), esp. 20, 24–25, 32.

87. Holmes, *Resistance*, 143–44.

88. Mattingly, *Armada*, 207–8.

89. *Somers Tracts*, ed. W. Scott (London, 1809–15), vol. 1, 149–60.

90. Holinshed, *Chronicles* 4:235; Rose-Troup, *Western Rebellion*, esp. appendix A, 411–14.

91. For Aske's interrogation, *Letters of Henry VIII* 12:1, 412, no. 901, item 73.

92. James, *English Politics*, 37–39. Given Darcy's plotting in 1534, and his association with Constable and the Durham faction and with the badge of Five Wounds, it may be going too far to say with James that Darcy belonged to a peace party. The difference between him and Constable was that Darcy set limits to his willingness to fight, being only prepared to justify violence against Henry if the king was proven to be a heretic; i.e., Darcy was prepared to join in a holy war, a crusade, but not in a civil secular rebellion; see note 57 above, and Dodds, *Pilgrimage of Grace*, 304. This revolt has provoked sharp controversy among modern historians, especially over the role of spiritual and political motivations. See in particular, C. S. L. Davies, "The Pilgrimage of Grace Reconsidered," *Past and Present* 41 (1968):54 ff., and G. R. Elton, "Politics and the Pilgrimage of Grace," *After the Reformation: Essays in Honour of J. A. Hexter*, ed. B. C. Malament (Manchester, 1980), 25–56. See now Davies's restatement of his views, and especially his interesting discussion of the religious symbols used by the rebels, in "Popular Religion and the Pilgrimage of Grace," *Order and Disorder in Early Modern England*, ed. A. Fletcher and J. Stevenson (Cambridge, 1985), 58–88. I am very grateful to Mr. Davies for allowing me to view a typescript of this article before publication, when I was first considering the problems he discusses so lucidly.

93. Dodds, *Pilgrimage of Grace*, 262, a hymn by the monks of Sawley.

94. Ibid., 274; Rose-Troup, *Western Rebellion*, 413.

95. Rose-Troup, *Western Rebellion*, 413; A. W. Pollard and G. R. Redgrave, *Short-Title Catalogue, 1475–1640*, vol. 1 (London, 1926), no. 13679 (I am grateful to Mrs. J. Loach and Dr. P. Slack for this reference).

96. Holmes, *Resistance*, 143.

97. Foxe, *Acts* 5:147.

98. *Somers Tracts* 1:190, 203, in tract *The Execution of Justice in England* (c. 1581–82).

99. *Letters of Henry VIII* 12:pt. 1, 402–3.

100. Dodds, *Pilgrimage of Grace*, 304.

101. C. Sharp, *Memorials of the Rebellion in 1569* (London, 1840), 204–5.

102. Ferguson, *Indian Summer*, ix, 34, 78, 162, 172, 188, 218–21.

103. J. A. Dop, *Eliza's Knights: Scholars, Poets, and Puritans in the Netherlands, 1572–86* (Leiden, 1981), 18, 156–76, chapter 5, passim; cf. R. C. Strong and J. A. van Dorsten, *Leicester's Triumph* (London, 1964).

104. Dop, *Eliza's Knights*, 2–4, 174; cf. Stukeley being condemned for lack of patriotism, not irreligion, in Peele's *Battle of Alcazar*, 262.

105. Dop, *Eliza's Knights*, 99 and note 2, 167; P. A. Jorgensen, "Theoretical Views of War in Elizabethan England," *Journal of the History of Ideas* 13 (1952):480.

106. *Somers Tracts* 1:447, in an anti-Spanish pamphlet couched in terms of a letter to Mendoza, the Spanish ambassador in Paris.

107. M. Walzer, *The Revolution of the Saints* (London, 1966), esp. 8, 91, and in general, chapter 8, "Politics and War."

108. B. Capp, *English Almanacs, 1500–1800* (Ithaca, N.Y., 1979), 99; cf. Firth, *Apocalyptic Tradition*, and Hill, *AntiChrist*.

109. *Diary of Abraham de la Pryme*, ed. C. Jackson, Surtees Society (Durham, 1870), 132.

110. Hill, *AntiChrist*, 182: Capp, *Almanacs*, 99, 176; cf. the doom-laden prophecy of Ralph Josselin, vicar of Earl's Colne, Essex, in his *Diary*, ed. A. MacFarlane (London, 1976), 653, on hearing of a Turkish victory in Transylvania in 1660.

111. A. I. Suckling, *The History and Antiquities of the County of Suffolk*, vol. 2 (London, 1846), 228.

112. *Henry IV*, Part 2, act 1, sc. 1, lines 19–21 (c. 1597).

Bibliography

This list is not intended to be exhaustive. For the chief sources and major secondary works on the crusades in general, readers should consult the bibliographies in the studies by Runciman, Mayer, and Riley-Smith. The aims here are to indicate the main sources upon which this investigation has been based and to note secondary works of particular relevance and use (and therefore not all works cited in the notes have been included here as well). To do otherwise would entail a complete bibliography of all medieval English and much of medieval European history; in short, a book in itself.

SOURCES

It will be seen that, where possible, I have noted translations of important chronicles. This is for the convenience of the nonspecialist. The serious researcher or student must, of course, rely upon the originals, but translations can engage the interest of those lacking linguistic expertise or confidence and perhaps may inspire the acquisition of the skills necessary to penetrate, understand and enjoy the subject more deeply.

Accounts Rendered by Papal Collectors in England, 1317–78. Ed. W. E. Lunt and E. B. Graves. Philadelphia, 1968.

Acta S. Langton. Ed. K. Major. London, 1950.

Adam of Bremen. *Gesta Hammaburgensis Ecclesiae Pontificum.* Ed. B. Schmeidler. Hanover, 1917.

Adam of Usk. *Chronicle.* Ed. E. M. Thompson. London, 1904.

Aelfric. *Lives of Saints.* Ed. W. W. Skeat. Early English Text Society. 2 vols. London, 1881–90.

Albert of Aix. *Liber Christianae expeditionis. R.H.C.Occ.*, vol. 4.

Allen, W. *Defence of Sir William Stanley's Surrender at Deventer, 1587.* Ed. T. Heywood. Chetham Society, 1851.

Ambroise, *The Crusade of Richard Lion-Heart.* Trans. M. J. Hubert and J. L. La Monte. New York, 1976.

Ancient Charters prior to A.D. 1200. Ed. J. H. Round. London, 1888.

André, B. *Vita Henrici VII: Memorials of Henry VII.* Ed. J. Gairdner. RS. London, 1858.

Anna Comnena. *The Alexiad.* Trans. E. R. A. Sewter. London, 1969.

Annales Cambriae. Ed. J. W. ab Ithel. RS. London, 1860.

Annales Gandenses. Ed. H. Johnstone. London, 1951.

Annales Londoniensis. Chronicles of Edward I and II, ed. W. Stubbs, vol. 1. RS. London, 1882.

Annales Monastici. Ed. H. R. Luard. 5 vols. London, 1864–69.

Annales Paulini. Chronicles of Edward I and II, ed. W. Stubbs, vol. 1. RS. London, 1882.

Annales Regis Edwardi Primi. William Rishanger, *Chronica,* ed. H. T. Riley. London, 1865.

Annales S. Albani a Johanne Amundesham monacho. Ed. H. T. Riley. RS. 2 vols. London, 1871.

Anonimalle Chronicle. Ed. V. H. Galbraith. Manchester, 1927.

Anselm. *Opera Omnia.* Ed. F. S. Schmitt. 6 vols. Edinburgh, 1938–61.

Baluze, E. *Vitae paparum Avenionensis.* Ed. G. Mollat. 4 vols. Paris, 1914–27.

Barling's Chronicle. Chronicles of Edward I and II, ed. W. Stubbs, vol. 2. RS. London, 1883.

Barnwell Chronicle. Memoriali Walteri de Coventria, ed. W. Stubbs. RS. London, 1872–73.

Bede, *Ecclesiastical History of the English People.* Ed. B. Colgrave and R. A. B. Mynors. Oxford, 1969.

Bedfordshire Wills. Ed. F. A. Page-Turner and M. McGregor. Bedfordshire Record Society. Vol. 2, 1914. Vol. 58, 1979.

Bekyngton, Thomas. *Official Correspondence.* Ed. G. Williams. RS. London, 1872.

Benedict XII. *Lettres closes et patentes intéressant des pays autres que la France.* Ed. J. M. Vidal. Paris, 1913–50.

Blaauw, W. H. "Letters of Ralph de Neville." Sussex Archeological Collections, vol. 3. 1850.

Bonet, H. *Tree of Battles.* Trans. G. W. Coopland. Liverpool, 1949.

Bracton, Henry de. *De legibus et consuetudinibus Angliae.* Ed. T. Twiss. 6 vols. RS. London, 1878–83.

————. *De legibus et consuetudinibus Angliae.* Ed. and trans. S. E. Thorne. 4 vols. Cambridge, Mass., 1968–77.

Bracton's Note Book. Ed. F. W. Maitland. London, 1887.

The Brut. Ed. F. Brie. London, 1908.

Brut y Tywysogion. Ed. J. W. ab Ithel. RS. London, 1860.

Brygg, Thomas. *Itinerarium in Terram Sanctum domini Thomae de Swynburne. Archives de l'Orient Latin* 2 (1884).

Cabaret d'Oronville, J. *La chronique du bon duc Loys de Bourbon.* Ed. A.-M. Chazaud. Paris, 1876.

Calendar of Chancery Warrants, 1244–1326.

Calendar of Close Rolls.

Calendar of Documents preserved in France illustrative of the History of Great Britain and Ireland, 918–1206. Ed. J. H. Round. London, 1899.

Calendar of Documents relating to Scotland. Ed. J. Bain. London, 1881–88.

Calendar of Inquisitions Post Mortem.

Calendar of Letters and Papers Foreign and Domestic of the Reign of Henry VIII. Ed. J. Gairdner. London, 1890.

Calendar of Liberate Rolls.

Calendar of Papal Registers. Ed. W. T. Bliss et al. 14 vols. London, 1893–1960.

Calendar of Patent Rolls.

Calendar of the Roll of the Justices in Eyre, 1227 (Buckinghamshire). Ed. J. G. Jenkins. Buckinghamshire Archeological Society, vol. 6. 1945.

Calendar of Select Pleas and Memoranda of the City of London, 1381–1412. Ed. A. H. Thomas. Cambridge, 1932.

Calendar of State Papers, Domestic.

Calendar of State Papers, Rome.

Calendar of State Papers, Spanish.

Calendar of State Papers, Venetian.

Canon of Bridlington. *Gesta Edwardi Tertii. Chronicles of Edward I and II,* ed. W. Stubbs, vol. 2. RS. London, 1883.

Capgrave, John. *De Illustribus Henricis.* Ed. F. C. Hingeston. RS. London, 1858.

Cartularium Abbathiae de Whiteby. Ed. J. C. Atkinson. 2 vols. Surtees Society. Durham, 1879–81.

Cartularium Monasterii de Rameseia. Ed. W. H. Hart and P. A. Lyons. 3 vols. RS. London, 1884–93.

Cartulary of the Augustinian Priory of Bruton. Ed. Bishop Hobhouse et al. Somerset Record Society, 1894.

Cartulary of Carisbrooke Priory. Ed. S. F. Hockey. Isle of Wight, 1981.

Cartulary of the Cluniac Priory of Montacute. Ed. Bishop Hobhouse et al. Somerset Record Society. 1894.

Cartulary of God's House, Southampton. Ed. J. M. Kaye. Southampton Record Series. Southampton, 1976.

Cartulary of Haughmond Abbey. Ed. V. Rees. Shropshire Archeological Society. Cardiff, 1985.

Cartulary of the Hospital of St. John the Baptist. Ed. H. E. Salter. Oxford Historical Society, vol. 68, Oxford, 1914–17.

Cartulary of the Knights of St. John of Jerusalem in England: Secunda Camera, Essex. Ed. M. Gervers. London, 1982.

Cartulary of Muchelney Abbey. Ed. E. H. Bates. Somerset Record Society. 1899.

Cartulary of Osney Abbey. Ed. H. E. Salter. Oxford Historical Society, vol. 89. Oxford, 1929–36.

Cartulary of the Priory of St. Denys near Southampton. Ed. E. O. Blake. Southampton Record Society. Southampton, 1981.

Cartulary of St. Frideswide's, Oxford. Ed. S. R. Wigram. Oxford Historical Society, vol. 31. Oxford, 1896.

Caxton, William. *Godeffroy de Boloyne.* Ed. M. N. Colvin. Early English Text Society. London, 1893.

La chanson de la croisade Albigeoise. Ed. E. Martin-Chabot. 2 vols. Paris, 1931–61.

Les chansons de croisade. Ed. J. Bédier and P. Auby. Paris, 1909.

The Chapter Act Book of the Collegiate Church of St. John of Beverley. Ed. A. F. Leach. Vol. 2. Surtees Society. Durham, 1903.

Charters of the Earldom of Hereford, 1095–1201. Ed. D. Walker. *Camden Miscellany* 22 (1964).

Charters of the Honour of Mowbray. Ed. D. E. Greenway. London, 1972.

Charters of Norwich Cathedral Priory. Ed. B. Dodwell. Vol. 2. London, 1985.

Chartes de prieuré de Longueville. Ed. P. le Cacheux. Société de l'histoire de Normandie. Vol. 89. 1934.

Chartularium Prioratus de Brinkburne. Ed. W. Page. Surtees Society. Durham, 1893.

Chartulary of the Priory of Boxgrove. Ed. L. Fleming. Sussex Record Society. Vol. 59. 1960.

Chartulary of the Priory of Healaugh Park. Ed. J. S. Purvis. Yorkshire Archeological Society Record Series. 1936.

Chartulary of the Priory of St. Pancras of Lewes. Ed. L. F. Salzman. Sussex Record Society. Lewes, 1932.

Chaucer, Geoffrey. *Canterbury Tales.* Ed. W. Skeat. Oxford, 1894–97.

Chronica Johannis de Oxenedes. Ed. H. Ellis. RS. London, 1859.

Chronica Johannis de Reading et Anonymi Cantuariensi. Ed. J. Tait. Manchester, 1914.

Chronica Monasterii de Melsa. Ed. E. A. Bond. 3 vols. RS. London, 1866–68.

Chronicle of Lanercost. Trans. Sir H. Maxwell. Glasgow, 1913.

Chronicle of Pierre de Langtoft. Ed. T. Wright. 2 vols. RS. London, 1866–68.

Chronicle and Political Papers of Edward VI. Ed. W. K. Jordan. London, 1966.

Chronicle of Walter of Guisborough. Ed. H. Rothwell. Camden Series. London, 1957.

Chronicon Petroburgense. Ed. T. Stapleton. Camden Society. London, 1849.

Chronique d'Ernoul et de Bernard le Trésorier. Ed. L. de Mas Latrie. Paris, 1871.

Chronique des quatre premiers Valois. Ed. S. Luce. Paris, 1862.

Civil Pleas of the Wiltshire Eyre, 1249. Ed. M. T. Clanchy. Wiltshire Record Society. Devizes, 1971.

Clement VI. *Lettres closes, patentes et curiales intéressant les pays autres que la France.* Ed. E. Déprez and G. Mollat. Paris, 1960–61.

Complete Peerage of England, Scotland, Ireland, Great Britain, and the United Kingdom. Ed. G. E. Cockayne. New ed., ed. V. Gibbs, G. H. White et al. 13 vols. London, 1910–59.

Cotton, Bartholomew. *Historia Anglicana.* Ed. H. R. Luard. RS. London, 1859.

Councils and Synods with Other Documents Relating to the English Church. Gen. ed. F. W. Powicke. Vol. 1. Oxford, 1981. Vol. 2. Oxford, 1964.

Cronica del Rey Don Alfonso el Onceno, Cronicas de los Reyes de Castilla. Ed. C. Rosell. *Biblioteca de autores españoles.* Vols. 66 and 68. Madrid, 1875, 1877.

Curia Regis Rolls.

Curia Regis Rolls, 1194–95. Ed. F. W. Maitland. London, 1891.

De Expugnatione Lyxbonensi. Ed. C. W. David. New York, 1976.

De Expugnatione Terrae Sanctae per Saladinum Libellus. Ed. J. Stevenson. RS. London, 1875.

"Dialogue between Henry de Lacy and Walter Biblesworth on the Crusade." *Reliquae Antiquae,* ed. T. Wright and J. O. Halliwell, vol. 1. London, 1841.

Dialogue of the Exchequer. Ed. C. Johnson. London, 1950.

Diary of Abraham de la Pryme. Ed. C. Jackson. Surtees Society. Durham, 1870.

Dictionary of National Biography.

Diplomatic Correspondence of Richard II. Ed. E. Perroy. Camden Series. London, 1933.

Diplomatic Documents, 1101–1272. Ed. P. Chaplais. London, 1964.

Documents of the Baronial Movement of Reform and Rebellion, 1258–67. Ed. R. E. Treharne and I. J. Sanders. Oxford, 1973.

Documents and Records Illustrating the History of Scotland. Ed. F. Palgrave. London, 1837.

Dubois, Pierre. *The Recovery of the Holy Land.* Trans. W. I. Brandt. New York, 1956.

Durham Annals and Documents of the Thirteenth Century. Ed. F. Barlow. Durham, 1945.

Eadmer. *Historia Novorum in Anglia.* Ed. M. Rule. RS. London, 1884.

Earliest Northamptonshire Assize Rolls. Ed. D. M. Stenton. Northamptonshire Record Society. Lincoln and London, 1930.

Early Yorkshire Charters. Ed. W. Farrer and C. T. Clay. Yorkshire Archeological Society. 12 vols. 1914–65.

Early Yorkshire Families. Ed. C. Clay and D. E. Greenway. Yorkshire Archeological Society Record Series. 1973.

Einhard. *Life of Charlemagne.* Trans. L. Thorpe, *Two Lives of Charlemagne.* London, 1969.

English Historical Documents. Gen. ed. E. C. Douglas. Vols. 1–4. London, 1955–75.

English Suits before the Paris Parlement, 1420–36. Ed. C. T. Allmand and C. A. J. Armstrong. Camden Society. London, 1982.

Enguerrand de Monstrelet. *Chroniques.* Ed. J. A. C. Buchon. Paris, 1836. Trans. T. Johnes. London, 1877.

Ephraim of Bonn. *The Book of Remembrance. The Jews and the Crusades,* ed. and trans. S. Eidelberg. Madison, Wis., 1977.

Epistolae Academicae Oxoniensis. Ed. H. Anstey. Oxford Historical Society. Vol. 36. Oxford, 1898.

Epistolae Cantuariensis: Chronicles and Memorials of Richard I. Ed. W. Stubbs. Vol. 2. RS. London, 1865.

Eulogium Historiarum. Ed. F. S. Haydon. RS. London, 1863.

Ex chronico anonymi Laudunensis canonici. R.H.F., vol. 18.

Expeditions to Prussia and the Holy Land made by Henry, Earl of Derby. Ed. L. Toulmin-Smith. Camden Society. London, 1894.

Extracts from a Yorkshire Assize Roll, 3 Henry III (1219). Ed. W. T. Lancaster. *Miscellanea.* Vol. 1. Yorkshire Archeological Society Record Series. Vol. 61. 1920.

Eynsham Cartulary. Ed. H. E. Salter. 2 vols. Oxford Historical Society. Vols. 49 and 51. Oxford, 1907–8.

Fasculi Zizaniorum Magistri Johannis Wyclif cum Tritico. Ed. W. W. Shirley. RS. London, 1858.

Feet of Fines for Yorkshire, 1232–46. Ed. J. Parker. Yorkshire Archeological Society Record Series. 1925.

Finke, H. *Acta Aragonensia.* Berlin and Leipzig, 1908–66.

Florence of Worcester. *Chronicon ex chronicis.* Ed. B. Thorpe. 2 vols. London, 1848–49.

Flores historiarum. Ed. H. R. Luard. RS. London, 1890.

Foedera, conventiones, literae, etc. Ed. T. Rymer. 3d ed. The Hague, 1745. London, 1816.

Foxe, J. *Acts and Monuments.* Ed. S. R. Cattley. 8 vols. London, 1837–41.

Froissart, J. *Chronicles.* Trans. T. Johnes. London, 1839.

Fulcher of Chartres. *Historia Hierosolymitanae.* Ed. H. Hageneyer. Heidelberg, 1913. Trans. R. Ryan and H. Fink. Knoxville, Tenn., 1969.

Gaimar. *Lestoire des Engleis.* Ed. T. D. Hardy and C. T. Martin. RS. London, 1888–89.

Geoffrey of Monmouth. *Historia Regum Britanniae.* Ed. A. Griscom and R. Ellis Jones. London, 1929. Trans. L. Thorpe, under the title, *The History of the Kings of Britain.* London, 1966.

Gerald of Wales. *De Rebus a se gestis.* Trans. H. E. Butler, under the title, *The Autobiography of Giraldus Cambrensis.* London, 1937.

———. *Journey through Wales.* Trans. L. Thorpe. London, 1978.

———. *Opera.* Ed. J. S. Brewer. 8 vols. RS. London, 1861–91.

Gervase of Canterbury, *Historical Works.* Ed. W. Stubbs. 2 vols. RS. London, 1879–80.

Gesta Abbatum Monasterii Sancti Albani. Ed. H. T. Riley. 3 vols. RS. London, 1867–69.

Gesta Francorum et aliorum Hierosolimitanorum. Ed. R. Hill. London, 1962.

Gesta Henrici Quinti. Ed. F. Taylor and J. S. Roskell. Oxford, 1975.

Gesta Stephani. Ed. K. R. Potter and R. H. C. Davis. Oxford, 1976.

Glanvill. *Tractatus de legibus et consuetudinibus regni Angliae.* Ed. G. D. G. Hall. London, 1965.

Great Rolls of the Pipe. Pipe Roll Society. 1884– .

Guillaume de Machaut. *La Prise d'Alexandrie.* Ed. M. L. de Mas Latrie. Geneva, 1877.

Hagenmeyer, H. *Die Kreuzzugsbriefe aus den Jahren, 1088–1100.* Innsbruck, 1902.

Hall, E. *Chronicles.* London, 1809.

Henry of Huntingdon. *Historia Anglorum.* Ed. T. Arnold. RS. London, 1879.

Herbert of Bosham. *Vita S. Thomae.* Vol. 3 of *Materials for the History of Thomas Becket,* ed. J. C. Robertson and J. B. Sheppard. RS. London, 1875–85.

Higden, Rannulf. *Polychronicon.* Ed. J. R. Lumby. RS. London, 1865–86.

Hill, R. *Ecclesiastical Letter-Books of the Thirteenth Century.* Oxford. B. Litt. thesis. 1936.

Histoire général de Languedoc. Ed. C. de Vic, J.Vaissete, and A. Molinier. 16 vols. Toulouse, 1872–1904.

Histoire de Guillaume le Maréchal. Ed. P. Meyer. Paris, 1891–94.

Historia Monasterii Sancti Petri Gloucestriae. Ed. W. H. Hart. 3 vols. RS. London, 1863.

Historical Manuscripts, Royal Commission on. *Second Report,* appendix. London, 1871.

———. *Fifth Report,* appendix. London, 1872.

———. *Eighth Report,* appendix 1. London, 1881.

———. *Fourteenth Report,* appendix 8. London, 1895.

———. *Report on Various Collections.* Vols. 1 and 2. London, 1901 and 1908.

Historical Papers and Letters from Northern Registers. Ed. J. Raine. RS. London, 1873.

Holinshed, Raphael. *Chronicles of England and Ireland.* 1587. Reprint, 1808–9.

Indentures of Retinue with John of Gaunt, 1367–99. Ed. N. B. Lewis. *Camden Miscellany* 22 (London, 1964).

Issues of the Exchequer. Ed. F. Devon. London, 1837.

Itinerarium peregrinorum. Ed. H. E. Mayer. Stuttgart, 1962.

Itinerarium peregrinorum et gesta regis Ricardi. Ed. W. Stubbs. RS. London, 1864.

James VI of Scotland. *The Poems of James VI of Scotland.* Ed. J. Craigie. Scottish Text Society. Edinburgh, 1955–58.

James of Verona. *Liber Peregrinationis.* Ed. R. Röhricht. *Revue de l'Orient Latin* 3 (1895).

Jean de Joinville. *Life of St. Louis.* Trans. M. R. B. Shaw. London, 1963.

Jocelin of Brakelond. *Chronicle.* Ed. H. E. Butler. London, 1949.

Johannis de Trokelowe et Henrici de Blandeforde: Chronica et Annales. Ed. H. T. Riley. RS. London, 1866.

John of Hexham. *Chronicle.* Symeon of Durham, *Opera Omnia,* ed. T. Arnold. Vol. 2. RS. London, 1882–85.

John of Longueville. *Modus Tenendi Curias. The Court Baron,* ed. F. W. Maitland and W. P. Baildon. Selden Society. London, 1891.

John of St. Victor. *Excerptae memoriali historiarum.* R.H.F., vol. 21.

John XXII. *Lettres communes.* Ed. G. Mollat. Paris, 1904–47.

————. *Lettres secrètes et curiales relatives à la France.* Ed. A. Coulon et al. Paris, 1906–72.

Josselin, Ralph. *Diary.* Ed. A. McFarlane. London, 1976.

Journals of the house of Lords.

Knighton, Henry. *Chronicon.* Ed. J. R. Lumby. RS. London, 1889–95.

Knights Hospitallers in England: The Report of Philip de Thame. Ed. L. B. Larking and J. M. Kemble. Camden Society. London, 1857.

Kohler, C. "Deux projets de croisade en Terre Sainte." *Revue de l'Orient Latin* 10 (1903–4).

Landon, L. *Itinerary of King Richard I.* London, 1935.

Le Strange, H. *Le Strange Records.* London, 1916.

Letter Book of William of Hoo. Ed. A. Gransden. Suffolk Record Society. Ipswich, 1963.

Letters and Charters of Gilbert Foliot. Ed. A. Morey and C. N. L. Brooke. Cambridge, 1967.

Letters of John of Salisbury. Ed. W. J. Millor and C. N. L. Brooke. Vol. 2. Oxford, 1979.

Letters and Papers of Richard III and Henry VII. Ed. J. Gairdner. RS. London, 1861–63.

Letters of St. Bernard of Clairvaux. Trans. B. S. James. London, 1953.

Libellus de Vita et Miraculis S. Godrici Heremitae de Finchale. Ed. J. Stevenson. Surtees Society. 1847.

Lincolnshire Architectural and Archeological Society. *Reports and Papers.* Vol. 3. Lincoln, 1945.

List of Ancient Correspondence. Rev. ed. Vol. 15 of *P.R.O. Lists and Indexes.* Reprint. New York, 1968.

Literae Cantuariensis. Ed. J. Brigstocke Sheppard. RS. London, 1887–89.

London Eyre of 1244. Ed. H. A. Chew and M. Weinbaum. London Record Society. London, 1970.

Lunt, W. E. "The Text of the Ordinance of 1184." *EHR* 37 (1922).

Malory, Thomas. *La Morte d'Arthur.* Ed. J. Rhys. London, n.d.

Mandeville's Travels. Ed. M. C. Seymour. Oxford, 1967.

Marsh, Adam. *Epistolae. Monumenta Franciscana,* ed. J. Brewer. 2 vols. RS. London, 1858.

Materials for the History of Thomas Becket. Ed. J. C. Robertson and J. B. Sheppard. 7 vols. RS. London, 1875–85.

Matthew Paris. *Chronica Majora.* Ed. H. R. Luard. 7 vols. RS. London, 1872–84.

————. *Historia Anglorum.* Ed. F. Madden. 3 vols. RS. London, 1866–69.

Monumenta Franciscana. Ed. J. Brewer. RS. London, 1858.

Murimuth, Adam. *Continuatio Chronicarum.* Ed. E. M. Thompson. RS. London, 1889.

A Northamptonshire Miscellany. Ed. E. King. Northamptonshire Record Society. Northampton, 1983.

North Country Wills. Ed. J. W. Clay. Surtees Society. Durham, 1908.

Odo of Deuil. *De Profectione Ludovici VII in orientem.* Ed. V. G. Berry. New York, 1948.

Ye Oldest Diarie of Englysshe Travell: The Pilgrimage of Sir Richard Torkyngton. Ed. W. J. Loftie. London, 1884.

Oliver of Paderborn. *Capture of Damietta.* Trans. in E. Peters, *Christian Society and the Crusades, 1198–1229.* Philadelphia, 1971.

Orderic Vitalis. *The Ecclesiastical History.* Ed. and trans. M. Chibnall. 6 vols. Oxford, 1969–80.

Ordinatio de predicatione S. Crucis in Angliae. Ed. R. Röhricht. *Quinti Belli Sacri Scriptores Minores. Société de l'Orient Latin* 2 (Geneva, 1879).

Paston Letters and Papers. Ed. N. Davis. Oxford, 1971–76.

Peele, George. *The Battle of Alcazar.* Ed. J. Yoklavich. *The Dramatic Works of George Peele,* ed. C. T. Prouty. New Haven, Conn., 1952–70.

Peter of Vaux-de-Cernay. *Historia Albigensis.* Ed. P. Guébin and E. Lyon. 3 vols. Paris, 1926–39.

Philippe de Mézières. *Epistre lamentable et consolatoire.* Ed. Kervyn de Lettenhove. *Froissart, Chroniques.* Vol. 16. Brussells, 1872.

————. *Letter to King Richard II.* Ed. G. W. Coopland. Liverpool, 1975.

————. *Le Songe du Vieil Pèlerin.* Ed. G. W. Coopland. Cambridge, 1969.

Pipe Roll 31 Henry I (1130). Ed. J. Hunter. London, 1833.

Pleas before the King or his Justices, 1198–1202. Ed. D. M. Stenton. Selden Society. 1948–49.

"Poésies du troubadour Gavaudan." Ed. J. Jeanroy. *Romania* 34 (1905).

Political Poems and Songs. Ed. T. Wright. RS. London, 1859–61.

Political Songs of England. Ed. T. Wright. Camden Society. London, 1839.

Pollard, A. W. and Redgrave, G. R. *Short-Title Catalogue, 1475–1640.* London, 1926, 1976.

Proceedings of the Privy Council. Ed. H. Nicolas. Vol. 3. London, 1834.

The Pylgrymage of Sir Richard Guylforde to the Holy Land in 1506. Ed. Sir H. Ellis. Camden Society. London, 1851.

Ralph Niger, *Chronicles.* Ed. R. Anstruther. Caxton Society. London, 1851.

———. *De Re Militari et Triplici Via Peregrinationis Ierosolimitano.* Ed. L. Schmugge. Berlin, 1977.

Ralph of Coggeshall. *Chronicon Anglicanum.* Ed. J. Stevenson. RS. London, 1875.

Ralph of Diceto, *Ymagines Historiarum, Opera Historica.* Ed. W. Stubbs. 2 vols. RS. London, 1876.

Raymond of Aguilers. *Historia Francorum qui ceperunt Iherusalem.* *R.H.C.Occ.,* vol. 3. Trans. J. H. Hill and L. L. Hill. Philadelphia, 1968.

Raynaldus, O. *Annales Ecclesiastici.* Lucca, 1747–55.

Records of the Templars in England in the Twelfth Century. Ed. B. A. Lees. London, 1935.

Records of the Wardrobe and Household, 1285–86. Ed. B. F. Byerley and C. R. Byerley. London, 1977.

Recueil des actes de Philippe Auguste. Ed. H. F. Delaborde. Vol. 1. Paris, 1916.

Recueil des historiens des croisades: Documents Arméniens. Ed. C. Kohler. Vol. 2. Paris, 1906.

Recueil des historiens des croisades: Historiens Occidentaux. Ed. A. Beugnot et al. 5 vols. Paris, 1844–95.

Recueil des historiens des Gaules et de la France. Ed. M. Bouquet et al. 24 vols. Paris, 1738–1876.

Regesta Clementis V. Ed. Monachi Orchinis S. Benedicti. 8 vols. Rome, 1885–92.

Regesta Pontificium Romanorum, 1198–1304. Ed. A. Potthast. Vol. 1. Berlin, 1874.

Regesta Regum Anglo-Normannorum, 1066–1154. Ed. H. W. C. Davis et al. 4 vols. 1913–69.

Register of Archbishop J. le Romeyn. Ed. W. Brown. Surtees Society. Durham, 1913–16.

Register of Archbishop Walter Giffard of York. Ed. W. Brown. Surtees Society. Durham, 1904.

Register of Archbishop W. Wickwane. Ed. W. Brown. Surtees Society. Durham, 1907.

Register of Bishop Geoffrey Giffard of Worcester. Ed. J. W. Willis Bund. Worcester Historical Society. 2 vols. Oxford, 1902.

Register of Bishop John de Pontissara of Winchester. Surrey Record Society. 9 vols. London, 1913–24.

Register of Bishop Robert Rede of Chichester. Ed. C. Deedes. Vol. 1 Sussex Record Society. London, 1908.

Register of Bishop William Ginsborough of Worcester. Ed. J. W. Willis Bund. Worcester Historical Society. Oxford, 1907.

Register of St. Benet of Holme. Ed. J. R. West. Norfolk Record Society. Nos. 2 and 3. 1932.

Register of St. Osmund. Ed. W. H. Rich-Jones. 2 vols. London. 1883–84.

Register of T. Bourgchier. Ed. F. R. H. du Boulay. Canterbury and York Society. Oxford, 1957.

Register of Thomas Langley. Ed. R. L. Storey. 6 vols. Surtees Society. Durham, 1956–70.

Registres de Boniface VIII. Ed. G. Digard. 4 vols. Paris, 1884–1935.

Registres de Clément IV. Ed. E. Jordan. 6 vols. in one. Paris, 1893–1945.

Registres de Grégoire IX. Ed. L. Auvray. 4 vols. Paris, 1890–1955.

Registres de Grégoire X. Ed. J. Giraud. 5 vols. in one. Paris, 1892–1960.

Registres d'Innocent IV. Ed. E. Berger. 4 vols. Paris, 1884–99.

Registres d'Urbain IV, Ed. L. Dorez and J. Giraud. 4 vols. Paris, 1899–1958.

Registres du trésor des chartes; Inventaire analytique. Ed. R. Fawtier. 2 vols. Paris, 1958.

Registrum Abbatiae Johannis Whethamstede. Ed. H. T. Riley. 2 vols. RS. London, 1872–73.

Registrum Ricardi de Swinfield. Ed. W. W. Capes. Canterbury and York Society. London, 1909.

Riant, Comte. "Pièces relatives au passage de pèlerins à Venise." *Archives de l'Orient Latin* 2 (1884).

———. "Privilèges octroyées aux Teutoniques." *Archives de l'Orient Latin* 1 (1881).

Richard of Devizes. *Chronicle.* Ed. J. T. Appleby. London, 1963.

Rigord. *Gesta Philippi Augusti.* Ed. F. Delaborde. Vol. 1 of *Oevres de Rigord et de Guillaume le Breton.* Paris, 1882.

Riley-Smith, L. and Riley-Smith, J. *The Crusades: Idea and Reality, 1095–1274.* London, 1981.

Rishanger, William. *Chronica.* Ed. H. T. Riley. RS. London, 1865.

———. *De Duobus Bellis.* Ed. J. O. Halliwell. Camden Society. London, 1840.

Robert Grosseteste. *Epistolae.* Ed. H. R. Luard. RS. London, 1861.

Robert of Torigni. *Chronicle. Chronicles of the Reigns of Stephen, Henry II, and Richard I,* ed. R. Howlett. Vol. 4. RS. London, 1889.

Roger of Howden. *Chronica.* Ed. W. Stubbs. 4 vols. RS. London, 1868–71.

———. *Gesta Regis Henrici Secundi.* Ed. W. Stubbs. 2 vols. RS. London, 1867.

Roger of Wendover. *Flores historiarum.* Ed. H. G. Hewlett. 3 vols. RS. London, 1886–89.

Röhricht, R. *Regesta Regni Hierosolymitani.* Innsbruck, 1893.

Rolls of the Fifteenth (1225) and the Fortieth (1232). Ed. F. A. Cazel and A. P. Cazel. Pipe Roll Society. London, 1983.

Rolls of Justices in Eyre, Gloucestershire, Warwickshire, Staffordshire, 1221, 1222. Ed. D. M. Stenton. Selden Society. London, 1940.

Rolls of Justices in Eyre, Lincolnshire, 1218–19 and Worcestershire, 1221. Ed. D. M. Stenton. Selden Society. London, 1934.

Rolls of Justices in Eyre, Yorkshire, 1218–19. Ed. D. M. Stenton. Selden Society. London, 1937.

Rolls and Register of Bishop Oliver Sutton, 1280–99. Ed. R. Hill. Lincoln Record Society. Vols. 3–5. Hereford, 1954–65.

Rolls Series: The Chronicles and Memorials of Great Britain and Ireland during the Middle Ages. London, 1858– .

Rotuli Curiae Regis. Ed. F. Palgrave. London, 1835.

Rotuli Hugonis de Welles episcopi Lincolniensis. Ed. W. P. W. Phillimore. Lincoln Record Society. No. 6. Lincoln, 1912–13.

Rotuli Litterarum Clausarum. Turri Londonensi asservati, 1204–27. Ed. T. D. Hardy. 2 vols. London, 1833–44.

Rotuli Litterarum Patentium. Ed. T. D. Hardy. Vol. 1. London, 1835.

Rotuli de Oblatis et Finibus. Ed. T. D. Hardy. London, 1835.

Rotuli Parliamentorum. 6 vols. n.d.

Royal and Historical Letters of Henry IV. Ed. F. C. Hingeston. Vol. 1. RS. London, 1860.

Royal Letters of Henry III. Ed. W. W. Shirley. 2 vols. RS. London, 1862–66.

Saewulf, *Pilgrimage of Saewulf to Jerusalem.* Ed. J. Brownlow. London, 1892.

————. *Relatio de peregrinatione Saewulfi.* Ed. T. Wright et al. Palestine Pilgrims Text Society. No. 4. London, 1896.

St. Alban's Chronicle, 1406–20. Ed. V. H. Galbraith. Oxford, 1937.

Salter, H. E. *Facsimilies of Early English Charters in Oxford Muniment Rooms.* Oxford, 1929.

Scriptores rerum Prussicarum. Ed. T. Hirsch, M. Toeppen, and E. Strehlke. 5 vols. Leipzig, 1861–74.

Scrope and Grosvenor Controversy. Ed. N. H. Nicolas. London, 1832. Collated by C. G. Young. Chester, 1879.

Select Cases for the Ecclesiastical Courts of the Province of Canterbury, c. 1200–1301. Ed. N. Adams and C. Donahue. Selden Society. London, 1981.

Select Documents of the English Lands of the Abbey of Bec. Ed. M. Chibnall. Camden Series. London, 1951.

Selected Letters of Pope Innocent III. Ed. C. R. Cheney and W. H. Semple. London, 1953.

"Sermo de cruce domini." *Textes inédits,* ed. M. T. d'Alverny. *Etudes de philosophie médiévale.* Vol. 52. Paris, 1965.

Sharp, C. *Memorials of the Rebellion in 1569.* London, 1840.

Siege of Carlaverock. Ed. N. H. Nicolas. London, 1828.

Smith, T. *English Gilds.* Early English Text Society. Vol. 40. London, 1870.

Somerset Medieval Wills. Ed. F. W. Weaver. Somerset Record Society. 1901.

Somersetshire Pleas. Ed. C. E. H. Chadwick-Healey and L. Landon. Somerset Record Society. 1897, 1923.

Somers Tracts. Ed. W. Scott. London, 1809–15.

Song of Lewes. Trans. *E.H.D.,* vol. 3.

Statutes of the Realm.

Stenton, F. M. "Early Manumissions at Staunton." *EHR* 26 (1911).

————. *Transcripts of Charters relating to Gilbertine Houses.* Lincoln Record Society. Vol. 18. 1922.

Storgursey Charters. Ed. T. D. Tremlett and N. Blakiston. Somerset Record Society. Frome, 1949.

Symeon of Durham. *Opera Omnia.* Ed. T. Arnold. 2 vols. RS. London, 1882–85.

Testamenta Vetusta. Ed. N. H. Nicolas. London, 1836.

Thame Cartulary. Ed. H. E. Salter. 2 vols. Oxford, 1947–48.

Tractatus de Regimine Principum. Ed. J.-P. Genet. *Four English Political Tracts of the Later Middle Ages.* Camden Series. London, 1977.

Trivet (or Trevet), Nicholas. *Annales.* Ed. T. Hog. London, 1845.

Turner, T. H. "Unpublished Notices of the Time of Edward I." *Archeological Journal* 8 (1851).

Tyson, M. "The Annals of Southwark and Merton." *Surrey Archeological Collections* 36 (1925).

Urban V. *Lettres secrètes et curiales.* Ed. P. Lecacheux and G. Mollat. Paris, 1902–55.

Vergil, Polydore. *Anglica Historia.* Ed. D. Hay. Camden Society. London, 1950.

Vetus Liber Archidiaconi Eliensis. Ed. C. L. Feltoe and E. H. Minns. Cambridge, 1917.

Victoria History of the Counties of England.

Vita Edwardi Secundi. Chronicles of Edward I and II, ed. W. Stubbs, vol. 2. RS. London, 1883. Trans. N. Denholm-Young. London, 1957.

Walker, D. "A Letter from the Holy Land." *EHR* 72 (1957).

Walsingham, Thomas. *Historia Anglicana.* Ed. H. T. Riley. 2 vols. RS. London, 1863–64.

—————. *Ypodigma Neustriae.* Ed. H. T. Riley. RS. London, 1876.

Walter Map. *De Nugis Curialium.* Ed. M. R. James, rev. C. N. L. Brooke and R. A. B. Mynors. Oxford, 1983.

Warkworth, John. *A Chronicle of the First Thirteen Years of the Reign of King Edward IV.* Ed. J. O. Halliwell. Camden Society. London, 1839.

Waurin, Jehan de. *Recueil des chroniques d'Angleterre.* Ed. W. Hardy and E. L. C. P. Hardy. RS. London, 1864–91.

Waterton, E. *MS Roll of English and Irish Knights Hospitaller.* 1903.

Westminster Chronicle. Ed. L. C. Hector and B. F. Harvey. Oxford, 1982.

Wey, William. *Itineraries.* Roxburghe Club. London, 1857.

Wilkins, D. *Concilia Magnae Britannicae et Hibernicae.* London, 1733–37.

William of Malmesbury. *Gesta Pontificum Anglorum.* Ed. N. E. S. A. Hamilton. RS. London, 1870.

—————. *Gesta Regum Anglorum,* Ed. W. Stubbs. 2 vols. RS. London, 1887–89.

—————. *Vita Wulfstani.* Ed. R. A. Darlington. Camden Society. London, 1928.

William of Newburgh. *Historia rerum Anglicarum.* Ed. H. C. H. Hamilton. London, 1856.

—————. *Historia rerum Anglicarum.* Ed. R. Howlett, in *Chronicles of the Reigns of Stephen, Henry II, and Richard I.* 2 vols. RS. London, 1884–89.

William of Poitiers. *Histoire de Guillaume le Conquérant.* Ed. R. Foreville. Paris, 1952.

William of Tyre. *Historia Rerum in Partibus Transmarinis. R.H.C.Occ.,* vols. 1 and 2. Trans. E. A. Babcock and A. C. Krey. New York, 1976.

Wills proved in the Consistory Court of Norwich. Ed. M. A. Farrow. Norfolk Record Society. Vol. 16. 1945.

Worcestre, William. *Itineraries.* Ed. J. H. Harvey. Oxford, 1969.

Wyclif, John. *Tractatus de Officio Regis.* Ed. A. W. Pollard and C. Sayle. London, 1887.

Wykes, Thomas. *Chronicon. Ann. Mon.,* vol. 4.

Yorkshire Deeds. Vol. 7. Ed. C. Clay. Yorkshire Archeological Society Record Series. 1932.

SECONDARY WORKS

Andrieu, M. *Le Pontifical Romain au Moyen Age.* Vatican, 1940.

Appleby, J. T. *England without Richard.* London, 1965.

Armitage-Smith, S. *John of Gaunt.* London, 1904.

Armstrong, C. A. J. *The Usurpation of Richard III.* Oxford, 1969.

Atiya, A. S. *The Crusade in the Later Middle Ages.* London, 1938.

————. *The Crusade of Nicopolis.* London, 1934.

Baldwin, J. W. "La decénnie decisive: les années 1190–1203." *Revue Historique* 266 (1981).

Barber, M. *The Trial of the Templars.* Cambridge, 1978.

Barlow, F. *William Rufus.* London, 1983.

Barnie, J. *War in Medieval Society.* London, 1974.

Bartlett, R. *Gerald of Wales, 1146–1223.* Oxford, 1982.

Bates, D. *Normandy before 1066.* London, 1982.

Beebe, B. "The English Baronage and the Crusade of 1270." *BIHR* 48 (1975).

Bémont, C. *Simon de Montfort.* Paris, 1884. Trans. E. Jacob. Oxford, 1930.

Bennett, J. A. W. *The Rediscovery of Sir John Mandeville.* New York, 1954.

Biddle, M., ed. *Winchester in the Early Middle Ages.* Oxford, 1976.

Bindoff, T., ed. *House of Commons, 1509–58.* Vol. 1 of *History of Parliament.* London, 1983.

Blaess, M. "L'abbaye de Bordesley et les livres de Guy de Beauchamp." *Romania* 78 (1957).

Borg, A. "Crusader Sculpture." *St. John Historical Society Newsletter* (December, 1985).

Braudel, F. *The Mediterranean and the Mediterranean World in the Age of Philip II.* Trans. S. Reynolds. London, 1973.

Brundage, J. A. "*Cruce Signari:* The Rite of Taking the Cross in England." *Traditio* 22 (1960).

————. *Medieval Canon Law and the Crusader.* (Madison, Wis., 1969).

————. "A Note on the Attestation of Crusaders' Vows." *Catholic Historical Review* 52 (1966–67).

Burleigh, M. *Prussian Society and the German Order c. 1410–66.* Cambridge, 1984.

Burnet, G. *History of the Reformation.* Ed. E. Nares. 4 vols. London, 1830.

Butler, L. H. "The Order of St. John and the Peasants' Revolt." *St. John Historical Society Pamphlets*, no. 1. 1981.

————. *The Seige of Rhodes.* London, 1980.

Cam, H. M., and Jacob, E. F. "Notes on an English Cluniac Chronicle." *EHR* 44 (1929).

Campbell, J. "Observations on English Government from the Tenth to the Twelfth Century." *TRHS*, 5th ser., 25 (1975).

Campbell, J., et al., ed. *The Anglo-Saxons.* Oxford, 1982.

Capp, B. *English Almanacs, 1500–1800.* Ithaca, N.Y., 1979.

Carpenter, D. "The Gold Treasure of King Henry III." *Thirteenth Century Studies*, ed. S. Lloyd. Woodbridge, 1987.

Cate, J. L. "The English Mission of Eustace of Flay." *Etudes d'histoire dédiées a la mémoire de Henri Pirenne.* Brussells, 1937.

Catto, J. "Religion and the English Nobility in the Late Fourteenth Century." *History and Imagination*, ed. H. Lloyd-Jones et al. London, 1981.

Cazel, F. A. "The Tax of 1185 in Aid of the Holy Land." *Speculum* 30 (1955).

Cazelles, R. *La société politique et la crise de la royauté sous Philippe VI de Valois.* Paris, 1958.

Chambers, R. W. *Thomas More.* London, 1935.

Cheney, C. R. "The Alleged Deposition of King John." *The Papacy and England.* London, 1982.

————. "The Eve of Magna Carta." *Bulletin of the John Rylands Library* 38 (1955–56).

————. *Hubert Walter.* London, 1967.

————. *Innocent III and England.* Stuttgart, 1976.

Chrimes, S. B. *Henry VII.* London, 1972.

Christiansen, E. *The Northern Crusades.* London, 1980.

Ciggaar, K. "England and Byzantium on the Eve of the Norman Conquest." *Anglo-Norman Studies* 5 (1982).

Clanchy, M. T. *England and its Rulers.* London, 1983.

————. *From Memory to Written Record.* London, 1979.

Clarke, M. *Fourteenth Century Studies.* Oxford, 1937.

Clifford, E. R. *A Knight of Great Renown.* Chicago, 1961.

Colvin, H. M., et al. *History of the King's Works.* Vols. 1 and 2. London, 1963.

Constable, G. "The Financing of the Crusades in the Twelfth Century." *Outremer,* ed. B. Z. Kedar, H. E. Mayer, and R. C. Smail. Jerusalem, 1982.

————. "Medieval Charters as a Source for the History of the Crusades." *Crusade and Settlement,* ed. P. W. Edbury. Cardiff, 1985.

————. "A Note on the Route of the Anglo-Flemish Crusaders." *Speculum* 28 (1953).

————. "The Second Crusade as seen by Contemporaries." *Traditio* 9 (1953).

Contamine, P. *Guerre, état, et société au fin du moyen âge.* Paris, 1972.

————. *La Guerre au moyen âge.* Paris, 1980.

Corner, D. "*The Gesta Regis Henrici Secundi* and *Chronica* of Roger Parson of Howden." *BIHR* 56 (1983).

Coss, P. R. "Cultural Diffusion in Medieval England." *Past and Present* 108 (1985).

Cowdrey, H. E. J. "The Anglo-Norman Laudes Regiae." *Viator* 12 (1981).

————. "Cluny and the First Crusade." *Revue Benedictine* 83 (1973).

————. "Pope Urban II's Preaching of the First Crusade." *History* 55 (1970).

Cowen, I. B., et al., ed. *Knights of St. John of Jerusalem in Scotland.* Edinburgh, 1983.

Cuttino, G. P. *English Diplomatic Administration, 1259–1339.* Oxford, 1971.

David, C. W. *Robert Curthose.* Cambridge, Mass., 1920.

Davies, C. S. L. "The Pilgrimage of Grace Reconsidered." *Past and Present* 41 (1968).

————. "Popular Religion and the Pilgrimage of Grace," *Order and Disorder in Early Modern England,* ed. A. Fletcher and J. Stevenson. Cambridge, 1985.

Davis, H. W. C. "Henry of Blois and Brian FitzCount." *EHR* 25 (1910).

Davis, R. H. C. *King Stephen.* London, 1977.

Delachenal, R. *Histoire de Charles V.* Vol. 3. Paris, 1916.

Delaville le Roulx, J. *La France en Orient au XIVe siècle.* Paris, 1885–86.

Denholm-Young, N. *Richard of Cornwall*. Oxford, 1947.

Denton, J. H. *Robert Winchelsea and the Crown, 1294–1313*. Cambridge, 1980.

Déprez, E. *La papauté, la France, et l'Angleterre, 1328–42*. Paris, 1902.

Dobson, R. B. "The Decline and Expulsion of the Medieval Jews of York." *Miscellanies* 11, in *Transactions of the Jewish Historical Society of England* 26 (1979).

———. *The Jews of Medieval York and the Massacre of 1190*. Borthwick Papers, no. 45. York, 1974.

Dodds, M. H., and Dodds, R. *The Pilgrimage of Grace and the Exeter Conspiracy*. Cambridge, 1915.

Dop, J. A. *Eliza's Knights: Scholars, Poets, and Puritans in the Netherlands, 1572–86*. Leiden, 1981.

Douglas, D. C. *The Norman Achievement*. London, 1972.

———. *William the Conqueror*. London, 1969.

Douie, D. *Archbishop Pecham*. Oxford, 1952.

du Boulay, F. R. H. "Henry of Derby's Expeditions to Prussia, 1390–91 and 1392." In *The Reign of Richard II*, ed. F. R. H. du Boulay and C. M. Barron. London, 1971.

Duff, E. G. *Fifteenth Century English Books*. Oxford, 1917.

Duncalf, F. "The Peasants' Crusade." *American Historical Review* 26 (1920).

Dyer, S. "The Weston Family and the Order of St. John." *St. John Historical Society Newsletter* (September 1983).

Edbury, P. W., ed. *Crusade and Settlement*. Cardiff, 1985.

Edbury, P. W., and Metcalf, D. M., eds. *Coinage in the Latin East*. Oxford, 1980.

Elton, G. R. "Politics and the Pilgrimage of Grace." *After the Reformation: Essays in Honour of J. A. Hexter*, ed. B. C. Malament, Manchester, 1980.

Erdmann, G. *Die Entstehung des Kreuzzugsgedankens*. Stuttgart, 1935. Trans. M. W. Baldwin and W. Goffart, under the title *The Origins of the Idea of the Crusade*. Princeton, N.J., 1977.

Eyton, R. W. *Antiquities of Shropshire*. 12 vols. London, 1854–60.

Ferguson, A. B. *The Indian Summer of English Chivalry*. (Durham, N.C., 1960).

Field, P. J. C. "Sir Robert Malory." *Journal of Ecclesiastical History* 28 (1977).

Finke, H. *Papsttum und Untergang des Templerordens*. Munster, 1907.

Firth, K. R. *The Apocalyptic Tradition in Reformation Britain, 1530–1645*. Oxford, 1979.

Fletcher, R. A. *St. James' Catapult*. Oxford, 1984.

Forey, A. J. "The Crusading Vows of the English King Henry III." *Durham University Journal* 65 (1973).

———. "The Military Order of St. Thomas of Acre." *EHR* 92 (1977).

Fowler, G. H. "The Beauchamps of Eaton." Bedfordshire Historical Record Society. Vol. 2. 1914.

Fowler, K. *The King's Lieutenant*. London, 1969.

Fox, A. *Thomas More*. Oxford, 1982.

Fraser, C. M. *A History of Antony Bek, 1283–1311*. Oxford, 1957.

Gervers, M. "Rotundae Anglicanae." *Acts of the XXII International Congress of Art History.* Budapest, 1969.

Gilchrist, J. "The Erdmann Thesis and the Canon Law, 1083–1141." *Crusade and Settlement,* ed. P. W. Edbury. Cardiff, 1985.

Gillingham, J. *Richard the Lionheart.* London, 1978.

Giuseppi, M. W. "On the Testament of Sir Hugh de Neville." *Archeologia* 56 (1899).

Godfrey, J. "The Defeated Anglo-Saxons take Service with the Eastern Emperor." *Anglo-Norman Studies* 1 (1978).

Goodman, A. *The Loyal Conspiracy.* London, 1971.

Grabois, A. "Anglo-Norman England and the Holy Land." *Anglo-Norman Studies* 7 (1984).

Graham, R. "Letters of Cardinal Ottobuono." *EHR* 15 (1900).

Gransden, A. *Historical Writing in England, c. 550 to the Early Sixteenth Century.* 2 vols. London, 1974–82

Grousset, R. *Histoire des croisades.* 3 vols. Paris, 1934–36.

Hamilton, B. *The Latin Church in the Crusader States: The Secular Church.* London, 1980.

Harris, B. E. "Ranulph III, Earl of Chester." *Journal of the Chester Archeological Society* 58 (1975).

Harvey, P. D. A. "The English Inflation of 1180–1220." *Peasants, Knights, and Heretics,* ed. R. H. Hilton. Cambridge, 1976.

Harvey, S. "The Knight and the Knight's Fee in England." *Peasants, Knights, and Heretics,* ed. R. H. Hilton. Cambridge, 1976.

Haskins, C. H. "A Canterbury Monk at Constantinople." *EHR* 25 (1910).

Head, C. "Pope Pius II and the Wars of the Roses." *Archivium historiae pontificae* 8 (1970).

Hehl, E.-D. *Kirche und Krieg im 12 Jahrhundert.* Stuttgart, 1980.

Hill, C. *Anti-Christ in Seventeenth Century England.* London, 1971.

Hill, G. F. *History of Cyprus.* Cambridge, 1940–52.

Hillgarth, J. N. *The Spanish Kingdoms.* Oxford, 1976.

Hollister, C. W. *The Military Organisation of Norman England.* Oxford, 1965.

Holmes, G. A. "Cardinal Beaufort and the Crusade against the Hussites." *EHR* 88 (1973).

Holmes, P. *Resistance and Compromise: The Political Thought of the Elizabethan Catholics.* Cambridge, 1982.

Horniker, A. L. "William Harborne and the Beginning of Anglo-Turkish Diplomatic and Commercial Relations." *Journal of Modern History* 14 (1942).

Housley, N. J. "Crusades against Christians." *Crusade and Settlement,* ed. P. W. Edbury. Cardiff, 1985.

————. *The Italian Crusades.* Oxford, 1982.

————. "The Mercenary Companies, the Papacy, and the Crusades, 1356–78." *Traditio* 38 (1982).

Hudson, A. *Lollards and their Books.* London, 1985.

Huizinga, J. *The Waning of the Middle Ages.* Trans. F. Hopman. London, 1938.

Hurnard, N. *The King's Pardon for Homicide.* Oxford, 1969.

Hyams, P. R. *Kings, Lords, and Peasants.* Oxford, 1980.

Iorga, N. *Philippe de Mézières et la croisade au XIVe siècle.* Paris, 1896.

James, M. E. *English Politics and the Concept of Honour, 1485–1642. Past and Present* Supplement 3 (1978).

James, M. R. "The Drawings of Matthew Paris." *Walpole Society* 14 (1925–26).

Jenkins, H. *Papal Efforts for Peace under Benedict XII.* Philadelphia, 1933.

Jones, E. " 'Othello', Lepanto and the Cyprus Wars." *Shakespeare Survey* 21 (1968).

Jones, T. *Chaucer's Knight.* London, 1980.

Jones, W. R. "England against the Celtic Fringe." *Cahiers d'histoire mondiale* 13 (1971).

————. "The English Church and Propaganda during the Hundred Years War." *Journal of British Studies* 19 (1979).

Jordan, W. C. *Louis IX and the Challenge of the Crusade.* Princeton, N.J., 1979.

Jorgensen, P. A. "Theoretical Views of War in Elizabethan England." *Journal of the History of Ideas* 13 (1952).

Kedar, B. Z. "The General Tax of 1183 in the Crusading Kingdom of Jerusalem." *EHR* 89 (1974).

————. "The Passenger List of a Crusader Ship, 1250." *Studi Medievali,* 3d ser., 13 (1972).

Keen, M. H. "Chaucer's Knight, the English Aristocracy, and the Crusade." *English Court Culture in the Later Middle Ages,* ed. V. J. Scattergood and J. W. Sherbourne. London, 1983.

————. *Chivalry.* New Haven, Conn., 1984.

————. *England in the Later Middle Ages.* London, 1973.

Kilgour, R. L. *The Decline of Chivalry.* Cambridge, Mass., 1937.

King, E. *Peterborough Abbey, 1086–1310.* Cambridge, 1973.

King, E. J. "A Letter to his Agent." *Order of St. John of Jerusalem Historical Pamphlets,* no. 4. 1930.

King, E. J., and Luke, H. *The Knights of St. John in the British Realm.* London, 1967.

Knowles, C. H. "The Resettlement of England after the Barons' War." *TRHS,* 5th ser., 32 (1982).

Knowles, D. *The Religious Orders in England.* 3 vols. Cambridge, 1948–55.

Lecoy de la Marche, A. "Le prédiction de la croisade au treizieme siècle." *Revue des questions historiques* 48 (1890).

Legge, M. D. *Anglo-Norman Letters and Petitions.* Oxford, 1941.

Le Patourel, J. *The Norman Empire.* Oxford, 1976.

Leyser, K. J. "Frederick Barbarossa and the Hand of St. James." *EHR* 90 (1975).

Linder, A. "An Unpublished Charter of Geoffrey, Abbot of the Temple in Jerusalem." *Outremer,* ed. B. Z. Kedar, et al. Jerusalem, 1982.

Little, A. G. *Studies in English Franciscan History.* Manchester, 1917.

Lloyd, S. "The Lord Edward's Crusade of 1270–72." *War and Government in the Middle Ages,* ed. J. Gillingham and J. C. Holt. Woodbridge, 1984.

Longnon, J. *Les compagnons de Villehardouin.* Geneva, 1978.

Loyn, H. R. *Anglo-Saxon England and the Norman Conquest.* London, 1962.

Lunt, W. R. *Financial Relations of the Papacy with England.* 2 vols. Medieval Academy of America. Cambridge, Mass., 1939–62.

————. *Papal Revenues in the Middle Ages.* 2 vols. New York, 1965.

461

Luttrell, A. "The Hospitallers at Rhodes, 1306–1523." *History of the Crusades*, gen. ed. K. Setton. Vol. 3. Madison, Wis., 1969– .

Mackay, A. *Spain in the Middle Ages*. London, 1977.

Mackenzie, H. "The Anti-Foreign Movement in England in 1231–32." *Anniversary Essays by Students of C. H. Haskins*, ed. C. H. Taylor. Boston, 1929.

Macquarrie, A. D. "The Ideal of the Holy War in Scotland, 1296–1330." *Innes Review* 32 (1981).

––––––––. *Scotland and the Crusades*. Edinburgh, 1985.

Marius, R. *Thomas More*. London, 1985.

Mason, E. "Legends of the Beauchamps' Ancestors." *Journal of Medieval History* 10 (1984).

Mattingly, G. *The Defeat of the Spanish Armada*. London, 1961.

Mayer, H. E. *The Crusades*. Oxford, 1972.

––––––––. "Henry II of England and the Holy Land." *EHR* 97 (1982).

––––––––. "Kaiserrecht und Heiliges Land." *Aus Reichsgeschichte und Nordischen Geschichte*. Kieler Historische Studien. Stuttgart, 1972.

––––––––. *Mélanges de l'histoire du royaume latin de Jérusalem*. Paris, 1983.

McFarlane, K. B. *Lancastrian Kings and Lollard Knights*. Oxford, 1972.

McHardy, A. K. "Liturgy and Propaganda during the Hundred Years War." *Studies in Church History* 18, ed. S. Mews. (Oxford, 1982).

McKisack, M. *The Fourteenth Century*. Oxford, 1959.

Mifsud, A. *Knights Hospitaller of the Venerable Tongue of England*. Malta, 1914.

Miller, E. *The Abbey and Bishopric of Ely*. Cambridge, 1951.

––––––––. "The State and Landed Interests in Thirteenth Century France and England." *TRHS*, 5th ser., 2 (1952).

Miller, E., and Hatcher, J. *Rural Society and Economic Change, 1086–1348*. London, 1978.

Mitchell, S. K. *Taxation in Medieval England*. New Haven, Conn., 1951.

Molinier, A. "Description de deux MSS." *Archives de l'Orient Latin* 1 (1881).

Morey, A., and Brooke, C. N. L. *Gilbert Foliot and his Letters*. Cambridge, 1965.

Morris, C. "Propaganda for War: The Dissemination of the Crusading Ideal in the Twelfth Century." *Studies in Church History* 20, ed. W. Shiels (Oxford, 1983).

Morris, W. A., and Strayer, J. R. *English Government at Work, 1327–36*. Cambridge, Mass., 1947.

Mortimer, R. "The Family of Rannulf de Glanville." *BIHR* 54 (1981).

Murray, A. *Reason and Society in the Middle Ages*. Oxford, 1978.

Nicol, D. M. "A Byzantine Emperor in England." *University of Birmingham Historical Journal* 12 (1969–70).

Nicholson, R. *Edward III and the Scots*. Oxford, 1965.

Owen, D. M. *Church and Society in Medieval Lincolnshire*. Lincoln, 1971.

Owst, G. R. *Literature and the Pulpit*. Oxford, 1961.

––––––––. *Preaching in Medieval England*. Cambridge, 1926.

Painter, S. *William Marshal*. Baltimore, 1933.

Palmer, J. J. N. *England, France, and Christendom, 1377–99*. London, 1972.

Parker, T. W. *The Knights Templar in England*. Tucson, Ariz. 1963.

Parsons, J. C. *The Court and Household of Eleanor of Castille in 1290*. Toronto, 1977.

Pennington, K. "The Rite for taking the Cross in the Twelfth Century." *Traditio* 30 (1974).

Perroy, E. *L'Angleterre et le grand schisme d'Occident*. Paris, 1933.

Phillips, J. R. S. "Edward II and the Prophets." *England in the Fourteenth Century*, ed. W. M. Ormrod. Woodbridge, 1986.

Powell, J. E., and Wallis, K. *The House of Lords in the Middle Ages*. London, 1968.

Powicke, F. M. *Henry III and the Lord Edward*. Oxford, 1947.

————. *The Thirteenth Century*. Oxford, 1962.

Prestwich, J. O. "Richard Coeur de Lion: *Rex Bellicosus*." *Academia Nazionale dei Lincei: Problemi attuali di scienza e di cultura* 253 (1981).

Prestwich, M. C. *The Three Edwards*. London, 1979.

————. *War, Politics, and Finance under Edward I*. London, 1972.

Ramsay, J. H. *A History of the Revenues of the Kings of England, 1066–1399*. 2 vols. Oxford, 1925.

Rawlinson, H. G. "The Embassy of William Harborne to Constantinople, 1583–88." *TRHS*, 4th ser., 5 (1922).

Richardson, H. G. *The English Jewry under Angevin Kings*. London, 1960.

Richardson, H. G., and Sayles, G. O. *The Governance of Medieval England*. Edinburgh, 1963.

Riley-Smith, J. "The Motives of the Earliest Crusaders and the Settlement of Latin Palestine." *EHR* 98 (1983).

————. "A Note on Confraternities in the Latin Kingdom of Jerusalem." *BIHR* 44 (1971).

————. *What were the Crusades?* London, 1977.

Ritchie, R. L. G. *The Normans in Scotland*. Edinburgh, 1954.

Röhricht, R. "La croisade de Prince Edouard d'Angleterre, 1270–74." *Archives de l'Orient Latin* 1 (1881).

Rose-Troup, F. *The Western Rebellion of 1549*. London, 1913.

Roskell, J. S. "Sir Richard Waldegrave." *Proceedings of the Suffolk Institute of Archeology* 27, pt. 3 (1957).

Ross, C. *Edward IV*. London, 1974.

Roth, C. *A History of the Jews in England*. Oxford, 1978.

Round, J. H. *Feudal England*. London, 1895.

————. *Geoffrey de Mandeville*. London, 1892.

————. "Some English Crusaders of Richard I." *EHR* 18 (1903):475–78.

Runciman, S. *A History of the Crusades*. 3 vols. Cambridge, 1951–54.

Russell, F. H. *The Just War in the Middle Ages*. Cambridge, 1975.

Russell, P. E. *The English Intervention in Spain and Portugal*. Oxford, 1955.

Sayers, J. "English Charters from the Third Crusade." *Tradition and Change: Essays in Honour of Marjorie Chibnall*, ed. D. Greenway, C. Holdsworth, J. Sayers. Cambridge, 1985.

Scammell, G. V. *Hugh du Puiset*. Cambridge, 1956.

Scarfe, N. *Suffolk in the Middle Ages*. (Woodbridge, 1986).

Scarisbrick, J. J. *Henry VIII*. London, 1968.

Schein, S. "Gesta Dei per Mongolos, 1300: The Genesis of a Non-Event." *EHR* 94 (1979).

—————. "Philip IV and the Crusade." *Crusade and Settlement*, ed. P. W. Edbury. Cardiff, 1985.

Setton, K. *The Papacy and the Levant*. 4 vols. Philadelphia, 1971–84.

Setton, K., gen. ed. *History of the Crusades*. 5 vols. to date. Madison, Wis., 1969– .

Shepard, J. "The English and Byzantium." *Traditio* 24 (1973).

Siberry, E. "Criticism of Crusading in Fourteenth Century England." *Crusade and Settlement*, ed. P. W. Edbury. Cardiff, 1985.

—————. *Criticism of Crusading, 1095–1274*. Oxford, 1985.

Smail, R. C. "Latin Syria and the West, 1149–1187." *TRHS*, 5th ser., 19 (1969).

Somerville, R. "The Council of Clermont and the First Crusade." *Studia Gratiana* 20 (1976).

Southern, R. W. *The Making of the Middle Ages*. London, 1968.

—————. *Medieval Humanism*. Oxford, 1970.

—————. "Peter of Blois and the Third Crusade." *Studies in Medieval History presented to R. H. C. Davis*, ed. H. Mayr-Harting and R. I. Moore. London, 1985.

Steel, A. *Receipt of the Exchequer, 1377–1485*. Cambridge, 1954.

Stenton, D. M. "Roger of Howden and Benedict." *EHR* 68 (1953).

Stenton, F. M. *Anglo-Saxon England*. Oxford, 1943.

Stones, E. L. G., and Simpson, G. G. *Edward I and the Throne of Scotland*. Oxford, 1978.

Strong, R. C., and van Dorsten, J. A. *Leicester's Triumph*. London, 1964.

Suckling, A. I. *The History and Antiquities of Suffolk*. London, 1846.

Sutherland, D. *The Assize of Novel Disseisin*. Oxford, 1973.

Tanner, N. P. *The Church in Late Medieval Norwich*. Toronto, 1984.

Throop, P. *Criticism of the Crusade*. Amsterdam, 1940.

Tipton, C. L. "The English and the Scottish Hospitallers during the Great Schism." *Catholic Historical Review* 52 (1966).

—————. "The English at Nicopolis." *Speculum* 37 (1962).

Town, C. E. "From the Crusades to Clerkenwell." *St. John Historical Society Newsletter* (September 1983).

Trabaut-Cussac, J.-P. "Le financement de la croisade anglaise de 1270." *Bibliothèque de l'école des chartes* 119 (1961).

Tristram, E. W. *English Medieval Wall Painting: The Thirteenth Century*. Oxford, 1950.

Tudor-Craig, P. *Richard III*. National Portrait Gallery. London, 1973.

Tyerman, C. J. "Philip VI and the Recovery of the Holy Land." *EHR* 100 (1985).

—————. "Some Evidence of English Attitudes to the Crusade in the Thirteenth Century." *Thirteenth Century Studies*, ed. S. Lloyd. 1987.

Vaughan, R. *Matthew Paris*. Cambridge, 1958.

Vidal, J. M. "La poursuite des lépreux." *Melanges de litérature et d'histoire religieuse*. Paris, 1899.

Wallace-Hadrill, J. M. *The Barbarian West*. London, 1969.

Walsh, R. J. "Charles the Bold and the Crusade." *Journal of Medieval History* 3 (1977).

Walzer, M. *The Revolution of the Saints*. London, 1966.

Warren, W. L. *Henry II*. London, 1973.

_____. *King John.* London, 1961.

Wernham, R. B. *Before the Armada.* London, 1966.

White, G. H. "The Career of Waleran, Count of Meulan." *TRHS,* 4th ser., 17 (1934).

Wightman, W. E. *The Lacy Family in England and Normandy, 1066–1194.* Oxford, 1966.

Willis, P. "Temple Sowerby." *St. John Historical Society Newsletter* (December 1983).

Wright, L. B. *Middle Class Culture in Elizabethan England.* Chapel Hill, N.C., 1935.

Wright, N. A. R. "The Tree of Battles of Honoré Bouvet." *War, Literature, and Politics in the Late Middle Ages,* ed. C. T. A. Allmand. Liverpool, 1976.

Wrottesley, G. *A History of the Bagot Family. Collections for a History of Staffordshire,* n.s. 11 (London, 1908).

Wylie, J. H. *History of England under Henry the Fourth.* 4 vols. London, 1884–98.

The following works came to my attention too late for consideration in this book:

Housley, N. J. *The Avignon Papacy and the Crusades.* Oxford, 1986.

Lloyd, S. "Gilbert of Clare, Earl of Gloucester, and the Crusade of the Lord Edward, 1270." *Nottingham Medieval Studies* 30 (1986).

Powell, J. M. *Anatomy of a Crusade, 1213–21.* Philadelphia, 1986.

Riley-Smith, J. *The First Crusade and the Idea of Crusading.* London, 1986.

Index